# EQUAL PAY FOR EQUAL WORK

*THE STORY OF THE STRUGGLE FOR JUSTICE BEING MADE BY THE WOMEN TEACHERS OF THE CITY OF NEW YORK*

BY

GRACE C. STRACHAN

1910

B. F. BUCK & COMPANY

160 FIFTH AVENUE

NEW YORK

Grace C. Strachan.

Mrs. Beverly Dabney Benson (*nee* Jean Strachan)

*To my sister, Mrs. Beverly Dabney Benson,* née *Jean Strachan,*
*who, though not a teacher herself, worked devotedly*
*and untiringly for "Our Cause," I lovingly*
*dedicate this book.*

# CONTENTS

## CONTENTS

# PREFACE

Salary—A periodical allowance made as compensation to a person for his official or professional services or for his regular work.—*Funk and Wagnalls.*

Notice the words, "a person." Here is no differentiation between male persons and female persons.

Yet the City of New York pays a "male" person for certain "professional services" $900, while paying a "female" person only $600 for the same "professional services." Stranger still, it pays for certain experience of a "male" person $105, while paying a "female" person only $40 for the identical experience. These are but samples of the "glaring inequalities" in the teachers' salary schedules.

Why is the male in the teaching profession differentiated from the male in every other calling, when his salary is concerned?

Why does the city differentiate the woman it hires to teach its children from the woman it hires to take stenographic notes, use a typewriter, follow up truants, inspect a tenement, or issue a license?

Why are not the appointees from the eligible lists established by the Department of Education, entitled to the same privileges and rights as appointees from Civil Service lists from other City and State Departments?

Some ask, "Shall the single woman, in teaching, be given the married woman's wage?" I do not know what they mean, but I say, "Why not the single woman in teaching just as much as the single woman in washing, in farming, in dressmaking, in nursing, in telephoning?"

Again, some ask, is there such a thing as "equal work" by two people?

Technically, no. No two people do exactly the same work in the same way. This is true of all professional and official work. Compare Mayor Gaynor's work with Mayor McClellan's. Will any one say their work as Mayor is "Equal Work"? And yet the pay is the same. Do all policemen do "Equal Work"? Yet they receive equal pay. So with firemen, school physicians, tenement house inspectors. The taxpayers, no doubt, believe that, judged by his work, Mayor Gaynor is worth a far higher salary than many of his predecessors. But a great corporation like the City of New York cannot attempt to pay each of its employees according to the work of that particular street cleaner or fireman or stenographer, and so must be content with classifying its positions, and fixing a salary for each. So should it do for its teachers. That is all we ask.

The male teachers argue for a "family wage" for the "adult male." Who ever heard a man who is a doctor or a lawyer or a plumber or a grocer or a baseball player or a barber or a janitor, advance such argument?

This is surely "special pleading." A logical interpretation would make it necessary for the Board of Education to base each salary on the individual worker's family. Manifestly on such a basis it would be unfair to pay the wealthy bachelor the same salary as the poor married man; or the married man with seven children and a mother-in-law to support, the same as the married man whose father-in-law supports him. Furthermore, the "family wage" restricted to "adult male" presupposes that the woman teacher has no family obligations. All intelligent people know that this is not true. But the chief objection to the "family wage" is that a just application of such a standard to any schedules, necessitates inquiry into one's private life, which is an intrusion to the extent almost of violating the Constitution.

What good citizen will deny that selling 1800 pounds of coal as a full ton is bad for both the buyer and the seller? The former is cheated, but the latter is a cheat.

Paying a man more money for teaching a class than is paid a woman for teaching the same class breeds two serious evils for men teachers. The lesser of these evils is the lessening of their chance of appointment.

But by far the greater evil to the man teacher in the unjust salary schedule, is the degeneration of his fine sense of truth, of honor, of justice. This placing of a false and inflated value on his services causes him to imagine he is something that he is not. It is as if a four-foot man propped up on stilts should think that he was actually a six-foot man, and eligible for a place in the "Broadway Squad." An unbiased judge would soon expose his masquerading and his true stature.

It is akin to all those deceptions exemplified in such sayings as "A lion in sheep's clothing." Not, however, that a male teacher who is opposing his sisters in the profession, is comparable to a lion.

It is inevitable that the male teacher having been put by the State in a special and privileged class based simply on the accident of sex, should come to think he is some strange and unusual creature that must be pampered and decorated and even fed and clothed at the expense directly of his sister workers and indirectly of the community which supports him,

A man who thinks he is funny when he is not, becomes a bore. A man who thinks he is serious when he is only trite, becomes a joke. But a man who thinks he is worthy when he is not, becomes an unconscious and potential hypocrite—a Pharisee, a " sounding brass and tinkling cymbal."

Is there not great danger that the person—who simply because he happens to be of the male sex receives twice as big a salary as another person in an identical position who happens to be of the female sex—will gradually become an undesirable citizen. In nine cases out of ten, he knows in his heart that the children in the woman's class are deriving greater benefit from her life and service than the children in his class are obtaining from his. Is he not taking unto himself things that are not rightfully his? And must it not follow, as the night the day, that his sense of truth is warped; his sense of justice, untrustworthy; his sense of right generally, unbalanced?

This very male teacher, however, whose perception of true values has been blunted and distorted by the false value put upon his services, is set up as the mentor and the model for our boys and girls. Does it not inevitably follow that our boys and girls must suffer? Their sense of true values, their fineness of judgment, in short, their whole moral nature, is endangered. You can not draw pure water from a polluted well.

Who will deny that a railroad track with one of its rails depressed three feet below the other is dangerous to all who travel on it? I hold that all who are connected with the enforcement and the operation of our unjust salary schedules are in danger of moral degeneration. Therefore, I hold that the entire community should fight the unjust salary schedules paid our teachers, as immoral and as a menace to the welfare of the State.

Let us all—those in the teaching system and those out of it—who are interested in making effective the purpose of our noble forefathers who planned our great and glorious Constitution "to establish justice"; and "to promote the general welfare," unite in the determination to bring about a speedy amendment to this dangerous law.

Senator Dolliver, Chairman of the Committee on Education and Labor, discussing a bill to prohibit child labor in the District of Columbia, said: "A strong feeling prevails in Congress that child labor regulation should be left to the states. One of the arguments that will be made for the proposed legislation for the District of Columbia will be that if Congress takes up child labor in the District of Columbia and handles it without gloves, it will set a good example for states that are slow in dealing properly with this subject."

Let New York City handle the "woman labor" trouble without gloves.

The facts set forth hereafter prove that the State of New York and the City of New York degrade and belittle their women teachers in a markedly unusual way, and to a markedly unusual degree. Do not the women teachers resent this degradation and this belittling? Yes, the women teachers do. But often they are afraid to voice their resentment. Some of them are intimidated by their superior officers. The women teachers of New York City, though, after years of private complaining and inward resenting, have formed themselves into a great united body whose voice is being heard 'round the world. There are so many of us—fifteen thousand and more—that the very strength of numbers has given us courage; and the timid, scattered cries of individuals have swelled into one great grand choral that reaches the hearts of the people. And the people rule!

The Interborough Association of Women Teachers of the City of New York sends greeting to all its sisters, and promises that the degradation and belittling will disappear "as mists of the morning." The recognition of women is but in its morning.

Statistics show that the number of male teachers is not decreasing in the City of New York, but that it is increasing at a rate higher than that of the rest of the country; that indeed it is upwards of 25 per cent. greater than City Superintendent Maxwell is said to think necessary.

The fetish of feminization is exploded by such authorities as Professor Dewey and Professor Thorndike of Columbia. It is upheld only by foreigners unacquainted with us, our customs, and our schools, and by a few misguided followers of such foreigners.

The much mooted law of "Supply and Demand" is really a boomerang argument in the hands of our opponents; for besides the exposition offered by "The Association of Unappointed Men Teachers," figures from Superintendent Maxwell's Tenth Annual Report show that instead of a scarcity there is an excess of teachers in our high schools.

"Equal Pay" for men and women teachers is the rule in the cities of the great, free, progressive West.

*"Equal Pay" was the rule in Brooklyn* until the passage of the Davis Law in 1900.

The chief obstacle in our path, is the *cost* of "Equal Pay" in dollars and cents. Think of that! Then remember that this is the country of Washington and Lincoln and Webster and Patrick Henry. Can any true American say, " I know you are not getting a square deal, but I won't help you because it would cost me a dollar or two? Was it because the tax on tea would cost a penny or two that our forefathers fought the War of the Revolution?

There is much said about "the proper calibre of men teachers," all of which propounds the theory that money is the only bait that will attract men to teaching, but little is said about the far more important thing—" the proper calibre of women teachers." Yet the facts are that the Board has for several years found it impossible to get a sufficient number of women teachers " of the proper calibre."

This unfortunate condition will persist while the Board of Education is encouraged by the state in the Davis Law, and is permitted by the city, to continue its unfair treatment of its women teachers. I would consider it a matter for regret, if one of my four nieces or eight nephews should feel called upon to teach under our present system. I want my nephews to be manly men, and my nieces not to be contaminated by an environment of injustice.

## JUSTICE

Blessed are they that hunger and thirst after justice; for they shall have their fill. (Matt. v.)

" When people quit believing in justice, there's nothing doing in making them better."—*Policeman John F. Foley, in Globe* May 23, 1910.

" A tower four square and impregnable is the just man. He is beacon and sanctuary for his fellows. He is panoplied in justice—that virtue which maketh for sterling character and which is one of the four strong hinges upon which the whole moral order turns. It is more than honesty, which is one of its features only, and it vitalizes honor, which is its bloom and fragrance. It giveth to every one—to God, to home, to country, to Caesar, to the man it sways—all that belongs to each. It respects every obligation and every right. The man who withholds theirs from his fellows is recreant to God and to Caesar and tears into shreds self-respect, without which there is naught left but degeneracy. What a benefactor of his race is the just man! His thoughts are of the loftiest and gentlest, his word is his bond and baffles bankruptcy; his deeds shine like stars in the blackness of life's wretchedness.—*Rev. P. A. Halpin, New Rochelle College, in New York Times,* April 24, 1910.

"The spirit of unrest is an inarticulate cry, it may be, for fair play. When that cry becomes articulate and vociferous, when the mighty American spirit is aroused, the bulwarks that protect special privileges and selfish interests will be battered down and the people once again will come into their own."—*Dr. Felter, at Congregational Church dinner, Brooklyn,*

"The people are beginning to feel that these questions are moral questions, rather than economic. The next great task for the Christian Church to undertake is to plead the cause of the poor and the weak against special privilege and legislation in the interest of favorites. There can be no political and social equality so long as there is industrial inequality through class legislation. There is but one solution of the social problem in the republic—that is, the application of the Golden Rule to the laws of the street."—*Dr. Hillis at Congregational Church dinner, Brooklyn.*

Wherever an injustice is done, evil will result. A great injustice is done the women teachers in our present salary schedules, and it is being perpetrated by the very department from which citizens have a right to expect the highest ideals of justice and morality.

The statutes of the State of New York may be read from beginning to end and there will be found no statute which deliberately places woman's service in a lower wage scale than man's, except Section 1091 of the charter of the City of New York—the "Davis Law."

The cause of Equal Pay has attracted widespread attention and support. When the women teachers of New York City made their first organized protest they addressed themselves to the local authorities but were accorded such contemptuous treatment that they found it necessary to appeal to the Legislature for a statute reading the principle into the charter. Equal Pay thus became immediately a question of widespread importance, and soon attained the proportions, the dignity and the momentum of a great social movement. The principle of Equal Pay is representative of the candid judgment of more than half the population, who are opposed to the present system as being a fundamental negation of their sense of fair play. They realize that long toleration and tacit acceptance of an injustice but increase their obligation to destroy it. The movement is gaining strength and ground every day.

The friends of Equal Pay insist that a more formal and specific statement of the inception, progress and prospects of the work should be made and it is because of their insistence that this book is written. Equal Pay has won support wherever its arguments have been fairly presented. I believe the day is not far distant when it will revolt the intelligence of everybody whose opinion is of any consequence to argue that there is any excuse for paying a woman less for the same work than is paid a man, whether that work be in a so-called profession or in the mechanical arts and trades.

I shall have utterly failed in my purpose if those who read this book do not realize that this struggle for "Equal Pay" is a fight for simple justice.

All intelligent people must acknowledge that injustice is immoral. All must agree that to practice or uphold injustice is dangerous to the individual, the corporation, the municipality, the State, the Nation.

It is the desire to assist in purging the profession, the city, the State, the Nation, to which I belong, of the great moral danger involved in the unjust practice of paying for service according to the sex of the servant, that has made me lead the fight of the women teachers.

I offer this book in the same spirit.

GRACE C. STRACHAN.

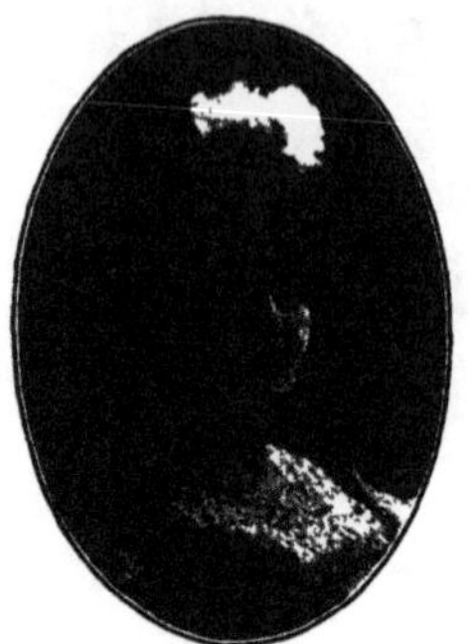

Miss Mary A. Curtis,
The Bronx.

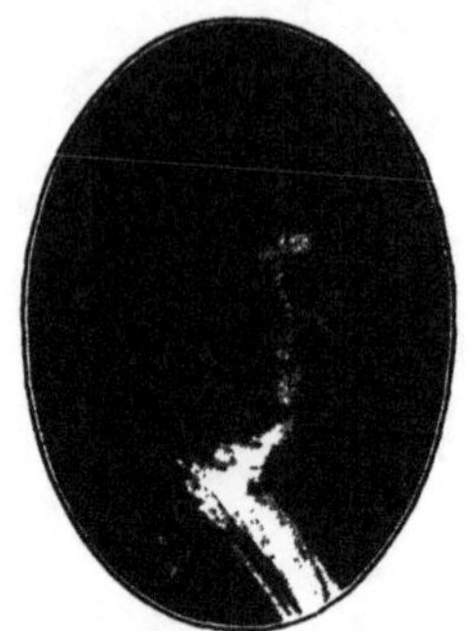

Miss Anna E. McAuliffe,
Queens.

Miss Annie B. Moriarty,
Brooklyn,
Chairman Organization Committee.

Miss Lina E. Gans,
Manhattan.

Miss Clara I. Walson,
Richmond.

VICE-PRESIDENTS, INTERBORO ASSOCIATION OF WOMEN TEACHERS, NEW YORK CITY.

MISS ISABEL A. ENNIS,
Secretary, Interborough Association of Women Teachers, 1906-1910.

MISS ELLEN T. O'BRIEN,
Treasurer, Interborough Association of Women Teachers, 1907 and 1908.

MRS. N. CURTIS LENIHAN KILLEEN,
Honorary President, Interborough Association of Women Teachers. Treasurer, 1906; President, October, 1906—October, 1907.

OFFICERS INTERBORO ASSOCIATION OF WOMEN TEACHERS, NEW YORK CITY.

# ORGANIZATION

OF

## The Interborough Association of Women Teachers

In the annual report of the National Educational Association for the year 1908, Prof. Ulysses G. Weatherby, University of Indianapolis, says that the "lower pay of women than that of men for equal work is due entirely to the lack of serious professional spirit and organization."

The Interborough Association of Women Teachers is the largest, most powerful, single organization of professional women in the world.

Early in 1907, the *Journal* said editorially: "In the Interborough Association of Women Teachers, the women of the public school system of Greater New York have developed an organization of ten thousand members, which is pledged and committed to the principle that the position should carry the salary in the school service. The injustices of the present salary schedules have been felt for years by these ten thousand women; but until the present organization was effected it was impossible for them to act as a unit. To-day the strength, energy and intelligence of every individual member are being utilized to a given end. Unity of action has been established, and the result is a campaign that has astonished the community and roused public conscience. The tremendous energy and devotion of these women and their thousands of friends have also created a moral force and an intelligent power that is to be recognized and that must be reckoned with by civic organizations, politicians and political parties."

There are various stories as to who was the first one to suggest that the women teachers should organize to secure "Equal Pay." All agree, however, that the credit of starting the organization is due to Miss Kate Hogan, a teacher of a seventh year class of boys in a Manhattan school. Miss Hogan was elected first President, Miss Anne Goessling, Vice-President, Miss Isabel A. Ennis, Secretary, and Miss Fannie I. Flanly, Treasurer. The latter was soon obliged to resign on account of death in her family, and Mrs. N. Curtis Lenihen was chosen to succeed her.

I attended the first meeting of the association in April, 1906, simply to show my sympathy with the movement. Learning that I was eligible for membership, I paid the fifty cents dues, and I have never missed a meeting since, except on account of death or official business. In May, 1906, at Miss Hogan's request, I accepted the chairmanship of the Executive Committee.

In November, the Association was shocked and saddened by the death of Miss Hogan. As the constitution made no provision for filling a vacancy caused by death, a special election was held at which Mrs. Lenihen was elected president, and Miss Ellen T. O'Brien, treasurer.

In 1907 the constitution was amended so as to provide for a vice-president for each borough. Miss Alida S. Williams was elected for Manhattan, but illness soon compelled her resignation, and she was succeeded by Miss Lina E. Gano, who has been unanimously re-elected every year since. Mrs. Annie B. Moriarty has always been the vice-president from Brooklyn. Miss Emma McCabe and Miss Mary A. Curtis have represented The Bronx; Mrs. Elizabeth A. Loughlin and Miss Annie E. McAuliffe, Queens; and Miss Rebecca Ludlum followed by Miss Clara I. Watson, Richmond.

Mrs. Lenihen was re-nominated for the presidency, but ill health caused her to withdraw, and I was elected president in October, 1907. Mrs. Lenihen (now Mrs. Killeen) was made Honorary President. Miss Ennis is the only one of the original officers still serving.

In 1907, an Organization Committee was founded with Mrs. Moriarty as chairman. Most effective work has been done by and through this committee. The vice-president of each borough is vice chairman for that borough, and is responsible for its organization. She must see that each Senate and each Assembly district has a competent and enthusiastic leader, and each school one or more delegates. The leaders and delegates of each district are expected to familiarize themselves with the boundaries of the district, the names of its representatives in the Legislature and the Board of Aldermen, and their attitude on "Equal Pay."

The association has grown from less than a hundred in April, 1906, to upwards of 14,000 to-day. Splendid work was done by Miss Ennis as secretary and Mrs. Lenihen as treasurer in rolling up the membership in the early days. Later, the Organization Committee workers carried it on.

Yeoman service has been rendered by all those named above from the beginning, but the brunt of the battle fell on Mrs. Lenihen, Miss Ennis, Miss O'Brien, Mrs. Moriarty and Miss Gano. I take this opportunity of telling all the members how much I appreciate their splendid united spirit and unselfish coöperation. The loyalty of the "primary teachers" is especially acknowledged because of the continuous attempts of our opponents to weaken or destroy it.

While the Interborough Association, in its fight has had a difficult task and some set-backs, *it has never been defeated.* Why? The leaders have never lost faith.

Robert Louis Stevenson, the Beloved, puts it this way:

> To feel in the ink of the slough
> And the sink of the mire
> Veins of glory and fire
> Run through and transpierce and transpire,
> And a secret purpose of glory fill each part.
> And the answering glory of battle fill my heart;
> To thrill with joy of girded men,
> To go on forever and fail, and go on again,
> And be mauled to the earth and arise,
> And contend for the shade of a word and a thing not seen with the eyes,
> With the half of a broken hope for a pillow at night—
> That somehow the right is the right,
> And the smooth shall bloom from the rough.

## HONORARY VICE-PRESIDENTS

Justice William Crane.
Justice Dittenhoefer.
Justice Stephen Stephens.
Justice Vernon Davis.
Justice J. W. Gerard.
Justice M. L. Erlanger.
Justice C. H. Truax.
Justice E. F. O'Dwyer
Judge George J. O'Keefe.
Ex-Justice Edward H. Hatch.
Justice Robert J. Wilkin.
Judge Frank O'Reilly.
Judge J. G. Tighe.
Judge Morgan M. L. Ryan.
Monsignor Lavelle.
Monsignor Edward McCarty.
Monsignor J. I. Barrett.
Rabbi Stephen S. Wise.
Rev. Charles Cassidy.
Rev. Joseph H. McMahon, D. D.
Rev. Percy S. Grant.
Rev. C. R. Duryee.
Mons. J. T. Woods.
Lieutenant-Governor White.
Hon. John H. McCooey.
Hon. William H. Edwards.
Sen. Thomas F. Grady.
Hon. James E. March.
Cong. William Sulzer.
Cong. Otto G. Foelker.
Hon. Julius Harburger.
Hon. Charles McCormack.
Hon. John B. Byrne.
Hon. John J. Cronin, M. D.
Ald. George Markert.
Walter T. Edgerton.
Hon. Timothy L. Woodruff.
Hon. Patrick F. McGowan.
Hon. William Leary.
Hon. Charles F. Murphy.
Hon. Robert Hebberd.
Hon. Walter Bensel, M. D.
Hon. Robert H. Elder.
Hon. John S. Shea.
Hon. Arthur Murphy.
Hon. Patrick Hayes.
Hon. William F. Sheehan.
J. Hampden Dougherty.
Anna B. Allan.
Miss Helen Varick Boswell.
Mrs. Lillie Devereux Blake.
Beatrice Fairfax.
Mrs. J. Borden Harriman.
Mrs. Carrie Chapman Catt.
Mrs. James W. Gerard.
Mrs. Martin W. Littleton.
Dorothy Dix.
Mrs. Harriet Stanton Blatch.
Mrs. Gilbert E. Jones.
Mrs. Charles H. Hyde.
Mrs. William A. Engemann.
Mrs. Forbes Robertson.
Miss Mary Drier.
Mrs. Cynthia Westover Alden.
Mrs. E. W. Townsend.
Dr. Anna Shaw.
Miss Ida Craft.
Mrs. Harry Hastings.
Mrs. Thomas J. Vivian.
Miss Margaret Lavelle.
Miss Margaret Schlessinger.
Mrs. Frederick Nathan.
Dr. Adelaide Wallerstein.
Mrs. Earl S. King.
Mrs. William H. Hotchkin.
Mrs. Helen Hoy Greeley.
Mrs. James Lees Laidlaw.
Miss Anne Morgan.
Lewis Nixon.
Caesare Conti.
Major Edward R. Gilman.
Clement B. Asbury.
John J. Harrington.
Antonio Zucca.
Harold B. Christensen.
Theodore Sutro.
Henry Batterman.
Nathaniel H. Levi.
George G. DeBevoise.
S. T. Hollister.
Cyrus Frederick Leubuscher.
George R. Crowly.
Howard Marshall.
C. V. Gould (James McCreery & Co.)
Alexander Della Paoli.

Hon. Mirabeau L. Towns.
Charles H. Strong.
George Foster Peabody.
Isaac H. Russell.
George W. Titcomb.
John Francis Yawger.
Hon. Robert H. Roy.
John Lorenz Cronin.
A. F. Lauterbach.
Col. Alexander S. Bacon.
Eugene Lamb Richards.
Charles F. Kingsley.
Edward McCrossin.
Charles V. Nellany.
Hon. James A. Donnelly.
Hon. Henry N. Tifft.
Hon. Joseph W. Keller.
George B. Hanavan.
Benjamin Blumenthal.
James Edward Gravilly.
Mrs. William J. Gaynor.
Mrs. Charlotte B. Wilbour.
Mrs. William Cumming Story.
Mrs. Mirabeau L. Towns.
Ella Wheeler Wilcox.
Mrs. O. H. P. Belmont.
Ida Husted Harper.
Mrs. Belle de Rivera.
Mrs. Charlotte Iranni.
Mrs. Egerton L. Winthrop, Jr.
Mrs. Edward Lauterbach.
Mrs. William M. Ivins.
Mrs. James Griswold Wentz.
Miss Margaret Grady.
Mrs. Cora Welles Trow.
Mrs. John S. Crosby.
Mrs. John Francis Yawger.
Mme. Katharine von Klemmer.
Dr. Frances Squire Potter.
Mrs. Alma Webster Powell.
Miss Eliza Macdonald.
Frederick Nathan.
Alfred B. Hall.
John W. Sawyer.
William S. Germain.
George P. Eckman.
Ezra W. Sampson.
W. A. Duke.
John Wanamaker.
William H. McAdoo.
Samuel Strauss.
John A. Wilbur.
Benjamin Blumenthal.
Edward F. Linton.
H. W. Lyall.
M. Peter Benedict.
Col. Alexander S. Bacon.
Henry Siegel.
John C. Sheehan.
George C. Boldt.
John C. Judge, Attorney.
D. T. Cornell.
E. W. Townsend.
Guy Loring Smith.
Edgar Smith.
Browne C. Hammond.
L. J. Fagan.
James P. Quinn.
James E. March.
Charles J. Adams.
Alfred I. Kirkup.
Andreas Dippel.
John Temple Graves.
Edwin Markham.
Theodore Dreiser.
Carl E Dufft.
William Dean Howells.
Ellis Parker Butler.
George W. Blake.
Ossian Lang.
Thomas J. Cunningham.
James C. Monaghan.
George Henry Payne.
Major E. T. McCrystal (Irish American.)
Alfred L. Manniere.

## MINISTERS

Rev. James Alyward.
Rev. James Burns.
Rev. William A. Ring.
Rev. Paul Reichertz.
Rev. J. J. Slattery.

Rev. John Braum.
Rev. Henry A. Braum.
Rev. Fred W. Blakesli.
Rev. William Blakes.

Rev. F. J. Castellano.
Rev. I. J. Conlon.
Rev. R. A. Cahill.
Rev. P. H. Casey.
Rev. John P. Chidwick.
Rev. James Lyon Caughey.
Rev. John C. Campbell.

Rev. William V. Dunwell.
Rev. John H. Dooley.
Rev. George F. Dean.
Rev. John Dolan.
Rev. Thomas Daly.
Rev. Joseph Donohue.
Rev. J. J. Durkin.
Rev. James Donlon.
Rev. Thomas F. Ducui.
Rev. J. Dunn.

Rev. Luke Evers.

Rev. James T. Fitzimmon.
Rev. James J. Flood.
Rev. Henry A. Fitzgerald.

Rev. Charles H. Grubb.
Rev. M. W. Gilbert.
Rev. J. C. Grimmell.
Rev. Walter A. Gardner.
Rev. Percy S. Grant.
Rev. C. F. Guntner.
Rev. Anthony J. Grogan.
Rev. D. W. Gill.
Rev. B. F. Galligan.
Rev Thomas F. Gregg.
Rev. C. L. Goddell.

Rev. R. Haepflin.
Rev. Nicholas J. Hughes.
Rev. J. H. Hinch.
Rev. M. J. Henry.
Rev. George Houghton.
Rev. Dr. Hutchins.
Rev. Jeremiah Heafy.
Rev. E. S. Hollaway.
Rev. John P. Hughes.

Rev. F. H. Justa.

Rev. J. M. Stanton.
Rev. M. A. Sheehan.
Rev. Samuel Schulman.
Rev. Talbot John Smith.
Dr. William Stinson.
Dr. George M. Searle.
Rev. Edwin Sweeney.
Rev. M. J. Scott.
Rev. H. T. Scutter.

Rev. M. Trathen.
Rev. Mathew A. Taylor.
Rev. T. D. Tempane.
Rev. S. W. Tumms.

Rev. George Van De Water.
Rev. W. H. Vaughn.
Rev. T. D. Van Wilderberg.
Rabbi Faulk Vidaver.
Rev. Michele De Vincent.

Rev. Drew T. Wyman.
Rev. J. A. Walther.
Rev. D. D. Whittier.
George Blake.
John C. Freund.
Reuben L. Gledhill.
James A. Foley.
Alfred E. Zass.
William J. Bolger.
Rev. W. W. Barringer.
Henry E. Chapman.
Thomas Freel.
Rev. Alexander Irvine.
Ezra Tuttle A.
Lawrence Gresser.
Miss Lewison.
Miss Woerishaffer.
Miss Mary Dreier.
Belle De Rivera.
Mrs. William Cununings-Story.
Miss Charlotte Wilbour.
Mrs. Harriet Johnston Wood.
Mrs. C. W. Fisk.
Mrs. Harry Hastings.
Mrs. John Francis Yawger.
Mrs. Gilbert Jones.
Miss Mary Garrett Hay.
Mrs. George B. Reid.
Miss Florence Guernsey.
Mrs. John Zimmerman.
Mrs. Root Francis Cartwright.
Rev. W. H. Lawrence.

Rev Alva E. Knapp.
Rev. William E. Katzenberger.
Rev. John J. Keoghan.
Rev. John J. Kellehan.
Rev. John J. Knowles.
Very Rev. Canon Knowles.

Rev. J. D. Long.
Rev. David Leahy.
Rev. L. J. Lockinger.
Rev. J. A. Lyons.
Rev. William Livingston.

Rev. C. B. Lutz.

Rev. Thomas F. McMillen.
Rev. C. H. McGrath.
Rev. A. H. C. Moorse.
Rev. J. S. Moran.
Rev. J. F. Molloi.
Rev. P. E. McCorry.
Rev. John McQuirk.
Rev. William H. Murphy.
Rev. P. J. Minogue.
Rev. P. H. Maher.
Rev. John J. McCahill.
Rt. Rev. Charles McCreedy.
Rev. Charles McKenna.
Rt. Rev. James H. McGean.
Rt. Rev. D. McMillan.
Rev. Matin A. Meyer.
Rev. Edw. McGuffey.

Rev. John O'Donovan.
Rev. J. F. X. O'Connor.
Rev. Daniel O'Dwyer.
Rev. J. F. O'Gorman.

Rev. John P. Peters.
Rev. Charles H. Parkhurst.
Rev. John F. Patty.
Rev. William L. Penny.
Rev. James W. Power.
Rev. S. Parin.
Rev. M. J. Phelan.
Rev. George S. Pratt.
Rev. Lindsay Parker.
Rev. John H. Pastoret.

Rev. Charles T. Ritter.
Rev. L. Rabe.

Hon. James B. McEwen.
Major McCrystal.
Miss Lillie Devereaux Blake.
John Meehan.
Senator Stillwell.
John Henry Payne.
Rev. William Parkhurst.
Joseph Hyman.
John Randolph.
Charles F. Kingsley.
Dr. N. J. Coyne.
Jacob Mariner.
Isaac Alden.
Saul C. Lavine.
Mr. F. Pitelli.
Robert H. Elder.
Judge H. Hylan.
J. Diner.
John Temple Graves.
Justus Ralph.
William A. Cokely.
Thomas Mulry.
Thomas I. Curtis.
M. McConville.
A. B. McStay.
James P. Holland.
B. Hannah.
Clement B. Asbury.
Richard Webber.
Nathaniel H. Levi.
Alfred I. Kirkus.
Dr. Robert F. Ives.
Dr. J. Edward Herman.
Rev. Robert N. Merriman.
Rev. George C. Groves.
Mrs. August Beyer.
George Millard.
George De Be Voise.
Charles Adams.
Charles Hollister.
John Whalen.
Terence P. Smith.
Edward Moloughuey.
Harold Dudley Greeley.
George F. Elliot.
Judge Morgan J. O'Brien.
Eugene Philbin.
Martin W. Littleton.
Frederick Nathan.
Rev. John Donaldson.
William Sulzer.

# Equal Pay for Equal Work

## CHAPTER I

## FOREWORD

Rabbi Wise pointed out in his speech at our mass meeting on March 6, 1908, that our subject lacks the one merit of being new, for as early as 1871, Wendell Phillips offered the following resolution at a meeting at Worcester: "We demand, that whenever women are employed at public expense to do the same kind and amount of work as men perform, they shall receive the same wages."

But the subject is older than that, for on July 29, 1862, the question of equal pay for equal work by teachers came up at the session of the New York Teachers' Association. The committee to which it had been referred reported against giving equal salaries to men and women teachers, although it was said that the salaries of women teachers should be larger. Miss Anthony (Susan B.) offered as a substitute for the committee's resolution another to the effect that "justice requires that the amount of compensation should not be regulated by sex, but by the amount of service rendered." After a sharp discussion, the previous question was ordered and the Anthony resolution was voted down.

Section 1091 of our city charter, familiarly known as the Davis Law, sets forth the only logical consideration which should govern the fixing and regulating of salaries of teachers, in the words, "and the salaries of all principals and teachers shall be regulated by merit, grade of class taught, length of service, experience in teaching or by a combination of these considerations"; but this is immediately negatived by the next sentence in which a new consideration, *that of sex,* is given an insulting and, to the women teachers, degrading prominence, in that it is made the basis for dividing the salary schedule for the same grade and class of work into two unfair and inequitable lists.

Horace E. Deming at one of our mass meetings said: "It needs no argument to convince any sane and reasonable person that a man or a woman, a city or a state, a corporation or an individual—any employer—that pays *A* a different price from *B* for doing the same work, is guilty of a mean act. Now, there is something inexpressibly mean in according treatment to a woman which one would not even contemplate in the case of a man. If the salaries of men teachers are too high, reduce them to the same figure as that paid to the women teachers. If the women are receiving too little pay, raise it to that of the men teachers. If neither is being justly paid, find a fair and equitable salary, *but under all circumstances pay the same price for the same work, irrespective of the sex of the worker.*"

When one considers that this is the twentieth century and that the struggle set forth in these pages is being fought by women, by women in America, by women of the greatest city in America, one is forced to doubt the much vaunted superiority of American men in their dealings with their women.

Yet we have been fighting for years to get *simple justice* for some of our women. "But," you say, "maybe these women are unworthy." Worthy or unworthy, they the entitled to justice; but it happens they are amongst our most worthy citizens. I believe that if the Mayor were asked to tell which of the city's servants he could spare least for all time, he would say the women teachers.

Is it not hard then to believe that four years have passed since we pointed out the injustice under which we are laboring, and that 15,000 of us are still appealing to the properly constituted authorities for relief. And yet we are not discouraged. We believe that the great majority of the citizens and taxpayers—fathers and mothers, brothers and sisters, of the 700,000 pupils in our public schools—will support and strengthen our appeal to our

Board of Education, our Board of Estimate and Apportionment, and—if need be—to "Albany."

And what is this appeal of ours?

Simply that our salary schedules be Civil Service schedules: that there be but one salary for one and the same position whose incumbent is selected from an eligible list after competitive examination—in more familiar terms, "Equal Pay for Equal Work."

Nor is this some wonderful, new idea of the women teachers.

The State as an employer pays but one salary for one and the same position.

The City as an employer pays but one salary for one and the same position.

The Board of Education as an employer pays but one salary for one and the same position under most of its schedules.

1. Vacation Schools. Principals and teachers.
2. Evening Schools. Principals and teachers.
3. Principals High Schools.
4. District Superintendents.
5. Assistant Directors of Special Subjects.
6. Model teachers, Training School for Teachers.
7. Principal of Model School.
8. Principal of Training School for Teachers.
9. Evening Recreation Centers. Principals and teachers.
10. Vacation Play Grounds. Principals and teachers.
11. City Superintendent.
12. Associate City Superintendent.
13. Board of Examiners.

## GENERAL OUTLINE

"Certainly, have the women, but not because they are cheaper. If women are put in the subway ticket offices, they must have equal pay with the men."

Mr. William G. McAdoo, President of the Hudson River Tunnels, spoke as above when his general superintendent suggested the employment of women as ticket sellers on the ground that besides being more expert than men, they would be cheaper also.

When later questioned by a reporter, Mr. McAdoo said among other things:

"I am not a champion for the great suffrage cause, but when Mr. Munger told me that women as ticket sellers were more nimble-fingered, more expert than men, I told him to take them on at full pay. The day is here when it is a necessity for large numbers of women to be employed outside the home, and it is only fair that there should be no discrimination in the matter of pay. Work is work, no matter who accomplishes it, and if women can do as well as men, they should have the same money."

Thus are the chains that have hampered women through all the centuries being broken by force of light. Forged by brute strength, pride, prejudice and passion, they are disappearing of their own rottenness. Mankind is realizing and is acknowledging that the parts played by the mother, the wife, and the sister in the game of life are often as important as those played by the father, the husband and the brother. In the world of work, it was so long taken for granted that the woman of the family should work "from sun to sun" in the dairy, the kitchen, the nursery, the field, the sewing-room, and at the spinning wheel, without pecuniary reward that when she appeared to work side by side with men in the public labor market, it was natural that any wages greater than nothing seemed munificent reward for her services. The woman, used to being treated as a slave or a plaything, accepted her smaller wage without murmur. But Progress never really stops on her upward path, though she sometimes seems to lose her way, and within the last decade or two vast strides have been made in the movements to better the conditions surrounding women who must work in the public mart. Thinking men realize that their own protection as labor units demands the removal of conditions which make them compete with cheap labor. That this competition is a menace to the men is shown over and over again in the apportionment of our teachers. Recently 200 women and only three men were appointed from the License No. 1 list. When the Chairman of the Committee on Elementary Schools was appealed to by the men for an explanation as to why more men were not appointed, he said in effect it was because women are cheaper.

*"Work is work, no matter who accomplishes it, and if women can do as well as men they should have the same pay."*

Mr. McAdoo has in these words voiced the slogan of the women teachers of the City of New York in their fight for a revision of the salary schedules. When the Mayor, the members of the Board of Education, and the members of the Board of Estimate and Apportionment of this great city hold the same just view of work and pay as does Mr. McAdoo, then indeed will the women teachers' fight be won.

"But," say the opponents of the women teachers, "it is not justice, but more money the women want." And apparently we have found it impossible to change this view in the minds of the male teachers and the members of the Board of Education that oppose us. Yet when the Interborough Association of Women Teachers submitted to its members the question: *Would you support a bill * providing an increase of 40 per cent in your salary but not embodying the principle of "Equal Pay,"* "No" formed 99.4 per cent of all the answers received.

The editor of the New York *Sun,* however, has shown that *he understands* the aim of women teachers in their campaign, in the following editorial on "The Equal Pay Veto" published May 15, 1909:

"Emphasis is laid by his Honor on the fact that, according to certain experts, the proposed change would add $6,000,000 a year to the budget. But, in spite of the other

* Such a bill was introduced in 1907 by Assemblyman Francis (Rep.), at the request of a man receiving $2400, as assistant to principal, though serving as principal of a school of *seven* classes, ranging in grade from Kindergarten to 3B. Needless to say, the bill provided an increase for him also.

fact that this side of the question was aired at the hearing, and on other occasions, it is clear that it is a very weak argument. 'Give us justice. That is all we ask,' say the women. 'Oh, but it would be so expensive,' say the men. A very lame and ridiculous rejoinder. Besides, sordid as the defense is, it would be more conclusive if we lived in a city and state in which strict economy was regarded as one of the things earnestly sought after by persons in office.

"Well, the ladies don't get the money, not just yet. They must go on paying a tax on the accident of birth. They may command in the schoolroom, but, when the time for remuneration comes around, must realize that in this best regulated of all possible worlds, doublet and hose is superior to petticoat.

"Now, in a case like this, the main thing is to get attention. The women court inquiry, investigation. From the beginning their appeal has been to the record of the work done. The mayor announces that he will appoint a commission to investigate the whole question in all its aspects. It is safe to predict this will cause jubilation in the camp of the women and gloom among the men in the department.

"In the meantime, the opponents of the measure might cast about for some new arguments, for there is reason to believe that they will be needed before long."

I quote the above because it expresses the facts so succinctly. It is a recognition of the truth that not only justice, but all arguments worth while are on the side of the women teachers. Ours is a question of *justice*—not of religion or prejudice or money. Yet there are many who claim that the opposition in some instances is racial, in others, religious. If we were to consider such criticism seriously, we would need to imagine ourselves back in the Middle Ages, centuries before our great wars of the Revolution and the Rebellion had been fought and won, instead of right here in the imperial city of imperial America in the twentieth century.

But Mr. McAdoo and the editor of the *Sun* do not stand alone. One of the most prominent judges in the United States, Hon. William J. Gaynor of the Appellate Division of the Supreme Court of New York, presided at a magnificent mass meeting held on behalf of the women teachers and spoke earnestly on the worthiness of their cause. Other judges of the same court, Hon. John Woodward and Hon. Luke D. Stapleton, presided at the first and second annual banquets of our great organization, and not only honored us by their presence, but strengthened our cause by their splendid addresses.

It would be a herculean task to name all the prominent men and women who have publicly espoused our cause, to say nothing of the thousands upon thousands of noble men and women who are ot in the "prominent" class, but whose encouragement has been very sweet, and whose assistance has been very valuable to us.

The remarkable majorities given our "Equal Pay" bills by Senate and Assembly of 1907, 1908, and 1909, have been striking evidence of the strength and popularity of our cause. Senator Horace White, the "father" of the "White Bill" of 1907 and of 1908, became the Lieutenant-Governor of 1909. Senator Gledhill, the father of the "1909" bill, was honored by appointment to a place on the Legislative Committee authorized to report on the proposed new charter for this city. Senator Thomas F. Grady has never missed an opportunity of supporting our cause. Our first bill was introduced by Senator Patrick H. McCarren (Dem.). This bill was not reported out by the Cities' Committee, the so-called "White Bill" being prepared and reported out instead. The Assembly bills of 1907 and 1908 were both fathered by Hon. Robert S. Conklin (Rep.), that of 1909 by Hon. James A. Foley (Dem.). Both Secretary of State John S. Whalen (Dem. and Ind.) and Secretary of State Samuel S. Koenig (Rep.) have rendered us valuable aid. Our bitterest opponents in Senate and Assembly, Senator Travis and Assemblyman Lee, have both said they believed in "Equal Pay," but have opposed our bill on account of its *cost in dollars and cents.*

What would have been thought of the colonist of 1775 who said he believed in the principle of "Taxation without Representation" but objected to the *cost in pence* of the tax on tea? We can feel respect for the man who opposes our bill because he is, on account of heredity, environment, mode of life, or some disappointment in mother, sister, wife or sweetheart, still of the opinion that a woman even when she does a piece of work as well as a man, should be paid less than a man simply and solely because she is a woman; but what respect can one have for him who says he believes a request is *just,* but refuses to grant it because it might cost each taxpayer *one cent* more on every thousand cents of the assessed valuation of his taxable property? Can such a one be a true citizen of the United States?

"But," some may ask, "why have the women teachers of the city of New York carried their fight to Albany. Why have they not appealed to their own Board of Education? To their own Board of Estimate and Apportionment? To their own Board of Aldermen?"

We answer: We have done all these things. We organized as "The Interborough Association of Women Teachers" in April, 1906, and at once formally and respectfully petitioned our Board of Education to revise the salary schedules so that teachers occupying the same position would receive the same pay. Our request was never acknowledged, but we learned through the minutes of a subsequent meeting of the board that the Committee on By-Laws and Legislation, to which our communication had been referred, asked "to be excused from further consideration of the matter."

We then began systematic work with the individual members of both the Board of Education and the Board of Estimate. In the interviews with these members, we found that few, if any, realized the enormity of the discrimination against women teachers in the present salary schedules. The mayor, George B. McClellan, persistently refused to grant an interview to me or any other member or any committee of our organization. This attitude

HON. PATRICK H. MCCARREN,

FATHER OF FIRST "EQUAL PAY" BILL EVER INTRODUCED, FEB. 6, 1907. STRONG, FAITHFUL, STEADFAST FRIEND OF THE WOMEN TEACHERS. DIED OCTOBER, 1909.

caused us much chagrin, disappointment, and sorrow; especially as we knew that members of the Board of Education, our strongest opponent, had access to his presence and his attention. We—in our simplicity, shall it be said?—felt that he was *our* mayor as much as he *theirs,* even though we were women and they were men; for are we not all citizens of the municipality over which he presided? Yet here is an organization comprising over twelve thousand of the women selected to be educators of the city's children, denied a word with the chief executive of that city, either as mayor or as President of the Board of Estimate and Apportionment.

In contrast to this attitude of the mayor, the Board of Aldermen had each year of our fight unanimously adopted a resolution in favor of the women teachers.

In the fall of 1906, a second appeal for a hearing was sent to the Board of Education, and this time the By-Law Committee fixed a date for such a hearing. *Two* of the five members of this committee and no other of the *forty-six* members of the board attended. It was evident that the plea of the women teachers fell on stony ground.

The work of this year made it clear to the women teachers that they themselves must go to Albany, the state capital, and seek the amendment to Section 1091 of the charter, which would eliminate therefrom the words "male" and "female" and cause teachers to be paid according to the position held and not according to their sex. Yet many citizens have criticized us for so doing. Personally, I see no good reason why the women teachers should not appeal to their legislators at Albany for relief from an injustice that was legalized by chapter four hundred and sixty-six of the laws of 1900. Governor Hughes in his veto message on our bill justified such appeal in these words: "The board of education is thus directly subject to the control of the Legislature, and whatever provisions may be found necessary or wise for the purpose of defining its powers or *prescribing its policy, must be prescribed by the Legislature. No other authority is competent to make such provision.*" Therefore, it is proven that while we had shown courtesy to our home officials in applying to them for relief, we might as reasonably have applied to the ice man for a ton of hay.

The campaign of 1907 was carried on mainly at Albany. The "Equal Pay" bill reported out by the Senate Cities' Committee, and familiarly known as the "White Bill," passed the Senate with a vote of 45 to 1, and the Assembly with a vote of 105 to 15. It was bitterly opposed by the Board of Education and some male principals and teachers. We expected Mayor McClellan to veto it. He did. It was re-passed by the Senate and Assembly with votes of 37 to 9 and 82 to 55 respectively. We did *not* expect Governor Hughes' veto, because we believed him to be a lover of justice and thought he would see that *justice* demanded this change in the state law. His veto ended the campaign of 1907.

The campaign of 1908 was also carried on at Albany. The White Bill again passed the Senate with more than a two-thirds vote, but was killed in the Committee on Rules of the Assembly. Apparently, the chairman of the New York County Republican Committee had more influence with the Rules Committee than did the Assembly itself, because although 104 of the 150 members of the Assembly signed a petition requesting that committee to report our bill out, their prayer availed naught. Furthermore, I was told that if the petition were signed by every member except the five forming the Committee on Rules, the bill would *not* be reported out on account of the approaching gubernatorial election. It was evident that the power of an organization comprising 12,000 women was given serious consideration. And so ended the campaign of 1908. We were encouraged by the indubitable evidence that had political exigencies not been in the way, our bill would have again passed the Legislature.

The campaign of 1909 had two new features—the "Conciliation Committee" and the Charter Revision Commission. The Conciliation Committee consisted of seven men and seven women, four of whom—two men and two women—were not members of the supervising or teaching force.

Of the "outsiders," the two men were ex-presidents of the Board of Education, while one of the women was a member of a local school board and the other of the Public Education Society. The report of this committee, signed by twelve of its members—the other two, both Manhattan male teachers, having resigned—became the text of the bill of 1909.

The legislative campaign of this year was short, because it was not until after we learned definitely that the new charter was not to become law this session, that the "Equal Pay" bill was introduced. It was passed in the Senate by a vote of 38 to 3, and in the Assembly by 126 to 14.

This year we did *not* expect the mayor's veto. We believed that both the mayor and the governor would study the history of this bill, would note its final vote in the Legislature after three years of public agitation both here and at Albany, would consider the number of members elected and re-elected after voting in favor of the women teachers, would appreciate the fact that many thousands of taxpayers had signed petitions in favor of the "Equal Pay" bills, would compare the judges, rabbis, ministers, priests, lawyers, business men and others speaking and writing in favor of the women teachers' cause, with the members of the Board of Education and of the male teaching force opposing these bills, and that they would consider such a demand from the people superior to any personal or private demand in connection with this legislation.

But the mayor *did* veto the bill. However, he recognized the importance of a matter which had for nearly four years demanded and received public attention by providing for a commission to investigate the question of teachers' salaries. That the dignity of our cause was also recognized is indicated by the personnel of the commission appointed: Hon. Joseph H. Choate, Mr. W. C. Brown, President of the New York Central Railroad, and Prof. John Bates Clark, of Columbia University. Mr. Choate declined the appointment and Mr. Brown at first accepted, but later resigned. Their places were filled by the appointment of Gustav Schwab, President of the North German Lloyd Steamship Company, and Charles Hallam Keep, President of the Knickerbocker Trust Company. Their report submitted in December, 1909, decided nothing, and added nothing new to the discussion, but made much of the "Law of Supply and Demand."

On December 17, 1909, a great mass meeting was held in Carnegie Hall, Hon. Mirabeau L. Towns presiding, which unanimously and enthusiastically adopted a resolution providing for Equal Pay in instalments covering five years, which was approved by Mayor McClellan in a letter in which he condemned the application of "the harsh rule of the commercial world—law of supply and demand" to "a condition so different from the average problems of daily life."

On December 22, 1909, a similar resolution was introduced in the Board of Education by Commissioner Arthur S. Somers, and hence is now called the "Somers' Resolution."

The introduction of this resolution by Commissioner Somers marks a great speech in our history—the championing of our cause by one of the members of our own board.

January 1, 1910, a new Board of Estimate came into power, and one of its earliest acts was to authorize the appointment of a new commission on teachers' salaries, on a resolution offered by Hon. John Purroy Mitchell, President of the Board of Aldermen, which provided that the commission consist of five members, two to be appointed by the mayor—Hon. William J. Gaynor, two by the comptroller—Hon. William A. Prendergast, and one by the President of the Board of Aldermen.

The following have been named: Mrs. Frank H. Cothren, Mr. Clinton L. Rossiter, Dr. Lee K. Frankel, Mr. Leonard P. Ayres, Mr. James M. Gifford.

We court inquiry along pertinent lines. The women teachers have nothing to fear from an investigation. We believe that the more thoroughly and more widely the matter is understood, the better it is for us. There is always, however, the danger that a commission will deal with a live, concrete problem as if it were a dead, abstract one. We would like the members of this commission to visit the schools, and see the teachers at work, we would like them to have the power to put those whom they call before them on oath, and to be sure that they were dealing with facts, not opinions; with conditions, not theories.

We consider all inquiries as to our "needs" as not pertinent. We hold that if the daughter of a millionaire, or even Hetty Green herself, should qualify and secure a position as teacher in our public schools, the city should pay her according to the position it permits her to hold, regardless of her "needs" as compared with those of other teachers, either male or female. Let it not be forgotten that 99 per cent of the women who work are doing so, because through inability, indifference, dissipation, illness, or death, some man—father or husband or brother—has made it necessary. And shall we be called upon to publish these facts? For instance, I know a teacher, ill herself, who pays the board of an insane uncle so that her mother's brother may not become a charge on the state. Should she be called upon to tell this? Has it any just bearing on the amount of money the city should pay her for teaching some of its children?

Meantime, we have been greatly encouraged by the attitude of the Charter Revision Committees. The Ivins Commission, 1908-9, provided for "like salaries" for "like positions." The Legislative Charter Commission—1909—recommended "The classes and grades and salaries of each class and grade of members of the supervising and teaching staffs shall be fixed with regard to the duties and responsibilities of the position and the fitness and experience of the appointee thereto or incumbent therein, irrespective of sex."

The Legislative Charter Commission bill—1910—contained a similar clause in parentheses with a note explaining that the vote as to whether or not it should be included in final report to Legislature, was a tie.

This clause was eliminated by the Assembly Cities Committee under the influence of Mr. Warren I. Lee, but on

May 23, 1910, was restored by the Assembly at the request of Mr. A. E. Smith, by a vote of 78 to 12.

Among the prominent advocates of "Equal Pay" we quote Mr. J. Edward Swanstrom: "The contention of the women teachers is that they are fighting for a principle and not merely for an increase in salaries. This principle may be briefly stated to be 'equal pay for equal work,' that is to say, for work of a given position women shall receive pay with men. This principle prevailed during the many years that I was President of the Brooklyn Board of Education, and there is much to be said in its favor. To pay a woman teacher a salary of $1,000 for doing the same kind of work—and doing it as well—for which a male teacher receives a salary of $1,500, seems very much like imposing a tax of $500 upon the woman teacher, merely because she is a woman. Miss Strachan, the able leader of the women teachers in their equal-pay crusade, characterizes such discrimination as degrading."

We point with pleasure to the following extract from the minutes of the Board of Education, City of New York, March 27, 1907:

"From the Secretary of the City Club of New York, stating that at a meeting of the trustees of said club, held on March 20, 1907, the following resolution was adopted:

"'Resolved, That this board recommend to the Board of Education that women teachers in the City of New York should receive the same salary as men teachers for the same amount and quality of work.'"

About the same time, the Public Education Association wrote to the Board of Education, telling them that the association favored paying men and women the same salary for the same positions, and submitting the opinion that the board should do all possible to get the Board of Estimate to endorse such a scheme.

The following quotations show that even our opponents are in favor of "Equal Pay":

Senator Fuller:—"I believe in the principle of equalization as fully as any other senator. I believe women should get the same salaries as men."—In Senate, Apr. 15, 1907.

Senator Travis:—"I desire to say to my colleagues that I have never opposed the principle of equal pay."—In Senate, 1908.

Assemblyman Lee told our committee he believed in the "Equal Pay" principle; but he opposed us on the ground of "expediency."

Edgar S. Shumway, at meeting of Presidents of Associations, Board Rooms, April 1, 1909:—"I am free to say that if the money were under my control, I would see to it that the woman who is first assistant in a High School, as I am, received as much money as I received."

Sidney C. Walmsley:—"We do not raise objections to equalization." (Hearing before Senate Cities Committee, Feb. 26, 1907.)

City Superintendent Maxwell, in Tenth Annual Report:—"With regard to women principals it must be quite clear to anyone familiar with the work of the board of examiners that it is quite as difficult to obtain women principals of the requisite scholastic and professional attainments and executive ability as it is to obtain men principals. On this ground I recommend that as soon as money is available the salaries of women principals be equalized with those of men."

Commenting on the above, the *Globe* of Jan. 10, 1908, said:

"The Board of Education has found it more difficult to obtain women teachers of the requisite ability than it is to obtain men teachers. Evidence of this fact is shown in the action of the board of examiners, in granting concessions in examinations to the women teachers in order to increase the supply. It has not granted concessions to the men. On this ground it would seem that the salaries of women teachers should be at least 'equalized with those of men.'"

One of the most regrettable features of the agitation has been an evident distrust of the Board of Education.

Mr. Harrison, member of board, at mayor's hearing, May 11, 1909:—"That is our first objection to this bill—

a four mills appropriation to the general school fund. Four mills on the assessed valuation would amount to $7,158,-190—that enormous sum. This amount would be placed in the hands of the Board of Education to disburse, and it is quite a general rule, quite the tendency of human nature, that anybody having seven millions of money to spend, finds some means to spend it." And

Mr. Stern:—"There has never been in the history of the Board of Education any year in which there has been any excess placed in the treasury and if this bill passes, I can assure you, acting in good faith, there will be so many activities presented to us that the taxpayers will find that there never will be any excesses paid back into the treasury."

And yet the records of the comptroller's office show that on May 22, 1903, the Board of Education returned a surplus of $1,000,000 from 1900 taken from the general appropriation school fund. On the same date they turned in $330,000 from the general school fund appropriation for 1910, to be turned into the general fund for the reduction of taxes.

Do I hear some reader ask: *What is the cause of all this agitation? What is it all about?* Let me cite a few prominent examples of the "glaring inequalities" and "gross injustices"—the words quoted are from Governor Hughes' message on our bill—existing in the present salary schedules.

Suppose a boy and a girl—they may even be twins—have been sent to the same schools, been taught by the same teachers, passed the same examinations, and finally been appointed to teach classes identical in grade and sex of pupils. Suppose both succeed to the satisfaction of their superior officers, and appear for their reward. Is it not the same for both? Oh, no! The one who was the boy, simply because of his sex, receives a yearly salary $330 higher than that of the one born a girl.

How long would a woman have to teach a similar class of boys in order to receive the salary a man receives the first year? *Seven years.* And not then even would she receive it, unless she had passed the examination by both principal and district superintendent for renewal of license at the end of the first year, again at the end of the second year, and for permanent license at the end of the third year. Her record being satisfactory, she would receive an increase of $40 each year, until the end of the seventh year. Her salary would then be $840, and would remain such unless she be rated as "fit and meritorious" by both principal and superintendents. Thus you see, a woman teacher must teach seven years and pass satisfactorily through four examinations before she receives a salary equal to that of a man teaching the identical class would receive the *first* year. But what would the man teacher be receiving in *his* seventh year? This is indeed interesting. Instead of an increase of $40 each year he has been receiving one of $105, so that his salary has mounted to $1,530. The percentage of increase in the case of the man is so much larger than in the case of the woman that the original discrepancy of 50 per cent grows from year to year until after twelve years of service he receives $2160, and she for the same work and the same sacrifice of years earns $1080, *or just one-half of what he receives.*

Take another instance. It is a well recognized principle that the supervisor should be paid a higher salary than the person supervised by him. Yet in our remarkable schedule of salaries the maximum salary of an assistant to principal, *if a woman,* is $1600, though she supervises male teachers who receive as high as $2160 and even $2400. Bear in mind that these male teachers are not eligible to hold the position she does, that she must have had at least eight years of experience before she is permitted to take the examination for license as assistant to principal, and that this examination is so difficult that sixty per cent of those who took it in 1907, failed.

Again, to be principal one must have had at least ten years of experience, must have passed an examination, which records prove to be very difficult, and must have waited often as long as four years for appointment from an eligible list. Supposing a most unusual case, that a woman becomes a principal in her twelfth year of service, her salary of $1750 as such, is $305 *less than that of a male teacher,* also in his twelfth year of service, who may be teaching a "baby class," and is $650 less than that of a male teacher of a graduating class. Her maximum salary of $2500 is only $100 more than that of a male teacher, who may have a small class of girls in the graduating class, while she may have the responsibility of a school of 3000 pupils and the supervision of sixty teachers. A male principal of the identical school would receive $1000 a year more than the woman.

Such examples as these indicate that a consideration incompatible with the principle that all citizens are equal before the law has been influential in determining that a position when filled by one person shall command a higher salary than when filled by another person, though the work is equally well done and equally satisfactory in results.

In spite of the importance attached to the question of cost in some quarters, it is a minor consideration in comparison with the equities of the situation. The constitution of the state provides that no citizen's property shall be taken from him without proper compensation; and it is to the honor of our government in all its divisions that complaint is seldom or never heard that private property is taken without paying for it all that it is worth. It certainly is not contemplated that in any phase of government, or any branch of the public service, citizens shall be required to work for less than their services are worth. It would be fatal to the future and the fame of any legislator or of any man in public life, to advocate a law which should provide that a woman teacher in the schools of New York City should work *twelve* hours and a male teacher *six* hours for the same pay. Yet that is an exact equivalent of what the present schedules do. The principle is identically the same as though a law were enacted compelling her to work two hours to his one in order to get the same compensation. To propose such a rule would excite derision and contempt. Why should the law now in existence not meet with the same derision and contempt, and be speedily amended?

The Interborough Association of Women Teachers of the City of New York predicts that it will.

Our Association early in 1908 gathered some statistics.* They showed 377 women—eleven of them married and six widows—supporting 707 others besides themselves. These teachers are all women, but the people depending wholly upon them or partly upon them are their mothers or their fathers or both or a brother or a sister or a niece or a nephew. These are actual figures collated from written answers to our questionnaire. You see, then, that here is an average of two people for every woman to support besides herself. Now, what salary is offered to these young women of twenty-one years of age, after they have spent all these years in preparing for the position of teacher? What salary is she being paid by the City of New York, the greatest city in the world, with the greatest public school system in the world? $11.53 a week. A woman in charge of one of the stations in the city gets more than that. Does the latter have to spend as much money on clothes? No. She can wear the same clothes from one end of the year to the other if she wants to, and not be criticised. But I know when I go into a classroom, among the things that I notice is the teacher's dress—whether it is neat, whether it is appropriate. She must be a model for her class. Besides, the teacher must live in a respectable neighborhood and make a good appearance at home and abroad, and she must continue her studies in order to give satisfactory service.

Another thing that we must not forget is that *a teacher has to eat and live on Saturday and Sunday and during the summer holidays.* A member of the Board of Education said to me that although $11.53 was not a big salary in the City of New York, that a teacher only worked five days.

* Our experience with this questionnaire showed us that the teachers resented—and we felt the resentment was justified—our inquiry into their family affairs. A few resigned because of it.
G. C. S.

Well, that is the number of days we are in school. But those who know teachers, know that we work other days and other nights and often all summer, preparing to make ourselves more valuable to our pupils and our employer. But whether we work or not, we must have something to eat and somewhere to sleep, and something to wear on those other days. And furthermore, the hours and the vacations are the same for the men teachers as for the women teachers. So that does not seem a very fair reason to give why salaries should not be equalized.

Another reason sometimes given for paying men more is that they are needed for special work in the schools. If they are, the Board of Education should classify those positions. We hear some talk about the need for athletics. We shall be glad if the men assist in the athletics. But I knew a school of 48 classes with no man teacher except the one in the shop, that graduated about 200 boys and girls a year, and during one term the athletic teams in that school beat almost every school they played with. And I knew another school of equal size and grade that had three men teachers besides the one in the shop, and it didn't win a single game—because it didn't have any athletic teams.

In evidence of the world-wide character of the subject of "Equal Pay for Equal Work," I quote the following:

New York *Times,* 1908—In Shaffhausen the women teachers have won the equal-pay fight in which New York women have failed.

Recently there was held in Nancy, France, the first congress of university women. All classes of public school teachers were represented, and many questions relating to the schools were discussed, but the most important was equal pay for the women teachers in the elementary schools.

This agitation for equal pay in France is of long standing, as on March 13, 1886, M. Goblet offered an amendment to the law fixing the salaries of the men and women teachers at the same rate. But the lack of sufficient funds prevented it from becoming a law. Another effort was made in 1889 and again in 1905. In 1907 a parliamentary commission declared itself in favor of the principle of equal pay for equal work, and it was decided to organize a campaign to secure legislation on this subject. At the following election this was the most important question in the provinces. This campaign has been carried on most earnestly for the past two years. Societies of university women have been founded in nearly every school district in France. These have been united in a very powerful federation, the secretary general of which is a brave teacher of Lorraine, Mlle. Marie Gueron of Laxoules—Nancy. A huge petition in favor of equal salaries has been circulated in all the public schools of France and tens of thousands signatures have been gathered.

"A dispute over the equal pay of women and men physicians has just terminated in Halifax. The dispute began by the issue of an advertisement by the Halifax Board of Guardians for a resident woman physician at a salary of $500 a year. Previously the position had been held by a man at a salary of $750 a year. The matter was taken up at once by the London School of Medicine for Women, which called the attention of the British Medical Association to it. The *British Medical Journal* got interested and as a result of its warning the woman physician who had applied for and received the place resigned. In July the Guardians appointed another woman to the place. This woman, when her attention was called to the dispute, asked to be released from the appointment and the bond of $250 which she had agreed to forfeit in case she failed to serve twelve months. This brought the Halifax Board of Guardians to terms and established the principle of equal pay for men and women physicians so far as they are concerned."

### TEACHERS' EQUAL PAY FIGHT

(New York *Press*)

"There is trouble about the salary of women teachers in New South Wales, Australia, almost paralleling the fight that the women teachers have waged for several years in this city for equal pay for equal work with men. The Australian women teachers also charged they were underpaid in comparison with the men teachers. The Women's Progressive Association of New South Wales took the lead in the fight, which has ended its first phase with complete victory for the women teachers. An appropriation of $300,000 for increase in teachers' salaries was made, and the men calmly proceeded to grab the entire amount. A vigorous protest was made by the association, but it was not until after a bitter fight that it was directed women teachers should share equally in the increase. The women, however, found argument and persuasion useless, and it was not until they threatened to make use of their voting privilege in a body that they won their point. Now the teachers are going on for equal pay all around, and they are confident they will score a second and greater victory."

### WHERE EDUCATION IS WORTH WHILE

(The *Globe* )

"Frequent expression is given to the view that teachers in New York City ought to be happy with their lot, for the reason that they are better paid than teachers elsewhere, and that conditions here are better. But evidence is growing to prove that these are not the facts.

"In Argentina, which is coming to be regarded as one of the most progressive nations of the earth, education and the 'business' of school teaching is put first of all duties. There they do not pay out their revenues for all sorts of things and divide what is left among the teachers.

"The teachers' pay is placed first among obligations. After a certain length of service the teacher is put on the retired list and her pay goes on till death. As high as $2,000 is paid to retired teachers. The close of a thirty years' service is made a great event, greater than the opening of an exposition or the inauguration of a governor. And New York is called progressive."

## EXPLANATORY NOTES

"I. A. W. T." or "Interborough" means Interborough Association of Women Teachers.

"Board" means Board of Education.

"Board of Estimate" means Board of Estimate and Apportionment.

In New York City, the course in the elementary schools covers eight years. Each year covers two grades. The first half is designated by "A," the second, by "B." Thus 5A grade means first half of fifth year; 8B, last half of eighth year.

Knowing that the public would be justified in thinking me prejudiced in favor of "Equal Pay," I have used so many quotations from authorities of far higher rank than myself that the book is almost wholly a compilation. I have included many of the speeches made at the hearings, mass meetings, and banquets where our "Cause" was discussed. I have also letters and articles that have appeared in the public press, as well as personal letters. Should I, by an oversight, have used any personal letter without the writer's permission, I hope I shall be pardoned. I wish I could have included every word that has been said or written in our behalf, every name that has been signed to a petition. We appreciate every one.

The book is in six parts.

Part I—History, story, and some arguments.

Part II—Addresses.

Part III—Editorial comment.

Part IV—Letters.

Part V—Endorsements: Board of Aldermen, Business, Editors, Artists, Literateurs, Educators, Judges, Lawyers, Doctors, Labor Unions, Political Clubs and Officials, Religious, Women's Clubs.

Part VI—Documents.

## CHRONOLOGICAL SUMMARY.

### 1906.

"Consolidation" and Need of Uniform Schedules for Greater New York.
Ahearn Law, 1898-99.
Davis Law, 1900.
Organization of Interborough Association of Women Teachers, 1906.
Petition to Board of Education.
Individual members of Board petitioned.
How Much Will It Cost?
Committee waits on President Winthrop.
Committee waits on Mayor McClellan.
Committee waits on other members of Board of Estimate.
Interborough Association of Women Teachers again asks hearing.

### 1907.

Hearing—Attended by Mr. Harrison and Mr. Stern—Board of Education.
Committee goes to Albany.
Committee sees Governor Hughes, Lieutenant-Governor Chanler and Speaker Wadsworth.
McCarren Bill introduced.
Conklin Bill introduced.
Report of Committee on By-Laws.
Hearing on McCarren Bill.
Hearing in Assembly on Conklin Bill.
White Bill passes Senate 45 to 1.
Hearing in Assembly on White Bill.
White Bill passes Assembly 105 to 15.
Hearing before Mayor McClellan.
McClellan Veto.
White Bill re-passes Senate 37 to 9.
White Bill re-passes Assembly 82 to 55.
Hearing before Governor Hughes.
Governor Hughes' veto.
First annual banquet.
Board of Education proposes increases.

### 1908.

Cooper Union Mass Meeting—Jan. 20—John Francis Yawger, presiding.
Association Hall Mass Meeting—Mar. 6th—Hon. William J. Gaynor, presiding.
"White" Bill passes Senate 35 to 8.
"White" Bill held in Committee on Cities, Assembly.
"White" Bill held in Committee on Rules, Assembly.
Committee appeals to Committee on Rules.

Petition to Committee on Rules signed by 104 Assemblymen.
Second annual banquet.
Board of Education proposes increases.

1909.

Ivins Charter Revision Commission reports "like salaries" for "like positions."
Conciliation Committee.
Report of Conciliation Committee.
Meeting of Presidents of Associations—President Winthrop, presiding.
"Conciliation Committee" schedules approved by vote of 15 to 7.
Apr. 6—Hearing on Educational Chapter at Albany, Charter dead.
Davis-Smith Bill introduced.
Gledhill Bill passes Senate 38 to 3.
Apr. 24—Third annual banquet.
Gledhill-Foley Bill passes Assembly 26 to 14.
Board of Education disapproves Gledhill-Foley Bill.
May 11—Mayor McClellan's hearing.
Mayor McClellan's veto.
Board of Education proposes increases.
Hearing—Charter Legislative Committee.
Hearing—Budget.
Dec. 17—Carnegie Hall Mass Meeting, Hon. Mirabeau L. Towns, presiding.
Dec. 22—Somers Resolution, Board of Education.

1910.

Board of Estimate Commission.
Jan. 22—City Club "Equal Pay" luncheon.
Report of Charter Legislative Commission carries "Equal Pay."
Mar. 16—"Equal Pay" meeting of Board of Education votes down Somers Resolution 23 to 16.
Brief on Constitutionality of Davis Law.
Additions to Charter Legislative Commission.
Mar. 20—Injunction against Board of Education to prevent promotion of man of 5 years experience to Graduating Class over the heads of many eligible women.
April 16—Fourth annual banquet.
April 18—"Equal Pay" clause eliminated by Assembly Cities, Assembly.
Injunction sustained.
May 23—"Equal Pay" clause restored to Charter by Assembly—78 to 12.

## CHAPTER II

### ARE MEN TEACHERS NEEDED?

The question, "Are Men Teachers Needed?" presupposes others:

(a) Is there some appreciable difference between men as teachers and women as teachers that justifies the placing of "Men Teachers" in a special and privileged class, paying them special and privileged salaries?

(b) Are there some special purposes for which men are needed?

(c) Are men better teachers than women?

As to the first, I am compelled to state that after a long and varied experience as pupil, teacher, principal and superintendent, in both day and evening schools, I am not able to answer in the affirmative except to state that the average woman teacher is superior to the average man teacher in all the qualities that go to the making of good and noble men and women.

### ARE MEN TEACHERS NEEDED?

I think no better answer to this question could be written than the following description of the Indianapolis schools by Associate City Superintendent Andrew W. Edson, of New York City, which appeared in the *Globe*, March 18, 1910. It must be remembered that the description is of elementary schools having an eight-year course, as ours have, and that the teachers and principals are all women, and—best of all—the classes are all mixed. When will New York City be so progressive as to do away with the Oriental custom of separating our boys and girls?

Mr. Edson says: "The average work of the schools is high. Some of it is about the same as may be found in New York, certainly not better; some of it is decidedly in advance. I wish to speak of a few aspects of the schools that may be of especial interest to New York teachers.

"In several schools algebra and Latin are taught in the eighth year of the elementary course. These studies are offered only to those pupils who show exceptional ability in mathematics and language studies. German, as an elective, is taught from the second to the eighth year. Opportunity is given all pupils who maintain a high standard in the elementary schools to gain one-half year's credit in the high schools in algebra, Latin, German, civics, and advanced English.

"Civics:—The study of civics takes place in history in the last half year of the elementary school course. The pupils are provided with copies of Dunn's 'The Community and the Citizen.' The author of this book is the director of civics in the schools of the city. Owing partly to the fact that the plan of the book and the effort of the teachers present the subject in such an interesting and practical manner, to the fact that some one supervises the work closely and supplies mimeographed copies of practical suggestions to the teachers from time to time, and to the further fact that sufficient time and attention are given to the subject, the instruction in civics was the most satisfactory of any I have ever observed.

The great aim seemed to be the creation of an interest in community relations and the formation of habits of civic thought and action. Teachers and pupils made the subject intensely interesting by the introduction of so much that was local and personal.

"Mathematics: The point of special interest in the teaching of arithmetic is an innovation attempted this year in dispensing with a text-book in the seventh and eighth years, and the substitution therefor of sets of problems prepared by a committee of the teachers. The problems all bear upon the prices of articles in the local meat markets, grocery stores, department stores and the manufacturing establishments in the city and state; the cost of running the city departments, including the schools, fire, police and street cleaning; the local improvements, tax rate, bond issues, railroad and bank issues; the cost of labor and production. The work is a novel attempt to make the study of arithmetic eminently practical to the pupils in the Indianapolis schools.

"English: There seemed to be a general agreement among the visiting superintendents that the one distinctive point of excellence in the Indianapolis schools is the study of English. The course of study and syllabus in this subject are very complete and suggestive. Much of the work in the seventh and eighth years is of a high school grade. In all the elementary grades special attention is given to good oral expression. In nearly every instance the pupils expressed themselves readily in correct English. There was a noticeable fluency of expression in several exercises observed. The attention of the pupils was directed to helpful criticism; the pupils were encouraged to note the use of choice English and the expressions deserving special commendation. A fine spirit prevailed.

"In several classes admirable teaching exercises were conducted, as follows: While the pupil was reciting, several pupils quietly arose from their seats. As soon as the pupil reciting had finished his statement, the pupils standing supplemented or challenged the statements made, or asked pointed questions of the one reciting. Often the statements of the supplementing or challenging brought others to their feet. The novelty of the plan, the alertness and intelligence of the pupils, and the fine spirit displayed, made these exercises intensely interesting.

"Manual Training: In the seventh and eighth years, the boys have shop work and the girls have cooking in special shop and cooking centers.

"In one school a modified course of study is arranged, and the boys and girls are given four and one-half hours per week in manual training; three hours in shop work, and one and one-half hours in mechanical drawing for the boys and one and one-half hours in cooking, one and one-half hours in sewing, and one and one-half hours in freehand drawing for the girls. The work of all grades appeared to be planned and carried out in lines eminently practical.

"Latin: In one of the schools Latin is made a live language. The teachers and pupils carry on the work by the conversational method—at least there is the freest exchange of opinions on the part of pupils in the use of Latin words and sentences to express thoughts. There is a constant challenge by the members of the class, with reasons for the same, on the form of expression, on the words that should be used in each particular instance.

"Pianola: In several of the schools pianolas have been secured through the efforts of the pupils or their friends. These pianolas are placed in the lower corridor, and once or twice a week, at the opening of the school, the classes throughout the building are entertained for some ten minutes. The doors of all classes are opened as some pupil operates the pianola. The name of the selection is written on the black-board in each room so that the pupils may become acquainted with the selection being rendered.

"Men teachers: The question of 'equal pay for equal work' is solved in Indianapolis, as men are entirely eliminated from the elementary grades, either as teachers or principals. All of the classes are mixed, so that no boys' 'bonus' classes are formed. And, if I was correctly informed, the salary schedule allows the same compensation in one elementary grade that it does in any other—a blessed relief in the assignment of teachers.

"I doubt if, all in all, a better school organization and better school work can be found in the United States than in Indianapolis."

I have quoted thus fully from Mr. Edson's letter, to show the excellence of the plans of work in all lines, and to call attention to the fact that all the teachers and even all the principals, are women.

In March, 1907, the Public Education Association sent a communication to the Board of Education, from which the following is quoted: "That the work of the women teachers is equal, if not superior, to that of the men engaged in teaching in the public schools seems not to be seriously disputed anywhere. It is also admitted that the women teachers in an increasing number make of their teaching a life work, while too many of the men regard it merely as a stepping-stone to be used only while they fit themselves for the law or some other profession.

"On the other hand, the changed economic conditions no longer justify paying the man a larger salary than the woman, on the ground that the support of a family is dependent upon his wage, inasmuch as a large proportion, at least, of the women teachers are devoting their wage to this identical purpose, while perhaps a majority of the men are still unmarried and looking elsewhere for a permanent support.

"While, for these reasons, the Public Education Association approves of the policy of 'equal pay,' it does not hold the teachers justified in going to Albany for legislation to make the adoption of such a policy mandatory upon the Board of Education. Not only is this step offensive to the policy of home rule, which in such a matter stands for the idea of local responsibility and self-respect, but it means the appeal from a body well informed to one less informed. The solution of the question rightly belongs, in our opinion, to the Board of Education, and we earnestly hope that it will take the matter up for the fullest investigation and consideration with a view to making an appeal to the city authorities for sufficient funds with which to pay salaries to both men and women commensurate with the work done."

This communication has been ordered "printed and filed" in the minutes of the board.

# CHAPTER III

## ARE MEN TEACHERS NEEDED FOR SPECIAL PURPOSES?

As to the second question, "Are men teachers needed for special purposes?" I am prepared to say that if the pupils are segregated in different buildings—which, by the way is a persistence of the monastic and nunnery ideas of the Middle Ages, that I, although a Catholic myself, deplore as abnormal and unnatural except for those who are specially called to the religious life—it would be consistent to select men as principals of boys' schools and women as principals of girls' schools. But, though our board does maintain many separate schools for boys and girls, it does not evidence this consistency in selecting its principals. While it is true that it has not appointed a woman as principal of an all-boys' school, it has put three of our largest girls' schools under the care of men, viz.—Wadleigh High School, Washington Irvine High School, and Girls' High School. This inconsistency has so affected the principal of the last named school that he apparently saw nothing inconsistent in his attitude when he attacked the schools of this city as being "feminized."

Another "special purpose" for which there is yet some ground to seek men rather than women, is the development of outdoor athletics. The education of our girls in outdoor sports is of such recent growth that there are not yet as many women as men prepared to take up this work. The time is not far distant, however, when this discrepancy will have disappeared. Meantime it is reasonable to select and pay the teachers—women as well as men—who do special work in this line. But it is not reasonable or fair to pay all men teachers—the majority of whom do not give any extra time to this special work—extra or special salaries on the plea that they are "needed for athletics." I have recently learned that the Board of Education *is* paying some men an additional bonus extra for "athletic work." This is explained in the following:

On September 25, 1907, the Board of Education adopted: "Resolved, That the director of physical training be empowered to designate teachers, either in the elementary schools or in the high schools, for after-school services, not to exceed one day at a time, for the purpose of aiding in the conduct of field days and athletic competitions of school children, and that the teachers so designated for such service receive $2.50 for an afternoon or for an evening, or for a Saturday morning."

On April 13, 1910, the by-law committee reported that in accordance with the above the custom has been to designate teachers to assist in the management of after-school athletics, and to reimburse them for services according to the above resolution, but a question having arisen as to the legality of paying the teachers referred to, in the absence of a by-law making specific provision for such payment, it submitted the following resolutions:

"Resolved, That section 42a. of the by-laws of the Board of Education be, and it is hereby amended by inserting therein a new subdivision to be known and designated as subdivision 2a, reading as follows:—2a. Subject to the committee on athletics, the director of physical training may assign persons holding licenses as teachers for the public schools to the control and management of after-school athletics; but no person so assigned shall serve for more than two days consecutively."

"Resolved, that schedule XIII, appearing in subdivision 18 of Sec. 65 of the By-laws of the Board of Education be, and it is hereby amended by adding thereto a new clause, reading as follows:—(f) Teachers assigned to the control and management of after-school athletics shall be paid $2.50 for service rendered in an afternoon, in an evening, or on a Saturday, this amendment to be considered as in effect from and after January 1, 1910." Adopted 26 to 5.

It is worthy of note that the whole trend of our board's treatment of the subject of athletics is to lay stress on the importance of athletics for boys. Now, I believe that the physical development of the girls, the future mothers of the race, is of far greater importance to the city and the state than the physical development of the boys. Moreover, it is more natural for boys to play games in the open air than it is for girls. Mother often wants Mary to "help with the dishes" or "mind the baby," when she is glad to have John "run out and play." Therefore, I hold that the city might much better be offering special rewards to its women teachers who give many hours in teaching its girls basket ball, football, folk dances, and other physical training exercises.

While I have heard much of the "special purposes" for which men are needed, the most diligent search of the City Charter and the By-laws of the Board fails to discover them; but Associate Superintendent Edson, in Mr. Maxwell's Tenth Annual Report, says:

"One of the most perplexing problems confronting the Committee and the Board of Superintendents at the present time, is the employment of men teachers. A few years ago, when there were many men and few women, on the eligible lists, and when the necessity for economizing in expense was not so pressing as it is at the present time, vacancies were filled by exhausting the eligible lists for both men and women. This gave many schools, especially in Manhattan, an unusually large proportion of men in the teaching ranks. Many of these men were assigned to work in the third, fourth and fifth years, as well as in the higher grades.

"This condition of affairs has continued to the present time with no definite policy established for determining the number of men that should be allowed each elementary school or the grade of work to which they should be assigned.

"There can be little question but that boys and even girls at some time in their elementary course need the oversight, instruction of manly men as well as of womanly women; men can teach and manage certain classes and can often teach certain subjects better than women can; and that they can be called upon to do certain lines of work more properly than women can, as for instance, to oversee the playgrounds and sanitaries, and to organize the athletics."

At last, the mystery is explained. At last the "special purposes," the "certain lines of work," are defined. "To oversee the playgrounds and sanitaries," "to organize athletics." And it is to be assumed that these are the "special purposes" which Superintendent Maxwell means when he says in the same report: "—men who are employed, not because on the average they teach the ordinary school branches better than women do, but for special purposes."

Think of it! The city is paying hundreds of men—all men teachers—from $300 to a $1000 a year bonus because a *few* of them police playgrounds, and a *few* others organize athletics.

With reference to this supervision of playgrounds and sanitaries, I can only say that every woman principal and every woman teacher should do her duty along this line. I must also say that I have seen poorer results in this direction in schools with men than in those without men. I do not assume that this is the rule or the probability. It may be that the man principal shirks his duty and responsibility in this particular the more, the greater number of men teachers in his corps. Furthermore, the board insists that a janitor engage a matron for the "girls' yard," and that he or a male assistant look after the "boys' yard." It is the principal's duty to see that the janitor does his duty. Surely, then, it cannot be reasonably maintained that a male teacher should be given several hundred dollars a year more for doing special "police" service for the relief of the principal.

Furthermore, if it is *necessary*—mind you, I say *necessary*—to have men "to oversee the playgrounds and sanitaries," is it not the duty of the Board to appoint at least one man teacher to every school? This it does not do. But if it is *necessary*—again, I ask you to note the word "necessary"—to have men for this purpose, the hundreds of schools without men teachers or even principals must evidence lack of this supervision of playgrounds and sanitaries. Do they? I can confidently say they do not; and it is plain that the board is of the same opinion, or it would not permit this lack. Even if more of this sort of supervision were necessary, the board might better hire a special assistant janitor in each playground than to pay *all* men teachers a large bonus for such purpose.

As to the boys and girls *needing* the oversight and instruction of men in their elementary course, I can do no better in refutation than to refer to Superintendent Edson's own statement on the elementary schools of Indianapolis, and to the records of many of our own schools which have and which want no men teachers. Out of an experience with the elementary school work probably at least equal to Superintendent Edson's, I say that there is great question of this necessity. Neither do I know of any subjects which authorities prove are better taught by *men*. Again it is a question simply of the *teacher*. But, even should it be granted that certain subjects are better taught by men, let us be fair and businesslike about it, and let us classify these subjects, and fix salary for teachers of such subjects; but when the teachers have been selected, let them be paid alike, whether they be all men or all women, or some men and some women.

# CHAPTER IV

## ARE MEN NEEDED BECAUSE THEY ARE BETTER TEACHERS?

Are Men Teachers Needed Because They are Better Teachers? I don't think so. But instead of setting forth some of my personal reasons growing out of my personal experience, I will rest content with submitting the opinions of others.

First as to discipline.

The *Evening Sun* of Feb. 14, 1908, says, editorially:—"The significant thing about the report made by the special committee of the Board of Education is to be found in the premises rather than the conclusion. The revival of the rod is suggested. There is nothing startling about that. What is important is the demonstration that conditions exist which cannot be met by the moral suasion, which is so characteristic of a soft and merciful age.

"No less than 208 of the principals and superintendents in this city are for the rod, while 181 oppose it. On the other hand, only 64 women favor corporal punishment, while 104 are against it. This may mean that the women are more successful disciplinarians than the men, even under present conditions."

The *World* of Feb. 15, 1908, commenting on the same report, says: "Does the sum of their replies confirm the common belief that women teachers are more successful in controlling children? That by tact, persuasion and moral influence they get better results than men? Otherwise, why is it that the men incline so much more than the women to the use of force?

"This is a fact that the Board of Education cannot afford to overlook in reaching a decision. In a way their demand for the whip reflects upon the efficiency of the men themselves. They would not ask for it if they knew they had succeeded without it."

### AS TO SCHOLASTIC RESULTS

Figures issued by Supt. Maxwell, bearing on the promotions to high schools, Jan. 1908, show that in Brooklyn, 90 per cent. of the pupils on register in the 8 B classes were graduated, while in the Bronx only 79 per cent. were successful. In the Bronx 16.4 per cent. of the teachers are male; in Brooklyn 10.9 per cent. It may be that more of the Bronx boys can win athletic prizes; but I know that any of my readers who have had sons and daughters "left back" after reaching the graduating class will not think that much of a compensation. In this connection, it is pertinent to quote the *Globe* of March 3, 1910, anent the "Athletic Scandal": "The school which has been hit hardest is No. ——, Bronx. The investigation showed that the Brooklyn schools, as a rule, followed the regulations."

There are several elementary schools with boys throughout all the grades that have had no male teachers. Those I know best are 3, 11, and 16 in Brooklyn (Nos. 11 and 16, since the death of Mr. Lewis and Mr. Dunkly, have some men teachers). Through the kindness of Miss Bliss, Miss McCalvey, and Miss Black, I am enabled to give the names of some prominent men who graduated from said schools. Can any four schools which boast as long a line of male teachers do better?

## PUBLIC SCHOOL No. 3, BROOKLYN

Hon. Alvah W. Burlingame, State Senator.
Borough President Alfred E. Steers.
Ex-Dist. Attorney James Ridgeway
Hon. William Berri.
Rev. George Hoyt.
Rev. Wilbur Caswell.
Dr. William Butler.
Mr. Conrad Keyes—Lawyer.
Mr. Homer Keys—Lawyer.
Mr. Gardner Dresser, Broker, in Wall Street.

## PUBLIC SCHOOL No. 16, BROOKLYN

Frederick L. Wurster, Ex-Mayor of the former City of Brooklyn.

Hon. William B. Hurd, Jr., Lawyer, formerly County Judge, Kings County.

Hon. William Cullen Bryant (Deceased), was Fire Commissioner of the City of Brooklyn and Publisher of the Brooklyn Daily *Times*.

Rev. John Donlon, Roman Catholic clergyman, well-known public speaker.

Almon Gunnison, President, St. Lawrence University.

Hon. Alfred Hobley, Ex-Sheriff Kings County.

Clarence Lyon, Secretary of the Williamsburgh Fire Ins. Co.—one of the largest insurance companies in the United States.

Morrison Gray, Custom House Broker.

Clarence H. Wandel, Lumber Merchant.

Herbert Ketcham, Brooklyn Surrogate.

Frank E. O'Reilly, City Magistrate, City of New York.

John McKee, of Cooper and McKee, Manufacturers of Refrigerators.

J. Wesly Rosengaert, Theatrical Manager, New York City.

David Myrtle, M. D., of Brooklyn.

Rev. Ralph Wood Kenyon, Episcopal clergyman in Brooklyn.

James A. Sperry, now publisher of the Brooklyn *Daily Times*, and a prominent newspaper man.

Daniel T. Wilson, Manager-partner of Flandraw and Co.—well-known carriage and automobile manufacturers. Ex-Pres., Hanover Club.

William J. Meyers, Manager, Union Stove Co., Beekman St. Largest concern of its kind.

T. W. Weeks, Sec. Barrett Manufacturing Co., of N. Y. City.

Luke O'Reilly, Prominent Criminal Lawyer.

PUBLIC SCHOOL No. 11, BROOKLYN

Mr. Seward Prosser, Vice-President of Astor Trust Co., 5th. Ave, and 36th. Street, N. Y.
Mr. Paul E. Bonner, Pres. North Side Bank of Brooklyn.
Arthur L. Smith, Cashier of Schermerhorn Branch of Mechanics Bank of Brooklyn.
Barent Van Beuthuysen, Paying Teller, National City Bank, Brooklyn.
Laurus E. Sutton, Brooklyn Savings Bank.
Blenhardt Burger, South Brooklyn Savings Bank.
Professor William J. Berry, Polytechnic Institute.
Wallace Gilbert, Editorial staff of *Tribune*.
Doctor Herbert C. Allen.
Dr. James Cole Hancock.
Mr. Frank Tyler, Real Estate.
Mr. James L. Brumley, Real Estate.
Mr. Edmund D. Fisher, Flatbush Trust Co., now Deputy Comptroller.
Dr. Edward Hopke.
Arthur Fitzhugh, Broadway Bank.
Edwin J. Kempton, Lawyer.
Dr. John Moffat.
Frank L. Sniffen, Guarantee Trust Co.
Charles H. Young, Lawyer.
Chester H. Beebe, School of Music Director.
William L. Perkins, Lawyer.
John and Edwin Watkins, Stationers.
Fred D. Edsall, Managing Supt. of Brooklyn Academy of Music.
Fred C. Williams, Advertising Agent.
Orlando H. Jadwin, Wholesale Druggist.
Lionel Moses, Architect.
Charles Brinkerhoff, Brooklyn Trust Co.
George P. Moffat, Fidelity Casualty Co.
Charles C. Miller, Lawyer.
Le Roy Harkness, Lawyer.

Harry N. Kellogg, Chairman of American Newspaper Publishing Co.
Eben Morford, Supt., Home for Blind.
Frank Williams, Steam and Water Heating Apparatus.
Walter Quackenbush, Manager of the North Western Miller.
Sidney T. Williamson, Member N. Y. Stock Exchange.
William H. Powell, Vice.-Pres. Atlantic Terra Cotta Co.
Clark Howard Great Eastern Casualty Co.
Arthur W. Forman, Importer of Diamonds.
Rev. William D. Street.

95 Fifth Ave., New York.

My dear Miss McCalvey,

. . . . .

If you will permit me to say so, your own thoroughgoing spirit of fair play was also a great element for good in that formative period.

. . . . .

Edgar B. Moore.

It is noteworthy that most speakers and writers on teachers almost unconsciously use the feminine pronouns, e.g.

Superintendent Maxwell tells a story about a teacher in an East Side district. She was going home from school when one of the people of the district stopped her and said, "Miss K., I cannot help seeing how the children love you. You know my Bennie and Rosie? They're in your school. You are such a help to me at home. Some time Bennie, he say, he won't. Then he quick stop and he say, 'All right mamma. Miss K. says I ought to obey you.' When you stand on that platform, lady, and say something, it is just like when God speaks. Do you know that?"

And Mrs. Clarence Burns, who has devoted years to the cause of children, says: "It is not only that a teacher's mental equipment should enable her to teach in the schools —that, on the face of it, is important—but she must have, to be a successful educator, a teacher in the best sense of the term, a personality that will tend to uplift those who come under her jurisdiction. It must be healthful, capable of imparting its wholesomeness, and stability, must radiate strength and self-reliance even while her pupils rely upon her. Her personality, whether it makes for good or ill, is bound to obtrude itself upon the less mature nature of those with whom she is brought in contact. One of her pupils will receive one impression from one of her characteristics; another will receive another. These, as the single drops of water make the ocean, are the particles of "which characters are formed."

Some may contend that men are needed for the more scientific, more exact subjects. But a study of the "Departmental Programs" in the Elementary Schools refutes that contention. For instance:

| MALE TEACHERS | | WOMEN TEACHERS | |
|---|---|---|---|
| Assigned to 8B Mixed. | | Assigned to 7A Girls. | |
| Salary | $2400.00 | Salary | $1440.00 |
| | Periods | | Periods |
| Grammar | 4 | Mathematics | 15 |
| Music | 1 | Grammar | 9 |
| Penmanship | 1 | Music | 1 |
| Reading | 22 | Study | 4 |
| Study | 4 | Hygiene and Spelling | 4 |
| Hygiene and Physical Training | 1 | Music and Physical Training | 1 |
| Spelling and Physical Training | 1 | Spelling and Physical Training | 1 |
| Unassigned | 1 | Unassigned | 3 |

Miss Clara W——writes: "On Nov. 12, 1909, I visited P. S.—Manhattan—a school consisting only of pupils of the seventh and eighth years—and asked the principal, Mr. ——, to let me observe his *best* classes in Mathematics. The classes to which I was sent were all taught by women teachers despite the fact that there were several men teachers of Mathematics in the school.

Miss Elizabeth H. Du Bois, in a letter to the *Evening Post*, Dec. 14, 1908, says:

"The following is a bald statement of facts and figures in which nothing is extenuated or aught set down in malice.

The statistics are made up from the high school with which the writer is most familiar, having been appointed as a teacher there in September 1897, the year in which the high schools were created.

With these exceptions, then, and not counting the annex (which has a principal and staff of teachers of its own), the departments of English, Latin, French and German, history, mathematics, science, drawing, and physical training, number 27 men and 49 women who are doing full work as first assistants, assistants or junior teachers. 450 hours of teaching per week are assigned to the 27 men; 941 to the 49 women. The average for each man, therefore, is 16 hours and 40 minutes per week, and for each woman 19 hours and 12 minutes. In the academic departments 7 women and 2 men are doing the maximum work, 25 hours per week.

Turning now to the matter of salaries, the sum of all the salaries paid to the 27 men, divided by 40 (because there are 40 school weeks in the year), is $1,528.25, making the average salary per week paid to each man $56.60. In the same way the sum of the salaries paid to the 49 women, divided by 40, is $2,111.75, making the average salary per week paid to each woman $43.10. So that each woman, for doing two and a half hours' more work per week receives $13.50 less pay.

In the different departments a comparison of the figures is illuminating.

In the English department, for instance, the seven women receive $100 less per year than the five men. In the German department, the six women receive but $200 more than double the amount paid to the two men. And in the Latin, although the head of this department is a woman, and therefore receives the maximum salary for a woman ($2500 per year), the five women receive $1,470 less than the 5 men.

Taking into account training and experience in teaching, of the forty-two women (drawing and physical training have been left out) eighteen hold a bachelor's degree, nine a master's, two the degree of doctor of philosophy, thirteen have no academic degree. Of the 25 men teaching academic subjects, sixteen hold the bachelor's degree, six the master's, one the degree of doctor of philosophy; two have no academic degree. In experience, the average for the men is fifteen years and ten months, for the women eighteen years and four months.

It cannot be said of the high schools, as it sometimes is of the lower schools, that there is any difference in the grade of work done by the men and the women. The work done by the men and the women in the high schools is identical in each department, the same grade of classes is taught by the two, the same books used, the same ground covered. The only difference is that two and a half hours' more of teaching per week is done by each woman for $13.50 less pay.

It seems unnecessary to speak of the proctoring of study-halls and of the girls' and boys' lunch rooms at recess, for these duties are shared equally by men and women. So, too, the care of books, and athletics, assigned to certain men, is quite off-set by the care of the literary and debating societies and the various art clubs, whose meetings after school must be attended by a teacher. This work falls largely on the women teachers. In addition to which, what is known as "escort duty" (*i.e.*, clearing the various floors of loiterers at three o'clock) is assigned only to women; each woman remaining for this purpose ten successive days in each half year.

The inequality of distribution, however, is greatest in the physical training department. There are, in the school, 869 boys and 1719 girls. But, although the girls number twice the boys (less nineteen) there are two men for the boys and just two women for the girls. On one day of the week, indeed, the two women together teach as many girls as there are boys in the whole school. The sum of the salaries paid the two women is $3,640 per year, to the two men $4,690. So that for almost double the work they receive $1,050 less pay.

"These statements may be verified by consulting the present programme of the school, the city records and those of the Board of Education."

And another teacher of experience writes:

"Why take it so completely for granted that the average man teacher can do more efficient work than the average woman teacher in developing ability to use knowledge for life purposes? What evidence have we for this except the ancient egotism of men that God must, by some hocus-pocus, have made them superior beings?

"I am a woman of much experience as a teacher and supervisor. I have had both women and men teachers under my supervision, and I have to admit, I started out expecting to find men far more proficient along just the lines emphasized by Mr. R. My disillusionment has been complete, and I affirm, from much careful observation, that men teachers, as a rule, not only fall far short of women in capacity for discipline among adolescent girls and boys, but also in skill in arousing genuine mental activity. I do not claim that this is due to any difference inherent in sex. I am not prepared to say as to this. I do say that as far as my own experience and observation go, and these have been somewhat extended, the average woman teacher does better work—including in "better" the ability to develop power of thinking in the upper grades than the average man teacher.

"Let him who doubts go as an unimportant stranger and visit the classes of women and men in the upper grades, high schools, and training schools of New York, and some surprises will await him or her, concerning the superior power of men teachers for older scholars.

"This, like the rib story, awaits demonstration.

Frances Isabel Davenport.

Brooklyn, Dec. 30.

## CHAPTER V

### ARE MEN TEACHERS NEEDED FOR THEIR MANLY INFLUENCE?

THOSE who claim that men teachers are needed in the elementary schools must prove:

(1) That the New York City boys who are taught by men in the elementary schools are superior in education, culture and manliness to those taught by women;

(2) That the men in New York City who are graduates from elementary schools having men teachers are far superior in education, culture, and manliness to the Up-State men, or men from Indiana, California, and other states having no men teachers in their elementary schools.

If this superiority be proven, it will go far toward justifying the extra millions that have been spent in order to give the New York boy some men teachers in the elementary schools.

We are told that these men teachers are needed for their "manly influence," and to serve as "models" for our boys.

Supt. Maxwell, in his Tenth Annual Report, says:

"Some men teachers are and should be employed in the higher grades for three principal reasons:

(a) "That the pupils may come under the influence of the intellectual and moral qualities that particularly characterize men, as well as under the influence of the intellectual and moral qualities that particularly characterize women;

(b) "That the pupils may be made to feel that culture and refinement are not the peculiar province of women, but should also be striven for and possessed by men;

(c) "That the larger boys may have guidance and leadership in athletic sports."

One naturally asks, what are the intellectual and moral qualities that particularly characterize men, and those other intellectual and moral qualities that particularly characterize women?

Dr. Wm. T. Manning, rector of Trinity Church, in his Baccalaureate address to Columbia University, discussing the question of larger attendance of women than men at church said:

"In the first place, men as a class are not more intellectual than women; but rather the reverse is true; and in the second place, history shows that the higher people rise in the scale of intellect, the more truly religious they become.

"The disparity between men and women in religious interests is due in large part to the fact that on the whole women lead higher lives than men do. Their lives are less selfish, less hardened by contact with the business of the world, less under the power of certain of the grosser sins."

The N. Y. *Journal of Commerce,* May 13, 1909, said editorially: "In some grades and branches masculine minds of the best order and training are eminently desirable to make the education what it should be"; but Professor Smith of London says that every year seems to show with increasing conclusiveness that "there is in the great mass of cases a practical equality in male and female minds.

Again, Supt. Maxwell says in his Tenth Annual Report: "At that age, however, at which boys begin to extend their intellectual horizon beyond the circle of childish amusement, it is pre-eminently necessary that they should have an opportunity of acquiring thro' imitation the characteristics of men as well as the characteristics of women; of following the example of men of character, as well as the example of women; and of seeing in men as well as in women illustrations of culture and refinement."

In a recent report made by the Male Teachers' Association of this city regarding the necessity for men teachers, this sentence appears: "And in this connection we plead for men who are men."

I am sure that we all agree that men who are men will be welcome as teachers in our public schools, to serve as models for our boys; but, I believe, also, that you will agree with me that the man who believes that it would be unmanly to pay his sister the same salary as is paid to him when she does the same work is not the type of man we want in our public schools, is not the sort of man we want our sons and our brothers to imitate.

Science has proven that a stream will not rise higher than its source. If the boys in our public schools had no other models of honor, culture and manliness than the male teachers in their fight for simple justice, the future male citizen of this city would be a sorry type.

That the tactics of these male teachers have often been despicable, deceitful and dishonorable, the following illustrations will show:

Having found that their plea for an increase of salaries for themselves had no friends except a few members of the Board of Education, and the Board of Superintendents, while practically the whole public was agreed that the women teachers were poorly paid; and knowing that the Women Teachers' bill, carrying a minimum salary of $720, had passed the Legislature three times and had been unanimously endorsed by the Board of Aldermen three times; knowing also that Superintendent Maxwell in his Ninth Annual Report had recommended a similar minimum salary; knowing furthermore that President McGowan had notified the Board of Estimate and Apportionment that he would oppose all increases of salary until the salaries of the women teachers were increased, the Association of Man Teachers and Principals in May, 1909, passed a resolution recommending to the Board of Education that the initial salary of a woman teacher be $720. The women teachers resented this action as a deliberate attempt on the part of these men to pretend to the public an interest in the welfare of the women, notwithstanding the fact that this very association was not only organized for the purpose of opposing the women teachers, but that it had been continuously active and maliciously bitter in its opposition to this day.

Mr. Maxwell in his last Annual Report says: "I am also of opinion that more systematic and detailed instruction is needed to the end that all the children of this great city may not leave its public schools without clearly defined notions of a right, of a duty, of virtue, of truth and falsity, of right and wrong, of honesty, and dishonesty, of the binding force of contracts, and of respect for law."

One of the most desirable attributes in man or woman is truth. But Mr. W. a male teacher opposing the Equal Pay bill in the Senate Committee on Cities in February, 1907, stated that of all the teachers in the system "only a pitiful *five* per cent." were men; though the figures in Dr. Maxwell's latest previous annual report showed that eleven and one-half per cent. of the teachers were men.

Another desirable attribute is respect for the rights of others. But many women teachers have been hampered and troubled by the oppressive tactics of their male superior officers. This is attested in the following letters received by me:

Received May 1, 1907: "In several schools here, notably School No. —— the principal has practically coerced the teachers into signing this opposition paper. (A petition against the White Bill.) He spoke for over half an hour, and in the end, as one teacher said to her sister, 'I felt if I didn't sign it, things would be very unpleasant for me.'"

Another:

"The enclosed notes are copies of ones circulated in P. S. —— this week. They were given to me by a teacher who is protesting, but who fears lest Mr. —— should harm her professionally. All matter concerning the Interborough is concealed, and therefore, I, as a delegate from P. S. —— have been asked to notify you."

Another:

"—— woman in the departmental system of —— would like very much to join, but is afraid to do so, lest it may serve as a pretext to force her out of her position in favor of the men. She is an exceptionally superior teacher, and I think if you could give me some assurance that nothing of that kind would result, that she would be glad to join. *She has been thoroughly intimidated by a former principal.*"

May 1, 1907, "—— told me that her aunt —— a teacher

in P. S. —— said that the boys in the —— High School are writing notes to the Mayor as taxpayers urging him to refuse to sign the 'White Bill.'"

Jan. 10, 1910. "On Friday, Miss ——, the head of department of P. S. ——, Manhattan, called to see me in regard to the I. A. W. T. As you are aware, the principal of that school, Mr. ——, has said repeatedly that there shall be no member of his force a member of our Association. No later than last week, he caused the teachers to sign as to whether or not, they were members of said association. So Miss —— and five associates, wish to join unknown to him. Please explain to the secretary, Miss Ennis, that under no condition can literature be sent to the school, as it will be confiscated and the offenders punished."

Do we want our boys to imitate such men teachers as:

Mr. X.—bachelor, receiving eight hundred and forty dollars a year more than woman teacher of same grade of boys, who said to woman he was entertaining at dinner, "I couldn't be taking you and other teachers out and giving you a good time, if I were getting a 'Woman's Wage.'"

Mr. Y. who said: "There is a little Miss 'Y'—now. That gives me an additional claim to the position."

"I said: 'If I were your wife and you held me or my baby up as a plea for favor or salary, I'd leave you and support myself and baby.' Does a doctor with a baby ask a larger fee than a doctor with no baby? Does a lawyer present his family as ground for larger fee? Why should male teachers be the only people—either in professional or laboring—classes to urge their family responsibilities as excuses for special salary favors? Consider the matter in another light. Think of the woman applicant for this position. She is teaching in both day school and night school to support herself and assist in the care and support of her family including a sister hopelessly ill of tuberculosis. She has to be an 'old maid.' She can have no child to grow up and assist her in her old age."

Mr. Y. "Well, I have a sister who is an old maid and I'm glad of it. She helps us."

Mr. A. who spoke to me one day with his mouth so

offensively dirty with tobacco that I had to turn away in in disgust.

The New York Evening *Sun* in an editorial Feb. 27, 1907, wrote: "The representatives of the male teachers of this city did not cut much of a figure at Albany yesterday. Poor Mr. Wellnesley, he could not help it. There was a suggestion of the dog in the manger when he argued as follows. 'This bill says that women teachers shall have equal pay for equal work, but it says nothing to prevent a woman being able to get more than a man.' (Loud laughter.)

"'We men teachers want to be protected so we can't be reduced.' But for true frankness Mr. Cort surpassed all his fellow protestants. He did not mince matters. 'If this bill becomes law,' he said, 'it will defer the increase in the men's pay.' In other words, the self-seeking male persons opposed what their opponents called a simple act of justice on the ground that it would tend to prevent the commission of a further injustice."

On the occasion of our Mass Meeting at Carnegie Hall, the Male Teachers had handbills distributed in front of the building which the *Irish-American* of Dec. 24, 1909, referred to thus:

"If men teachers in some combination are responsible for the trashy circular handed to persons going to Carnegie Hall, they ought to be ashamed of themselves. After some two or three false statements as to what the women demand, the circular winds up with the following rubbish:

"'How is your bread buttered. The cat's paw pulled the monkey's chestnuts from the fire. Who's the cat?

"'Who is being buncoed?

"'How many guesses will it take to explain this?'

"It will not take many guesses to explain that the City of New York is being buncoed by some of the men teachers, if this is a sample of the stuff their brains are made of. The movement for equal pay will not be retarded by such contemptible asininity.

"The women teachers' claim is based upon justice. So long as their work measures up to the same extent and efficiency as the work of the men, there is no reason for penalizing them by a lower salary."

But probably the most deadly danger to the moral nature of our boys is that which has been exposed to the public recently—the dishonorable practices of some men principals and teachers in connection with athletic competitions. Superintendent Maxwell reports: "—— From such investigations as I have been able to make, I find that from about fifty school boys were certified who should not have been certified. I am fully convinced that this certification was the result of nothing worse than carelessness. There are some instances, however, in which the explanation offered by the principal is not satisfactory to me. I feel, therefore, that this is a matter which should be investigated by a committee of the Board of Education——"

*Globe,* Mar. 24, 1910: "Principals from about fifty schools have been before a sub-committee of the Committee on Elementary Schools to explain their actions in certifying ineligible boys as eligible. When it is considered that only about 100 schools competed, in the elementary school indoor championship games, the seriousness of the scandal is apparent.

"As has been intimated, the seriousness of the situation lies not so much in the fact that a few school trophies have been withheld as in the revelation of the ethical standards that obtain among some of the principals. For in certain instances it seems the principals, with the knowledge of the pupils, permitted ineligibles to compete. The effect of such an example on the future moral standards of the pupils is obvious."

The inquiry, it transpires, was granted. One district superintendent, in speaking of the results of the investigation, said:

"The irregularities seem to have been pretty general all along the line, and while in many instances it may be explained away, in at least two cases there was direct connivance on the part of the principal in permitting ineligible boys to compete. If they are going to teach ethics and morality in the schools, it would seem they might at least follow their own precepts."

"The athletes, many of whom have not yet reached the age of discretion, entered the contests because they were certified by the teachers and principals, and won prizes. Then they found that they were ineligible to compete, and were forced to return the prizes. The effect is most unfortunate. As one of the most prominent teachers of the city said yesterday: 'For goodness sake, keep at the evils in schoolboy athletics. Of what possible use all this athletic movement, if the moral fibre of the boys is to be weakened by the knowledge and example of the moral weakness of their principals and teachers!'"

The *Globe*, of March 23, 1910, published an example of another kind of moral astigmatism:

"Charles Kothe, a teacher in Public School 29, East 126th Street, and Justice Zeller in the Children's Court, disagreed yesterday on the subject of psychology. The justice threatened to stir the Board of Education into activity, and criticized the principal of the school.

"Several weeks ago Walter Uhl, a pupil in —— class was arrested, paroled and, —— ——, principal of the school, and the teacher were instructed to inform the court as to the boy's parole record. A few days ago the principal reported like this: "The boy's attendance is poor, and lessons very poor."

Justice Zeller asked for the teacher's report, and got several cards, indicating a fine record for Uhl, who was pronounced "perfect" in his studies. The justice subpoenaed K——, when he would not respond to a request to appear, and in court Justice Zeller yesterday showed K—— a card concerning Uhl. Kothe admitted none of the entries on the cards was correct, and Zeller wanted to know why.

"I made those entries for psychological reasons," K—— said. "I gave the boy good marks because I did not want to inculcate in his mind any antagonism."

"I am astonished at this revelation," said Justice Zeller. "I am going to transmit these papers to the Board of Education, and I want to say to you also, Mr. Principal, that your conduct in this case has been very unsatisfactory to the court. I'll see whether these teachers certify to reports correctly or incorrectly with the connivance of their principals. This is a disgrace to our system of education."

And the following from the *Eagle* of Feb. 24, 1910, shows another type of man whom we do not want our boys to imitate:

"The Bureau of Municipal Research gives out some remarkable facts in connection with the case of M—— J. D——, principal of Public School No. ——, Manhattan, who was yesterday fined by the Board of Education $500 for absenting himself from the school and devoting his time as a commissioner in condemnation proceedings. Controller Metz maintained that the penalty was inadequate and he declared that the board would agree with him if all the facts were brought out in the case.

Abraham Stern, chairman of the committee on elementary schools, objected to Mr. Metz's proposition. He said there were no more facts to be considered, because Principal D—— had admitted the charges.

According to the Bureau of Municipal Research the following facts were not considered by the committee:

1. That D—— for years falsely certified his school payroll.

2. That he made false statements to the president denying the absences that he now admits.

3. That he made false statements to the press.

4. That he was fined one-thirtieth of the amount of the fees earned from his double relations.

5. That he falsely certified to street opening pay receipts.

6. That he admits having received 451 full payments of $10, when he should have received one-half, $5 had he not certified falsely.

7. That Judge Dowling dismissed and rebuked him for the worst form of abuses disclosed in street opening proceedings.

The bureau's statement continues.

"With respect to Judge Dowling's dismissal of D—— December 15, last (as recorded on page 1099 of the Law

Journal for December 17) the following facts are given for the first time:

"'Commissioner D——, L—— F——, and P—— G. C——, acting as commission concurred on awards for sixty-two pieces of property, aggregating $245,013.73. Later D—— and F—— agreed upon preliminary awards at $328,356.25 for the same pieces of property, and finally recommended for those same pieces of property $256,649. This 'boosting' of awards Commission C—— objected to and made a minority report which led Justice Dowling to dismiss and rebuke D—— and F—— and to throw the case out. D——'s fees for this proceeding alone will be, unless cut, nearly seven times his fine, and, besides, the city must spend several thousands more on new proceedings.'

. . . . .

"At yesterday's meeting Commissioner Stern maintained that the Board of Education could not take cognizance of the conduct of a school principal on condemnation proceedings. Commissioner Metz maintained that the Board of Education was duly bound to take cognizance of offenses against public welfare that were a matter of court record, especially when the school principal concerned had not only falsely certified to school payrolls and diverted school time, but had perjured himself by making a false affidavit to the Board of Education himself regarding his connection with condemnation proceedings."

. . . . .

Commenting on this case, the *Globe* of Feb. 24, 1910, said: "Efforts were made by Commissioners Metz and McGowan to have a further investigation made by the committee on elementary schools of the charges preferred against Principal M—— E. D—— of P. S. ——, Manhattan, in connection with condemnation proceedings when the report of the committee on elementary schools was presented to the board at its meeting yesterday, but without success. The board approved the recommendation of the committee that Mr. Devlin be fined $500.

"In its report the committee stated that the particular charge was that Mr. Devlin had been absent from school on seventy-nine occasions between January, 1906, and Sept. 30, 1909, attending such proceedings, and that he had failed to note his absence on the payrolls. It reviewed his excellent record in the schools and cited that in view of that record and of the fact that he had pleaded guilty and that it was his first offense, the fine of $500 was regarded as adequate punishment.

"Mr. Metz declared that he believed that this was an instance where severe action ought to be taken. There had been a great deal of talk about condemnation proceedings, and when a man in the employ of the city was involved an example ought to be made of him. It was a bad precedent to make the punishment so light.

"Those members of the board who were not members of the committee which had heard the trial, explained Mr. McGowan, were in ignorance of many of the facts and were therefore not good judges. He suggested that an opportunity might be given to the members who so desired to go over the evidence.

"Chairman Stern of the committee on elementary schools explained that it would do no good, as there was no evidence. The charges had been read and Mr. D—— had admitted them. They were as given in the report, and as they had been proved it was for the committee to determine the punishment. In doing so it had considered Mr. D——'s excellent record.

"Mr. Metz wanted to know if the committee had considered Mr. D——'s affidavit that he was not in the employ of the city, and Mr. Stern said that it had and that the affidavit was correct, but it was not included in the charges as preferred and the committee could not have considered it if it had so desired.

"I believe," replied Mr. Metz, "that there ought to be a fuller investigation. All related facts ought to be taken into consideration."

"This brought Mr. Stern to his feet with a severe arraignment of the Bureau of Municipal Research. There were certain matters which they as members of the board were not required to investigate. This was not a legislative investigating committee, and it was not its duty to investigate outside matters. The powers of the committee were limited to the consideration of the charges enumerated in the charter, and all facts material to the charges had been considered and investigated. If it was to be the policy to go outside and investigate what teachers, principals, and commissioners did outside of their particular lines of work it would be a strange proceeding.

"He characterized the statements being circulated by the Bureau of Municipal Research as maliciously misleading. That bureau, he said, was probably acting from good motives, and it ought to consider that other boards also acted from similar motives. The statements made concealed part of the truth. For instance, it was stated that on fifty-nine occasions Mr. D—— received pay in two outside positions at the same time. The impression was given that this was in school hours, but there was no evidence to show whether it was or not. What difference did it make to the board how many jobs he had if they were not within school hours?

"Another allegation was that 447 times he was recorded as being at commissions at 3 P. M., giving the impression that he was neglecting his school work. The facts presented were that he was recorded wrongly, for he had reported at ten minutes or quarter after three, but he was recorded as being on duty at three and had neglected to have the record corrected. These were the type of malicious allegations which were being circulated.

"The committee had extended to the bureau the unprecedented courtesy of having a representative present. He attended the first hearing, which was adjourned, but at the second he did not appear until the trial was over. As to the affidavit that Mr. D—— was not an employee of the city, Mr. D—— was correct. Were the city not to pay him and were he to sue he would have to sue the board and not the city under a ruling of the court.

"The allegations came down to those seventy-nine times he was away during school hours, and it was upon them that the fine was computed. Allowing two to three hours for each of the sessions, it would be seen that the fine was

HON. WILLIAM J. GAYNOR,

MAYOR OF THE CITY OF NEW YORK.

CHAIRMAN OF BROOKLYN MASS MEETING HELD BY INTERBOROUGH ASSOCIATION OF WOMEN TEACHERS, MARCH 6, 1908. HE WAS THEN JUSTICE, APPELLATE DIVISION, SUPREME COURT.

much in excess of the time lost to the city by the principal. The statements of the bureau were made for the purpose of influencing the members wrongly. Mr. Devlin's long connection with the system, his high standing and excellent record must be considered. He had made a misstep and had admitted it. The punishment was sufficient to prevent a recurrence of the evil.

"It was a principle for which he was contending, Mr. Metz declared. Mr. D——'s record on commissions had been traced back for years and he had been misstepping during that time. Every one knows that appointments on commissions depend upon pull and a man ought to be above that or not be a principal. He believed the punishment should be nothing short of dismissal.

"Mr. McGowan said that Mr. Stern's review of the facts had made the members acquainted with the details. He did not regard the statements of the Bureau of Municipal Research as misleading, but as setting forth what they had found to be the facts. The report was then adopted."

Can we expect the boys brought up under the influence of Mr. D—— to have a fine sense of truth and a high ideal of honor?

Is it not conceivable that such loose notions of truth and honesty and honor in our public schools must inevitably taint the whole nation? If our boys and girls are reared in such an atmosphere can we hope for better things from them?

And again I quote:

"Thieving weighers of the Sugar Trust." There has been so much debauchery, such glaring dishonesty in public officials, that we come to hail a man with decent instincts as a prodigy of virtue! Is it not a shocking comment upon our institutions? Somebody will be wanted who will hang a few public "grafters." We shall have a national vigilance committee. The same processes that were found to be most salutary in San Francisco during the early 50's of the last century will be tried again in every large city of this land! There will not be any temporizing. Short weight will get a "short shrift." Stealing from the general government will be placed upon the same plane as stealing from one's butcher or baker.

" By that time we shall have reached a point at which every official tried and convicted of robbing the people of the United States will be branded in some indelible manner. As Anna Katherine Green suggests in her latest "thriller," this brand ought to be put upon the cheek. There it could be seen of all men.

"How much better than a perfunctory punishment!" —Julius Chambers, *Walks and Talks,* Jan. 11, 1910.

## CHAPTER VI

### ARE MEN TEACHERS NEEDED TO PREVENT FEMINIZATION?

It is sometimes claimed that men are needed to prevent the feminization of our schools.

This claim has been made by Herr Munsterberg, Alfred Mosely and other foreigners whose opinions must be discounted on account of their lack of long and familiar acquaintance with us and our institutions.

This claim is also made by some male teachers and their friends, whose opinions must be considered in the light of their great desire to secure the appointment of more men to teaching positions. Their condition is like that of a vendor of jet beads, for instance, who has an over-stocked market, and is naturally anxious to create a demand for jet beads. In opposition to their opinion, I quote some American authorities. The first is Prof. John Dewey, who as an American and a scholar, is worthy of greater consideration than any one hitherto mentioned.

Prof. Dewey was head of the Department of Philosophy at the University of Chicago from the foundation of that institution. Five years ago he accepted the chair of philosophy at Columbia. He is one of the best known English-speaking teachers of his subject, and is Past President of the American Philosophic and Psychological Association.

Only recently William L. Felter, head of the Girls' High School in Brooklyn, returned from a trip abroad with dark and gloomy views on the American School System. The press quotes him as saying: "Too many women teachers are at the root of a large part of the evils of our public schools," he asserted sadly. "I thought so once and now I know it—I have been talking with Alfred Mosely. The preponderance of women teachers is swiftly and surely feminizing our boys."

Prof. Dewey, who has happened to make a point of lecturing on women in the public schools, was shown Mr. Felter's published convictions. And Prof. Dewey smiled—very dryly—and said:

"There is no more efficient body of workers in America than the great army of its women teachers. They feminize boys? Nonsense! Where are our effeminate boys, if you please?"

"I wish," he remarked by way of casual beginning, "that I could happen on some of these effeminate school boys. Somehow, I've never been able to discover them. Strangely enough, the people who lament their ascendency, don't seem to produce the article. Now, I am so constituted that whenever I examine any sort of new theory, I want proofs to back me up. Where are they? Where are our effeminate boys?

"The notion that our splendid women teachers are making mollycoddles of their boy students is utterly absurd. Why, women themselves are anything but mollycoddles in these days of basket-ball and athletic 'stunts' without number! They'd be the first to despise the 'feminine' boy—instead of petting him into being.

"The whole notion is an English pipe dream. Girls in England are an absolutely different sort from the American type. They are brought up to wait on their brothers by inches—just as they are afterward supposed to wait on their husbands. Very likely a course of education under such gentle young women would tend to 'feminize' boys—or make them bullies.

"But Mr. Alfred Mosely and his fellow commissioners should not judge other girls by the kind they happen to know at home—and then, to cap the climax, implant their own preconceived impressions on impressionable Americans. That's adding insult to injury. Luckily, the big, common-sense majority of Americans prefer to judge with their own eyes.

"That they don't believe women teachers are making weaklings of their sons is shown by the multiplication, instead of subtraction among the ranks of those same teachers. American fathers and mothers want the best—and insist on having it. They simply would not stand for the great majority of women who instruct their children unless they believed in those women. That their belief is fully justified is my unhesitating assertion.

"There is absolutely no reason why women should not occupy the executive as well as other positions in the educational system. Chicago proved itself more progressive than New York, when it placed a woman at the head of its immense school system—because she was the fittest one for the place. She has done splendid work in the past—she will continue to stand for even finer accomplishments in the future, because her field is larger. But she is no glaring, lonely exception. There are probably women right here in New York who are as fit, or fitter, to hold the important administrative positions in educational matters now occupied by men. Fitness should be the only requisite of choice. Is it?

"It is perfectly true that the public is not disposed to appreciate very highly that which can be had cheaply. The very fact that the salaries of the women teachers have been kept down for so long is doubtless at bottom responsible for the spasmodic waves of discontent with them and their works—such as the criticism that they are making our boys feminine. For the sake of our own self-respect, in our attitude to those to whom we entrust our children, we should not consent to load them with the incubus of cheapness.

"I believe that women do excellent work in the more highly salaried teachers' positions that already exist. It has been contended that with all the advantages of their higher education, women have not proved themselves the equals of men in intellectual accomplishments. I believe that they have not been given the chance to do this. Positions of responsibility and power have not been open to them. They have been denied the highest opportunities of scientific research, for example. When they have been granted such, well, even Mme. Curie's own husband admitted that his wife was as much the discoverer of radium as himself!

"I should like to see more women in professors' chairs in our colleges and universities. In the women's colleges they have long done work of the highest order. Why should they be less able to do such work in colleges not devoted entirely to women?

"Prophecy is rather a foolish and thankless task, but I believe that before many years we are going to see women occupying professors' chairs in our co-educational colleges at least. I am positive that women could do most excellent work in such positions. Why not? The woman's brain and the man's brain are both capable of equal achievement. The only reason for the apparent discrepancy between the work each has so far actually performed, is that one has deliberately handicapped the other with narrow opportunities and conventionally restrained outlook. If you take two equally healthy babies and tie the arms of one of them till both of them grow up, of course you'll have a weaker physical development in the case of the one who has been bound. For centuries men have been tying women's brains and the result is a weaker mental development. That will all be remedied when the bandages are removed. And a new one is being taken off every day.

"I would see the teaching system equalized—more women among the college instructors, more men in the public schools. I would have a fair contest of brains, without regard to sex. And let the best man—or woman—win!"

Also opposed to the feminization theory is Prof. Edward L. Thorndike, also of Columbia University, who has made an investigation of the high school statistics of the country and in the January, 1910, number of the *Educational Review* published his conclusions. They are that the influence of the male teachers upon the proportion of male students is very slight, and that the proportion of boys who go over to or even stay through the high school does not at all depend upon the percentage of men on the staff of the school.

"It always is, or should be, interesting to put speculations about education to the test of facts," says Prof. Thorndike. "The result often is, or should be, a warning to us against the intellectual crime of giving mere opinions where indolence is our only excuse for failing to verify them.

"In the present article I propose to seek light on the very common opinion that the ratio of boys to girls in high schools, and particularly in the later grades of high schools, can be largely increased by increasing the percentage of men teachers in these schools.

"To answer the question, 'Do the high schools which, while roughly alike in other respects, differ greatly in the proportion of male students?'"

The tables he prepared revealed only a "very, very slight" direct relation between the proportion of male teachers and male pupils. In 184,000 students recorded, the percentage of boys is less than 4 per cent. more among the 84,607 in schools with from 40 per cent. to 91 per cent. of men teachers than among the 81,527 in schools with from 0 per cent. to 35 per cent.

"The central tendency is to have three out of eight teachers men and to have 142 girls for every 100 boys enrolled. For 33⅓ per cent. increase in the proportion of male teachers, one finds an increase of less than one per cent. in the proportion of male students; for 66⅔ per cent. increase in the former proportion, one finds an increase of 2 per cent. in the latter; and for an increase of 100 per cent. in the former, an increase of 4 or 5 per cent. in the latter. Where the former proportion is halved the proportion of male students drops only about 1 per cent. and where it is reduced to a third, the drop in the latter is less than 2 per cent."

Taking forty-two schools of thirteen or more teachers having a percentage "of male teachers of 24 or under and the forty-one such schools having a percentage of male teachers of 47 or over. Although on the average the latter group have two and a half times as high a percentage of male teachers, they have a percentage of male students hardly any higher and a percentage of male graduates which is decidedly lower than is found in the schools with few men teachers."

"Evidently," says Prof. Thorndike, "the influence of

the proportion of male teachers upon the proportion of male students, even when combined with whatever unreasoning tendency there is for school boards to provide a larger share of men teachers when the enrollment consists largely of boys and with the tendency of certain communities to look with disfavor on feminization of both the teaching profession and the school populations, is very slight."

Taking up the equally interesting question whether high schools differing greatly in the proportion of male teachers show corresponding differences in the proportion of male graduates, Prof. Thorndike declares that "the proportion of male teachers thus makes even less difference in the proportion of male graduates than in the proportion of male students as a whole. It appears then, that the influence which made the slight correlation between the sex ratio of the staff and that of the student body was not in the main the attractiveness of men teachers to boys. For, in so far as it was that, the relation should be closer for graduates upon whom the supposed attractive force would have acted from one-half to three and a half years longer.

Another prominent American educator who flouts the "Feminization" theory is Alexander T. Stuart, Superintendent of Public Schools, Washington, D. C. In the *Sunday Tribune* for March 22, 1908, one of his articles appeared which was part of a discussion started by G. Stanley Hall. Following are some extracts from said article: "I can read little else in Doctor Hall's article on the 'Feminization of Boys' than a plea for the return to corporal punishment at home and in school, and as such I believe it will have few defenders.

"It is true that there has been a noteworthy decrease in the number and in the proportion of men teachers in the United States within thirty years; but that the results of this growing influence of the woman teacher and of the mother upon the character of the individual boy and eventually upon the nation, are now, or are to be as described, I do not for a moment accept.

"In the reports of the eminent English educators who constituted the Mosely commission, which investigated the

American school system in 1903, the absence of the man in the schoolroom was repeatedly deplored; but I fail to recall that any of these experts claimed to have discovered in the discipline, bearing or scholarship of the American boy at school, or in the behavior or achievements of the American man, as found participating in the great social, political, and business movements of this country, any tangible evils that might rightly be traced to the undue influence of woman in the education of boys. On the contrary, their reasons for wanting more men seemed to consist in the fact that men teachers were the fashion in England, supported by the general statement that perhaps boys, after a certain age, would better be under a man. It is unfortunate that this startling plea for the transfer of the control of our boys at home from the mother to the father, and at school from the woman teacher to the man teacher, by so eminent a student of childhood as Dr. Hall, could not have been made without his frank avowal that the all too sympathetic methods of women must now be abandoned to the sounder ministrations of a 'good stick or ferule.'"

I quote from still another American educator on this point. President James M. Green, of the State Normal College at Trenton, New Jersey, in a speech delivered on the occasion of the Regents' Convocation at Albany, N. Y., October 29, 1909, said:

"The claim that we should have men teachers in any considerable numbers in the elementary grades will not be taken very seriously by the parents of the country. There are a number of more or less fanciful theories about the race becoming effeminated, etc., that are gotten up and that sound learned; but, seriously speaking, there is no worry. There are some men who would be adapted to elementary teaching and would do it well, but women show an especial adaptation to this grade of work, and they do it so successfully that the large part of it may safely be left to them."

Coming to the authorities in our own system, Associate Superintendent Davis in Superintendent Maxwell's 6th Annual Report says:

"I am inclined to believe that this conclusion is based on theory and not upon fact. It is not my experience, extending over twenty-four years, that the boys of this city show, either in school life or out of school life, this lack of masculine characteristics."

Dr. Luther H. Gulick, then, Director of Physical Training, and supervisor of athletics in New York Public Schools:

"City conditions prevent that precise form of manifesting the combative element in the boy which is brought out in smaller districts where he has more freedom, but the city-trained boy has never proved himself to be a quitter." Dr. Gulick is of the opinion that most of the athletes in this country had received their elementary training under women teachers. He suggests that this might prove to be true of most of the athletes on the Olympic team. "Theoretically it would seem that the boy who received practically all his early training under a woman teacher would become somewhat effeminate," said Dr. Gulick, "but the facts, as we can judge them in the New York public schools, do not justify such a conclusion. The New York boy goes into athletics with an aggressiveness and spirit of combativeness which is sometimes difficult to keep within reasonable bounds. That is our trouble—it is hard for us to keep him from fighting too much, and in that very particular, I think, lies the best test we have of his manliness."

On the general proposition of feminization, the following is interesting:

Jno. K. Le Baron, writing for the New York *World:* "Most great men have had noble mothers. Many who have attained enduring distinction have been the sons of weak, dissolute and obdurate fathers.

"The story of Cornelia, daughter of Scipio, wife of Tiberius the elder and mother of the Gracchi, is one of the luminous pages of history. True, the Gracchi had a remarkable father, but, dying when they were young, he left his sons to their mother's care. The Gracchi were the noblest Romans of their day.

"The mother of Confucius was 'a woman of rare mental

and spiritual worth.' The great philosopher constantly sought her companionship and counsel.

"The father of Savanarola was an indigent profligate. It was from his mother that he received his sublime courage, and her teachings were the basis of his character.

"Pope, a cynic and a sage, bitter in his resentments and cruel in his cynicisms, was devotion itself to his mother and owed much to her restraining influence.

"'It was to his mother,' says Mathews, 'a woman of great energy and rare accomplishments, that Bulwer was indebted for the formation and guidance of his literary tastes.'

"Andrew Carnegie, speaking to boys in a school in Pittsburg, said recently: 'Woman raises man to the highest standard. My mother and my wife made me all that I am.'

"Our own great and beloved Lincoln declared: 'All that I am and all that I hope to be I owe to my mother.'"

## CHAPTER VII

### SUPPLY AND DEMAND

I TALKED at the City Club one afternoon, and I believe I shocked them very much by not treating this "economic law" with more reverence. I said it made me think of the vegetable market. When it is applied to men and women, it seems silly. I happened to say—trying to be funny in order to hide my weariness of the oft-heard arguments—the only market I would consider would be the matrimonial market. And one of the speakers that followed me criticised me as being "flippant." I appeal to my married readers: Is that a flippant subject?

One is prone to think primarily of a building—an insensate mass of matter. But truly, a school is complete without a building. Wherever there is one to teach and one to be taught, there is a school. Some of the greatest schools in history were without buildings. But to bring about the greatest good to the greatest number, and to put into effect the opinion that the welfare of the State depends on the education of its citizens, buildings are provided. That they are not absolutely necessary to school keeping, however, was proven in San Francisco recently, when the city, after the earthquake, kept school in open fields while its buildings were being restored.

Now, of the two necessities for a school—teacher and pupil—which is more necessary? The answer to this is largely forced by the much misused law of Supply and Demand. A State is not a State without a natural supply of pupils; a State may be a State without a natural supply of teachers. So that the teacher is the greater necessity to the State.

Therefore, the State must see to it that it get a sufficient number of teachers to supply the natural demand made by its millions of children and its duty to promote the general welfare. Suppose all the teachers of the State rebelled against some injustice—fancied or real—and agreed to stop teaching. Can you imagine the condition of the State at the end of a week? How much worse at the end of a month? A year? Ten years? But it is doubtful if in these days a State could stand ten years without schools. One might ask, What would the teachers do? How would they earn a living? But is it not inevitable that the demands for policemen, for matrons and nurses in hospitals, insane asylums, prisons, and other houses of detention, for lawyers, for doctors, would all increase with the millions of children left without teachers? It would not take a State very long to realize how much it needs its teachers—how much it owes its teachers. Suppose it was only the men teachers that became dissatisfied and gave up their positions. Would the State find it impossible to get women to do their work? But again, suppose it was only the women teachers that left their classrooms and their pupils? Could the State fill their places as readily as they might those of the men? The task would be far more difficult.

Much has been written about the decreasing number of men teachers in the schools of the country and the threatened feminization of boys by reason of the large and increasing proportion of women teachers. Examination of the statistics of the Board of Education of this city show that the conditions here are directly opposite to those in the rest of the country. Here the proportion of men has been increasing since 1902. Not only that, the school authorities now claim that the elementary schools have almost all the men teachers they need.

The report of the United States Commissioner of Education shows that in 1901-2 the percentage of men to women teachers in the country at large was 27.4, while in 1906-7 it had dropped to 22.3. In this city, however, the percentage in high and elementary schools in 1902 was 8.3 per cent., while in the year ended July, 1908, it was 11 5/14 per cent.

Comparing the figures for the separate schools, even more interesting deductions are possible.

In 1902 there were in high schools 284 men and 346 women, a total of 630, or 45 1/12 per cent. men. In 1908 there were 530 men and 592 women, a total of 1122 and a percentage of 47 3/11 men.

In elementary schools in 1902 there were 10,181 teachers, of whom 617, or 6 1/20 per cent., were men, and 9564 women; but in 1908 the total number of teachers was 13,354, of whom 1113, or 8 4/13 per cent., were men.

In his Tenth Annual Report, Mr. Maxwell says: "The majority of the class teachers in the public schools are women for two reasons: (a) for the younger children who constitute the larger number in the schools, women make the better teachers; (b) the services of women teachers may be obtained more cheaply than those of men." And further on he says: "In order to obtain the services of even a small number of men, it has been found necessary to pay considerably higher salaries than those paid to women."

Yet statistics prove that this "small number" is greatly in excess of the average for the United States.

Superintendent Maxwell's Report for 1907-8:

| | |
|---|---|
| Total number of teachers | 1,7177 |
| Total number of women teachers | 15,003 |
| Total number of men teachers | 2,174 |
| Percentage of women teachers | 87.3 |
| Percentage of men teachers | 12.7 |

In a speech at the 20th Anniversary Dinner of the Midwood Club, May 21, 1909, Superintendent Maxwell said, in speaking of men teachers, "Ten per cent. is as much as we need."

Why then load up the system with 12.7 per cent., nearly 25 per cent. more than the City Superintendent thinks necessary?

I have enough of the political-and-social economist sense to recognize and acknowledge that the ratio of the normal or natural supply of any commodity to the normal or natural demand for such commodity is a valid basis for regulating the cost or selling price of same. But I have also enough of common sense and good judgment to differentiate the supply-and-demand arguments which are forced, abnormal, spurious and inapplicable from those that are real and applicable. A mustard poultice is a good thing to apply to an inflamed chest, but the most rabid supporter of the mustard poultice remedy would not insist on applying it to an inflamed eye!

Now, I claim that the argument of "Supply and Demand" is *not applicable* in the consideration of the "Equal Pay" question raised by the Interborough Association of Women Teachers. I base my claim on the following facts:

1. Said teachers are not in the open market; but, on the contrary, the supply is limited to those who secure places on an eligible list.

2. The qualifications and requirements to be met by candidates are fixed, not by God's or Nature's laws, but by the laws of the State and the by-laws of the Board of Education.

3. The supply of such eligible candidates is dependent on the *number, frequency,* and *regularity* of the examinations, and is therefore largely in control of the Board of Examiners and Board of Education.

4. The demand for teachers depends on the supply of pupils.

5. The supply of our pupils in grades below the seventh year of the Course of Study is nineteen times as great as the supply of pupils in all grades above the sixth year of the Course of Study.

6. All authorities agree that the best interests of the children demand women teachers in these lower grades.

7. Principals demand women teachers in these lower grades.

8. Superintendents demand women teachers in these lower grades.

9. Our Board of Education provides two regular examinations a year—January and June—for teachers of these lower grades.

10. Our Board of Education provides examinations for

license for higher grades and positions at irregular, unknown, infrequent periods.

The following are but samples: *Globe,* January 11, 1910: "It is doubtful if an examination of teachers of Mathematics in High School will be held before March or April. Probably not for a year."

Another: "No date has been set for the next examination for women teachers of history in high schools. One will not be held before next fall."

Who knows when the next examination for candidates to teach Music, Physical Training, Mathematics, Latin, Biology or any other special or high school subject will be held?

Who knows when there will be an examination of such people as desire to be Model or Critic Teachers in our Training Schools?

Ask any high school principal, any director of a special subject, any one of the 46 members of the Board of Education, any one of the 230 members of the local school boards, any one of the students in our high schools or colleges, any Civil Service Commissioner, any of the other officials of the city, any of the citizens of the city, any taxpayer, and see if you will receive a satisfactory answer?

In a letter which I wrote to a clerk of the Board of Education in January, 1910, I asked these questions:

"Can you tell me when the next high school examination will be held?

"The date of the last previous examination in the same subject?

"When was an examination for Model teacher or for Critic teacher in training school held, and when will the next one be?"

Following are the answers received:

"High school examinations are held twice each year in such subjects as there is a demand, when the lists of such subjects are exhausted or likely to be exhausted. It is likely that the next examination will be held about April first.

"The examinations for licenses to teach in training schools are held only when there is a vacancy."

If college graduates knew that there would be an examination every June or every September, or at some other regular, stated time, when they were free to get to New York and take the examination, there would never be any scarcity of candidates.

In face of these conditions, I question the good faith of any who apply the general argument of Supply and Demand to the solution of the question which the women teachers have raised.

But admitting, for the sake of argument, the good faith of the advocates of Demand and Supply as applied to this question, let us try to demonstrate the

Theorem: The men teachers of New York City should be paid more than the women teachers thereof because the supply of the women teachers is greater than the supply of men teachers.

Granted: (a) That there is an Association of Unappointed Men Teachers demanding places in these public schools.

(b) That there is no Association of Unappointed Women Teachers, nor are women teachers making any formal demand for such places.

(c) That the number of men teachers holding License No. 1 who have waited one, two, or more years for appointment is far in excess of the number of women holding similar license who have waited six months.

(d) That a man teacher has brought mandamus proceedings against the Board of Education to compel his appointment because his percentage was upwards of 90, while women with only 70 per cent. were appointed to places for which he was eligible.

(e) That no woman teacher has ever brought such proceedings on similar grounds.

*Therefore:* Men teachers should be paid *more* than the women teachers, because the supply of *men* teachers is *greater* than the supply of women teachers. Reductio ad Absurdum!

Furthermore, the highest educational authorities hold that women are the best teachers for the younger children.

City Superintendent Maxwell is an educational authority, and Mr. Maxwell states in his Annual Report, 1907: "Experience doubtless shows that women teachers teach younger pupils, *boys as well as girls, better* than men."

Horace Mann is recognized as one of the foremost educators in the history of our country, and Horace Mann said he would as soon place an elephant to brood chickens as he would a man to teach little children.

Yet, the city of New York is paying a man who teaches little children from one and a half to *two times as much* as it pays a woman who teaches these same little children, and it makes the woman serve seven years before it pays her what it gives the man in his first year of service.

Finally, we must not lose sight of the fact that the cry that men teachers are needed comes from prejudiced sources, that is—according to the petition blank of the Unappointed Men Teachers—"certain members of the Board of Education," "remarks of principals," and "statements of the Association of Principals and Male Teachers." Where is the cry from the pupils? (See Professor Thorndike's conclusions.) Where is the cry from the public? Where is the cry from the representatives of the people—the Board of Aldermen, the Legislature?

Compare the demand for Equal Pay:

From the people of the city represented by the Board of Aldermen. Unanimous vote.

From the people of the city represented by the Legislature, 80 out of 86 New York City votes for it.

From the Labor Unions representing hundreds of thousands of our citizens. Unanimous.

From the hundreds of Organizations of women and men.

From the thousands of individual citizens who have used voice or pen in our behalf.

## CHAPTER VIII

### SCARCITY OF WOMEN TEACHERS BREEDS DETERIORATION IN QUALITY OF TEACHER AND OVERCROWDED CLASSES

WHEN we went to Albany in January, 1907, there were 633 actual vacancies in the public schools of New York city. When you realize that that is about the number of teachers in the city of Rochester, its significance will sink deeper. Imagine the city of Rochester failing to supply teachers for its public school children. No Legislature or Governor would hesitate long over enacting a mandatory law to make her do so. Yet here in our own city, with its millions of foreigners, was a number of school children equal to the total number of public school pupils in one of the first-class cities of this State, equal to the total number of public school children in the State of Louisiana, greater than the total number of all the people in the State of Nevada, without regular teachers: to-day in the care of a pupil; to-morrow in the hands of a male substitute, at three dollars a day; next day in charge of a female substitute, at two dollars and a half a day. Is it any wonder we have thousands and thousands of backward children?

And what has the State done about it in these four years? Nothing. It is true the Legislature passed two bills, one effect of which would have been to increase and improve the supply of teachers, but Governor Hughes's veto killed one and Mayor McClellan's the other.

And what has the city done about it? Apparently has not noticed it. If these vacancies were all in the North Side section, or the Flatbush section, or the Bushwick section, the Board of Trade and the Taxpayers' Association of that particular locality would be "up in arms"; but they are scattered through the five hundred schools, and so the danger does not seem acute in any one spot. Through all our fight, I have heard only one man speak on this phase of the question, pointing out his right and that of all citizens to have good teachers for their children and emphasizing this need in the case of the children of laboring men who may have to leave school early. This man was James L. Gernon, speaking at a meeting of the Central Labor Union, Brooklyn, at which we were permitted to state our case.

And what has the Board of Education done about it? Held a special and extra examination in April, 1908; extended the age limit of candidates for license No. 1; made certain concessions in ratings.

High school teachers have told me their best girls are not taking up teaching. They are learning that the city offers far better salary inducements in other positions; and all who know anything about teaching, acknowledge there is no occupation that calls for so much self-sacrifice. When a girl who is employed as clerk or stenographer or telephone operator goes home at night, her work is over. Not so with the girl who is a teacher. Some may say that the teacher has shorter hours and longer vacations. That is true, but the shorter hours and longer vacations are not fixed out of consideration for the teacher, but for the pupil. It is true the teacher could not stand the strain, either; but if the pupils could, the teachers might be allowed to break down if that did not also entail a loss to the pupil.

### SCARCITY OF TEACHERS BREEDS DETERIORATION OF QUALITY OF TEACHER AND OVERCROWDED CLASSES

One of the inevitable results of a short supply is deterioration of quality. The demand for women teachers has been so much greater than the supply that the standards of qualifications and requirements and rating have been lowered. Nearly all those who complete the courses for teachers at high and training schools have been granted licenses to teach. For the special examination for license No. 1 given in April, 1908, concessions were made to induce teachers from outside this city to compete.

Commenting on this, the *Evening Journal* of December 31, 1908, said editorially:

"Why Not Teachers Better Paid Instead of Teachers Less Intelligent?

"The New York public schools have issued a circular which lowers the standard of candidates for public school positions.

"Women that ordinarily would be required to pass certain examinations before being accepted as school teachers are now exempt from parts of examinations or allowed to pass and become teachers on a lower percentage than formerly.

"The explanation is simple—there are not enough public school teachers.

"There are now seven hundred vacancies in the public schools. Seven hundred more teachers are needed.

"This lowering of standard follows closely upon a fight to prevent the women in the schools from getting fair play —the same pay as men for the same work.

"It is interesting to observe the school authorities fighting against decent pay for the women, struggling to keep women teachers on an inferior wage plane, and then inviting women of inferior ability to become teachers because not enough able women can be hired on an unjust basis of pay.

"But this question ought to force itself on the school authorities:

"Why have you a shortage of seven hundred among your women teachers? Why are you compelled to change your examination standards? Why not pay the women fairly? Wh not give them what you give men for the same work? Why not make of the teachers a satisfied, dignified, well-paid, thoroughly appreciated body of public officials? Their work is the most important work that is done in the world.

"Why insist on treating them as though they were 'hands' in a factory to be kept down to the lowest possible wages? Why not consent to pay an intelligent woman in the public schools, a woman to whom fifty young human souls are confided, as generously as you treat the man who sweeps out the halls in the Court House or the janitor who feeds the furnace, or even the policeman who handles the criminal?"

Other press comment was:

"A little while ago the *Delineator* was asking the question, 'What is the matter with the public schools?' There were a number of suggestions that developed from that investigation. There are a number of things the matter. Out of them all one defect in our educational system stands out glaringly. It is most tersely told in the last report of the United States Commission of Education. It's a simple statement of the salaries that American cities pay their school teachers.

"And that, ladies and gentlemen of the school boards, is what is the matter with our public schools, says the *Delineator.* We pay our unskilled street laborers something like a dollar or a dollar and a quarter a day. We are paying our school teachers some less and some a little more. It is the wages that a dull brain and a primitive mind are worth.

"In return for such wages we are requiring a service that should be entrusted only to a mind and heart enriched with all that literature and art and science can contribute to a perfect culture. It should be only such a personality into whose training we give the future citizens of the nation. Can we get personalities like that to serve us in our public schools? Not any longer than they can help it. Just as soon as their force of character and intelligence and initiative enable them to reach a better-paying position, one that will allow them to buy books and hear music and have the other good things of life that their large natures crave, they go after it.

"Until we realize with a conviction that reaches our pocketbooks that the school laborer is worthy of her hire, we aren't going to keep the best school laborers in the public employ. And there will continue to be something the matter with the public schools."

New York *Tribune,* December 31, 1907: "In making it somewhat easier for women teachers to secure places in the

New York City schools Superintendent Maxwell takes cognizance of actual conditions. The present shortage of more than seven hundred teachers indicates the practical impossibility of maintaining ideal standards of scholarship, and the Superintendent considers it far wiser to furnish seven hundred schoolrooms with teachers of moderate attainments than to deprive some thirty thousand pupils of proper facilities."

*Herald,* January 23, 1909: "The Pay of Teachers." "'There has never appeared any reason why teachers' salaries should be so small when compared with the importance of the work they are called to do, but it has been so since the old Greek peripatetics used to dispense philosophy in exchange for a crust.—Washington *Post.*' But how inevitably the laws of compensation works. Poor pay means mediocre teachers as a rule; mediocrity in teaching means inferior education, and in the train of the latter follows inefficiency and poverty among the masses. Fortunately American States and cities are learning the lesson that great economic waste results from poor pay for teachers."

Hon. Lewis Nixon, speaking at our Carnegie Mass Meeting, supported the contention of the women as a business proposition. He did not consider that the law of supply and demand was applicable, and declared that equal pay ought to be granted for business reasons. It had been his experience that whenever a product is sold for less than it is worth there is deterioration in the product. It was conceded that the women were not being paid what they were worth, for the city was paying men more for identically the same service. He added that if the inequalities were not rectified the result would be in the long run the impairment of the efficiency of the teachers.

Associate Superintendent Davis said in Superintendent Maxwell's 6th Annual Report: "It seems to be impossible to find an adequate number of properly qualified persons to fill all vacancies."

City Superintendent Maxwell in his 10th Annual Report says: "I feel constrained to say from my intimate acquaintance with the work of the Board of Examiners that the salaries now paid to women teachers are not sufficient to attract to our schools the best women teachers in the country." Mr. Maxwell had previously made some salary recommendations on which the *Standard-Union* of January 10, 1908, thus commented: "The advocacy of equal pay for men and women teachers is taken out of the field of sentiment by some common-sense observations of Superintendent Maxwell, who recommended increasing the minimum for women from $600 to $720, that the maximum be not less than $1500, and that all the principals shall receive the same salaries. He suggests there are some special purposes for which a few men teachers are essential. If so, and it really costs more to get them than it would to get women for the same places, an exception to the principle of equal pay might be made here—but it is to be noticed that the shortage of teachers over which such an ado is made just now is a shortage of women teachers. There is much reason to suspect the notion that a qualified man for a man's place is harder to get than a qualified woman for a woman's place is more or less a myth."

District Superintendent Richman reported: "An almost insurmountable obstacle to real progress is due to the fact that not a few teachers lack definite knowledge of the subject matter to be taught."

On account of the dearth of women teachers it was announced, "In the oral examination for license No. 1, a standing of 62 credits will be accepted in the case of women who have received a sufficiently high rating in the written to bring the average up to 70."

If we grant that our high schools and training schools are graduating only such as are fit scholastically at least, should not the "Oral Examination," including as it does ratings on "Personality," "Record," and "Use of English," form the most important part of the examination for teacher's license?

Some of the reasons for the scarcity of women teachers in the public school system are given in the address of Abby Leach, professor of Greek, Vassar College, before the Collegiate Alumnæ, Boston, November, 1907. She said: "Girls are now turning away from teaching as their work and seeking other occupations, and this is right, for few are fitted to be teachers. But the real reason is that the life of a teacher does not attract them, and without question they do come into much more human relations in other lines of work. Philanthropy is popular, and anyone who allies herself with any philanthropic or charitable work is better paid, and brought into pleasanter social relations than a teacher. Yet there is often no comparison between the value of the work in each case. The teacher is training the mind and character, the other is frequently ministering only to bodily needs; the one works for the immaterial, the other for the material. Why is the one valued so highly and the other undervalued? Does it mean that the age is so given over to material things that it does not really care for anything else? If parents did care deeply for the mental development of their children, were in earnest for them to have the best possible education, would they allow the profession of teaching to be so poorly paid as it is now? Would they submit to such poor teaching as is found too commonly now?"

That the scarcity still persists is proven by the fact that all of the women teachers on the eligible list for license No. 1 were appointed February 24, 1910. At that date there were still over 100 men waiting for appointment.

### SCARCITY OF TEACHERS BREEDS OVERCROWDED CLASSES

But the most serious result of the scarcity of teachers is the overcrowding of classes and the resultant crop of average pupils. Associate Superintendent Davis reported November, 1906: "The scarcity of teachers prevailing at the time of the present writing warns us that we cannot increase the number of classes and thus reduce the number of pupils to a class faster than is warranted by the supply of trained teachers. With few exceptions, at various times during the year the several eligible lists for teachers in the elementary schools have become exhausted."

The *Globe* made this pertinent comment:

"Large classes, one of the worst evils of any public school system, bid fair to remain in the New York schools for many months. Being unable to get enough regular teachers for the local schools, the Board of Education has instructed the board of superintendents not to further decrease the number of pupils to a teacher. This means that even the largest classes cannot be reduced in size, and that no more special classes for over-age and foreign-born children can be organized for the present.

"There are thousands of classes in the public schools which have from forty-five to sixty pupils all in the care of one teacher. It is evident that with so many pupils the teacher cannot do his or her work justice. Furthermore, the classrooms have been planned to accommodate not more than fifty pupils, and to crowd more than that number into a single room means a decrease in the air space per child and less healthful conditions. . . . Under such circumstances the pupils cannot do their best work."

Mr. Joseph M. Rogers, in the March number of *Lippincott's,* says in an article on "Educating Our Boys": "No teacher is physically or mentally competent to give proper instruction to forty children, which is the average size of a division in the public schools. It is amazing that so much is accomplished under such diffiulties. It is because the average teacher—usually a woman—gives of her vitality and sympathy and mental force to an extent which is abnormal and deplorable."

These conditions are not exaggerated. I know of two school districts in this city which had recently 187 classes with registers greater than 50, and 18 classes with registers of 50. This out of a total of about 650 classes.

Yet in a report to the Board of Estimate, President Winthrop of the Board of Education quotes Dr. Maxwell in the following manner: "Fifty pupils is too large a number to occupy any room or for any teacher to teach, no matter how numerous the sittings."

And Dr. Maxwell, in an article in the *City Record,* said: "I have made a study of this subject for years and have reached the very definite conclusion that the limit of a teacher's most successful work is reached with the following number of pupils in the respective grades:

| | |
|---|---|
| " Kindergarten | 30 |
| 1 A—4 B | 40 |
| 5 A—8 B | 30 |
| Defectives | 10." |

Yet the average number of pupils to a class in the grades from 1 A to 8 B, inclusive, according to Mr. Maxwell's 10th Annual Report, is 42. Is it surprising that the same report states that there are tens of thousands of over-age or retarded children in our schools?

Is this economy? Scarcity of teachers breeds large classes. Large classes breed over-age children. Over-age children cost the city to educate from two to four times what normal-age children cost.

At a meeting of the Flatbush Taxpayers' Association January 6, 1910, Commissioner Frank Meyer of the Board of Education said: "It is an outrage to place 60 children in a room and ask a teacher to instruct them. It is a shame to burden teachers in the grammar grades with more than 45 pupils at the most. . . ."

I am sure we all agree with him.

Wisdom says: "Hire more teachers."

Market replies: "Can't supply them at present rates."

Wisdom answers: "Offer higher rates."

# CHAPTER IX

## SCARCITY OF TEACHERS BUT UNAPPOINTED MEN

The press of yesterday, December 16, 1909, informs us that "having made unsatisfactory progress in their fight to induce the Board of Education to appoint more men teachers in the Elementary Schools, the men who are on the eligible list waiting for appointment have decided to take the matter to the courts. They hope to secure a decision which will declare illegal the practice of the Board of Education of making two eligible lists—one for men and the other for women teachers."

Thus are the men teachers unwittingly, I think, and unwillingly, I believe, assisting us. We, too, want one eligible list as the result of one examination, but we also want one salary for the position to which the license thus gained entitles its holder."

Again the press states: "The Association of Unappointed Men Teachers will hold a meeting December 17, 1909, at which committees will be appointed to continue the work with members of the Board of Education in order to convince them that men ought to be appointed."

In Superintendent Maxwell's report for 1906-7, Associate Superintendent Davis, then Chairman of the Superintendent's Committee on Nomination, Transfer and Appointment, discussing the supply of teachers, says: "The scarcity of regular class teachers has continued during the past year. Each eligible list has been exhausted as soon as received, in order that every available teacher might be placed in the schools at once. The cause of this scarcity as related to the sources of supply and to the conditions giving rise to an increased demand, was explained in the annual report of the City Superintendent. The number of declinations of appointment has added to our difficulties in this matter, there having been 72 declinations by men and 117 by women during the year."

In the same report, Superintendent Davis said: "The number of men teachers as compared with the number of women teachers employed in the public schools will always remain small because of the natural restrictions upon their employment. Men should not be assigned to schools that are exclusively for girls, nor should they be assigned to teach little children in classes of the first three years, even when these classes are composed entirely of boys. As these restrictions shut man from the vastly greater part of the school system it should be plain that the opportunities for their appointment must be comparatively few."

"In making nominations the Board of Superintendents has considered only the conditions in the individual schools; and when these have required the services of men, nominations have been made accordingly."

"Every request made by principals for men teachers has been complied with, and whenever in the judgment of the committee the services of a man teacher seemed desirable in any school a nomination was made without such request."

On December 11, 1907, in order to find out the reasons for the shortage of teachers, the Board of Education passed the following resolution, offered by Mr. Cosgrove: "Whereas, The city superintendent has heretofore reported to this board that a number of classes have been deprived of teachers, both regular and substitute, for some time; therefore be it

"Resolved, That the committee on elementary schools be requested to inquire into the causes leading to this result, and report the result of such inquiry to this board, together with such recommendations as it may deem advisable to remedy the situation."

On January 25, 1908, the *Globe* stated: "Usually the list from the January examinations is not announced until April, this year conditions regarding vacancies are such as to demand a speedy remedy. Heretofore it has been the custom of the board to appoint the teachers from the January eligible list for service in the fall, but this year the list will be immediately exhausted."

Associate Superintendent Edson in Superintendent Maxwell's Tenth Annual Report writes: "The usual scarcity of teachers prevailed until near the close of the school year, when a special examination was held in the month of April, 1908, to accommodate teachers from outside the city."

"On the other hand," says Superintendent Edson in Mr. Maxwell's Tenth Annual Report, "the employment of men involves greatly increased expense. As a business proposition, therefore, it does not seem wise *or necessary* to have a large number of men in any teaching corps. As far as any *necessity* exists, *a few will do as well* as more."

All in all, one is forced to the conclusion that Superintendent Edson is not worried bv the "lack of men teachers."

It is often stated that "Equal Pay" will drive men out of the schools. It is evident that "Unequal Pay" is *keeping* them out. The daily press for over a year has contained letters from these men teachers, complaining that they are not appointed, and the men on the eligible list have now organized into what is called "The Association of Unappointed Men Teachers." They have compiled facts showing that since June, 1908, 1500 women and only 39 men have been appointed. This Association has recently presented a petition to the Board of Education, praying for appointment.

Following are some samples of their plaints:

Letters to *Globe:*

October 13, 1909: "Since February, 1908, 196 have passed the examination. Only 15 appointed." "To see over 1000 women and young girls (many of whom had barely succeeded in getting the necessary rating of 70%, and had not yet demonstrated their capability) appointed before them. To bitterly realize that most of these girls appointed had passed the examinations later than they."

May 17, 1909: "Three men out of a total of over 100

were appointed last month. And as it happened, one of the three was a reinstated teacher at that. The merging of the present and the coming eligible list will mean that some of us, already despairingly distant from the top will be pushed still farther down into the realm of almost utter hoplessness." "By education and training they (the male teachers) *are fitted for no other work.*" "Yet an examination for License No. One for both men and women will take place in the early part of June. Such a state of affairs strikes me as paradoxical. Why create a large supply when there is no demand?"

Matthew J. writes: "The men on the No. One list this year seem to be singularly fortunate(?). They were notified of their having passed way back in July. . . . The schools open and no men are appointed. They wait two months, and have the pleasure of witnessing the enlivening spectacle of 250 women appointed and no men. They wait another month and see the entire list of women appointed and still no men, etc."

Causal Pugntndo Habemus, June 29, 1909: "I learned from your paper that the board refused to appoint men because of lack of funds? *Are we* caused to suffer because we are men? If, then, men are needed, but are on the other hand, 'more expensive than women,' why not apportion appointments according to the expense? Why not appoint three women to every two men? etc."

Men teachers are quite willing that women should suffer because they are women, but what an outrage that *they* should be caused to suffer because they are men. Apparently C. P. H. does not realize that his plan would not fill so many vacancies. But what does it matter whether the children have teachers or not, so long as more men teachers get places?

And a citizen writes: "Apropos of the recent letters in the school columns of *The Globe,* it is not edifying to note how ardently men will long for harmony 'in the face of danger' when they are the ones to whom danger has her face turned.

"I write as a citizen who has taken a keen interest for

moths in the brave struggle of the women teachers against the blatant injustice done them in the present salary schedule.

"Throughout that time I have seen few statements from men teachers of sympathy toward the women in their fight for justice. On the contrary, in spite of the fact that the women sought in no way to injure the men, the attitude of the latter has openly been and intentionally hostile to the women's cause.

"Now that they 'are facing danger' these gallant gentlemen are growing tired of 'the sad story of contention' that is injuring the dignity of the profession. It would have seemed more in keeping with their dignity and that of their profession had they come to this conclusion when they had favors to confer instead of favors to gain.

"Manhattan, Dec. 18. FRANK MAYNARD."

That the Board continued to be concerned over the shortage of teachers appears in a report submitted to the Board of Education, November 10, 1909:

"The committee on elementary schools respectfully reports that it has given careful consideration to the motion offered by Mr. Cosgrove at the meeting of the Board of Education on October 13th (1909), to the effect that this committee be requested to report to the Board the number of vacancies which exist in the elementary schools at the present time, how many of these vacancies can properly be filled by men, and also as to the advisability of appointing men thereto. The number of vacancies existing at the time was about 300, most of which were filled by the appointment at the last meeting of the Board of 250 women and 24 men, to take effect November first, not counting thirty-five teachers of special subjects. It has been the policy of the board of superintendents to assign men teachers only to boys or mixed classes, with which policy your committee has been and is in accord."

## CHAPTER X

### FALSE CRY OF SCARCITY OF HIGH SCHOOL MEN

In view of the facts presented herewith, it is difficult not to believe that there has been deliberate and wilful misrepresentation by those who have been clamoring for increased salaries for high school men teachers on the ground that there is a scarcity of such teachers.

The figures in the following table are taken from Superintendent Maxwell's Annual Report for year ending July 31, 1908. (See table next page.)

It is plain, therefore, that while only 44 per cent. of the pupils in the high schools are boys, that 47 per cent. of the teachers in the same schools are men. What authorities demand more men? Many of us think that if the percentage of high school men teachers equals the percentage of boy pupils, any reasonable demand should be satisfied.

The preponderance of men cannot be justified on the ground that men are better prepared because according to eminent authority men have less education as a preparation for teaching in the secondary public schools of the United States than women, and they remain in teaching very little longer than the opposite sex. Professor Edward L. Thorndike of the Teachers' College, Columbia University, reached these conclusions as the result of a careful investigation into the subject, and presented them in a publication entitled "The Teaching Staff of Secondary Schools in the United States," made at the request of the United States Bureau of Education. Professor Thorndike presents a variety of significant facts with reference to education, experience and salaries of teachers in our secondary schools. The report develops the fact that over five-ninths of the women have as long an education as has the median man, and not quite two-fifths of the women have taught as long as the median man.

Further evidence of the spuriousness of this cry of "Scarcity of High School Men" is given by Examiner

NUMBER OF HIGH SCHOOL PUPILS AND TEACHERS, JUNE 30, 1908.

| School | Men Trs. | Women Trs. | Boys | Girls | | |
|---|---|---|---|---|---|---|
| Morris | 35 | 59 | 904 | 1829 | that is 37 % men teachers to | 33% boys |
| Manual Training | 50 | 51 | 1448 | 1779 | that is 50 % men teachers to | 45% boys |
| Erasmus Hall | 44 | 42 | 711 | 1990 | that is 51 % men teachers to | 26% boys |
| Eastern District | 21 | 31 | 593 | 1505 | that is 50 % men teachers to | 28% boys |
| Bryant | 6 | 26 | 341 | 480 | that is 18 % men teachers to | 41% boys |
| Newton | 6 | 10 | 182 | 288 | that is 37½% men teachers to | 50% boys |
| Flushing | 12 | 12 | 208 | 310 | that is 50 % men teachers to | 40% boys |
| Far Rockaway | 3 | 5 | 68 | 110 | that is 60 % men teachers to | 38% boys |
| Jamaica | 10 | 15 | 194 | 468 | that is 40 % men teachers to | 30% boys |
| Richmond Hill | 8 | 11 | 196 | 324 | that is 42 % men teachers to | 37% boys |
| Curtis | 15 | 17 | 334 | 449 | that is 47 % men teachers to | 43% boys |
| Totals | 534 | 575 | 13834 | 17183 | 47 % | 43% |

Walter L. Hervey, who was in charge of the high school teachers' examinations in an appendix to Dr. Maxwell's last annual report, that the plentiful supply has "made it possible to apply a correspondingly rigid principle of selection not only in respect of scholarship and teaching ability, but particularly in respect of use of English and personality."

"It is a fortunate thing for the schools that such a situation exists. It is always unfortunate when, in order merely to supply an urgent demand for teachers, it is necessary, as it sometimes has been necessary, to license candidates who for any reason are doubtful or 'on the line,' or who have an insufficient command of English; or who, in dress, manner or personal habits, are careless or unrefined; or who, though satisfying these and many other requirements, lack those traits of responsibility, public spirit and devotion, without which a teacher may indeed give instruction in a subject, but cannot be an effective and loyal member of the faculty of a school."

In April, 1908, the board was forced by scarcity of teachers to hold a special and extra examination for teachers for elementary schools. In striking contrast was the condition affecting high schools. For years it has been the custom to hold an examination for high school teachers in April and another in October. In 1908, however, there there were so many teachers available that the April examination was abandoned, and the October examination advanced to September. Furthermore, the announcement for the September examination showed that it would cover but few subjects, as in the others the supply was sufficient.

*The Globe,* January 10, 1910, said: "There is no dearth of applicants for positions as teachers in the local schools now. The November high school tests brought out nearly five hundred applicants." Yet Superintendent Stevens is quoted as saying: "We must either offer better inducements or lower our standard for high school men."

Other evidence is given in press comments as: On October 20, 1909, the *Globe* published the following:

"At the recent hearings on the budget statements have been made frequently which tended to show that the supply of teachers for high schools was much less than the demand and that such condition did not exist in the elementary schools. Certain facts appear to have been overlooked. Examinations for elementary school teachers are held regularly in January and June each year, irrespective of the condition of the eligible list. Examinations for teachers in the various subjects in high schools are held only when the list in that particular subject is nearly exhausted. Thus at the present time when the high school teachers are so much in demand, the examination for such teachers to be held in November will cover only a few subjects. The limited demand is due in large measure to failure to hold examinations.

"Under date of October 27, City Superintendent Maxwell announces that the November examinations will also include tests for library assistants and for men teachers of stenography, mechanical drawing, English and joinery, and for men and women teachers of commercial branches and freehand drawing.

"Need more be said?"

And later,

"Hundreds of college graduates and experienced teachers are anxious to teach in the local high schools at the salaries now paid. At the examinations for licenses to teach in those schools last week there were present 460 applicants, the largest number which has taken such examinations in years.

"One hundred and nine took the test for teachers of German, while 86 wanted to teach Latin. The figures for the other licenses were: Biology 47, French 17, English 57, chemistry 35, stenography and typewriting 14, wood turning 2, forge work 1, joinery 3, mechanical drawing 6, freehand drawing 17, music 8, commercial branches 18, clerical assistant 31, and library assistant 9.

"These facts seem to bear out the contention of *The Globe* that the seeming scarcity of teachers for high schools is due to failure to hold examinations at regular intervals. It has been the custom to defer examinations for high school teachers until the existing lists are nearly exhausted."

But most significant of all is the action indicated in the following from the *Globe* of February 8, 1910:

"Plans for increasing the supply of high school teachers without in any way lessening the qualifications or lowering the standards were blocked at a Board of Education meeting recently by Chairman A. Stern of the special committee on increase of teachers' salaries. The reasons given were that he feared that the standards might be lowered and that to increase the supply of high school teachers *would result in doing away with the chief argument used to secure higher salaries for the men in the high schools.* Dr. Maxwell's assurance that the standards would not be lowered and that experienced local teachers now in their prime would be secured, was of no avail. Mr. Stern withdrew his signature from the report, which, he stated, had been presented to him only fifteen minutes before, and as he made the third member whose signature made the report possible it had to be withdrawn from consideration.

"The report from the by-law committee provided an amendment to the qualifications for eligibility for license as assistant teachers to the effect that the requirement of two years experience in grades of the 'last two years' of the elementary school course for persons not college graduates should be changed to 'last *four* years' of the elementary school course.

"Will not the change," said A. Stern, "result in securing a poorer kind of teacher?"

"It is my deliberate judgment," replied Dr. Maxwell, "that the change will not result in inferior teachers. It must be remembered that they are to come from our own schools. In the upper grades are most of the older teachers in the system, and under this plan an opportunity will be given to those who have served from seven to twelve years in the schools, to those just in their prime, to secure positions in the high schools. The examiners will not let down the bars. This board can well trust them to see to it that only those well qualified for the work are licensed."

"This reply was a disappointment to Mr. Stern, who explained that the change was more serious than he thought when he signed the report. 'It was presented to our committee only about fifteen minutes ago, and I signed it, but on further consideration I believe we should go slow. *Can't the members see how dangerous it would be just at this time when we are trying to secure increases in salaries to do anything to increase the supply?* We have repeatedly sought increases for the men teachers in the high schools, and one of the main reasons for doing so was the inability to get teachers, and now it is proposed to do away with the demand by stating that we can get teachers and will get them at a cheaper rate. I do not believe we will get the proper type of men if we alter the qualifications. At any rate, let us wait a while before we act.' "

## CHAPTER XI

### THE FAMILY-TO-SUPPORT ARGUMENT

It is rather a sad commentary on our profession that its men members are the only men who object to women members of the same profession getting the same pay for the same work. Who ever heard of a man lawyer fighting a woman lawyer in this way? A man doctor arguing that another doctor should give her services for less pay simply because she happened to be a woman? And leaving the professions, what attitude do we find the men who form our "Labor Unions" taking on this question? They form a solid phalanx on the side of "Equal Pay." The most powerful of all unions in many respects—"Big Six"—has a By-Law making it a misdemeanor to pay a woman less than a man working at the same form. All Labor Unions fight "two prices on a job."

Is it not sad to see men, American men, shoving aside, trampling down, and snatching the life preservers from their sisters? I say life preservers seriously and mean it literally. For to the woman obliged to support herself, is not her wage earning ability truly a life preserver. How can any man except one whom she is legally privileged to assist, take from a woman any part of the wages she has earned, and remain worthy even in his own eyes? The excuses he makes to himself and to others in the attempt to justify his act, tend to belittle him more and more.

And yet some men whose blood sisters have by teaching provided the money to enable them, their brothers, to become teachers, oppose those very sisters in their efforts to obtain "Equal Pay for Equal Work." Can one ask for stronger proof of the insidious danger to our manhood which lurks in unjust standards of salary for service rendered? The true man, the good man, ought to put the woman who earns a respectable living, on a pedestal, as a beacon of encouragement to other women to show them one who wanted clothes to wear, and food to eat, and a place to live, and who obtained them by honorable labor.

### THE FAMILY-TO-SUPPORT ARGUMENT

I must say at the outset that in my opinion considerations of family responsibilities have no place in the fixing of Salary Schedules. I hold that *salary is for service,* and should be measured by the service rendered, irrespective of the size, weight, color, complexion, race, previous condition of servitude, height, length of nose, location of ear, character of costume, religion, size of shoe, height of heel worn, hair or lack of hair on the face or head, number of children, nephews, nieces, aunts, grandfathers, parents—real or in-law—or other dependent relatives, of the person rendering the service. I'm sure if a man comes to sweep off the snow from your front stoop, you do not ask him if he is married and how many children he has, in order to fix the price for his work.

But for the sake of argument and of the opportunity to ask a question or two, we will consider this—the most common and persistent of the arguments proposed by our male opponents. A man who is a teacher should be given a higher salary than a woman who is a teacher, because a man has—or may have—a family to support.

Notice, I say "a man who is a teacher." I do this because I have never heard a man who is a doctor, or a lawyer, or a plumber, or a grocer, or a baseball player, or a barber, or a janitor, propose said argument.

Now, if salary is to be measured by the size of the salary receiver's family, why do we give Mayor Gaynor with six children the same salary we gave Mayor McClellan with no children? Or why does our Board of Education give Superintendent X. with no children as much salary as it gives Superintendent Y. with nine children? Again, has not Miss M., who has to support an invalid father and an uncle in an insane asylum, the same right to consideration as Mr. N. who has a wife and a son to support?

As a matter of fact, if these considerations have any place in the fixing of salaries, Miss M. should be given the higher salary, because, as has been well put by Miss Ennis, Secretary of the Interborough Association of Women Teachers, every child is in the nature of an endowment policy for his parents, as he is a potential wage-earner, while the relatives dependent on the woman teacher are, as a rule, those from whom she can look for no assistance in her old age.

Another member of our Executive Committee, Miss Clara Calkins, disposed neatly of this argument, by suggesting to a member of the Board of Education who interposed this objection to "Equal Pay," that the Board fix a salary for a position and then add a bonus for each child or dependent.

The "Family-to-Support," or "Family-Wage" argument ranks above even the "Supply-and-Demand" argument in the age and the frequency of its use by our male teacher opponents.

Is it not pitiful to find the very men who are reputed to be hired for their "Manly Influence" so unmanly? How any self-respecting wife and mother can permit her husband to go around publicly begging because he married her and with her became the fortunate possessor of children, is beyond my comprehension. Why is she satisfied to be on a different plane as a wife than is the girl who married a doctor, or a lawyer, or a merchant, or a plumber, or a street sweeper?

I can only account for her attitude by assuming that she thinks as her husband does, and I account for his attitude by believing one of three things:

(1) that he did not take up the sacred profession of teaching because he found it to be his true vocation, but rather because it was an easy road to an assured income;

(2) that he belong to a race whose traditions have always always placed woman on a lower plane than a man; or

(3) that he is of the conservative type, dead to all progress, that believes because a condition "has been," it should continue to be.

I am firmly convinced that while teaching is a natural vocation for most women, it is rarely the true vocation of a man. And that those who enter the profession without the love for it which overshadows even the pocket returns, invariably deteriorate. Their lives are spent largely among those whom they consider their subordinates—in position or in salary, if not in intellect—the children and the women teachers. They grow to have an inordinate opinion of themselves. No matter how ridiculous or absurd or unfair may be the attitudes they take and the things they say, there is no one to say, "Nonsense!" as would one of his peers in the outer world. The novelist David Graham Phillips in the following description of one of his characters expresses my opinion better than I can myself: "Peter was not to blame for his weakness. He had not had the chance to become otherwise. He had been deprived of that hand-to-hand strife with life which alone makes a man strong. Usually, however, the dangerous truth as to his weakness was well hidden by the fictitious seeming of strength which obstinacy, selfishness and the adulation of a swarm of sycophants and dependents combine to give a man of means and position."

Recently in one of our schools, a male assistant to the principal resigned. The vacancy thus caused was filled by a woman. This woman is doing the same work as the man did, but with greater satisfaction to the principal. *But* she is being paid $800 a year less than the man was.

In another school I know there was a woman assistant to principal. As a grade teacher she had married and resigned, expecting—as most girls do when they marry—that she wouldn't have to work outside the home any more. But her husband became a victim of tuberculosis, and they went to Colorado in search of health for him. Time passed, their funds were exhausted, the invalid was unable to work, and so they came back, and the wife—after certifying, as our by-laws require, that her husband was unable to support her and had been so for two years—was reappointed. Later she secured promotion to assistant to principal. During the day she labored in a large, progressive school, composed almost wholly of children born in Russia, or of Russian parentage. At night she taught a class of foreign men. Now, although she actually had a family to support, she was receiving $800 a year less than a man in her position would receive. A married man? Oh, no, not necessarily. He might be a millionaire bachelor, or the pet of a wealthy wife—it is only necessary for him to be a "male" assistant to principal. Possibly on account of her family responsibilities, probably because she was ambitious, she strove for a principalship. During the school year, she traveled to Columbia University and took post-graduate courses after school and on Saturdays; during the summer, when she should have been resting, she was studying with Professor This and Professor That. Last September she took the examination for a principal's license: in October, she died—typhoid, the doctors said. The husband she had cheerfully and lovingly supported for years survived her but a few weeks.

Why have I dwelt on this? To show the absurdity of the "family wage" argument of the male teacher.

A circular recently issued by some of our male-teacher-opponents evidenced this pitiable state of mind. Following are some quotations with comment:

3. "To the employee that wage is just which furnishes the living wage—understanding thereby living in accordance with the physical, mental and moral standards of the class of laborers."

One is forced to ask, Who will set the physical, mental, moral standards that differentiate a teacher from a preacher, doctor, lawyer, artist, engineer, etc.?

4. "To the Adult man teacher that wage is just which furnishes such a living wage for the average family."

Again the male *teacher* is segregated in a pitiful class of mendicants.

6. "A mandatory wage greater than that is unjust to the employer. His liberality must be limited by considerations of the *quality only of the work.*"

Pity the average male teacher if this were made the actual standard of wages.

8. "It follows that from the standpoint of the employer the necessary masculine wage is an unnecessary feminine wage. This is, I believe, cold-blooded economic law. Salaries are not 'rewards of merit.' They are the *market price of labor.*"

In what new dissertation on logic and economics shall we find accepted definitions of "the necessary masculine wage," "unnecessary feminine wage"? Senator F., in opposing our bill, quoted, "Shall the single woman, in teaching, be given the married woman's wage?" I ask, Why not?—just as the single woman in washing, in farming, in millinery, in nursing, in telephoning, and writing.

9. "Equalization must be on (1) basis above, (2) equal to, or (3) lower than the necessary masculine wage."

Again the masculine wage. On this point the following letter from Mr. Arthur Gibb, proprietor of Frederick Loeser & Co., one of the largest department stores in the city, employing thousands of men and women during the year, is pertinent:

"Brooklyn, March 5, 1908.

"Miss GRACE C. STRACHAN.

"*Dear Madam:* The movement has my entire sympathy and I hope you will be successful in your endeavor to have the salaries of men and women teachers equalized. To claim that a man should have more pay than a woman because he may have more people dependent upon him is as absurd as to claim that a man with six children should have more pay than one with none. *Neither the city nor any other employer should consider anything but whether the person is fitted to fill the place, salary being based on the work performed and not on sex.*

"Yours very truly,

"ARTHUR GIBB."

10. "If on either of the first two theoretical possibilities, it is unjust to the employer, so far as the present corps of women teachers are concerned; it is unjust to women candidates, as only the very exceptional women will be taken; unjust to the schools, *as women will be replaced by men.*"

We appreciate the acknowledgment that the schools would suffer if women should be replaced by men. We note the continued expression of distrust of the Board of Education.

The men who are opposing "Equal Pay" seem incapable of "seeing true": witness the crooked reasoning of the following:

"To the Editor of the Brooklyn *Eagle:*

"Several labor unions have indorsed the female teachers' plea for equal pay. The men teachers want to submit through the *Eagle* that these indorsements have been secured without a fair consideration of facts. Notwithstanding that the male teachers are making a distinctly labor union fight to maintain a high standard of salary, the unions have in no instance called for the men's side. Therefore, we must come out in the open and declare our position.

"Everybody knows that the mission of women in the labor world has been to lower wages. Hence the hope of every labor idealist: the elimination of women from the competitive field. And how? By making work too attractive for her to ever want to leave it or by fixing the man's salary according to the low standard that obtains everywhere for the woman? Does any labor unionist want his salary measured by the standard his boss is willing to adopt for his girl laborers? Would labor unionism be doing its duty by the millions of men toiling to support families if it were to send throughout the nation the edict that wherever a woman was employed, in public or private service, she should be paid as much as her male co-worker—and more pernicious still—that no man should be paid a dollar more than the woman employed in similar service. Wouldn't this be a blow at the very vitality of unionism? Wouldn't it everywhere regulate the man's salary by the universally lower woman's salary? Ought any labor unionist demand that the Legislature of New York enact this precedent? The essence of unionism is antagonistic to class legislation. Why, then, do the unions demand laws for the female school teacher that they would deny their own female co-workers?

"The men teachers of New York are not making a fight to hold their grip on the dollar. Few of them—an insignificant minority—will lose a cent by the proposed legislation. Our fight is not for those that are in, but for those who are to come in. We don't want a $2,160 maximum cut to $1,635 for the young man entering the profession now. We don't believe that the salary of any man in any public activity should be regulated by the low rate that time and custom have universally fixed for women.

"M. T.

"Brooklyn, March 18, 1907."

---

"'M. T.' is evidently unfamiliar with the principles governing trade unions, or he would have known that they have always strenuously objected to low-priced labor, whether it is of men, women or children; that they have for many years done their utmost to drive children out of the factories, mills and mines; that they have everywhere lent their aid and assistance to women to organize for higher wages and less hours of labor. Typographical Union No. 6 at one time had to compete with woman labor for which employing printers paid less per thousand ems than for that of men. When the 'matter' set up by the women was corrected and ready for the forms, it was just as valuable as was that set up by the men. As a rule women took longer to set a thousand ems, and sometimes their proofs contained more errors; but as they had to make the corrections the loss was theirs. They, therefore, could not earn as much as men, even though they had received the same price per thousand. There were women, however, who were exceptions to that rule, and could do as much and as good work as the average man. Of late years, women have received in union offices the same rates as the men for piece work.—Editor Brooklyn *Eagle*."

Yet, I would not be understood as despising all men who choose the teaching profession, or as belittling the value of good men in our public schools. There are some splendid men in our system, men contact with whom is beneficial to associates and pupils alike. Needless to say, they all love justice, and are therefore all warm advocates of "Equal Pay" schedules.

Nevertheless, I pray that no one of my eight nephews shall feel a "call" to teach while the present conditions, deadly to the finest moral and manly virtues, exist.

One of the best things that has been written in connection with our fight, is the following editorial. It was the leader in the New York *Press* of February 21, 1910:

"MORAL ASTIGMATISM

"We imagine that disinterested people will read with a feeling of mixed censure and amusement the statement made by the men teachers of the elementary schools, in a pamphlet addressed to the Board of Education, in regard to the subject of equal pay for men and women teachers.

"They, the men, have come out against equal pay. Perfectly natural action, based on naïve selfishness, is likely to provoke a smile, mixed with unfavorable criticism. The men are afraid, no doubt, that if the women receive more pay, they (the men) will not receive so much, or that, at any rate, their pay will not be so likely to be raised.

"One of the arguments used by the men teachers against equal pay is that such a system would tend to prevent the women marrying, that it would 'involve the establishment of a preferred celibate class.' In other words, these men fear a system by which women may no longer feel themselves forced to marry for economic reasons. They say, in effect, 'keep down the salaries of women, for if we give them an opportunity for independence they won't marry us.'

"Any action such as this on the part of the men teachers which tends to limit the growing independence of women is reactionary and short-sighted. The fact that so many women are led to marry in order to improve their material condition is hateful to our ideals. It is probably true, that under a system of equal pay, where services should be paid for irrespective of sex, some women who now marry would remain single. But there are some men to-day who remain single because of relative economic independence, which they desire to maintain. These men are, however, relatively few. Women are as instinctive and as normal as men are, and independence, which they feared to lose, would prevent very few from marrying when they could make marriages which were attractive to them. Independence of women would improve marriage, since fewer women would marry because of necessity. By the same means divorce would be decreased, and human happiness would have a boom.

"But these wide considerations do not appeal to a body of men teachers whom their 'interests' have made morally astigmatic. Especially from teachers, perhaps, we should demand some element of altruism and sympathy with social progress."

The following was the result when I tried to outline a debate on the resolution: That men teachers should be paid a higher salary than women teachers, because they have families to support.

*Affirmative:*

Granted (a) That it is the fashion to look upon the man as the support of the family.

*Negative:*

Granted (a) That salary is for service rendered.

(b) That 500,000 women of our country are wage-earners.

(c) That the public schools are not included in the eleemosynary institutions of the city, county, or State.

(d) That a man teacher who has no one dependent on him is paid the same salary as one who has many dependent upon him.

(e) That the man teacher whose wife is worth $100,000 is paid the same salary as the man teacher who marries a poor school teacher who has no money or property income.

HON. GEORGE B. McCLELLAN,

MAYOR OF THE CITY OF NEW YORK WHO VETOED THE "WHITE" AND THE "GLEDHILL-FOLEY" "EQUAL PAY" BILLS—1907 AND 1909.

(f) That most women teachers have many dependent on them.

(g) That only a fraction of one per cent. of the women teachers have no one dependent on them.

(h) That our own school records contain evidence that some women teachers are supporting even their husbands.

(i) That men doctors do not demand a higher fee than women doctors.

(j) That men typesetters do not get higher pay than women typesetters.

(k) That men attendance officers in our public school system do not get more pay than women attendance officers. (I have one woman officer who supports herself and three children and contributes to the support of her father. I have one man officer, who is a young bachelor and contributes to the support of a widowed mother.)

(l) That men who teach in our evening schools are not paid more than women who teach in the same schools.

(m) That men who teach in our summer schools are not paid more than women who teach in the same schools.

(n) That the United States does not pay the man teacher more than it pays the woman teacher.

(o) That no State in the Union except New York fixes by statute a salary for a man higher than that for a woman occupying the same position.

(p) That New York State nowhere fixes a salary for a man higher than that for a woman except in Section 1091 of the Charter of the City of New York, which sets the minimum salaries for "female" teachers and for "male" teachers.

## CHAPTER XII

### CIVIL SERVICE AND SALARY SCHEDULES

ALL we ask is to be paid on the same basis as other Civil Service employees. That sex of worker is not considered either by the city or the State in other departments is amply proven by the following:

"New York, January 31, 1908.

"*My dear Miss Strachan:*

"Replying to your letter of the 26th instant, I have to say that among Civil Service employees sex is not made a basis for difference in salary when the position held is the same.

"I am sending you, under separate cover, a copy of the Rules and Classifications of the Municipal Civil Service Commission.

"Yours sincerely,

"ARTHUR J. O'KEEFE,

"J. G. C. (Civil Service Commissioner)."

The quotations below are interesting in this connection:

"On Wednesday, Nov. 4, the Civil Service Commission will conduct an examination for typewriting copyist, second grade, for the Board of Water Supply. The examination is open to both men and women. The requirements are identical. The salary is the same for both sexes.

"This is a recognition of the principle of 'equal pay for equal work.' This is the principle which the women teachers ask be applied in the public schools.

"The city recognizes it in one branch of the city government, why not in the schools?"

Another:

"'Equal pay for equal work' is not a new principle in

New York City government. Ample evidence of this fact is presented in the recent announcements of future Civil Service examinations.

"On Jan. 22 an examination will be held for the position of dietitian, and it is open to both men and women on equal terms, and the salary ranges from $720 to $1,500 per annum, there being no discrimination on account of sex.

"On Jan. 25 an examination will be held for bacteriologist. It is open to both men and women, and the salary is $1,200. There is no sex discrimination here.

"Why should there be discrimination in the pay of teachers?"

Another:

"Since the agitation started by the Interborough Association of Women Teachers, that the position of public school teacher be placed under the jurisdiction of the Municipal Civil Service Commission, subject to all regulations of civil service, the interest throughout the city is centering around the women holding any and all governmental positions. The transfer on Thursday of Miss Anna Murphy from the Department of Public Charities to the License Inspector's Department has occasioned considerable comment.

"The salary paid Miss Murphy is the same as that paid to any of the men holding a like position.

"There are now three women holding the position of Inspector of Licenses, each at a salary of $1,500—all appointed by Commissioner Bogart, who believes that in every position, be it public or private, appointments should be made irrespective of sex, provided the incumbent is capable of holding such position. . . .

"The appointment of Miss Murphy is a further incentive to the women school teachers to have all positions of the Department of Education placed under the civil service jurisdiction."

Extract from our Memorandum to the Ivins Charter Commission:

"*Sirs:* The twelve thousand members of the Interborough Association of Women Teachers of the City of New

York, representing every grade and department of the public school service from kindergarten to district superintendent inclusive, is unanimous in its petition that you recommend such a revision of the Chapter on Education as will secure:

"A.—Salary for position, regardless of sex of incumbent.

. . . . .

and in support thereof we beg you to consider:

"1. The recent opinion of Judge Gray of the New York Court of Appeals in the case of State vs. Williams, in which he says:

"'The right of the State to restrict or regulate the labor and employment of children is unquestionable; but an adult female is not to be regarded as a ward of the State, or in any other light than the man is regarded when the question relates to the business pursuit or calling.

"'In the gradual course of legislation upon the rights of a woman in this State she has come to possess all the responsibilities of the *man, and she is entitled to be placed on an equality of rights with the man. Considerations of her physical differences are sentimental and find no proper place in the discussion of the constitutionality of the act.*'

"2. That in Section 1091 of the Charter, the State in effect said to the Board of Education, it is the policy of the State to pay women teachers less than men teachers; and yet a careful study of Chapter 577, Laws of New York, 'An Act making Appropriations for the Support of Government'—the only other Act in which the State appears as an employer of labor—fails to disclose a single indication that the State as an employer considers *sex* of the incumbent in fixing the salary of the position. For instance, on pages 19 and 20, we find:

"'*Department of Education.*

"'Commissioner's Office.

"'For the salaries:

of the *commissioner* of education, seven thousand five hundred dollars ($7,500), and for his traveling and other expenses, one thousand five hundred ($1,500), pursuant to chapter forty, laws of nineteen hundred four.

*secretary* to the commissioner, one thousand five hundred dollars ($1,500);

*of the employees according to grade:*

sixth grade, two employees, one thousand dollars each ($2,000);

"'Administration Division.

*chief,* three thousand dollars ($3,000);

*cashier,* two thousand five hundred dollars ($2,500);

*of the employees according to grade:*

seventh grade, one employee, one thousand five hundred dollars ($1,500);

sixth grade, two employees, one thousand two hundred dollars ($2,400); two employees, one thousand dollars each ($2,000);

fifth grade, three employees, nine hundred dollars each ($2,700);

fourth grade, one employee, seven hundred twenty dollars ($720).'

"On Page 27:

"'*Teachers' Institutes.*

"'For the salaries:

of *five institute conductors,* three thousand dollars each ($15,000);

of a *special instructor in drawing,* two thousand two hundred dollars ($2,200);

of a *special instructor in primary work,* reading and literature, two thousand dollars ($2,000);

of a *special instructor in English,* one thousand two hundred dollars ($1,200).'

"Page 53:

"'*State Commission in Lunacy.*

"'For the salaries:

of the *medical commissioner,* seven thousand and five hundred dollars ($7,500);

*legal commissioner,* five thousand dollars ($5,000);

*lay commissioner,* five thousand dollars ($5,000);
*medical inspector,* four thousand five hundred dollars ($4,500);
*secretary,* four thousand dollars ($4,000);
*auditor* of the state hospital estimates, four thousand dollars ($4,000);
*of the employees according to grades:*
eighth grade, one employee, one thousand seven hundred dollars ($1,700);
seventh grade, three employees, one thousand five hundred dollars each ($4,500);
sixth grade, four employees, one thousand and two hundred dollars each ($4,800);
fourth grade, one employee, seven hundred dollars ($700);
second grade, one employee, four hundred twenty dollars ($420).'

"Page 55.

"'*Rochester State Hospital.*

"'For the maintenance of the Rochester state hospital, two hundred forty thousand dollars ($240,000), or so much thereof as may be necessary.'

"Page 58.

"'*Prison Department.*

"'For the salaries:
of the *superintendent* of state prisons, six thousand dollars ($6,000);
*superintendent's clerk,* four thousand dollars ($4,000);
two stenographers, one thousand dollars each (2,000);
messenger, one thousand dollars ($1,000);
one parole officer, one thousand five hundred dollars ($1,500);
two parole officers, one thousand two hundred dollars each ($2,400).'

"3. We pray you to consider also in this connection whether the Civil Service Laws are not being violated when persons who have complied with the *same* requirements as to qualifications and examinations in competing for a position, are not then placed in order of standing on the *same* eligible list, and paid the *same* salary when appointed to the same position.

"In conclusion, we reiterate: The Interborough Association of Women Teachers of the City of New York, prays that in your report you will recommend such a revision of the Chapter on Education as will remove the injustices to women in the salary schedules incorporated in Section 1091 of the Charter of the City of New York, without, however, removing from the teachers of this city the protection of having their minimum salaries fixed by the State."

### SALARY BASED ON SEX-SALARY BASED ON DRESS

Alfred Hall in a letter to the North Side Board of Trade (Bronx), under the date of March 1, 1908, wrote:

"Our women teachers are not asking for charity; they only ask for the same pay as the male teachers receive for doing identically the same work.—Woman disguised as man has done duty in army, navy and various other positions, and always received the salary that went with the position, and if one of our girls in man's attire, applied for a position as teacher in our public schools and passed the necessary examinations, she would receive a man's pay. Woman should need no disguise to get justice in a civilized country.—The man, in cap and gown, sits on the bench to dispense justice, and his salary is not reduced on account of his wearing the frock. The emblem of justice is a female figure holding the scales, but her sex, alas! is denied justice because of that sex."

That woman has been accepted as man because of her dress, and has been paid wages as a man, is proven by the following:

St. Louis, February 16.—"James" Davis, who deceived as to sex even Del Brown, the man who shared "James's" room at a boarding house were both employed as men servants, is really Mabel Davis, of Waverly, New York.

Miss Marion Hamilton Gray, who dressed as a boy and posed as a boy ever since childhood, according to the story she told Magistrate Kernochan in Night Court last night, is going to don petticoats.

The Magistrate advised her to, and she said she would. Until about two years ago she had found her masculine disguise perfectly comfortable and her masculine life, including cigarettes and pipe, very agreeable. She crossed the ocean as a cabin boy without detection. She had a goodly income from somewhere in Great Britain. She was accepted as the son of Colonel Hamilton-Gray of the British Army, and kinsman of the noble Scottish family of that ilk.

Butte, Montana, December 12.—"The sudden death yesterday, at Manhattan, of 'Sammy' Jones, aged 80, disclosed the fact that instead of being a man, as everyone in the vicinity of Manhattan for the past eighteen years had believed 'him' to be, Jones was a woman."

St. Louis, February 15.—"'William' Winters, a handsome, rosy-cheeked boy, was transformed to Miss Lillian Winters to-day. 'My first job was at Quincy, Ill., posting bills, and I continued the work for two years. I wanted to live in a larger city and came to St. Louis in the latter part of 1902. I have lived here all this time as a man and not one person has suspected that I was otherwise. The best job I ever had was while I drove a wagon for a foundry and that only paid $12. The impulse has always been strong with me to break away from the men I was thrown in contact with, and while I behaved as one of them I hated it all. I wanted to be a girl.'"

If any of the above had succeeded in getting a license to teach in the city of New York without having her disguise discovered, she would have received a male teacher's salary—"a family wage."

# CHAPTER XIII

## WOMEN TEACHERS AND OTHER WOMEN CIVIL SERVICE EMPLOYEES

In this connection the difference in the requirements for eligibility must be considered.

The character of the work required, the years of preparation involved, the necessity for constant study, the vital importance of maintaining a good social position in the community should all be taken into consideration when the matter of fixing a fair remuneration for a teacher is at issue.

Under the Compulsory Education Law, a girl may leave school when she has reached the age of fourteen years, and has satisfied certain scholastic requirements in elementary subjects—fixed by the Board of Superintendents as those of the 5B grade; while in order to be eligible to teach in our elementary schools, a girl must have graduated from a four years' course at a high school and a two years' course at a Training School for Teachers, and must also have passed the examinationn given by the Board of Examiners of the Department of Education, of New York City.

It will thus be seen that a girl who desires to serve the city as a teacher in our public schools must first serve an apprenticeship of at least nine years: because in addition to fulfilling the requirements which would entitle her to "working papers" she must complete successfully the work of the sixth, seventh, and eighth years of the Elementary School Course, of the four years in the High School Course, and of the two years in the Course of the Training School for Teachers, before she is eligible even to take the examination for License No. 1, which she must pass before she is eligible for appointment as a Teacher in our Elementary Schools.

On the other hand, the girl who decides to serve the city as a Stenographer, a Typewriter, a Telephone Operator, a Tenement House Inspector or an Attendance Officer, must fulfill no requiremennts as to scholarship, and must pass no examination other than that given by the Civil Service Commission for the particular position desired.

## STATISTICS TAKEN FROM CITY RECORD, 1905-6.

All positions under Civil Service Commission.

Number of women about 5000.

No salary discrimination against women—position carries salary, without regard to sex of person holding it.

*Mayor's Office*

| | |
|---|---|
| Carolyn, private sec., /06. | $1800 |
| Carrie, clerk, /02. | 1200 |
| Henry, clerk | 1200 |
| Rose, sten. bk. and typ. | 1200 |

*Com. of License*

| | |
|---|---|
| Rena, sec., 6/9/04. | $ 900 |
| Marion, inspec., 9/27/05. | 1500 |

*City Clerk's Office*

| | |
|---|---|
| Lillian, sten. & typr., /04. | $1050 |
| Francis, messenger | 1200 |
| Anna, sten. to pres., /02. | 1200 |

*Dept. of Finance*

| | |
|---|---|
| Agnes, clerk, /01. | 900 |
| Sophie, clerk, /04. | 900 |
| Mary, sten. and typr., /00. | 1350 |
| Mary, sten. and typr., /99. | 1050 |
| Anna, sten. and typr., /93 | 900 |
| Lizzie, cleaner, /98. | 540 |
| John, watchman, /01. | 900 |
| Eliz., /02 | 1200 |
| Mary, sten. and typr., /02 | 900 |

Positions under Board of Education.

Number of women about 15,000.

Great salary discrimination against women, in most of the positions.

Teachers of grades from kindergarten to 6B must teach 16 years and have the $60 bonus for boys, before receiving $1300. This is the maximum.

Schedule III

| Years | |
|---|---|
| 1 | $ 600.00 |
| 2 | 640.00 |
| 3 | 680.00 |
| 4 | 720.00 |
| 5 | 760.00 |
| 6 | 800.00 |
| 7 | 840.00 |
| 8 | 880.00 |
| 9 | 920.00 |
| 10 | 960.00 |
| 11 | 1000.00 |
| 12 | 1040.00 |
| 13 | 1080.00 |
| 14 | 1120.00 |
| 15 | 1160.00 |
| 16 | 1200.00 |
| 17 | 1240.00 |

Annual increase $40.
Bonus for boys' classes $60.

Gladys, sten. and typr., /03 900
Lillie, sten. and typr., /99 1050
And nine others.. 720 and 1200

Telephone operators appointed Dec., 1905.....$1300
Other telephone operators from .........$600 to $1500

Clerks $ 750, 900, 1050, 1200, 1500

Annual increase not less than $150.

Medical examiners who have other practice besides school inspection..$1200

Secretaries to heads of departments, $1300, $1500. $1800.

Stenographers and typewriters, $750, $900, $1050, $1200, $1350, $1500, $1600.

Tenement house inspectors, $900, $1050, $1200, $1350, $1500, $1800.

(Unclassified)
Cleaner, $450, $640, $750.

Seamstress, Truant School, $780.

Attendance Officers, men and women, Department of Education, $900, $1050, $1200, $1350, $1500.

A woman teacher must have taught three years and passed examination for license for promotion and be assigned to class of the 7A, 7B, or 8A grade, before she is placed in the schedule which pays $1320 at the end of 15 years, with $60 bonus for boys' classes.

A woman teacher must have taught at least eleven years, must have secured two higher licenses, and be assigned to a graduating class of *boys,* before she receives $1500.

When one considers the difference in the nature of the work and the requirements for eligibility between teachers, and the artisans mentioned below, the following facts are interesting:

| | | | |
|---|---|---|---|
| Laborers receive from | $2.00 | to $3.50 | per day |
| Cartmen | 3.50 | to 4.00 | per day |
| Truckmen | 4.50 | to 5.00 | per day |
| Drivers | 4.00 | | |
| Painters | 4.00 | | |
| Blacksmiths | 4.00 | | |
| Carpenters | 4.00 | | |
| Stablemen | 3.00 | | |
| Plasterers | 5.50 | | |
| Tinsmiths | 4.00 | | |
| Stokers | 3.00 | | |
| Hod carriers | 3.40 | | |

Figures below taken from Superintendent Maxwell's Tenth Annual Report:

717,250 Net Enrollment of Pupils in all Schools—year 1907-8.

$18,596,874.70 for salaries of teachers.

Total sum per year for teachers' salaries per pupil, $25.92.

Total sum per school day for teachers' salaries per pupil, 13 cents if reckoned on 197 days; 7 cents on 365 days.

Total sum per school hour for teachers' salaries per pupil, 2 cents if reckoned on 197 days; 1 cent on 365 days.

Prevailing rate of wages per hour for carpenter is 80 cents.

Prevailing rate of wages per hour for plumber is 80 cents.

There were 197 school days in school year of 1907-8.

A teacher's "hours" are reckoned here as six.

*N. B.*—Of course, it is well known that a teacher has to eat and dress throughout the whole 365 days, and that her hours of labor do not end at three.

## OTHER COMPARISONS

Statistics of the largest ten cities in the U. S. show the average maximum salary paid elementary school teachers to be $1373.

| Teachers Salary in First Year | | | | Street and Sewer Laborers | |
|---|---|---|---|---|---|
| Boston........ | $552 = | $10.61 | per week | $12.06 | per week |
| Cincinnatti.... | 400 = | 7.69 | " | 9.87 | " |
| New Orleans.. | 315 = | 6.06 | " | 9.62 | " |
| Providence.... | 400 = | 7.69 | " | 9.20 | " |
| Los Angeles... | 540 = | 10.40 | " | 12.00 | " |
| New York.... | 600 = | 11.53 | " | | .. |

CITY PAYS BETTER SALARIES TO OTHER WOMEN WORKERS

New York City cannot get enough teachers for its public schools, and one reason is that it offers better inducements to women to seek other city positionns. It grants "equal pay" to the typewriting copyists, and the salaries are as good, often better, than those paid to teachers, although the requirements for eligibility are not so high and the examinations prescribed are not so difficult as those prescribed for teachers.

The Civil Service Commission has just issued the following call for an examination for "typewriting copyists":

"Public notice is hereby given that applicationns will be received from Monday, Dec. 16, until 4 P. M., Monday, Dec. 30, 1907, for the position of typewriting copyists, second grade (male or female). The examination will be held on Monday, Jan. 20, 1908, at 10 A. M. The subjects and weights are: Speed test, 6; tabulation, 3; arithmetic, 1. The salary is $600 to $1,050 per annum, inclusive. Candidates may also qualify as graphaphone operators. The minimum age is eighteen years. For further information apply to the secretary."

From this it will be seen that the city recognizes the principle of "equal pay" or salary for position so far as typewriting copyists are concerned. Comparison with the requirements, etc., for teachers' licenses shows that it is much easier to secure the $600 salary of a stenograher than it is to get the $600 paid to woman teachers.

First as to requirements. The minimum age limit is

eighteen for teachers and for typewriting copyists. The preliminary education required, however, is not the same.

A candidate for a teachers' license must at least have completed a high school course and two years in the training school, or else have been graduated from the Normal College.

The candidate for the position of typewriting copyist is required to have only an elementary school education and need not necessarily have had experience or training in stenography.

The examinations which the candidates for teachers' licenses must pass are much more difficult than those required of the typewriting copyists.

Applications for teachers' licenses must pass written examinations and practical tests in the following subjects:

History and principles of education.

Methods of teaching.

Constructive work and drawing.

Music.

Physical training.

Sewing.

In addition they must pass an oral examination.

The subjects and weights in the examination for typewriting copyists are:

Speed test, 6.

Tabulation, 3.

Arithmetic, 1.

As regards the salary, both begin at $600, but the women teachers are granted an automatic annual increase of $40; however typewriting copyists do not receive an automatic increase, their increase being determined by the department heads, but the amount is usually $150 each time. It is evident, therefore, that the typewriting copyist will reach the maximum at an earlier date than the teacher.

Under such conditions it is not surprising that there should be a scarcity of teachers.—*Globe,* Dec. 20, 1907.

*N. B.*—Some of the work done by typewriting copyists is "piece work." I know a girl who could make as high as $200 a month. She often made $150.—G. C. S.

Miss Isabel Ennis, secretary of the Interborough Association of Women Teachers contributed the following interesting comparisons:

Telephone operators are paid $5 a week for six weeks while learning the handling of a switch-board; $6 a week when put at work, and, if proficient, receive increases of a dollar a week every three months till they become senior operators at $10 a week. An attentive girl can become a supervisor within two years at $12 a week. Assistant chief operators get $15 a week; chief operators, $25 a week.

Girls have to serve an apprenticeship of nine years without pay to earn $11.47 a week as teachers.

This states the case of the public school teacher as compared with the telephone operator in the matter of salaries, and accounts in some degree for the shortage of 704 teachers in the public schools of this city, and for the fact that in October, 1907 there were 1498 classes without teachers at different times.

But besides these facts, there is the further circumstance that telephone operators trained by the company and paid during their schooling are in demand for private switchboards at wages varying from $10 to $15 and even $20 a week.

These facts bear upon the disclosures made by *The Evening Mail,* on Saturday, when it was shown that there was a serious famine in school teachers and that one of the causes for this shortage of supply was that as stenographers, after one year's training, girls could earn $780 a year, while it took nine years' schooling to fit a young woman for a $600 a year position in the public schools.

The exposure of the way the supply of school teachers is diminished by the rewards offered by other lines of business has aroused the liveliest interest among the friends of the public schools and among the teachers themselves.

One of the teachers, who has been long enough in the service to be well on toward the $1000 mark, through $40 a year additions to her stipend, said:

"The dollars in the great big $600 per year paid by the city have lost their cartwheel size to teachers from out of town, for they know by experience they cannot meet their expenses with any such salary. Again, advancement is slow, and the munificent $1240 after seventeen years' experience no longer attracts as it did, when $1240 had a $1600 purchasing value.

"Apropos of your comparisons of stenographers and teachers, let me give you the story of two graduates of mine, Miss A. and Miss B., both fourteen years old. Miss A. had secured a position in the telephone service. Miss B. was to be a teacher because they 'got such nice wages.' I calculated on the blackboard for them that Miss A. at $6 per week for seven years of fifty-two weeks each, would earn $2184. Miss B. spends four years at high school, two years at training school, possibly a year to 'get located,' and as yet has not earned a dollar. Miss B. will teach several years before she can be 'even' with Miss A.

"Compare the stock in trade of the telephone operator, who is paid while she is learning, and that necessary for the teacher, and then let any one in the system dodge the question as to whether or not the famine in teachers is connected with the fact that 'teachers get such nice wages.'

"Nor is this all. Last spring I collected some statistics, among which was the salary paid to twenty telephone operators, all former pupils of mine. The youngest was sixteen, the oldest twenty. I found:

| | |
|---|---|
| Four received, per week | $ 8 |
| Four received, per week | 10 |
| Six received, per week | 12 |
| Four received, per week | 14 |
| Two received, per week | 20 |

"The average was $12 per week, 50 cents per week more than is paid a teacher. I found the averarge wages among those who became stenographers much higher."

# CHAPTER XIV

## COST

In considering the "Cost" of "Equal Pay," we are dealing with the greatest obstacle that has stood in our way. Simmered down, the facts are:

(*a*) Some male teachers have opposed us because it would cost so much to give the women just salaries that there would be less chance of the men getting a further raise in their salaries.

(*b*) Some male taxpayers have opposed us because they believed it would raise their taxes.

(*c*) The Board of Education has opposed us we do not know why.

(*d*) The Mayor opposed us (1) because his Board of Education opposed us; (2) because he would not listen to our side; (3) because the money was wanted for something else.

It has been noted with gratification by women teachers that not one woman taxpayer has ever opposed them on the ground of increased taxes. It has likewise been noted with amusement tinged with scorn that the male taxpayers who have opposed us as such, have evidently assumed: (1) that all taxpayers[1] are men; (2) that the women

[1] The public press of January 10 and 11, 1910, in articles commenting on the report of the Board of Taxes and Assessments for the year, show that a woman heads the personal tax list, and one tax list printed, showed 135 men assessed on $30,495,000 and 146 women assessed on $31,365,000.

teachers themselves are, of course, not taxpayers; (3) that the women teachers are their beneficiaries.

In the various estimates that have been published, the most glaring and inconsistent misrepresentations have been made.

As a matter of fact, it has not been possible to give a definite and exact estimate of the cost of the "White Bill"—the bill passed in 1907 and vetoed by Mayor McClellan and Governor Hughes—because the cost would absolutely depend on the schedules made by the Board of Education. The bill made mandatory, (*a*) the raising of the minimum salary from $600 to $720; (*b*) an annual increment of at least $105; (*c*) equal salaries for men and women occupying the same position; and (*d*) no salary reduction. It is true that it also made mandatory the increase of the three mill appropriation (Sec. 1064, Charter) to four mills; but to say that this meant an arbitrary increase of the proceeds of one mill, is palpably false because there has not been a year since the original four mill appropriation was reduced to three that the Board of Estimate has not been obliged to allow more than the amount produced by the three mill provision, this extra allowance sometimes exceeding a million dollars.

### UNRELIABILITY OF ESTIMATES

In proof of the unreliability of the estimates, note the following:

(*a*) Auditor Cook of the Board of Education, in a communication addressed to Hon. Abraham Stern, April 26, 1907, says: "*In accordance with your instructions* I have prepared and present herewith a statement of the approximate cost of equalizing salaries of teachers in the public schools, so far as relates to the fiscal year 1908. In preparing this statement, and in the absence of any actual or tentative schedules of salaries formulated by the Board of Education under authority of the "White" bill, *it becomes necessary to assume* certain conditions in anticipation, and such conditions, as stated and explained by you at a recent interview, are understood to be as follows":

(*b*) Mayor McClellan in his veto message on the "White Bill," dated May 10, 1907, said: "As to the question of the additional expense which will be forced upon the City by this measure, there is considerable differance of opinion."

(*c*) Comptroller Metz in letter to me dated March 25, 1908 said: "I beg to acknowledge your communication of the 12th instant requesting me to answer certain questions, as indicated below, concerning the several so-called women teachers' 'equal pay bills,' which have been presented to the Legislature during the present and the preceding sessions, and to reply as follows:

"'1. Has the Department of Finance made a formal estimate of the amount of money necessary to put into effect the Conklin Equal Pay Bill of 1908?'

"*It has not.*

"'2. Has the Department of Finance made a formal estimate of the amount of money that would be required to put into effect the Women Teachers' Equal Pay Bill reported by the Senate Cities Committee on March 3, 1908?'

"*It has not.* But *on the figures submitted by Auditor Cook* on April 26, 1907, representatives of this department have estimated the minimum cost thereof to be not less than the amount stated therein $9,109,354, and probably a substantial amount greater than that sum.

"'3. Has the Department of Finance asked for a legal opinion on, or a legal interpretation of, any of the so-called Women Teachers' Equal Pay Bills?'

"*It has not.* This department has been requested, at different times, to furnish an estimate of the amount of money that would be required to establish the equal pay salary schedule proposed by one or another of said bills but so far no attempt has been made to make such an estimate, and for the reason that, in my opinion, *no such estimate can be made with any approach to exactness because the cost of any one of the proposed equal pay bills would depend largely upon the salary schedules which the Board of Education might see fit to establish in compliance with the provisions thereof.*"

(*d*) Mayor McClellan's Commission—Messrs. Schwab, Keep and Clark reported: "Your commission find it impossible to make any computation of the probable additional cost to the city, which would follow the adoption of the provisions of the 'White Bill.'"

It will be noticed that the Auditor of the board of education did not address his communication to the Board of Education but to Mr. Abraham Stern; and not to Mr. Stern as chairman of a committee of said board, or even as a member of said board, but simply "Mr. Stern." Yet, these are the estimates, confessedly based on assumption, that have been presented as the estimates of the Board of Education, and have been used by the Mayor, the Comptroller, various other officials and individuals and associations in opposing "Equal Pay" on account of its cost.

On March 23, 1908, I sent the following to Mr. Cook:

MR. HENRY R. COOK,
Auditor, Board of Education.
My Dear Mr. Cook:

Notwithstanding your reply to a recent communication, I again write you, and I hope that you will give me direct answers to the following questions:

1. In making your estimate as to the cost of the "White Bill" last year, did you have any legal opinion to guide you in interpreting such Bill?

2. Is it not true that in making said estimate, with its

total of $9,100,000 and upwards, you worked on an imaginary set of schedules, which would pay all the teachers in the system as if they were male teachers under the existing schedules?

3. Acknowledging that the two clauses "The Board of Education shall establish uniform schedules" and "No salary of any member of the supervising or teaching force shall be reduced," do not compel the Board of Education to make schedules which shall include all the individual salaries, is it not possible for the Board of Education to comply with all the requirements of the "White Bill" without going beyond the proceeds of the four-mill tax?

4. Is it not true that the Davis Law protects the salary of a male teacher in grades below those of the seventh and eighth years in the Elementary Schools only in an initial salary of $900 and an annual increment of $105?

5. Is it not true that the Board of Education is free today to divide Schedule VI. and make a new schedule for male teachers in the grades of the first six years, with a maximum to be reached at the end of the fifth, sixth, seventh, eighth or ninth year, as it might choose?

I beg for an early reply to this communication and for direct answers to these questions, because the estimate which you made of the "White Bill" of last year is being constantly used against us by the opponents of our bill, and we believe that you do not wish to be responsible for supplying said opponents with this false charge.

Yours very truly,
GRACE C. STRACHAN,
President Interborough Association
of Women Teachers.

I received the following in reply:

March 30, 1908.

Dear Miss Strachan:

I beg to acknowledge receipt of your communication of March 23, asking me to answer specifically five questions which you propound in relation to teachers' salary legislation.

On February 17, 1908, in response to your letter of February 3 bearing on this same subject, I advised you that it had been suggested to this Bureau that it is inadvisable to issue any official statements, in regard to the teachers' salary bill now before the Legislature, except on request of the Board of Education or its committees. I now beg to advise you that it has been conveyed to me that a continuation of such attitude on the part of this Bureau is expected.

Yours very truly,

HENRY R. M. COOK,

Auditor of the Board of Education.

It is thus easily seen that the responsibility of the estimate of the cost of Equal Pay rests on Mr. Abraham Stern and Auditor Cook. Let us read the following in this connection:

The New York *Tribune* of Friday, May 4, 1900, contained an article in which it was stated that Auditor Cook estimated that "under the Davis Law, principal's salaries would in fifteen years become $8,500 for men, and $6,700 for women." Now, we all know the Davis Law has been in effect ten years and no man principal is receiving over $3500, or woman, over $2500.

The *Eagle* of March 18, 1910. "The vacillating attitude of the Board of Education in deciding which parts of the city require the erection of new school buildings resulted in the laying over of a resolution at the meeting of the Board of Estimate to-day, authorizing the issue of corporate stock in the sum of $1,845,000 for new buildings. Controller Pendergast had submitted a report recommending the appropriation but at his own request the board deferred action. President Winthrop could not explain the budget, and Henry Cook, the auditor of the board, was mystified just as much."

Mr. Stern said in opposing the Davis Law, it would cost "$26,000,000," but Mr. Maxwell's 10th Annual Report contains the following table:

*Payments From General School Fund For Salaries Of Teachers In Elementary High and Training Schools*

| Year. | |
|---|---|
| 1898-99 | $ 8,059,958.89 |
| 1899-1900 | 10,583,133.64 |
| 1900-1901 | 12,587,011.56 |
| 1901-02 | 13,395,882.38 |
| 1902-03 | 14,350,802.94 |
| 1903-04 | 14,885,891.42 |
| 1904-05 | 15,574,005.00 |
| 1905-06 | 16,870,891.47 |
| 1906-07 | 17,582,067.32 |
| 1907-08 | 18,596,874.70 |

The Davis Bill became law July 3, 1900. It appears that the salary increase for 1901 was $2,003,877.92.

Though Borough President Coler and Comptroller Metz rarely agreed while members of the same Board of Estimate and Apportionment, there is striking agreement in the attitude of Mr. Coler on the Davis Bill in 1900, and the attitude of Mr. Metz on the White Bill, in 1907, as the following quotations prove:

Comptroller Cole on Davis Bill:

"It imposes an enormous and unnecessary burden on taxpayers;"

"Its provisions and the manner in which it became a law are bound eventually to demoralize the school system;"

"It was opposed by Board of Education;"

"It was opposed by many newspapers;"

"It was vetoed by Mayor Van Wyck;"

"It was forced on city by Republican legislation;"

"It was signed by a Republican governor;"

"Belief has become common that the organized schoolteachers of this city are a political force which it is dangerous to oppose no matter how extravagant their demands may be;"

"The bill is a raid on the city treasury; it takes from the control of the Department of Finance $20,000,000 which is hereafter to be disbursed by irresponsible clerks."

*"It is inevitable that not a few teachers will be found drawing higher salaries than Cabinet officers, college presidents or the Governor of New York."*

Comptroller Metz on White Bill:

"I am and have been of the opinion at all times that the proposition to equalize salaries in the Board of Education would cost the city about $13,000,000."

This is nearly $4,000,000 more than even Auditor Cook's extravagant estimate.

Mr. Coler and Mr. Metz have also agreed in opposing the "Equal Pay" bills.

### STUDY OF SCHEDULES

One of the first questions that was asked us when we began our agitation was, "How much will it cost?" And so our Executive Committee, carefully selected to represent every grade and special subject, worked many weeks in the preparation of "Equal Pay" schedules. We were unanimous in the opinion that the minimum salaries established for men teachers by the Davis Law should be preserved. So the $900 salary, the minimum fixed by the Davis Law for a "male teacher" we made the minimum salary for a teacher of boys' or mixed class. The committee was unanimous also in the opinion that the present bonus of $60 for teachers of boys was insufficient and did not attract the necessary supply of women teachers, so we fixed $120 as the least, and $180 as the greatest difference between the salaries of a teacher of a girls' class and that of a teacher of a boys' class of corresponding grade. The minimum annual increment for a male teacher fixed by the Davis Law we made the annual increment for all classes. So far all had gone smoothly. But at this point we found ourselves confronted by a discrimination other than salary, and in trying to explain this discrimination is that we have found the greatest difficulty in making those unacquainted with the technical terms and intimate details of our system and of the Davis Law understand.*

The Davis Bill became law May 3, 1900. The committee of the Board of Education which prepared the schedules under the new law was headed by Abraham Stern. This committee prepared schedules in strict conformity with the provisions of the Davis Bill, in every instance but one, which exception favored the men, it is embodied in Schedule VI, Section 65, of the By-Laws of the Board of Education. The way in which this has effected women teachers will be easily understood from a consideration of the provisions of the Davis Bill, which provided that:

(a) "No kindergarten or female teacher of the grades of the first six years of the elementary schools shall receive less than $600 a year;"

(b) "No male teacher shall receive less than $900 a year;"

(c) The annual increment of female teachers as described in (a) shall be not less than $40;

(d) The annual increment of a male teacher shall be not less than $105;

(e) No female teacher as described in (a) shall after sixteen years of service receive less than $1240;

* Two months later, I was elected Associate Superintendent by the Brooklyn Board of Education. As principal, I had received the maximum salary of $2500. The committee appointed to make schedules unler the new law, Mr. Abraham Stern, chairman, recommended a salary of $2500 for a "female" district superintendent, and $5000 for a "male" district superintendent. Miss Whitney had been elected a superintendent in Brooklyn, a year before, and was receiving the same salary as the men. It was the manifest purpose of the committee to deter women from seeking the position of superintendent by making the salary less in reality than that of a principal. I gave up my vacation and brought to bear all the social, political and religious influence I could to have the salary fixed for district superintendents without the qualifying words "male" and "female." The committee's final report included a uniform salary of $5000, the amount then being paid to the district superintendents—all men—in Manhattan.

(f) No female teacher of the grades of the last two years of the elementary schools shall after fifteen years of service receive less than $1320;

(g) No male teacher of the grades of the last two years of the elementary schools shall after twelve years of service receive less than $2160;

(h) No female teacher of a graduating class shall after ten years of servicel ess than $1440;

(i) No male teacher of a graduating class shall after ten years of service receive less than $2,400.

The compliance with these provisions produced the present schedules of the Board of Education as tabulated below:

Schedule III. Women.

Kindergartens and Teachers of Grades 1A-6B.

Mandatory minimum ..$ 600.00

Mandatory increment .. 40.00

| Year | |
|---|---|
| 1 | 600.00 |
| 2 | 640.00 |
| 3 | 680.00 |
| 4 | 720.00 |
| 5 | 760.00 |
| 6 | 800.00 |
| 7 | 840.00 |
| 8 | 880.00 |
| 9 | 920.00 |
| 10 | 960.00 |
| 11 | 1000.00 |
| 12 | 1040.00 |
| 13 | 1080.00 |
| 14 | 1120.00 |
| 15 | 1160.00 |
| 16 | 1200.00 |
| 17 | 1240.00 |

Schedule VI. Men.

Mandatory minimum ..$ 900.00

Mandatory increment.. 105.00

| Year | |
|---|---|
| 1 | 900.00 |
| 2 | 1005.00 |

(Number of increments left to the discretion of the Board of Education.)

Present schedule IV. Grades 7A—8A.

16th year .............$1320.00

Present schedule V. Grade 8B.

11th year ............$1440.00

Present schedule VI. Grades 7A—8A.

13th year ............$2160.00

Present schedule VII. Grade 8B.

11th year ............$2400.00

The schedules also provided that the female teacher of a boys' class or of a mixed class having at least forty per cent. of the register, boys, shall receive a bonus of $60 a year. The male teacher in charge of a girls' class would receive as much as for a boys' class, but it is the practice not to place men over girls' classes although there is no law or regulation against such procedure, and there has been a male teacher of an 8B girls' class.

The above figures show the cause of the great disparity in the estimates of the cost of equal pay. There are three definite schedules fixed for female teachers; there are not three definite schedules fixed for male teachers. *The Davis Law failed to fix a minimum-maximum salary for male teachers in grades of the first six years of the course,*—in other words, a minimum-maximum to correspond to the $1240 of Schedule III.

Now I believe that Mr. Stern's Committee either did not notice this lack or they failed to grasp its full significance. They realized that under the law there was for male teachers a minimum salary of $900; a minimum increment of $105; a minimum after twelve years of $2160; but they appear not to have realized that the last mentioned salary was mandatory only in the last two years of the course, namely, in 7A, 7B, 8A, and that they were at liberty in grades of the first six years (1A-6B) to cease adding the increment of $105 wherever they chose to do so. Instead, therefore, of making Schedule VI correspond to Schedule III for women, and fixing a maximum in the grades of the first six years, less than the $2160 fixed for male teachers of the grades of the last two years—just as the $1240 for women in the lower grades is less than the $1320 fixed for female teachers of the grades of the last two years—Mr. Stern's Committee made Schedule VI cover *all male teachers of grades below the graduating class.* This is why when we asked the Legislature at Albany to have salaries fixed for "teachers of boys' classes" and "teachers of girls' classes," instead of for "male teachers" and "female teachers," our opponents were able to state that there was a male teacher of a 2B grade—a grade of the last half of the second year of the course, where the normal child is seven and a half years old—who was receiving $2160 a year. Mr. Stern held that to comply with our request would cost the city of New York over nine million dollars because every female teacher in the kindergarten and grades 1A to 6B inclusive, would after twelve years of service have to be given $2160 a year. This statement he must have known to be false for the Board of Education is at liberty under the Davis Law to fix any maximum it pleases for male teachers of the grades of the first six years, limited only by the Davis Law restrictions that the minimum be not less than $900 and the annual increments not less than $105.

Our schedules known as the "McCarren Schedues" provided that the increment be added seven times, the following schedule resulting therefrom:

*Teachers of Boys' or Mixed Classes*

*(Grades 1A-6B)*

| Year. | | |
|---|---|---|
| 1st. | (Minimum as fixed by the Davis Law) | $ 900 |
| 2nd. | (Increment of $105 as fixed by the Davis Law) | 1005 |
| 3rd. | | 1110 |
| 4th. | | 1215 |
| 5th. | | 1320 |
| 6th. | | 1425 |
| 7th. | | 1530 |
| 8th. | | 1635 |

## INTERBOROUGH ESTIMATES COMPARED WITH BOARD ESTIMATES

That our estimates were correctly made is evidenced by the fact that except for the item involved in the foregoing explanation, our figures correspond almost exactly with those of Auditor Cook.

*Estimate of Interborough Association of Women Teachers*

| | | | |
|---|---|---|---|
| (a) | 10,012 | Women Teachers of Kindergarten and grades of first six years | $4,116,915 |
| (b) | 1,044 | Teachers of 7A, 7B, and 8A | 742,327 |
| (c) | 329 | Teachers of 8B | 259,180 |
| (d) | 192 | Principals | 191,500 |
| (e) | 345 | Assistants to Principals | 298,000 |
| (f) | 571 | High and Training School Teachers | 219,130 |
| | 12,493 | Total | $5,827,052 |

*Estimate of Auditor Cook*

| | | | |
|---|---|---|---|
| (a) | 10,077 | Women Teachers of Kindergarten and grades of first six years | $5,869,550 |
| (b) | 1,049 | Teachers of 7A, 7B, and 8A | 707,970 |
| (c) | 323 | Teachers 8B | 251,840 |
| (d) | 191 | Principals | 191,000 |
| (e) | 345 | Assistants to Principals | 276,000 |
| (f) | 564 | High and Training School Teachers | 230,580 |
| | 12,549 | Total | $7,526,940 |
| Sub. | 10,077 | Teachers below 7A | $5,869,550 |
| | 2,472 | Teachers and supervising officials above 6B | $1,657,390 |

In estimating item (a) Auditor Cook used a maximum of $2160 for all teachers, including kindergarten teachers, below 8B. We used $1635 for teachers below 7A. Our estimates for the remaining items give an average of $689.29 for each of the 2,481 teachers and supervising officials above the 6B; Auditor Cook's give an average of $670.46. Thus it is seen that our estimate on these items is exorbitant according to the method of computation followed by the Board of Education to the extent of $18.83

per teacher, or $235,243.19 for the 12,493 teachers included in the estimate.

To the above total of

| | | |
|---|---|---|
| | $7,526,940 | the auditor's estimate added: |
| (g) | 188,530 | For women appointed since June 1, 1906. |
| (h) | 810,084 | For cost of mixed and boys' classes. |
| (i) | 120,000 | For cost of female substitutes. |
| (j) | 79,000 | For cost of filling vacancies. |
| (k) | 481,000 | For cost of difference in increment. |
| (l) | 248,000 | For cost of enlargement of system. |
| | $9,483,454 | Total. |
| (m) | 374,100 | Approximate saving on outgoing system. |
| | $9,109,354 | Estimate which was quoted by the Mayor and others as the "cost of the bill." |

It is evident that items (g) to (l) inclusive being also computed on the $2160 basis are all exorbitant, and greater than for the "White Bill" or any other plan of "Equal Pay."

It appears that the auditor did not consider the above estimate correct at all times, for the *Evening World* of October 5, 1908, in an article on the "Budget Hearing" of the Board of Education said: "Mr. Metz then wanted to know how the salary increases suggested compared with the increases proposed in the teacher's bill last year. With Auditor Cook's help Mr. Winthrop placed the figures at $6,500,000 for the bill and $3,500,000 for the budget estimate."

### $9,000,000 INCREASE NEGLECT OF PRIMARY TEACHER

There have been many inconsistent arguments made by our opponents, and many inconsistent platforms borrowed for special occasions, but no inconsistency has been so flagrant in its baldness or so contemptible in its use as that involved in this "$2160 estimate."

The Board of Education, the Association of Male Principals and Teachers, Mayor McClellan, Comptroller Metz, and the pitifully small number of citizens' associations that opposed us, all used the "Cost"—$9,000,000 and upwards (even to $13,000,000 by Mr. Metz) as one reason for their opposition, and in the next breath announced as another reason—that it, the "Equal Pay" bill, did not provide an increase for the "primary teachers." Thus to make one false argument, they boosted the estimate to $9,000,000 by figuring on paying all teachers from kindergarten, to 8A inclusive, under the $2160 schedule; and then for another false argument they claimed that the "primary teachers" were neglected by the Interborough.

In this connection the following item is pertinent: "December 17, 1909. The Bureau of Municipal Research has asked the press to state that neither it nor its representatives have ever declared that an equal pay schedule would cost $11,000,000 or of necessity disregard the need of 14,000 teachers; no scheme which entirely ignored 14,000 teachers could cost $11,000,000. Thus far it has contained itself to seeking facts.

The primary teachers who attended our meetings and read our literature knew that almost the whole struggle of the Interborough was in their interests. If the "Equal Pay" fight concerned only the 2500 women who occupied the positions above the 6B grade, it would have been won easily. The cost would have been less than $2,000,000. Indeed, City Superintendent Maxwell in his report for the year ending July 31, 1907, recommended "Equal Pay" for women principals.

But most of the primary teeachers knew that the leaders of the Interborough themselves opposed the "White Bill" until they succeeded in having incorporated therein the amendments: (1) "and that the difference between the salary of a teacher of a boys' class of corresponding grade shall not be more than $180:" and (2) "at least ninety-three percentum of the amount appropriated for the general school fund shall be set aside for the payment of the salaries of the members of the supervising and teaching staff of the regular public day schools of the City of New York." The leaders of the women teachers knew that without the first amendment above, the board could make the "Equal Pay" clause almost ineffective and wholly ridiculous by making the difference between the salaries for boys' classes and girls' classes as great as or even greater than the present difference between the salaries for male teachers and for female teachers. They insisted on the second amendment to prevent the dissipation of the proceeds of the additional fourth mill in evening, summer, and lecture activities and increasing salaries of workers therein, other officials and attendance officers. They knew that equalization would up to the Davis Law Minimums require less than thirty per cent. of such proceeds, thus leaving upwards of seventy per cent. of same for teachers below the 7A grade.

The following resolution adopted by The Interborough Association of Women Teachers of the City of New York, indicates the attitude of the great majority of the "Primary tachers":

"At a meeting held at City College, March 20, 1908: Whereas, We know that Mr. Melvin R. Hix, Mr. Bernard Cronson, Mr. Edward S. Shumway, and other male teachers and principals who are opposing us in our campaign for Civil Service Salary Schedules, are giving as one of their excuses for their indefensible attitude toward the women teachers, that our bill now before the legislature does not protect 'the primary teachers,' and

"Whereas, We believe that this expressed interest in the welfare of the primary teacher is insincere, and is evidenced for the purpose of blinding the members of the legislature, the taxpayers, and others to the true motives behind the actions of these male opponents; and

"Whereas, No 'primary teachers' have authorized or engaged said male opponents of our bill to enter any plea in behalf of said 'primary teachers,' therefore

"Resolved, That the Interborough Association of Women Teachers of the City of New York, resents this unwarranted reference to any of its members by the opponents of the bill which said Association is seeking to enact into law, and brands as unworthy a manly man the motives that impel said opponents to hide their true colors behind the plea that they see in our bill lack of protection for the 'primary teacher.'

"Primary teachers: Emma Osterndorff, P. S. 93, Manhattan; Emma McCleary, P. S. 16, Brooklyn; Emma Weber, P. S. 62, Queens; Margaret Killion, P. S. 39, Bronx; Marie Sweeney, P. S. 17, Richmond.

"Kindergartner: Martha Poucher, P. S. 32, Bronx."

### IF INCREASES BEFORE EQUAL PAY BEGIN WITH THOSE RECEIVING LOWEST SALARY

Though our male teacher opponents in their attempts to weaken our ranks, have tried to make it appear that a few of our higher salaried members are actuated by selfish motives, our work in decrying the increases for women principals and for district superintendents proves the contrary.

Mrs. Moriarty has always said when "Equal Pay For Women Principals" or even increase for principals, was under discussion: "Let the principals wait; begin with the lowest salaries."

The increase of the salary of district superintendent from $5000 to $6000 was defeated by only one vote.

The following letters bear on the subject of this increase:

The regard in which the proposed increase is held is shown by the following letter, written by Grace C. Strachan, herself a district superintendent and president of the Interborough Association of Women Teachers. A copy of this letter has been received by every member of the Board of Education:

"Although I believe that the arguments in favor of paying District Superintendents a higher salary than that of any principal are sound, just and reasonable, I take the liberty of strongly urging you to postpone your approval of the proposed amendment of Section 65 of the By-Laws for the purpose of increasing the salary of District Superintendents, until such section is amended for the benefit of the grade teachers.

" The higher salaried members of the Interborough Association of Women Teachers have always held that if the adjustment of salaries prayed for by said association cannot be secured for all members at one and the same time, that the beginning shall be made with the lowest salaried teachers, namely, the teachers that are paid under Schedule III."

To the Editor of the Brooklyn *Eagle:*

While it is true that I objected to the increase of the district superintendents' salaries, I do not wish to be misunderstood in this connection or to receive any credit to which I am not entitled, and so I feel constrained to state that I believe the salary of a district superintendent should be greater than that of any principal. At present the principal of a high or a training school is paid the same salary as a district superintendent. Yet no one will deny that a district superintendent has greater responsibility, heavier labor and greater official expenses. For instance, during the past summer I had twenty-six vacation schools, vacation playgrounds and evening playgrounds, which I was obliged to inspect and report on formally, including in my report a rating for each individual teacher.

If a high school principal works in one of these vacation playgrounds or schools he or she is paid a regular per diem salary. In like manner, I am obliged to examine the evening schools in my districts and report on them at least twice in the year and rate each principal and teacher. Should a high school principal take the principalship of an evening school, he would receive $7 a night.

The traveling and restaurant expenses absolutely incumbent upon district superintendents are naturally much greater than those of a high school principal. While the high school principal has but one school to reach every day and can have a permanent luncheon place, the district superintendent has often twenty or more schools. Besides all this, a district superintendent is elected for a limited time, while a principal has a permanent tenure after the first three years.

For all these reasons I think that the salary of district superintendent should be higher than that of high school principal. I think further that it should be a higher salary than that of a member of the board of examiners, and I hope that the necessary adjustment may soon be properly made. However, I shall continue to object to any increases in the salaries of the higher paid officials until the salaries of the teachers—especially the teachers in the schedules running from $600 to $1240—have been increased, according to the schedules approved by the Interborough Association of Women Teachers.

GRACE C. STRACHAN.

Brooklyn, December 28, 1909.

### EQUAL PAY IN INSTALMENTS

The Bureau of Municipal Research has said: "If the Board of Education has been wasting hundreds of thousands of dollars in paying extra ' salaries to men for work which women could have done just as well, this should be frankly admitted.' I have elsewhere shown that in one school with 126( ?) boys in seven classes, seven men were employed. I know of another school which with 74 boys in classes above 6B, was costing the city $3500 for a male principal, and $2400 for a male teacher in the 8B class of 15 boys and 19 girls."

Furthermore, that our Association has been not only willing but anxious to lessen to the taxpayer the burden of establishing our "Equal Pay" principle, is proven by our Gledhill-Foley bill (1909) and the Somers' resolution (1910.) The former provides "that each member of the teaching and supervising staff shall at once become entitled to all the emolument in accordance with above schedule to which said person is entitled by reason of merit, experience and position held; *but the Board of Education may limit the expense of putting these schedules into effect by making the highest salary to be paid to any teacher or supervisor in the year* 1910 *and each year thereafter until the maximum salary shall have been reached, the salary in the proposed schedule which is equal to or next higher than the amount that would be obtained by adding two of the annual increments in said schedule to the salary due said teacher or supervisor under the present schedule.*"

The Somers' resolution provided: "That such revised schedules be put into effect as soon as funds sufficient therefore are provided by the Board of Estimate and Apportionment, and that pending full financial ability, the increases in women teachers' salaries be paid *in annual instalments which shall be not less than twenty per cent. of the difference between the maximum salaries now fixed for men and the maximum salaries now fixed for women occupying the same position,* except that for the year 1910 there shall be a flat increase of not less than $120 per annum for all women teachers below the 7A grade and not less than $120 for all women teachers of special subjects."

That this has been the disposition of the Interborough from the beginning, is shown by an article that appeared in the *Globe* of March 11, 1907.

Later, I called on Mr. Abraham Stern and told him we were willing to spread the increase over three or four years, and that we would like to incorporate a clause making such provision in our bill. He said such a clause would probably render our bill unconstitutional, and realizing that he was a lawyer, we dropped the matter.

The *Globe* article described a meeting of our Executive Committee and said: "Serious consideration was also given to an amendment which *would limit the immediate increase in expense to the city.* The question was raised as to whether such amendment would not invalidate the bill, and pending a legal opinion on this point, action has been postponed.

"If it is found that such a provision can be incorporated in the bill without invalidating it, an amendment will be prepared. Just what the amendment will be it is impossible to state definitely at this time. It is agreed that every teacher now in the system receiving less than $900 should on January 1, next, be raised to the minimum provided in the law, and that thereafter should receive an annual increase of $105. Although opinions differ, there are many who believe that those who would receive an immediate increase of more than a certain sum—probably $400—should receive such increase in two or more annual instalments according to the amount of the increase. It is also agreed that any teacher having served twenty years or more on January 1 should be immediately raised to the minimum maximum fixed in the law. Nothing definite has been decided as yet regarding this matter."

## *ANALYSIS OF BOARD'S SCHEDULES*

### THE BOARD OBJECTS TO 4 MILL TAX, BUT ASKS FOR $5,060,-469.02 IN EXCESS OF 3 MILL TAX

An anomaly has been presented by the board's opposition to the four mill clause in our Equal Pay bills and its presentation of schedules in the budget of 1909 calling for an increase in the general fund which required $5,060,469.02 in addition to the three mill tax. Of this increase $3,273,163.52 was for increases in salaries.

Ever since Governor Hughes in his veto message on the "White Bill," declared that in the present schedules there are "glaring inequalities that clearly should not be permitted to continue," the board has been on record as asking for increase in salaries. The public generally has always supposed that their action in this connection indicated a great victory for the women teachers, but that this supposition is not borne out by facts and figures, the following shows:

### REPORT OF AUDITOR OF THE INTERBOROUGH ASSOCIATION FIGURES

To the Board of Education:

I have the honor to comply with your directions of January 26, 1910, (see Journal, page 224), to verify the figures contained within a communication of the Interborough Association of Women Teachers relating to the tentative schedules of teachers' salaries adopted by the Board of Education in 1907 and 1908, and included within the annual budgets submitted to the Board of Estimate and Apportionment for 1908, 1909 and 1910.

The statements containing said figures follow in categorical order:

1. "The maximum of the kindergarten teachers is raised $20, while the maximum of the male first assistant of the high school is raised $500." (Statement by I. A. W. T.)

The above statement is literally correct, but it is only a small part of a full comparison of these two extremes of the teaching corps. A more complete analysis shows:

The minimum salary of a kindergartner is raised from $600 to $660 per annum, or $60, an increase of 10 per cent. The maximum salary is raised from $1240 to $1260 per annum, or $20, an increase of 1.61 per cent., but such maximum salary is reached in sixteen years under the proposed plan as against seventeen years under the present method. The annual increment of $40 is unchanged.

A hypothetical person serving for seventeen years under this schedule would earn $15,640 under the present method, and $16,620 under the proposed plan, an increase of $980, or 6.26 per cent.

The average annual salary of the 739 kindergartners now employed is, under the present method, $823.38, and, under the proposed plan, $882.73, an average increase of $59.35 per person, or 7.2 per cent. There are now but twelve kindergartners in the maximum salary year, and these would be increased from $1240 to $1260 per annum.

The 727 remaining kindergartners would each receive an increase of $60 per annum. The aggregate annual increase for kindergartners is $43,860.

The minimum salary of a male first assistant in high and training schools is raised from $2500 to $2900 per annum, or $400, an increase of 16 per cent. The maximum salary is raised from $3000 to $3500 per annum, or $500, an increase of 16.66 per cent., but such maximum salary is reached in four years under the proposed plan as against six years under the present method. The annual increment is increased from $100 to $200, or 100 per cent.

A hypothetical person serving for six years under this schedule would earn $16,500 under the present method and $19,800 under the proposed plan, an increase of $3300, or 20 per cent.

The average annual salary of the eighty-seven male first assistants affected by the change of rate is, under the present method, $2,795.40, and under the proposed plan, $3,311.49, an average increase of $516.09 per person, or 18.46 per cent. The aggregate annual increase for these persons is $44,900.

2. "The annual increment of the primary teacher is raised $8; that of the teacher of the seventh and eighth years, $0; while the annual increment of the male first assistant in the high school is raised $100." (Statement by I. A. W. T.)

This statement is literally correct, but, as a basis for judgment, it is insufficient.

The minimum salary of a woman teacher of grades from 1A to 6B, inclusive, is raised from $600 to $720 per annum, or $120, an increase of twenty per cent. The maximum salary is raised from $1240 to $1440 per annum, or $200, an increase of 16.12 per cent., but such maximum salary is reached in sixteen years under the proposed plan, as against seven years under the present method. The annual increment is increased from $40 to $48 an increase of twenty per cent.

A hypothetical person serving for seventeen years under this schedule would earn $15,640 under the present method and $18,720 under the proposed plan, an increase of $3,080, or 19.69 per cent.

The average annual salary of the 10,768 women teachers now employed in Schedule III (grades from 1A to 6B, inclusive) is, under the present method, $913.69, and, under the proposed plan, $1,088.85, an average increase of $175.16 per person, or 19.16 per cent. The aggregate annual increase for these persons is $1,886,108.

The minimum salary of women teachers of grades from 7A to 8A inclusive, is raised from $600 to $720 per annum, or $120, an increase of twenty per cent. The maximum salary is raised from $1320 to $1440 per annum or $120, an increase of 9.09 per cent. The life of the schedule remains the same, namely, sixteen years. The annual increment of $48 is unchanged.

A hypothetical person serving for sixteen years under this schedule would earn $15,360 under the present method, and $17,280 under the proposed plan, an increase of $1,920, or 12.5 per cent.

The average annual salary of the 1380 women teachers now employed in Schedule IV (grades from 7A to 8A inclusive) is, under the present method, $1252.97, and under the proposed plan, $1373.14, an average increase of $120.17 per person, or 9.59 per cent. The aggregate annual increase for these persons is $165,840.

The schedule for male first assistants in high schools is analyzed under Statement 1, preceding.

3. "Even the annual increments of the clerical assistants and library assistants in high schools are raised $50—that is, 100 per cent.—in contrast to the twenty per cent increase given to the primary teachers, and the 0 per cent. given to kindergarten teachers and those of the seventh and eighth years of the elementary schools. Contrast the $20 increase in the maximum of the kindergartner to the $400 increase

in the maximum of the high school library assistants." (Statement by I. A. W. T.)

This statement is literally correct but, as a basis for judgment it is insufficient.

The minimum salary of a woman clerical assistant in high and training schools remains at $700 per annum. The maximum salary is raised from $1000 to $1200 per annum, or $200, an increase of twenty per cent., but such maximum salary is reached in six years under the proposed plan as against seven years under the present method. The annual increment is increased from $50 to $100, an increase of 100 per cent.

A hypothetical person serving for seven years under this schedule would earn $5950 under the present method and $6900 under the proposed plan, an increase of $950, or 15.96 per cent.

The average annual salary of the ten women clerical assistants affected by the change of rate is, under the present method, $899, and, under the proposed plan, $1050, an average increase of $151 per person, or 16.79 per cent. The aggregate annual increase for these persons is $1510.

The minimum salary of a male clerical assistant in high schools is raised from $900 to $1000 per annnum, or $100, an increase of 11.11 per cent. The maximum salary is raised from $1200 to $1500 per annum, or $300, an increase of 25 per cent., but such maximum salary is reached in six years under the proposed plan, as against seven years under the present method. The annual increment is increased from $50 to $100, an increase of 100 per cent.

A hypothetical person serving for seven years under this schedule would earn $7350 under the present method, and $9000 under the proposed plan, an increase of $1650, or 22.44 per cent.

The average annual salary of the five male clerical assistants affected by the change of rate is, under the present method, $1120, under the proposed plan, $1400, an average increase of $280 per person, or twenty-five per cent. The aggregate annual increase for these persons is $1400.

The minimum salary of women library assistants in high and training schools is raised from $700 to $800 per annum, or $100, an increase of 14.28 per cent. The maximum salary is raised from $1,000 to $1,400 per annum, or $400, an increase of 40 per cent. The life of the schedule remains the same, namely, 7 years. The annual increment is increased from $50 to $100, an increase of 100 per cent.

A hypothetical person serving for 7 years under this schedule would earn $5,950 under the present method and $7,700 under the proposed plan, an increase of $1,750, or 29.41 per cent.

The average annual salary of the 31 women library assistants now employed is, under the present method, $950, and, under the proposed plan, $1,300, an average increase of $350 per person, or 36.84 per cent. The aggregate annual increase for these persons is $4,550.

There were no men library assistants included in the budget for 1910.

The schedules for kindergartners and male first assistants in high schools are analyzed under statement 1, preceding, but it is necessary, in the interest of particularity, to again state that, of the 739 kindergartners now employed, only 12 have reached the maximum year. These 12 would receive increases of $20 each.

4. "Again, this budget includes an average increase of $363.14 for each of the 560 men in the high schools, while the 9,971 women in the elementary schools would receive only an average increase of $177.07." The budget of the Board of Education for 1910, showing the teachers actually employed May 31, 1909, has been used as a basis for preparing the two tables of analysis presented herewith."—(Statement by I. A. W. T.)

The budget shows that 14,751 women of all classes would receive an aggregate increase of $2,639,762, representing an increase of average salary from $1,033.42 to $1,212.37, or $178.95 per person, or 17.31 per cent.

The budget also shows that 582 men of all classes would receive an aggregate increase of $206,215, representing an increase of average salary from $2,144.34 to $2,498.66, or $354.32 per person, or 16.52 per cent.

The statement regarding 9,971 women and 560 men is, therefore, incorrect. There is a wide discrepancy between the number of persons referred to in this paragraph of the circular and the actual number as found in the budget.—(The 9,971 is the number of women in grades 1 A—6 B. Inclusive. The 560 is the number of men high school teachers.—GRACE C. STRACHAN.)

5. "In the special subjects we find teachers of music, sewing, drawing and physical training with an increase in their maximum of $300 to $400, while the teachers of cooking receive no increase—that is, the teachers of music and physical training receive $600 more than the teachers of cooking."—(Statement by I. A. W. T.)

This statement is imperfectly framed and thus leads to seeming ambiguity. (The statement refers to maximums and is absolutely correct regarding them.—GRACE C. STRACHAN.)

In the schedule for women teachers of music and drawing the minimum salary remains the same, namely, $1,000 per annum; the annual increment also remains the same, namely, $100 per annum. The life of the schedule, however, is extended from 5 years to 9 years, making the maximum salary $1,800 per annum, instead of $1,400 per annum.

In the schedule for women teachers of sewing and shopwork, the minimum salary remains the same, namely, $900 per annum; the annual increment also remains the same, namely, $100 per annum. The life of the schedule, however, is extended from 4 years to 7 years, making the maximum salary $1,500 per annum, instead of $1,200 per annum.

In the schedule for women teachers of physical training the minimum salary is increased from $900 per annum to $1,000 per annum. The annual increment remains the same, namely, $100 per annum; but the life of the schedule is extended from 4 years to 9 years, making the maximum salary $1,800 per annum, instead of $1,200 per annum.

In the schedule for men teachers of music and drawing

the minimum salary remains the same, namely, $1,200 per annum; the annual increment also remains the same, namely, $100, but the life of the schedule is extended from 5 years to 9 years, making the maximum salary $2,000 per annum, instead of $1,600 per annum.

. . . . .

| | | |
|---|---|---|
| 14,764 | women teachers receive increase of | $2,639,927 |
| 581 | men " " " " | 206,050 |
| 15,345 | | $2,845,977 |

Average of women's increase $178.80
Average of men's increase $354.65

These figures are substantially correct.

Permit me to point out that neither the figures of the Teachers' Association as to difference of minimums, maximums, and increments, nor the comments of this bureau thereon, should, of themselves, be accepted as either proof or disproof of the correctness of the basic principles of either or both the present method or the proposed plan of fixing teachers' salaries. Such figures are infallible only in the restricted sense that they are correct arithmetical results; such figures are not conclusive as to the fundamental correctness or incorrectness of either of the factors used, namely, the present method, on the one hand, or the proposed plan on the other.

The point to be borne in mind is that, granting the basic salaries for the several classes of teachers to be equitably determined after consideration of all appropriate factors, then any mere recital of the resultant differences between the present method and the proposed plan is simply an expression or statement of previous "inequalities" reduced to arithmetical terms. In other words, the principle involved is not what is the increase in the minimum or the maximum salary of one class of teacher as compared with another class, nor, again, as to whether the annual increment is increased or not; the question is solely as to whether the proposed schedules are equitable and just, and, if that be demonstrated, then the increase of the proposed plan over the present method is simply a matter of mathematics and not of argument—that is, the increase merely represents the cost of making perfect that which is imperfect.

Respectfully submitted,

HENRY R. M. COOK,

Auditor of the Board of Education.

February 18, 1910.

And yet the schedules are presented as being "For the women teachers." And because we tried to make the facts clear to the Board of Estimate and the public, and because we appeared before said board to present the following resolutions, Senator Travis, in the speech in which he tried to excuse his vote against our bill in 1908 after voting for it in 1907, and still insisting that he believed in "Equal Pay," asked: "Who were the people that opposed the adjustment of these inequalities? They were the women teachers, represented by their leader, Miss Strachan, who demanded that the Board of Estimate veto the appropriation." A study of our resolutions will show that this was not any more accurate than the same senator's expressions on the cost of our bill.

October 3, 1908.

At the regular bi-monthly meeting of the Interborough Association of Women Teachers the following resolutions were adopted:

"Resolved, That the action of the Interborough Association of Women Teachers on the new salary schedules which the Board of Education has included in its budget for the year 1908, be as follows:

"1st. Approval of all parts of such schedules as reduce the present discriminations against women teachers and supervisors.

"2d. Disapproval of all parts of such schedules as increase the salaries of men already receiving more than women occupying the same position.

"3d. Disapproval of all parts of such schedules as tend to impair the value of the Kindergarten and of Domestic

Science in our School System; and be it further resolved: That this action of the Interborough Association of Women Teachers be presented to the Board of Estimate, either personally, through one of its officers, or in written form, on the occasion of the public hearing set by said Board on the Budget of the Board of Education for the year 1909; and be it further resolved,

"That the Interborough Association of Women Teachers prays the Board of Estimate to take such action as will cause the said salary schedules to be so amended that men and women occupying the same position in the public schools of our city shall receive the same pay."

The resolution was adopted unanimously October 3, 1908. 790 delegates present. Similar resolutions were adopted October 9, 1909.

On October 15, 1908, we sent the following letter to the Board of Estimate:

"*To the Members of the Board of Estimate and Apportionment:*

"The Interborough Association of Women Teachers submits the following specific instances of ways in which the Educational Budget may be decreased, by denying the proposed increases to male teachers in High and Training Schools:

| | | | |
|---|---|---|---|
| "High Schools— | | | |
| Male Clerical Assistants, | 4— | Total increase, | $ 1,000 |
| Male Library Assistant, | 1— | " " | 330 |
| Male Junior Teachers, | 17— | " " | 1,100 |
| Male Assistant Teachers, | 439— | " " | 145,420 |
| Male First Assistants, | 64— | " " | 33,300 |
| Total for High School Teachers......... | | | $181,150 |
| Training School for Teachers— | | | |
| Male Assistant Teachers, | 9— | Total increase, | $ 2,620 |
| Male First Assistants, | 8— | " " | 3,100 |
| Total for Training School Teachers...... | | | $ 5,720 |

"It will thus be seen that the sum of $186,870 can be deducted from the Budget by denying these proposed increases to male teachers, whose salaries without said proposed increases will still be greater than the salaries of women occupying the same position, even should the increases proposed in the women's salaries be granted.

"The Interborough Association of Women Teachers respectfully suggests that a further saving could be made, while the city continues to pay women teachers less than men occupying the same position, by replacing male teachers in charge of girls' classes in the elementary schools by women teachers. It is well known that in at least one school in Manhattan, there are no women teachers in the grades of the last two years, although there are many girl pupils in such grades.

"Respectfully submitted,

"GRACE C. STRACHAN,

"President."

In the discussion resulting in the Board of Estimate, October 4, 1908, on the presentation of these schedules, the following facts were emphasized:

| | |
|---|---|
| The per capita cost of pupil in high school, . . | $90.00 |
| The per capita cost of pupil in College of the city of New York,. . . . . . . . . . | $185.50 |
| The per capita cost of pupil in Normal College, . | $5.13 |

Mr. Maxwell's Tenth Annual Report shows:

| | |
|---|---|
| Per capita cost of pupil in Elementary School, . | $31.61 |
| " " " " " " High Schools, . . | $92.30 |
| " " " " " " Nautical School, . . | $338.27 |
| Per capita cost of pupil in Training Schools (Theory Department), . . . . . . | $102.69 |
| Per capita cost of pupil in Truant School, . . | $58.03 |

This is estimated on average daily attendance, and includes only the cost based on salaries. When it is considered that the salaries of superintendents, examiners, directors, and other attendance officers are all classed with the expenditures for elementary schools, and when it is further considered that the cost per pupil of scholastic supplies, including library books and apparatus, is less for the elementary schools than for any other, it is evident that the cost of a high school pupil is three times that of an elementary school pupil, while six pupils could be paid for in elementary school with the cost of one boy in New York City College. Even the boy in the Truant school costs 83.8 per cent. more than the boy in the elementary school, although the salary of the truant officer is added to the other expenses of the elementary school boy. As for the Nautical school, that is a record breaker indeed. Almost eleven boys could be taught in elementary school for the average cost of one boy on the School Ship, based on expenditures for salaries of officers, for sustenance and crew.

Poor elementary school pupil and poor elementary school teacher! And yet what is the reason for our public school system? Is it not the education of the elementary school pupils? Should not our first thought be of them? Should not our greatest efforts be toward perfecting our system in regard to them? Yet the contrarry is true. The course of study is planned not for the ninety-five per cent that never even finish the elementary school course, not even for the five per cent that do graduate from the elementary schools, but for the pitiful fraction of one per cent that enter college.

And yet we are treated to false appeals for more money to get "more men teachers in the high schools" when statistics show there are already more men for the high school boys than there are women for the high school girls!

### MONEY FOR OTHER INCREASES

Speaking of Mayor McClellan's excuse for his veto of the Equal Pay for Teachers Bill—that it would cost $13, 000,000 and the city could not afford it—Mr. Towns commented caustically upon the record of the present adminis-

HON. JAMES W. WADSWORTH, JR.,
SPEAKER OF ASSEMBLY DURING THE FOUR YEARS OF "EQUAL PAY" FIGHT.

tration, stating that it was the first time the Mayor had shown timidity in spending the people's money freely.

"Beside the amount of money he has spent," said Mr. Towns, "this teacher's increase apportionment might be compared with an attempt to start a fertilizing factory with one small canary bird on the highest peak of Mount Chimborazo."

During all this time that we were being opposed on the ground of greater expense to taxpayer, employees of other departments were receiving increases.

In a pamphlet by Comptroller Metz, entitled "Cost of Government of the City of New York," with an analysis of the Budget for the year 1909, appears on page 34, "the necessity for this action I personally regret, for some provision, I believe, should have been made for the increase of the salaries of the teachers in the elementary schools, of Police Lieutenants and Sergeants and fourth grade firemen and Patrolmen, and there should have been allowances for the increase of salaries of many worthy employees in the various Departments, but in the interests of economy I joined with my associates in the Board of Estimate and Apportionment for a Budget which should contain no salary increases whatever."

Being myself a taxpayer as well as a school teacher, such press articles as the following naturally had a special attraction for me during the years that the Board of Estimate was denying our appeal.

The Brooklyn *Eagle,* May 28, 1909. "The city may be too poor to build subways. The debt limit may always be conveniently used as a bugaboo. But, to use a vernacular expression of a Tammany man, there was a 'jail delivery' of salary increases on the calendar of the Board of Estimate to-day.

"Here are a few of the increases which Controller Metz seeks to make. They were all reported upon favorably by the select committee on salaries, of which Mr. Metz is a member. The first two fix the grade of examiner in the Finance Department at $5,000 a year for two incumbents. One of the men whom the controller intends to favor was receiving a salary of $1,050 when Mr. Metz came into office.

"That is not all for the Finance Department. For the chief bookkeeper, Mr. Metz has provided a $1,000 increase. The chief auditor is similarly favored. The head of the law and adjustment division is also given a $1,00 increase.

"There are two other examiners in the Finance Department, whom Mr. Metz evidently believes should be favored with an increase in salary. For them he intends to fix $3,000 each. The deputy collector of assessments and arrears in Manhattan also finds it hard to get along on his present salary, so Mr. Metz has decided to raise it to $4,000. Then there are two accountants to whom Mr. Metz proposes to give salaries, respectively $2,400 and $2,500.

"President Coler is just as lavish as Mr. Metz. He proposes the establishment of clerk to the local improvement boards at $3,000 per annum. So that some of the inspectors of plumbing in the Building Department may receive an increase he proposes the fixing of a grade at $2,400. To the man who drives Mr. Coler's automobile he has decided to give a $300 increase, fixing his salary at $1,500.

The chief engineer of the bureau of sewers, Mr. Coler believes, is being underpaid unless he receives a salary of $6,000. A resolution fixing the salary at that amount was accordingly introduced. The same opinion evidently is entertained by Mr. Coler toward the chief engineer of the bureau of highways and the chief engineer of the bureau of sewers. The salary of both officials is fixed at $6,000.

Then comes the superintendent of Mr. Coler's municipal asphalt plant. Mr. Coler proposed to fix his salary at $2,500. But for the man who is known as the searcher in his office, Mr. Coler also proposed an increase. His salary in the future will be $1,800.

Altogether 139 salary increases were on the calendar. Besides Mr. Metz and Mr. Coler, the health department and the other borough presidents divided the honors."

The *Eagle* of June 5, 1909, said editorially: "Increases for 139 city employees passed the Board of Estimate and Apportionment. For example, $3,000 is a good fat salary for the clerk to the local improvement boards of Brooklyn. Engineers of the Bureau of Sewers and of Highways, are, of course, technical positions, but you can hire pretty good engineers for less than $6,000, the salary fixed for those positions. Nobody wants the city to be niggardly in its pay, but between that and wholesale extravagance there is room to draw the line of justice tinged with generosity."

The total sum of the increases in the municipal departments, exclusive of fire, police and school departments, for the six months' period, commencing Jan. 1, 1907, to July 1, 1907, was $633,021.70.

Coler's Bulletin:

. . . . .

"But there are other specifications.

"Not to mention the Kissena Park land purchases, the purchase of waterfront property for ten millions, whose assessed valuation was only one-fifth that amount, and a dozen other little real estate deals of that kind, there is the astounding waste in the Catskill watershed, where land commissioners are paid fifty dollars a day, and where a contract bid is thrown out for no apparent reason than that it is two million dollars lower than the bid which is accepted.

"There is the nine million dollar subway made useless by reason of the failure of the city to complete it.

"There is the Queensboro Bridge, built at a cost of twenty million dollars, and so overloaded with steel as to make it dangerous and to involve an admitted waste of two million dollars. In order to make this bridge safe the steel had to be taken off again, and the provision for elevated railroad service had to be abandoned. This reduces the capacity of the bridge one-half. It was of this bridge that the Scientific American said, it was the greatest engineering blunder in bridge construction. It was at the celebration of this bridge opening that an observer remarked: 'Could there be anything more absurd than the parade of the bridge engineers. It is like a procession of doctors at the funeral of a victim of their blunders.'

"The reduction of its capacity one-half and the actual cost of the excess steel on this bridge make a total of waste amounting to $12,000,000.

"Another item is the construction of a three-and-a-quarter-million terminal of the Brooklyn Bridge, instead of adopting the simple Poulsen plan of bridge relief which can be installed for a quarter of a million."

. . . . .

Mr. William M. Hoge says: "We are only getting on the fringe of it" in Article on "How New York City is fleeced out of Millions," written for *Eagle,* Dec. 5, 1909, by Frederick Boyd Stevenson.

The New York *American,* Dec. 30, 1909, said: Comptroller will show it up in Report—Some prices quadruple—Yearly waste $50,000,000.

The statement of Supreme Court Justice Wesley O. Howard of Troy, that 40 per cent of money appropriated for public use is lost in graft, was echoed yesterday by President-elect John Purroy Mitchel, of the Board of Aldermen, and by Comptroller Metz. Justice Howard was provoked to the declaration by the size of a bill presented to him by condemnation commissioners on the Catskill watershed.

"It is impossible to fix an average percentage of graft," said Mr. Mitchel, who, as Commissioner of Accounts, has exposed graft continuously for three years. "In some cases, the graft is more than 40 per cent," and in other cases less. It's as high as 200 per cent, and even more, in some of the transactions we have uncovered. I don't think it is possible, though, to average graft."

"Graft in condemnation proceedings exceeds 40 per cent," said Comptroller Metz. "Judge Howard is talking about a graft I have been showing up ever since I became Comptroller. I'll show you in a day or two, when I make my report on condemnation public just how much condemnation graft there has been in this town. In some pieces the graft is 1000 per cent; in others it isn't more than 10 per cent.

"There is waste in some contracts and graft in others, but there is no estimating the amount. All I know is that the city finds itself 'stuck' to the tune of millions each year. On small things, where open order contracts are given by some department heads, I have found the size of the bills tripled and quadrupled. If that ain't graft, what is it?

"Testimony taken by the Legislative Investigating Committee last winter showed that an average of 25 per cent of the money spent by the city annually is wasted. The annual expenditure for all purposes exceeds $200,000,000, so the annual waste which might come under Judge Howard's classification of graft is $50,000,000."

### UNPAID TAXES

I think that it would be better for the taxpayers who oppose our bill to divert their energies toward assisting the city to collect its unpaid taxes. It must be realized that whatever the cost of "Equal Pay," it is simply the measure of the injustice the women teachers are laboring under. Those who emphasize this cost, including the Board of Education, seem not to realize that the greater the estimate placed on this injustice, the greater the crime exposed. But even the nine million, eleven million, thirteen million dollar estimates sink into insignificance when compared with the estimate of Unpaid Taxes.

The State Board of Tax Commissioners in annual report for 1906, stated in connection with unpaid franchise taxes: "In Greater New York alone these unpaid taxes reach the large total of $18,476,585.54."

The *World*, December 17, 1908: "By request of Gov. Hughes, the new charter commission made to him yesterday a special report upon city finances. After showing that the city on Nov. 1, was within $8,582,705 of the limit of its borrowing capacity, the report that the borrowing capacity at the moment is so limited is manifestly due, among other things, to the fact of the city's failure to collect its taxes and assessments. There was due the city on Nov. 1, 1908, for unpaid taxes and assessments for the year 1906 and prior years, the following:—

| | |
|---|---|
| Reai Estate Taxes, ........................ | $ 9,418,708 |
| Special Franchise Taxes, .................... | 17,964,830 |
| Personal Property Taxes, .................... | 32,346,528 |
| Assessments (to date) about ................ | 26,000,000 |
| | $85,730,066 |

In 1909 Mr. Ivins wrote Gov. Hughes that New York City had exceeded its debt limit by more than $5,000,000. Gen. Tracy, as referee, fixed the debt limit at 106 millions and upwards.

### OUR TAXES COMPARED WITH OTHERS

That our taxes are not abnormally large is shown by the following from the New York Evening *Post*: "The average annual burden (of taxation) on the head of every Japanese family amounts to 1.5 of his average income. A comparison of 20% in Japan is made with England 9.9; France 12.2; Germany 7.9; America 3.2; Italy 20.3; Austria 20.6." Compare an annual average burden of taxation on the head of every American family of 3.2 per cent with England 8.9; France 12.2; Germany 7.9; Italy 20.3. Many Americans are content with this system of economy that to a great extent results in the over-crowding of school-rooms and the overwork and underpay of school teachers."

The *Globe*, of October 18, 1907, in an article on the meeting of the State Department of Superintendents said: "The general question of teachers' salaries was discussed at the afternoon session, when Supt. R. A. Taylor, of Niagara Falls, presented the results of his investigations as to 'Prevailing Methods of Grading the Salaries of Teachers.' It was something of a surprise to those present, particularly the people from New York City, to learn that New York City is not the banner salary city. It devotes only .776 per cent of the money raised by taxation to teachers' salaries, whereas Mechanicsville gives .857, Newburgh .810 and Salamanca and Elmira .780 each. It was also reported that the minimum salary in a number of the small cities is the same or higher than that in New York City. Cities registering less than 1000 students devote 28 per cent of their school money to teachers' salaries; those having from 2000 to 3000 pupils devote 63.3 per cent; those having from 3000 to 5000 devote 70.9 per cent; those over 5000, 67.3 per cent. The state average is about 65 per cent.*

This from the *Eagle* of March 18, 1910, makes us hope that something will be left for us next time:

The comparative statement of payrolls prepared by Controller Prendergast was presented to the Board of Estimate and Apportionment at the meeting to-day. The months compared were December, the last under the McClellan administration, and January and February, the first two months under the present administration. Mr. Prendergast's figures go to show that the January payroll was $252,109.02 less than the December payroll, and the February payroll compared to the last month of the previous administration shows a decrease of $552,409.62.

As I said at the beginning of this chapter, we started out with the determination that we would do nothing to reduce any salary fixed by the Davis Law, but the male teacher opposition to us has been so unfair and insulting that now we are prepared to insist that whatever money is allowed by the Board of Estimate and Apportionment for teachers' salaries shall be divided equitably, *i.e.*, if the board of education has $1,500 for the hiring of two teachers for two positions exactly the same, it should divide it

* One "Taxpayer," wrote to the *Globe* that if the White bill became law he expected to raise every one of his tenants from $3 to $5 a month. As one correspondent answered: "A landlord like that doesn't need the passage of a 'White Bill' to cause him to raise your rent. He would do it if he found a little fresh air coming into your apartment." Said correspondent proceeded to show how her landlord with property valued at $32,000 would have to pay $32 more if one mill tax were added, and that this would mean only 26⅔ cents per month for each of the tenants.

into $750 and $750 instead of $600 and $900; and if it has $6000 for two principals of the same kind of school, it shall divide it into $3,000 and $3,000, instead of $3,500 and $2,500.

Our McCarren-Conklin bills of 1907 and Gledhill-Foley bill showed we are ready to have the board establish a salary for a principalship of a boys' school, higher than that of the principalship of a mixed or a girls' school; and for a mixed school, higher than that of a girls' school. Likewise, as to assistants to principals and other positions. Nor do we look for an obstacle in the Davis Law, because if Charter Revision does not soon eliminate the objectionable features of that law we are prepared to test its constitutionality in the courts. The following brief shows that steps have already been taken along this line.

# CHAPTER XV

## IS THE DAVIS LAW UNCONSTITUTIONAL?

In the matter of the Application of the Interborough Association of Women Teachers to the Board of Education for a Revision of the By-laws of the Department of Education relative to the salaries of men and women teachers.

### I

The obligation to equalize salaries in the schools is legal as well as moral.

A legal as well as a moral obligation is upon the Board of Education to equalize the salaries of men and women in the School system of New York. Section 1091 of the charter under which these salaries have been fixed while ostensibly a protective bit of legislation is in reality discriminatory and makes a distinction between the men and the women of the schools based solely upon sex in spite of the fact that it recites, that "salaries shall be regulated by merit, grade of class taught, length of service, experience in teaching, or by a combination of these considerations." There is nothing in this unctuous introduction to indicate it is about to declare that a man teacher after a certain number of years of service shall receive a salary of 100 per cent greater than a woman who does the same work.

After reciting the considerations which shall regulate the salaries of the teaching force the law goes on to establish different minimum rates of compensation for men and women in the same positions, and the difference is based upon the fact of sex and nothing else.

This is discriminatory legislation and it is in violation of the Constitution of the United States and of the Constitution of the State of New York. There is no warrant for such discriminatory legislation and there is abundant reason for declaring it null and void.

The 14th Amendment of the Federal Constitution is as follows:

All persons born or naturalized in the United States, and subject to the jurisdiction thereof, are citizens of the United States and of the State wherein they reside. No state shall make or enforce any law which shall abridge the privileges or immunities of citizens of the United States; nor shall any State deprive any person of life, liberty or property, without due process of law, nor deny to any person within its jurisdiction the equal protection of the laws.

If the section of the Charter of New York, under which the Board of Education has the authority to make by-laws regulating salaries is protective in its character, it is evident that it does not give the men and the women of the school system the equal protection to which all persons, all citizens, are entitled under this amendment. If it is discriminatory, as the women teachers know it is, then it is in direct contravention of this declaration. Section 1091 of the charter is either protective or discriminatory. In either case it is a violation of the greatest of the Constitutional guarantees added to the organic law after the Civil War.

The right to equality under the law is insured to the citizen by a triple guarantee. These are the fourteenth amendment of the Federal Constitution and Sections 1 and 6 of Article 1 of the Constitution of the State of New York. The State guarantees are as follows:

Section 1, No member of this State shall be disfranchised, or deprived of any of the rights or privileges secured to any citizen thereof, unless by the law of the land, or the judgment of his peers.

Section 6. . . . No person . . . shall be deprived of life, liberty or property without due process of law.

As briefly as is consistent with the magnitude of the subject and the dignity of the cause we shall discuss these guarantees and their application to the subject of Equal

Pay by taking them up in inverse order and ascertaining and quoting the judicial definitions necessary to demonstrate that the Charter provision regulating salaries is in direct violation of the Bill of Rights, (Article 1, Section 6, Constitution State of New York) and the fundamental law of the nation as well.

It is necessary then to know the meaning of the word liberty as set forth in the Bill of Rights, the interpretation of the phrases "due process of law" and "Law of the Land" and the application of the declaration "Equal Protection of the Laws."

In the People *v.* Marx (99 N. Y., 386), known as the Oleomargarine case, the Court of Appeals thus declared the broad application and the inviolability of the Constitutional guarantees:

. . . The Constitution of the State provides (Art. 1, Sec. 1), that no member of this State shall be disfranchised or deprived of any of the rights and privileges secured to any citizen thereof, unless by the law of the land, or the judgment of his peers. Section 6 of Article 1 provides that no person shall be deprived of life, liberty or property, without due process of law, and the Fourteenth Amendment to the Constitution of the United States provides that "No State shall make or enforce any law which shall abridge the privileges or immunities of citizens of the United States, nor shall any State deprive any person of life, liberty or property, without due process of law, nor deny to any person within its jurisdiction the equal protection of the laws." These constitutional safeguards have been so thoroughly discussed in recent cases that it would be superfluous to do more than refer to the conclusions which have been reached, bearing upon the question now under consideration. Among these no proposition is now more firmly settled than that it is one of the fundamental rights and privileges of an American citizen to adopt and follow such lawful industrial pursuit not injurious to the community as he may see fit.

(1 Abb. U. S. 398; 16 Wall. 106; 4 Wash. C. C. 380; 98 N. Y. 98.) The term "liberty," as protected by the

Constitution, is not cramped into a mere freedom from physical restraint of the person of the citizen, as by incarceration, but is deemed to embrace the right of man to be free in the enjoyment of the faculties with which he has been endowed by his creator, subject only to such restraints as are necessary for the common welfare. In the language of Andrew, J., in Bertholf *v.* O'Reilly (74 N. Y. 515), the right to liberty, embraces the right of man "to exercise his faculties and to follow a lawful avocation for the support of life," and as expressed by Earl, J. in *re* Jacobs, "one may be deprived of his liberty, and his constitutional right thereto violated, without the actual restraint of his person. Liberty in its broad sense, as understood in this country, means the right not only of freedom from servitude, imprisonment, or restraint, but the right of one to use his faculties in all lawful ways, to live and work when he will, to earn his livelihood in any lawful calling, and to pursue any lawful trade or avocation."

A denial, therefore, of the equal protection of the law is an invasion of the liberty of the citizen. And when that denial is of such a character that it compels one citizen to sell product or service to the government for less than another, it amounts to a serious invasion of a fundamental right, which cannot be excused or explained by the assertion that there is freedom of choice as long as there is no actual physical conscription. The fallacy of this argument is illustrated by supposing that the Metropolitan Street Railway Company were permitted to charge different rates of fares. The citizen discriminated against would not be physically seized and compelled to ride, and would at all times have the right to walk, but he would, nevertheless, be the victim of an unequal and unconstitutional law. The argument that women have the right to refuse to teach at the present salaries is beside the question. They always had that right and they always will have it. In refusing to accept employment they have equal right with men. In preparing for their work as teachers they must have the same or equivalent qualifications as men. In this they are equal, too. What they want now is equality of protection under the law, equality of opportunity; equality of pay.

*What constitutes the law of the land.*

It may be urged that what the Legislature has decreed is itself the "Law of the Land" or "Due Process of Law." And that, therefore, Section 1091 of the Charter and the inequitable by-laws of the Board of Education enacted thereunder are valid. Let us see then what these phrases mean.

An early case in the judicial history of this State is that of Taylor *v.* Porter (4 Hill, 145), in which occurs this definition:

"The words 'Law of the Land,' as here used, do not mean a statute passed for the purpose of working the wrong. That construction would render the restriction absolutely nugatory, and turn this part of the constitution into mere nonsense."

In People *v.* Toynbee (20 Barb., 169), it was held:

. . . By "the law of the land" is meant a proceeding according to the course of the common law; a trial and judicial sentence, and not merely a statute passed for accomplishing the wrong. . . . The power of the Legislature in the enactment of laws (whatever it may be in other countries), is not unlimited in this; but is restricted both by the written constitution, and by the generally received principles of practice and right.

## II.

*Legislation dealing with persons similarly situated must treat them alike.*

It is not denied that the Legislature had the power to authorize the Board of Education to fix salary schedules as it saw fit, provided these schedules applied equally to every teacher eligible for a given position in the School Department. It had the power and the right to deal with the teachers as a class. It had the power to enact liberal or penurious laws as it saw fit. But after it set the teachers apart for special legislation it had *neither the power nor the right to authorize a special classification within the general classification.* A law relating to a class which affects members of that class unequally, whether as to privileges or penalties, is necessarily in violation of the guarantee that every citizen shall have the equal protection of the law.

It is not claimed that any citizen, even a school teacher has a natural or inherent right to public employment, or that the city has not the right to refuse his services for reasons which may seem sufficient to the representatives of the Department of Education. But it is asserted that when the city sets up a standard of eligibility and declares all who have measured up to it successfully are fit and capable, it has not the right to make arbitrary distinctions between those whom it employs for the same work. If the teachers are worthy of their hire, it is because they have proved themselves qualified for the work and have done it acceptably. If a man teacher is worthy of his hire it is because he has done his work well and not because he is a man. A similar rule applies to the woman teacher. Merit, grade of class taught, length of service, experience in teaching, or a combination of these considerations should regulate compensation, as the Charter says they shall, though it does not follow these brave words.

## III

*Laws relating to persons similarly circumstanced which affect them unequally are a violation of the guarantee of civil rights.*

The Hon. Archibald R. Watson, Corporation Counsel of New York, and one of the most erudite law writers in this country, has discussed the subject of "Civil Rights" in Vol. VI of the American and English Encyclopedia of Law, in an essay noteworthy for clear reasoning and well-considered conclusions. Here are three of them:

"Under the Fourteenth Amendment discriminating or partial legislation favoring or discriminating against particular persons or classes, or particular persons of the same class, is prohibited.[3] And, it has been said, equality of protection implies not only equal accessibility to the courts for the prevention or redress of wrongs and the enforcement of rights; but equal exemption with others of the same class from charges or burdens of every kind[4] (p. 78)."

"Though a law be not discriminating in terms, yet if it is applied and administered by public authority so as practically to make unjust discriminations between persons similarly circumstanced in law, in matters affecting their substantial rights, the law will be held invalid as being, in operation, such a denial of equal protection as is within the prohibition of the Constitution[6] (p. 79)."

"It is immaterial, therefore, that legislation is general in terms, and that the persons at whom it is directed are not particularly designated. If the intent of the law was that it should affect a certain class with unequal harshness, which object is accomplished in its operation, the law contravenes the equal protection clause of the Fourteenth Amendment, and is void.[7]"

Let us see what the Supreme Court of the United States has said in upholding the principles set out by Mr. Watson, that whenever there is class legislation, every member of that class shall be treated alike.

In Hayes *v.* Missouri (120 U. S., 68; 30 L. E., 578) it declared:

"The Fourteenth Amendment to the Constitution of the United States does not prohibit legislation which is limited either in the objects to which it is directed or by the territory within which it is to operate. It merely requires that all persons subjected to such legislation *shall be treated alike, under all circumstances and conditions,* both in the privileges conferred and in the liabilities imposed."

And in Barbier *v.* Connolly (113 U. S., 27; 28 L. E., 923) it had already said:

"Class legislation, discriminating against some and favoring others, is prohibited, but legislation which, in carrying out a public purpose, is limited in its application, if within the sphere of its operation it affects alike *all persons similarly situated,* is not within the amendment."

Throughout these decisions, both of the Supreme Court of the United States and the Court of Appeals of this State, it is repeated over and over again that classifications are legal only when every person similarly circumstanced is treated alike. It will be observed that the words *person* and *citizen* are used, that no distinction is made because of sex. In the case of the Missouri Pacific Railroad *v.* Mackey (127 U. S., 205; 32 L. Ed., 109) the Court repeated, Justice Field writing:

"And when legislation applies to particular bodies or associations, imposing upon them additional liabilities, it is not open to the objection that it denies to them the equal protection of the laws, if all persons brought under its influence are treated alike under the same conditions.

". . . Such legislation is not obnoxious to the last clause of the Fourteenth Amendment, if *all persons* subject to it are treated alike under similar circumstances and conditions in respect both of the privileges conferred and the liabilities imposed."

Coming down to a later day, Justice Brewer, in Cotting *v.* Goddard (183 U. S., 79), wrote for the same Court:

"But while recognizing to the full extent the impossibility of an imposition of duties and obligations mathematically equal upon all, and also recognizing the right to classification of industries and occupations, we must nevertheless always remember that the equal protection of the law is guaranteed, and that such equal protection is denied *when upon one of two parties engaged in the same kind of business and under the same conditions burdens are cast which are not cast upon the other.*"

To the same purpose was the eloquent decision of Justice Brewer in Gulf, C. L. S. F. R. Co. *v.* Ellis (165 U. S., 150; 41 L. Ed., 666). In this case the Court said:

"While as a general proposition this is undeniably true, yet it is equally true that such classification *cannot be made arbitrarily.* The State may not say that all white men shall be subjected to the payment of the attorneys' fees of parties successfully suing them, and all black men not. It may not say that all men beyond a certain age shall be alone thus subjected, or all men possessed of certain wealth. These are distinctions which do not furnish any proper basis for the attempted classification. That must always rest upon some difference which bears a reasonable and just relation to the act in respect to which the classification is proposed, and can never be made arbitrarily and without any such basis. . . . The first official action of this nation declares the foundation of government in the words: 'We hold these truths to be self-evident, that all men are created equal, that they are endowed by their Creator with certain inalienable rights, that among these are life, liberty and the pursuit of happiness.' While such declarations of principles may not have the force of organic law, or be made the basis of judicial decisions as to the limits of rights and duty, and while in all cases reference must be had to the organic law of the nation for such limits, yet the latter is but the body and the letter of which the former is the thought and the spirit, and it is always safe to read the letter of the Constitution in the Spirit of the Declaration of Independence. No duty rests more imperatively upon the courts than the enforcement of the Constitutional provisions intended to secure the equality of rights which is the foundation of free government. . . ."

## IV

*Arbitrary and fanciful classifications and discriminating legislation affecting persons of the same class unequally are condemned by the Courts.*

Numerous decisions in the Federal and the State Courts hold that legislation applying to well defined classes of persons is constitutional provided there is valid reason for the classification and every one in a given class is equally subject thereto. In legislating for the teachers of New York it was impossible to discriminate between men and women teachers in respect to salaries without producing an inequitable and unequal situation. The Legislature enacted a law for the protection of the teachers of New York. This it had a right to do and its legislation would be beyond criticism on Constitutional grounds if it dealt equally with all teachers similarly situated, similarly circumstanced. The law knows no distinction of persons, and this salutary rule must be kept in mind. Section 1091 of the Charter and the By-Laws enacted under it show a sharp distinction between persons as such. They distinguish between teachers occupying the same position in the matter of salary. They provide that a man occupying a given position shall have 50 per cent. more than a woman at the beginning of service and that after a certain number of years he shall have 100 per cent. more. This is a distinction between members of the same class not contemplated by the Constitution and not tolerated by the laws of New York in regard to any other public servants appointed under the merit system.

Confusion is caused in considering this question by the fact that the Constitution of the State of New York and the Constitution of the United States, as interpreted by the courts permits classification, so long as the individuals in a given class are subjected to the same treatment. Of course this rule has sharp and well defined limitations. There can be no arbitrary or fanciful classifications. Legislation which applied solely to redhaired persons would not be Constitutional. Legislation providing different schools for white and colored children would not be constitutional unless the schools were made just as good for the children of one race as for the children of the other. Women lawyers would upset a law providing that their costs in lawsuits should be 50 per cent. of the costs collected by men lawyers and they would do so under these clauses of the fundamental law providing for equality of all citizens before the law. A law which should prescribe that women physicians should be paid half the fees paid men physicians would not be constitutional. And such a law would be upset even if it were couched in the specious and apparently protective phraseology of Section 1091 of the Charter. The Courts would hold it a limitation upon their earnings, and intended as such, no matter what the wording might be.

When the Legislature passed the Law now forming Section 1091 of the Charter it was legislating on behalf of the teachers of New York as a class. The statute so far as it increased the salaries of the teaching force by providing minimum amounts that should be paid by the Board of Education was a distinct step in advance, but so far as it permitted discrimination against women teachers, it was a distinct retrogression, and the fact was pointed out by Governor Roosevelt who signed the bill. It was an especially retrogressive measure so far as the teachers of Brooklyn were concerned for they had equal pay before consolidation and this law took it away from them.

A rule of equal treatment of pupils in the public schools was enunciated by the Court of Appeals in the case of People *et rel.* Gallagher *v.* King (93 N. Y. 448), in which it was said:

"The design of the common school system of this State is to instruct the citizen, and where, for this purpose, they have placed within his reach means of acquiring an education with other persons, they have discharged their duty to him and he has received all that he is entitled to ask of the government with respect to such privilege."

This case arose from the establishment of separate schools for colored pupils in Brooklyn. It holds that the benefits of the public school system must be offered equally to all pupils. Is it conceivable that a rule of equality applying to the pupils may be legally denied to the teachers. The law declares that there must be practical equality of efficiency between schools in the same grade. If the inequality of salaries is excused by saying that men are better teachers than women, how can the equal efficiency of these schools be maintained when changes and transfers take place in the teaching force from time to time?

## V

*Recent statutes and decisions in this state indicate that the Legislature and the Courts regard men and women as equal before the law.*

Significant legislation and significant decisions have been enacted and written in this State recently regarding the equality of men and women before the law. The Domestic Relations Law (Chapter 19, L. of 1909) makes the rights and the liabilities of husband and wife equal and re-enacts the law that a married woman and an unmarried woman shall have the same contractural business and property rights. The legislation of this State declares equality, of the civil rights of men and women generally. Section 1091 of the Charter of New York is the *only bit of legislation in which the principle of equality is ignored.*

In sustaining equality of the contractural rights of men and women, Justice Gray of the Court of Appeals writing for that tribunal in People *v.* Williams (189 N. Y. 131) in which a law preventing women from working in factories at night was declared unconstitutional, made these sweeping declarations:

"The fundamental law of the State, as embodied in its Constitution, provides that 'no person shall * * * be deprived of life, liberty or property without due process of law.' (Art. 1, Sec. 6.) The provisions of the State and of the Federal Constitutions protect every citizen in the right to pursue any lawful employment in a lawful manner. He enjoys the utmost freedom to follow his chosen pursuit and any arbitrary distinction against, or deprivation of, that freedom by the legislature is an invasion of the constitutional guaranty. Under our laws men and women now stand alike in their constitutional rights and there is no warrant for making any discrimination between them with respect to the liberty of person, or of contract. * * * It is clear, as it seems to me, that this legislation cannot, and should not, be upheld as a proper exercise of the police power. It is, certainly, discriminative against female citizens, in denying to them equal rights with men in the same pursuit. * * *

"An adult female is not to be regarded as a ward of the state, or in any other light than the man is regarded, when the question relates to the business pursuit or calling. She is no more a ward of the state than is the man. She is entitled to enjoy, unmolested, her liberty of person, and her freedom to work for whom she pleases, where she pleases and as long as she pleases, within the general limits *operative on all persons alike,* * * *

"So I think, in this case, that we should say, as an adult female is in no sense a ward of the state, that she is not to be made the special object of the exercise of the paternal power of the state and that the restriction here imposed upon her privilege to labor, violates the constitutional guarantees. *In the gradual course of legislation upon the rights of a woman, in this state, she has come to possess all of the responsibilities of the man and she is entitled to be placed upon an equality of rights with the man.*"

And this opinion had the concurrence of the entire court with the exception of Justice Cullen, who was absent.

No extended argument is necessary to demonstrate where the Legislature stands in regard to this question of "Equal Pay." Its action at three successive sessions indicates how it now regards Section 1091 of the Charter and the By-Laws enacted thereunder. The Legislature is willing to right the wrong it sanctioned, and the highest Court of the State has indicated that it will favor neither special privileges nor special disabilities for women whatever their walk of life. The duty of the Board of Education is as apparent as its power is ample.

The By-Laws of the Board of Education have in general used the minimum salaries prescribed by the Charter as the maximum salaries of the school system. The Board of Education, is not prevented by the Charter from making schedules that are just and equitable. It has abundant authority both in natural justice and the fixed Law of the Land.

CHARLES F. KINGSLEY,
Attorney-at-Law.

## CHAPTER XVI

### GLARING INEQUALITIES AND INCONSISTENCIES

*Principals of Elementary Schools*

Maximum ........Women . $2500 Men . $3500

*Grade Teachers*

| | | | | | |
|---|---|---|---|---|---|
| Women— | 1st | Year....$ 600 | Men— | 1st | Year....$ 900 |
| " | 7th | Year....$ 840 | " | 7th | Year....$1633 |
| " | 12th | Year....$1080 | " | 12th | Year....$2160 |

A man gets first year same as woman eighth year.

Woman Teacher's Annual Increase, $40.00. Man's, $105.00.

*Secondary Schools*

| | | | |
|---|---|---|---|
| | Women..$ 936.00 | | Men..$1500.00 |
| Maximum | " ..$1440.00 | Maximum | " ..$2400.00 |

*Graduating-Class Teachers*

*(8th Grade)*

Women..........$84.00 Men............$150.00

*High Schools*

| | | | |
|---|---|---|---|
| Men Principals..........$5,000. | | No Women. | |
| 1st. Assts. | Maximum—Women..$2500 | Men..$3000 | |
| Assistants | " " ..$1900 | " ..$2400 | |
| Junior Teachers | " " ..$1000 | " ..$1200 | |

*District Superintendent*—$5,000. 21 *Men*—3 *Women*

Woman Principal—72 Classes—3,200 Pupils—Salary $2500
Man Principal —12 Classes— 480 Pupils—Salary $3500

The woman assistant to principal (she must have a special license) will receive in the eleventh year $1,600; a man teacher in school supervised by this assistant receives $2,400, or $2,160. That is, though *not eligible* to position held by the woman, he may receive fifty per cent. more salary.

A man teaching in lowest schedule receives in his *sixth* year a salary higher than that paid a woman who is head of a department in her *ninth* year.

A woman must be teaching boys and in her seventh year of experience before she receives the salary a man has from the very beginning.

A man teaching a graduating class is receiving $650 *more* than a woman principal of a school, say of 77 classes, when both are in their eleventh year of service. Her maximum finally is only $100 more than his.

A woman principal *never* receives, no matter how large her school, no matter how excellent her record, as much as a man principal in his *first* year.

We could cite case after case of a woman principal in charge of a school of from 40 to 77 classes receiving $1,000 *a year less* than a man principal in charge of a school of from 12 to 40 classes.

*Assistants to Principals or Heads of Departments, 8B Grade*

| Years of experience. | Women. | Men. |
|---|---|---|
| 9 | $1,400 | $2,100 |
| 10 | 1,500 | 2,250 |
| 11 | 1,600 | 2,400 |

A woman may supervise a department in which there are men teaching grades receiving salaries 50 per cent. higher than hers. Yet (1) the man, not having Head of Department license, is not eligible to the position the woman holds; (2) a man in the lowest grade, holding lowest license, is receiving in his *sixth* year $1,425—a salary higher than that of a woman Head of Department in her *ninth* year of service. These women often have charge of 25 classes, with the responsibilities of training the teachers, disciplining the pupils, making laborious reports, interviewing parents, and so on.

| Years of Experience. | Principals. Women. | Principals. Men. | Men in Grades below 8B. | Men in Grade 8B. |
|---|---|---|---|---|
| 11 | $1,750 | $2,750 | $1,950 | $2,400 |
| 12 | 2,000 | 3,000 | 2,055 | 2,400 |
| 13 | 2,250 | 3,250 | 2,160 | 2,400 |
| 14 | 2,500 | 3,500 | 2,160 | 2,400 |

It will be seen that women, after serving the required ten years satisfactorily, passing the very difficult examination for a principals' license, and securing a position as principal (usually after weary waiting), (1) receives in her first and second years as principal a lower salary than a man who may be in even the lowest grade (see schedule VI.); (2) serves three years as principal at a lower salary than a man in the 8B is receiving when the by-laws permit her to *begin* service as principal; (3) *never* receives, no matter what her experience, the salary a man receives in his *first* year as principal; (4) never receives a salary more than $100 in excess of that received by a man in the 8B grade having ten years' experience, and not having either the license for or the responsibility involved in her position.

In a recent circular issued by the Association of Men Principals and Teachers, the statement is made that "Women teachers should note with interest that a 'complete, accurate and scientific statement of the increased cost of living' proves that 'every dollar you receive in salary now will buy not more than what 80c. would have bought in 1899.'"

It has not been necessary for the women teachers to make any scientific inquiry to find out that at all times and at any time since 1899:

(*a*) In her 13th year of service in grades below the 7A, the woman teacher has been receiving only 50 to 73⅓ cents for every dollar paid to the male teacher of same grade and experience;

(*b*) The woman assistant to principal has been receiving only 66⅔ cents for every dollar paid the male assistant to principal;

(*c*) The woman principal has been receiving only from 63 to 71 cents on every dollar paid the male principal;

(*d*) The woman teacher of a graduating class of boys has been receiving from 62 to 64 cents for every dollar paid to the male teacher of same grade and experience.

Not long ago, acting in my capacity as District Superintendent of Schools, I examined Mr. B., who was nearing the end of his third year of teaching, and so had to be passed upon as to his fitness for a permanent license. I found his work generally unsatisfactory, and I could not recommend that his license be made permanent. Yet he was receiving fifty per cent. more salary than Miss B., who was appointed at the same time as he was and assigned to the same kind of class. In fact, Miss B. would have to teach eleven years to get as much as he was receiving. Furthermore, she would need to have passed the examination for a permanent license at the end of her third year, and the examination as to fitness and merit at the end of her seventh year of service.

Is not such a state of affairs bad for Mr. B. as well as unjust to Miss B., and a disgrace to the community?

Mayor McClellan, in his letter, read at our Carnegie Mass Meeting, said:

"For the teaching of little children *there can be no question but that women are far superior to men,* and that they are therefore entitled to a higher rate of compensation."

In his Ninth Annual Report, Superintendent Maxwell said: "Experience has doubtless shown that women teachers teach younger pupils, boys as well as girls, better than men."

Yet the men teaching these very "younger pupils" are paid from 50 to 100 per cent. more salary than the women who teach them "better."

*Glaring Inconsistencies in the Attitudes of Our Opponents*

The cry that the salaries of men teachers will be reduced—yet.

The cry that "Equal Pay" will cost nine to thirteen million dollars.

The cry that "Equal Pay" will drive men out, and again

The cry that "Equal Pay" will drive women out.

The cry that the "Equal Pay" bills are mandatory—yet

The cry for the retention of the Davis Law.

The statement that women are superior to men as teachers of young children, yet

The demand for the Davis Law which pays men from 50 to 100 per cent. more than women in the primary grades.

The statement that men must be offered a higher salary than women in order to get "men of the proper calibre," yet

The fact that hundreds of men now in the system are the same men that were engaged in Brooklyn on "Equal Pay" salaries. Among them are the City Superintendent, three Associate Superintendents, six District Superintendents, four High School principals, and numerous elementary school principals. Now young men are appointed direct from City College.

# CHAPTER XVII

## THE WHITE BILL OF 1907

It is painfully significant that the majority of the arguments advanced by the opponents of this bill, when they get down to the question of feasibility, are based upon a profound distrust of the Board of Education. It seems to be taken for granted that wherever the law leaves a loophole for the Board of Education to wiggle away from its mandate and do the wrong thing, prompt advantage will be taken thereof. The brief of the Men teachers and Principals amounts to a petition to the Legislature not to pass the White bill, because they will be turned over to the tender mercies of the Board of Education. The pleas put forward by Mr. Stern in behalf of the primary teachers is in effect a prophecy that they will fare badly at the hands of the Board of Education, because the Legislature has not specifically stated all that may be done for them. Mrs. Leveridge, who appeared before the Assembly Cities Committee in opposition to the bill, made an argument amounting to an attack upon the Board of Education, which she feared would discriminate against the primary teachers. Miss Davidson and Miss Reardon both evidenced such fear of the Board of Education that they are willing to continue working under the unjust and inadequate schedules of the Davis law rather than be left to the "discretion of the Board of Education," with a prospect of a share in the proceeds of the "extra mill." Miss Davidson was so excited about this taking from her "the only safeguard and protection given me by a State Law" that she added 586 to 565 and made a total of eleven thousand and fifty-one as the number of "primary teachers" opposed to the White bill. Incidentally I know that many of these protestants are *men* below the 7 A Grade.

In a statement made by the Senate Committee which reported this bill through Senator White, appears some comment upon the course of the Board of Education in not heeding the petition of the women teachers for justice. It is easy to see that these men accepted with some reluctance the conviction that the Board of Education had not done its duty in this matter and that they proceeded only after a careful examination of the situation. Bygones should be bygones. The slate has been wiped clean and the Board of Education is now free to go ahead and discharge the responsibility put upon it by this bill, sure of the loyal co-operation of those who have urged its enactment, sure that the only suspicion breathed against it comes from the men who are opposing the White bill.

### NO POLITICS IN THIS BILL

There is no politics in this bill. An examination of the entire work of the Legislature would reveal no measure so free from politics as this one. Senators and Assemblymen without distinction of party supported it. They agreed that it was right in principle and they had no hesitation in saying that they were glad to support it when they learned positively, after consultation with the members from the counties composing Greater New York that it did not violate the principle of Home Rule. Certainly these members of the Legislature were justified in the conclusion that they were endorsing the principle of Home Rule when they realized that practically the entire legislative delegation from Greater New York favored the bill. And they were right. It is inconceivable that any bill violating the principle of Home Rule could have practically the unanimous support of the delegation from this city without regard to party, without stimulating some observant lawmaker to a political argument against it. There is no politics in this measure. There can be no politics in it. Legislation so just that it appeals to the sense of fairness of members of both parties so strongly that they refuse to entertain the thought of attempting to make political capital out of it, requires no defense against such a charge. It would be as sane to assert that the unanimous vote by which Congress declared war against Spain was tainted with politics. The passage of this bill by the Legislature marked one of those occasions in the life of the State when the lawmakers said, "It's just. It's right. Why have these women delayed so long in asking for justice? Let us do all that we can to right the wrong, without quibbling, without pettiness. Let us do our part to right the wrong."

The same reasons which actuated the Legislature to pass this bill ought to secure its endorsement by the Mayor of New York. Better than any member of the Legislature is he acquainted with the fact that the women of the schools have been unfairly treated. More than any member of the Legislature is he responsible to these women who now appeal for justice. He is the first citizen of the community where the wrong has been tolerated; and now under the Constitution and the laws it becomes his duty to pass upon their petition, a petition which the Legislature has stamped with its approval with practical unanimity. As Mayor of New York and a fellow-citizen of these women, he is more completely their representative than any member of the Legislature can be. They have asked the Legislature to clothe him with power to give them the justice they seek. The Legislature has done its part. An army of 13,000 women, without one exception, believe that he will do his.

The brief submitted by the President of the Interborough to Mayor McClellan urging his approval of the White bill, contained the following:

"Those who approve the bill beg you, Mr. Mayor, to consider this bill not as you would *original* mandatory legislation over which you had no control; and furthermore, as an amendment which restores in large measure powers taken from the City seven years ago. Viewed in this light, there seems to be no ground left on which you would justify a veto, except that this bill establishes a principle which your Board of Education has disapproved—the principle of 'equalization.'

"We beg you to believe that many members of said Board approve this principle, that public sentiment is overwhelmingly in favor of it, that all Civil Service standards demand it, and that we pray *you* to agree with us in the opinion that 'the position should command the salary' irrespective of color, size, weight, race, religion, politics, or *sex* of the person occupying same.

"*Further Reasons for Approval of Senate Bill* 1218:

"It secures *justice* to 13,000 of the citizens of the great city—to 13,000 of the city's most necessary, valuable and worthy employees.

"It gives a far greater measure of Home Rule than does Sec. 1091 of Charter it amends.

"The great majority of the best citizens of the city request it—witness:

"Over 100,000 names on petitions representing hundreds of millions of taxable property.

"Over 5,000 telegrams sent you by citizens requesting its approval.

"Over 5,000 individual requests of Primary Teachers for Approval of bill.

"State Representatives approve it:

"Witness: 21 Senators, 1 against; 63 Assemblymen, 3 against.

"City representatives approve it: witness unanimous resolutions of Board of Aldermen.

"Over 5,000 petitions of Primary Teachers as against the few who seek to defeat the bill."

Some of the men employed in the School Department banded themselves together to oppose this measure. From them and from them alone have emanated several statements purporting to give reasons against this measure. Let us examine these "reasons."

1. Women always have earned less than men.

2. It would belittle the men to earn the same salaries as the women.

3. Men would not get ahead in the school system.

4. Men are better teachers than women.
5. Men have families to support.
6. Men have a contract which this law would break.

The first reason is a recapitulation of the old argument used by the defenders of every hoary wrong. It amounts to saying that a custom is good and should be perpetuated because it is old. Slavery, polygamy and brigandage relied for ages upon this argument.

To the second declaration that it would belittle the men to receive the same salaries as women, it is enough to answer that it is infinitely more belittling for them to support an unjust system whereby women are paid only one-half as much as men for doing the same work with equal faithfulness, fidelity and success.

Another link in their chain of argument is that men would not get ahead in the school system as fast as they do now. They may be right in this conclusion, if they mean that favoritism and discrimination in their favor because they are men would no longer be factors in promotion. But if they mean that hard work, attention to duty, competency, satisfactory results, are not to receive recognition, they are profoundly mistaken. These elements of service will be the factors in determining promotion in the future. The merit system will obtain instantaneous recognition in the School Department as never before in its history, and ambitious, progressive men will have a better chance and a wider range of opportunity than ever before.

Men are better teachers than women, they say. This is the fourth reason. If that is so, men will soon dominate in the school system of New York, for salaries will be as attractive for all in a given grade or schedule as they are now for a chosen few in that grade or schedule, a chosen few whose claim to special financial recognition by the city is the fact that they are men. That argument answers itself. Of course there is a further fact that those of us who have attended school and who have had an opportunity to judge, do not come to the same conclusion as to the relative ability of men and women teachers as do these sapient gentlemen.

But what can we say in response to the statement that men have families to support? Granting this as an argument, it must be acknowledged that it costs a woman just as much to support a family as it costs a man. They know that while she may be compelled to accept a salary fifty per cent. less than his salary she is not given a corresponding reduction in anything she buys. They know that she must pay as much for clothing and board and car fare and theater tickets and medical attendance and shoes and the other necessaries of life as they. She must endure the humiliation of accepting fifty cents on the dollar when drawing her wages, but she finds no corresponding reduction in the price of anything she buys through all the wide range of possible purchases. Is it not true that in thousands of cases, right here in the school system of New York, women are supporting families or aiding brothers and sisters to obtain an education and to embark in a profession? This is true in even a larger degree than might be supposed at first thought. The old order changes. Years ago the son was the reliance and the mainstay of aged parents. He devoted himself to the old folks and stayed at home and remained single in order to provide for them. Now the burden is frequently shifted to the daughter. The son marries and has a family of his own, while the daughter remains at home and cares for her parents. This is a phase of social conditions in New York city to-day which represents a changing sense of family loyalty and duty. It is not easy to explain; but it exists, nevertheless.

What about the implied contract the men say in their sixth objection to this bill they have with the city? They have no contract either expressed or implied which depends for its validity upon denying their women associates in the School Department the right to equal pay for equal work. There is no law, no contract, no bond guaranteeing to them the right to advance at the expense of their fellow teachers of the female sex. But the women teachers have a guarantee by virtue of their citizenship, both from State and nation, that they shall have equal treatment before the law with all other citizens and that no disability shall be attached to them by reason of race or creed or sex. And this bond is paramount and perpetual.

The Association of Men Teachers and Principals evidently believe in the present Charter provision called the Davis law because it *does not* observe the principle of Home Rule with such breadth and sweep as does the White bill. In their circular entitled "Why Senate Bill No. 1162 cannot accomplish its purpose," they say: "The Davis law lacks the broad generalization of the White bill. . . . If it is wise to regulate the salaries of policemen and other city officials by statute, there would seem to be no well-founded reason against the retention of similar legislation in the case of schools. To substitute for fixed, definite salaries, guaranteed by the State, a fluctuating system, changing from year to year, sensitive to financial depression, and responsive to the caprice and whim of municipal political fortune, would seem a long step backward. It is earnestly hoped that very careful consideration will be given before so revolutionary a bill is made a law."

The Men Teachers and Principals, it is apparent, are opposed to the White bill, not because it violates the principle of Home Rule, but because it refers the whole question of salaries, subject to a few general principles, back to the Board of Education, thus recognizing Home Rule. They are opposed to the bill which they call "revolutionary" because it recognizes the principle of Home Rule and gives back to the Board of Education certain broad and sweeping powers which the Davis law took away. The Legislature in passing this act was so careful to confer full authority upon the Board of Education under the general declaration of equality, a sentiment in no sense local or limited, that the Men Teachers and Principals opposed the bill. They cried out against it because full authority under the declaration of equality is bestowed upon the Board of Education, an authority which the male opponents of the measure denominate the "caprice and whim of municipal political fortune." The Legislature has passed an act containing a declaration of a principle as broad as humanity and as enduring as justice; under which it restores to the

Board of Education the power of which it was deprived seven years ago. At the same time it has furnished ample funds to readjust the salary schedules on an equitable basis.

The Board of Education, through its apparently authorized spokesman, Mr. Abraham Stern, absolutely refused to consider any request involving "equalization." This was the only ground on which our organization could, under its Constitution, stand.

Furthermore, the Interborough realized that no officer or body of officers of the *City* government could eliminate the words *"male"* and *"female"* from Section 1091 of the City Charter.

Thus was the appeal to "Albany" justified.

MR. ABRAHAM STERN'S OBJECTIONS: "Bill is a violation of 'Home Rule.'" We grant that the bill is mandatory in some of its provisions; but it is evident to every fair-minded student of this bill that it gives to the Board of Education a far greater measure of "Home Rule" than does Sec. 1091 of the Charter which it seeks to amend.

Mr. Stern is right in saying it compels the raising of the lowest salary $600 to $720, and the reduction of a 16-year term to 12 years. For seven years the Board has failed to see the unfairness in the present conditions. Our State representaives were amazed to find our teachers so meanly paid.

Mr. Stern's arguments and Mr. Maxwell's letter both showed a failure to grasp the true situation. There is nothing in the "White" bill which would make it necessary to transfer "all men (519) in grades from 2 B to 6 B" (Mr. Maxwell's letter) into grades above the 6 B between now and January 1, 1908, for the purpose of avoiding the necessity of paying all teachers of boys' classes below the seventh year salaries according to $900 . . . 2160 schedule. That schedule is secured to men below the 7th year grades only by a by-law of the Board of Education, and therefore it can be amended at any meeting of said Board. Suppose, then, that the "McCarren schedules" were adopted by the Board. No men would need to find places in "the grades of the last two years" (Davis law) in order to secure continuance of $105 increment to $2,160 except those who had completed eight years in the lower grades. This number at present is 53, that is 466 less than the 519 mentioned in Mr. Maxwell's letter. It will thus be seen that even those who believe that men are needed below the 7 A grade need have no fear.

Mr. Stern said where there are men in the grades the "schedules must be different" from the schedules of grades where there are no men. This does not appear in the "White" bill. There is nothing in the "White" bill to prevent the Board of Education from making *uniform schedules* for all grades below 7 A. Then, where is there ground for all the wild and unfounded fears of "the primary teachers" and their recently discovered friends? Surely not in the "White" bill; but rather in the distrust of the Board of Education.

Mr. Stern contrasted the salary of a teacher in the 4 A and that of a teacher in the 4 B, intimating that the latter would receive 50 per cent. more than the former, and claimed that here was "the most pernicious and vicious feature of this bill." This arbitrary division between the 4 B and the 4 A is absolutely unjustifiable by any provision of the "White" bill.

We are surprised to have Mr. Stern compare the teachers with the employees of the business world. The teacher's is a Civil Service appointment. She is taken out of the conditions which prevail in the open market, and after having complied with all the requirements, and having passed a competitive examination, she is placed on an eligible list; then she must await appointment in order of standing.

## CHAPTER XVIII

### THE WHITE BILL—1908

The White bill of 1908 was practically the same as that of 1907, which had passed both houses of the Legislature twice; but it had been carefully redrawn by Horace E. Deming, who had represented us at the Governor's hearing in 1907, and who was familiar with the objections which had been made against it.

Two of the reasons given by Mayor McClellan for his veto, namely, that the principle of Home Rule was violated, and that the bill was mandatory, had been rendered null and void in the following words by Governor Hughes in his veto message on the bill:

"Apart from the power of the Mayor to appoint and remove as stated, and the duty of the city to supply the funds as required, the Board of Education exercises its powers independently. It is not subject to control by the city authorities. There is no contract or official relations between the teachers and the city."

"The Board of Education has the management and control of the public schools and of the public school system of the city, subject only to the general statutes of the State relating to public schools and public school instruction and to the provisions of the charter."

The Mayor's third reason, the expense, we held to be entirely covered by the provision of our bill which increased the three-mill tax to four mills, and we believed that unless a majority of the taxpayers of the city objected no one else should.

The Governor in his veto message had said:

"The Board of Education is thus directly subject to the control of the Legislature, and whatever provisions may be found necessary or wise for the purpose of defining its powers or prescribing its policy must be prescribed by the

Legislature. No other authority is competent to make such provision." The Governor also said, "But while the Legislature has power to deal with every phase of the matter, the course which experience approves is that certain general principles of action should be laid down, and that within these principles, freedom with reference to details of management should be left to the subordinate body acting with peculiar knowledege of local conditions."

We were asking the Legislature to lay down the general principle, "There shall be no discrimination in salary on account of the sex of the incumbent of a position." This principle had prevailed in Brooklyn until the Legislature, by passing the "Davis Bill" in 1900, instituted the schedules which we were seeking to amend. The "Davis Bill" had put upon thousands of the best citizens of the city a degrading discrimination. The Legislature of 1907 becoming aware of this injustice twice had voted to remove it.

Some have said, "Your Board of Education has power to amend these schedules as you desire." This is true. But after repeated appeals, our Board of Education has failed so to amend them. Governor Hughes, in his veto message of our bill, states "under the by-laws adopted by the board (referring to the Board of Education) glaring inequalities now exist." Again Governor Hughes, in the same message, says, "It is proposed by legislative enactment to establish the proposition that for work of a given position women shall receive equal pay with men. It is for this principle the supporters of the bill contend, and not for mere increased pay. The gross inequalities which have been permitted by the Board of Education, and which clearly should not be continued, are pointed out for the purpose of emphasizing the principle in question."

Impelled probably by these opinions so clearly expressed by the Governor, our Board of Education had prepared salary schedules which reduced to some extent the "glaring inequalities," and which called for an additional appropriation of about $3,000,000. But the Board of Estimate and Apportionment refused to allow money for this proposed increase. All this in the face of the undeniable fact that upward of 20,000 of the city's children, and therefore of the children who, under the constitution of the State, must be given an education, are without regular teachers.

But we found a special reason for appealing to Albany again in the last sentence of Governor Hughes' message, which ran as follows: "The matter should be left to the Board of Education to be dealt with locally, as it may seem best, *unless* the Legislature is prepared to lay down the general principle for the entire State and the entire public service."

We believed that the Legislature, in again passing our bill, would give proof that it was "prepared to lay down the general principle for the entire State and the entire public service." But as New York City is the only city in which the State has fixed salaries for teachers, and our appeal was therefore for an amendment to the Charter of the City of New York, we did not feel justified in making our bill a State bill. Furthermore, the State, in its appropriation act, does provide salaries for positions regardless of the sex of the incumbent.

Our bill was passed by the Senate with more than a two-thirds vote, the longest speech against it being made by Senator Travis of Kings, who insisted that he believed in "Equal Pay," praised women teachers, spoke of the unemployed and the cost of the bill. The eight Senators who voted against us were all so-called "Hughes' Senators."

When the bill reached the Assembly it became evident that it was of sufficient importance to be considered in connection with the approaching gubernatorial and presidential election.

The following letter, written while the bill was being held in the Cities Committee, is offered in evidence. I submit it without names at the request of the recipient:

"Albany, N. Y., March 12, 1908.

"I have your letter of the 10th inst. and wish to say that I do not believe that you mean to refer to me when you speak of a 'hold up.' I have never been accused of such action on legislation nor do I believe that the other members of the committee of the Affairs of Cities who have taken the same action as I, do so from any such motives. If there were no other reason for my opposing the bill I would do so for the protection of Governor Hughes.

"I helped to give the teachers an opportunity to present their cause to him last year. He has stated his opinion which he has not yet changed. I consider their efforts this year one intended to put him in as bad a position as possible. Because of the politicians who are behind this matter, I consider that it has developed into a political game of the meanest kind.

"I trust that you will consider the above remarks not as directed against the women school teachers, whom I consider a very deserving class and whom I would like to aid, but rather at the methods being used to further the political designs of certain politicians.

"With kindest regards, I am,

"Very truly yours,

"(Signed) ——— ———."

In the issue of March 30, 1908, a New York morning paper printed the following from its correspondent in Albany: "Speaker Wadsworth accorded the school teachers an hour's interview, and the bill in all its phases was discussed in his private room. Politics now figure in the passage of the bill. It is said that Governor Hughes does not want the bill to be put up to him a second time. His friends say that a veto of it on the eve of a Presidential election might be injurious to him. For that reason the 'Hughes Senators' voted against it. The Hughes men on the Rules Committee are taking this view of the political end of the bill and it is still hanging fire there."

The inference to be drawn from the above is scarcely complimentary to the Executive of a great Commonwealth where 12,000 of its law-abiding citizens—without the franchise—are trying to have a recognized injustice corrected by the body that enacted it.

While the bill was pending in the Rules Committee, we made the following appeal:

"In the name of the Interborough Association of Women Teachers, consisting of over 12,000 of the women in the Supervising and Teaching force of the public school system in the City of New York, I do pray you to report out Senate Cities Committee Bill 686, familiarly known as the 'Women Teachers' Equal Pay Bill.' I base my petition on the following:

"1. Because the Bill is a Senate Cities Committee Bill;

"2. Because the Bill passed the Senate by more than a two-thirds vote;

"3. Because the Bill is similar to, but an improvement on the Senate Cities Committee Bill 1218 of the last session, which passed the Assembly first by a vote of 105 to 15, and second, after Mayor McClellan's veto, by a vote of 82 to 55;

"4. Because the Board of Aldermen representing the people of the City of New York, has unanimously endorsed the measure;

"5. Because the Bill is endorsed by nearly 300 civic, religious, political, social, business and labor organizations in the City of New York, and throughout the entire State, representing hundreds of thousands of voters and many millions of capital;

"6. Because thousands of individual citizens and taxpayers, fully cognizant of the meaning and cost of this particular piece of legislation, have added their endorsement to our petition;

"7. Because at two very enthusiastic Mass Meetings, resolutions praying the Legislature to pass this Bill were unanimously adopted. At the Cooper Union Meeting, the resolution was moved by Rev. Henry A. Mottet, Pastor of the Church of the Holy Communion, New York; and at the Brooklyn meeting, by Rev. Lynn P. Armstrong, Rector of the Cuyler Presbyterian Church;

"8. Because the Legislature owes this measure of relief and justice to the women teachers of the City of New York, since it was by an act of the Legislature in 1900 that the unusual and unjust discrimination against women on account of sex was fixed by statute;

"9. Because the passage of this bill will purge the statutes of the Empire State of the only law which discriminates against woman in the labor market simply on account of her sex;

"10. Because all the evidence tends to show that if the relief sought by the women teachers could be granted directly by the voters of the City of New York, the women would be immediately successful;

"11. Because if we are to go down to defeat in the Assembly, we would like our friends in said body to have an opportunity of showing their loyalty to our cause.

"12. Because *it is right.*

"Do not kill us like rats in a trap. Give us a chance, at least, in the open field."

In addition to this, a petition begun by Assemblyman Conklin—the "father" of the Assembly bill—and circulated among the members of that body, was signed by 104 of the 105 members not on the Rules Committee. But the committee did not report the bill. This seemed so contrary to the true spirit of a democratic government that I was not surprised to hear Mary Chalmers—one of our most conservative members—say: "Now I know how anarchists are made."

# CHAPTER XIX

## CONCILIATION COMMITTEE AND SIX-AND-SIX PLAN

In the fall of 1908, a committee of men and women, which came to be known as the Conciliation Committee, was organized, with Henry N. Tifft, a former president of the Board of Education, as chairman, and Charles Dewey, president of the Male Principals' Association, as secretary. The other members were:

Katharine D. Blake, principal elementary school;

Katharine A. McCann, principal elementary school;

Annie B. Moriarty, principal elementary school and vice-president Interborough Association of Women Teachers;

Kate Turner, first assistant, high school;

Grace C. Strachan, district superintendent of schools and president of Interborough Association of Women Teachers;

Mary Moore Orr, Local School Board;

Miriam Sutro Price, president Public Education Society;

J. Edward Swanstrom, author of the "Swanstrom Six-and-Six Plan," ex-president Borough of Brooklyn, ex-president Board of Education;

Walter B. Gunnison, principal high school;

Magnus Gross, teacher of 8 B and president of New York City Teachers' Association;

James J. Sheppard, principal high school and president Interborough Council, and,

Frank L. Perkins, principal elementary school and president Brooklyn Teachers' Association.

Before the work of this committee was completed, Mr. Gross and Mr. Sheppard resigned. The final report contained a schedule of salaries in which there was no difference in salary based on the sex of the teacher. The report was adopted by representatives from a majority of all the teachers' associations in the city by a vote of 15 to 7.

This meeting of the presidents of the Board of Education and the various associations of teachers and principals of this city was held in the Board Rooms, Hall of Education, at 8 P. M., on Thursday, April 1, 1909.

Hon. Egerton L. Winthrop, Jr., president of the Board of Education, was asked to preside, and Mr. Charles O. Dewey, president of the Principals' (Male) Association of the City of New York, was elected secretary.

Among those present were Egerton L. Winthrop, president of the Board of Education; Commissioners A. Stern, Barrett, Kanzler, Haupt, and Katzenberg; President Grace C. Strachan of the Interborough Association of Women Teachers, President J. J. Sheppard of the Interborough Council, President Mary Curtis, Association of Women Principals of New York City; President W. A. Boylan of the Principals' Club, President Charles O. Dewey of City Principals' Association, President Magnus Gross of the New York City Teachers' Association, President F. K. Perkins of the Brooklyn Teachers' Association, President E. S. Shumway of the Male High School Teachers' Association, President J. S. Tildsley of the High School Teachers' Association, Principal Fanny S. Comings of the Brooklyn Heads of Departments, President Mary Lilly, New York Heads of Departments; President Fred Paine of the Association of Male First Assistant Teachers in High Schools, President Edgar Vanderbilt of the Male Principals' Association of Manhattan and the Bronx, Henry Moore of the Male Teachers of Brooklyn and Queens, President Alice Gray of the Brooklyn Class Teachers' Association, President Lina E. Gano of the Women's High School Teachers' Association, Miss Katherine D. Blake, W. B. Gunnison, Miss Kate E. Turner, President Van Evrie Kilpatrick of the School Garden Association, S. C. Walmsley, R. Richardson, M. D. Quinn, Mrs. A. B. Moriarty, Miss Clara C. Calkins, representing the Women Principals' Association of Brooklyn.

Among the most interesting statements made in the discussion preceding the vote on these "Conciliation Schedules," were the following: Miss Alice Gray, president of the Class Teachers' Association, approved "particularly the clause relative to class teachers' salaries, and more particularly those additional salaries given to teachers of boys' and of mixed classes in the lower grades, increasing from the first and second years to the third and fourth and then again to the fifth and sixth"; and Mr. Edgar S. Shumway, president of the Male Teachers' Association, said, "I am free to say that if the money were under my control, I would see to it that the woman who is first assistant in high school, as I am, received as much money as I received."

The committee was unanimous in its opinion that a kindergarten class could not be a true kindergarten class unless it consisted of both boys and girls, and therefore that the teacher of such a class should receive no bonus. The statement that the elasticity of schedules is endangered by the new law is also misleading.

The schedule is uniform for all teachers in the grades of the first six years, except for the variance in bonuses for mixed and boys' classes. The Conciliation Committee was also unanimous in its opinion that the best interest of the children of the city would be conserved by having all classes in the first six years mixed classes, and therefore the bonuses were so planned, as to make it cheaper for the Board of Education to make two classes mixed classes, rather than one a girls' class and the other a boys' class. For instance: in the group where the bonus for the mixed classes is $60 the bonus for a boys' class is $132. Therefore, the Board would save $12 on every two classes that it organized as mixed classes, rather than as one a girls' class and the other a boys' class.

This plan also makes it possible for the Board to offer some special inducement to men teachers, as the salary for a boys' class, even in grades of the first six years, is from $60 to $180 higher than the salary for a girls' class. All who are familiar with the workings of the system of the public education in this city, know that it is much more difficult to get teachers for mixed and for boys' classes than it is for girls' classes, and in this particular the committee believed that the law of supply and demand was properly recognized in offering a larger salary for the teacher of boys.

In the grades of the seventh and eighth years, the departmental system is now quite generally used, and it often happens that a teacher assigned to a grade of the 7 A girls in charge of the mathematics, spends half her time teaching boys of various grades, including, frequently, boys of the graduating classes. We believe that it is manifestly unfair then to pay such a teacher only the salary of a 7 A girls' class. We believe that this work should be treated practically the same as that in high schools, where a teacher is in charge of a special subject. In high schools there is but one salary, and therefore in the new schedules but one salary is provided for teachers of the grades of the seventh and eighth years, excepting that there is the bonus for teachers in mixed and in boys' schools. Again, this is to meet the contention that in order to get teachers of boys, a higher salary should be offered.

The statement that the new bill adds a year to the elementary school course is also wrong. At present there is an eight-year elementary school course and a four-year high school course. The committee was in favor of dividing those twelve years according to the Six-and-Six plan, or rather Six-and-Three-and-Three plan. This subdivision has been approved by the City Club, by the State Department of Education, by the Department of Education in France and Japan, as well as in ten of the large cities in this country.

The report of the Conciliation Committee includes practically all of the "Swanstrom" and "City Club" Six-and-Six plan. I regret that lack of space prohibits my including all the opinions of prominent educators that have been expressed on this plan. All reports agree that there is something wrong with our present Course of Study, particularly in what it does for the majority boy or girl that leaves school at fourteen—the compulsory school age in this State. Personally, I feel very strongly on this point; and were there no other element of great value in the Six-and-Six plan, I would favor it because its adoption would *force* a revision of the Course of Study that would benefit this majority boy and girl.

Briefly, the Six-and-Six plan provides that the twelve years now divided into an eight-year elementary course and a four-year high school course be divided into a six-year elementary and a six-year high school course; and that this latter be subdivided into a three-year " junior " or " sub " high school course to be taught in one or more buildings in each school district, and a three-year full high school course preparing for college, professional, or advanced vocational work; that the first two years of the junior high school have elective trade courses, the third to be a double course, one part consisting of subjects now taught in the first year of the present high school and the other of trade classes—an arrangement permitting the pupil intending to leave school at the end of the junior high school to take, if he chooses, a full trade course.

In an address before the International Congress of Arts and Sciences at St. Louis, September 23, 1904, City Superintendent Maxwell advocated practically the identical plan now " proposed " by the City Club. In the course of that address Dr. Maxwell said: " School life above the kindergarten age should be divided into two equal periods. . . . Each period would provide for six years of school work—the elementary from six to twelve; the secondary from thirteen to eighteen."

The National Educational Association has had a committee working on this problem for several years, and in its report for 1908 says:

" It is well to note that within the present year, J. Edward Swanstrom, for some time president of the Board of Education in Brooklyn, and later a member and president of the Board of Education of Greater New York, published in the Brooklyn *Eagle* an argument for the adoption of the six-year course of elementary study, to be followed by three years of work in the lower high schools plus three years in the upper high grade or specialized high schools. In that article Mr. Swanstrom argues forcibly that his plan would not only increase the educational efficiency of the schools, but would be highly economical for the City of Greater New York.

"At least ten cities in the United States, for several years, have employed the proposed six-year division and believe it to be more economical."

The following evidence dissatisfaction with our present courses:

Schools have been mapping their courses to prepare pupils for the professions in spite of the fact that only 10 per cent. ever take up such work. Over 90 per cent. of the population enter industries and the schools provide little or no training. This education of the few to the neglect of that of the many was the theme of an address by Arthur Dean, chief of the Division of Trade Schools of the State Department of Education, Albany, at the Washington Irving High School yesterday. He made a plea for revision of the course. In part he said:

"Do you girls know what per cent. of our population is engaged in industrial occupations? Ninety per cent. Do you know what per cent. is engaged in the so-called learned professions—teaching, preaching, doctoring, etc.? Ten per cent. What is now beginning to seem strange and unfair to the American citizens is that the education offered to boys and girls of from thirteen years of age upward has been conducted entirely for the 10 per cent. The movement into which America is now entering is to adjust secondary education to the lives of all, not a part of its people. Culture must and will exert its influence upon American life, but if anyone asserts that culture is to be obtained only or even especially in the high school courses now in vogue, he is no longer to be believed. There is no culture superior to that which comes from doing things which one can see the use of."

## REORGANIZE THE SCHOOLS

"I would give no less attention to graduating lawyers and physicians, but would give a great deal more to turning out of our public schools young men with a good,

HON. ALFRED E. SMITH,
STRONGEST AND HARDEST FIGHTER FOR THE "EQUAL PAY" BILLS IN THE ASSEMBLY CITIES' COMMITTEE, THE CHARTER LEGISLATIVE COMMITTEE AND ON THE FLOOR OF THE ASSEMBLY.

common school education plus a year's practical training at some useful trade. I would have a first-class manual training school attached to every high school and to every college and university, where young men could be turned out good, practical journeymen, blacksmiths, boilermakers, carpenters, cabinet workers, plumbers or skilled workmen at some other useful trade. I would increase the capacity of these schools to accommodate every child in the community and then I would make attendance compulsory.

"If we adopt Germany's system of technical training, her research and thoroughness, and combine them with our inventions, the combination would dominate the world. Without these fundamental qualities, it is only a question of time when this country must surrender its place as a leader among the great manufacturing nations of the world."—*President W. C. Brown* of the New York Central.

*Standard-Union,* March 16, 1909:

"A NEW PLAN FOR THE SCHOOLS

"Of the various plans for settling the differences between the men and women teachers on the question of pay, a proposal which may go into the administrative code of the charter offers the best prospect of bringing about agreement. It divides the twelve years of school work into two periods of six years each and provides that all teachers in the lower six years shall be women. In the upper six years all teachers shall be graduates of colleges, and there shall be no distinction of sex in the pay schedules. If this should receive the assent of the majority of both men and women teachers, it would settle the salary question permanently.

"There are some other features in the plan which will commend it to the public; and this in spite of the fact that any breaking up of the accustomed system of high school education will do away with many cherished associations and require a good deal of personal adjustment to new conditions by meritorious educators. For a long time it has been sought to make the system more flexible, so as to meet the various needs of the young in so large a community. It is true that under the present methods the high schools are all overcrowded; but that is a problem by itself. While the large attendance shows that present opportunities are appreciated, it does not prove that more variety in opportunity would not be welcomed. Under the plan proposed the upper six years would afford this in greater measure than now. The first three years, a sub-high school course, would lead either to three years more of work in the regular high schools preparing for college or to a like period in trade or manual training high schools.

"It is this principle which will have to receive more consideration in the future, whether it comes through the plan involved in the somewhat precarious chances of the proposed charter or whether it is attained in a more gradual manner. Industrial and commercial education has now become an absolute necessity. There is absolutely no lack of agreement that the great progress made by the German nation recently in a country very poor in natural resources and maritime facilities, is due more than anything else to its marvelously thorough education in handicrafts and business. The need is met here in a very haphazard and imperfect way at present. Some great manufacturing concerns have their own schools, which means a withdrawal of boys from the advantages of public school education for the sake of industrial training the State is just as much bound to give as it is to teach Latin or Greek. Many young men have practically no training at all which directly fits them for what they will have to do in life. The effect on the nation's prosperity is bound to show in time. The world's business which is a subject of fierce international competition, is not done by untrained men. There are some observers who take the matter very seriously. Mr. Frank A. Vanderlip, now at the head of the National City Bank, reports with something like alarm that in recent international exhibitions, he saw no American manufactured goods which excelled in merit; they were superior only because made more cheaply by the aid of automatic machinery. Mr. Vanderlip preaches the need of industrial training in schools, and of financial and business courses in the universities, on this text.

"Obviously, it is the unskilled man who in time of business depression swells the list of unemployed, burdens charity and government relief and lowers the whole tone of the community.

"Now, if the boys and girls who are going to work with their hands, the great majority of the population at all times, ought to be educated for their work, the education should be in the public schools and should begin at the earliest possible date. For such, at present, there is a pitifully large number of things they spend time in learning which they will proceed immediately and necessarily to forget. If at the age of twelve, when the rudiments of knowledge and mental discipline have been attained, they could be switched into a course of education designed directly to fit their needs through life, the benefit to them and to the community would be instantly apparent, and the provision for the classical courses of study would not be harmed by their absence."

The following was sent in reply to a letter received in May, 1908:

June 4, 1908.

MR. HENRY C. WRIGHT,
Secretary, City Club of New York,
55 West 44th Street, New York.

*Dear Sir:*

In reply to your communication of May 29th, asking for my opinion on the so-called "Six-and-six" plan recommended by Mr. J. Edward Swanstrom, I submit the following:

I myself and the Interborough Association of Women Teachers, of which I am president, heartily endorse Mr. Swanstrom's plan in so far as it establishes the principle that the positions in the school department should be carefully graded, that one salary should be attached to each grade of position, and then that the person occupying any of these positions should receive the salary attached to the position, regardless of sex.

I agree with the general opinion that our High School Course as at present planned and conducted is practically a failure, and I would welcome any change that would tend to keep more of the 600,000 pupils attending our public schools in school until they have completed some so-called High School Course.

It may be that what may seem to be a trifling expense, viz: the weekly carfare and luncheon account necessary when pupils have to travel long distances to High Schools, is keeping quite an appreciable number of pupils from continuing their education. Mr. Swanstrom's plan would, to a large extent, overcome this objection,—if it be one—since the beginning years of the secondary course would be carried on in various elementary school buildings more convenient to the pupils of the various neighborhoods. I think there is no doubt in the mind of anyone who has given much thought to the subject that many pupils, both boys and girls, would remain longer in High School if they found it possible to carry on their work which would fit them for business or industrial life, and did not—as they now do in a great majority of cases—find themselves compelled to follow a course designed especially to fit pupils for college.

I have never suggested or requested that men be confined to any particular grades in our schools. I have said and I do say that the Elementary Schools, even as constituted today, can be splendidly managed without any men teachers. In proof of this assertion, I refer to Public Schools, Nos. 3, 11, and 44, Brooklyn, under my own supervision, as schools having no men teachers, and yet ranking, as they have ranked for many years, among the best schools in the city. I agree, however, that men are least desirable in the lower grades of the elementary schools. But in any case, I believe that the city is always able to do justice, and that justice in the salary schedules will not prevail until people occupying the same position, under the same restrictions and requirements, receive the same pay.

. . . . .

Though I have not had time to make even an approximate estimate of the cost of establishing Mr. Swanstrom's plan, I know that it would be more expensive than the adoption of the schedules submitted by our Association. The schedules suggested by Mr. Swanstrom have the same minimum as ours,—$720, and the same maximum within $15, his being $1620, and our $1635. There is a difference in the increment, however,—Mr. Swanstrom's being $75, and ours $105, which is the present increment for male teachers in the lower grades of the elementary schools. His bonus of $120 for boys is the same as that suggested by us. His minimums for heads of department and principals of elementary schools are the same as in our schedules. Therefore the great mass of teachers would be paid under Mr. Swanstrom's plan very nearly the same salaries as were incorporated in our original "Equal Pay Bill," but the salaries suggested in the high school are higher than those which we asked for. I therefore must object to the statement that the "Six-and-six" plan will be a lighter burden for the taxpayers than the plan proposed by the Interborough Association of Women Teachers.

While it is true that the auditor of the Board of Education prepared a detailed estimate "which shows that to equalize the salaries of the sexes on the basis of the salaries paid to men teachers will increase the budget of the Board of Education by the amount of $9,100,000 a year"; it is also true that the women teachers at no time asked that the salaries for teachers in the grades of the first six years be increased to the salaries paid by the Board of Education, but not required by the Davis Law, to the male teachers in grades of the first six years. We believe that the adoption of the salary now paid to the men in those years, from the first year through the eighth year of experience, would form an equitable and satisfactory schedule for all teachers in those grades. In this connection we do not acknowledge the criticism that we were thus reducing the salaries of men teachers as a just one, because while any male teachers in those years receiving more than $1635 could not have their salaries reduced, all male teachers in those grades not yet receiving the $1635 would be free to seek promotion into grades where the higher salaries could be obtained under the State Law, and the beginner would have eight years in which to seek and obtain such promotion.

In conclusion, while I cannot speak formally for the 12,000 women teachers in my Association, I have every reason to believe that they would agree with me in approving on the whole Mr. J. Edward Swanstrom's new plan for schools.

Yours very truly,
GRACE C. STRACHAN,
President, Interborough Association of Women Teachers.

## CHAPTER XX

### GLEDHILL-FOLEY BILL

We deferred an appeal to the Legislature of 1909 until the fate of the report of the Charter Revision Commission, of which William M. Ivins was chairman, had been settled. This report, while making no reference to salaries in the chapter on Education, elsewhere provided for "like salaries" for "like positions." Early in April we were definitely informed that the "Ivins Charter" would not pass. Then we prepared a bill containing the schedules included in the report of the Conciliation Committee and also a clause restoring the "fourth mill." This was introduced by Senator Reuben L. Gledhill, Republican, of Kings, and Assemblyman James A. Foley, Democrat, of New York, and so became known as the "Gledhill-Foley" bill. It passed the Senate by a vote of 38 to 3, and the Assembly, 126 to 14. It was vetoed by Mayor McClellan after a hearing on May 11, 1909, and as the Legislature had then adjourned, it could not be re-passed. It is worthy of note that only *6* of the *86* members of the Legislature from New York voted against the bill.

It was opposed by practically the same people with practically the same arguments as the White Bill of 1907.

The Board of Education's meeting hastily called as shown by the *Globe*, May 6, 1909:

"Last Monday the by-law committee of the Board drew up a report in opposition to the bill, and it was agreed that a special meeting should be held at 4.30 o'clock this afternoon to adopt it.

"Whether or not it was because of fear of opposition to the report or whether or not it was to prevent the women teachers from learning of the contemplated action and looking to forestall it, has not been disclosed, but it is known that it was agreed to keep secret as long as possible the fact that the meeting was to be held. The notices of the meeting were not sent out until yesterday, many of the commissioners not receiving them until this morning. A public announcement of the meeting was not made. So well were the plans laid that those who are directing the fight upon the bill do not anticipate any opposition to the report to-day."

And the *Globe* of May 7, 1909, said:

"Without any discussion, the Board of Education at a special meeting held yesterday adopted resolutions condemning the teachers' salary bill now before the mayor as revolutionary and detrimental to the schools, and asking the mayor to veto it.

"As told in *The Globe* yesterday it had been decided last Monday to hold the meeting, but the decision was kept a secret and few of the members were notified until yesterday morning. Everything had been carefully planned and was carried out without a hitch, although the members had to wait until long after five o'clock to get a quorum. The telephone was called into requisition and the desired members were secured. Twenty-seven were present.

"They include Messrs. Aldcrofft, Barrett, Coudert, Bruce, De Laney, Dresser, Cunnion, Ferris, Francolini, Greene, Higgins, Hallick, Katzenberg, Kanzler, Lazansky, May, Man, McCafferty, Harrison, McDonald, O'Donohue, Sherman, A. Stern, J. E. Sullivan, Wilsey, Wingate, and Winthrop. When the motion to adopt the report was put there was a division. Probably six or eight members opposed it, leaving less than a majority of the entire board in favor of it. President Winthrop declared the report adopted."

The Board in its report of disapproval, said: "An analysis of said bill shows that it contains thirty different schedules of salaries for members of the supervising and teaching staff in elementary schools, and nine schedules for members of the supervising and teaching staff in high and training schools." (Extract from report of Committee on By-Laws and Legislation.)

As a matter of fact the said bill contains only *four* different schedules for elementary schools as at present organized, with specific "bonuses" for teachers of "mixed" and "boys'" classes and schools; while it contains only *four* schedules for high and training schools, with an addition of $150 in mixed schools and $30 in boys' schools.

The apparent increase in the number of schedules is really an increase in the number of "bonuses." The present schedules provide a bonus of $60 per annum for female teacher of mixed boys' classes.

What the Board makes to appear like eight different schedules for grades below 7A, is really one schedule—$720 to $1620, with bonuses as follows:

Kng. 1A—2B Mixed, no bonus; 1A—2B Boys, $60; 3A—4B Mixed, $60; 3A—4B Boys, $132; 5A—6B Mixed, $72; 5A—6B Boys, $180.

Our present schedules give a principal or an assistant to principal of an all girls' school the same salary as a principal or an assistant to principal of a mixed or a boys' school. Now it is well known that it is more difficult to manage a boys' school than a girls' school: it is harder (*a*) to keep the classes all supplied with good teachers, (*b*) to keep the buildings and playgrounds in good condition, (*c*) to maintain discipline. And so the Conciliation Committee decided to extend the "bonus" policy established by the Davis Law for teachers in the elementary schools, all through the system. This is indicated in their schedules which follow:

*Assistant to Principal Supervising Grades of the First Six Years*

(Increment, $150)

| Year | Girls' School | Mixed School | Boys' School |
|---|---|---|---|
| 1 | $1,800 | $1,950 | $2,100 |
| 3 | 2,100 | 2,250 | 2,400 |

*Principal of at least Twenty Classes in Grades of the First Six Years*

(Increment, $250)

| Year | Girls' School | Mixed School | Boys' School |
|---|---|---|---|
| 1 | $2,450 | $2,600 | $2,750 |
| 4 | 3,200 | 3,350 | 3,500 |

*Assistant to Principal Supervising in Grades of the Seventh and Eighth Years*

(Increment, $150)

| Year | Girls' School | Mixed School | Boys' School |
|---|---|---|---|
| 1 | $1,950 | $2,100 | $2,250 |
| 3 | 2,250 | 2,400 | 2,550 |

*Principal Having Twenty-Five or more Teachers in the Grades of the Seventh and Eighth Years*

(Increment, $250.)

| Year | Girls' School | Mixed School | Boys' School |
|---|---|---|---|
| 1 | $2,700 | $2,850 | $3,000 |
| 4 | 3,450 | 3,600 | 3,750 |

In our brief to Mayor McClellan on Gledhill-Foley bill, we said: "Mr. Harrison and Mr. Stern intimated by their remarks on variations in salaries of teachers according to whether they taught girls' mixed, or boys' classes, and on variations in the salaries of principals according to the number of classes supervised, that such bases of variation in salaries would be an innovation. We respectfully submit that the present charter of this city (See Sec. 1091) and the By-laws of the Board of Education (See Sec. 65, sub-division 8, "Principals of schools of not less than *12* classes—," "A principal of a school with a high school department, having supervision of not less than 25 teachers in the aggregate (elementary and high) shall receive, in addition to the salary provided in Schedule I, the sum of $500 per annum"; sub-division 9, "Teachers in charge of schools of the fourth order (less than 12 classes but not less than 6 classes,"—"less than 6 classes"; sub-division 14 (a) "A principal of a high school having supervision of not less than 25 teachers,—" (b) "A principal of a high school having supervision of less than 25 teachers"; and sub-division 11, "A female teacher of a boys' class, or of a mixed class as defined in sub-division 1 of this section, shall receive the sum of $60 per annum in addition, etc.") prove that *it is the settled policy of the Board of Education* to pay principals according to number of classes, and to pay teachers of mixed and boys' classes higher salaries than teachers of girls' classes. It therefore seems unfair to charge that this bill in continuing this policy will cause more political scrambling for promotion than there is now.

"It is charged by some that Senate Bill 1210 does not provide 'Equal Pay' and by others that it provides more than 'Equal Pay.' We have found the spirit of our campaign embodied most tersely in the expression 'Equal Pay for Equal Work"; but what we are actually seeking is "*Salary for position* without regard to the sex of the *incumbent.*" The Gledhill-Foley schedules are based on this principle.

"This bill has been approved by:

(1) The Interborough Association of New York, comprising over 12,000 members;

(2) The New York City Teachers' Association, consisting of thousands of men and women teachers, principals, and superintendents;

(3) The Association of Women Principals of the City of New York;

(4) The Association of Assistants to Principals, Brooklyn;

(5) The Class Teachers' Association.

*It has been endorsed by*

(1) The Brownsville Taxpayers' Association;
(2) The Central Flatbush Taxpayers' Association;
(3) The Central Federated Union, representing over 200,000 voters;
(4) The Central Labor Union, representing many thousands;
(5) The City Federation of Women's Clubs;
(6) Thousands upon thousands of individual taxpayers;
(7) Scores of firms and business houses.

"But above and beyond all in importance, unless we deny our own political institutions and principles, must we value the endorsement given by *The People* through their regularly elected representatives in our State Legislature, after *three years* of public agitation on the question of the discrimination against our women teachers.

"Opposed to this vast majority striving to give the women teachers the relief they seek are a few men who represent only themselves as individuals, or the minority that constitutes a majority vote at meetings of a few self-constituted organizations, not authorized to represent any taxpayers but themselves.

"The Interborough Association of Women Teachers furthermore asks you to consider the trustworthiness of the statements made by Mr. Abraham Stern, representing the Board of Education in opposing this bill; because ten years ago in opposing the bill which became the "Davis Law," he claimed that the cost of said bill would be $26,000,000—it cost about *five million.* He claimed that it was revolutionary, arbitrary, dangerous; and he characterizes Senate Bill 1210 in the same way. Yet after ten years' experience of the Davis Law *he and the other members of the Board of Education are unanimous in their appeal for the retention of the Davis Law.* Is it not fair to believe that if you sign our bill and it becomes law, that its beneficent effects on our school system will be such as to cause a similar change of heart?

"We do not admit that the number of basic schedules

is increased by the new law, while admitting that basing the salaries on the *sex of the pupils taught* instead of on the *sex of the teacher,* has increased the number of 'bonuses' for mixed and boys' classes.

"It is true to-day that in Brooklyn nearly all of the children in the first year of high school, which is the 9th year in this 12-year course, are housed in elementary school buildings. We believe that the children will be greatly benefited by having the course of study so readjusted as to make an intermediate or sub-high school for children of the 7th, 8th, and 9th years, this intermediate or sub-high school being, in many cases, vocational or trade, in others commercial, and in others purely literary; thus leaving the last three years of the twelve for a true high school course to be followed by such pupils as intend to go on to college or go on to complete their studies in the profession or calling chosen. It is a matter of general criticism that the present course of study is prepared for those who are to enter college, although over 95 per cent of the children who are taught under it never even enter high school.

"However, though the Committee was strongly in favor of the Six-and-Three-and-Three plan, variously known as the 'Swanstrom Plan,' and the 'City Club Plan,' and the 'Six-and-Six Plan,' there is nothing in the bill which forces any such reorganization on the Board of Education. True, there is a schedule of salaries provided for schools, consisting of grades of the 7th, 8th and 9th years, but until such schools are established, such schedule of salaries is inactive.

"Still, there is no law or principle that makes an increase in the number of schedules undesirable. The intimation made by both Mr. Harrison and Mr. Stern, that the proposed bill would compel the Board of Education to reorganize the school system is not borne out by fact. There are at present girls' schools, mixed schools, and boys' schools. It is true that under the present law, principals and assistants to principals and teachers are paid under various 'male' and 'female' schedules, *i.e.,* schedules varying according to the *sex* of the principal, assistant to principal and teacher

—e.g., Miss O'C, principal of a school of 60 classes of boys and girls receives $1000 less a year than Mr. O'M, principal of a school of 12 classes, while the bill under discussion proposed to pay said teachers and supervisors according to the sex of the pupils taught and supervised, and so provides bonuses for those in mixed and boys' schools.

"In making this readjustment, the Board of Education would decide what constitutes a mixed school, just as it has decided that a 'mixed class' for purposes of bonus salary must have 40% of boys on register.

"This bill is objected to on the ground that it is mandatory. It is true that the bill is mandatory, but how, in the nature of the case, could it be otherwise? Do we expect the child of Irish parents to be Hindoos, for instance? Do we look for sweet apples on a sour apple tree? Or, as Senator McCarren has put it: 'If you wanted to mend a hole in a granite wall, you would not use a Charlotte Russe.' So, we admit that these provisions that we are asking you to approve as an amendment to the 'Davis Law,' are mandatory. But we beg you not to consider this amendment as you would *original* mandatory legislation, but as an amendment to mandatory legislation over which you had no control.

"Likewise, in considering the 'four-mill' provision, we appeal to you to remember that

(1) The Board of Education prays that the present mandatory provisions in the city charter, fixing salaries and a minimum tax rate, be continued;

(2) All the teachers unite in asking for the restoration of the fourth mill;

(3) Over 90%—all the women teachers and many of the men teachers—approve the Gledhill-Foley Teachers' bill;

(4) Fully 90% (165 out of 182) of the members elected to the State Legislature by the voters of this city, after three years of public agitation on the question, voted in favor of this bill;

(5) We are supporters and defenders of a government in which "*the majority*" rules;

And therefore, we pray that you will agree with us that respect for "Home Rule," "Fair Play," and "The Majority" demands your approval of this bill.

GRACE C. STRACHAN, President.

*But*—the Mayor did veto the bill. He however, in his veto message this time recognized the importance of the measure by promising to appoint a commission to investigate the question of teachers' salaries. He later indicated that he realized that the problem was one worthy of serious and dignified consideration, by naming as members of such commission, Hon. Joseph H. Choate, ex-Ambassador to Great Britain; Hon. William C. Brown, president, New York Central Railroad, and Professor John Bates Clark, of Columbia University. The first named declined the appointment and the second resigned after one meeting because he could not spare the time he believed such an investigation would require. Their places were filled by the appointment of Joseph M. Schwab, president of the North German Lloyd Steamship Company, New York, and Charles Hallam Keep, president of the Knockerbocker Trust Company. The report submitted by this commission to Mayor McClellan just prior to the close of his term of office stated that they had not been able on account of lack of time, to make such an investigation as would justify a definite report. They made several alternative suggestions which added nothing to the previous discussions and arguments connected with the great struggle of the women teachers.

The matters to be investigated by the special commission are explained by the mayor as follows:

"First, the average rates of living of teachers, both male and female, in this city, and to ascertain, if possible, the general trend of responsibilities which they have to meet on the salary offered to them by this city.

"Second, to compare, as near as possible, the salary rates in other cities with those offered to teachers in this city.

"Third, to investigate and accurately determine what increase to the budget such recommendations as they may deem proper to submit will make."

The New York *World,* of May 29, 1909, said the following editorially:

"New York's public school teachers naturally object to the proposed public inquiry into the method and the cost of their living. We have gone to great lengths in our sociological bookkeeping, but always it has been in the wrong direction. We invade the privacy of the *self-respecting poor* on the slightest provocation. Admonished on every hand to look after certain elements at the other end of the social scale, we do nothing.

"The worst possible use of publicity is to expose *respectable poverty* or *modest thrift* to the gaze of the multitude. The best possible use of publicity is to throw daylight upon all those supplicants who, aided by favoring laws, are reaping where they have not sown.

"Every beneficiary of privilege should be held to a strict public accounting, but none is exacted of him. Every self-supporting American is entitled to exemption from the inquisitorial activities of students, theorists and meddlers, but he alone is probed, measured and tabulated."

*Democracy,* of same date, commented as follows in its leading editorial:

"The equal pay bill of the school teachers has been vetoed by Mayor McClellan, but the teachers have the encouragement of knowing that their battle is further advanced than it ever was before. Indeed, it has progressed so far that they will, without question, win the next battle, which will be next year. They cannot fail again. A commission is to be named to investigate the average rate of compensation received by teachers in other communities and the cost of living. The results of this investigation will undoubtedly show that the teachers here are underpaid, and that at the end of the year they are worse off than the same class of public workers in other sections of the country. The women school teachers are educated and refined women. They have been accustomed to refined surroundings. And it is absolutely necessary that their environment should be refined, for if this were not so, their usefulness as teachers of the young would lose greatly in value. Clothing, food and rent are dearer in this city than in any other place in the world. And amusements and luxuries are dearer too, and every rational human being knows the absolute need of amusement and luxuries. Any person receiving only the necessaries of life is soon reduced to the level of beasts. They fail mentally and physically. They retrograde instead of advancing. In nearly every other calling a trade or a profession is learned, and then the work of study, save the study of experience, is over. But a teacher has to keep on studying and learning. She cannot say that her profession is learned, for it is never mastered. No matter how far ahead she goes there is still more ground to traverse. She is not permitted to wait and rest, for there is always a steady pushing from the rear, and she has to fight to keep in the lead or she will fall hopelessly behind. Besides studying books she has to study human nature. She must be patient, and tender, thoughtful and forbearing. She has no time for the nursing of her own woes, for she is always attending to the woes of others. There is no chance on earth for her to get more than she earns, and none of our public men need fear that she will be overpaid. But all of our public men, and every man of public spirit ought to do what he can to see that she is not underpaid. We are sure that the commission to be named by the Mayor will be an excellent commission, and that its report will end in giving the women teachers the same pay as that received by the men teachers, and this will be done, we believe, without troubling the legislature."

*And again on June 12, 1908:*

"Miss Smith may be able to live as well as she wants on ten dollars a week, while Miss Jones would require twice as much to secure only those things which she would consider absolutely necessary. Nor does a teacher's responsibilities enter into this subject any more than do the questions of charity, sympathy, or love. The whole question is purely a business one. To say that a person ought only to receive enough compensation to enable him to live is absurd. He is entitled to the sum he earns whether it be ten dollars a week or a thousand dollars. Do the women teachers labor as long and as truthfully as the men? Are they as necessary in the schools as the men? Would the city be better off if there were no women teachers? These, it seems to us, are the salient points.

"And if these questions are answered favorably to the women, then comes the question of compensation. And it would be impossible to thresh out this question carefully enough to separate the chaff from the grain without also discovering whether the compensation of the men teachers is just. If this is answered in the affirmative, then the question whether the women teachers ought to receive the same pay as the men, for the same work answers itself. And the result would be that when the Board of Estimate meets to consider the budget of 1910, the school appropriation will be big enough to place the women on the same plane as the men in the matter of pay."

## CHAPTER XXI

### THE SOMERS RESOLUTION

On December 22, 1909, Commissioner Arthur S. Somers, presented the following resolution in the Board of Education:

"Resolved, That it be referred to the Committee on By-Laws and Legislation to consider the advisability of amending the By-Laws as follows:

"That Section 65 of the By-Laws of the Board of Education be amended so as to provide but one salary for one and the same position, except that the teachers and supervisors of boys may receive an additional salary or bonus not to exceed $180;

"Resolved, That it also be referred to said Committee to consider the advisability of amending said section in the following manner:

"That such revised schedules be put into effect as soon as funds sufficient therefor are provided by the Board of Estimate and Apportionment, and that pending full financial ability, the increases in women teachers' salaries be paid in annual instalments which shall be not less than twenty per cent. of the difference between the maximum salaries now fixed for men and the maximum salaries now fixed for women occupying the same position, except that for the year 1910 there shall be a flat increase of not less than $120 per annum for all women teachers below the 7A grade, and not less than $120 for all women teachers of special subjects."

The I. A. W. T. submitted in this connection the following:

If the "Equal Pay" principle is recognized, the Interborough Association of Women Teachers is willing that the increases necessary to establish this principle be paid in three or four annual instalments.

To establish the "Equal Pay" principle the Board of Education would need to classify its positions, and fix but one salary for each class of position; except that teachers, assistants to principals, principals and other supervisory officers of boys may receive an additional salary or "bonus," said bonus not to exceed $180 for teachers in the elementary schools.

Pending adoption of "Equal Pay" schedules, the following increases are suggested as the first instalment:

ELEMENTARY SCHOOLS

*N. B.*—The numbers of principals, assistants to principals, and teachers indicated below are those submitted to the Board of Estimate, October, 1909, by the Board of Education for the year 1910.

*Increase for Women Teachers based on Twenty Per Cent.*

| | | |
|---|---|---|
| 196 | Principals, 1/5, ($3500-$2500), *or $200 | $ 39,200 |
| 380 | Assts. to Principals, 1/5, ($2400-$1600), *or $160 | 60,800 |
| 20 | In charge of Schools, 1/5, ($2400-$1600), *or $160 | 3,200 |
| 11 | Senior Teachers in Charge, 1/5, ($2160-$1540) *or $124 | 1,364 |
| 607 | | $104,564 |

**N. B.*—The difference between the present maximums for men and women.

*Present Schedule III.*

739 Kindergarten.
837 1a grade.
1,024 1b grade.

Salaries for women range from $600 to $1240.
Annual increment, $40.

860 2a grade.
962 2b grade.
881 3a grade.
Salaries for men range from $900 to $2160. Annual increment, $105.
918 3b grade.
870 4a grade.
871 4b grade.
805 5a grade.
According to year of service, limit: 12 for men, 16 for women.
777 5b grade.
611 6a grade.
565 6b grade.
It is suggested that maximum in these grades be $1635 for boys' classes and $1515 for girls' classes, to apply to both men and:
40 Miscellaneous women teachers;
62 Ungraded;
205 More than 1 grade;
65 C.,
Special English Class to Foreigners;
90 D.,
Special "Working Paper Class";
361 E.,
Special "Over Age" Children Class.

11,533

11,533 teachers scheduled at $120 equals $1,383,960.

*All Women Teachers under present Schedule IV.*

550 7a grade.
437 7b grade.
363 8a grade.
25 Miscellaneous.
9 More than 1 grade.

1,384

1,384 Women Teachers under present schedule IV at ⅕, ($2160-$1320), or $168 equals $232,512.

*Women under present Schedule V.*

298 8b grade.
9 More than 1 grade.
1 C.
1 D.
1 E.
4 "In Excess."

314

314 under present schedule V., at ⅕, ($2400-$1440), or $192 equals $60,288.

---

| | | | |
|---|---|---|---|
| Total | 607 | Principals, etc .................. | $ 104,564 |
| Total | 11,533 | Teachers, Kgn. to 6B, etc. ...... | 1,383,960 |
| Total | 1,384 | Teachers, 7a-8a, etc. ............ | 232,512 |
| Total | 314 | Teachers, 8b, etc. .............. | 60,288 |
| | 13,838 | Elementary School. Total ...... | $1,781,324 |

HIGH SCHOOLS

Women

| | | |
|---|---|---|
| 2 | (Lib. asst.), ⅕, ($1200-$1000), or $40....$ | 80 |
| 10 | (Cler. asst.), ⅕, ($1200-$1000), or $40 .... | 400 |
| 10 | (Lib. asst.), ⅕, ($1200-$1000), or $40...... | 40c |
| 29 | (Jun.), ⅕, (($1200-$1000), or $40 ....... | 1,160 |
| 570 | (Asst.), ⅕, ($2400-$1900), or $100 ....... | 57,000 |
| 21 | (First asst.), ⅕, ($3000-$2500), or $100 .. | 2,100 |
| 642 | | $61,140 |

TRAINING SCHOOLS

Women

| | | |
|---|---|---|
| 1 | (Cler. asst.), $\frac{1}{5}$, ($1200-$1000), or $40 .... | $ 80 |
| 3 | (Lib. asst.), $\frac{1}{5}$, ($1200-$1000), or $40 .... | 120 |
| 63 | (Model Tr.), $\frac{1}{5}$, ($2400-$1500), or $180... | 11,340 |
| 13 | (Critic), $\frac{1}{5}$, ($2400-$1500), or $180 ...... | 2,340 |
| 52 | (Asst.), $\frac{1}{5}$, ($2400-$1900), or $100 ....... | 5,200 |
| 8 | (First), $\frac{1}{5}$, ($3000-$2500), or $100 ...... | 800 |
| 141 | | $19,880 |

*Special Teachers.*

| | | Women | Men |
|---|---|---|---|
| 39 | (Music) .................... | $1400 | $1600 |
| 52 | (Drg.) .................... | 1400 | 1600 |
| 23 | (P. Trg.) .................. | 1200 | 1600 |
| 115 | (Cook.) .................... | 1200 | |
| 62 | (Sew.) .................... | 1200 | |
| 3 | (Shop.) .................... | 1200 | *2160 |
| 6 | (French) .................. | 1400 | 1600 |
| 27 | (German) .................. | 1400 | 1600 |
| 327 | | | |

327 Special Teachers at $120 equals $39,240.

About 450 Clerks or additional Teachers increase 25 cents per day for 194 days of 1910 equals $21,825.

*Additional for those who have reached Maximum in Present Schedules.*

| | | |
|---|---|---|
| 180 | Women principals, $200 additional........ | $ 36,000 |
| 1,500 | Kng.—6B, $120 additional .............. | 180,000 |
| 912 | 7a-8a, $168 additional .................. | 153,216 |
| 340 | 8b, 192 additional ..................... | 65,280 |
| 160 | Special, etc., $120 additional ........... | 19,200 |
| 13 | Jun., $40 additional .................... | 520 |
| 261 | Asst., $100 additional .................. | 26,100 |
| 10 | First, $100 additional .................. | 1,000 |
| 3,376 | | $481,316 |

SUMMARY

| | | Based on 20% |
|---|---|---|
| 196 | Principals. Total increase instalment...$ | 39,200 |
| 380 | Asst. to Prin. To increase instalment.. | 60,800 |
| 20 | Asst. in Charge, 6 to 11 classes ........ | 3,200 |
| 11 | Teachers in Charge, less than 6 classes.. | 1,364 |
| 11,533 | Teachers, Kgn.—6B and others paid under present Schedule III. ........ | 1,383,960 |
| 1,384 | Teachers, 7a-7b-8a and others paid under present Schedule IV. ......... | 232,512 |
| 314 | Teachers, 8b and others paid under present Schedule V. .................. | 60,288 |
| 642 | Teachers, High Schools ............. | 61,140 |
| 141 | Teachers, Training School for Teachers. | 19,880 |
| 327 | Teachers, Special Subjects ........... | 39,240 |
| 450 | Teachers, Additional or Clerks ........ | 21,825 |
| 15,398 | | $1,923,409 |
| | If possible allow 3,376 having reached maximum .................................. | 481,316 |
| | For Principals, teachers and others to fill vacancies and provide for increase in system .... | 95,275 |
| | | $2,500,000 |

*To the Board of Education:*

The Interborough Association of Women Teachers of the City of New York respectfully submits the following statements in connection with the report made to your Board by the Committee on By-Laws and Legislation at the meeting of January 12, 1910, on the resolution offered by Mr. Somers, December 22, 1909.

The report referred to states that "the principle of Equal Pay for men and women teachers occupying the same position is the principle involved in the first of the resolutions offered by Mr. Somers. It further states that "the Board of Education disapproved Senate Bill No. 893," the so-called "Equal Pay" or "White Bill" on March 22, 1907, and that on May 6, 1909, your committee presented a report in opposition to Senate Bill No. 1210, known as the "Gledhill-Foley Bill," which provided salaries for teachers in various grades without regard to sex, which report was approved by the Board of Education.

Our Association admits all the above but it is surprised at the following: "Your Committee is aware of no change in the situation up to the present time which would justify it in recommending that the Board reverse the action taken by it on the occasions above referred to."

We respectfully submit that the Committee must know that since May 6, 1909, the following members have been appointed to the Board of Education:

Miss Olivia Leventritt,
Mr. Herman A. Metz,
Mr. Frank L. Polk,
Mrs. Helen C. Robbins,
Mr. John Whalen,
Mr. Patrick F. McGowan,
Mr. Antonio Pisani, M.D.,
Mrs. Alice L. Post,
Mrs. Christine Towns.

In view of the fact that these nine new members have been added to the Board and that there are still two vacancies, it is inconceivable to this Association that the Committee on By-Laws and Legislation should be "aware of no change in the situation up to the present time, etc."

We submit further, that at the meeting of May 6, 1909, at which the so-called "Gledhill-Foley Bill" was disapproved, there was not a majority of the whole Board of Education recorded against it. Only twenty-seven Commissioners answered roll call, and members of this Association who were present at said meeting heard several "Noes" when the negative vote on the report of the Committee on By-Laws and Legislation was called for by the presiding officer. Besides, the meeting of May 6, 1909, was not a regular meeting of the Board of Education, but was a special meeting, the notices of which were not received by some members until the very day of the meeting and by most of the members only the day previous. Furthermore, said meeting was not in session five minutes, and we believe that many of the members of the Board of Education are prepared to give more time than that to the consideration of this vital subject.

In contrast to such hasty action as the above, we respectfully submit that during the past three years the Senate, the Assembly, the Governor of the State, the Mayor of the City of New York, and the citizens assembled in various Mass Meetings, have given several hearings on the principle involved in the "White Bill," the "Gledhill-Foley Bill" and the resolutions offered by Mr. Somers, and in no case has the hearing been shorter than two hours. When said bills have come before either house of the Legislature for final decision, the vote has always been taken by recording each individual member's vote either for or against, and the vote has always followed a full and free discussion, lasting on several occasions upwards of three hours. In contrast to an attendance of 27 members out of a board of 46—an attendance of 58.7 per cent.— was the attendance of the Assembly Committee on Affairs of Cities at the hearing on the "White Bill" when 13 out of a committee of 13 sat throughout a hearing lasting three hours—100 per cent. of attendance.

We submit also that in disapproving the "White Bill," the Board of Education faced a complex proposition, because beside the principle of salary for position without regard to sex, the "White Bill" involved the four-mill tax, a minimum salary of $720, a minimum annual increment of $105 and a maximum number of increments of twelve. A similar statement is true of its action on the "Gledhill-Foley Bill," as this bill involved not only the same salary for men and women teachers occupying the same position, but the so-called Six-and-Six Plan, and fixed salaries in detail, varying for girls', mixed, and boys' schools.

Therefore, we submit that the Board has never placed itself on record as approving or disapproving the simple principle, *"That men and women teachers occupying the same position shall receive the same pay"*; and we therefore beg that your Board, without referring the said proposition to any Committee, let the teachers and the public generally who are striving to have this principle embodied in all the salary schedules of our teachers, know the attitude of the Board of Education on this simple proposition.

Respectfully submitted,

THE INTERBOROUGH ASSOCIATION OF WOMEN TEACHERS,

GRACE C. STRACHAN, President.

ISABEL A. ENNIS, Secretary.

## CHAPTER XXII

### DISCRIMINATIONS OTHER THAN SALARY

SINCE we began "agitating" for Equal Pay, we have experienced discriminations other than salary. By far the most unjust of these is that connected with the assignment and promotion of teachers.

In one school, this attitude was indulged and permitted to such an extreme, that there was not a woman teacher on the "top floor" although the classes were as follows:

| Grade. | Boys | Girls | Teacher |
|---|---|---|---|
| 8b. | 24 | 16 | ...........Joseph ——— |
| 8A. | 23 | 15 | ...........Robert ——— |
| 7B. | 18 | 12 | ...........Michael ——— |
| 7B. | 18 | 13 | ...........Pat ———— |
| 7A. | 26 | 14 | ...........Fred. ——— |
| 7A. | 27 | 13 | ...........Ernest ——— |
| | — | — | |
| Totals | 136 | 83 | |

It is probable that if this school had been located in an "American" district, the parents of the girls would have expressed dissatisfaction; but it was in an Italian section and the parents were more or less unacquainted with the language and life of the country. So the principal continued to carry out his intention as expressed to one of the women teachers, "I would put up the most incompetent man before I would put you up," until our association brought the facts to public notice. Finally one woman was promoted. Surely, even those who hold that men are needed for "growing boys" will not hold that "growing girls"—especially girls from an almost tropical clime —need men teachers to the absolute exclusion of women.

The unfairness that consists in assigning a woman teacher to a girls class in a department, so as to deprive her of the bonus of $60.00, though her program makes her teach boys a large portion of the day, promises to bring about another legal suit against the board. On this point, the *Globe* recently printed a letter of which the following is a part: " . . . under the rules of the board a teacher whose class has more than 40 per cent. boys receives $5 a month extra pay. But the officials have decided that this bonus shall be determined, not by the classes taught, but by the class for which the teacher calls the roll. By separating boys and girls at roll call a few teachers keep the register for all the boys and get the extra pay and the others lose it, even though during the rest of the day they may devote their teaching hours wholly to boys' classes.

"One teacher in a certain school has for four years received the bonus for a boys' class. She taught twenty-nine of the thirty-two class periods a week, and last year had altogether 470 boys and 510 girls. Under the new schedule she is given a girls' class. She is teaching in the classroom thirty-one full periods a week, and has a total of 515 boys and 460 girls. She loses the extra pay, as do two other teachers, simply because she keeps the registry for a girls' class, though her teaching hours are increased and she is teaching a larger proportion of boys than before. Two of the four teachers in this school now in charge of boys are men. Incidentally (this for those who maintain that boys need the instruction of men), one of these men teaches girls' classes more than one-half his time each week, and has more girls than boys in his total, while the other has each week eight hours respite from teaching, while no woman teacher has more than two hours and some only forty minutes outside the classroom."

The editor of the *Globe* in his reply to the above, said: "Such a plan is of doubtful legality. The teachers who believe that they are being deprived of the bonus illegally should file a claim for it with the By-Laws Committee of the Board of Education. The charter is explicit. It says 'and no female teacher of a boys' or a mixed class shall receive less than $60.00 per annum more than a female teacher of a girls' class of a corresponding grade and years of service.'"

Some propose that men should be assigned only to higher grades. I am opposed to the limiting of the places to which men shall be appointed, just as I am opposed to limiting the places to which women shall be appointed. History shows in the lives of Frobel and Pestalozzi that men have been successful teachers even in the kindergarten and history of more recent date shows in one of our American cities that a woman can be a successful superintendent of schools. In this connection, the following editorials anent this woman superintendent are interesting:

New York *World,* July 30, 1909. "Mrs. Young, though she follows many distinguished educators in the place, is probably better equipped for the service than any of them."

New York *Tribune,* August 1, 1909. "There are several reasons why a woman should be especially fitted for the position of school superintendent. . . . Chicago, always daring in its innovations, has chosen a woman for superintendent of its public schools. There can be no question of her high qualifications for the place. . . . That she was unanimously chosen in competition with men is either a high tribute to her personal worth or to the intelligence of the members of the Board of Education, who decided the case on its merits, eliminating entirely the question of sex."

New York *Globe,* July 30, 1909. "What will the educationists who have sounded an alarm against the feminization of our schools have to say of the selection of a woman as superintendent of the schools of the second largest city in the country? . . . But, after all, it is not the educationists who will be most disturbed. Whatever her intellectual gender, it is clear that Mrs. Young has been chosen because of her superior fitness for the position."

Brooklyn *Times*. "Chicago contains a population only a little less than that possessed by the Borough of Manhattan. She is the second city in size in America. Her school problems must be something like those of Greater New York. The Chicago Board of Education is composed of men. This woman must possess unusual ability and force of character to have won to her support a body that would naturally be prejudiced against her sex. Given a man of equal ability in opposition, he should easily have been the victor, with only men acting as judges. But Mrs. Young through her own inherent abilities, broke down all these old-time prejudices and carried off one of the highest prizes in the educational world."

Again we read, "Mrs. Agnes Knox Black has just been appointed professor of elocution in Boston University. She was chosen from among several score of candidates most of whom were men.

"Miss Ruth Carrell has been appointed assistant professor in department of bacteriology in the University of Michigan. She is looked upon as one of the most brilliant young women in the country.

"Miss Margaret E. Cross is professor of education in Tulane University."

### DISCRIMINATIONS OTHER THAN SALARY

In contrast, is the experience of those who have opposed Equal Pay. Many of them have been rewarded. Mr. S—— was made teacher in charge of annex to Manual Training School. Miss G—— who publicly stated that she did not believe in "Equal Pay" was given a district superintendency; as was also Mr. E—— the first president of the Association of Men Teachers and Principals, organized to oppose the women's association. Mr. T—— was given the principalship of a high school. The following also is significant:

"Holders of Permanent License No. 1 (Men only)

whose records are satisfactory, and who desire to serve as teachers in charge of study room (teachers of English) in the recreation centers during the season of 1908-1909, should present themselves at this office (Room 422), on Wednesday, November 4, or Thursday, November 5, or Friday, November 6, 1908, at 4 P. M. The compensation for this work is $2.50 per session. No examination, written or oral will be required."

Neither in law, in logic, nor in fact, is there any ground for holding that the proposed legislation infringes in any way upon the principle of home rule, or is mandatory legislation in the sense that it interferes with the accountability of any local authority to the people of the locality.

## I

What is municipal home rule? It is a local government accountable to the people of the locality. What does this mean? It means a government conducted by officials accountable to the people of the city for their official conduct.

This is fundamental and elementary.

It was to accomplish this result in the case of city government in New York and Brooklyn that, after twenty-five years of effort, we at last secured a mayor, elected by the people, with full authority to appoint and remove at his pleasure heads of city departments; and in the last charter of New York no head of a department holds office for any fixed term whatever. This is home rule as far as it has yet gone in the government of the City of New York. We can at least hold the Mayor responsible for the conduct of his heads of departments. If our street cleaning commissioner does not do his duty, or our police commissioner is derelict, we can appeal to the Mayor, and the Mayor can remove him at pleasure.

Now, in what sense is the Board of Education accountable to the people of New York City? Its members hold offices for fixed terms of five years, and are irremovable except upon charges and a regular trial. What this means we know from abundant experience in New York, where for years and years the heads of departments held office for fixed terms and were not removable except on regular charges and after a trial at which they were entitled to be represented by counsel. They never were removed, and each one managed his department as he pleased.

Suppose the people of New York are dissatisfied with the way in which the Board of Education manages educational affairs, what can the people do about it? Suppose the Mayor is dissatisfied, what can he do about it? The charter in terms excepts the Board of Education from the control of the Mayor. They are neither elected nor are they removable by any elected official. They hold an utterly irresponsible position, accountable to nobody but themselves for their official conduct.

How, then, is the principle of home rule infringed when this irresponsible, independent body is given more or less power? It may be wise to give them more, it may be wise to take some of their power away; but there is no more home rule involved than there is when the Legislature says what the duties of the superintendent of prisons should be. I suppose the superintendent of prisons would feel that his "home rule" was interfered with if the Legislature decided that it was for the best interests of the State to change its regulations with regard to his office.

How, then, either as a matter of law, of logic or of fact can the Board of Education, which is not accountable for its acts to the people of New York City or to local officers elected by the people of New York City, be regarded as an illustration of the principle of home rule?

## II

From time immemorial education has been in the special care of the State. Education is a State function. No State in the Union has ever surrendered this function, or has abdicated the right to exercise the function.

The Constitution of the State of New York, in Article

IX, declares that the Legislature shall provide for the maintenance and support of a system of free common schools wherein all the children of this State may be educated—all the children of this State; not some of them, but *all* of them. Whether the children happen to be residents of New York City or of Chemung County, the Constitution says that the Legislature shall provide for the maintenance and the support of schools in which they shall be educated.

And there is no member of the Board of Education who does not know that the Board is not a city department. It is an independent corporation, created such in terms, as the agent of the State, to carry out and administer whatever policy the State determines in the matter of education in New York City. The City of New York, as such, has absolutely no control whatever over the Board of Education. It has no superior except the New York Legislature. If the Board of Education does wrong, if it has too much power, or if it has too little power, there is no authority to which to appeal to right the wrong, to diminish or to increase the power, except the Legislature. The Mayor has nothing whatever to do with either the grant or the exercise of any power by the Board of Education. Its members are not his subordinates. His opinion with regard to the conduct by the Board of Education of its affairs is of no more legal consequence than that of any other citizen of the State.

In my opinion, the sending of this bill to the Mayor of New York for his acceptance, after its passage by the Legislature, was of very doubtful necessity. It hardly seems a special city law under the definition in Article XII, section 2, of the Constitution, which says, "Special city laws are those which relate to a single city or to less than all the cities of a class." This was a bill affecting, not the corporation of the City of New York, but affecting a special corporation created by the Legislature to perform a special task, namely, to carry out and administer the legislative policy as to education within the physical area of the City of New York.

The Gunnison case, decided by the Court of Appeals in 1903 (176 N. Y., 11), states very clearly the precise legal status of the Board of Education. The decision is by a unanimous court, consisting of Chief Judge Parker and Judges Gray, Bartlett, Haight, Cullen, Werner and O'Brien, unanimously affirming a decision of the Appellate Division, Second Department, made by Goodrich, *P. J.*, and Bartlett, Woodward, Jenks and Hirschberg, *JJ.*, Justice Hirschberg writing the opinion at the Appellate Division and Justice O'Brien in the Court of Appeals.

A teacher sued the Board of Education for salary. Demurrer was interposed on the ground that the City of New York was the proper party to be sued, because the Board of Education was a city department, like the Dock Department, for example.

"It is apparent from the general drift of the argument that the learned counsel for the defendant is of the opinion that the employment of the teachers in the public schools and the general conduct and management of the schools is a city function, in the same sense as it is in the case of the care of the streets or the employment of police and the payment of their salaries and compensation. But that view of the relations of the city to public education, if entertained, is an obvious mistake. The city cannot rent, build, or buy a schoolhouse. It cannot employ or discharge a teacher, and has no power to contract with teachers with respect to their compensation. There is no contract or official relation, express or implied, between the teachers and the city. All this results from the settled policy of the State, from an early date, to divorce the business of public education from all other municipal interests or business, *and to take charge of it as a peculiar and separate function through agents of its own selection and immediately subject and responsive to its own control.* To this end it is enacted in the general laws of the State that all school trustees and boards of education shall be corporations, with corporate powers, which, of course, includes the power to sue and be sued in all matters relating to the control and management of the schools (School Law, title 8, section

7). These corporate powers are expressly conferred upon this defendant by the City Charter (Section 1062). . . . The only purpose for which the defendant was created a corporate body was to conduct a system of public education in a designated division of the State, and manage and control the schools therein. This obviously includes the employment and payment of teachers, and none of these powers or functions are conferred upon the city as such. The only relation that the city has to the subject of public education is as the custodian and depositary of school funds, *and its only duty with respect to that fund is to keep it safely and disburse the same according to the instructions of the Board of Education.* . . . If the State has departed from the settled policy that has prevailed since its organization of keeping the work of public education and the control and management of its schools separate and distinct from all other municipal interests and business by the selection *of its own agents* and clothing them with corporate powers to represent the schools, such as school districts and boards of education, and has devolved these powers and duties directly upon the city, we would naturally expect to find such a departure and notable change expressed in language so clear that no doubt could arise as to this change of policy. If the Board cannot be sued for teachers' wages, and the teacher must resort to a suit aginst the city, then surely the Board must have sunk into a mere city agency, and it no longer has any use for independent corporate powers. Public education then becomes a *city* function, exposed to the taint of current municipal politics, and to any and every mismanagement that may prevail in city departments. . . . We have seen that the policy of this State for more than half a century has been to separate public education from all other municipal functions, and to entrust it to independent corporate agencies of its own creation, such as school districts and boards of education, with capacity to sue and to be sued in all matters involved in the exercise of that corporate power. . . . The learned counsel for the defendant must, therefore, be able to point to some new and plain provision of the present charter that abolishes the long-settled policy of the State and reduces the Board of Education to a mere city agency, incapable of being impleaded in the courts as a defendant upon one of the contracts it made for the employment of teachers in the schools."

The Court of Appeals then holds that there are no such provisions in the charter, but that, on the contrary, the Board of Education remains what it always has been, an independent corporation, the agent of the State for the maintenance and support of such system of education as the State decides shall be supported and maintained within the physical area of The City of New York.

Nor is this all. The State has never hesitated, either in New York or in the other States of the Union, to take effective measures to compel a given locality to raise by taxation sufficient funds to maintain a proper system of education. When the State standard of what should be expended for education, in view of the general interests of the public, is higher than the local standard the locality sometimes fails to raise enough money by taxation to support the schools according to the State standard. To meet this niggardliness on the part of the local taxing officers, resort is sometimes had to the conferring of direct powers of taxation on boards of education, or to mandatory legislation directing that such and such a per cent. of the annual tax levy in the locality shall be devoted to school purposes.

When the Greater City of New York was created the experiment was tried of having the Board of Estimate and Apportionment act upon the budget which the Board of Education prepared, setting forth the needs of the department of education. Experience soon made it clear that the Board of Estimate and Apportionment would not willingly allow a sufficient sum adequately to support education in New York. The Legislature was compelled, therefore, to state a minimum figure and to order that at least that amount should be collected in The City of New York and devoted to the purposes of education. This is the origin of the four-mill provision contained in the so-called Davis

Law of 1900, now incorporated in section 1064 of the New York Charter.

When the city authorities announced that property in New York would thereafter be assessed at one hundred per cent. of its market value, it was thought that the four-mill provision would produce more money than was needed, and the city authorities asked the Legislature, therefore, to reduce the four mills to three. This was done in 1903. But the raising of the assessed values to one hundred per cent. of the market value never really materialized, and the three-mill provision has proved insufficient. This proposed bill, therefore, restores the original four mills to be spent for purposes of education.

Since, therefore, both law and logic and the actual existing facts require that if any change is needed in the policy or method of administration of education in New York City, the State and State only can compel the change, to what authority except the State, shall those appeal who believe that the present policy of the Board of Education in New York City is unjust? The Mayor cannot change the policy and the Board of Education announces that it will not change the policy.

## THE CRITICISM OF THE PROPOSED BILL BECAUSE IT IS MANDATORY

The proposed bill is criticised because it is mandatory. It is hard to speak of this criticism with respect. The Board of Education is the mere agent of its principal, the State. All the powers of the Board are and must be granted by mandatory legislation. There is no other way.

It is a familiar principle of the law of agency, and a maximum of common sense, that when the principal employs an agent it is the principal, and not the agent, who determines the terms and conditions of the power of attorney given the agent. That is precisely the situation here. The Board of Education is the agent of the State, acting for the State, not under an irrevocable power with terms so broad that the agent is left free to work his own will.

Such a situation would be absurd. It would be an abdication by the State of one of its fundamental duties. All legislation in regard to the Board of Education is necessarily a command, a mandate. The real question is whether the mandate which the State gives is wise. In the year 1900 the State gave the Board of Education a certain mandate under which the State has now become convinced gross injustice has been committed. It now revokes that mandate and declares another policy which in its opinion is unjust. Up rises the agent, the Board of Education, and says: "This is mandatory legislation which undoes the injustice, and therefore the legislation is unwise. You are interfering with our right to do what we please."

### THE HOME RULE AND MANDATORY LEGISLATION ARGUMENTS

Mayor McClellan's veto messages of both the "White Bill" and the "Gledhill-Foley Bill" included "Home Rule" Objections. On this point, Horace E. Deming in his Memorandum in support of the White Bill after the Mayor's veto, said:

Governor Hughes in his veto message said: (Gov. Hughes Veto pp. 1, 3, and 4 to parenthesis).

"The Board of Education of the City of New York consists of forty-six members, appointed by the Mayor for terms of five years respectively. They are excepted from the general provisions of the charter authorizing the Mayor to remove public officers holding office by appointment from him, whenever in his judgment the public interest shall so require, and are removable only on sustained charges. While styled the head of an administrative department, the Board of Education, by the terms of the charter, possesses the power and privileges of a corporation. As such, it sues, and may be sued. It has 'the management' and control of the public schools, and of the public school system of the city, subject only to the general statutes of the state, relating to public schools and public school instruction and the provisons of the charter."

GOVERNOR HUGHES' CLEAR AND DECISIVE NEGATION TO THE HOME RULE OBJECTION

"Apart from the power of the Mayor to appoint and remove as stated, and the *duty* of the city to supply the funds required, *the Board of Education exercises its powers independently.* IT IS NOT SUBJECT TO CONTROL BY THE CITY AUTHORITIES. *There is no contract or official relations between the teachers and the city. The* CITY CANNOT BE SUED *upon the contracts made by the board.* This results, as the Court of Appeals has said, from 'the settled policy of the state from an early date to divorce business of public education from all other *municipal* interests or business,' and from the creation of the Board of Education as a corporate body 'to conduct a system of public education in a designated division of the *state* and manage and control the schools therein.'" (Gunnison v. Board of Education, 176 N. Y. on pp. 16, 17.)

"*The Board of Education is thus directly subject to the control of the Legislature,* and whatever provisions may be found necessary or wise for the purpose of defining its powers or prescribing its policy, *must be prescribed by the Legislature. No other authority is competent to make such provision.*

"But while the Legislature has power to deal with every phase of the matter, the course which experience approves, is that certain *general principles,* of action should be laid down, and that within these principles, freedom with reference to details of management should be left to the subordinate body acting with peculiar knowledge of local conditions.

"(N. B. The 'White Bill' sought to lay down the general principle, 'that, where men and women are both employed under any particular schedule, there shall be no discrimination in salary on account of the sex of the incumbent.'—G. C. S.)

"When the so-called Davis law was passed in 1899 (signed by Governor Roosevelt, May 3, 1900), it was thought important to the educational interests of the city that certain minimum salaries for teachers should be prescribed, as well as minimum annual increments, presumably to improve the service. In these prescribed minima, wide differences appear between the amounts payable to men and to women. These control the Board of Education only as minimum requirements, but the practice has been to pay women less than men, and under the by-laws adopted by the board *glaring inequalities* now exist.' "

City Superintendent Maxwell speaking at Milwaukee, 1905, said: " The best means hitherto found to enable the state to reinforce without discouraging local authorities is the enactment by its legislative branch of the laws laying down minimum requirements and making of regulations by its educational officers, which shall have the force of laws. These laws should embrace at least the following provisions: A minimum salary for the teachers that shall be in some degree commensurate with their training, etc."

### HOME RULE AND THE DAVIS LAW

From Report of the New York City Superintendent of Schools, 1900:

" It may be inferred that there must have been something extraordinary in the local conditions to call for the enactment of this Statute (the Davis Law) by the Legislature. Such indeed was the case. Stated briefly, the most obvious reason why the teachers had the support of the press and the public and the sympathy and co-operation of the Governor was that the Board of Estimate and Apportionment *had failed to provide the funds necessary to carry into full effect a comparatively mild measure regarding teachers' salaries* which the Legislature had passed in 1899 (the Ahearn Law.) This statement is the exact truth, and it was the truth that appealed so strongly to the press, the public, and the legislative authorities.

" In 1897 the New York Board of Education came to

realize the absurdities and injustices of the system of paying teachers, and made many honest and strenuous efforts to remedy abuses by adopting new salary schedules. Every one of these efforts was rendered abortive by the failure of the Board of Estimate and Apportionment to provide the funds necessary to carry the revised schedules into effect. Even the attempt of the Legislature in 1899, known as the Ahearn Law, to cut the Gordian knot was nullified in the same way—*the Board of Estimate and Apportionment did not supply sufficient money.*"

From report of the New York City Superintendent of Schools, 1907.

"We struggled along for three or four years under very great financial difficulties, which caused serious injury to the school system, and kept up constant irritation and agitation among the teaching force. These difficulties reached their culmination in the school year 1899-1900, when for months no salaries were paid to teachers in the Boroughs of Queens and Richmond, when the salaries of many teachers were arbitrarily reduced.—So great was the unrest—that a comprehensive measure was introduced into the legislature by Senator Davis.

"It (the Davis law) put an end to an almost intolerable condition with regard to teachers' salaries.—Under these circumstances I cannot but regard the Davis law as having been of very great advantage to the schools. I sincerely trust that it will be maintained on the statute book as a defense against capricious changes in teachers' salaries, until something better is provided."

### THE GOVERNOR'S REASONS FOR SIGNING THE DAVIS BILL

On signing the bill May 3, 1900, Governor Roosevelt attached a memorandum containing this statement: "The general purpose of the bill is admirable, and the best educators, the men most interested in seeing the schools of

Greater New York put upon a thoroughly efficient basis, most thoroughly favor the measure. The Ahearn Law was rendered nugatory by the action of the Board of Estimate and Apportionment. This action plunged affairs into chaos and rendered legislation absolutely necessary; the present bill being drawn primarily merely to meet the pressing necessity created by this action and by the chaos into which it threw the schools. The general purpose of the bill is so good, the change so vitally good, and the provisions as a whole will tend so much to the betterment of the schools that I deem it best to sign the bill."

That the Board of Education itself has not hesitated to go to Albany for relief, appears in the Minutes of said Board, e. g.

The minutes of the Board show that in 1887, when Hewitt was Mayor, the Board under the presidency of J. Edward Simmons, appealed to the Legislature to re-open the budget. This request was granted and $150,000 obtained for the relief of financial stress in the New York school system.

Similar action was taken in 1902.

The appended extract from the minutes of the meeting of February 24, 1904, shows exactly how the Board appealed for relief when it found itself facing a deficit of $381,343.72—$250,000 of which was needed to operate the recreation centers and playgrounds. At this meeting a special committee comprising Felix M. Warburg, Jacob W. Mack, A. Stern and William Lummis, submitted the following report:

"After careful consideration of the needs of the system and possible methods of raising money to meet existing and threatened deficiencies, your committee is of the opinion that there is but one practical way of securing funds. THIS IS THROUGH AN ACT OF THE LEGISLATURE, which permits the re-opening of the Budget. For this action there is ample precedent in the year 1902. It has been learned that such a bill has been introduced, at the behest of the City Administration, into both houses of the Legislature."

The committee then offered the following resolution, which was adopted:

"Resolved, That Senate Bill No. 498, which has for its purpose the granting of power to the Board of Estimate and Apportionment to reopen the Educational Budget for the year 1904, in order to provide moneys necessary for the unimpaired maintenance of the public schools, and which has been introduced, be, and it is hereby approved, and that the city's legal representative be requested to take active steps to further the passage of this measure."

This information is of value in refuting arguments that the Board has never appealed to the Legislature.

That New York state is not unique in this matter appears from the following:

### MORE PAY FOR TEACHERS IN UTICA

The bill which will enable the School Board of Utica to increase the salaries of the school teachers has been passed by the Legislature and after being approved by the mayor and Common Council will be returned to Albany for the signature of the governor. The measure raises the limit for school appropriations.

*Governor Hughes signed this bill.*

### PLAN TO GET MORE MONEY FOR SCHOOLS

Legislation is being sought in Tennessee which will provide that twenty-five cents on $100 of taxable property in Memphis shall be set apart for school purposes. This with the state appropriation, will create a fund sufficient to meet the current expenses of the schools, but it is claimed by the Board of Education that the funds for the new school buildings that are imperatively demanded to meet the needs of the situation as it is now presented to them must be provided by a bond issue.

From Milwaukee—"With a view toward enabling the teachers to receive the full increase contemplated by the committee on rules (of the school board) *the legislature* at its ensuing session will be asked to enlarge the amount that may be raised by taxation beyond the present limit of 3½ mills on each dollar of assessed valuation.

### WORKING FOR A STATE SCHOOL SYSTEM

"A state, rather than a local, school system, is proposed for Pennsylvania by the Educational Commission appointed by Governor Stuart, two years ago, and bills putting it into effect are now before the legislature of that state. The control of the schools is taken from the cities and towns and lodged in the state, which will direct them through a board of seven regents, appointed by the governor. Provision is made for a state superintendent.

"Cities, towns and villages are classified into three divisions, according to population, and the school boards thereof are to be elected. In the cities the boards will consist of fifteen members, appointed by the courts; in second class districts the boards will have nine members, three elected every two years for six-year terms, while the smallest districts will elect boards of five, one member being chosen each year for five years. Board powers in conducting the schools are given to these boards, subject to the general regulations of the state regents.

"Methods of taxation are to be uniform, the boards being limited to levying not more than 10 mills on the dollar in the big cities. Textbooks cannot be changed oftener than five years, and the lists of such will be prepared by the state. Provision is made for the education of all children and for their transportation where necessary. Compulsory education laws modelled after those of this state are included.

"Colleges of education in Pittsburg and Philadelphia are to be opened and normal schools throughout the state will be incorporated in the school system."

## CHAPTER XXIII

### HOME RULE AND MANDATORY LEGISLATION

All the opponents of the Women Teachers forget the "Home Rule" and "Mandatory" arguments when the proposition to omit the "Davis Law" from the revised charter is under consideration. Witness the following extracts from Mr. Shumway's pen as printed in the *Eagle,* Dec. 20, 1908:

To the Editor of the Brooklyn *Eagle*:

"Do the people of New York realize that in the proposals of the Charter Revision Commission is involved no less danger than the placing of the public schools under political control? That this a real and not a fancied danger is made plain in Chairman Ivins' testimony before the Cassidy Committee. Mr. Ivins said:

"I am a home ruler; I do not know any reason why the Legislature should be called upon to fix the salaries of teachers or firemen or scrub women or policemen, or anything else . . . The theory of the Charter Commission is that all salaries hereafter should be fixed by the Board of Estimate and Apportionment . . . Our commission believes in the doing away of the fixing of any minimum or maximum salaries by the Legislature."

It is worth while to compare with the above the words of the Court of Appeals, quoted approvingly by Governor Hughes in his veto of the White Bill:

"The settled policy of the state from an early date has been to divorce the business of public education from all other municipal interests or business." (Gunnison vs. Board of Education, 176, N.Y.)

With the Board of Estimate in absolute control of school finances, what is there to prevent a return to the conditions described by Superintendent Maxwell in his report, as follows:

"We struggled along for three or four years under very great financial difficulties, which caused serious injury to the school system, and kept up constant irritation and agitation among the teaching force. These difficulties reached their culmination in the school year 1899-1900, when, for months, no salaries were paid to teachers in the boroughs of Queens and Richmond, when the salaries of many teachers were arbitrarily reduced . . . So great was the unrest . . . that a comprehensive measure was introduced into the legislature by Senator Davis.

"It (the Davis Law) put an end to an almost intolerable condition with regard to teachers' salaries . . . Under these circumstances, I cannot but regard the Davis Law as having been of very great advantage to the schools. I sincerely trust that it will be maintained on the statute book as a defense against capricious changes in teachers' salaries, until something better is provided."

"There are real dangers to pupils and teachers in the proposed revision of the educational chapter of the city charter.

"First, as to tenure of office. Is it understood that teachers are not protected by civil service rules? That if the present charter protection were repealed, the teacher of long, 'fit and meritorious service' may, at the end of any year, be simply "not re-engaged?" That retention may be conditioned not on school service, but on political serviceableness? That the chief victim of such a condition will be the child?

"Second, as to salaries. Is it understood that the salary of one year will furnish no assurance regarding that of the ensuing year? That the salary of $1,300 one year may be reduced the next year to $1,000 or $900? That this would be true even if the provision guarding tenure were retained, or even if teachers were put under civil service rules? The case of Walters vs. City of New York (119 Appellate Division Reports 464) decided in May, 1907, clearly establishes this point. Judge Gaynor's concurring opinion expressly states: 'The said board (Estimate and Apportionment) has the power to reduce as well as increase salaries, to readjust the scale of salaries in any department on the recommendation of the head thereof, and the courts have no right to hamper it in the exercise thereof."

Is it understood by parents and teachers that the repeal of the Davis Law (carrying down with it, of course, the mandatory three mills) signifies a relapse to the old conditions when tenure, salary and promotion hung absolutely on the will of the machine boss? When the teacher who gave "the right party" a liberal "rake-off" on his salary was the favored one, and no parent could secure fair treatment of his child as against such "influence?" Is it understood that the schools have a way of "going to the dogs" under such "home rule" in New York City?

E. S. SHUMWAY.

Brooklyn, Dec. 19, 1908.

Now, of course, the repeal of the Davis Law would not, of necessity, "carry down with it, *of course,* the mandatory three mills," as the "three mill" law constitutes Sec. 1064 of the Charter, while the "Davis Law" as now understood is Sec. 1091. Neither is the "tenure of office" affected by the Davis Law. As to the closing statements of Mr. Shumway's letter, I can only say that I was in the Brooklyn schools six years before the "Davis Law" was enacted, and I consider such aspersions on the Board of Education totally unwarranted. It is unfortunate reflection on the one who confesses knowledge of such illegal transactions.

The *Globe* of May 7, 1909, commented thus:

"In the report of its By-law committee in opposition to the teachers' salary bill, adopted yesterday by the Board of Education, one of the reasons given for opposition to the bill was that the proposed schedules 'provide not minimum rates of salary, but absolute rates which the Board of Education can neither increase nor diminish', thus depriving the Board of Education and the city authorities of all rights

SENATOR GRADY, "EQUAL PAY" ORATOR.

which inhere in them in the matter of fixing salaries of members of the supervising and teaching staff.

BUT—

In the report on charter revision, adopted by the board, the fixing of salaries by the State was favored in the following declaration:

"Your committee is of the opinion that the principle embodied in section 1091 of the present charter (state protection of teachers' salaries) should be embodied in the new charter or the proposed administrative code."

The Board of Education again in May, 1910, petitioned the Legislature to retain the Davis Law in the revised charter. While Women Teachers need not Fear the Abolition of the Davis Law, because:

1st. Governor Hughes's references in his message on our bill, to the "glaring inequalities," and "gross injustices" of the present salary schedules, and the public sentiment aroused during the past two years, practically guarantees the women teachers against reduction in salary.

2nd. The only salaries that have been increased since the adoption of the Davis Law have been those of teachers and supervisors not protected by the Davis Law, namely:

(a) Male teachers in grades below 7A.—(For such the Davis Law provides no minimum or maximum after a specified term of service.)

(b) Teachers and supervisors of special subjects.

(c) District Superintendents, Associate City Superintendents, and City Superintendents.

(d) Members of the Board of Examiners.

N. B. Even the Attendance (Truant) Officers—the only employees other than members of the supervising and teaching force who are paid out of the general fund—have had their maximum salary raised from $1200 to $1500.

3rd. City Superintendent Maxwell in speeches at the conventions of the National Educational Association and at other meetings, has taken the stand that the State should fix and protect minimum salaries of teachers in its public schools.

4th. All teachers agree in the belief that the best interests of the schools will be served by state protection of their salaries;

But the following resolution was unanimously adopted at the general meeting of our association, December 5, 1908:

Whereas: The Interborough Association of Women Teachers of the City of New York believes that the best interests of the schools are being preserved by the state laws which protect the teachers' tenure of office and the teachers' pension fund; and

Whereas: Said Association while not advocating the so-called Davis Law as such, believes that inasmuch as the State makes mandatory provision for the common school education of all its children between the ages of four and twenty-one years, it is but reasonable and logical for the State to make mandatory provision for the payment of teachers and other officers required to carry out such mandatory provisions, therefore

Resolved: That the Interborough Association of Women Teachers of the City of New York exert all its powers toward securing such action by the Charter Revision Commission, the State Legislature, and the State Executive as will secure to teachers:

(a) Just salary schedules in which there shall be no discrimination in the salary of a position because of the sex of the incumbent;

(b) The present State protection of the tenure of office of teachers;

(c) State protection of teachers' pensions, which shall not vary with the sex of the teacher or officer pensioned; and

(d) The moneys necessary to carry out such schedules as may be established under (a) above, by providing that the city shall set aside an amount not less than four mills on every dollar of assessed valuation of the real and personal estate in the City of New York, liable to taxation.

## CHAPTER XXIV

### SOME FEATURES OF HEARINGS BEFORE MAYOR MAC CLELLAN

THE Mayor, contrary to all legislative practice, called upon the proponents of the measure first. This naturally put us at a disadvantage. At the first hearing we were surprised by this proceeding, because our experience at the three hearings in Albany had led us to expect that the opposition would be called for first. Before the second hearing, I wrote Mayor McClellan, asking him to reverse the order at this time; but he did not. He even refused us a minute for rebuttal; but that, too, was denied.

At the hearing on the White bill, we thought it best to have members of our own Association present our case: so our speakers were Mrs. Curtis Lenihen, as assistant to principal; Miss Lina E. Gano, as high school teacher, Mrs. Annie B. Moriarty, as principal; Miss Isabel A. Ennis, as grammar grade teacher; Miss Emma V. McCleary, as primary grade teacher, and myself.

At the hearing on the Gledhill-Foley bill, we decided to have representative citizens speak on our behalf, and more than seventy appeared to do so. Their names follow, but time permitted only a few to voice their approval. Among them were:

Sen. P. F. McCarren.
Mr. John C. Freund, Editor and taxpayer.
Mrs. Belle de Rivera—President of City Federation of Women's Clubs.
Mrs. William Cumming Story—as a taxpayer.
Rev. Alexander Irvine.
Lillie Devereux Blake.
Thos. Freel, a born New Yorker and a taxpayer.
Senator Gledhill.
Assemblyman Foley.

Commissioner Holland, of the Board of Education, representing Central Federated Union.

The opposition has been the same at both hearings: members of the Board of Education; male teachers; and representatives of Taxpayers' Associations. I submit some extracts from their speeches. The speeches of our advocates appear in Part II. Be sure to read them.

## *Types of Opposition.*

Mr. De Muth, President of the West Side Taxpayers' Association.

Executive Committee Greater N. Y. Taxpayers' Association.

United Real Estate Owners' Association.

"We have with us a representative of the City of New York, and one of the members of the Board of Education. Here are the underlings of that department, the superior officers having refused to give them what they believe they were entitled to, etc."

Mr. Shumway.

"We are asking that the economic law be regarded, because we believe that any violation of this law will react to the injury of the schools."

Mr. Abraham Korn.

I represent the Harlem Property Owners' Association. "Now we all know that men have, since the creation of the world, been on a footing a little above the female sex."

The "Taxpayers' Association" representative, who says: "We have educated these young ladies." "We have guaranteed them a position the very day they graduated from Normal School." "The *taxpayers* feel that they have treated these young ladies very magnanimously, by guaranteeing to them as soon as they graduate, a profession in which they can earn a livelihood, the opportunity to enter the public schools of this city and earn their living as teachers." "*We* have, by legislative enactments, taken them out of politics," "*we* have made provisions for taking care of these teachers; they draw their salaries even during sickness under certain circumstances, and their position is waiting for them when they return and are able to do their work again." "And there is another provision whereby, after twenty years of service, they are allowed, by reason of old age, to retire on a certain per cent. of their salary." "If they reach the age of thirty years of service, they are compelled by law to retire on a certain per cent. of their salary." "This illustrates once again the generosity with which the teachers of this city are treated by the *citizens* of the city." "The *citizens* . . . have been very careful to go to Albany and carefully legislate our public schools out of politics entirely, and thereby safeguard the public schools against political influence and interference and against all uses of privilege and all of those things." *

Imagine how hard it is to have to sit and listen to this "We," "We," "We," "the citizens," "the taxpayers." As if "these young ladies" "these teachers" were brought into the City like sparrows or fish spawn from some foreign country, instead of being the daughters, sisters, and in some few instances the wives and mothers of our taxpayers. Hundreds are direct taxpayers. All are indirect taxpayers through their landlord or boarding-house keeper.

As to our pensions, one would think Mr. Levey and some other men put their hands in their pockets and gave us the money. Instead of which, we ourselves contribute to the pension fund from the day we begin to teach under a regular appointment, one per cent. of our salaries; and to this, are added all deductions for unexcused absences—during 1907 these deductions amounted to $274,743.13—and five per cent. of the excise taxes. Neither is a teacher allowed to retire "by reason of age" after twenty years, nor is she "compelled to retire" after thirty years of service. Not until she is 65 years old can a teacher be "compelled to retire" and not then unless she has served thirty years.

Like his companion in opposition to fair play, Mr. De-

* These are extracts from Mr. Levey's speech at the Mayor's hearing on the Gledhill-Foley bill.

Muth, Mr. Levey was astounded by our conduct in daring to go to Albany in search of relief. He said, "we are confronted with this proposition of the school teachers banding together, and going down to Albany to increase their salaries; they have entered upon a systematic campaign in Albany for this purpose."

But the footless part of all such argument as Mr. Levey and his ilk is that they don't touch the point at issue at all. They all jag holes in the field outside even the outside ring, without once getting near the bull's eye. Everything they say is as true of the men teachers as of the women teachers. Is it impossible for them to see that we are simply seeking "equal pay for equal work?"

## CHAPTER XXV

### TEACHERS AND POLITICS

Much has been said about the "women teachers and politics."

To begin with, I think the woman teacher has as much right as a man teacher or any other citizen to take an active interest in politics—in other words in the government of her country.

The Constitution says, "All persons born or naturalized in the United States are citizens thereof and of the State in which they reside." The officials "elected by the people" are elected to represent the women and girls as truly as the men and boys. It is their duty to conserve and preserve the rights and interests of the women and girls as fully as they do those of the men. The women and all minors are counted among those who are enumerated for the purpose of fixing the number of representatives a State shall have in Congress. It is the duty of women teachers to be acquainted with the forms of government, the governmental policies, and the public history of government officials. Why should woman not be free to express her views on all these subjects, and to do all that she properly can to influence the election of such officials as she prefers shall represent her?

On October 27, 1908, the City Vigilance League of New York, addressed a circular letter "To the Female School Teachers of New York City:—" in which it said, "The school teachers of our city compose one of the strongest moral forces. They are shaping the characters of our children. We must depend upon them to give to many thousands their only teaching in veneration for law and love for the Constitution and its spirit," and yet because members of this league thought that some of the women teachers were opposing the re-election of Governor Hughes, they in the same letter made several absolutely false accusations against the women teachers, which led Rev. Mr. Parkhurst, the honorary president of said League, and other ministers to attack us in a most unwarranted manner.

As a matter of fact, the Interborough Association of Women Teachers as an association never took any official stand one way or the other in the gubernatorial election of 1908. There were some members in favor of Governor Hughes' candidacy. Naturally, however, there were more in favor of Lieutenant Governor Chanler's. My personal attitude was expressed in the press at the time, in these words, "I am not one who believes in trying to carry water on both shoulders, and I openly declare that I am working zealously as an individual for the success of Mr. Chanler. Besides, we do not believe that there is a great moral issue in this campaign. Mr. Chanler's attitude on the gambling bills is as clear as Mr. Hughes's. Those who favor his election can hardly be accused of playing into the hands of the professional race-track gamblers, since Mr. Chanler's vote, as presiding officer of the Senate, was the decisive vote which brought about re-consideration of the bills, and so insured their ultimate passage. Furthermore, since his nomination, he has openly declared that he will veto any attempt to repeal the Hart-Agnew law.

We have been accused of contributing to the Chanler campaign fund. Like all the other accusations made in this unfair attack, this is false. Nor do I know of any members being asked to contribute. On the contrary, some of our members have received the following letter. It has been addressed in each case to *Miss* ———, indicating that those who were sending out the letters were making a direct appeal to women teachers to contribute to the Hughes campaign fund."

HUGHES ALLIANCE
non-partisan
34 West thirty-third Street, New York.
Telephone, 781 Madison Square.

Chairman,
Hon. Charles A. Schieren.

Vice-chairmen.
R. Fulton Cutting.
Darwin R. James, Jr.
Col. Henry W. Sackett.
Ansley Wilcox.

Treasurer,
J. Adams Brown,
President New Netherland Bank,
41 West 34th Street.
Secretary,
Major F. M. Crosset,
30 West 33d Street.

New York, October 28, 1908.

"As College men, we are fundamentally interested in the fight of Governor Hughes to maintain an independent and efficient State administration as against a threatened return to the old methods of favoritism and inefficiency.

"This is not a new fight. Columbia men have stood on the right side of it since the beginning.

"The forces which stand behind the opposition to the Governor hoping to profit by his defeat, are not playing fair. So far, the anti-Hughes campaign has been one of misrepresentation, and we are catching up as rapidly as possible with the fanciful stories with which the enemies of constitutional government are appealing for support, and forcing home a truthful statement of facts.

"There are a dozen or more of these stories in circulation. The absurd scare that the Governor's re-election would mean Blue Law legislation and an attempt to interfere with the legitimate enjoyments and recreations of the people, is one you have doubtless heard. Petitions are being sent out to work up anti-Hughes sentiment on just such "issues." Each bubble bursts before the first gust of truth that blows on it. We hope to do enough truth telling to make the Hughes plurality a record-breaker and thus vindicate the honor of our State.

"The undersigned address you on behalf of the Hughes Alliance, an organization of Democrats, Republicans and

Independents, embarked on a campaign of truth-telling in support of Governor Hughes. We feel that a failure to uphold the purpose of the present administration would be not only a reflection on the good name of the State, but severe reverse to the cause of good government, and that years would be required to regain the ground lost.

"Can we count on your assistance to the extent of a subscription of $10, or more if possible, to carry on this work. We further want your actual support in your own election district, and hope you are taking an active part in this campaign.

"Will you 'line up' with us in order that the good work of Governor Hughes, so well begun, may be carried forward?

Very truly yours,
Francis S. Bangs, '78.
Benjamin B. Lawrence, '87 Mines
Herbert L. Satterlee, '83.
Albert W. Putnam, '97.
George W. Kirrhwey, L. S."

The board of education at this same time tried to pass what became known as the "Gag Law." Commissioners Freifeld, Wingate and Jonas in urging this resolution confined their criticisms to the women teachers and especially to me, as evidenced in the following resolution presented by Commissioner Jonas on October 14, 1908:

"Whereas, In the public press recently appeared statements to the effect that Miss Grace C. Strachan, a district superintendent, had publicly urged employees of the Board of Education to electioneer for or against certain candidates for office because of their attitude toward the so-called equal pay bill; and

"Whereas, This Board of Education found it necessary not long ago to criticise and reprimand this same employee for political activity and inattention to duty, which mild action and warning has had no apparent effect, be it therefore,

"Resolved, That the attention of the City Superintendent

of Schools be called to the matter, with the request for a report to this board."

The *Eagle* of October 15, 1908, had this to say of the matter:

"The resolution might have been adopted without question but for the opposition of Samuel B. Donnelly,* who was always ready to defend the women in the matter of their agitation for equal pay." Mr. Donnelly wanted to know what the City Superintendent was expected to report: Was it as to whether Miss Strachan had a right to exercise her privileges? It was an inadvisable resolution. If she had neglected her duties, then charges should be preferred against her; but if she was doing her duty as district superintendent she had a right to exercise her privileges in her own time. She was not the only one taking part in the campaign or movement. There were others, but she was the most successful. He was opposed to the resolution in the present form in which it was presented.

" Mr. Jonas replied that when the matter was up before, he had called the attention to the actions of Miss Strachan and others, and it struck him that because of their inaction on that occasion they were to blame for the present situation.

" Abraham Stern said it was a question whether the board had a right to interfere if there was no misconduct. Instead of investigating Miss Strachan, they should first find out if the board had the power to do anything in the premises. If there was no misconduct on the part of an employee, the board was powerless. He moved that the matter be referred to the committee on by-laws and legislation.

" With a request that it report at the next meeting," put in Mr. Jonas.

" Robert L. Harrison, the chairman of that committee, pleaded with the board not to refer it to him. He wanted to know what they were to find out. Were they to read the papers to ascertain what Miss Strachan had said? Were they to summon witnesses? It would take six months

* Mr. Donnelly is now Public Printer.

to find out what Mr. Jonas wanted. He should be more definite.

"Mr. Jonas said his intention was plain. If warranted, charges ought to be preferred against Miss Strachan. It was that he meant.

"Again Mr. Donnelly entered a protest, saying that Miss Strachan was assigned to certain districts, to which he and Mr. Schaedle were also assigned. If she was not doing her duty they would know it, and would prefer charges against her for it; but they could not prefer charges against her for what others were permitted to do. There were clerks and other employees of the Board of Education who were active in political work. They had a right to be.

"After Mr. Kanzler asked whether the newspaper clippings to which Mr. Jonas referred, were attached to the resolutions, which provoked some laughter, the resolution was adopted as amended, and the matter is now in the hands of the committee on laws.

"Miss Strachan was informed last evening of the resolution and what had been done, and she was astonished. She said she had received permission yesterday afternoon from the president of the Board of Education to attend, to-day, the hearing upon the educational department budget for herself, Miss Gano, and Miss Curtis, two vice-presidents of the Interborough Association of Women Teachers, and did not suppose any fault was to be found with the action of the association.

"I have not neglected any of my duties," said she, "and therefore do not fear what the Board of Education will do to me. As to taking political action, I believe I have the right of an American citizen, secured to me by the Constitution of the United States, even if I am not a voter."

"Why does not Mr. Jones find out what the men employees of the Board of Education are doing? And why does he not ask that charges be preferred against them?"

The By-Law Committee, at the next meeting of the board, recommended the following amendments:

"Section 1. No member of the supervising or teaching staff shall be permitted to join or become a member of any club or association or to take part in any movement intended or undertaking to affect legislation for or on behalf of the Department of Education, or any officials or members thereof, or to contribute any funds for such purpose.

"Section 2. Any combination or concerted effort among the employees of the Board of Education to elect or defeat any candidate for public office by reason of his having agreed or refused to agree to favor or oppose any legislation affecting the salaries of said supervising or teaching staff or other employees shall be deemed to constitute gross misconduct and insubordination.

"Resolved, That copies of the foregoing amendment to the by-laws be transmitted to the principals of all training, high and elementary schools with the instructions that the same be read to their teachers immediately."

"The report was signed by Commissioners Harrison, Freifeld and Wingate, Mr. Stern refusing to concur with the others. He said he did not approve of the teachers electioneering, but that the matter was one which needed careful consideration, and asked that the matter be put over. Mr. Stern pointed out that no reference was made to salaries in the resolution as he thought there should be, as there might be other matters which teachers could work for or against with impunity. For instance a bill might be introduced in the Legislature providing for a different way of appointing principals, when he thought the principals would be perfectly justified in raising a protest. He tried to show how many persons would be affected by the by-laws by saying that the Department of Education did not consist of only forty-six members but of the entire clerical and teaching staffs and 650,000 pupils as well. In conclusion he asked that six members stand with him in asking that the matter be put over.

"Mr. Stern got his six men, but Gen. Wingate moved to suspend this by-law for the meeting, saying that the matter was an important one, and that the Board was confronted with an emergency which should be acted on at once. He told of how a delegation of Brooklyn teachers had on Tuseday visited the home of a candidate for office and asked him to pledge himself in their behalf, with the threat that if he refused to give it they would work against him. He declared that the 13,000 teachers who had banded themselves together were hurting the Board irreparably, and as Election Day was so near immediate action should be taken.

"George Freifeld expressed himself as being amazed at the stand Mr. Stern had taken, and said that the 650,000 children he had spoken of were being affected at the present time worse than they would be if the by-laws were adopted. He said that only recently during school hours the teachers in a school had collected money for the purpose of trying to defeat a certain candidate. Mr. Freifeld told of a secret meeting of the Interborough Association held last Thursday even after the matter had been taken up by the Board.

"Robert Harrison, Chairman of the Committee on By-Laws, had a little fun over the remarks that Mr. Stern had made, and said that the members of the Board might as well resign, and let the teachers run the affairs. After several more had spoken, Mr. Stern took occasion to defend his attitude, and said that the proposed by-law did not prevent action by individuals. He thought this point was one that ought to be remedied. Gen. Wingate withdrew his motion and the matter went over until the next meeting."

The New York *Commercial*, not, I believe, friendly to the women teachers' cause, made this editorial comment, November 5, 1908:

"Opinions will differ as to the propriety of public-school teachers engaging actively in politics and especially in those political matters which have to do with State and municipal legislation on educational affairs. But as to defining such political activity as an offense carrying with it a penalty, why, that is a proposition almost too absurd for discussion."

Yet some members of the board of education of New

York, annoyed at the electioneering and speech-making by Miss Grace C. Strachan, a Brooklyn public-school teacher, seriously propose to "put the law" on her and her kind. The board's committee on by-laws has just made a report advising that nothing be done to Miss Strachan and her co-offenders, inasmuch as there is no by-law at present prohibiting such political work, but recommending that a new by-law be passed that would make it gross misconduct and insubordination for any member of the teaching or supervisory staff to join an organization that undertakes to influence educational legislation. This by-law would also forbid opposing or seeking the election of any candidate who voted for or against the bill to raise the pay of the teachers. The matter went over to the next meeting, but not until a warm discussion had been had on the proposition. Commissioner Abraham Stern's protest was timely and forcible. "Every teacher," he said, "has a right to express his or her opinion upon all things relating to the board of education and you are going too far in making it insubordination to exercise that right." Commissioner Wingate complained that over in Brooklyn a committee of public-school teachers went to a certain candidate for public office and said that the thirteen thousand teachers of Greater New York would put a boycott on him and on his business unless he would pledge himself in advance to vote for higher pay for the teachers. "It is time that we stopped this sort of thing, this outrage," declared the commissioner. By "we" he meant the board of education presumably. But what has the board got to do with it? The Brooklyn candidate ought to be able to handle the matter himself. There is law enough already that he can "put on" every member of the teachers' committee who threatened him—and he ought to do it. But the board can't muzzle the teachers. If they choose to make fools of themselves it is nobody's business but their own."

At the following meeting, held on Nov. 11, 1908, the committee had modified its resolution to the following:

"Resolved, that the by-laws of the Board of Education

be, and they are, hereby amended by inserting therein a new section to be known and designated as section 57A with the caption: "Electioneering Prohibited" reading as follows:

"Section 57A. No member of the supervising or teaching staff shall individually or otherwise, by any means or methods, publicly advocate the election or defeat of any candidate for public office or instigate or take part in any movement to elect or defeat such candidate, by reason of such candidate's attitude toward legislation affecting the salaries of members of the supervising or teaching staff."

On this form the By-Law Committee had been a unit, but the women teachers succeeded in preventing its adoption. The vote was 20 to 16 in favor of the amendment, but a majority of all the members, that is 24 votes, were needed. The following is from the *Eagle* of Nov. 12, 1908.

"Robert L. Harrison, the chairman of the committee, in moving the adoption of the by-law, conceded that there had not been unanimity in the committee when the previous proposed by-law was adopted, but that now the committee was a unit.

"Nathan S. Jonas, who introduced the original motion by which the matter came before the committee admitted that he had had some unpleasant correspondence since that time but he had had no quarrel with any of the teachers, nor did he have a preference for the male over the female teachers. What he had done was to stop insubordination in the system. He felt that the board of superintendents in charge of the teaching staff should have enforced discipline. He wanted to make his position clear. In the future he would endeavor to hold the superintendents responsible for the discipline among the teachers.

"Hugo Kanzler hoped the by-law would not be adopted, because he did not want to abridge the freedom of speech. He agreed that during the recent election the action of some teachers was highly improper, and he was so impressed with the dignity of the office of teacher that he did not want any of them to stand on a par with ward heelers. There was no reason, however, to pass any drastic measure, which would curtail the right of the teachers to pass an opinion, individually or collectively.

"Mr. Kanzler took the opportunity, too, to reply to the attack made on the women teachers by Dr. Parkhurst, although he did not mention the clergyman by name. He denounced the charge that they were in an unholy conspiracy with the gamblers. The teachers of the city were of such a character that they could not nor would they form any such conspiracy. He saw no objection to their agitating for an increase of salary, if they did not neglect their duty in the classroom. It would come pretty close to hanging a padlock on the mouths of the teachers and putting the key in the hands of the Board of Education. He wanted American fair play for all.

"General Wingate protested that the resolution would not close the mouths of the teachers. It was intended solely to prohibit electioneering, and was confined to that prominent evil. They were meeting a great public evil, which should be stopped.

"Samuel B. Donnelly championed the women teachers. During the month of October the newspapers had much to say about the active participation of the women teachers in the campaign, he said, and members of the Board of Education had asserted that they had received complaints from candidates to the effect that women teachers were actively opposing them. The press reports, however, contained little if any reference to the political activities of the men teachers, and the actions of the men teachers were not criticised in the meetings of the board. It was therefore fair to conclude, said he, that the restrictive by-law was aimed directly at the women teachers only. There was antagonism between members of the board and the women teachers and between men and women teachers, and Mr. Donnelly asserted that the responsibility of this antagonism rested principally with the men. The speeches of the leaders of the men teachers and the circulars which had been issued by them were indicative of a spirit that merited condemnation by the members of the board. In his opinion the proposed by-law was improper, and in opposition to the state constitution. The board should take steps to harmonize the differences between the men and women, and should do nothing to aggravate the situation.

"John C. Kelley wanted to be put on record as being opposed to the resolution. The proposed by-law was opposed to the right of free speech, which was guaranteed to every free American. If the same things of which the complaint was made had been done by men nothing would have been said or done. If the women were doing their duty in the schools properly and fittingly, then it was all that the board should require of them.

"Abraham Stern defended the resolution and proposed by-law. There was nothing in it to prevent free speeech; there was nothing in it to prevent the teachers signing any petition in behalf of any principle. Every constitutional right was retained, but it would prevent electioneering and would uphold the dignity of the profession of teaching, and the majority of the teachers would be in favor of it. He did not think there would ever be any occasion when the by-law would have to be enforced. It was done for the protection of the women teachers themselves.

"Men who voted for and against the resolution.

"Yeas—Messrs. Barrett, Bruce, Coudert, Delaney, Dresser, Freifeld, Greene, Haase, Harrington, Higgins, Ingalls, Jonas, Man, May, Schaedle, A. Stern, C. J. Sullivan, Suydam, Wingate, Winthrop.—20.

"Nays—Messrs. Aldcroft, Cosgrove, Cunnion, Donnelly, Ferris, Haupt, Hallick, Kanzler, Katzenberg, Kelley, McDonald, O'Donohue, Partridge, M. S. Stern, M. J. Sullivan. —16."

On the vote on this proposed by-law the New York *Commercial* said in an editorial, Nov. 13, 1908:

"It is almost unbelievable, but it is nevertheless true, that twenty members of the New York board of education have by formal ballot registered their approval of a proposition to put gags in the mouths of the public-school teachers, to withdraw from them the right of free-born American citizens to express their personal opinions. The matter came up in the form of a motion made at the last board meeting to amend the by-laws by the adoption of a section forbidding teachers to take part in movements seeking the defeat or the election of any candidate for public office because of that candidate's attitude toward legislation for fixing teachers' salaries. The proposal was aimed, as everybody in and out of the board knows, at those women teachers who have organized for the purpose of securing the passage of a law increasing the salaries of women teachers in this city.* As to the proprieties or the good taste involved in all this there is a question, of course. Some people may approve it, others may condemn it, and others still may hold no opinions on the subject. It all depends on circumstances and the point of view. But to seriously attempt to stop it by a board-of-education-by-law, violation of which would furnish ground for the making of charges that might cost a teacher his or her position, is preposterous. It is on all fours with a proposition for the adoption of an ordinance forbidding holders of municipal office to vote in city elections or to join political clubs or other political organizations. It reeks with intolerance and narrow mindedness. It is unthinkable. Yet only one more vote in the board of education would have carried this proposition through. Most members of the board of education very naturally and properly resent the action of those women teachers who seek to go over the board's head for the regulation of salaries by law—a matter strictly within the board's jurisdiction and control—but to take any official notice of it at all is beneath the dignity of a school commissioner. Give the public school teachers all the tongue latitude and all the rope they want—they will gag themselves or hang themselves in good time without the aid of by-laws."

A similar policy is indicated in the following extract from the *Sun* of October 17, 1908:

* The *Commercial* is mistaken in the purpose of our organization, which is to establish the principle of one salary for one and the same position regardless of the sex of the incumbent.

"Mr. Robinson gave out copies of a letter he had written to William H. Maxwell, Superintendent of Schools, in which he said:

"Referring to your conversation with me over the telephone to-day in which you stated that you considered our action in having invited Miss Grace C. Strachan to address the budget was improper, I beg to say that the matter of the teachers' salaries and of the entire school budget is one in which the taxpayers of the city are vitally interested.

"We want to know both sides of the question and we propose to seek every means in our power to ascertain what the truth is. If Miss Strachan is able to present any reasons why such increase should properly be made we have the right to know what these reasons are. I feel very strongly, therefore, that your attitude in condemning us for asking her to address the meeting to-morrow is very extraordinary."

The *Call* of November 12, 1908, contained an article which read:

"In connection with the reported attempt of the Board of Education of New York City to throttle the public school teachers, it occurs to me that there is much more to be considered than the rights of the teachers, important as these rights are.

"Unless our teachers have initiative, individuality and culture, they cannot impart these qualities to the children. Since in many if not in the majority of cases the children's parents, victims themselves of the present unjust economic conditions, have not and therefore cannot impart these qualities, the importance of having teachers who can do so is at once obvious and overwhelming.

"If culture, as Bosanquet says, is 'A habit of mind instinct with purpose, cognizant of a connection and a tendency in human achievement, able and interested in discerning the great from the trivial,' and if, as Professor Zeublin says, 'Our culture cannot stand up face to face with contemporary problems, it is a contemptible culture,' then indeed must we realize how important it is that our teachers should have every possible stimulus to its development. What greater stimulus can there be than that afforded by the opportunity for the teachers to become a positive element not only for the betterment of their own condition through their organized political effort, but indirectly, as a consequence of this, the elevation, morally, mentally, physically and politically of the public at large?

"Does the Board of Education think that its undemocratic assaults upon the freedom of speech and action of the teachers will encourage people of character and conviction to enter the profession? Do they wish to inflict upon this community, instead of sturdy educators with the character and individuality, a generation of pedagogic jellyfish, sans culture, sans character, sans individuality, and sans brains. If so, let it pursue, its high-handed policy of Russianizing our educational system.

"I should like to see my own children become fine and useful and self-respecting educators of the coming generations, but if they must abdicate their intellectual and moral sovereignty, then it were better that they should take their chances in the fratricidal struggle called private capitalism, bad as it is.

"School teachers of New York, do you intend to be men and women or mollycoddles and mollusks.

"W. W. PASSAGE.

"411 Adelphi St., Brooklyn, Nov. 7."

And a friend wrote:

"I am no encourager of 'insubordination,' if such there be anywhere, in the course pursued by certain 'teachers' in New York City, in the recent State Election politics. But I am quite clear in my own mind that converting 'teachers' into helots will not help them make their boys and girls into free, self-reliant, independent and tolerant American citizens. I am personally a great admirer of both Governor Hughes and Superintendent Maxwell. I hoped for the election of the former. I consider the latter the greatest executive yet produced in American Education, and one of the greatest reformers. Nothing, however, that has occurred outside of my own experience has given me more genuine personal satisfaction than to see you and your associates stand honestly and openly for the rights even of teachers to be equal citizens with others in this Republic. In other words, I consider that the board of education in New York City and its officers are offending against the best interests of the democratic nation that is to be when they say to the women of New York City schools 'Silence: we are the thinkers and the lords,' and to the men of the schools, 'Splendid: work all you care to as long as you work in line with the powers that are.'

"Knowing fairly well the historic inferiority of teachers and their isolation from 'going' affairs, knowing also the present inferiority of women, political and legal, I am not surprised at the attitude of the school authorities toward the women who do the work of education at direct contact with the children and youth. I have long been a convinced equal suffragist; and as such welcome the present movement.

Yours sincerely,
(Signed) William E. Chancellor,
Superintendent, Norwalk Union (City)
School District.

Nov. 11, 1908."

In connection with all the foregoing, the following letter was sent:

City of New York, November 10, 1908.

To the Members of the Board of Education:

The Interborough Association of Women Teachers respectfully submit the following:

The City Vigilance League of New York, whose officers are Charles H. Parkhurst, Honorary President, Frank Moss, President; Matthew Beattie, Vice-President; F. W. Block, Treasurer, and Thomas L. McClintock, Secretary, recently circulated a printed circular letter addressed to the 'Female School Teachers of New York City,' which contained various misstatements. We quote some extracts, and state the facts:

"*a.* 'Last Friday evening the women teachers held a meeting at No. 5 West 125th Street. At that meeting there was distributed a circular which advised voting for Mr. Taft and Mr. Chanler,—showed how it could be done, and giving reasons for the doing of it.'

"No such literature has ever been seen or discussed or distributed by the Interborough Association of Women Teachers.

"*b.* 'Women teachers are going among their friends . . . and are urging them to vote against Mr. Hughes. . . . They say that their instructions are to do this ungracious work very quietly.'

"The Interborough Association of Women Teachers has never offered or passed any resolution affecting the candidature of Governor Hughes, nor has the Association given instructions to work quietly for any candidate. It is respectfully submitted that individual members have the same rights as other citizens under the Constitution of the United States and of the State of New York.

"*c.* 'When our women teachers are lending themselves to such a movement . . . seeking to obtain votes for the ticket for which the gamblers are frantically working;—when it is all being done, not for love of gambling and gamblers, not for unbridled license;—but simply for more pay . . . they put their argument on the sole ground that their pocketbooks would be benefited; the principles involved are overlooked. . . .'

"The Interborough Association of Women Teachers is organized for the purpose of establishing the principle that for 'work of a given position women shall receive equal pay with men.' Governor Hughes recognized this in his message on the 'Equal Pay Bill' when he said: 'It is for this principle the supporters of the bill contend and not for mere increased pay.' The association at all public hearings has made its position on this point definite and clear and it has never sacrificed any other moral principle in its efforts to establish this one.

"The Interborough Association of Women Teachers believes it to be necessary and proper to submit the above statement to your Board because, as your employees, its members desire you to know the truth, and also because resolutions criticising the women teachers and based wholly or partly upon press items and indirect information, have been presented and discussed at recent meetings of your Honorable Board. During said discussion it has been charged that the women teachers were raising a campaign fund.

"The Interborough Association of Women Teachers has never raised any contribution for campaign purposes. Neither has it contributed to any campaign fund. Furthermore, the only request for contributions to a campaign fund received by any of its members, so far as it is known by this association, came from the Hughes Alliance, and asked for a subscription of '$10, or more if possible,' for the purpose of aiding in the re-election of Governor Hughes.

"In conclusion, the Interborough Association of Women Teachers respectfully submits that it is its intention and desire not to violate any by-law of the Board of Education, while relinquishing none of the rights and privileges secured to all citizens by the Constitution of the United States, and that it believes the women teachers are justified in looking to the Board of Education to defend them against such unwarranted and unjust condemnation.

"EXECUTIVE COMMITTEE,
"Interborough Association of Women Teachers."

Throughout this controversy so much had been said in meetings of the Board and reported in the public press about me and my work, that I deemed it due myself and my reputation to memorialize the Board with the following statement:

"October 27, 1908.

"Whereas, at two recent meetings of the Board of Education, held on October 14 and October 28, my name was used in a formal resolution and in formal discussion in such a way as to give my employer and the public ground for thinking that I am neglecting my duty as district superintendent of public schools, I respectfully submit the following report of the work I have done since my assignment to Districts 33-35 and the commencement of my duties in said districts on September 11, 1908:

"1. Made sixty visits to the nineteen public schools and the three evening schools located in these districts.

"2. Examined ninety-three teachers in their classrooms for report on approval of license.

"3. Examined eleven teachers in their classrooms for report on approval of service.

"4. Inspected seventy-six classes, meeting teacher in each class, in three evening schools.

"5. Held four formal conferences with principals in office of district superintendent after 3 P. M.

"6. Attended four meetings of local school boards.

"7. Conducted eight formal hearings after 2.30 P. M., in suspension cases.

"8. Conducted thirty-one formal hearings after 3.30 P. M., in truancy cases.

"9. Transferred the whole organization of School No. 49 to the building occupied by No. 117, as the building of the former had to be closed during the process of repairs. This action necessitated putting P. S. No. 117 entirely on part time, giving the organization of the latter school the A. M. session and No. 49 the P. M. session. And

"10. Encompassed changes in organization in ten of the ten schools in District No. 33, and in six of the nine schools in District No. 35.

"(N. B.—Of the three schools not reorganized, one P. S. 74 consists of grades of the fifth, seventh, and eighth years only, and two—P. S. 75 and P. S. 86—will be the subjects of many changes in the near future, due to the opening of addition to No. 75.)

"11. The net results of reorganization already completed are:

"(1) Reduction in number of pupils on part time from 6560 to 3687—that is, a decrease of 2893.

"(2) Increase in number of over-age pupils receiving special instruction and care from 959 to 2532—that is, an increase of 1573.

"These improvements were made possible by:

"(1) The opening of the addition to P. S. No. 24, giving up to date 768 more sittings. The total number of additional sittings in both districts, however, is only 732, because of the decrease of 36 in P. S. 21 by reseating made during summer vacation.

"(2) Changing school district boundaries and transferring hundreds of pupils to neighboring schools where there were vacant sittings.

"(3) Rearranging classes in schools so as to make better use of sittings.

"It will be seen that after allowing 1464 as the number of part-time pupils placed on full time by the 732 additional sittings the number of part-time pupils relieved by means of other changes in organization amounts to 1429.

"In conclusion, I respectfully ask that you protect my reputation and usefulness as an employee of the Board of Education from unjust attack and undeserved injury."

This, however, was not the first time that the women teachers had incurred the displeasure of the Board, but it is noteworthy that not once in the four years' struggle has the Board criticised the male teachers.

The Bronx *Star* of September 12, 1907, contained the following:

"By adopting a scathing report of a special committee, the Board severely rebuked the teachers, who, during the agitation for 'equal pay for equal work' last spring, absented themselves from school without permission and went to Albany to force through the Legislature their salary bill, which Governor Hughes and Mayor McClellan both vetoed.

"No 'positive disciplinary action, even against the chief offenders,' is recommended by the committee in its report. It is 'content to call emphatic attention to the inherent impropriety of the acts themselves and to the mischief and injury developed in the system by their practice, and to sound a fair warning against their repetition.' The committee takes this stand 'because of the fact that in the past absence from school duty for similar purposes, although never so flagrant as during last winter, was usually passed over in silence, and consequently the idea has developed that condonation would follow the offense.'

"To prevent the recurrence of 'a demonstration fraught with such large possibilities of evil to the system,' the committee recommends certain drastic reforms. These will be put into operation as soon as possible, for the Board feels that the system must be disciplined. The recommendations of the committee are as follows:

"'First—That the Committee on By-Laws and Legislation be requested to frame immediately more stringent rules governing the absence of teachers, principals, supervisors and superintendents for causes other than those specified in Section 44 of the By-Laws. In the opinion of this committee the present deductions are wholly inadequate, and have no deterrent effect. It is recommended that a larger portion of the pay of an absentee be deducted.

"'Second—That absence without justifiable cause should be immediately followed by charges of neglect of duty or insubordination to be preferred against the offender by the City Superintendent or other proper supervising officer or member of the Board of Education. Such action is earnestly recommended, but to abridge the constitutional right of petition, which is abundantly secured, but to preserve the integrity of an equally important institution, known as the public school system, from the effects of disorder and demoralization, if not disruption, at the hands of agitators.'

"District Superintendent Grace C. Strachan, who managed the teachers' campaign, and Mrs. Nora Curtis Lenihen, and Miss Isabella Ennis, president and secretary of the Interborough Association of Women Teachers, which backed the salary bill, are severely critcised in the committee's report, as follows:

"'There are instances of neglect of duty which call for special mention, Miss Grace C. Strachan is a district superintendent in receipt of a salary of $5,000 per annum from the city. Her absences, as reported, aggregate thirty-four days. The place she holds and the duties she is called upon to discharge are especially important and delicate and preclude the possibility of performance by a clerk, nor can neglect of them be cured by "over-time." She is the official supervisor of twenty-two principals and about 700 teachers, all of whom are under her supervision, and they have a right to assume that she is moved by the highest ideals of fidelity to duty.

"'Her official report of her absences, containing the reasons for the same, reads as follows: *"Work in a cause destined to uplift the moral standards of the school system, and hence of the community, the State, the nation, and the world*—the establishment of justice for the women workers in our public schools." She was so engaged during fully one-fifth of the school year, and during that time she rendered but little, if any, service in supervision of the schools, teachers and scholars in her district, for which part service she drew her salary in full.

"'Mrs. N. Curtis Lenihen admits an absence of twenty-nine days since January 1, 1907, and Miss Isabella Ennis admits eleven and one-half days. Neither deigns to assign any cause for the same. Both are the recipients of ample salaries from the city and the system, against whose interests they persistently agitated for legislation that was notoriously unjust to a large number of teachers.'

"The number of days of absence acknowledged to have been spent in Albany by various members of the teaching and supervising staff exceeds 500," the report continues. "This equals an absence for a single teacher of over two and a half school years. It also appears that upward of 300 of the supervisors, principals and teachers were thus actively engaged." By these absences, in the opinion of the committee, "the service was demoralized."

The average reader of the foregoing report would form the conclusion that there was wholesale neglect of duty by the women teachers. As a matter of fact, it was rarely that more than one teacher was absent from any one school at the same time for the purpose of "going to Albany." It must be remembered that there were then 511 public schools. There were only two occasions when large delegations of women teachers went to Albany. The first of these was the hearing on the McCarren bill before the Senate Cities Committee, and the second, the hearing on the Conklin bill before the Assembly Cities Committee. Most of the schools sent delegates. With only one from each school, it will be seen the total would have been over 500. It must be remembered also that every teacher so absent lost her day's pay, and was expected to supply a substitute.

In my own behalf, I sent the following communication to the Board:

"*To the Board of Education:*

"Sirs—Before adopting any by-law which is the outcome of the report presented last month by your special committee on absences, and approved by your Honorable Body, I respectfully request that *you reconsider said report for the purpose of correcting it.* I am not willing to believe that your Honorable Body would knowingly permit a false or even misleading statement to become a permanent part of your records. While there are several parts of said report which in the interests of justice and fair play are susceptible of alteration, I ask for the correction of only one part, to wit: that which in effect states that my absence of thirty-four days constitutes an absence of one-fifth of a school year. To begin with, *thirty-four* is one-fifth of only 170. During the past school year, the *day schools* were in session 193 days. Therefore, even in the case of a teacher whose duty required her to be present during only those 193 sessions, a statement that an absence of 34 days constitutes an absence of *one-fifth* of a school year, is manifestly incorrect. But in the case of a district superintendent, the incorrectness of such a statement is far greater.

"As district superintendent, I was on duty not only during the 193 days that the day schools were in session, but also during the 120 nights that the night schools were in session, and the 48 days that the Vacation Playgrounds were in session, and the 30 days that the Vacation Schools were in session, and also during the hours between 3.30

P. M. and 5 P. M. on Mondays and Wednesdays and 9 A. M. and 11 A. M. on Saturdays that the City Superintendent has assigned as office hours, and also during the hours of the day and the night that the Local School Board of my districts were in session, and also during the many hours before 9 A. M. and after 3 P. M. when I was in conference at my home and office and the Hall of Education with parents, principals, superintendents and teachers, and also during the many hours on Sundays and holidays which I have devoted to my work as district superintendent. In connection with the above, I respectfully submit that on July 1, 1907, I informed the City Superintendent that I wanted to be absent fifteen days for the purpose of attending the Annual Convention of the National Educational Association at Los Angeles, California. On the ground that I was on duty in connection with the Vacation Schools and Playgrounds, the City Superintendent refused to permit such absence. And although I pointed out that the Vacation Schools would not open until July 8, 1907, and would be in session until late in August, and that therefore I would have time to inspect the schools assigned to me after my return, the desired approval was withheld. Furthermore, during the *eight* summers since my election as district superintendent I have been on duty part of July and August. From the foregoing it is evident that any statement to the effect that an absence of 34 days in one year on the part of a district superintendent constitutes an absence of one-fifth of a year, is manifestly incorrect and unjust.

"I am now serving my fifteenth year in the public schools of the City of New York. Never once have I been absent for trivial or selfish reasons. Personal illness or illness and death in my immediate family, with but one exception that I can recall, have been the only causes of absence on my part prior to January 1, 1907. The records of this department will show that I have never received one cent refund on account of absence. It is true that during some of my absences my salary has been paid in full, but my case in this respect is not unique.

"The report referred to in this communication, also referred to a previous prolonged absence on my part. It is true that from October 6, 1904, to February 19, 1905, I was a hospital patient with a broken arm. During all that time, though submitting to an anesthetic thirty-two times, and suffering almost constant and agonizing pain, I was in daily touch with my office and the affairs in my twenty-one schools. Principals, teachers and parents came to the hospital to confer with me. Miss de Buck or some other clerk brought me the mail and other matter from my office. I dictated letters and reports and signed thousands of requisitions, reports, and other official documents. The Committee on Supplies, learning of the pain and difficulty under which I was laboring, very kindly passed a resolution permitting my stamped signature to take the place of my personal signature on requisitions. Therefore, reference to this absence, in the report of Mr. Jonas's Committee, seems ungracious, if not unfair.

"In conclusion, I pray your Honorable Body to reconsider the report.

"Very respectfully yours,

"GRACE C. STRACHAN."

The latest action of the Board in connection with our going to Albany is told thus by the *Herald* of April 29, 1909:

"The question came up as to whether permission should be granted to Miss Grace Strachan, district superintendent, and seven women teachers to be absent from school and go to Albany to hear the decision of the Legislature in regard to the Teachers' Equal Pay Bill the latter part of the week.

"Abraham Stern, chairman of the Committee on Elementary Schools, said:

"'The teachers want to go to Albany to buttonhole the members of the Legislature and this Board should not allow any lobbying by school teachers.'

"Joseph E. Cosgrove defended the women. 'The trouble with this Board is that more sentiment is needed.

What is eight teachers out of 16,000? I think the Board shows narrow mindedness if it denies their request. And I think it highly improper to characterize these women teachers as "lobbyists" and to say that they want to go to Albany to "buttonhole" members of the Legislature.'

"Thomas J. Higgins, chairman of the Committee on the Care of Buildings, said there has been too much sentiment shown by the Board to the teachers and that the request should not be granted. Alrick H. Man declared the teachers who absent themselves to go to Albany should be fined, and George Freifeld said:

"'The attitude of the women teachers is a sordid striving after more money.'

"Nicholas J. Barrett, chairman of the Committee on Supplies, said that no courtesy could be shown to Miss Strachan, 'who, though she is the highest salaried district superintendent, does not seem to have much to do, but can go to Albany while the other district superintendents are kept busy all of the time.'"

The following day, the Gledhill-Foley bill passed the Assembly with a vote of 126 to 14, and during the discussion Charles F. Murphy, though voting "No," said:

"I sympathize with this great body of our public servants who are forbid to present to our committees in this House their views upon this bill. They should have the same rights which are accorded to the corporation of the City of New York, the Public Service Commission, the railroad interests, the telephone interests, the Charter Revision Commission and all other interests, whether public or private.

"I desire to take off my hat and pay my respects to that band of masterly women who have for the past few years been fighting the battle which they consider just and right. The women teaching the lower grades are working for woefully insufficient compensation, and they are leading clean and wholesome lives under adverse circumstances. I know many of them who are working for six or seven hundred dollars a year and endeavoring to repay a serious indebtedness incurred in securing their education.

"The chivalric spirit of man cannot but be inspired by the plucky battle which is being waged. I have not opposed these bills for political effect, and I deprecate the cheap politics of candidates for office who will arrange a plant or mill in public meetings so that an issue may be raised for campaign purposes against women who have no forum in which they may make an effective defense of their principle."

He was frequently applauded.

On November 12, 1908, I sent the following letter to the *Eagle,* after a personal interview with Hon. St. Clair McKelway, editor, about the editorial and news article referred to in my letter, and after securing a promise from him that my reply would be given the same prominence as the articles to which it referred. The promise was not kept, though the letter was published:

"To the Editor of the Brooklyn *Eagle:*

"Many of the women teachers who read your recent editorial on 'Should Keep Out of Politics' and the news article entitled 'Women Teachers' Aid Hoodoo to Candidates' ask that you show your good will toward all your readers by setting before them in unprejudiced statements both sides of the argument. And they ask particularly now that you publish this letter in full and give it as conspicuous position as was accorded the articles above referred to.

"These articles stated that Senator Travis received in the recent election a plurality of 4,015 votes, as compared with 1,636 two years ago, and implied that this increase is due solely to the opposition of the women teachers.

"In this connection we call attention to the fact that two years ago Chanler, as Democratic candidate for lieutenant-governor, carried Kings County by over 25,000, while this year Taft, as Republican candidate for President, carried it by 23,085. How does the *Eagle* explain the fact that Senator Travis, a Republican, ran 2,564 behind Taft in his own district?

"The *Eagle* of November 4 said, 'Harman (Travis'

opponent) made a remarkable run. Harman ran ahead of Bryan 2,564.'

"The *Standard-Union* (Rep.) of same date gave Harman 2,692 more than Bryan. Harman had declared himself in favor of the women teachers.

"From Senator Travis, who opposed the women teachears, let us turn and consider the case of Assemblyman Conklin (Rep.), who introduced the Equal Pay Bill in the Assembly both in 1906 and 1907. The *Globe* says: 'This year the women made a stronger fight than ever before in favor of Conklin.' He received last year a plurality of 334. This year he was re-elected by 1,719—five times his plurality of 1906.

"What is the conclusion here? Did the aid of the women teachers prove a hoodoo to Mr. Conklin? He again leads all the local candidates in his district, as he did last year.

"The case of still another friend of women teachers is that of Senator White—the father of the 'White' Equal Pay Bill. As a candidate for lieutenant-governor on the Republican ticket he carried Brooklyn by 4,777, although Chanler as candidate for governor on the Democratic ticket carried this borough by 4,368—a difference of 9,145 in favor of Senator White.

"We hold that it would be just as reasonable to claim that Senator's White's lead was due to the assistance of the women teachers as to claim that the lead of Senator Travis was due to the opposition of the women teachers. The *Globe* says: 'No doubt the active support of the women was a great help to him' (Senator White).

"The *Eagle's* figures also show that though Lee, Murphy and Colne, all opponents of the women teachers' bill, have increased pluralities this year, they ran behind the head of their ticket by 945, 812, and 963, respectively. Although Taft carried Kings County by 23,085, Green's (Rep.) plurality dropped from 2,287 in 1906; Chanler (Dem.) carrying Brooklyn by about 25,000, to 1,071 in 1907 and 927 in 1908. He ran 670 behind Taft. DeGroot (Rep.), also an opponent of the women teachers, ran 1,071 behind the head of his ticket. These figures are significant when it is considered that other Republicans, who did not antagonize the women teachers, ran well along with their tickets—Weber and Surpless, for instance, running only 57 and 71, respectively, behind Taft.

"Another Assemblyman, George V. Sheridan (Dem.), Bronx, who has been conspicuous as an opponent of the women teachers, suffered a decrease in his plurality from 1,122 in 1907 to 786 in 1908, though his Republican opponent had come out openly in favor of the women teachers."

Sheridan was defeated in 1909.—G. C. S.

Mr. Brady's letter on same editorial is interesting:

"To the Editor of the Brooklyn *Eagle:*

"As an old reader of your valuable paper and one of the many thankful for the stand you took for Taft and Hughes, I was somewhat surprised to read your editorial in last evening's edition, under the heading, 'Should Keep Out of Politics.' You give several sets of figures, showing the probable effect of the school teachers' opposition, which, on examination, prove exceedingly misleading and show an erroneous conclusion.

"If your statement that 'the opposition of the Interborough Teachers' Association will soon equal in value the indorsement of one of the minor parties' is true, how do you account for the showing of candidates for re-election in whose Assembly districts no organized effort was made at all by the teachers? For instance, Charles G. Weber, in the Fifth Assembly District (who, by the way, voted for the teachers' bill), ran behind Mr. Taft, the proper candidate to use as a standard for comparison, only 57 votes, and Thomas J. Surpless, in the Sixth Assembly District (who voted against the teachers' bill), ran but 71 behind Mr. Taft. Senator Travis, in his district, ran 1,567 behind Mr. Taft, and Messrs. Lee, DeGroot, Colne, Murphy and Green ran, respectively, 945, 1,071, 963, 812 and 670 behind Taft.

"From the foregoing comparative figures Messrs.

Weber and Surpless, with no opposition from the teachers, made a much better showing than any of the other candidates whom you mention as being opposed by the teachers; so that, on your own basis of computation, the teachers' opposition must be deemed effective. . . .

"HARRY J. BRADY.

"426 De Kalb Avenue, November 7, 1908."

Two other correspondents who resent suggestion that women instructors attend to their knitting:

"To the Editor of the Brooklyn *Eagle:*

"On November 6, in an editorial supporting the thesis that women teachers should keep out of politics, you named a number of instances in which local candidates, opposed by the women, were elected by increased pluralities, and you somewhat plainly implied that such increases showed added strength as a result of the teachers' opposition.

"Brooklynites are proud of the willingness with which the *Eagle* is accustomed to present both sides of a question. I am relying on that willingness in asking you to give publicity to one or two facts which seemed to have been overlooked by the writer of the article referred to.

"A local candidate's strength is probably shown quite as clearly by the comparison which his plurality bears to that of the head of his ticket as it is by a comparison of his plurality at one election with that at another. In the Sixth Senate District, according to the revised city vote published on November 4, Mr. Taft received a plurality of 6,579, as against Mr. Travis' plurality of 4,015. In the same district, Mr. Harman ran 1,300 votes ahead of Mr. Bryan. In the Eighteenth Assembly District, Mr. Taft's plurality was 5,304, Mr. Lee's 3,759. Here Mr. McGann ran 425 votes ahead of Mr. Bryan. In the Fourth Assembly District in Queens, Mr. Taft had a plurality of 2,625; Mr. DeGroot of 1,554, while Mr. Robinson ran 500 votes ahead of Mr. Bryan.

"Though the Taft 'landslide' could not keep the pluralities of the local Republican candidates in question up to those of the head of their ticket, it would hardly be unfair to assume that it had somewhat more to do with their increased pluralities than had the opposition of the women teachers. It would hardly be unfair to believe that one of the factors which helped these gentlemen's opponents to run ahead of their tickets was the support of the women.

"Whether the teachers' recent political activity was wise or otherwise, justice would seem to demand a consideration of all the facts of the case in an impartial discussion of its bearing on election issues. Justice might even suggest a reference to the fact that such activity was quite undoubtedly a factor in the success of the candidates for whom it was most employed. I refer, of course, to Mr. Conklin of the Twenty-first Assembly District, Manhattan, and to the present Lieutenant-Governor-elect, Horace White.

"A Friend of the Women Teachers.

"Brooklyn, Nov. 7, 1908."

Anent the same election, the New York *Globe* said:

"It is in the minor contests that the influence of the teachers is more likely to be felt. The men teachers presented united, determined and ceaseless opposition to the re-election of Assemblyman Conklin. Last year he received a plurality of only 400. This year the women made a stronger fight than ever before in support of Conklin, and he was re-elected by over four times this plurality, or 1,719. In the same district White received a plurality of 1,765, and Hughes only 1,585.

"As White and Conklin were the particular objects of attack of the men who were repeatedly to 'kill White and bury Conklin,' the women teachers feel that they have won a great victory in the election of two of the chief advocates of 'Equal Pay.'

"John Harman, who was supported by the women, 'made a remarkable run,' according to the Brooklyn *Eagle,* which adds that 'the number of Republican ballots split in favor of Harman varied from 10 to 30 in the different election districts.'

"There are two facts, however, which confuse calculations in this district. The men teachers also favored Hughes and opposed White, but Hughes received only 2,510 plurality, while White got 3,565."

After the election of 1907, the *Eagle* printed an article along the same lines. I wrote to the men whom they described as having suffered on account of their allegiance to the women teachers. Following is a characteristic reply:

"Albany, April 10, 1908.

"*My Dear Miss Strachan:*

"Replying to your letter in regard to the statement recently published that my action in connection with my vote on the Equal Pay bill had cost me a thousand votes or more, I do not hesitate to say that the statement is absolutely false. The reduction in vote was due entirely to local conditions. The first year I ran I had the endorsement of the Independence League and my name was on two tickets. This year the Independence League endorsed my opponent and his name was on two tickets. The number of votes influenced for or against me by the male teachers . . . amounts to zero.

"Yours sincerely,

"JAMES J. HOEY."

It had been clear throughout that the animus of all those who attacked the women teachers for political activity in this gubernatorial campaign was the fact that they believed the women teachers were working against Governor Hughes. Proof of this is shown by the fact that not one reference was made by them to the pernicious activity of the men teachers. I use the word "pernicious" deliberately, because I believe their literature distributed during this same period, copies of which appear below, justifies its use.

"MEN TEACHERS' AND PRINCIPALS' ASSOCIATION OF THE CITY OF NEW YORK.

"*To all Delegates,*

"Gentlemen:

"Lest there be some man in your school who is not apprised of the exact situation, we ask that you circulate this notice among all men in your school, including the Principal.

"Governor Hughes vetoed the 'Equal Pay' Bill. Your association stands pledged to support him to a man in his race for the Governorship. You certainly must all know that but for his courageous veto the bill would have become a law, and every young man in the system would have suffered a decrease in his maximum; and all men have lost forever any possibility of increase.

"The least you can do is to

"VOTE for HUGHES

irrespective of party affiliation.

"Urge this upon all your friends now and on Election Day. You men can do a lot if you try!

"Senator White, who fathered the 'Equal Pay' Bill in the Senate, is running for Lieutenant-Governor on the Republican ticket.

"VOTE AGAINST WHITE."

The following appeared in the Brooklyn *Eagle,* October 28, 1908:

"As you probably know, the association is making its crucial fight against Conklin in the Twenty-first Assembly District. We have laid our plans carefully and now need men, good men, to aid in a whirlwind campaign. Your school has always ranked as one which I do not hesitate to count on. We need every man in your school for every afternoon and evening, beginning Monday evening, the 26th, only until election. There is quiet, dignified work for each, according to his tastes.

"It is vitally important to beat this man. To those inclined to hesitate let me say that it is better to be vigorously aggressive now and by beating Conklin, end it all, than to let this dissension drag along in the schools, ruining the efficiency of the service, sapping the energies of the teachers and dragging the schools back into politics and all that that entails.

"Let us be men, courageous and far-seeing, believing that in the end all will see that we have served the schools more than ourselves in this fight.

"Will you to-day urge upon your men ready response to this call. I want every available man to meet me at the Shenandoah Club, 2305 Seventh Avenue, New York, on Monday evening. If they cannot come Monday evening, then at their first opportunity. I shall be there continually until election. Take Subway to One Hundred and Thirty-fifth Street; walk west to Seventh Avenue and around the corner. Send me, in the enclosed envelope, a list of the men in your school who will come forward, the days and evenings they can give and their residences.

"We are all working very hard for the interests of all. Will you help us?"

Two copies of a paper called "The New York School Master" were distributed. The matter they contained appears below:

"THE NEW YORK SCHOOL MASTER
More culture and more men in the schools.

---

Vol. I  Brooklyn, N. Y., October 20, 1908.  No. 3.

---

VOTE FOR HUGHES!

Republican Candidate for Governor

Because:—

Governor Hughes saved every young man $525 on his maximum salary by his veto of the White ("Equal Pay") Bill.

Governor Hughes saved every man his chance of ultimate increase in salary. Had the "Equal Pay" Bill become a law, the necessity of raising ten women's salary to every man's increased, would have forever precluded the possibility of any increase.

Governor Hughes will lose a few votes because he vetoed the White Bill. WE MEN should respect his manly stand for what he considered his duty, and irrespective of party affiliation, cast our votes for Hughes. An American Executive should be encouraged to fearlessly perform his duty, irrespective of the interests he may injure.

It is reported that Mr. Chanler if elected Governor, will favor an "Equal Pay" Bill. Can YOU support your FAMILY on a woman's salary.

VOTE FOR DEGROOT.

Candidate for Assembly in Queens.

His action, last session, as a member of The Assembly's Cities' Committee, AGAINST the "Equal Pay" Bill, has marked him for defeat by the Interboroughites (to say women teachers would be too comprehensive).

Page 2.

VOTE AND WORK AGAINST CONKLIN, Republican candidate for Assembly in the 21st Assembly District.

BECAUSE:—

He has insulted every MAN in the schools, in public debate and in private conversation.

He introduced The "Equal Pay" Bill in the Assembly, which would have lowered every young man's maximum by $525; and which would have forever prevented any man's schedule being increased.

He believes that men should not be employed as teachers. He thinks them out of place in the schools—elementary especially.

A vigorous campaign is being waged against this man. If you live in his district or are willing to work against him, send your name to Austin H. Evans, 44 West 128th St., Manhattan.

VOTE AGAINST WHITE—Republican candidate for Lieutenant-Governor.

Because,

He is a scheming politician of the worst order, entirely antagonistic to every reform Governor Hughes has attempted to inaugurate.

He put through the Senate the White ("Equal Pay") Bill, which swept away every safeguard provided by The Davis Law, thereby willfully seeking to throw the schools back into politics.

VOTE FOR TRAVIS.

He made a cogent argument in the Senate against Miss Strachan's unjust bill. Was, in consequence, upbraided by her in the press. On Thursday she ordered her association to defeat him.

Page 3.

Published Monthly by
The Association of Men Teachers
and Principals of the City of
New York.
Under the direction of the
Press Committee.
BERNARD CRONSON, Ex-Officio.

| | |
|---|---|
| James J. Sheppard | John L. Hulshof |
| Charles O. Dewey | Roy L. Richardson |
| Esle F. Randolph | Chas. H. Davis |
| Edgar S. Shumway | F. E. Odell |
| John Liebermann | D. D. Wallstein |
| Frederick H. Paine | Hadley C. Case |

R. P. Ellis, Chairman,
E. 49th St., Mill Lane, Brooklyn.
Wm. E. Barhite, Secretary.
Address all communications to the Chairman.

EDITOR'S NOTE:—

Numerous letters have been received by the Editor, requesting that a list of Assemblymen and Senators who voted for the "Equal Pay" Bill be published. Inasmuch as the sentiment in favor of "equal pay" is waning greatly, the Editor suggests that each man visit his Assemblyman and Senator, and their opponents if possible, and ascertain how they intend to stand this year. Many changes will be found.

Here is a task for every man in the system. As soon as a candidate has declared himself for or against us, we shall be very glad to be apprised immediately of the fact, and due publicity will be given. *The Schoolmaster* will be issued weekly during the campaign. If you do not get your copy, write us at once.

Our Civic Duties.

Schoolmen should take an interest in civic affairs. We are failing in our duty as representative citizens in the community, if we do not evince the same intelligent interest and participation in the administration of our representative form of government that we seek to impress upon coming generations as its inalienable heritage and duty.

This does not mean that we are to become politicians or ward heelers. It does mean, however, that you should know your representatives in the Assembly, the Senate and in Congress, and that they should know you, as a teacher living in their district, and as a man who will give their actions the close scrutiny they deserve.

Therefore, make it your business, whatever your party affiliations, to meet your present Assemblyman and Senator. They can always be found at their political clubs over the week-end. Introduce yourself—give them your card. And even if you do not discuss questions with them, give them occasion to observe that you are about and exercising your civic rights."

Other literature sent out by the male teachers is equally illuminating.

For example:

"DEPARTMENT OF EDUCATION
THE CITY OF NEW YORK

"THE STUYVESANT HIGH SCHOOL
"226 East 23d Street

"FRANK ROLLINS, *Principal.*

"408 West 150th Street, N. Y. City.
"October 28, 1907.

"*Dear Sir:*

"Assemblyman Conklin of the 21st Assembly District must be defeated or badly scared this fall by men teachers. Some are working day and night to do so. Your interest last spring encourages us to ask you to help now. Please visit evenings, Saturday and Sunday afternoons—before election, the Republican voters whose names and addresses are on the inclosed list. The names on the back (cross marked) are not in your section. Names of known supporters of Felix are crossed off. You can paste this on stiff paper for more convenient use. If you meet with other teachers, get them to help. If you can't visit all voters—the most effective influence—or even if you can, it would be well to leave a statement of points for each voter. Some lines of attack:

"1. Property holders and rent payers don't want a man who joined with McCarren and White and trying, through a reckless political bill, to add from 10 to 13 millions to the city budget.

"2. Conklin, with Brough of the 19th, alone among Republican Assemblymen from Manhattan, refused to support the Mayor's veto of the White Bill and to uphold home rule last spring.

"3. To judge from this record, a vote for Conklin is not supporting Hughes.

"4. A 30-year-old Assemblyman has more 'nerve' than wisdom, to insult the Board of Education as he did in several speeches, and is unfair to cast ridicule, for political advantage, upon a few men teachers who are facing 500 women teachers in an Assembly hearing.

"5. Felix, the Democratic candidate, is a school teacher. As a Hebrew, he is influential and a member of the synagogue. These points for teachers and Hebrews.

"6. If you can't meet an objection to Tammany, at least dissuade from voting for Conklin. Scheppler, the Ind. League Candidate, is a leader in the printers' union and a strong man—considerations attractive to labor men.

"Remember, even if you do not change many votes in the strong Republican section in which you will work, much will be gained for our cause, if you can get a number of Republicans to express to Conklin their disapproval of his course last spring.

"Don't fail us. We have a great chance this fall to show that we are not a negligible political factor.

"Yours respectfully,

(Signed) "AMBROSE CORT—Capt. 19th Sen. Dist."

Mr. Conklin ran ahead of his ticket by over 300.

"On two different occasions within the space of one week, the association made attempts to have a number of men teachers meet the candidate for Assembly in the 21st Assembly District, who is favorably disposed to us.

"Both attempts were failures. Impression made upon the candidate was not one to inspire political respect for the men teachers.

"Another meeting is called for next Monday, October 19th, at 4 P. M. at Y. M. C. A., 5 West 125th Street.

"It is important for the success of the coming campaign of your association that you attend, just to show that you are once in a while awake to your interests, and that you can spare an hour to attend to them yourself, instead of by proxies who are themselves absent from the meetings.

"Come and bring as many friends as possible.

"Sincerely,

"BERNARD CRONSON.

"Monday, Oct. 19, 4 P. M., Y. M. C. A., 5 West 125th St."

APPEALS FOR MONEY.

"We, the undersigned, teachers of P. S. No. ...., Brooklyn, hereby agree to contribute one dollar each per month for the months of February, March and April, 1908, for the purpose of an educational campaign, the same to be applied to dues and assessments in the Association of Men Teachers and Principals of the City of New York.

| "Name. | Feb'y | March | April |
|---|---|---|---|
| ........................ | ....... | ......... | ...... |

"May 11, 1907.

"The Association of Men Teachers and Principals of the City of New York

"Dr. WM. L. ETTINGEN, *Pres.*

"To the Delegate:

"The White Bill has been vetoed by the Mayor. This means:

"*That* an attempt will be made to have the Bill passed over His Honor's veto.

"*That* a committee from our Association must proceed at once to Albany and stay there for an indefinite number of days.

"*That* the committee will incur expenses which the Association must meet.

"*That* the Association has no endowment fund and no money outside of what it receives from the men teachers and principals.

"*Conclusion:*

"Please collect from all who have not yet paid their membership dues and assessments; *then fill out the blank sent to* you several days ago, and send money and blanks to

"BERNARD CRONSON,
"129 W. 136 St. Man.

"* A number of schools have already paid up in full and sent in blanks. A *printed list of members, the amounts paid by each and membership cards will be sent at the earliest opportunity.*"

"Association of Men Teachers and Principals of the City of New York

"Brooklyn, October 26, 1908.

"To the Delegates and Men:

"*Gentlemen:* It is very important that the dues be forthcoming at this time. Will you kindly collect on receipt hereof and transmit your report on the enclosed blank to the Treasurer, Dr. David H. Holmes, in the enclosed envelope. He will issue you a receipt.

"If it is not convenient to pay all just at this time collect all you can and give date of payment of balance in the column provided on the blank.

"We are in the midst of a most aggressive campaign and need these funds. To those few who may not favor aggressiveness, say that it is better to end this dissension now, once for all, than to allow it to drag along sapping the energies of teachers, perpeutating lack of harmony and ruining the efficiency of the service.

"Let all men support their organization in this fight. A decisive victory means the end of 'equal pay.' Fear not to ACT, trusting that in the end all shall see that we have labored more for the good of the system than for ourselves.

"Faithfully yours,

"BERNARD CRONSON,

"President.

"DAVID H. HOLMES,

"Treasurer.

"*Dues,* $2.

"R. P. ELLIS,

"Chairman Press Committee."

"Principals' Association of the City of New York.

"April 21, 1910.

"To the Men Principals of New York City.

"*Gentlemen:* At the last meeting of the Principals' Association, the members present voted that each male principal of the city be requested to contribute five dollars to a fund for advancing the interests of the schools.

"This fund is not to be used in defraying the routine expenses of the association, but it is intended to satisfy a special and very important claim upon the resources of every man in the schools.

"Please send your contribution to Mr. J. J. Driscoll, P. S. No. 16, Richmond.

"Yours very truly,

"RUFUS A. VANCE,
President.

"CHARLES B. JAMESON,
"Cor. Secretary."

Editorial, Richmond Hill *Record*, Saturday, October 31, 1908:

"DEGROOT AND THE TEACHERS.

"William A. DeGroot's reply to attacks upon his conduct as a legislator will be found in another column. In the course of the week the *Record* has received many letters from its friends among the male school teachers asking that this reply be published.

"Really, the *Record* must admit that it does not know what, at present, is Mr. DeGroot's attitude toward the equal pay bill, so called. The *Record* is not even sure that the desire of the male teachers to have Mr. DeGroot's reply published indicates that they regard his candidacy favorably.

"But, taking it for granted that the male teachers believe the publication of Mr. DeGroot's reply will help and not hurt his candidacy, their interest in the matter would seem to show that Mr. DeGroot has made his peace with those of the school teachers who have votes, and that he is, now, opposed to the so-called equal pay bill.

"Into the merits of that bill the *Record* will not enter. Like all similar bills, it had good and bad features.

"Some time ago an organization of school teachers—the kind that have votes—was formed to bend Mr. DeGroot's stubborn will to theirs. Apparently he bent before he broke.

"Some time ago the organization referred to was

HON. HORACE WHITE,
FATHER OF "WHITE" "EQUAL PAY" BILLS OF 1907 AND 1908.
LIEUTENANT-GOVERNOR OF NEW YORK, 1909 AND 1910.

formed. It had all sorts of officers and committees. The printing was done in this office. The path of the weekly newspaper is not bestrewn with roses, and even publishers must eat sometimes. It costs money to print long letters, but the *Record* prints Mr. DeGroot's willingly. One of the members of the teachers' organization who did not communicate with this office was the treasurer. We would be pleased to have him do so.

" There's a reason."

Richmond Hill *Record,* October 3, 1908:

" MALE TEACHERS ARE ANGRY.

*" So Is the Record, with Much Greater Reason.*

" Conspiracy, did you say? Oh, worse! Simply awful! A dozen letters have been received at the *Record* office during the week, of which the following is a fair sample. Strange as it may seem, all are from male school teachers, and each has some grievance as a pretext for the letter and each winds up with the same comment on Mr. DeGroot in almost exactly the same words. Some remarked, ' Not for publication,' so the names of the writers will not be given.

" Last year was organized the Male Teachers' Association and had ' captains ' in every district. The *Record* did some printing for the association, and even at this late date would not object to something other than far-fetched ' grievances.'

" Last year DeGroot was not quite sure about his vote on the equal pay bill for school teachers. This year Robinson, the Democratic candidate, has declared himself in favor of the women. Do the letters to the *Record* indicate that DeGroot has made promises to the men?

" As for the charges of the unfairness of the *Record,* they are twaddle. The columns of this paper are always open to both sides on any question. This week Mr. DeGroot takes up more than his share of space, all of which was arranged for before these indignant school teachers got their heads together.

"Here is the complaint:

"'Editor Richmond Hill *Record*.

"'Dear Sir: About a year ago I was disgusted with your estimate of local real estate values—encouraging readers to buy, saying that property would soon be worth double its then value, etc. Any intelligent man cognizant to the least degree of the real estate situation must have known that such an estimate was unwarranted. You have treated other matters in a way equally biased, it seems to me. Yet a newspaper is supposed to present all subjects to its readers, without prejudice or bias.

"'Recently you have criticised Mr. DeGroot. Have you been fair to him? Have you enumerated all that he has done for Queens? In the matter of his Commissioner of Records bill, and the Hammitt letter, have you stated his side of the case or requested him to do so? If not, why not?

"'W. E. HENDRIE.

"'Lester Ave., Richmond Hill.'

"As proof that there is a 'nigger' somewhere, it is only necessary to state that the criticism of Mr. DeGroot did not in any way refer to the Equal Pay bill, and yet every letter received by the *Record* comes from a male teacher."

Contrast the circular sent out by the women teachers:

"NOTICE.

"Let us be noted for our appreciation and gratitude.

"Mr. Robert S. Conklin, Republican, was our standard-bearer in the Assembly. He is seeking re-election in the 21st Assembly District, Manhattan, being the territory embraced in the following:

"Beginning at the foot of West 133d street, to Amsterdam avenue, to West 130th street, to Convent avenue, to Morningside avenue E, to West 123d street, to Eighth avenue, to West 127th street, to Fifth avenue, to West 135th street, to Lenox avenue, to West 136th street, to Seventh avenue, to West 141st street, to North River.

"Mr. John V. Sheridan, Democrat, renominated in the 35th Assembly District, New York, and Mr. Warren I. Lee, Republican, renominated in the 18th Assembly District, Kings, are the only Assemblymen from the City of New York in the last Assembly, who are seeking re-election, who did not vote for our bill either before or after the Mayor's veto.

"INTERBOROUGH ASSOCIATION OF SCHOOL TEACHERS.

"N. B.—All other Assemblymen who have been renominated voted for our bill."

As evidence that our course in taking an interest in politics was not disapproved by all, I print with the writer's permission, the following from a letter written me by Hon. Clarence R. Freeman, Alderman Thirty-first District, New York.

Extract from letter of October, 1907:

"In my opinion, the teachers can do a very great deal in forwarding their legislation, if they find out what districts are the so-called close districts, and in such sections ask the candidates on either side for an expression of opinion upon 'Equal Pay' platform, and whether they would be willing to support that platform, if elected. By way of convincing candidates that it is worth while to answer such questions, you might tabulate the names and addresses and total number of women teachers and sympathizers residing within a given district.

"Personal letters written by the teachers to their friends asking for the support of some special candidate, are very effective. Also, the enlistment of the active aid of the male relatives of all such teachers. From experience, I can say that a handful of workers, if determined, can make 300 or 400 votes for any reputable candidate."

New York *Globe,* October 31, 1909.

*School Editor of the Globe:*

"Sir: Will you kindly inform me where I can get a ballot to conform to the wishes of 'Equal Pay for Equal Work?' I want to vote for those who favor the idea and scratch those who do not. I also protest against the action of the Board of Education in attempting to deprive their teachers of the rights of citizens.

"Manhattan, Oct. 29. 'A CITIZEN."

("You could probably secure the information by addressing the president of the Women Teachers' Association, Miss Grace C. Strachan, Brooklyn. You reside in Assemblyman Conklin's district. He introduced the women teachers' bill. Governor Hughes vetoed it. Messrs. Chanler, Whalen, Hauser and all the present state officers, except Governor Hughes, gave assistance to the women during their campaign. Senator White, the Republican candidate for lieutenant-governor is the author of the 'White Equal Pay' bill vetoed by Governor Hughes. The women are not allied with any party, but are supporting those persons who aided them in their campaign or who favor the 'equal pay' principle."—School Editor.)

NEW YORK, October 9, 1907.

"*Dear Madam:*

"The part that I took during the last session of the Legislature in promoting the interests of the New York City school teachers is no doubt still fresh in your mind. At all times I had charge of the Equalization Bill, and twice succeeded in passing it in the Assembly. In addition, I frequently acted as advisory counsel to the Interborough Association in its campaign.

"I have been renominated for Member of Assembly by the Republican organization of this 21st Assembly District, and I am writing to ask your support, and through you that of your friends and relatives. As this is what is sometimes described as an 'off' year, many citizens will not register and vote unless urged to do so. I am depending upon you to do all you can to bring about my re-election. We need every vote we can get. If citizens do not register they cannot vote. Ask them to register and vote. Last day of registration is Monday, October 14, 1907.

"Very truly yours,

"ROBERT S. CONKLIN,

"Member of Assembly,

"21st Assembly District."

Department of Latin,
The Morris High School,
166th Street and Boston Road.

May 1, 1907.

"*Assemblyman Conklin,*

"Dear Sir:—I am writing you again with reference to the White Bill for which you voted for reasons best known to yourself. The enclosed clipping voices the sentiments of sane and fair-minded citizens. Furthermore, the male teachers in your district have organized and are about to pledge their support to the men who favor their interests in this bit of legislation. I am captain of the High School division of about thirty men, who represent five times as many votes. There is hardly a man among us who is not a member of some fraternal order or organization in which he can influence votes. It might pay you to bear this in mind when the bill comes to you after the mayor's veto—if such a joke bill ever does come back.

"Very truly,

"AUSTIN HALL EVANS."

"44 W. 128.

"May 3, 1907.

"*Mr. Austin H. Evans, Esq.,*

"44 *West* 128*th St.:*

"I have before me your letters of April 29th and May 1st, respectively. In courtesy I should answer the former, the discourtesy of the latter requires that it should receive some attention. Permit me to suggest that if you desire to influence members of the legislature you are adopting extremely injudicious methods in attempting to do so.

"It is not unusual to find among people of a low order of intelligence and morality a conception of public officials as men so lacking in decency and courage as to be swayed in the discharge of duty by threats as to their political welfare.

"We have, however, a right to expect a more wholesome attitude to prevail among people of education and culture to which class your position and language would seem to indicate that you belong. And in the most friendly spirit, I suggest that before writing any other letters of like character to other legislators, you and your associates carefully read Sections 46, 67 and 127 of the *Penal Code.*

"In the matter in which you are interested as in all other matters that have come before the legislature, I have acted according to my best judgment and conscientiously in the interests of the public at large rather than in the interests of any particular class. With all due respect to your political power, I shall continue to act according to my best judgment and ask no support from those who would require anything else of me.

"We have carefully considered this school question and given a most respectful hearing to the male teachers. We have been unable to see, from any argument presented, wherein the men's present financial position would in any way be affected.

"I think on sober reflection that you will come to realize that there has been a rather unwise show of temper in the matter.

"Just what will be done in the event of a veto by the mayor, I am not now prepared to say. But you can rest assured that threats will have a tendency to facilitate the bill's passage over the mayor's veto rather than to retard it. It will have to be considered in a somewhat different light than on its original passage, but in the interests of wholesome civil spirit, I assure you that whatever action is taken, will be taken irrespective of its vote getting or vote losing influences.

"Very truly yours,

(Signed) "ROBERT S. CONKLIN."

"April 3, 1908.

"MISS GRACE C. STRACHAN,
"293 Henry St.,
"Brooklyn, N. Y.

"*My dear Miss Strachan:*

"I regret to inform you that at the last session of the Cities Committee last night I could not secure the report of the Teachers' Bill. We were in session until half-past one o'clock. I do not think it will be in violation of our pledge to say nothing of proceedings in executive session for me to tell you that you have a very strong ally in Mr. Smith; he has made a very vigorous fight for the bill and it has at times looked as if we would carry the proposition. I have all along thought that the Committee would release this bill towards the end of the session; it now appears that I was mistaken. If there had been a full attendance of the house this morning I should probably have moved to discharge the Committee from further consideration of the bill because this was the last day on which that could be done. There were not over seventy (70) members present in the house, however. It may possibly be that the Rules Committee will report the measure. The Rules Committee will be guided of course by the attitude of the Speaker. Senator White, if he takes a vigorous stand on this proposition, has powerful influence in this branch of the Legislature. He may be able to get it out. The only other member of the Rules Committee besides the speaker on whom you can probably make any impression is Mr. Merritt.

"Again expressing my regret and disappointment at my inability to bring about results satisfactory to yourself, I remain,

"Very truly yours,
(Signed) "ROBERT S. CONKLIN."

"Oct. 10, 1908.

"*Dear Miss Strachan:*

"In response to a notice sent out by A. H. Evans, the Vice-President of the men teachers of Manhattan, a meeting was held yesterday afternoon at the Harlem Y. M. C. A. It was well attended by these gentlemen. The news I get is to the effect that they are much better equipped with funds this year than they were last, and that they are to work with better organization than they have heretofore. It was stated at the meeting that I was to be the particular object of attack in order that an example might be set to other evil-doers. I believe that they have some scheme for trying to operate in the negro districts, of which we have several.

"I do not think, in view of the fact that this is a national election, that any of the local candidates will be in any danger if the district goes for the national ticket. For the present I simply wish to call the proceedings at this meeting to your attention in order that you may consider them in your deliberations.

"Very respectfully yours,
(Signed) "ROBERT S. CONKLIN."

"New York, Oct. 29, 1907.

"*My Dear Miss Strachan:*

"As one of the registered voters of the —— district. I received the circular sent out by the Interborough Teachers and am very much pleased with the same. The men teachers have, I understand, had a meeting which was attended by invitation by my opponent, —— —— ——, whose card I enclose. They are working openly against me now and are preparing, I understand, to send out matter in opposition to me this week.

"Assemblyman —— had a good idea. He sent to each teacher in his district a list of the voters in the house in which she lived, and asked her to see everyone of them. If it had occurred to me, I should have had the circular you sent the teachers make the same suggestion and enclosed a list of voters from the City Record. However the matter may turn out, I want to thank you for the way in which you have 'made good" in my behalf.

"Very truly yours,
"—— —— ——."

Extract from letter of Oct. 2, 1907:

"As you are aware, I am again a candidate for the Assembly and hope to be re-nominated on Friday. My District is the * * *

"I intend writing to every teacher living in that neighborhood and I hope that you and your friends will be able to assist me in not only getting out the registered vote, but by the votes of your friends. I shall be very glad to have a letter from you that I could use to the teachers of my district.

"Yours sincerely,

"—— ——."

In the campaign of 1909, we sent the following letter to each Alderman, Member of Assembly, and any candidate for city office which involves membership in the Board of Estimate and Apportionment:

Brooklyn, October 11, 1909.

To —— —— ——,

Candidate for ——.

*Dear Sir:*

The Interborough Association of Women Teachers is an organization whose membership comprises more than twelve thousand women in the public schools of the City of New York.

Since April, 1906, this Association has been striving to secure such amendment of the salary schedules under which the teachers are paid, as will abolish the discriminations against women.

The Department of Education is the only city department which is excepted from the provisions of the Civil Service Law.

*In no other department does the salary of a position vary with the sex of the incumbent.*

This Association is naturally and properly desirous of knowing your attitude on this matter, and begs a reply to the following question:

*Do you believe that all city employees whose appoint-*

*ment is made from an eligible list, should be paid according to the position held, without regard to the sex of the employee?*

Should you so desire, a committee representing our Association will be pleased to call upon you at your convenience, outside of school hours.

Very respectfully,

ISABEL A. ENNIS, Secretary.

Please send reply to:
MISS GRACE C. STRACHAN,
1308 Pacific Street,
Brooklyn, N. Y.

The following are some of the replies in whole or in part:

"October 15, 1909.

"MISS GRACE C. STRACHAN,
"1308 Pacific Street,
"Brooklyn.

"*My Dear Miss Strachan:*

"I have your circular favor of the 11th instant in which you request an expression of my views on the subject of equal payment for equal service to school teachers of both sexes.

"I am glad to inform you that I am very much in sympathy with your contention on this subject, and I fully feel with you that all city employees whose appointment is made from an eligible list should be paid according to the position held without regard to the sex of the employe.

"If the committee which you so kindly say will be pleased to call upon me can offer any practical suggestion by which I can aid your Association to bring about that result, I shall be very glad indeed to see the committee at its own convenience.

"Sincerely,

"JOHN H. MCCOOEY."

"As a matter of principle I do believe that municipal employees should be paid without regard to the sex of the employe. Without ever having made a study of the application of this principle to the public school teachers of New York City, my convictions have always been upon the side of equal salaries for men and women teachers.

"Before passing upon the question finally, however, and certainly before taking any official action upon it, should it be my good fortune to be elected to the office for which I am now a candidate, I wish to have before me all the facts bearing upon the question, as, for instance, the character of work done by the teachers of both sexes.

"Yours very truly,

"JOHN PURROY MITCHELL."

"*My Dear Miss Strachan:*

"I have received one of your circulars wanting to know where we stand. I presume it was sent to me because I am on the list of candidates—in other words, am enjoying a little distinction for a few brief weeks—but you know where I stand—don't you? I have not changed my views one iota from what I said at the meeting in March, 1908.

"With very best wishes, believe me,

"Yours very truly,

"WILLIAM A. PRENDERGAST."

"New Brighton, N. Y., Oct. 16, 1909.

"*Dear Miss Strachan:*

"In reply to your circular of October 11th, 1909, I desire to say, in answer to question asked, that I believe that all city employees, whose appointments are made from eligible lists, should be paid according to the position held, without regard to sex of the employee. This has always been my stand in this matter, and anything that I can do in my humble way towards helping you I will be pleased to do.

"Wishing you success, I am,

"Yours truly,

"CHARLES J. MCCORMACK,

"Democratic Candidate for Borough President of Richmond."

*Democracy* of November 6, 1909, said:

"With Mayor-elect Gaynor, John Purroy Mitchell, President-elect of the Board of Aldermen, and William A. Prendergast, as the next Comptroller, the women teachers of Greater New York are more than ever confident of success in their campaign for equal pay. All three men are known to be in favor of the equal pay bill.

"At a meeting of the Interborough Association held in May of 1908, Judge Gaynor was the presiding officer, with Mr. Prendergast as the speaker of the evening.

"Practically all the candidates for either Alderman or Assemblyman, who have pronounced themselves in favor of the equal pay bill, have been re-elected, Assemblyman Conklin, who twice introduced the Equal Pay bill, was re-elected, as was Assemblyman Foley, the introducer of the Gledhill-Foley bill. Assemblyman Sheridan of the Bronx, who has for three years in succession voted against the bill, was this year defeated. Assemblyman Warren I. Lee, who is known to be against the bill, has been re-elected. Thomas P. Peters, Republican candidate for Register, and one of the women teachers' greatest opponents, was defeated by a greater majority than any candidate on the Kings County Republican ticket."

"I am heartily in favor of the equal pay movement. I believe that women should get the same pay as men for the same work. If a woman is considered competent enough to be placed in charge of certain work, her sex should not be considered, for really that has nothing to do with the matter. She should be paid for the work, not because she happens to be a woman, but because she is entitled to the standard of wages, whatever that be.—ROBERT R. MOORE, Democratic candidate for Comptroller."

One hundred fifteen answers were received. Only one, that of Cyrus C. Miller,* was unfavorable. Three were

* Mr. Miller's letter appears in Part IV.

noncommittal. One hundred eleven, that is, 96.5 per cent., were favorable. Mr. Miller was elected President of the Bronx, but his success was largely due to the fact that Mr. Louis Haffen split the Democratic vote by running on an independent ticket. The only New York City Democrat in either house, who voted against the Equal Pay bills, Mr. John V. Sheridan, of the Bronx, was defeated in this election. Thirty-five of the candidates for Assembly had previously voted for the Equal Pay bills, thirty-one were re-elected. Of the four who were defeated, two were in Queens districts, and as the Queens County Republican organization has always been most friendly to the women teachers' cause, we had to be neutral. Another was Mr. Cuvillier, of the 30th district, New York, who was prevented by a serious attack of pneumonia from taking any part in the campaign, and whose opponent, Peter Donovan, was on the Fusion ticket and was an avowed friend of "Equal Pay." The fourth was Adolph Stern, of the 6th district, New York.

## CHAPTER XXVI

### BIRD STORY

Once upon a time a plain, ordinary Woman Teacher went to see a Lady of High Degree. She wanted to make the Lady understand the "Women Teachers' Cause." She cared not that the door was opened noiselessly by a noiseless liveried man and that she was conducted noiselessly up a beautiful staircase to a beautiful library wherein was the Lady of High Degree. She cared not for the big blazing log fire, cared not for the perfectly appointed tea table that a flunkey in satin knee breeches and white stockings and buckled shoes rolled into proximity to her—the plain, ordinary woman teacher—and the Lady of High Degree. She cared not for the tea and the cakes and the bonbons, so charmingly served by so charming a Lady, though she could not but take note of the beautiful, perfect hands as they daintily flitted among the tea things or lay on the folds of the pretty blue silk negligee the Lady wore, and she thought, "I suppose, she need never even wash those hands of her very own, if she doesn't want to." But indeed she cared not for all these trifling things. Hers was a serious mission. This Lady of High Degree had power to assist the thousands of women teachers whom she represented. Nor was that all: to assist them was to uplift all womankind. The Lady of High Degree would herself be uplifted. So the plain, ordinary Woman Teacher talked and talked and strove to put into her words all that she felt and all that she meant—labored hard to make that Lady of High Degree *see* why she and fifteen thousand other women teachers had banded together and were waging a war against existing laws. She answered many questions and tried to clear up many doubts. And when a long time had gone by, and she was hoping the day was won, the Lady of High Degree said: "I thank you very much. I am most interested. But I am not sure that women can do the same work as men. I am not certain that it is in nature for them to do so. Now, I am very much interested in birds. In fact, I have an aviary on my top floor and I spend much time there. And I have been watching those birds, and I must say, *I notice that the work of the male birds is very different from the work of the female birds.*"

And that night as the tired Woman Teacher lay awake, she thought, "What's the use! We don't speak the same language."

## PART TWO—CHAPTER ONE

### IN ASSEMBLY HEARING, MARCH, 5, 1907

ROBERT S. CONKLIN:—In behalf of 10,000 to 15,000 citizens who don't consider it reprehensible to favor this question I present these petitions signed by them in refutation of the position that has been taken by Judge Butts.

I can't hope to answer all of the arguments that have been advanced by so many speakers on the other side, but only rise to defend my own position in having introduced this bill in the Assembly. I think one of the speakers on the other side has referred to a college professor as authority for his own position. There is another one of the foremost authorities on municipal government in the world, one under whom I studied, one whose works are read and are a basis for study in every college throughout the country—Professor Goodnow, of Columbia—and I may say that he is one of the foremost home rulers in America to-day? Yet, on pages 83 and 84 of his book of municipal problems, I find this quotation:

"Experience has shown that the common schools could not, with due regard to their best interests, be left in the controlled management of local bodies. In some states, as in New York, the powers of the central authority are very large. There is no question that the adoption of the central administration of control has been of the greatest benefit in the field of education."

Some twenty-five years ago there came to this chamber a young man from New York City, and he at that time laid the foundation of his great reputation as a reformer. He was one who was always fighting for the best that could be had for cities, for government at large, for the interests of the people. He laid the foundation of his reputation at that time. Subsequently, when he was Governor of this State in 1899, this man, notwithstanding the fact that he was the earnest advocate of home rule for cities, made the initial step in the question of education, and provided that the board of education, or rather the City of New York, would be compelled to pay to the teachers in the educational system something like living compensation. The ratification of that man's position is seen in the fact that he has since been advanced from the position of Governor to the Executive of the United States—Theodore Roosevelt.

It was he who first had enacted into law, who himself signed this Davis law, which we are only seeking to amend. We are not seeking for any further encroachment upon the powers of the city authority than is authorized by this Davis law. Now let us see wherein the justification lies.

It has well been said by Judge Butts that the State Legislature has not so far attempted to interfere with the conditions in any other city throughout the state. But are not the conditions in New York City such as to warrant the interference of the legislature? Why, this legislature here to-day is bending and swaying at times, under public opinion generated in New York City, by the public school children of some ten or fifteen years ago. Isn't it within the province of this legislature, to see that that public opinion is properly formed, and how is it to see to it unless it provides for the proper education of those children?

It seems to me that the main matter for this committee to consider is whether this legislature has the right to butt in and try to regulate salaries in the City of New York. As to the qualifications of men teachers or women teachers, we have two exhibits here. Look at this picture (pointing to women teachers); and then on that (pointing to men teachers). And I must submit the case without argument.

Now, the question to be considered is whether the City of New York is doing its simple duty. It has the money to spend. Year after year they are increasing salaries down there. And what have they done for the teachers? . . . They are increasing salaries in other departments, and isn't it time for the State of New York, which has so much at stake, to say that this money—this increase in the city budget, if increase there shall be—that some of this increase shall go to the teachers? The board of estimate and apportionment has refused to appropriate the necessary money. Isn't it up to this legislature to say that in this matter of education at least, it is going to see that a proper compensation is received by these teachers in the New York schools? Look at the responsibility that is laid upon them. Yesterday I was riding down Third Avenue and saw a school in flames at 96th Street. I got out of the car. Mothers and fathers were running everywhere to find out what had become of their children. There was a teacher in that school teaching one of the lower grades, who by her own action was responsible for getting out those 2500 children in safety from the danger that menaced them. The teacher was Miss Blakeslee, I believe. I don't know what salary she was receiving, but I know she was in one of the lower grades. This teacher, with the responsibility of those 2500 lives, was receiving from $600 up to $1300, according to the time she had been in the service. Is this a proper compensation for anybody with such responsibilities upon her?

That is the reason I stand here as an advocate of this bill, because I don't believe the City of New York is doing the right thing by them. Do you know anything about what the problem is in the public schools? Have you ever seen these immigrants pouring in as they come over from Ellis Island—these hundreds of thousands that come in and take up their residence in New York City? It becomes the duty of the teachers of the New York public schools to light in those faces the soul that has been blotted out.

The city authorities have refused to take advantage of the privilege that is given them by the Davis law, and give to these women anything like what seems to be a proper compensation. And yet these children are going home and these parents are being educated by the children who are sent out by the public schools. This great party of immigrants who have done so much towards the shaping of policy in New York City, are receiving their impressions through their children, and those children are being taken care of by the public school teachers. Now, it seems to me that this is a state matter. It is a matter in which the state has a right to take a hand.

We don't care so much about, as far as we legislators are concerned,. these controversies between men and women. We simply tried in this bill to determine what is the proper compensation for women. Where the compensation had been fixed by the legislature, so far as the men were concerned, we determined that that compensation once being fixed (and it has never been questioned) is a proper compensation; that this compensation once being fixed was a proper criterion to go by; and we have tried to provide in this bill that these women shall receive that compensation.

Lyman A. Best:—When Governor Roosevelt signed the Davis Bill, which this bill proposes to amend, he made the statement that there was one thing about the bill which was wrong, and that was that it discriminated against the women. He was urged, however to sign the bill, although there was a discrimination against the women, and the statement was made that the evil would be corrected. A gentleman who was in the room said that when the time came this evil could be corrected, and the women who were doing the same work as men, properly recognized and given the same compensation as men, and he would be the first one to come up here and urge that that error be corrected. That gentleman was the first one to get up before the Senate Committee on Cities last week, and he was the first one to get up before this committee this afternoon in opposition to these ladies.

I represent an association of 4500 people. At a meeting of the representatives of said association at which every school was represented, and at which there were present over 50 men, a vote was taken as to whether we should sustain the women in this fight for equal pay. The vote was in favor of the women. Two-thirds at least of the men teachers and principals of Brooklyn are heartily in favor of paying the women the same salaries if they are doing the same work.

The claim is made that the city must pay these larger salaries to a man because he has a family or a prospective family. According to that, he should pay a certain pension to the city for the privilege of teaching school. The city is not employing teachers for the purpose of furnishing support to their families. They are not called except for the purpose of educating the children. We put in charge capable and competent men and women, and if the women do the same work, we believe that the laws of right and justice demand that they should receive the same salary. I am getting no increase of salary by this proposition. I favored the increase before the Interborough Association of Teachers was formed. If we wanted to do so we could give you a hundred cases where women have the burden of the support of families on their shoulders. I know you will find many more women than men in the grades who are supporting families.

We are asking you to give the extra salary to these women because they are doing the work, and they are doing it as well as the men. I am principal of one of the largest schools in the city, at one time with 70 teachers under me. In that list, I am sorry to say that there has been a much larger percentage of failures among the men than the women. They are not men that have prepared themselves to be teachers or that care to be teachers; they are using it as a stepping stone to something else. Their heart is not in their work. A man teacher came to me some years ago, and said that he had tried hard and yet he knew he was a failure. I said:—Will you follow my advice? There is a piece of paper and there is a pen; write out your resignation. He did so. To-day he is an engineer, getting a larger salary than he could ever get as a teacher. And there are other men of the same class. There are women teachers, too, who are failures, undoubtedly. The percentage is not equal to that of men. They go into the profession with the idea of making it their life work. The best men do not go into the work unless they have a missionary spirit and are not looking for results in salary only.

When a man says here that this is going to cost ten or twelve million of dollars, he is saying that which he knows is not true. Careful estimate shows that it will be under six millions of dollars. Under the provisions of the Davis law, the cost was larger than that. The time has come when the evil which has been upon these women for the past seven years should be rectified. If it costs twenty million dollars for the purpose of rectifying an injustice, let it. I sincerely trust that you will report this bill absolutely unamended.

MR. O'LOUGHLIN (speaker not known to women teachers):—If you only knew my position you would appreciate the opportunity that the chairman has given me here—and I begged it of him—to say a few words.

In the first place, my mother was a school teacher. In the second place, my sister was a school eacher. In the third place, a sister-in-law of mine was a school teacher. In the fourth place, another sister-in-law is a school teacher. And, to cap the climax, I married a school teacher. Now, if my folks should find out that I was here in Albany to-day, and went back to Kings County and did not stand here and raise my voice for this bill, which is honest, and true, and just, why there would be nothing left of the hair on my head, that is all.

I am here merely to bring a message to the committee. A week and a half ago, an organization was formed and called "The Independence League of the 12th Assembly District of Kings." This organization of 800 men met and adopted a resolution favoring this bill, and calling upon the members of the legislature to give the teachers what really belonged to them. When this subject came up in our organization of workingmen, I didn't quite understand it at first, and I said, "Just what is this thing?" They said it is a mere matter of some fellow doing his work on the job and doing it right, and if he does it right he ought to get pay for it. A man got up and gave some of this kind of talk, and before he got through all the men were backing him. Another fellow from another union said: "It is simply this: Here is a woman who does a certain amount of work and gets $600; here is a man who does the same work, and he gets $900. If this is allowed to continue, the first thing you know it will be allowed to come into the union." All agreed in declaring it a scab game, and said: "We are not going to stand for it."

One man said he was in a cigar factory; it had about 50 men employed; they were all expert cigarmakers. After a while the boss put in two machines. The boss said, "These machines do the work, we will give that job to a woman: you men wouldn't want that, you are all experts; that is a woman's job; being a woman's job, you don't want a woman's wages; we will give the women half." And so the women got half. After a while they put in another machine, and out went five more men, and so on until they all had machines. This man returned, and the boss said: "There is a machine idle; go to work." He started it? "How about the wages?" He said: "Whatever the machine pays." "That is a woman's pay." "Oh," they said, "things are different now; with the machines the pay is all alike—man, woman or child."

Since I was assigned to come and bear this message, I have been trying to find out who is opposing this measure. I find it is a handful of men teachers. What do you want—you men teachers? What is your argument? What can a man gain by trying to keep a woman down? If a woman does the same kind of work he does, it is to his benefit that she get the same pay. In a short time, as I understand it, from an economic standpoint they will employ more men.

The point is simply this. I was coming up in the train. I heard a man say, "I don't consider any of those women in there as good a teacher as I am." I says: "Why?" "Well, I am a man and she is a woman." I said: "She is doing the same kind of work." He said: "No." "Then," I said, "the city is not doing the right thing, putting somebody on that job when they can't do the work right; they ought to put one on there who will do the work right."

I came up here, not to make a speech; I came because I was asked to bear this message. There are 900 men in the 12th Assembly District of Kings County who favor this bill. If that amounts to anything, I offer it to you.

Miss Ellen T. O'Brien, Treasurer Interborough Association of Women Teachers:—The statement has been made in the press that the qualifications required of women are not the same as those required of men. I stand here, gentlemen, to refute that statement. When I took the examination for the principal's license, a man sat in front of me, a man on one side. All went into the examination at the same time and answered the same questions. If the board of examiners discriminated between men and women in examining those papers they were not true to their charge.

The statement has been made that in emergencies women fail. I deny that from personal experience. I am principal of one of the lower East Side schools composed of 2500 children. Last June, during the course of some special work being carried on by the Board of Health, the parents came to the school suddenly in great excitement and created almost a riot. They thought that their children's throats were being cut. They rushed into the school to save their children. My grade teachers—all women—braved that crowd, led those children out, showed them to the parents, and got them back again into the school in five minutes.

A few months ago an explosion of one of the steam pipes occurred in my school. Through the ignorance of some one of the immigrants in the neighborhood a false alarm was sent in; and before I knew what had happened my school was thrown into a panic by the fire department coming and rushing to our aid. My women teachers cleared the school in three minutes. Can anyone say that a woman is not equal to an emergency after that?

One of the speakers (Mr. Cronson) has referred to Ladd's Physiological Psychology. I studied in the same University, in the same class with the gentleman who spoke about Mr. Ladd. Everybody knows that nobody can tell what Ladd means.

## IN SENATE ON WHITE BILL, APRIL 15, 1907.

Senator White:—Mr. President, I would ask the indulgence of the Senate and its attention for a few moments, as this is a very important bill, and I believe every one about this circle will be interested to hear the facts in relation to it.

The Senator from the Seventh (Senator McCarren) early in the session, introduced a bill to correct what had seemed to many of us a very unjust condition of affairs in the public schools of the City of New York. The fact is that in 1900, after a long struggle in the legislature, a bill arbitrarily fixing salaries and arbitrarily fixing the annual increase or increment for teachers' salaries in the City of New York, was passed. It has since been recognized that it was an injustice for a woman occupying a position of trust and importance equal to that held by a man to receive a salary different and much less than the salary of that man.

That simple statement illustrates the general principle which has been recognized, I think, by nearly all who have viewed this subject in a fair and impartial light . . . in other words that it was a just thing that the position should command the salary, and not have salary determined on the basis of sex.

The Senator from the Seventh introduced a bill to obliterate this apparent injustice, and as to the merits of that bill I have no criticism to offer. The bill was earnestly considered in the Cities Committee, and while the Senator from the Seventh was naturally tenacious of the principles of his bill, I found nothing but encouragement from him in my effort and in the effort of the committee to reach a just and fair conclusion. Some of us spent days in New York City and elsewhere trying to get the best opinions we could, and the best advice we could, to the end that a bill might be adopted by this legislature that would meet the needs of the community, and do justice to all. As the result of that, a bill was prepared which gives to the local authorities, the Board of Education, the absolute power to fix the salaries of the teachers in the public schools, subject simply to two or three different provisions which were regarded as essential in the interests of and in justice to that vast body of men and women who have done so much to uplift and strengthen that great community.

Now, Mr. President, there has been no discrimination here as between men and women; there has been no member of that committee who has sought to do justice to any one at the expense of any other, or in recognizing any class to do injustice to any other. Our purpose has been solely to mature a bill which would do justice to all, and be based upon sound principles of legislation.

This bill provides that the Board of Education shall fix the salaries; it provides that there shall be an annual increment, an annual increase in the salaries of all the teachers. It provides that the lowest salary for any grade shall be $720 per annum—and the committee felt that that was not too much—that the services of any man or woman worthy to occupy that position were not overpaid by a such a salary. . . .

Now, after great consideration and after many days, and after consultation with what we believe to be the best thought among the women, and the best thought among the men—and I want to say

Mr. President, that we consulted men and women whom we regarded as disinterested and as well equipped to judge as any on this proposition—this is the final form in which the bill has been placed before the committee. Now so much for the general proposition. I may say that the committee, after consideration and deliberation, practically agreed—I won't say every Senator's views were fully met in all particulars, but I will assert that every member of the committee finally agreed—that probably all things considered, this was as fair and as equitable a bill as we could reach.

SENATOR GRADY:—I hope the day will come when the principle embodied in the McCarren-Conklin bill will be the law, not for teachers alone, but for every public servant, and that not the question of sex, but the question of position and of merit shall rule; and I am prepared to defend that as a general proposition, and I am prepared to defend it all the more earnestly as a special proposition applicable to the schools. "He who seeks equity must come into the court with clean hands" and I want to say to the Senator from the 8th (Senator Fuller) speaking figuratively, that his clients haven't clean hands. Theirs are colored with the crime of rank injustice as shown before the Committee and written out in every line of the Davis bill. . . . And ever since the Davis bill was passed that injustice embodied in the law by that form of deceit which conceals the truth rather than the fault, has been accentuated and made more grievous by the system of legislation adopted by our Board of Education, until it became necessary for these women teachers to organize in self defense.

And they have organized, and they have 11,000 members in their organization, and they have had representatives here from the beginning of the session, with not a single word uttered against the men, the salaries they were receiving or the increases they were obtaining. And the men, preparing for a second betrayal of the women, came here and stated that they favored the design of the bill, but they added "Our advantage must be preserved; before you do justice to the women you must see that the men are preserved in all their rights and privileges." . . .

I want to say that there are several positions in which the men have stood where they have added nothing to their standing as men engaged in teaching the youth of our city.

They have not been frank; they have not been fair; they have not been honest in the statement of their position; they have delayed this bill; they have suggested amendments which have been passed upon; they have insisted that they were in favor of the White bill as it was first reported by the Cities Committee and then when that White bill was amended as a compromise, they began again repeating the amendments, one of which is now before you, which they had relinquished when the first bill was reported from the Cities Committee.

Now I am in a position of thorough accord with that taken by the Senator from the Seventh (Senator McCarren). The men ought to be glad that this bill does not go further. We are not equalizing salaries now—I wish we were—but we are in a measure repairing the wrong done by the male teachers in the Davis law and before we need to be generous with the men teachers let us do partial justice to the 11,000 women teachers employed in the public schools.

That is an old worn-out, threadbare "chestnut"—if I may indulge in a colloquial—that of the men being in their position for life, not because they love to be teachers, entering into a contract the end of which is their highest aim, but that the women are transitory figures in the drama and seek some other profession as soon as opportunity presents. Statistics will show that in proportion to the number employed in the public schools of New York more of the women adopt the profession as a lifelong profession than do the men.

And so it is with the other suggestion—you drive the men out of the schools. This is stated before us by men who if driven out of the schools would have to look to high Heaven and Eternity for some other place to go. We do not propose to drive the men out of the public schools. They are protected not only by the law, but by the scheming legislation of the Board of Education. . . .

Just as to beat the Ferry bill I made the fare too small, just so to beat this bill the men who are in favor of equalization or who say they are, want to make the cost of it too high; they want to beat it by indirection; to beat it not by answering the arguments urged in its favor, not by controverting a single statement made in support of the legislation proposed, but to beat it by just such another betrayal as they accomplished in the original act.

Now those who believe in a more radical bill have yielded as far as men could yield; and those who believe in a conservative measure have gone as far as they can go, and linked together they propose that this bill shall pass this legislature.

Let me conclude with an illustration of the rank injustice that the present law now imposes. This letter is from one of the male principals. Here is what he says: "I have 32 teachers under my direction. Of these 22 are women. Out of the 22 women I could readily pick a dozen for whom I would not take in exchange a dozen high-priced men teachers. The assistant to the principal in my department is a woman. If I desire to be absent from school for any cause for any length of time she would take charge of the school by official designation of the Board of Superintendents, and for the time being would to all intents and purposes be Principal." "Yet three of the men teachers under her would draw salaries respectively of $2400, $2250 and $1845, while her salary would continue at its present figure $1600.

Now the bill you are voting on provides that such great, inexcusable, indefensible discrimination shall be leveled down.

I have some interests in the public schools of New York City, and some views on education similar to what Artemas Ward said exemplified his participation in the civil war, when he said he had lost two uncles and a cousin. I had two brothers and a sister in the teaching force of the public schools under the condition that prevailed before the passage of the Davis law, at the time when all the public school teachers were underpaid. I get my information at first hand. I am not giving you what any teacher said to me; I am giving you the views of those who have lived and worked up to the time that their work was too irksome. I learned what they have to say upon this bill, and I have behind that the sentiment of the great City of New York.

Votes on passage of bill, Ayes, 45; Noes, 1.

SPEECHES IN SENATE, MARCH 24, 1908. Preceding passage of White Bill.

SENATOR WHITE:—The bill before us does simply this: its striking feature is contained in the few words which require that the School Board of New York City shall make no discrimination in salary on account of sex. That is the essential and striking feature of the bill. There are certain other changes in the present law. I am not aware that they are particularly significant, and I doubt if anyone would oppose the bill on any other ground than that I have stated.

The measure has been criticised because it is said that this is establishing a new policy for the State. It is difficult for me to see how any man can contend that this is a correct statement in regard to the bill. If the State has any policy on that subject at all, it is well settled; but it is settled the other way. There is no discrimination permitted in regard to sex, so far as I know, except in this particular instance. Under the Civil Service law of the State, there is no discrimination permitted as to sex, and successful competitors reach their places on the eligible list, each in his place, entitled to receive the same salary for the same work irrespective of sex. Therefore, if there is any policy of the State on this subject, beyond doubt it is all the other way.

It has been said that this bill violated the principle of home rule. Well, the truth about that is this: The present law violates the principle of home rule. The present law is a mandatory provision, the so-called Davis law, whereby the Legislature sought to determine absolutely within certain very narrow limits, the salaries of the teachers of the City of New York, and to prescribe in various ways, by mandatory provision, how that Board of Education should govern that department in this particular. This bill wipes out very largely the mandatory provisions and gives almost unlimited discretion to the Board of Education in determining these problems. It is true that cognizance is taken of the great evils that had existed, of the admitted unfairness and of admitted wrongs; it is true that this bill prescribes certain mandatory provisions in relation to those things; but there is no sense in the argument that it is a violation of home rule,—that is, there can be no consistent argument because it is certainly a correct statement that this bill seeks to alleviate the situation by giving the Board greater discretion, although it does seek to correct the few evils of which those affected justly complain.

There is no dispute among disinterested men and women as to these evils; and I call attention to the fact that in the Governor's message of last year when he vetoed a bill of similar character—in that message the Governor very distinctly called attention to the evils and abuses, and particularly urged the correction of those evils. But a deaf ear has been turned to his appeal. The public knows perfectly well—whatever humbug and sophistry may be injected into this discussion—the public knows perfectly well that the present conduct of the schools of the city of New York has been subject to the most grave and just criticism; and this criticism has called forth a very earnest movement to reform and reorganize the Board of Education of that city.

It is known of all men, I think generally admitted and conceded, that there have been abuses which have required legislative consideration. Anyone familiar with such attitude as I have been able to take on city questions knows that I have struggled against mandatory legislation, struggled against the attempt of the legislature to regulate local affairs; but there are times and conditions when this Legislature has been called upon to do that very thing. I repeat this bill gives greater discretion and greater opportunity for the exercise of judgment on the part of the Board of Education, than does the present law it seeks to amend.

Although it must be admitted that it does prescribe certain definite principles under which the board must act.

Now then, it has been urged in criticism also that in addition to being a violation of home rule, it is mandatory in character. I may say in conclusion that what this bill does is to prescribe that there shall be no discrimination in regard to sex—that equal work shall receive equal pay; and in order to accomplish that, existing schedules are wiped out and three or four general principles are laid down under which the Board of Education must act. To summarize, this bill fixes a minimum salary of $720 a year; it provides for a minimum annual increment; it prescribes that no salary shall be reduced as a result of the operation of this bill; and finally, it prescribes that a tax of four mills shall be given to the Board of Education for salary purposes.

I shall be glad to try to discuss any particular objections that may be raised to the bill.

Senator McCarren:—I understand that practically this is the same bill the Senate passed last year. I do not believe it is necessary to explain to the Senators outside of the City of New York what provisions the bill contains. In brief, they simply provide that the female teachers shall receive, where they perform the same work, the same salaries that the male teachers receive. That is a simple proposition and, divested of all the verbiage employed in the discussion of this bill, you will in the last analysis have to decide for yourselves as to whether the female teachers who do the same work as the male teachers do, are entitled to the same pay.

It seems to me there can be no sensible refutation of that position.

The Senator from the Sixth (Senator Travis) expressed the situation in a nutshell when he called attention to the fact that there are male teachers in primary work, and that in order to bring the salaries of all the female teachers employed in teaching primary grades to the same point, it will be necessary to add to the salary list of the Board of Education, about $4,000,000. If that be so, it should be done.

Why should a male teacher doing less effective work in primary grades receive more than a female teacher?

Every man and woman who knows anything about human nature, knows there should be no male teachers doing primary work at all. We know that they cannot do teaching in the primary grades as well as a woman; and why should not a woman be paid as much as the men for doing better work than the men?

I am somewhat amazed by the question suggested by the Senator from the Sixth with reference to the economic proposition involved in this bill. He is much disturbed about the financial condition of the City of New York, and he very properly calls attention to the many needs of the city. We are constantly developing and our needs are growing, and we need more schools, sewers, and fire houses and greater police and fire protection. We need an increase of everything incidental to the development of the city. These needs cannot be prevented from multiplying as we go along, and of course the expenses must be multiplied to meet these conditions.

We need more transportation facilities? That is admitted. But that is no reason why the city should become a paternal government, and distribute its fund about to the unemployed. . . .

There is no reason in the world why these worthy school teachers, these women, should not receive the same pay as men. I graduated at a public school, and no man teacher could get me to do anything. It was the female teachers who gave me what education I received. A woman can get more out of boys than a man. I was ready to fight the man teacher, but I was always ready to do what the woman teacher wanted me to do; and whatever education the majority of young men of the City of New York received in the public schools, is entirely due to the honest, painstaking efforts of the women. It is their natural vocation—the training of the juvenile mind.

I want to say, Mr. President, that the finances of the City of New York will regulate themselves. It may be necessary to increase the valuation of the property in order to get the necessary money, but that will be attended to by the officials of the City of New York. But the proposition that we shall consider is one that should be considered solely on its own merits, and not in connection with any paternalism now in the mind of the Senator from the Sixth. I hope the Senators outside of the City of New York will bear in mind that this is a mandatory bill in all its provisions. It was passed after consultation with a number of men interested in educational matters in the City of New York. You are dealing with a mandatory law in the Davis law, and hence the necessity for the mandatory character of this bill. That is all there is to the proposition and I assume that the justice of that question will address itself to the intelligence of every Senator here who has given the subject any thought. I think the bill should pass unanimously.

SENATOR GRADY:—The first question to be determined by the Senate is as to whether or not for the redress of this admitted wrong, the women teachers of New York City have consulted the proper tribunal. That is, as to whether they should present their petition here to the legislature, or to the local authorities of the City of New York.

Upon that point, the Governor of this State in his message vetoing the bill last year used very clear and precise language. He said that the Board of Education is thus directly subject to the control of the Legislature; and whatever provision may be found necessary or wise for the purpose of defining its powers or prescribing its policy, must be prescribed by the Legislature. No other authority is competent to make such a provision.

The Governor went on to say that the suggestion of the Mayor of the City of New York, that the provisions of this law, the original law, known as the Davis Law, and the amendments known as the White Bill, in any way violated home rule, was not to be entertained for a single moment. He said that the indication of its use was a matter of State concern, and that the teachers had applied to the proper authorities for the redress of their grievances.

The Senator of the Sixth (Senator Travis) is in favor of equal pay for equal work, but requires an enormous amount of other things to be done, or requires that this injustice—admitted upon all sides,—must continue. . . .

The opposition to this bill comes from the male teachers. The male teachers—bless their dear good hearts—they are wonderfully exercised for fear you will withdraw the masculine influence from the schools, forgetting in their excess of interest in this bill, that in many of our schools we had absolutely withdrawn the masculine element.

We have schools going up to the 8th grade in which there is not a man teacher. Just think of the injustice we are doing to these children now when we are running big schools in New York without a male teacher. And they are fearful lest if you attempt to do justice to the woman teacher, you won't be able to deal generously with them.

Now that is the position of the male teacher in New York City. Remember, he came here when the Davis Bill was passed, and he saw that his minimum wage was fixed, generously fixed. Remember that the woman teacher depending on that bill, giving to her the same generous wage and a proper annual increment, found herself deceived, and now they come and tell you that to do what is acknowledged to be simple justice to the women, means that you cannot afford to be generous to them, and that this bill, therefore, should not become a law.

What was the Governor's objection to the bill? The Governor's objection was that if adopted for the City of New York, it should be adopted throughout the State.

In taking that position the Governor overlooked the fact that New York City had been singled out of the cities of the State for special treatment under the provisions of the Davis law, to which the White bill is an amendment. But we accepted the Governor's veto, and we sought relief from the Board of Education, which he said he was sure could be relied upon to redress the grievances of the woman school teacher, and they did undertake to redress them to a degree; and then our Board of Education found itself as powerless as the school teachers had found themselves. They asked for an increase from the Board of Estimate and Apportionment, which would have permitted some measure of justice. The suggestion that that increase was defeated by the action of the women school teachers or of any woman teacher or any representative of the women teachers, is entirely gratuitous; and is not borne out by the facts.

They went to the Board of Estimate and Apportionment and asked for an additional allowance. The women teachers went before the board and asked for a larger amount that would enable the Board of Education to equalize their salaries. But to say that they opposed the lesser amount is entirely gratuitous, and has no foundation in fact whatever; and the Board of Estimate and Apportionment refused them a dollar, refused them a dollar, so they are powerless, this Board of Education, just as the women teachers are powerless or any other tribunal of the city government under the provisions of the Davis bill.

Now, Mr. President, it is not for me to voice the justice that is behind this bill. I never went to the public schools. I never for an hour had the benefit of the teaching of any woman. But I know that the glory of the educational system in this State, as reflected in its public schools, belongs to that sex, and it never can be taken from the women teachers who have taken charge of the children of the people and have inclined the twig as it should go. Never was the work of women teachers such a contribution to the safety and to the welfare of the State as it is at this precise moment.

Think of the character of the population which is daily coming to New York at this time. I am speaking now of that population that intends an absolute and ready acquiescence in every provision of your law. Entirely unacquainted with our language, coming to these shores with the wrongs and oppressions of the governments under which they have lived, fresh in their memory and active in their recollections—these foreigners and their children are crowding the schools and are being taught by these women teachers.

First, they are taught the language of the country, and then they are made acquainted with the difference in conditions which changes their very nature from opponents of existing government to honest, faithful and law-abiding citizens.

I tell you if it were not for the work of the women teachers in the City of New York within the last ten years we would have growing up now, fast approaching manhood and womanhood, an element of your society that no influence known to government could restrain.

You would have brought up an element that believed the government must harass them; you would have brought up an element that would regard officials as the privileged and idle class; you would have brought up an element that would have regarded every condition consistent with the republican form of government as simply a continuation of the intolerable conditions from which they fled. Instead of that, you will find you have that element engaged to-day in every work that is intended to count for the betterment of their fellow man.

Who is directing the great settlement work on the east side of New York City? Who are the active men that are bringing to those of their own race knowledge of the difference between a republican and a monarchial form of government? Who are the active men in social life of New York City? Mainly, the men who but a few years ago from our women teachers of New York City were learning the primary principles of the English language, and were being made acquainted with our laws and customs.

I do not know of any element opposed to the passage of this bill except the male teachers; and they oppose it because they do not want their contract with the city disturbed; and they claim that they have continued in employment under the guarantee of an advance in the Davis bill; but they have nothing to say about the contracts between them and the city when the Davis bill was passed. They are willing that that little agreement should not be regarded with the same dignity as applies to a contract. They have a better thing now.

I want to say to you that all that we do as far as expense is concerned is to restore the provisions of the original Davis law. Do not be deceived about that. You would think we were robbing the public treasury of its last dollar. We are only restoring the provision that four mills of our own taxes shall be dedicated to the salaries of teachers. That was the original provision, and when we increased our assessments and found that four mills provided means enough to pay the good salaries to the men teachers and the miserable salaries to the women, instead of directing our efforts towards equalizing the salaries with the remainder of the four mills, our gentlemen friends were good enough to come to the Legislature and say that they thought they could get along with three mills, now, and let the women teachers continue under the inequalities and the injustice of their present existence.

So if you restore the four mills of the original Davis bill, in other words make the appropriation for teachers' salaries which was made in the original bill, then we will take care of the rest. We will see that the identical wage is paid for the identical work. We will see that the unanimous wish of our Board of Aldermen is carried out, and we will restore something of the equality that existed in the Borough of Brooklyn up to the time that the Davis law was passed; and we will do an act of justice to as hard working and as efficient a corps of public servants as is to be found within the confines of this State.'

Bill passed 35 to 8.

## HON. E. A. MERRITT, JR., MAJORITY LEADER, ASSEMBLY

In Assembly, April 29, 1909.

GLEDHILL-FOLEY BILL

I think that it is fair that this bill should be tested on its merits. If it is the pleasure of the house to pass the bill, let us pass it without amendments—without by indirection killing it.

It is a curious thing that this question of home rule should be brought up by gentlemen on the other side of the House. The Republican party in the Legislature has been obliged for many years to study the questions involved in the government of the cities of the State, including the great city of New York, and following the suggestion of the gentleman who last occupied the floor, do for those municipalities and that municipality the things which the people there desire. If the people of any of the cities of the State want any real reform they naturally come to the Legislature, which under Republican administration has always listened to the demands of localities and given them the things which they desired and needed.

There is a lot of nonsense talked about this home rule proposition. No city wants home rule. No city in this State wants to bear its burdens unreservedly by itself. And beyond and above that, our civic organizations prescribe that power and authority shall come from the people of the whole State.

Now here is a question. Why should we have interfered years ago in this matter of the salaries of teachers in the City of New York, passing a bill which regulates it? It was done, as this is to be done, at the demand of the taxpayers upon the Republican majority of the State Legislature. Having once assumed this responsibility, this bill or any bill of this sort naturally comes before the Legislature. There is a good deal of force in what my friend, Mr. Oliver, said. Primarily the people most affected are those who teach the youngest children, and it is an old saying that "the hand that rocks the cradle rules the world."

I think the bill ought to be passed, in its form here, properly authenticated as it is by title and in other ways. I do not care if it adds four million dollars to the expense of running the City of New York. They want it there. I know there is a feeling that it ought to be, down there. I know that when the administration of the City of New York wants to, it can easily save, without increasing the tax budget, the amount necessary to make this increase. I know that they do not want to do it—at least I am afraid so, and it is a thing I do not quite understand. But they seem—they don't seem to be quite eager to economize as they ought to be. But here is something that the people want, and I undertake to say to you, gentlemen, that if the administration of New York City wants to do it, they can do it and not spend one dollar more than they do now; and after they have paid this charge, if it is six million dollars, they could have another six million and still do this if they want to. . . .

## MAYOR'S HEARING, May 11, 1909.

SENATOR McCARREN:—The opponents of the bill hold that since this bill is of a mandatory character, it therefore should not be accepted by the Mayor.

Now let me call the attention of Your Honor to the genesis of the so-called Davis Law under which the system is now operating. After the consolidation of the old City of New York and the old City of Brooklyn, and the other territory, a great deal of agitation was set on foot for the purpose of establishing and fixing the salaries that should be paid to the public school teachers. There was considerable difference of opinion, and those who contended as to the right of local authority to regulate the salaries of the teachers did so on the ground that it was a question that affected this locality and following out the principle of home rule, the local authority should be permitted to fix the salary for the place. I have no quarrel with that proposition.

After considerable effort and many attempts on the part of the local authorities to fix satisfactorily the salaries of school teachers, they discovered they could not do it because of the conflicting views and of the different interests, and their inability to come to a unanimous agreement. So that the question was brought to the legislature. After a great deal of conference over it, and more or less agitation, the so-called Davis bill was evolved which arbitrarily fixed the schedules under which the school teachers are now being paid. So I would like to have Your Honor keep in mind this fact that we are operating under an arbitrary law. Yet, there is no proposition to repeal the Davis Law. . . .

Now, therefore, we must take into account and keep in mind that this is an amendment of the Davis Law and the Davis Law is an arbitrary measure, and inasmuch as we are dealing with an arbitrary measure, there is no other way we can deal with it than to amend the arbitrary measure. Now that is what we are trying to do; and those who say that we are opposing the idea of Home Rule must keep in mind the fact that we must either repeal the Davis Law or amend the Davis Law which is a mandatory measure; and this is, of course, a mandatory bill because it amends a mandatory statute—so much for that,

I want to say also, to Your Honor, that while it may cut no figure with you, I desire to call your attention to the fact, that this bill has practically twice passed the legislature by a very large majority. Once vetoed by yourself and the Governor and passed over your veto and failing to pass over the Governor's veto because the attempt was not made.

Now with reference to the equity in the bill. I want to say that everybody here will thoroughly agree with me when I say that if we owe anything at all to the scholastic system, we certainly owe a great deal to the efficacy and to the method of the female teachers in the public schools.

I cannot say too much in praise of the women teachers in our public schools. We know how by nature they are equipped to train and rear and direct the young minds. We know that the women teachers in our public schools are in every way equipped, and they give more time and they are, too, to a great extent, more deeply interested in their work. We know that to-day we have a class of young men who are teaching in our public schools for the purpose of earning a sufficient amount of money to enable them to enter some profession—the medical profession, or the profession of the law,—consequently they are there only temporarily; the women are there permanently, and not a single one of them ever hopes to better herself so far as an opportunity of earning a livelihood is concerned and she knows that she is there for life unless she fortunately or unfortunately gets married. Now that is the only way a woman teacher ever leaves the public school. So to that extent they look upon it as a life work. It is a labor of love with them. . . .

Now another point, it is contended that this bill if enacted into law, will cost the City four or five or six millions of dollars more than is now paid for educational purposes.

In answer to that I want to say that those who take that position calculate that the City will be saving money by the non-acceptance of this bill. That may be true, but it is also true, that the City can save money by reducing these salaries. If you take 50 per cent. off the salaries at the present time, that is a method of saving money. There are a great many different ways in which you can save money for the City, but that is not the question. The question is: Shall the City adequately pay its teachers?

I cannot understand how anybody can attempt to talk over the proposition that where equal work is done why equal pay should not be forthcoming. This bill provides elementally that there shall be equal pay for equal work, and it seems to me that it should not be necessary for one moment to contend for the acceptance of that proposition.

Now I simply want to emphasize to those who contend that this is a violation of a sort of home rule—that stereotyped expression—that you must remember that you are amending a mandatory act.

There is no other way that you can get at the solution of this proposition except by amending this mandatory act, for the system that we are to-day operating under is a mandatory one. The same thing could be said of the Fire Department and the Police Department. The salaries of every member of the uniformed force in both of these departments is arbitrarily fixed. It is provided by law, that when a fireman is appointed, he shall receive so much and that as he goes on in his graduation, he shall reach the maximum. The same is true in this bill, where the school teachers are asking for nothing more than is really due to them in their public service as public servants.

Ezra A. Tuttle:—Mr. Mayor: I don't come here to beg for justice. We may beg for mercy, but justice is a thing to demand and to fight for.

This bill is the embodiment of pure justice and nothing else, so far as it provides for equal pay for the women teachers for doing the same work that the men do.

If your Honor is about to ask me if I read the bill, I will answer it by saying, "No." It is sufficient for me to have Senator McCarren assure your Honor and this audience that the bill does provide for equal pay for the teachers both male and female, women and men.

Your Honor is familiar with history, and you know that from

the time of earliest history, down,—we will start with the English people, with King John—the teacher element in society, the downtrodden element in society, has always had to fight for its rights, for equality. And here we are, face to face, on the same proposition in this bill. It is the same in this 20th century of civilization,—that men, simply because they are strong physically, simply because they have relegated to themselves the right to govern, shall practice an injustice upon women merely because they are weaker.

Mr. Mayor, I was trained in the normal schools of this State as a teacher. I have taught school. I have practiced law in this city for twenty-five years and more, and I want to say to you, and I am not ashamed to acknowledge it, that I said to Miss Strachan, "You may think that moral suasion is all that is necessary in this fight, but I think before you win it, you will find that moral force as well is necessary."

Mr. Mayor, if I had been ashamed to confess that I said if the women teachers do not get justice out of our officials or your Honor, and the Governor of this State, that I would like to see the 15,000 teachers in this great city strike.

The Mayor—You are the Man!

Yes, I am the man, and I am not ashamed of it,—thank God I am not ashamed of it. I want to say to you, that strikes and boycotts are the means by which the downtrodden, the weaker element in society have always gained liberty, equity and justice; and it is not a thing to be ashamed of. They are despicable in the eyes of those who will not grant justice when only peaceful means are used. The labor men of America have raised themselves to their present position, higher than that of any other classes of laboring people, probably, by asserting forcefully their rights, and demanding justice.

The Mayor: Do you think that the teachers will strike if I now exercise my constitutional and legal powers in vetoing this bill?

Mr. Tuttle: No, sir, I do not; I am sorry to say I do not.

The Mayor: You would encourage them?

Mr. Tuttle: Yes, I am sorry to say it—I don't think they will. But I want to say to you that if you continue in the office of mayor for another term——

The Mayor: God forbid. (Laughter.)

Mr. Tuttle: Amen, amen, or any mayor that succeeds you, shall continue this process of declining and refusing to do justice to these teachers, the time will come when you will see that the teachers will assert their rights.

Mr. Curtis (The Central Federated Union):—Mr. Chairman, and Mr. Mayor, Your Honor: We are here on behalf of the teachers' bill. This is a committee of five appointed by the Central body, of which I am the chairman.

The body was unanimous in the endorsing of the school teachers' bill and we believe as organized men, that when women do the same work—the same class of work—as men, they should get the same pay.

We also believe if there is a tax that has to be made up by the taxpayers, it is the working men that, as a general rule, feel it. We are in favor of this bill, and we are willing, if it is necessary, to pay a little more taxes, and see that the school teachers get equal pay.

MR. HOLLAND: Mr. Mayor, I am not representing the Board of Education this morning; I am representing the Central Federated Union. Our Federation has endorsed this bill, and it is the belief of our association that for equal work there should be equal pay.

In mechanics, in electrical work, in typographical work, a woman doing the same identical work is given the same identical pay; in a machine shop where women are working alongside of men, they receive the same pay for the same kind of work. . . . I would not care if I was not on the Board of Education twenty-five seconds, but I am going to try to be honest while I am there.

This city was put on record some time ago as a model employer. I believe that here is the place where we can apply the principle of being a model employer and an impartial employer; and I hope your Honor can see your way clear at this time to sign this bill and give the women teachers the same opportunities as the men have at the present time.

MRS. BELLE DE RIVERA:—Your Honor, I represent the New York City Federation of Women's Club, an organization which comprises a membership of twenty-five to thirty-five thousand women. We held our semi-annual convention last Friday. I have here an official list of the Credential Committee from which it appears that 191 votes were cast, and it was a unanimous vote, in favor of the Teachers' Equal Pay Bill.

MR. FREEL:—Your Honor, I am here as a taxpayer of the City of New York. I also came here as a man who was born and brought up in the Lower East Side of the City of New York, over fifty years ago, and who has remained in his own city constantly for all that time; a man who, whatever in an educational way he possesses, owes it to the common school system of the City of New York; a man who is clear-eyed and a typical representative of the Lower East Side of the city, a man who has had to fight his way through and up, a man who has no misconceptions. He understands his New York, because he keeps his ear to the ground, and bumps elbows with conditions.

I want to say that among the women that I recollect that have been helpful to me in my various fights in the battles of life, I place the women teachers who helped me when I was practically unable to help myself, on the same plane and in the same position exactly, as I do my mother.

I believe that every man that has been born in the City of New York, and every man who has struggled as I have struggled, and has come into close relations with the teachers of the City of New York, are with me squarely on this proposition, and I believe that they are by far the large majority of the representatives of the taxpayers and residents of the City of New York.

We are in favor of this measure—the people; we have no other alma mater than the public schools of the City of New York. They know very well the teachers of the City of New York, they have confidence in them, and they ask you and they look to you to approve this and forward it for the signature of the governor, and I believe that if you do that, you will satisfy the larger majority of men and women who have been born and lived all their lives in the City of New York.

You may, and I have no doubt you will, dissatisfy and disgruntle some people who have come to the City of New York from outside of it, to improve conditions that they do not and never will understand; but you will satisfy the residents who live in the City of New York if you approve this mesure.

SENATOR GLEDHILL:—I will be very brief, Your Honor. I am very proud to be the sponsor of this bill. I have been identified with organized labor for over 25 years, and I am a firm believer——

The Mayor: Are you a member of the Central Federation?

No, sir, I am a member of the International Plasterers.

I am a firm believer in high wages. I believe that when all classes of people who are banded together into an organization receives the highest consideration possible, we receive the best products from them.

I feel that the school teacher is the ideal. I feel that all the inspiration and all the intelligence that the average youth to-day has, has come from these women, or some other woman who has taught them.

Now, someone has said that these teachers receive plenty. Well, when you think of the janitor downstairs who gets $200 a month, there is not much inspiration for the teachers upstairs who receive $60.

Organized labor, and organized movements such as these women are carrying on have been the means of uplifting humanity and making conditions better all the world over. These women are only asking for the addition of the one mill, it does not amount to anything very great. They simply ask that so much be set aside; and they are entitled to it.

These male teachers, who are fighting these women and who ought to be ashamed of themselves—they ought to be working for them. Practically, let us say, they ought to be out erecting building, or ought to be working at some physical labor for which they are better fitted than for that which the women are doing and which they are willing to do. If they are not willing that others shall get the same pay that they themselves get for the same work, let them show us why that is not the right spirit.

I trust, Your Honor, that you will see it in this way, and that you will sign this bill.

ASSEMBLYMAN FOLEY:—Your Honor, I desire to state that I have read this measure, and that I introduced it in the Assembly. I believe if you had asked that question last Thursday of the members of the Board of Education, you would have been startled by the number that answered: "No."

The Mayor: What question do you mean?

Assemblyman Foley: Have the members of the Board of Education read or seen the bill which passed both Houses?

Now, the most important phase of the measure to my mind, after the explanations that have been given of the equal pay part of it—and Your Honor appreciates that the words male and female have been eliminated from the Davis law and are not contained in the measure now before you—is that it increases the minimum salary of the women teachers from $600 to $720.

That the Board of Education has realized the injustice in the conditions as they now exist, appeared in their estimate submitted to the finance department; the governor recognized it in his veto of the measure two years ago; and I believe Your Honor has recognized it.

I hope Your Honor will sign this bill. In so doing you will render a great service in the cause of justice and do more good than it is possible for you now to appreciate.

## A TYPE OF OUR OPPONENTS

MR. DE MUTH:—I wish to speak as a representative of the taxpayers' association; I am a real estate dealer.

May it please Your Honor, as the president of the West Side Taxpayers organization, and as an executive member of the United Real Estate Owners' Association of the City of New York, I want to enter a protest against Your Honor's signature being placed to the teachers' bill. . . . To be properly named, it should be named the most gigantic grab bill that ever was put through a legislature, for that should be the name of the bill instead of the equal pay bill.

We have with us a representative of the City of New York, and one of the members of the Board of Education. Here are the underlings of that department, the superior officers having refused to give them what they believe they were entitled to, because their superior officers didn't think they should be entitled to the amount paid to these men.

The Board of Education of New York has endeavored as far as possible to increase the salaries as much as possible.

We have found here a condition of affairs existing here in this city that never existed in this town before. We have an attempt here to get out of the treasury of the City of New York, over the heads of the department, by the employees of the department, money that they believe they are entitled to. Now what have they done. We find these various organizations of teachers, combining themselves into bodies, discussing the question of how and devising means and ways in which they shall get this amount of money.

They hope to equalize the salary by making the women's salary equal the men's salary. If you will go carefully over the bill, you will find I am right in my contesting it. I don't care to argue that particular point, Your Honor, I am arguing it from a standpoint of the fact that the ladies have taken a peculiar course to arrive at a conclusion, that they have banded themselves together as members of an organization. . . . It has been said this organization went to Albany last year, I know that they were up there. The way they thought to pass legislation at Albany was the most peculiar system——

The Mayor: That is not before me either.

Mr. De Muth: I simply want to show you how the bill was passed with such an enormous majority.

The Mayor: That is surely of academic interest, the bill is before me.

Mr. De Muth: We will get down to the teachers?

The Mayor: I wish you would, because time is running on.

Mr. De Muth: I want to get down then to the purposes of the teachers coming before us as men of the city department. They have seen that they could not get what they wanted in New York City from their superior officers——

The Mayor: That is not before me——

Mr. De Muth: They go up to Albany to get——

The Mayor: One moment. Will you please discuss the bill that is before me. I have already read the title twice, this bill is before me and there is no question involved as to whether the teachers ought to be here or ought not to be here. Miss Strachan is here with the permission of the Board of Education, I take it.

Mr. De Muth: I hope so. I wish to say just this, Your Honor, we will get down to the point of it without any further argument.

Our associations are entirely opposed to this proposition simply because it is going to raise a fund of three million a year, we do not know for how long. . . .

The Mayor: Have you worked that out?

Mr. De Muth: We have done it on that proposition.

The Mayor: Will you give it to me as you have it there?

Mr. De Muth: We have not had any expert accountant here to go over this matter and figure it out as the other side have, but we have arrived at our figures as best we might.

The Mayor: You must have those figures before you.

Mr. De Muth: We have approximately these figures.

The Mayor: Well, give them to us.

Mr. De Muth: I have nothing with me, but this bill extends over a period of three years, this increasing—the figures are ready to be presented and will be presented in the course of argument this morning, but I have not the figures.

This bill from the start to the finish is really a salary grab bill. I believe Your Honor . . .

## ANOTHER TYPE OF OPPONENT

A Male Teacher:—I come to you as a man school teacher, as I have spent some years in the profession of teaching schools. . . . I was quite interested in what the man said from the teacher's side, telling about his school days and how he regarded the teachers that taught him in his school days in the same light as his mother. I, for myself, place no teacher in the same class with my mother. I remember two men teachers that I went to—I went to a mixed school composed of both boys and girls. I remember very distinctly of having one man teacher, who——

The Mayor: You place them in the same class with your father? (Laughter.)

Speaker (continuing): Your Honor, sir, I place the men teachers as men—they have an influence which is most important over the youths. This reminds me of a time—I am willing, perfectly willing to answer a direct question, and I think that a man teacher is an essential—in the lives of the youth of to-day——

I remember a distinct occasion when I had a man teacher who did the work which a woman teacher could not do for me—it was not in the City of New York, I admit, very likely on account of the lines they have to-day.

On the idea of discipline, it is absolutely necessary that there should be men teachers, as I think that is one of the great assistance to the women teachers which should not be considered too lightly.

Inevitably, the young man of to-day in schools, getting his early school training, needs the influence he gets bunking up against a man who is able to answer questions in a way a woman cannot. The uses of the men in the public schools are therefore more than simply to teach from books; the younger generation is training them up to feel that usefulness. They expect to be something more than what they are when they leave school. There are many branches of business open to them that are not open to the female.

A girl that is turned out from our schools to-day is fitted for a teacher and nothing else, but a man when he has grown up, he has many professions open to him—he may be mayor of the City of New York—do not understand me, Your Honor, that I mean any discredit, but I am simply mentioning the many activities of life which are open to a young man and which should have some other inspiration other than the women teachers in his younger days.

Another thing, a woman teacher may teach the boy so he can say "Good-morning," "Good-night," "Good-by," "I hope you will come again," "Am glad to meet you, glad to know you," and many of those little polite phrases, but show me the boy that has been taught by a woman teacher and knows enough and has manners enough, and knows how to act in going into a public office and applying for a position, knows how to address himself to a prospective employer, knows how to do a thousand and one things that a man can teach that a woman cannot. I mention that so as to illustrate why there should be men teachers whereby the boys may have some one to go to to get the information which they really need, which cannot be supplied by the excellent work of the lady-teachers. I say the New York schools need the men teachers. I have taught besides two years in New York, three years in other States, and know something about the conditions that exist here and elsewhere.

## IN SENATE ON MAYOR'S VETO OF WHITE BILL, 1907

SENATOR GRADY:—There is a wonderful deal of misinformation floating about concerning this bill, and as suggested by the Senator of the 38th (Senator White), it proceeds from the men teachers who up to the present time have had their full and sufficient salaries, but who are little in fear that if this bill passes that fullness and sufficiency will not be increased to overflowing.

Now let us go back a little while, before 1900, when the legislature commenced, at the request of the men who oppose this bill—understand that—at the request of the men who oppose this bill—when the state first undertook to regulate the salaries of the teachers in the City of New York. Prior to that time there was in Brooklyn no distinction as to the salary paid to male or to women teachers. The salary went with the position, and there was no distinction whatever made on account of sex up to that time.

Now that did not suit an organization then existing on the part of the men teachers. They came to the legislature and they asked the legislature first to provide a definite fixed sum that must be appropriated from the budget to the uses of the Department of Education; and they fixed that sum at four mills. That was the provision of the original law, that four mills of our annual taxation should be given to the Board of Education. To do what? To meet the mandatory provisions of the law which fixed the minimum salary for their position, which fixed the annual increment, and which determined the number of years in which the maximum should be reached. And I want to say in reply to the suggestion of His Honor, the Mayor of the City of New York, that if this bill should be defeated, the effect of that defeat would be to leave upon our statute books in full force a measure which is much more mandatory in its character than the measure now before the Senate, and if it was not for the high character of the mayor, I would charge him with bad faith in urging, as one of his objections, that the bill was mandatory in form.

The mayor then tells you that another objection—and by the way, remember that there is not in the mayor's message a single original idea. I can take the speech made by Mr. Harrison, and the speech made by Abraham Stern before the Committee of Cities, and pick out line for line every word contained in the message of His Honor, the Mayor. I do not say the mayor did not write his message, but I do say he compiled it from the speeches made before the Assembly Committee on Cities by two opponents of the bill. Now that is a fact.

What is the situation we are dealing with? By this mandatory bill now in operation, every provision of which was suggested by the men teachers, they have $900 a year to start with and $105 of annual increment, with a maximum salary of $2160. Now they decided that $900 was the lowest sum that should be paid to a male teacher; but when they came to deal with the women teachers they said: " She can get along on $600; and she doesn't need any such liberal increase as $105 annually; she would not know what to do with the money; so we will make her increment in the way of salary $40 annually as against our $105."

Now what is the position of those who favor passing this bill notwithstanding the objection of the mayor? They start out with the proposition that there should be no teacher, man or woman, in the public schools working for $11 a week. If there is any man that believes that $11 a week is proper compensation for a teacher in the public schools, man or woman, let him vote to sustain the mayor.

We do not believe it is, and as compared with salaries paid in any union free-school district of the State of New York, in proportion to expenses of living, this $600 is the meanest salary paid to any school teacher in the State of New York. We believe that at least $720 should be paid to any teacher, and we have not disturbed the minimum sum for the men from $900.

Now you have heard from Mr. ................ you have had pamphlets sent to you just as I have—that this bill only provided for increase of the compensation of the highest class of women teachers. That is a statement that was intended to prejudice you against the bill. But we had in this bill, as the Chairman of the Cities Committee knows, put in at the suggestion of the women, a provision that 66⅔% of all money paid for salaries, should be given to the teachers below the grade of 7A. But that was stricken out, not at the suggestion of the women, but stricken out at the suggestion that it involved too great a strain upon the discretion of the Board of Education.

Now the Senator from the ........... asked if we ever knew a Board of Education to pay any heed to the suggestions of the teachers. I have known such. Make your Board of Education responsive to the people and they will give heed. We have a Board of Education that cannot be reached, and if they could be reached they would be scourged from their places long since.

What is the truth about it? One year ago last February the women organized, just as the men teachers had organized long before; and exercising the greatest diligence that was possible from February, 1906, to February, 1907, they succeeded in interviewing many Commissioners and in securing a hearing by the Board. But this hearing was attended by only two of the whole Board of 46. . . .

Do you ask us to leave this matter with the Board of Education? —By defeating this bill you do not do it. Yes, but by repealing the Davis bill you do. Can you repeal that bill? I would like to see the phalanx of male teachers that would come up here in opposition to a proposition to repeal the Davis law. The Davis bill is their bonanza. They never have complained of the Davis bill nor will those who are on duty twenty-four hours after judgment day complain of it. That is the trouble with our Honorable Mayor—and if I do not lay sufficient emphasis upon the Honorable it is not my fault. He asks you just what the men principals and teachers ask you; just what Mr. Stern and Mr. Harrison of the Board of Education ask you. He asks you to let the Davis bill alone and allow the advantage to continue with the men.

Now suppose that the defeat of this bill did relegate the matter to the Board of Education, it would simply leave in force a much more mandatory enactment. The Board of Education from 1900 had the power to adjust these salaries. The Board of Education could have made the salary of every woman teacher more nearly the salary of the men teachers; the Board of Education knew it could not be justified either in economy or in morals that a woman teacher should have $40 annual increase and the men teachers $105; and it knew that the maximum salary for men teachers in grades superintended by women was greater than that paid to the superintendent over them. All these wrongs and injustices have been known to the Board of Education for seven years, and yet not a single move was made by them to adjust or correct the wrong. Not a single step was taken by them; and that statement cannot be successfully contradicted. But now at the fifty-ninth minute of the twelfth hour the Board of Education says: "We asked the women teachers and the men teachers to leave the matter with us, and they refused; they insisted that they were fighting for a principle of equal pay for equal work, and this principle they would not relinquish."

When the Board of Education asked that the matter be left with them they knew what the women teachers knew, and what the men teachers ought to have known, namely: that leaving the matter with them, under the existing law, permits them no discretion except to improve the condition of the women teachers—and to do that they have had seven years time; and yet during those seven years they did not address themselves to that question; and now in the face of legislation almost unanimously adopted by both chambers of the legislature they come and tell you that they should not be interfered with; that their discretion should not be encroached upon; that the expenses of government would be increased beyond measure: as to this latter they know you are simply restoring in this bill the four mills fixed in the original Davis act.

I have criticised school expenditures when I thought they were excessive, and I expect to be called upon to do so again. I am not prepared to say that there might not be great economies worked out in our department of education. But I will say this,—and it will be proven at the first opportunity there is to prove it, that to give justice to the women teachers the citizens of the City of New York are willing to be taxed whatever may be required. There is no man from Greater New York on this floor, representing a constituency that will justify $600 as the salary of a teacher in our public schools. He may think he does, but as soon as that can be tested it will be discovered that he does not. If you fail to pass this bill over the veto of the Mayor you will leave in operation a law that fixes that as ample compensation for the women teachers while at the same time it fixes $900 as the minimum compensation for the man teacher.

If this imposes burdens upon the people of the City of New York, the cause for which the burden is imposed is one of such complete justice that the people will gladly bear the burden. I do not know how some of my colleagues think, but you must remember that these teachers appealing here to-day for justice are not strangers in New York. By every fireside there can be found the boy that they taught and the girl that they taught. The parents do not have to take this question on suspicion, they have the work of the women teachers as evidenced in the education of their children; and they do not believe that there should be the discrimination in wages that is maintained by these present schedules—framed, not by our local authorities, but by the Davis bill. They do not believe it. There is no question of women's suffrage here; there is no question of equal rights. There is no question as to whether the saleswoman in a dry goods store is paid as much as the male salesman; there is no question as to whether the girl who is a cash girl is paid as much as the cash boy. There is only the simple question: Here we are dealing with trained educators—and don't make a mistake when you come to consider trained educators, for you will find equally brilliant examples among the women as you could possibly find among the men—the question is whether the trained educator who has taken every step required to equip her for the difficulties of her position in teaching a class, and in the management of a school, and as the superintendent of a district, whether she is because of sex to be penalized under the law for part of her salary. That is what is involved in this bill, and if you vote to sustain the Mayor you will vote to sustain the present law under which men will maintain their advantage and the woman teacher will continue to be at a disadvantage; but remember that will only be for a very little while.

IN SENATE: June 3, 1907.

ORDER OF BUSINESS: Reports of Standing Committees.

SUBJECT: Message of the Governor, in re Teachers' salary bill.

Senator Grady:—Mr. President, we are confronted with a most unfortunate condition of affairs regarding this most important piece of legislation. The reading of the message of the Governor discloses that he labors under a very erroneous idea that the principle underlying this bill is a novelty in the legislation of this State,—that for the first time it is suggested that for work of a given position women shall receive equal pay with men; and the veto proceeds from the expressed disinclination of the Governor to have that important governmental policy adopted by means of a local bill applying that principle to a single locality, and in that locality to a single element of the Civil Service—the teachers in our public schools.

He suggests to us in this message that instead of the mistaken course we have pursued that a policy of such importance should be adopted only after further consideration and with reference to an application of that principle to both the State and the municipal divisions of the State.

We can only ascribe to the Governor's lack of experience in purely governmental affairs, a position so unsound, and the lack of information upon which that mistaken opinion rests, to the fact that in the five months that he has been at the head of affairs in this State, he has not had the opportunity to acquaint himself with the details of our governmental policy, else the vote never would have issued from the Executive Chamber: for, that for work of a given position women shall receive equal pay with men is—and it has long been—the policy of the State, the policy controlling every department of the State, the policy which shapes every appropriation bill which has been presented to you in years; for here you will find in a bill making an appropriation for the support of government the appropriation going to the petition, regardless of the sex of the occupant.

Let the Secretary of State to-day name a woman for his Deputy, and under the law of the State the pay of that woman in that position is the same as is provided by law for the pay of any man who may hold it. Let the Attorney-General name a woman as his first or second deputy, and under the operation of the laws of this State as they are to-day, the pay of that woman in that position is precisely the pay given to the man who now holds it. In your appropriation bills you have your stenographers graded, and you have your clerks graded, and for these several positions, according to grade, there are established schedules of salaries to be paid to men and women alike, whoever may hold the position. So that in presenting to the Governor a bill which was intended in another municipal divison and toward another set of public employees, to vindicate this sound principle—that for work of a given position women shall receive equal pay with men—we were not as the Governor says, proposing to "*establish*" that proposition, but we were proposing to *apply* a proposition *already established* and vindicated in the State Civil Service, to the greater City of New York and to its school teachers. It might have been expected that in criticising the principle which we sought to make applicable to a local educational department, the Governor would have inquired as to the situation so far as the State Educational Department was concerned. The State Educational Department is a part of the Government of this State, and, subject to the general principle which dominates the entire State Government, has in operation the very principles which the Governor regards as a novelty, namely, *that for the work of a given position women shall receive equal pay with men.*

Now, what is the situation which this bill sought to meet? This bill proposed to rectify two injustices, one of which the Governor recognizes, and the other of which he ignores. That you haven't equalization of salaries in the Borough of Brooklyn is due not to any action taken by that particular constituency. They had equalization there up to 1900, and then you passed the Davis bill and *you destroyed the equalization that they had enjoyed,* and under which no complaint had ever been made that some novel principle was at work in government as far as that Borough was concerned. That injustice of the Davis bill the Governor entirely ignores, *failing to see in what is known as the White bill an attempt to re-establish as far as that bill is concerned the equality which the Davis bill destroys.*

The other injustice the Governor recognizes and deplores; and when I read that part of his message I was reminded of the chorus of the popular song:

"All I get is sympathy, and it ain't a bit of use to me;
When I was broke and hungry my friends all said
'Don't worry, Bill; there's lots of fish down in the brook;
All you need is a rod, a line and a hook.'
Ain't it funny, when you look for money,
All you get is sympathy."

He recognizes that there are glaring inequalities which should not be permitted to continue; and what is his fatherly advice? You will find it in the last paragraph—"The matter should be left to the Board of Education to be dealt with locally as may seem best, *unless the Legislature is prepared to lay down the general principle for the entire State and the entire public service.*"

Now, you will understand that for eight years these glaring inequalities have existed; that for eight years these glaring inequalities have been "permitted to continue"; that ample opportunity has been afforded to the Board of Education to put an end to them; that under the original levy of four mills for "the general fund" in the Department of Education budget they could have equalized the salaries of teachers in all of Greater New York; but instead of using the surplus derived from that four mill tax for the equalization of salaries, they permitted it to be reduced to *three* mills in order that they might have an excuse for not performing their duty.

You will understand that for eight years, eight years spent in a constant struggle to restore the equalization which the Davis bill destroyed, eight years spent in a fruitless struggle to have the salary go with the position rather than with the sex of the occupant of the position, that now they are asked to go back again to where for eight years they have been denied any sort of relief.

It is true the Governor gives us an alternative; and it is to that alternative I propose to address myself, and then to close. The alternative is in this language: "Unless the Legislature is prepared to lay down the general principle for the entire State and the entire public service." This is another way of repeating the objection which the Governor urges, that we have undertaken to deal with the matter by a local rather than by a general bill,—to use the precise words of the Executive, "There is no reason why the principle should be applied to teachers in New York and not to those in Albany, Syracuse, Rochester, Buffalo and elsewhere in the State."

Now, is the Governor sound in that? Are Albany, Syracuse, Rochester, Buffalo and the other municipalities subjected to the operation of the same principle in educational matters as obtains in New York?

Let us see! The Legislature in its wisdom has applied to Greater New York the unique principle of commanding its citizens to raise annually for the general educational fund such a sum as a tax of three mills upon every dollar of real and personal estate within that municipality—three mills upon every dollar liable to taxation within Greater New York.

Here is a distinct principle at work, applying exclusively to Greater New York, not shared in by either Albany, Syracuse, Rochester or Buffalo. And then the State has gone further, and it has prescribed for New York City and for New York City alone of all the municipal divisions of the State, the minimum salaries that shall be paid to teachers, men and women, and the maximum, and the number of years in which the maximum should be reached. So it cannot be for a moment argued that the Legislature having created this inequality by the application of two distinct principles to this particular constituency, cannot redress the inequality it has thus created unless it establishes an inequality for all. It is a plausible argument, as has been said. As an abstract proposition it may be sound; but we know in its practical application it is not entitled to a moment's consideration. We can point the Governor to one hundred laws on the statute books applicable to New York and New York City alone, establishing, regulating and continuing for that constituency a condition defended because of the peculiar character of that community and because of the peculiar circumstances that surround such a community.

But with greater force it has been said that if you are not going to address yourself to this question at all until you are prepared to deal with it as a whole, why then you have secured an indefinite postponement of the entire matter.

The Governor is not so well acquainted with affairs around and about the Capital as I thought he was, when he suggests for a matter of this importance "that the consideration of such a matter should be under circumstances directing the attention of every Member of the Legislature to its importance, with reference to his own constituency and to the State at large, and not upon the assumption that it is a question of purely local concern."

No one has ever claimed it was a question of purely local concern. No one who has addressed an argument in favor of the passage of this bill has ever suggested it was a question of local concern. It certainly did not lack any consideration when on this the 3rd of June we are discussing the message vetoing the work which began with the introduction of the bill on the 6th of last February. The measure was heard in public hearing before the Senate Committee on Cities; twice was it heard in public hearing before the Assembly Committee on Cities. Nor was that all: for after the difficulty and the perplexities of the situation, the possibility of injustice and the necessity for an absolutely equitable treatment of the question was made apparent, the Chairman of our Senate Cities Committee, not trusting even to his own ex-

HON. WILLIAM A. PRENDERGAST,
COMPTROLLER OF THE CITY OF NEW YORK.
SPEAKER AT "EQUAL PAY" MASS MEETING, MARCH 6, 1908.

perience, not satisfied with the embodiment of his own views, not willing that it should be taken simply as a measure, the friends or the opponents of which were to be satisfied; but regarding it as of immense importance to the educational interests which affect at least one-half of the State, brought to his assistance the best minds that he could consult and the best talent procurable. At the expenditure of days of his time outside of this Chamber and after official cares should have fallen from him, he then prepared what I am glad to have called "The White Bill." Not that I would detract one iota from the credit that belongs to the Senator from the 7th and to the Honored Member of the Assembly who originally introduced this bill; but I am glad to have it called "The White Bill," for it represents the best efforts of the directing force of our Committee on Cities; and he need not be ashamed to have his name attached to that measure of justice; and I hope it shall live to be his monument.

But, better yet, there never was a whiter bill presented to the Legislature of this State, whiter in the justice which it attempted to do to all; whiter in the character of those in whose behalf it was largely urged.

I hope no friend of the measure is either disheartened or dismayed. If a campaign of education is necessary upon the next floor we can have it there as well as we have had it on this floor since February last.

The principle underlying this bill is simple justice, simple justice itself, namely: "that for the work of a given position"—again to adopt the language of the Governor—"women shall receive equal pay with men." That is the principle at stake; that and that only is the principle to be vindicated; and the struggle for it will never end until it is written in the statute books of this State, not as now, applying to every State Department; not as now, applying to the State Educational System; but until it finds its place in the statutes of the State, there to testify to the sense of fairness, there to testify to the sense of justice, and there to vindicate the intelligence, of the entire State.

There may be a temporary set-back to our hopes and to our ambitions in this regard. We may yet have to chase the miserable pretext by which we are met in seeking the vindication of a great principle, that in private employment men can take advantage of the needs of the applicant for any place; that there are conditions in the labor market whereby you can extract from a man $12. of work for $8.; that generally speaking the women who seek private employment are those whose needs require to be immediately satisfied in order that their honor may be protected and their homes preserved; and that with such classes it may be possible for some employing wolf to discriminate between what the wage earner is entitled to and what her necessities will compel her to receive. But why take such illustrations with which to meet the unassailable and well established principle, as far as this State is concerned, that for the work of a given position the pay of women shall be the same as men, and the pay of men shall be the same as the pay of women. For one whose heart is bound up in the vindication of this just principle in order that the worthiness of every father and every husband and every son and brother of the mothers and the wives and the sisters of the land may be proven, I am willing to watch and wait; and to that struggle I promise the best effort of whatever of public life may be left to me.

## SPEECHES AT MASS MEETING—COOPER UNION

January 30, 1908.

Presiding, JOHN FRANCIS HARRISON.

ADDRESS BY SENATOR PATRICK H. MCCARREN:

*Ladies and Gentlemen*: My appearance here this evening would seem to be something like an effort on my part to reaffirm my allegiance to the cause. I assume that there is no necessity for me to say that I am as loyal to the cause that has brought this large audience here to-night, as I ever have been. (Applause.) And to repeat what the last speaker has said, I am of the opinion that ultimately the cause will triumph, because I believe that the cause is of that character so often referred to and so graphically described by Shakespeare—it is one that is thrice armed, because it is a just one.

There are two features in connection with the bill which was passed by the last Legislature, and which I understand will be introduced this year, substantially the same. The two features are the question, in the first place, of the principle of home rule, and the other feature is the question of the right of the female teacher to receive, when she performs the same work, the same wages that a male teacher receives for performing the identical work.

Now with reference to the question of home rule. I have been chided by many of the opponents of the bill for the seeming inconsistency in my attitude. I have always been regarded as a home ruler. And I have been moved to put forth my best efforts in the cause of home rule in my occupation as a legislator, because I have been obliged to confront the efforts of my Republican opponents in the Legislature to divest our community of its right to govern itself. Now I have stood conspicuously for the principle of home rule. And a few evenings ago I was brought to task by the Superintendent of Schools, Mr. Maxwell, who happened to be at a dinner where I was, and commenting on what I had said, he called the attention of the audience to my inconsistent attitude in my fathering of the so-called equal pay bill, and my insistence on the right of the City to govern itself, and my advocacy of the greatest amount of latitude in the City for the government of itself. Now that is a sort of specious argument. It is necessary to understand the origin of the so-called Davis law, which now governs our educational system in the City of New York. After a great deal of agitation, and after a considerable effort on the part of the legislators to frame such a bill as would bring about an equality of conditions, and a maximum of satisfaction, the so-called Davis law was framed and passed by the Legislature, and since its passage it has been practically in operation with very few slight changes. Now you want to bear in mind that the Legislature took to itself the power to regulate the salaries of the teachers in the City of New York, and in most all of the other Departments of the City government. Under recent amendments to the Charter, the City government is given the right to regulate the wages of its employees. But it is as specifically provided that the wages of the employees in the public school system shall be regulated by a State Act.

Now, inasmuch as there is no possibility of the entire repeal of the Davis law, there is no other way in which you can accomplish the purpose which you have in view, *except by an amendment to the Davis law.* So that, in order to accomplish the purpose of the school teachers and the friends of the school teachers who believe in their cause, *it is necessary to amend the Davis law.* Now sometimes a man may appear to be inconsistent, but his inconsistency at the time is the only way in which he can be consistent. (Applause.) If the opponents of the bill, or those who contend against the purpose of the teachers, would advocate the entire repeal of the Davis law, and give to the local authorities the right to fix the minimum and the maximum salaries, and the schedules in between, why, there might be some consistency, and there might be some force, in their position. But they insist on the retention of the Davis law, and oppose the proposition to amend it. So for that reason, the man who charges a proponent of the teachers' bill with inconsistency can be said to be more inconsistent himself. (Applause.) For that reason I feel that I am justified in my attitude in favoring the bill that has been put forth in the interest of the teachers.

I think that on the principle of equality, on the principle of equity, on the principle of justice, and on every other principle that appeals to the fairness in the composition of every individual, it must be admitted that where the female teacher does the same work that the male teacher does, she is entitled to the same compensation for her work. (Applause.) . . . We are confronted at the outset of the attempt this year to pass the bill in the Legislature and have it become a law, with the fact that we have in the Executive Chamber the same Governor that we had last year. There is no way in which we can change the Governor. (Laughter.) I mean by that, there is no way in which we can change his personality. There is a possibility of changing his mind. Now, of course, we know that Governors are liable to change their minds and political exigencies make almost every man in public office occasionally change his mind. (Great laughter.)

There may be some doubt about the force that might be brought into play to bring about a change of mind, inasmuch as we are dealing with non-voters. (Laughter.) But be that as it may, it seems to me that the position of the Governor last year was somewhat untenable, his argument against the bill being substantially one of justification on the theory that it was a local measure, and did not affect all the territory within our commonwealth. It seems to me this argument is one that cannot be maintained with that force and with that justice with which an argument should be equipped when it is intended to bring about the defeat of such a measure as Governor Hughes vetoed.

Now, many instances might be cited to show the inconsistency of the Governor. The Governor favored, and I suppose he had in his own mind good reasons for favoring, the proposition to pass and place upon the statute books the so-called "Public Utilities Bill." The principle of that bill, it seems to me, is just as repugnant to the mind of a man who is in favor of home rule as is the principle embodied in the teachers' bill. The public utilities bill provides that the City of New York, in the matter of the treatment of the Commission in the so-called first division, shall be mulcted to the extent of $1,250,000 per year for the expenses of that commission. Now, the Governor is not a local official, he is a State officer; and yet the Governor is responsible for the proposition that that sort of an act shall be passed and that sort of a burden shall be placed on the people of the City of New York, notwithstanding the fact that the local authorities have had no hand or part in the fixing of the salaries, or the amount of money that the people of the City of New York must annually pay for these officials. (Applause.)

It seems to me that inasmuch as nearly all the representatives of the City of New York in the Legislature in both branches were substantially in favor of the Teachers' Bill, that it might be said that the local authorities are in favor of the principles involved in the bill. As to whether the Governor will take another view of the bill or not, I cannot say, I am not in a position to speak for the Governor (laughter); but I want to say that I believe the bill will receive the same favorable consideration at the hands of the Legislature this year that it received last year. (Great applause.)

Now in this busy life that we are obliged to lead, whether we will or not, it is well for us to economize time. Time is money—no matter how many people may believe that it is not—time is money, and time can be saved by the friends of this measure if they will bring all their influence to bear upon the Governor and if they will busy themselves in the work of convincing the Governor that he was wrong. In order to economize time and in order to direct your efforts, so that they will have the most beneficial results, and so that they will bring to you the greatest amount of satisfaction, it is always best to know at the outset at what particular spot you should aim, so as to accomplish your purpose; and the purpose of the friends of this bill should be to bring, as I say, all the influence that can be brought to bear upon the one man who stood between the teachers and consummation of their object. That is, it seems to me, the work that you have in hand, and that is the direction in which your efforts should go.

I can only say to you that so far as the friends of the bill in the Senate of last year are concerned, that it can be safely said there will be no question at all about their attitude; and assuming that there will be very few changes, if any, in the bill, that the bill will speedily pass the upper branch of the Legislature. I want to assure you all that whatever efforts may be necessary to put forth in whatever work the teachers may think necessary to do, will be done by the friends of the bill in the Legislature of this year as cheerfully, and as happily and I think as victoriously, as last year. (Applause.)

### Address of Senator Thomas F. Grady

*Mr. Chairman, Ladies and Gentlemen*: You will see with what a regard for the eternal fitness of things the ladies manage. It was necessary that someone should stay up as late as this, and they made up their minds that it was more in line with my usual hour. (Laughter and applause.) My presence here is to inspire you with confidence that the justice of your cause is bound to triumph, and to regard such adversity as we have met with in the struggle as more of accident than design. In the few remarks that I addressed to my associates of the Senate upon the subject of the Governor's veto of the bill, my enthusiasm betrayed me into what I was afterwards convinced was a mis-statement, and I may say that that is not an unusual thing with me at all. (Laughter.) I charged that the Governor had not investigated the question. I have since discovered that he did; and now I am forced to take the other position that he was misled. *He was misled into supposing that he was dealing with a bill that provides the same salaries for similar work, whereas he was dealing with a bill that provides the same salaries for identical work.* (Laughter.) . . . *The policy of the State as embodied in every appropriation bill, is that the salary shall go to the position and not to the person occupying it; and every position in our State Civil Service to-day under the law pays to women precisely the same salary as it pays to men in that identical position.*

The governor was misled, I believe, when it was shown to him that women nurses in women's hospitals did not get the same pay as men nurses in men's hospitals, and that women keepers in women's prisons did not receive as high pay as men keepers in men's prisons; and that you will see is as wide of the question as it is possible for one to go. There can never be men keepers in women's prisons with any degree of success, and there would be no great ambition on the part of women to fill places as keepers in men's prisons. The positions are not interchangeable; there is no succession of grade; so that while I give to the governor credit as he deserves, because he is a busy man, a little more busy this year than he was last (applause), while I give to him credit, I still maintain the position—and I maintain it not with reference to this bill alone—I still maintain the position that so far as the State of New York has adopted any policy, it has been one of absolute equality for man and woman in the public service.

And then again, as Mr. Deming so clearly explained, the suggestion which the governor made that this great boon should not come to New York until we were ready to give it to all of the State—*we are ready to give it to anyone who asks for it.* I make that proposition now, and although it takes Conklin to tell you what is going to be done, I am the best authority in Albany for what is not going to be done; *and I say to you that no application from any locality to establish equality of pay for identity of service in any part of the public service will be refused by the legislature.*

Now remember that when the governor wrote his message, there were but two first-class cities in the State of New York—Buffalo and New York; and to-day Buffalo, without a legislative enactment, pays the salary for the positions. I have myself a very decided feeling as to what I regard as the unwarranted extension of the veto power. It was never so deeply impressed upon my mind as last year when all my bills were vetoed. (Laughter.) I want to suggest in all seriousness to the governor that there is no purpose in this meeting of antagonism to anybody. We have a higher aim than antagonizing the governor, or opposing the Board of Education or paying our respects or want of respect to our male opponents of last year.

*We are here in the cause of justice,* and being engaged in that cause, we have a right to believe we can convince any fair-minded man that lives, that he ought to be with us. I would like to ask when it was considered a part of the executive power not to review, but to defy the legislative mandate. *What becomes of the division of the departments of government, if when you pass a bill against the justice of which not one word can be said, about the constitutionality of which there is no question, but which is advocated in the very message of the governor himself, I want to ask, when you come to such extension of the veto power, that a governor can write across the act of Senate and Assembly, simply because he does not like the way in which it was done?*

Not for the reason that we have been discriminated against in a thousand other ways, but for the special reasons concerned and connected with this question, do we have a right to ask that this be made a special case.

Did the governor realize that it was the bill which we sought to amend that destroyed the equality that had always obtained as between men and women teachers in the Borough of Brooklyn (applause)? That for years in that Borough, the salary went to the position, regardless of the sex of the individual holding it? *That it was the Davis bill and what followed under it that destroyed that absolute equality, and that we have an absolute right to seek by amendment to that particular act to remedy the injustice that it works?* If that is not so, then I have a very poor knowledge of what legislation ought to be and how it can be accomplished. *I am not looking for the veto of the governor this year* (great applause), *because in so far as it is possible to meet his views without compromising the principle involved, every friend of this bill is prepared to go to the utmost limit* (applause). *But let there be now or hereafter no compromise as to the principle* (applause). There shall be no compromise as to the principle, because there can be none without an injustice that means, not the settlement of the great question, but its treament in the most vexatious manner possible.

I want to assure you that you have not lost a friend among the members of either House of the Legislature. (Applause.) There is, of course, a feeling of loyalty on the part of those identified with the executive, which makes them hesitate in taking any position towards which he may have expressed opposition. But can there be any question as to the governor's duty in the premises? Not that I am in a position to tell the governor as to his duties. (Laughter.) In his veto he said that he was confident that the Board of Education would correct the present existing glaring inequalities and he committed us to their tender care. I expressed some doubt as to what would happen. *Well, the Board of Education addressed itself to the "glaring inequalities" (from governor's message), and found they had no more power to correct them than we had, that they might recommend, but that that did not produce the coin;* and that a board which made no pretension whatever as educators in the strict and narrow sense, must pass upon the question as to whether it would be a good thing or a bad thing for our schools to have teachers in the same position receive the same pay. After giving us that long journey for nothing, when we come to the governor and say, "We have tried your plan and it did not work," would it not seem as if for a year at least, he would try our plan. (Great applause.) Not only have we suffered from that inconvenience, but see the position in which we find ourselves to-night—the Board of Education passes a resolution that the teachers shall not go to Albany, and as a consequence we have to bring Albany down here. (Great laughter and applause.)

I want to say while some of us are down here not entirely upon the business before the House, that *there is no journey so long or so difficult, but that a majority of the legislature will take it, in order, as was suggested, that the chivalry of the manhood of this imperial state may be vindicated.* (Applause.) I mean just that. *If the women received more salary than the men, I could find an excuse for it, but I tell you it takes away something from a man's dignity as a citizen and it adds an element of meanness to a man's position as a legislator, when he faces a condition in which injustice is worked against and upon the women folk, and he must stand with arms folded unable to offer any assistance or to redress the grievance under which they suffer.*

As an indication of the dignity of the manhood of the state, I would have such law as may be necessary passed now to correct the wrong—and that is the word I came here to speak to-night. *Do not weary of the contest; there cannot be a doubt among you of ultimate success*—those to whom you have entrusted your interests in the official positions in your association are capable, and better than that, unselfish, and better than that, devoted, and whatever may be your experience, standing together in the might and in the majesty of the influence which 13,000 good women command in any cause, you *just stand up for your principle until it is a part of the law of your state. I believe the relief will come this year.* (Applause.)

Now as I said to you, every effort will be made by those who are interested in your work to promote the bill, amend the bill, fix the bill—of course you don't know what that means—so that it may receive the executive sanction; but I have only to repeat the words of that experienced statesman and politician, as he himself would have me call him, Senator McCarren, that the important work is to get all the influence we can upon the governor now. We may not be able to reach him as handily in a little while.

It is most appropriate that this meeting should be held in this hall, the gift of one of the best friends, if not the best friend, that education ever had in this land, Peter Cooper; a hall in which all the great meetings of our citizens have been held—meetings to inspire enthusiasm and courage in the cause of the Union and defense of the flag; meetings to protest against the injustice which has been worked against our fellows in other climes and under other governments; meetings intended to be productive of the betterment of social political conditions in our own metropolis—*but never in all times has it held a meeting more worthy of the hall than the meeting it holds to-night.* (Applause.) *Never was cause more justly proclaimed from this platform, and never was cause more worthy of success than this cause, and of its ultimate success there can be no doubt.* (Applause.)

ADDRESS BY HON. ROBERT S. CONKLIN, MEMBER OF ASSEMBLY

There is one sort of political proposition on which we all can agree, and that is, that it was of great value to the teachers and to the community at large for the teachers last year to come into such close contact with the various departments of government, both municipal and state. I do not suppose, since the organization of the schools in New York City, that the teaching staff has had such a thorough comprehension of civil government as administered in the city and in the state as it has to-day. That was good, and it was valuable at that time because of this—that there has been a noticeable tendency on the part of the American people during the last score of years to lose confidence in the legislative department of their government, and to belittle it, and to insist that it shall be subservient to the executive.

Last year confidence in the legislative department of the government reached its lowest ebb. You could scarcely hear a good word for the legislature anywhere. It was the executive in both the state and the nation that commanded the people's confidence; and I say that at such a time as that, if nothing else came of this proposition, it was an excellent thing for the teachers—the trainers of the children, the educators of the future voters, to learn at first hand the spirit of earnestness and conscientiousness, of justice and integrity that pervades legislative halls.

I have here the report of the Charter Revision Commission of 1907. "The so-called Davis law, which fixes mandatorily the minimum salaries and annual increases to be paid to the supervising and teaching staffs of the Board of Education, should be repealed, as should all other mandatory provisions relating to appropriations for and expenses of the Board of Education. This recommendation is made, not because the Commission objects to the schedule of salaries fixed in the Davis law, or because it does not believe that there should be suitable and ample provision for paying the expenses of the Board of Education. *On the contrary, it is convinced that the element of certainty in the schedule of salaries should not be contravened.* This recommendation is made, however, because the Commission believes that all of such matters should be regulated by the Board of Estimate and Apportionment. In other words, that the principle of home rule should be applied to the management of this department in no less degree than to the management of every other department of the city government."

It is seen from this that the Board of Education is still a separate and distinct entity, over which the city exercises practically no control—there is no fault found with that—but in another place is a statement to the effect that the principle of home rule should be applied to this matter in no less degree than in the other.

They attempt to justify their position on home rule. I am a

home ruler, the same as my Democratic friend who preceded me. I believe thoroughly in home rule. I had almost forgotten that there is a justification for state control of teachers' salaries in ancient history. Here it is: "The Emperor Grattan, in 306 A. D., established a fixed schedule for teachers throughout the Empire. While professional chairs in these schools were filled for the most part through election of the municipal government, some were appointed direct through Emperor Julian, he claiming the right to fill all appointments." There is surely a worthy precedent. Now, I am going to sum up this home rule proposition so far as I am concerned in as few words as possible. In the country and smaller cities the training of the child is in the charge of a trinity, the home and the church and the school, and each bears its burden well. In New York City, unfortunately, in many districts, this trinity—is three in one—and that one is the school—the duties that are administered by the clergyman, by the parent in other cities, too often fall in this great city where the home and the church is so much neglected, upon the teacher; and she not only becomes a teacher, but she shoulders the burden of moral guidance, and of the parent as well.

Now, New York is the great gateway of the nation. Into it pour the immigrants from every land, and it is of vital importance, not alone to the municipality, but to the state and nation as well, that these children immigrants should be well taken care of. Why, it is the teacher that takes these children of the tenements and lets into their souls the only light that their poor stunted childhood shall ever know. (Great applause.) It is because this proposition in New York City is so much broader than it is in any other city, that even though we did concede, *which we do not concede*, that education in those cities was a matter to be administered solely by the local authorities, we could not concede that in this city, where the welfare of the young is of such vital importance to the state and to the nation, that New York City alone should have the right as to what should be done with these children and what should be done with the trainers of these children.

Now what shall the harvest be? We don't know just how these salaries are going to be administered. They tell us that New York City is poor—poverty-stricken. (Laughter.) Well, it is a matter of grave concern. The city budget we have seen advance in the last ten years from $70,000,000 to $143,000,000. New York City is the prodigal son among the municipalities of the country. Because it is a prodigal son, though it has some just debts, there is no reason why those just debts should not be paid. That is what we are trying to do—make the city, prodigal son as it is, pay its just debts.

I can say what some of the other gentlemen possibly will not venture to say: One of my reasons for advocating this is, that the City of New York during the last ten years has been increasing salaries. It has exhibited an enthusiasm over the advancement of salaries in every department except the Department of Education. In many cases—and we noted them—has the Board of Estimate and Apportionment advanced salaries in various other city departments recklessly and without regard for the just deserts of those who received the advance. Now, when this goes on year after year, it must some time or other reach a limit, and some time or another it is proper for the legislature to take notice of it and to say, that if the City of New York shall raise and shall spend millions annually in salary increases, that all of those salary increases shall not go to those whose principal claim upon them is the fact that they are voters, but that some proportion of it shall go to those who if they are not voters, are trainers of future voters. (Applause).

I don't know what is going to become of the bill. I hope for the best this year. But those of us, while we may differ sometimes as to ways and means to bring about a result, *those of us who have given this subject careful, earnest, studious consideration,* are all united upon this one proposition anyway—that we hope sooner or later that you will be victorious whatever methods you may pursue; and in your fight, the fight that we are waging for you and the fight that you are waging on your own behalf, we wish you Godspeed. (Great applause.)

## Address by Hon. James A. Donnelly, Deputy Attorney-General

*Mr. Chairman, Ladies and Gentlemen*: It is not mere gallantry which actuates me to declare that my presence here to-night affords me the utmost satisfaction and the keenest pleasure. The only alma mater I ever knew is the public school. Whatever regard for learning I possess was instilled in me by the women teachers who directed my youthful energies, and I should be worse than ungrateful indeed if I neglected the opportunity which this occasion affords me of paying my poor tribute to those who are laboring so earnestly and so faithfully to make our public school system successful. (Applause.)

When this republic was established among the nations of the earth, it was confidently predicted by its enemies that the new experiment in government based upon the equality of all before the law, must inevitably end in disappointment and failure. Government, contended those wiseacres, was a matter which required special skill; it could never be successfully conducted by permitting the uneducated rabble to share in its functions. The history of our country for the past century and a quarter gives the lie to those gloomy prophecies. The idea which infected the founders of this republic has been realized. But common candor compels the statement that the lofty purposes by which they were animated, must indeed have ended in disappointment and failure, if it had not been for the work performed by the public schools of America. (Applause.) Nearly two centuries ago there was published in England, a pamphlet, one sentence of which is enough to entitle it to enduring fame, for in that sentence there is to be found the most sensible expression of political philosophy that has ever proceeded from the mind of man. It was written by that eccentric genius Jonathan Swift. Swift's literary fame is more fairly established than his reputation for statesmanship, and yet, about a half a century before Thomas Jefferson gave to the world his immortal Declaration of Independence, the dean of St. Patrick's was urging that that government that did not derive its powers from the consent of the governed was the very definition and essence of slavery.

The framers of the American Constitution were not merely patriots inspired by love of their own country, having builded not merely for their own generation, but for all ages to come. And they observed that there would be erected upon this continent a government dedicated to the principle of the equality of all before the law; a government which should be an inspiration and encouragement to the oppressed of all time to come. And the history of this country amply attests the wisdom of the establishment of that principle.

The Irishman, bowed down beneath the yoke of oppression that has lasted with hateful persistency for over seven centuries, has here found a refuge from oppression. The boy driven from pillar to post, in this country of ours finds a haven—and an opportunity to enjoy the fruits of his industry undisturbed—likewise the Italian, the Russian, the man from every clime and from every country, fleeing from a government which exacts for the best of their lives a term of enlistment in the military service. These foreigners speedily become American citizens. And their children are as proud of their American nationality as the proudest descendant of those who voyaged across the seas in the *Mayflower*.

Now and then we hear the voice of the timid urging that immigration to these shores be restricted; but I say to those who fear for the safety of the Republic if the influx of foreign populations to these shores be not restricted or impeded, Democratic institutions have nothing to fear. If those who entertain that fear will go into the public schools of this metropolis any day of the week when they are in session, and see the manner in which the women teachers are making those children splendid American citizens, they will quickly abandon their fears. (Applause.)

*The principle involved in this bill is so simple and so plain that to state it is to prove its justice. It is that for the same kind of work there shall be paid to women teachers the same amount of compensation as is given to the men.* When a similar bill passed the legislature last year, the governor of this state vetoed it upon the ground, as I understand it, that it applied only to the City of

New York, and not to the other cities of the State. Our esteemed executive seems more desirous of maintaining and upholding the principle of equality of locality than the principle which animates the friends of this bill, to wit: equality of opportunity. *He seems to be more bent on preserving an abstract principle of uniformity than in upholding a concrete proposition of justice.* (Applause.) My friends, it seemed to me, that among the very first to come forward as the warm advocates of this bill would be the men teachers of New York. When Marie Antoinette was made the subject of execration and ignominy in her own country, I should have thought ten thousand swords would have leaped from their scabbard to resent the insult to her Majesty. Is chivalry dead in New York? (Applause.) Have our men become so blind—blinded by the love of gain—that the ancient spirit which would fight for a ribbon and die for a smile, has become completely obliterated? (Applause.)

But women teachers of New York, the principle upon which this bill is to succeed is not one of chivalry or of manly generosity towards the female sex. To the everlasting credit of the so-called weaker sex be it recorded that whenever she has entered the list to compete with men, she has demonstrated her capacity of doing that work, as good as that done by the men themselves. (Applause.) And the women teachers of New York, with the capacity of doing that work, to every one's satisfaction, ask for this consideration—not begging it as a boon—but demanding it as a plain and simple proposition of common honesty and common justice. (Applause.) *And because there underlies this bill a plain and simple proposition of justice, and because it finds an echo in the heart of every American citizen, who after all is a lover of fair play, I think I am safe in predicting for the fate of the bill this year an overwhelming success, and that it will at last find its place upon the statute books of the State of New York.* (Applause.)

HORACE E. DEMING, ATTORNEY, AT COOPER UNION, Jan. 30, 1908

In listening to Miss Strachan, I could not help thinking that after all the first purpose and the main purpose of government, the reason we need government at all, is in order to have justice. If we could all do justice, all have justice, without any government, what a happy rule it would be. But you cannot have justice unless the government does justice. And that is why so often we appeal to government. It needs no argument to convince any sane and reasonable person—there is quite a difference, you know, between a *reasonable* and a *reasoning* person—it needs no argument to convince a sane and reasonable person that a man or a woman, a city or a state, a corporation or an individual, any employer that pays A a different price from B for doing precisely the same work, *is doing a mean thing.* (Applause.) Now, there is something ineffably mean in treating a woman worse than you treat a man. (Applause.) And so you get rid very simply and very easily of the complicated economic arguments that have been put into the public prints in connection with this Teachers' Bill. The treatment of the teachers in New York has been ineffably, unspeakably mean. If the men are paid too much, reduce them to the women's salary. If the women are paid too little, raise them to the men's salary. If neither salary is just, find a salary that is just, but *for the same work pay the same price.* (Applause.)

But I wish to talk of something else. I do not know whether one felt more amused or more exasperated at the long, learned editorials—ignorant editorials, if the editor did not know—I presume he did not—to the effect that the great and sacred principle of home rule was violated when the teachers of New York appealed to the State Legislature. (Laughter.) And now, ladies and gentlemen, *what is home rule?* It is something we need very much in this city, and if we had it, don't you think the teachers would get their rights? I do. (Applause.) Home rule means a government of the city directly responsible to the people of the city over whom it exercises the power. We have not that in New York yet. I hope we may have it. Do you know what the Board of Education is? *Do you suppose the Board of Education is responsible to the city?* Have you any idea, any of you here—editors or reporters, men, women, visitors, anybody—have you any idea that the Board of Education in this city is responsible in any way whatsoever to the people of this city or to any elected officers of this city? *Do you think there is any earthly way by which the people of this town or any elected official of this town can hold the Board of Education responsible for its acts? Well, there is no such way;* and they call that *home rule.*

There are about four dozen men in the Board of Education, each one of whom is in for a five-year term, and he cannot be removed except on charges, and he has the right to be represented by counsel. Those of you who are over forty—perhaps there are some who will confess to that—will recall that when the heads of our city departments were appointed in that way, we never could remove them, if we tried. The mayor could never get rid of them. The Board of Education is in that unrootable class. They are there, and they are there to stay, and *the mayor has no more power, no more influence, no more right over them than you, or you, or you.* They are entirely outside of his jurisdiction. All he does is to name them, and that ends it as far as he is concerned. *He cannot veto their acts;* he cannot influence their conduct, they are an utterly irresponsible outside authority, and you cannot hold them accountable for anything they do as members of the Board of Education, as long as they do not steal or do something of that kind; and then it is a Criminal Court process, and not your affair or mine; *and that is home rule.* And so, when the teachers applied to the Board of Education, and the Board of Education would not even acknowledge the receipt of the communication, and incidentally a good while afterwards in the corner of the minutes, it was found that the committee whom the communication had been referred to, asked to be excused from further consideration of the communication—*there was no remedy at home, absolutely none.* Now, what are you going to do? *Did you know that the Board of Education was not a city department? Did you know that the city cannot control it in any way? Did you know that the Board of Education makes its own contracts, that the city does not make them? Did you know that the teachers, if they are not paid, have to sue the Board of Education, that they cannot sue the city?* It is a wholly independent corporation, just as independent as the New York Central Railroad is, and that is pretty independent. It is not like the Dock Department; it is not like the Street Cleaning Department or the Bridge Commission. Once in a while the mayor removes one of them—did you ever hear of his removing a Commissioner of Education?

Now, to be perfectly plain about it, the Board of Education is an independent corporation, organized under state law, *subordinate to nobody on earth but the legislature,* having in charge the *state function of education,* within the locality of New York City; and there is *no power under the sun superior to the Board of Education* within its functions of education, *but the New York State Legislature; and there is absolutely no other power to which the school teachers could appeal* (applause), and there is no other place now, either.

We convinced our masters, the legislature, that it was their proper function to grant this increase of pay to women teachers—that an injustice was being done—but *the governor vetoed the bill. He said it was a State Function. He said that injustice was being done, but he also said that the state could not undertake to do justice in one corner of it, and that everywhere in every State Department this principle of justice should prevail; and so he vetoed the bill. I trust that he will see that for once he did not see correctly. In its essence, his veto meant—you shall not have justice anywhere if you cannot have it everywhere.* Now, there is a fallacy there; and I am disposed to believe that if we are so fortunate as to reconvince the legislature, that we will have an additional argument to present to the governor. Following what the legislature did last year, the Board of Education attempted to correct some of the injustice and they recommended to our Board of Estimate and Apportionment a budget that would have increased the salaries and other expenses of the Board of Education by some $2,000,000 or $3,000,000. What happened? Exactly what happened in 1900. They would not have it, and they never will have it, and they never have given a proper appropriation. They always have other use for their money than spending it for the education of our children. *I think when the governor's attention is called to that, that we shall find an additional argument for the passage of our bill.*

### Address by Harriet Stanton Blatch

Teachers, as I have watched your great battle I have thought what a tremendous weight upon us tradition is. How it cramps us; holds us tight. What else, teachers, than that once upon a time clear back in the middle ages, women were paid less than men, and so you are going to be paid less to-day. But now I am going to give you a little optimistic message where there is no tradition in regard to women, and tell you that there are women who are not faced by this *question of unequal pay for equal work.* For instance, when young Dr. Crawford this last summer passed her examinations and at last won a place in one of our great city hospitals, and came to the hospital door, she was not told that she must take one-half of the pay of the man who had preceded her in that work. When Dr. Barringer, then Emily Dunning, was appointed the ambulance surgeon at Gouverneur Hospital, she was not told that she must take only part of her pay. *When my daughter, Nora Blatch, step by step passed her examinations, until she reached her goal as far as she, a girl of twenty-four, could go, and became an assistant engineer in the Board of Water Supply* (applause), *she was not told that she was to have only a fraction of the pay that she was worth to the city.* Now, my dear teachers, I feel your mother just as I feel the mother of that girl, and the intimate loving friend of these other women that I have mentioned to you. I feel your mother, and through every inch of my body goes rebellion at the injustice done you women. (Applause.) I have not quite liked to mention these very personal and dear examples to me, but your great leader, Miss Strachan, told me I must; and when Miss Strachan commands, I obey; and you have to obey also. (Applause.) Now, just one more example I am going to give, and then I will have done. A few years ago one of the very high positions in a great city department was vacant. A woman held the next position below that high position. She did all the work of the high position for some years and a half or two years. At last they thought they would fill that upper position and they advertised the examination for men only. Three women in this city were at once alert. We went down to the offending person and began to argue that question with him as to making that examination for men only, and we argued and argued with him, and the argument got hotter and hotter, the beads of perspiration stood out on his forehead, as first one woman and then another, and then another, took her turn at him; and finally he put down as his trump card, "Ladies, do you realize the salary cannot be changed, and it is $3000 a year?" "Yes," we said, "we realize it, and if a woman can stand up under that examination she can stand up under the $3000 a year." (Laughter and applause.) The results? It was exactly like the first international yacht race. You know we had to go to England the first time—we have never had to go again—and the race was around the Isle of Wight. Queen Victoria was interested in the race, and as the Yankee yacht came footing up to the finish, she asked a man who was standing there watching the race through a field glass, "Well, what boat is second?" "Your Majesty, there is no second." Our woman had no second; she was supreme. There was not a second nor a third to appoint from; they had to give it to her, and she got the $3000 a year. (Applause.)

*Women teachers, why should your profession be discriminated against in the whole range of the Civil Service examinations,* in the placing in positions and the paying of salaries? If I were a tyrant—some people say I am—but I mean a great big tyrant able to do things, and if the gods came to me and held in their hands the world and said to me: "What will you take to rule?" without a moment's hesitation I would say: "The schools." For I would know that the future lay within the hollow of my hand. For weal or woe, you teachers are making the to-morrow in our nation. Oh, not to do you justice! Think of it—a great community discriminating and making their teachers feel discontented, disloyal! We must win your loyalty and content by doing you justice. (Applause.)

### Address by Rev. Edward McGuffey, Episcopal Cathedral, Newtown

*Mr. Chairman and Ladies*: I presume the only reason why I have been invited down here to-night is that, as I look on the program, I am the only representative of any of the churches. And as the Church of God in all its branches has been most interested not only in women but in education, I am very glad indeed to come down here from the Borough of Queens and to add what my word and influence may do for the betterment of women in this regard. Although accustomed to preaching sermons and occasionally to engineering the taking up of collections (laughter), it is very seldom that I am called upon to face so many people; and so if I am troubled by any embarrassment, I trust that you will lay it to the circumstances of the case. But I would like to say as connected with my interest in education for seventeen years in the old town of Newtown, I have assiduously worked with those interested in education, and with some fair degree of success. I may say that the love of education runs in my veins, because I am the son of that old man McGuffey who wrote all the McGuffey books; and if you will do me the honor to come to my rectory I will open my fire-proof safe and show the original contract for the original McGuffey rhetorical guide for which my father received $500, payable quarterly during the year. But as my mind goes back to those old times, I feel as if I were borrowing my father's plumage; somewhat as Tom Hood felt when he went to Paris and went up in a balloon, and went up so high that when he looked down in the streets of Paris, it looked as if all his uncles were ants. (Laughter.) Mr. Chairman, and ladies and gentlemen, I have examined this matter of the equal pay of teachers with a great deal of care and I will not go over the ground which Miss Strachan and others have so fully covered; but I may say in one point I think Governor Hughes is right. I think what we propose that he shall do for the women teachers of New York City, it would be well for him to propose to do for the teachers of every city of this state. There can be no question about that. God, who gave women the duty of bearing children, knew into whose hands to place their education. The best teachers of the elementary schools, if not of the high schools in the world, are the women of to-day; and if God had intended men to be such superlative teachers, He would have caused them to bear some of the women's burdens. I myself am a graduate of the public schools of Cincinnati. I remember some of those teachers there. In the early course, the best teachers we had were the women. The best teacher in the Woodward High School, was Miss McIlvoy, whom I remember well—the best teacher of one of the best high schools west of the Alleghanies. My old teacher when I was in the fourth reader, Mrs. McGill, I think of now with great pleasure. She was a Scotch woman who had very bright red hair and a fiery temper; but she was the best, the kindest, the strongest teacher. I remember I had been sent out on numberless occasions to buy the rattan with which I was to receive my own punishment; and yet at the end of my year there, we boys got together and my father wrote a poem, which is still in my mind.

There can be no question about the justice of your cause, and it will prevail in the end. Mr. Chairman, and ladies and gentlemen, what would you think if I should go up here to the horse market and buy a horse and be very much pleased, and agree to pay $200, and then discover the horse was a mare, and say, "I will only give you $150?" (Great laughter.) And if my horse was a mare, Mr. Chairman, ladies and gentlemen, I would not say, "Because you are a mare you should only have three quarts of oats, while the gelding in the next door gets four" (laughter.) If an author should come with a good book, through the mail, send it to one of our publishers, and the publisher should agree to pay a price, say $500 or $600 for it, and then find that the author was a woman, would he be justified in saying, "You shall have but $250 for the book?" If a woman should paint a portrait, is she to get but $250 for a portrait for which a man would get $400? Does a woman pay less taxes than a man, because she is a woman? If she owns a piece of property, are her assessments less than they would be if she were a man? There can be no question about the justice of your cause; and it will prevail. I am glad to come down here to let you know that the best elements of the Borough of Queens are in this struggle with women for equal right, for equal pay. (Great applause.)

RESOLUTION OFFERED BY REV. HENRY A. MOTTET AND SECONDED BY EX-JUDGE WILLIAM H. WOOD.

Rev. Mottet:—Ladies and Gentlemen: As an ex-public school teacher, and, thank God, as a public school boy, too, I esteem it a very great pleasure to offer you for your consideration hereafter the following resolution:

*Resolved,* That the citizens of the City of New York here assembled in Cooper Union, January 30th, 1908, do endorse the "Equal Pay Bill" presented by the Interborough Association of Women Teachers of the City of New York, and urge the legislature to pass, and the Mayor of New York City, and the Governor of the State of New York to approve the same.

The Chairman: The Hon. Judge W. H. Wood will second the resolution proposed.

Judge Wood: Mr. Chairman, Ladies and Gentlemen: It was not until I arrived in the hall to-night that I learned for a certainty that I should be called upon to address this large and splendid audience upon the question which had called it together, in any of its aspects. A few weeks ago a couple of ladies interested in the movement asked me if I would come here to speak in favor of the measure, and I told them I should very gladly do so, because I was a believer in equality. (Applause.) I have been preaching democracy all my life, *and democracy, as I learned it, knows neither race, creed, sex nor color.* (Applause.) It welcomes beneath its broad banners all human beings as equal in civic rights and privileges. And because I believe in these doctrines, Mr. Chairman, ladies and gentlemen, it is with the greatest of pleasure that I second the resolution which has been offered before you for your action.

It seems to me that it is utterly unnecessary for anyone to offer arguments here in favor of the doctrine of equal rights for all human beings. *The logic of the adversaries of this measure to me resembles the Peace of God in that it passeth all understanding.* (Laughter.) The only objection apparently which is really made to the measure is that it in some way violates the doctrine of home rule. That point has been answered in various ways by the gentlemen who have addressed you, very logically and very completely, and yet it seems to me that they have all omitted the underlying principle upon which our public schools are founded. *The public schools of this State are not local institutions anywhere.* The

Public School system of our state is embodied in its constitution as a state policy and there is not a single rural school district anywhere from Lake Erie to Montauk Point that has the right to build a schoolhouse except by permission of the authority of the State of New York; and, therefore, when people tell you that regulating salaries of public schools in any portion of the state is a violation of the doctrine of home rule, you have but to point to the constitution of the state and to the decisions of the Court of Appeals to furnish them with a complete and satisfactory answer.

I am very much impressed with the speech of the gentleman who preceded me, who so eloquently described this Republic founded upon the consent of the governed. It is needless for me to say that I am thoroughly in accord with the spirit of Miss Strachan when she says that no matter whether this contest wins this year or not, the teachers are in it to win. (Applause.)

Resolutions passed unanimously.

## SPEECHES AT MASS MEETING—ASSOCIATION HALL, Brooklyn, March 6, 1908.

Presiding, Hon. William J. Gaynor, Justice, Appellate Division, Supreme Court.

### Address by the Hon. William J. Gaynor *

Presiding at Mass Meeting held by Interborough Association of Women Teachers, in Association Hall, Brooklyn, New York, March 6th, 1908.

*Ladies and Gentlemen*: I feel very much honored at being called here to preside over this meeting. I feel, however, as a presiding officer ought to feel, that it is my place to say very little. I feel, in fact, as Lord Eldon did, when Horne Tooke, on trial before him, not liking the interference of his Lordship in the trial, told His Honor that his business was to help the tipstaffs keep order in the court room, while the jury tried the case.

I suppose that I am not very well informed on the subject of the salaries paid to teachers of this city. There are others here who are well informed, and are able to speak on that question. I do know from my boyhood up that teachers in this country have been very miserably paid. I was brought up in the country and went to what we called in the country the "Deestrict School." I remember the poor teachers—sometimes a girl and sometimes a young fellow—who taught the school, and for pay boarded around among the poor people of the community in which I was brought up, and in addition to their boarding around they received a very pitiful compensation. In fact, if they received no more year by year, for

* Hon. William J. Gaynor was then Justice Appellate Division, Supreme Court. He is now Mayor of the City of New York.

all their lives, their heirs would not have any great squabble after their death over what was left. That has been the case all my life among the teachers in our common schools—meaning common to all, and open to all.

The teachers have been very poorly paid in this country, and that holds good all the way up and down through all scales of teachers and professors. Those in our colleges are paid poorly. I do not know that there is a head master in this country who is receiving $10,000 a year. There are head masters in England receiving much more than $10,000 a year. As a general proposition, I think it may be said that the payment of teachers in this country is lower than that of any of our other public servants, and I think the country comes to no good by being too niggardly in regard to the compensation of its public servants. They should be paid at least fairly well.

I am told that you girl teachers have to begin with $600 a year. That is little enough, it is less than a policeman has to begin with, and the men in my court, to keep order, begin with double that, and I am sure they do a great deal less than you do; in fact, I have a strong suspicion that I could keep order without them (laughter), not that I want to cast any reflection on them. They sometimes make more noise than the whole courtroom (laughter). $600 is not a large sum in these times when it costs so much to live.

Now, as I understand, the object of this meeting is to assert the proposition that girls and women are entitled for the same work, to the same compensation as the men. Now, I suppose that all the men in the public schools are of the same opinion (laughter), and if they are in your favor I think somebody has been playing a practical joke on me. Yesterday, at the breakfast table, an envelope was handed to me, containing 24 reasons why the salaries of the girls and women who are teachers should not be increased. If it is true that they are against you it seems to me very singular that your male comrades in the schools should not be with you in this movement. Certainly, it cannot hurt them if justice be done you.

Now, of course, to a large extent, it is an economic proposition. It is a proposition involving a question of justice and a question also of economy. On its face, it would appear that if a woman does the same work as a man, and does it as well as a man does it, that she should get the same compensation. In fact, it is recognized all over this country that women are doing more efficient work in our common schools than the work being done by men. (Applause). At all events, it would appear that if they are doing the work, at least, as well as the men, they should be paid an equal compensation, unless there be a good reason to the contrary, if that be possible.

Now the other side of the proposition is that it is said that it costs you ladies so much less to dress yourselves, and to live (laughter) that you ought to get less than the men get. I hope that is so, as I am bringing up several daughters myself (laughter). If that is so, and it takes so much less for a lady to live than it does a man, then it may be that as much should not be paid to you as is paid to a man. But, is that so? They say the men are all married and have big families to support. Is that so? I understand there are a lot of bachelors in the public schools who might well be married.

Mr. Byrne, the clerk of my court, told me this afternoon that from his knowledge and experience in life, he could say, that as to women—that it is a known fact that the girl who goes out into life in the schools as a teacher or as a stenographer, or into any work, sticks by the rest of the family and by the old folks at home, and that the women in this great city that go out to work have as many, if not more, people dependent on them for support as the men in the same occupation have. (Applause.) Now, I have not the statistics to verify that, and I have known all my life that it does no good, in a moment of enthusiasm or rush of blood to the head, to make exaggerated statements. It is better to have the statistics; and the matter for consideration is whether the salaries paid to the lady teachers of this city are too low from the beginning to the end, and whether they are fair in comparison with the salaries paid to the men for the same service, and you are all in the service of the State. The State would have nothing to do with education any more than keeping grocery stores except that the State derives benefit from education. The State maintains a system of free schools for that reason, to educate people sufficiently to keep government from tumbling down. Our free government rests on the intelligence of the many—on universal intelligence. In this country, where you have manhood suffrage, you will come out pretty poorly in the end, unless you have a fairly well educated moral *man* behind every vote, or the great majority of votes. Intelligent men are what count. The majority of the men who vote should be able to vote properly. If it were not for that interest which the States have in the matter, the government would leave education to the different religious denominations, and to private management, just as many other things are left in that way.

I will not dwell upon it further, but introduce those who are to speak to you.

## Address Made by the Hon. William A. Prendergast *

*Ladies and Gentlemen*: The few of us men who are left, and it is quite surprising that there are so many of us left after the

* Hon. William A. Prendergast was then Register, County of Kings. He is now Comptroller, City of New York.

severe trouncing that mere man has had to-night (laughter) I will not keep this up. If I moved uneasily on my seat it was because I wanted to jump up in defense of my luckless brothers who are about this building. While I am not going to dissent from any of the decisions, I am going on record to the extent of saying that I would like to hear this question or many of these questions regarding my sex discussed in a meeting like this, where only my sex was represented (laughter). I think that if such a meeting could be arranged, you would have before you a very forcible demonstration of moral influence.

I have been asked to-night to say a few words on the subject of civil service and equal pay. My friend, Colonel Bacon, made some reference to the superior moral suasion of women, and to coming into office or going to jail. Now I never had anything but a woman teacher, and I have at last gotten into office (laughter). I mention this in order to assure you ladies that tutelage under you is no disqualification or barrier to reaching the high esteem of the people (applause). It would have been a remarkable thing if your campaign had resulted in a complete victory. The truth is that there exists throughout this community an honest belief on the part of many men—influential men—that there are good, strong, moral, economic reasons why there should be a difference between the wages paid to women and the wages paid to men; and your victory will not be fully achieved until you have succeeded in convincing that element of the error of its reasoning.

Years ago the requirements of the man as the source of earning capacity exceeded those of the woman. The necessity of acquiring, of earning, really devolved upon him; but because that was true many years ago is no reason whatever why it should be regarded as economical at this time, but because it is economically false, and I believe Judge Gaynor was absolutely correct when he said that this question was an economic one. The great difficulty is in inducing men to acknowledge that times have changed since several hundred years ago. Woman has come to be a very considerable element in the earning capacity of the nation, because economic changes and economic requirements have compelled her to take that position. This being the case, it is idle to attempt to array against an argument like this, economics of a hundred years ago.

A few weeks ago, the women teachers were warned that they were proceeding on a dangerous course. It was claimed that just as soon as they forced any condition where the wages that would be paid them were much higher than those that had been originally paid, the men would immediately look to secure these positions themselves, and in the competition they would win. This argument was fallacious. In the first place in the business world, no matter what moral argument you may try to introduce, the law of supply and demand regulates the question of wages, and the only reason why larger wages are paid to men than to women is that there are more available women than men. But in this case we are not dealing in a field where the law of supply and demand applies. We are dealing with a question that is a civil service question. I believe, and I am sure, that everybody entertains this belief, that where the law can evoke its authority there should be absolutely no discrimination whatever between men and women in any position where women can give the same service as men; and if they cannot, they should not be permitted to occupy the position at all.

During the last couple of months I have had occasion to become a little familiar with the Civil Service; and I have observed that the person who seems most familiar with that law is not the counsel of that department, but the Civil Service employee.

We have certain laws passed in pursuance to the constitution of this state regulating the wages or salaries in Civil Service positions. In the department where I am,* we have women employees. They are paid exactly the same wages as are paid to the men. It is the same throughout the entire state, although I notice in one of to-night's papers that someone contends that in many parts of the state women are not paid the same salaries as men under the Civil Service law. If this condition really prevails, it only prevails because there has been a successful effort to get around the Civil Service law and disqualify women from occupying certain places.

I took occasion this afternoon to look over a Civil Service examination list, in which the competitors were called upon to display their efficiency in six studies. There were on that list, as a result of the examination, 53 names of people who had received 85% and over. Thirty-six of them were women's names (applause) and a woman led the list. So much for the argument that women do not rise to the occasion of competitive examination when they have men as their competitors. *The fact lives; a generality dies almost at its birth. There has been discrimination against women even under the Civil Service law, but it has always been caused by men in office, preferring to do what they thought was the popular thing rather than the essentially right thing.* For instance, in a campaign in this county last fall, a candidate for office in which women had been employed stated publicly as an argument with which he, no doubt, hoped to propitiate the men voters, that if he was elected he would appoint no women in his office. He was not elected. (Applause).

In other parts of the state, women have been disqualified, not because the law intended they should be, but solely because some individual exercised his personal influence, and in that way violated their rights. Now, this whole question resolves itself into two parts: one is the question of law, upon which I do not attempt to pass, because I am a layman; the other is the issue of elementary justice. That is a fundamental question.

I know a large number of men who teach in public schools. I

* Mr. Prendergast was then Register of the County of Kings.

have talked this question over with them, and *I think that their position in regard to this bill rests mainly upon the fact that they have a fear that the authorities, if required to spend quite so much money on the schools, might make an effort to cut down the salaries of all in an effort to economize;* and while they give twenty-four reasons why this bill should not be passed, I think with that *fear* removed, there would be comparatively little opposition by the men.

This is a question of justice, and *justice rises above all other considerations. Teachers come and teachers go, but justice is forever.*

I said to a man teacher of my acquaintance the other day, "I think they will win," and I have some glad tidings to make known to you. He said: "I think they will myself."

### Rabbi Stephen S. Wise, at Association Hall,

Brooklyn, March 6, 1908

In the matter of the Davis schedule, which the White bill aims to repeal, I take my stand with Superintendent Maxwell, who declares it to be "unjust to the women in many respects," with Mayor McClellan, who admits that there "is much force in the contention that the present law is unjust," and with Governor Hughes, who declares that "glaring inequalities now exist." To all of this I say amen,—and something more.

As one listens to the objections which are urged against the repeal of the Davis law and the introduction of the White schedule, one would imagine that it had been proposed to repeal the Ten Commandments or the Sermon on the Mount, and substitute some base maxim in the place thereof. What is it that we would do? Merely repeal a law which is unjust, unrighteous and arbitrary, which provides unequal pay for unequal work, and substitute therefor a fundamentally just and righteous measure, Equal Pay for Equal Work. The burden of proof, needless to say, rests upon those who favor inequality. The just demand of the women teachers of New York, Equal Pay for Equal Work, is radical only in the sense of being radically right. It lacks the one merit of being new, for as early as 1871, Wendell Phillips offered a resolution at a meeting at Worcester: "We demand that, whenever women are employed at public expense to do the same kind and amount of work as men perform, they shall receive the same wages."

One of the grounds of the Mayoral veto last year was the putative violation of home rule. Governor Hughes, on the other hand, maintains the very reverse, and vetoes the bill, alleging that the matter involved is not a question of purely local concern, but one of general principles and, therefore, generally to be established, if at all. For one thing, mandatory legislation touching educational affairs in the city of New York cannot truly be called violative of home rule, seeing that the Board of Education exercises a State function and operates as an agent of the State, so that the State by its Legislature is at home throughout the State in matters educational. Again, the principle which is embodied in the White bill is really established and recognized in many departments of the State. If it were not, I can think of no better way to bring about its establishment than through the enactment of such a measure as yours, which seeks to establish the principle in the largest city of the State, containing nearly half of the entire population of the State. In this connection, as one who has lived outside of New York, I would point out the moral value to the nation of our great city taking the lead vigorously and resolutely in such high causes as that for which you are battling. It is not enough that Greater New York leads the nation in its weekly Clearing House statements; we would have "Greatest" New York lead the nation in causes which make for national weal and national righteousness.

If the White bill were, and it is not, in violation of *home rule,* technically speaking, then I say we must choose between home rule and the golden rule. Violate, if you must, the political policy of home rule, but touch not the moral principle of the *golden rule.*

The gravamen of many honest objections to the White bill is that it would necessitate an enormous increase of expenditure which New York is unable to meet. I find it disingenuous to oppose the bill because of the present financial stress, seeing that the same objection was urged, and no less vociferously and persistently, before the advent of the present financial stringency. One is tempted to believe that the antagonism is due not so much to hard times as to hard heads.

If it be necessary to practice economy, then, in the name of common honesty, why should the citizens of New York suffer the wastefulness and profligacy which attend the mismanagement of the city's affairs and cry a halt not to extravagance, but only when an outlay is proposed which is dictated by elementary principles of justice and fair play? Who will venture to say that economy in the matter of pay to women teachers of New York would be proposed if women were voters? Unequal pay for equal work is the foundation of the Davis schedule, represents an injustice which, it is imagined, can be perpetrated upon non-voters with political impunity.

New York cannot afford this "enormous increase of expenditure," —is dinned into our ears. Poor little New York with its annual budget of nearly one hundred and fifty millions! One thing New York cannot afford to do is the wrong. One thing New York cannot afford to be is unjust. New York can afford to do the right. "The right thing is always in the long run the best thing."

Two further objections to the White bill, which were voiced by the Mayor, are: first, that it is mandatory legislation; next, that it endangers the elasticity of the school system. The right ought ever to be mandatory. The Davis schedule is no less mandatory. How long is the Board of Education to be suffered to do the wrong before we are to agree that the right should be made mandatory upon it? As for the so-called elasticity of the educational system of New York, I have heard of elastic currency and of elastic political consciences, but why should an educational system, of all things, be elastic? It is more important that it be right, that it be just, that it be moral. The present salary schedule is undeniably elastic, seeing that it is stretched into giving twice the wage to men that it awards to women for the same work.

Upon one ground alone might it be admitted to be just that men and women should receive a differing wage, namely, if men and women perform different work and if, moreover, the work of one is more important than the work of the other. But not even the most rabid glorifier of man makes that claim. We are solemnly told that boys need men teachers at a certain age. We ask in turn, do not boys and girls need women teachers before arriving at a certain age as truly as boys need men teachers at a certain age? The distinguished Superintendent of the City schools has stated: "Women teachers teach younger pupils, boys as well as girls, better than men." So that the summary of the matter is that men and women teachers may be said to perform work different in kind but not in quality,

It cannot be said too often that no one would lessen the number of men teachers in the schools or lower their salaries. The White bill aims solely to raise women teachers' salaries to the end that the principle, equal pay for equal work, may be realized. Such men as will not wish to teach in the schools if women are to receive the same salaries, the schools of New York can very well afford to do without. Our children will be the gainers by their retirement. It is urged with apparent seriousness that "the services of women teachers may be obtained more cheaply than those of men," that it is "not necessary to pay the same salaries in order to obtain a sufficient supply of women teachers." First, the injustice is perpetrated and then its results are pointed out as excuse for the continuance of the reign of injustice. What if the women teachers of New York could, because of their needs, be compelled to accept one-half of the present salary which is allowed them? Shall that course, too, be adopted? That is exactly what we have done under the operation of the Davis schedule. It is that which we are resolved shall no longer be possible in our city.

Your struggle is farther-reaching than you know. It is against legislation which rests upon the shifting sands of inequity and inequality that you stand. The battle of the American Democracy must ever be against the injustice of caste and the menace of privilege. The Davis Law represents the old and perishing order: the proposed White Law represents the new and abiding order.

The contest in which you are engaged is but a skirmish in the war in which the supreme victories are yet to be won,—a war that will not be ended until justice shall have been done to woman. "Justice, Justice shalt thou pursue"—justice to man, justice to woman.

### ADDRESS BY THE HON. ROBERT H. ELDER

*Ladies and Gentlemen*: I suppose Judge Gaynor's suggestion that the Mayor's veto in question was last year's veto, was intended to convey the implication, that therefore it was hardly worth discussion. Well, I have read the message and I heartily concur with him,—it is hardly worth discussing. *I did not find in it a single reason that would induce me to think for a minute that the women teachers of this city are not entitled to as much pay as the men. On the other hand, I could not help being impressed with the fact that the arguments put forth as reasons were merely subterfuges to hide the real reasons why justice is not awarded to the women teachers of this city.*

He had something to say in this message, for example, about home rule. Why, the question of home rule has nothing to do with this issue whatever. He also said that the enormous expense would be something that taxpayers would be unable to bear. Well, I think there is no question here of enormous expense. When you come to think of that reason, you must remember that, with political safety, there is only about a certain amount of money that can be collected in this community, through taxes. The real question is "*Who is going to get it?*" (Laughter and applause).

On this money question, I feel inclined to say something, probably under pressure of exuberant youth (I am still a boy) and I don't know whether I should; but I know of so much money being wasted in this community through government influences, simply on this question of "divide," I know that so much graft went out with the opening of Livingstone Street—money expended needlessly—spent in converting that alley into a wide street; I know of so much money that is wasted every year through the Real Estate Department of the Comptroller's Office; I know of so much money that is wasted ever year in the building of sewers and other improvements,—that I cannot believe but that the Mayor knows it, and others know it; and that when they talk about keeping this money from the women teachers (when they know you deserve it) that the whole question is simply *who shall get it?* (Applause). I believe this, too, that if you women had the right to vote *you* would get it. (Applause). If you had that political value, you would find out that the Mayor would be the first one to veto his veto; and after all, this question here of equal pay is really a political question.

I know that His Honor, Judge Gaynor, has said that it is an economic question. The only economic principle that could be applicable to a case of this kind, is the economic principle that things of equal value should bring the same price; and that the service and value of the work of women teachers in our public schools is the same as that of men teachers, no sane person can deny. (Applause). In certain departments of the school, there is work that only women can do: the kindergarten, for instance. It is not that women teachers' work is not as good as the men's, but because you are not worth as much to the politicians, that you are here. So this is not an economic question, but a political question.

Well, I said that "home rule" had nothing to do with it. Now, let us see if that statement will bear the examination and analysis which Judge Gaynor said was a good thing. We do not get enough of home rule, that is, in the City of New York, as a political community. The locality, of course, should be permitted to say what teachers shall be paid, but the issue here is not a question of what teachers should be paid. The question is whether women shall be discriminated against in favor of men. Do you mean to tell me that any small body of men,—like the Board of Education, any single community like the city of New York,—should be given the exclusive power to say whether it shall do right or wrong in a great fundamental question like this? Should it not rather be written down in the Bill of Rights, with the provision for due process of law, and with those provisions that protect and safeguard the individual liberties of men, and those provisions that are intended to establish equality before the law in favor of all human beings—there should it be written that equal services shall beget equal pay. Unfortunately, this principle is not there. But do you not agree that this question really is for the bill of rights and not for a small legislative body? Instead of being referred to the Mayor or to the Board of Aldermen, it should be written down in the fundamental law, in the Constitution itself, that women should not be discriminated against. So I do not think it is a question of home rule. It is just like many of those questions concerning women that came up years ago, and which, with the advance of civilization, were cast aside as unworthy the thought of Christian people.

Once, you know, woman was not allowed to draw any salary at all. If she went out and earned a wage the husband drew it. (Laughter). Those were pleasant days for the men (laughter) and they would have opposed the passage of any bill to give her the right to draw her own wages. It was a long time before the law allowed woman to own property and control it, and only within recent years in the State of New York has woman been given the right to control her own property. This question to-night is right in the line of evolution and it must be solved,—probably not now,—possibly not through this bill, but it will come sooner or later—that you will get the same pay as the men for the same work.

Now, I received one of those circulars that Judge Gaynor spoke about, giving 24 reasons evolved by the men against this measure. I did not believe that any man, born of woman, could oppose this bill; and what made it worse to me was the fact, as I afterwards learned, that although the men are attacking the women on this bill, the women have made no attack on the men at all. (Applause). The women have not asked that the men's wages be reduced, and have not asked that no increase be given to them. Indeed, they have been generous enough and careful enough to put a clause in the bill providing that the pay now given to the men should not be reduced. Yet the men are flooding the city with these circulars against this bill. It is impossible to describe to you the feeling that came over me, when I read that circular. I just got the sensation of seeing a big strong man striking at a woman, and I felt that I would like to do just what any real man would feel like doing under such circumstances (laughter), and I did come pretty near demolishing the circular. This action on the part of the male teachers is, to me, one argument in favor of the bill.

I certainly thank you, my friends, for this opportunity of appearing before you and speaking in behalf of so just a measure. It is the first time in my life that I have ever spoken authoritatively to school marms. (Laughter). As a rule they have spoken with authority to me (laughter), and when they did I learned to sit up and listen. Let us hope that this bill will become law, and also that in time to come, other benefits and immunities under the constitution, that should come to woman, will be freely accorded and actively enjoyed.

### Address by the Hon. Alexander S. Bacon

A very respectable sprinkling of mere men.

You are very brave, and if you are brave, what do you think of me? My title is secure, and yet I must begin by stating to you: "Equal Pay for Equal Work." It is not true. It is "Equal Pay for Better Work." Woman is peculiarly fitted for the training of the young. Man is not. There must be a moral element in training to make a good citizen. A man may be very learned and very wicked, and unless he has instilled in him very early in life a respect for woman he will be a bad citizen.

Miss Strachan says you voted 99.4 for principle. Men would not have done it. They would have taken the money every time (laughter). Therefore, women are like ivory soap—99.4 pure (laughter), and if the men had been voting it would have been 99.5 for the increase and let the principle go. I am shocked to hear from Mr. Elder that there is politics in this matter. I never knew that there was any politics ever suggested to the mind of the District Attorney, and he has even suggested that some of the revenues of this great city have been misapplied. (Laughter). In the opening of an alley into a street, he has even suggested that bosses have been privately enriched. Far be it from me for suggesting such a thing—the necessity of a new party where such bosses do not exist. (Laughter).

This is a subject of abstract justice. No voter has a right in a republic to vote against his ideals, for in a republic, where the people rule the people, the people would be the victim and the republic would fall. The strong arm of a despot may control an entire nation of criminals; but in a republic where the people rule, the people must live up to their ideals or the republic would fall. Therefore, the girls and the boys should be trained with respect for law and morality, and woman, therefore, is far better fitted to instill in the minds of the young the high ideals that form the 99.4 of her life. (Applause). Our form of government does not permit religious instruction in the schools, but does permit moral instruction, and moral suasion by women is of the very highest quality. If there be a class of unruly boys who have to have the discipline of a man teacher, give to that position a higher salary that you may get a competent teacher; but if the man fails and Miss Strachan be placed in that place, and succeeds, she earns the same salary.

We demand the highest qualities in our teachers. They must be graduates of the High School and the Training School. Any man with that training thinks himself competent to be President of a Bank at $25,000 per year (laughter); and the same moral qualities, intelligence and learning would receive a higher remuneration in any other department of the public service. You therefore ask nothing but strict justice.

I do not see how the man is as well fitted, or why he should be used at all in our public schools. Their muscles are of no value. I occasionally got the benefit of that side of instruction and behold what a model citizen it made out of me. (Laughter.) Inasmuch as the male teacher is not permitted to wield the rod, since all discipline must be by moral suasion, who so competent to use it as the women present? The moral qualities of the teacher are more important. The great masses of our boys and girls never get beyond our grammar departments. During that formative period their morals must be given a good start, or they will land in the penitentiary or in office. (Laughter). Therefore it is necessary that they should have surrounding them during their tender years the beneficent influence of women, and it is the moral influence of the common people upon which the republic must depend.

We would have had no republic after a century of trial had it not been for the public school and the good influences of old New England. You have a great mission to perform, and it is only common justice that you should have wages that are equal to the demands that are necessary for that position. Let there be no wrong distinction.

### Address by Carrie Chapman Catt

I regret indeed that this Male Teachers' Association did not send me one of its documents. Perhaps I might have found something more important to say to you to-night.

Of one thing I am sure, although they may have found 24 *excuses,* they have not found 24 reasons.

Our public school system exists in this country solely as the protector of the greatness of this American republic. In these days, we Americans have mighty problems to solve, problems which have no precedents, and yet when those problems arise for discussion the invariable decision is that the solution is to be found in the public schools. We have a mighty problem of immigration, and this is also a problem which may be solved in the public schools. Leave the matter to our teachers and they will train the children so that in the coming generation they will be as loyal to the stars and stripes as children born on our own soil. Within a little time, four great men, whose names are known the wide world over, have written on the question as to why patriotism was upon a decline in this country. They all held that it was declining, and each one declared that there was but one solution for this question, and that was to teach patriotism in the public schools.

We hear upon all sides of graft in connection with corporations and institutions. The solution of these difficulties lies with the public schools. We of this generation postpone the settlement of these problems, and lay the burden upon our army of public school teachers. If we are to put upon them this responsibility, why should they get less salaries in many cases than men whose only duty is that of manual labor? What shall we say when the question is raised as to whether women should be paid less than men? *That the question should be raised is an outrage.*

I am a woman taxpayer, and I have glad news to give to you, and to-night is the first time I have been glad about it. The taxes have been raised and raised enormously, and for what possible purpose could they have been raised but that the powers that be know that this bill will pass the legislature, and pass if necessary over the mayor's and the Governor's veto, and so they have made ready to pay those salaries when the time comes. I intended to be mournful about my increased taxes, but now I see it clearly, because I know the reason why and I congratulate you upon the success which is yours in advance.

### Address by George Frederick Elliott

*Mr. Chairman, Ladies and Gentlemen*: Most of you are cognizant of the fact that this is not my first appearance on a public platform to speak in behalf of woman's supremacy in educational matters and especially do I feel it an honor to speak before this splendid assemblage of ladies and gentlemen in behalf of the "Equal Pay" bill, in the interest of all the women teachers of the greater City, which, when passed, will eliminate, for all time, the distinction in salary between the sexes.

I look upon this meeting as very auspicious—auspicious in that we have one of the most distinguished jurists of this country as our presiding officer—Mr. Justice William J. Gaynor; that we have met in a hall notable for great meetings in this borough,—meetings that have been held for the uplifting of our fellowmen; and that we have met here to make history.

This "Equal pay for equal service" bill, in my judgment, is bound to become a law in this State, and this presence, from platform to audience, will enter largely into the influences which will eventually bring about its passage.

The clear and comprehensive addresses you have listened to by the gentlemen who have preceded me have embodied almost every phase of thought and argument that could be presented on behalf of this "Equal Pay" bill, and I hardly know that I can say anything that would add to the strength of their argument.

It has been suggested that I review some of the encouragements in the Governor's veto message, and, if possible, give some sound reasons for renewing the work for the re-passage of the bill. May I say, almost at the outset, that I am a great admirer of Governor Hughes, and I think the people of this State are singularly fortunate in having such an executive at the helm. No one doubts his purity or strength of character, his courage or his ability. They have all been demonstrated to the satisfaction of thinking men and women. In the reasons he has assigned for vetoing the "whitest bill that ever passed a Legislature," he had no words of censure of the women teachers or their methods, and I think that the press and the public fully appreciated this. He tells us, among other things, that "the glaring irregularities and gross inequalities that now exist in the present law clearly should not be permitted," and he disposes almost in a word of the question of "home rule," for he tells us that "the Board of Education is directly subject to the control of the Legislature, and whatever provisions may be found necessary or wise for the purpose of defining its powers or prescribing its policy must be prescribed by the Legislature, and no other authority is competent to make such provision."

If the people will get clearly into their minds the fact that the Board of Education is an arm of the State government, deriving all its power from legislative enactment of the State, and is in no wise subject to the control or direction of the city authorities, they will better understand our contention here.

The Davis law was enacted, as I have stated, to meet the needs and requirements of the City of New York, and we simply ask the

Legislature to fix the salaries of men and women on the supervising the teaching staff, and regulate said salaries by merit, the grade of class taught, length of service, and experience in teaching cr supervising, and that no discrimination or difference in the amount of salary paid men and women shall be made on account of their difference in sex in the schools of Greater New York.

It is not a question of salary or wage that we are agitating at all. It is purely the question of service. In plain Anglo-Saxon, the broad question is asked, "Is a woman, because she *is* a woman, to receive less pay for service which she actually renders than a man shall receive for the same service?" For my part, I say, most emphatically, no, and a thousand reasons might be advanced to support my belief, but we can do no better than to take the language of His Excellency, the Governor of the State, and say that the present law presents "gross inequalities" which must be remedied by the Legislature of this State.

I think it must be conceded that the Governor is in a very much better position to determine the equities of this bill after a fourteen months' incumbency of his office than when he was called to pass upon it before, when he had been but six months at the helm. He now has the added knowledge of the vast amount of labor that has been performed in spreading the matter, in all truth and fairness, before the citizens of this great city; in the number of meetings that have been held; the vast correspondence and the petitions that have been prepared and forwarded to him and to those interested in the matter, and the large amount of literature that has been distributed among the taxpayers of our city; the number of addresses that have been made and published upon the subject, not only by members of both houses of the Legislature but by some of the most distinguished citizens of the State, both men and women.

Governor Hughes is a learned and far-seeing man, and, as I have said, he has the courage of his convictions and dares to do right at all times, and I am sure that, with the added information before him with regard to the inapplicability of the principle for which we contend to the entire State, his knowledge of the law, and his oft-times admitted justice of our cause, he will have no hesitation in reversing his former decision, and when the Legislature again passes the "White bill," which it certainly will do, he will append his signature thereto, and thus become a part of this great historical movement which will forever redound to the honor and credit of our Empire State, of which he has proven himself to be so distinguished an Executive.

I think that when the law is placed upon the statute books, it will seem to add a few inches to the height of every female in the State, and the members of the Legislature will be proud of having taken part in the legislation which has stricken from the statute books the words "male and female," for all time, as affecting servants of public education, and that both sexes will hereafter stand or fall on their merits alone, and that position, and not sex, will, for all time, determine the value to be attached to it.

Our cry has been and ever will be "Equalization or nothing," and the "White Bill" will give us the consummation of our hopes. I know the women are willing, nay, anxious, to take their chances with such a law, and why should the men be afraid of their competing with them? Let the battle begin, and may the most capable competitors win, and I have no hesitation in saying that, both sexes being put to the test of their best ability, the standard of our public schools will be second to none in the world.

I cannot close this somewhat rambling talk without propounding the query: "What woman, aye, or man, either, can read or hear mentioned the following names of distinguished women without feeling proud of what they have accomplished for the world's best good?

Harriet Beecher Stowe, George Eliot, Elizabeth Barrett Browning, Jane Austen, Clara Barton, Maria Mitchell, Julia Ward Howe, Florence Nightingale, Madame Curie, Susan B. Anthony, Elizabeth Cady Stanton, Mary A. Livermore, Lucy Stone, Pauline Wright Davis, Sarah Tyndale, Mathilda Joslyn Gage, Mary Wollstonecraft, Anna Dickinson, Amelia, Bloomer, Frances Wright, Lucretia Mott, Emma Willard, Laura Curtis Bullard, Lillie Devereaux Blake, Mrs. Lyons (Holyoke, Mass.), Nora Blatch, Grace C. Strachan, Dr. Elizabeth Blackwell (the first woman to receive the degree of M. D. in 1849 in Geneva, N. Y.), Dr. Barringer, Dr. Crawford, Harriet Martineaux, Emily Faithful, Hannah Longshore. &c., &c.

## A LETTER

I count it a personal misfortune that I am too ill to go to your meeting to-night, for I should be proud and glad to testify in behalf of your cause of most obvious justice. Perhaps it is as well, however, for it is difficult to speak with restraint on such a subject. The idea that a certain piece of work deserves a smaller rate of compensation if it be done by a woman than it would deserve if done by a man *is a monstrosity.* That in this age it should find any excuse is inexplicable, and that an enlightened community should tolerate it to the vast injury of some of our hardest-worked and worst-paid public servants, is enough to make us all ashamed and sorry. It is time we should cease to pick the lean purses of those to whom we commit the most important of all our interests and it is time we should say to them that if we will pay teachers what their services are worth, we shall at least cease to take advantage of any teacher for the savage's reason that she is a woman.

The other idea that this community cannot afford this act of justice is still less endurable. As a matter of fact it cannot afford to do anything else. On the cold basis of business economy there is nothing but waste and loss in fraud and injustice. The suggestion that this, the richest city in the world, cannot raise the comparatively small sum required is absurd. We have never seemed to find it difficult to raise money to buy rotten fire hose, nor to pay for the removing of snow that is never removed, nor to help the poor but deserving paving contractor. Then we can certainly raise it to pay these women something remotely approximating a living wage. A just enforcement of the taxation laws upon corporations and other great interests would bring into the public funds a sum very much greater than that required here. The thirteen million dollars that the Metropolitan Street Railway Company owes at this moment and has long owed to this city for unpaid taxes would go some distance towards paying our defrauded school teachers. A very small percentage of the amount wrung from us annually by the watered stocks and fictitious bonds of our public utility corporations would give us the money needed. If, therefore, we can afford as a community to supply the funds for the watered stock luxury, and if we can afford to let the corporations dodge their taxes, we can afford to pay public school teachers some fraction of what they earn.

Of course there is no question that you will win. No cause of absolute and eternal justice was ever long defeated. But when you have won I should like to suggest one thought to you. You see how hard it is for disfranchised women to secure even a modicum of obvious justice. Here and there one body of women or another may secure a single concession like this, but do you really think that it is possible for women as a class to secure economic justice except by securing political justice? For do you really imagine that if the women teachers had been voters the politicians would dare to trample upon such a cause?

With every hope for your speedy and complete triumph,

Yours very truly,

Charles Edward Russell.

March 6, 1908.

## RESOLUTION

Adopted at Mass Meeting Held by Interborough Association of Women Teachers at Association Hall, Brooklyn, Mar. 6, 1908.

Whereas, Section 1091 of the Charter of the City of New York is the only statute in the laws of the State of New York that discriminates against women; and

Whereas, The Women Teachers' Equal Pay Bill seeks to amend Section 1091, commonly called the "Davis Law," so as to abolish the discrimination against the women teachers of the City of New York,

Be it Resolved, That we, citizens of the City of New York, assembled here in Association Hall, 502 Fulton Street, Brooklyn,

Friday, March 6, 1908, do unanimously endorse the Women Teachers' "Equal Pay" Bill, and urge the Legislature to pass, and the Mayor of the City of New York and the Governor of the State of New York to approve the same.

Resolution offered by Rev. Lynn P. Armstrong, Rector, Cuyler Presbyterian Church, Brooklyn.

Unanimously adopted.

## CARNEGIE MASS MEETING

### The *American* Editorial

At our Carnegie Hall Mass Meeting, Dec. 17, 1910, Hon. Mirabeau L. Towns said:

"I assert here that there has not been a man born of woman who, by his intelligence or great activity of individuality and mentality created a new epoch in human affairs that was not indebted primarily and above all things to the influence and instruction which he received from his mother or some other woman up to the time of his adolescence.

"When we get away from the Garden of Eden and Eve, the first milestone is Moses.

"And as we advance step by step, the occasions being too numerous to mention here to-night, I will refer to a few modern instances such as the mother of Henry IV. and Jean d'Albret, not forgetting Alfred the Great of England, whose youthful stepmother, married at the age of 16 years to his old father, instructed him in music and all of the sciences and knowledge which at that time were known and gave him the inspiration to start that country which at the present time rules over so many lands that the sun never goes down upon them.

"And then comes the mother of Goethe, and the mother of Humboldt; especially of Humboldt, who started a new era in geology and natural history and who proclaimed hundreds of times that he owed all his knowledge to his mother's teachings. The great Napoleon received his first instructions in manliness, in virtue and honesty from his mother, and he never, in the moments of his utmost greatness, forgot the debt that he owed to her and had her around him until he lost his scepter.

"And if we come down to the history of our own beloved land, Washington and the memorable Lincoln, both men who made epochs in history, founding and cementing this country, got all that they knew up to the period of their early adolescence from the wisdom and teachings of their mothers.

"This would seem to ordinary intelligence to refute the argument that women are not qualified to teach boys. If other instances are necessary, we might cite Charles the Great, Charles XII. of Sweden, the great Gustav Adolph, Wesley, Pope Clement, all stars in the firmament of great attainments. But is it necessary? Right in our midst from day to day we see the little mothers in our schools instilling the idea of morality, obedience and manhood into the minds of the conglomerate masses which receive the blessings of our educational system."

HUDSON & MANHATTAN RAILROAD COMPANY.

(HUDSON RIVER TUNNEL SYSTEM.)

W. G. McADOO EXECUTIVE OFFICES.
President.

HUDSON TERMINAL

30 Church Street.

New York, December 17, 1909.

My dear Miss Strachan:—

A severe cold prevents me, much to my regret, from participating in your meeting to-night.

You are contending, as I understand it, for the principles that for the same work, executed with equal efficiency, women should be paid as much as men.

I don't see how there can be any difference of opinion on this point. The fact that a given service is performed by a person who wears breeches does not make that service less valuable if equally well performed by a person who doesn't wear breeches. It is the character and quality of the service itself that determines, or should determine, its value, no matter what the sex of the person who renders it. And it makes no difference, or should make no difference, whether the performer has or has not somebody to support; nor is it a question of the "emotions," except in so far as the emotions inspire fair play and justice.

If a woman teaches the same classes in the same grades as the man, and does it just as well, she should have the same pay as the man.

If a woman sells tickets on a railroad just as well as a man, she should receive the same pay as the man. We voluntarily recognized this on the Hudson Tunnel System, where women are employed as ticket sellers. It was an act of common justice,—nothing more. It is unnecessary to multiply examples. The principle is sound beyond question. It is only a matter of its application.

If this be admitted, how can we refuse to equalize the pay of men and women teachers? If women are discriminated against, why should it be continued? The only argument I have heard against it is that it will increase taxes. Even if this be true, can we continue to perpetuate injustice merely to keep taxes down?

We can't afford to measure justice in dollars. It should be meted out at any cost. When the stricken people of Cuba cried out to us for justice, we didn't hesitate to make war on Spain because it might increase taxes. We didn't count the cost in blood and treasure when we decided that justice should be done. While we must be practical and reasonable in the application of every sound principle, we should not be deterred from correcting, within the limits of our means, inequalities or insufficiencies in the pay of men or women teachers because it may increase taxes. I do not know how far such inequalities or inadequacies exist, but they ought to be promptly ascertained and corrected.

Modern economic conditions have forced women to work in the same fields as men. That, of itself, is hard enough. No good citizen should be willing to put woman at a disadvantage or to discriminate against her in the matter of pay or opportunity in the struggle for existence.

With best wishes, I am,

Very sincerely,

W. G. McADOO.

## CITY OF NEW YORK

### Office of the Mayor

Dec. 17, 1909. m

Hon. Mirabeau L. Towns, Chairman,
Mass Meeting, Interborough Association of Women Teachers,
Carnegie Hall, City.

Dear Sir:

I regret exceedingly that a previous engagement deprives me of the pleasure of addressing the meeting of the Interborough Association of Women Teachers this evening.

I have long been in hearty accord with the movement to improve the condition of women teachers in the school system of the City of New York. It was with great regret that I found it my duty last May to veto the so-called Teachers' Equal Pay bill. It was in violation of the principle of home rule, and mandatory. I could obtain no satisfactory estimate of its probable cost, the figures submitted running all the way from four million to eight million dollars increase. I have, since then, received more carefully prepared estimates that show that the increase to the annual budget would have been about thirteen million dollars.

I did not feel that the financial condition of the City justified so large an increase at one time. In my veto message I promised to appoint a commission of representative citizens to ascertain what could be done in behalf of the women teachers of the City. This commission has not yet reported.

It will be remembered that the Governor in vetoing one of the equal-pay bills stated that in his opinion this State had not yet accepted the principle of equal pay for men and women,* and that one department of one city should not be singled out to test the new theory.

In the development of the child a woman's care, supplementing the love and solicitude of the mother, has always been recognized as the ideal influence under which our future citizens should be trained in their youth. The acknowledgment of the fact that women teachers are the best, if not the only agents of the State, to educate the younger children, is nothing but a recognition and endorsement of our early training.

For the teaching of little children there can be no question but that women are far superior to men, and that they are therefore entitled to a higher rate of compensation.

I do not believe that the harsh rule of the commercial world—the law of supply and demand—should be applied to a condition so different from the average problems of daily life.

The proposed plan to raise the salaries of women teachers of the lower grades by a certain annual increase to be determined by the local authorities and controlled by the Board of Estimate and Apportionment seems to have been carefully thought out and to be worthy of the most respectful consideration. It will do away with the greatest objection to all previous plans—that of at once increasing the annual budget by many millions of dollars.

I believe that a gradual increase of the salaries of the women teachers, beginning with those receiving the lowest pay, is the best plan to suggest to the incoming administration, and I wish you all success in conquering this first step in the right direction.

Respectfully,

GEO. B. McCLELLAN,
Mayor.

## ABSTRACT OF SPEECH OF JUSTICE JOHN WOODWARD AS TOASTMASTER AT THE FIRST ANNUAL DINNER OF THE INTERBOROUGH ASSOCIATION OF WOMEN TEACHERS OF NEW YORK CITY, AT THE WALDORF-ASTORIA, SATURDAY EVENING, JUNE 22, 1907.

I am glad to preside at this, the first, annual dinner of the Interborough Association of Women Teachers of New York City. It is, I understand, the first public banquet ever given by an organization of professional women, and it may rightly be termed the beginning of a new social era. It is, therefore, no common occasion. It is, in fact, as distinctive, as important, as the annual

* The Governor made no such statement. He implied this, but he was mistaken. G. C. S.

dinner by the New York Chamber of Commerce, for it is significant not only of the widening of woman's sphere but also indicative of her achievement.

The times have changed and we have changed with them, and as we look around us and contemplate this distinguished gathering, he must be blind indeed who does not see evidence of the triumph of the New Idea and of the progress of civilization. It was not so long ago when such an event would have been accounted one of the seven wonders of the world. Less than a hundred years ago the legal status of woman was as insignificant as the condition of a serf during the Middle Ages. Not only did the law deny to woman the free disposal of her property and surround her person with a Chinese wall of prejudices and restrictions, but she was not even permitted to own her own children. What a married woman earned became the property of her husband. She could neither make a will nor enter into a contract. She had no rights, no privileges, save through courtesy. For ages woman had been excluded from the professions. Denied almost every opportunity to become her highest self, she merely existed. One by one, however, these various disabilities, these rusty fetters of legal and economic injustice, forged by ingorance, have been cast away until *to-day we see her exalted to that divine equality with man which was the evident purpose of evolution.* The law of the survival of the fittest has never been more successfully demonstrated. Though the Society of Friends had long before proclaimed their belief in spiritual equality, it was, I believe, Mary Wollstonecraft who, in the latter part of the eighteenth century, first began the agitation for the rights of women. Since then there have been many champions, many martyrs. To mention Elizabeth Cady Stanton and Anna Dickinson is to call up a hundred other names. With what success their labors and their lives of self-sacrifice have been crowned, this occasion is eloquent evidence. It is also a splendid tribute to the fact that such freedom as woman has achieved has been won against almost overwhelming opposition by woman herself. Gradually but surely she has widened her sphere and extended the boundaries of her influence until to-day she is man's rival and competitor in almost every calling. In 1840 there were only seven occupations open to women. To-day she is distinguished in four hundred distinct lines of endeavor. No longer is she pitied because she labors, no longer does she eat the bitter bread of dependence. She not only holds her own, but she has gained, while advancing, the esteem and the admiration of man. She has added a dignity to labor; she has transfigured life; she has transformed our whole civilization. We have seen her enter the learned professions, Law, Medicine and Theology, and she has proved not unworthy. When in 1850 Dr. Hannah Longshore opened her office in Philadelphia, the doctors, much alarmed by this strange innovation, mocked at her attempt and opposed her with petty persecutions. Even the druggists refused to fill her prescriptions. To-day over 10,000 women are practicing medicine in this country alone.

Once, and that was not so long ago, either, woman was thought altogether incapable of high thinking. She can never, it was said with all the emphasis of masculine arrogance, compete with man in the severe mental discipline of the college. To-day more than 20,000 young women are enrolled in our higher institutions of learning, and it is conceded, no longer grudgingly, that they have no cause to be ashamed. Of what woman has accomplished in authorship, of her efforts for social purity and the amelioration of suffering, of her discoveries in science, of her eloquence and of her contributions to freedom, it is not necessary for me to speak.

To mention Elizabeth Barrett Browning, George Eliot, Florence Nightingale, Harriet Beecher Stowe, Clara Barton, Emma Willard, Maria Mitchell and Madame Curie, is to say more than volumes! But it is in the field of education that woman has reaped her finest laurels. Of the public school teachers to whom the State confides the instruction of the rising generation more than half are women. And such women! You have only to look around to admire.

Here then is a force, an irresistible force which, as it can no longer be opposed, must be conciliated. Ladies, we capitulate, I bring you the white flag. After a century of unceasing agitation woman has at last lifted herself to her true sphere. She has discovered that in union there is strength, and this democracy of her mind, this confederation of her sympathies, this concentration of her powers is, I am persuaded, about to become the greatest human force in our civilization. She has exalted herself and has lifted man with her. She is the very heart of progress. Surely it is not too much to say that she deserves her successes, and that wherever she labors she has proved worthy of her wage. And he must indeed be blind to truth and deaf to every tenderness who, gazing on this brilliant assemblage of fair women, could say that her intellectual triumphs have marred her beauty or lessened her charm.

## BANQUET 1909

Congressman Sulzer: "If the Governor vetoes your bill then next year I'll run for Governor, and it is certain that I won't veto it."

Hon. Samuel B. Donnelly, Public Printer: "Equal Pay has absolutely nothing to do with supply and demand. It is not because women demand the same salary as men do that so few are employed in the printing business, but because of the very great use of machinery, which in many cases demands the strength of a man.

"Woman is by nature a better 'mother' to little children left in her care during the greater portion of the day than men are. Then why shouldn't she receive the same salary?"

Lewis Nixon: "It is due to their (women teachers') efforts that the local schools have had such rapid development. Pupils taught by women have a much better understanding of human nature than have men, and are in that sense much better adapted for the business world."

## ADDRESSES DELIVERED AT FOURTH ANNUAL DINNER, INTERBOROUGH ASSOCIATION OF WOMEN TEACHERS, CITY OF NEW YORK, SATURDAY, APRIL 16th, 1910, HELD AT WANAMAKER BANQUET HALL.

HON. WILLIAM SULZER: Miss Strachan, Ladies and Gentlemen: This is unexpected, but not embarrassing. I knew when I came here I would be asked to make a speech, and I was glad to observe I was down at the end, so that I would come last; but I see the teachers are close students of the good book, and believe those who are last shall be first.

It is a great pleasure for me to be with you again to-night. I came over from Washington especially to be here. (Applause.) And these are troublous times at the Capital. If the House is in session, and there should be a call of the House, a warrant for my arrest has been issued for being absent without leave; and the Speaker has the right to take away my pay. (Laughter.) But I am chancing all that with Uncle Joe. I am against him and I am with the teachers. (Applause.)

I am here to-night to testify again to what I have frequently said during the twenty years I have been in public life—and that is, that I never could comprehend why any man who was a lawmaker, should discriminate so far as justice is concerned, between man and woman. (Applause.)

They call me a Democrat; and I am a Democrat, not so much in the political sense, as many people believe, but I am a Democrat in the generic sense. (Applause.) I believe in equal and exact justice to all. (Applause.) And that little word "all" includes all sorts and all conditions of men and women (applause) here, there and everywhere.

My sympathy is with the struggle the teachers of this city have been making for years for justice, for equal rights and for equal pay. (Applause.) I congratulate the teachers upon this magnificent assemblage, and the success of this great banquet. There are within the confines of the City of New York, many great organizations, but I undertake to say there is no other organization in the City of New York that could bring together so many distinguished, brilliant and representative people as the Teachers' Association. It speaks volumes for your cause.

I looked forward ever since the last banquet, a year ago, to this occasion, to be with you, to congratulate you that your struggle had been won; that your cause had triumphed; that your law had been put upon the statute book. But I regret to-night to learn that no further advance of the bill has been made during all the year. And someone is responsible for that. I hope that the brilliant minds of the men here, who wield the facile pen,—I know they do—will see to it that when the next year rolls around, and another banquet is given, the law will be upon the statute books. (Applause.) That is the way you men of the press—that is the way you men of the magazines—and no one can pay the writers on the magazines a greater tribute than myself, because within three years they have worked in America the greatest revolution of modern times—I hope you will turn you thoughts and your attention to the struggle of these women; and see to it that they get their rights, that they get justice. And for justice all magazines should be a temple, and for justice all the newspapers should be altars.

Now, my friends, just a word more. I am a believer in the school; and I am a believer in school-teachers, men and women. I believe that the mightiest force on earth is the little red schoolhouse on the hill; and next to that—the dominating influence of the school—the teacher in it. No one knows the debt the Republic of America owes to the schools and to the teachers.

God bless the teachers of New York and of America. (Applause.) And may their efforts be crowned with success; and their struggle for equal rights, and for equal pay for equal work be won in the coming year. (Applause.)

COMMISSIONER WALDO: Miss Strachan, Ladies and Gentlemen: To education more than any other factor, America owes her great advance in civilization, in commerce and in industry. The training of the mind of Young America is a profession on which the future of the Union most depends. I congratulate you as teachers of the greatest and largest school system in the world. I believe that you should have equal pay for equal work. I am a strong believer in adequate compensation for public school teachers, who devote their lives to the education of our future citizens. On the school teacher devolves the task of instilling in the coming generations a love of patriotism, the traditions of our country, and a love of liberty.

I am glad to be here to-night with you, and again I congratulate you upon this magnificent dinner. (Applause.)

COMMISSIONER ARTHUR S. SOMERS: A year ago I had not taken any position, as far as the question was concerned, one way or the other. I had been thinking some, however, and endeavoring to make up my mind as to what was the proper attitude for one who was engaged in public work, and who might have to deal with this question sooner or later. I recall that during all this time, though many of the lady teachers believed that I was not their friend, inasmuch as I had failed to advocate their cause, that I found one of the most charming conditions that a man can possibly realize; my friends among the women teachers,—and I had quite a number I am proud to say—when this question arose, never for a single instant wavered in their friendship for me, even though in their hearts they believed I was not friendly to "Equal Pay." There is a lady here to-night (Miss Ennis) who called at my house on school business, and as she was going, in some manner or other, we just touched on the question of equal pay; and she said to me: "The one thing that has pained me more than anything else is the fact that you who have been one of my oldest and best friends, is not on our side." And I simply smiled,—but her words set me thinking somewhat harder, and after having weighed the question, after having debated it, after having met all the arguments against it that I could raise within myself, I came to the conclusion that this question resolved itself down to a matter of simple justice. And when I reached that conclusion, I felt it incumbent upon me, as one of your representatives, as a representative of the citizens of this city in the Board of Education, to ask the Board of Education to declare itself one way or the other on this vital issue; and if possible to give color to the efforts of the women teachers—to show their sympathy for the efforts being made by these teachers in the name of justice; and to do this not for sentimental reasons, but simply because it is right.

I voice these few personal remarks only that my position may be clearly understood; that all may know that when I introduced my resolution I did it with all the consciousness of the justice of the position that I felt I was impelled to take. I have absolutely no apology to offer to anybody for my act, and if I were the only man in the great city to stand up in favor of that resolution, I would be willing to count as that minority of one.

My best wishes go with you. I sincerely trust that your efforts within a short time will be fruitful in successful results. The cause itself must win. There can't be any doubt about that. (Applause.) If we don't settle it; if this Board doesn't settle it, another administration will. If this legislature doesn't settle it, another legislature will. Because it is one of the things that is bound to move on; and if we don't get on the band-wagon and move with it, it will go on without us. But I assure you I give you my very best wishes, and I sincerely hope and trust that no effort will be spared to keep alive this vital issue, and to educate still further, as you have been doing in the few years you have been engaged in this work, the people of our great city and our great State. (Applause.)

MRS. KATE UPSON CLARK: I was a teacher myself, years ago; so when I say "we" I count myself in with you. And we are to-night in the position of the Irishman, of whom you all have heard, who, when he drew his weekly envelope uttered an ejaculation of pain and grief. One of his friends nearby said: "What is the matter, Mike; didn't you get as much as you were expectin'?" And he said, "I am working for the stingiest man I ever worked for. Yes, I got as much as I was expectin', but I was countin' on gettin' more than I was expectin'."

My friends, we were counting on getting more, and we didn't get it; but, as the speakers before me have said, you are bound to get it.

I wonder if you ever considered how the position of the teacher to-day is different from what it was in the beginning. In the olden time, the middle ages, and since then, the position of the teacher was very low. You remember that almost all great teachers were then looked down upon. Look back to Quintilian, who was the first to oppose corporal punishment; and you remember Socrates was put to death—and Quintilian was killed too because of his teaching, although he was a good man and a good teacher. And so on through all ages, the teachers have had hard work, and they have not been respected You doubtless remember that passage in one of Scott's novels, where it is said, "What do you want with reading and writing? Leave that to the women and the monks; it is no use to a man; all he wants to know is how to control a hawk, ride his horse and shoot with a bow." That was all the man prized in those days, and if he learned to read he was ridiculed for it; it was considered a silly thing for a man to do.

But as time has gone on the position of teacher has become more honorable, and teachers have been paid more and more; the teachers have come to have a social position, and a business position, and from the present outlook, my friends, I believe in the course of time this trouble that we are having about equal pay will disappear.

Of course there is no argument whatever against equal pay for equal work. (Applause.) It comes down simply to a question of expediency. Is it possible to do it? or isn't it possible to do it? You know in the olden time a married woman had to go to her husband if she wanted money, and ask for it; or steal it out of his trousers' pocket. (Laughter.) And she would be asked "what did you buy with that last quarter I gave you." (Laughter.)

Now the question is a matter of money. Are we worth all this money? If we were only a subway we could get millions. (Laughter.) But we are not worth as much money as parks, subways and sidewalks. We are just women. As Miss Strachan has said, we buy where we can get our things cheapest, and it seems to be good policy that women come cheap. We are poor, and we are glad to get almost anything. It is very silly, and very poor policy in us. We ought to get our prices higher and perhaps we could enhance our value. I don't blame these women who are going into business. You know all the rich people are merchants. Over on the other side the French are merchants. They are hard headed, and keen and shrewd. You can't fool them; you can't get ahead of them. And I tell you we have lots of head for business—I haven't any—but some of the rest have—and I want to see these business women going into business; going in with nerve and going in to win, and becoming great in finance. and making these men sit up and take notice. That is all that will make them look up to us—to make a lot of money. And I believe we are going to get it; and then women won't have to worry about earning their own living. (Applause.)

I am not afraid of the feminizing of the schools. There has been a lot of talk about that. The men who are talking that way don't understand us women. To them we are most mysterious things. We have nearly come up to them in a few years. They don't understand us. They don't know anything about us; we are mysteries. But, just the same we have the same feelings as they have; and if they will only take us as they do themselves, and treat us as they do another fellow, they will find we are all right. (Applause.)

Somebody in defining the law of progress, said "we get along by having the old hardshells die off." Now, my friends, we don't want anybody to die before his time; but if a few of these people opposing this bill will die off, we will get it. (Applause.)

HON. JAMES A. FOLEY:—In the public press about a month ago, appeared a statement of one of the Commissioners of the Board of Education, who said in the debate on the resolution of Commissioners, that he fixed the limit of efficiency, intellectually and physically, of the women teachers of this city at five years. As I glance over the audience to-night, in which I see so much evidence, so many living documents refuting that statement, I am sure that that gentleman knows very little about educational matters—far less than he knows about one of the Southern boroughs of the city. He was entirely wrong.

As the father of the equal pay bill last year, I naturally felt an interest in it this year; although it appears to have been kidnapped from Albany and transferred to New York City, to the tender mercies of the Board of Education. I have been wondering in all this talk of investigation, why the male teachers have not demanded an investigation of the popularity of the equal pay bill in the Legislature for the last three years. (Applause.) We have heard a good deal about bribes in Albany, of the thousands that are supposed to be in certain measures that have been introduced there; but let me tell everybody here, and let me assure the members of any male teachers' association, that the only reason, and the only foundation for the success and popularity of the equal pay bill at Albany, was the earnest desire on the part of legislators to correct an injustice that had been done to the women teachers of New York City, and to remedy an inconsistency which existed in the salary schedules in the school system of this city.

I feel that the women teachers of this city are the most efficient and loyal and effective servants that the city has. We hear a good deal of American fair play and the protection of its laws—and it is due mainly to the teachers of this city that the principle has been inculcated in American manhood. But if the treatment the women teachers have been receiving from the city authorities is American fair play, then let there be reform immediately along those lines.

The Board of Education seems to be awakening to the inevitable; and I think that if the vote for equal pay, as evidenced in the March meeting of the Board of Education, indicates anything, it indicates that the increased pay for the women teachers of this city, and the broad principle of equal pay, will soon be a reality. (Applause.)

Hon. Reuben L. Gledhill:—My dear Miss Strachan and ladies and gentlemen: "While the hour is late, it is but early to some of the nights we have spent fighting for your cause. (Applause.) The last remembrance I have is of being on the firing line, with my colleague, Assemblyman Smith, at something like three o'clock of a Sunday morning in the Murray Hill Hotel battling to put your proposition in the New York Charter; and we succeeded in doing it. (Applause.) This wasn't a place for oratory relative to your bill. We were alone; and while others slept, we were working for you. We expect to win, and we expect you to win.

Remember this: he is not the best general that wins the most victories; but he is the best that survives defeat after defeat and organizes victory at the end from the experience of those defeats. (Applause.)

You will in the end, I think, be very much like the warriors that Napoleon lined up for inspection. One of the inspectors said: 'These must have been heroic men; some have no arms, others are without limbs, and others are blind. What became of the men that inflicted these severe injuries on these noble warriors?' And the French general touched his hat and said: 'They are all dead, sir.' (Applause.)

And so will all our opponents be dead when we have finished with them. (Applause.)

Hon. George S. Davis,
Father of State-wide "Equal Pay for All Civil Service Employees," 1909.

HON. MIRABEAU L. TOWNS:—Madam President, ladies and gentlemen; and indomitable Amazonians:

I believe that you all know where I stand on this question. It will be unnecessary here to elaborate my opinions and convictions as to what salary a woman should receive for doing the same work that a man is called upon to do. What I wish to speak about in the few moments I shall consume, is, first, to give you my congratulations for the most excellent organization which you have perfected for the purpose of spreading this propaganda of simple justice. The aggregation of intelligence, and beauty, and courage, which is congregated here to-night to attend this festival cannot be matched anywhere in this country; and that means anywhere in the world. History does not recall an assembly, or an association similar to that which graces this occasion to-night. Where would you find so much intelligence, so much modesty, so much true female worth and beauty, as the most contracted vision would have beheld here this evening?

This question of equal pay is one which the mind of this community is not exactly prepared to receive; and it is one which you must expect to have slowly inculcated to that conviction which will result in a majority which permits public opinion siding with you. Now, you can only do that by organization. Miss Strachan said here in her remarks, that on the first occasion when you requested an audience of the members of the Board of Education to listen to the demands of the school teachers of this city, only two attended. Afterwards, and only after the very short campaign in which the Interborough Association transferred its base of operation from Albany, and came to front its enemies right at their very hearthstone, after a short preparation—only one meeting having been held at Carnegie Hall, and that meeting having been shunned by the Chief Magistrate of the City at that time, after he had given us a solemn promise to appear—we were able to go again before the Board of Education with far different results. Our only regret is that we had induced the Mayor to appoint four women upon the Board in the expectation that they, at least, would appreciate the seriousness of the subject which concerned their sisters. We found that three of them were not equal to the occasion, and could not rise to the emergency. From some influence which no person can define, they cast their votes against you, still it is recorded that sixteen fearless members of the Board stood up for right and justice, and had their names counted in favor of this vital question. (Applause.)

If that was defeat, it was not dishonorable. I cannot recall any great public question involving the expenditure of millions of dollars, that has within the last year come so near its success as this question of equal pay, which came before a Board that had been picked, I might almost say, for three years, ever since you began your agitation, for the purpose of defeating this very question. But so eloquent had been your argument and so just was your cause, that some of these very members turned at the vital moment in your favor, and but for the desertion of those whom you naturally counted to be your friends, you would have had a settlement of this question.

Now, I notice that those whom you seem to think are opposing you, and who have the power to give you this success, are so afraid of the gentle influence, the persuasive influence that you will exert over them, that they shun and avoid you. For they know that if they come within the circumference and periphery of your influence, and listen to your plea for justice, simple justice, and equality, they will be convinced.

And as it is to some extent a political question, and as our affairs are presided over by politicians, and as it is not exactly settled whether the majority of public opinion is on your side or not, and as it involves an expenditure of some millions of dollars which must be raised by taxation, these people, although convinced of the justice of your cause, are afraid to advocate it at this moment. Therefore, I say to you, as you have not the power of suffrage, as you have only the power of organization, and as you have perfected an organization that is not afraid to maintain your rights in good or evil report, that you still further perfect that organization. Only in work—indomitable and unwearying work—can you achieve success.

I believe that the next time the votes of the Board of Education are counted, if you will keep on working as I have suggested, and keep the propaganda before the people, and spread the light, that the majority will be just as great on the other side as it was against you at the last vote. (Applause.)

Everybody is agreed that there is something in the gentler sex which peculiarly fits it to instil instruction into the infant or unformed mind; to awaken in the children the noblest sentiments, to inspire them on the road which ambition selects; to give them gentle character; to give them respect; all of which go to make up good citizenship. From time immemorial, from the time of Moses,—our friend here stated a few examples, many more might be stated—the gentle influence of woman's mind and woman's hope and woman's unselfish, undying work has produced the greatest products in efficient and useful men—men whose lives have made mile-posts on the road of human progress. And nowhere is that influence on character encountered with such convincing force as in America—as seen in the history of our progress, our wealth, our prosperity, and our almost unlimited power. So that, although our opponents in the Board of Education may say in their fear, and in their grasping for feeble arguments, that men are more efficient in instructing the youthful man, they are refuted by thousands of instances in history; refuted by the very facts which form the foundation of the progress, of the development and wealth of this country.

So those arguments will be finished in this way, and there will be nothing left but the miserly argument that it will increase the budget. Now, that amounts to nothing, because, ladies, I say that you are the budget, that you train the citizen, that you take these rough masses of humanity that come from foreign shores without any ethical development, that you take them and give them ideas of morality, that you develop their minds, that you make of them the citizens of the future, that you give to them that power to discriminate in their citizenship which makes for their happiness, their virtue, and their manhood. It is to you women teachers of this community and other communities, but mostly of this community—this doorway of foreign immigration—to whom these young people come whose minds have, I might say, lain fallow for generations. They come here oppressed by poverty, to find the doors of education open to them. They go home at night and see the squalor and poverty of their parents; and next morning they go into our palatial schools and come within the influence of refined and cultivated women; and are inspired to nobler endeavors. And if there is one spark of manhood in them, if they have any of the attributes of the Creator, it is you who form and mold them into the perfection of action.

So, as I said before, you can count absolutely on your success. Keep up your organization. Present boldly your ideas before Mayor Gaynor, as you did before Mayor McClellan, and if he shuns you for fear of the gentle influence and convincing propositions that you place before him, see that he does not escape you, even though he take refuge with Mr. Frey, the ratcatcher. (Laughter.) Because this is only one of the great questions that confront us, and as the reverend gentleman very properly said, in its achievement and in the action that you take for its achievement, perhaps greater things will come than the mere sanction of equal pay for equal work. Woman will go up one step higher in power and in the respect of her fellow-men and sisters, and that, I say, is a thing for which we may devoutly wish. (Applause.)

MR. DANIEL FRISBIE, Democratic Leader of Assembly:—It will give me great pleasure to aid you in achieving what undoubtedly is your right, and is a measure of justice too. No citizen of this country of ours, and least of all a legislator or a statesman, can be insensible to the splendid service which the teachers of our country have rendered through all its long and glorious history. Three great influences are building up the framework of the character of our American citizen. The church, naturally and properly first; the school, and the press. I am proud to belong to the latter, and I believe that we are doing something each day to aid in the cause. But no one can be insensible of the powerful influence which you exert,—an influence which affects not only the individual student as you train and develop his powers of reason, his faculties, his grasp of those principles which underlie the success of every young man; but, my friends, there is more to it than the benefit of the inspiration which you give to the individual. The founders of our government, realizing that its success through all time must rest upon the intelligence, ability and integrity of its citizens, wisely provided for our school system. And from that day until this, they have liberally and generously supported it. In the legislature of the State of New York, a proposition for schools elicits no objection from any man. The more liberal they are, the more fully we feel we are doing our duty to our State. And now, my friends, if that be true, it must equally be true that those who have in charge the youth of our State, are entitled to the greatest consideration, and our high respect and esteem.

I think there is no American who does not look with pride upon the past history of his country. Certainly we in the great City of New York, and in the State of New York, have reason to feel proud of our accomplishments during the past century. But, my friends, much as we have advanced in commerce, in manufactures, in the building up of a city which is fast becoming the great financial center of the world; in the endowment of our libraries, of our art galleries, in the advancement of science, and education; there is one acme of greatness which we are yet to achieve. I believe that we are to develop here and that it will be our greatest test of greatness, the typical ideal citizen. The citizen who will have as his inspiration the elevation of womanhood; and the realization of the fatherhood of God and the brotherhood of man. And in that development, in that glorious elevation of our state, no one will render greater influence toward that desired result than the women teachers of the City and State of New York. (Applause.)

Hon. Timothy Healy:—Ladies and gentlemen: You certainly have my sympathy, for fair play and justice. I have been fighting for twenty-five years for that principle; and I want to see the teachers of this city get a fair deal; which they are not getting. I know probably more of the situation, not here alone, but in Chicago—where a namesake, Margaret Healy, is doing sterling work—and in other cities, than you. And you ladies are to be congratulated on the splendid organization that you have.

I am in favor of equal pay, and better pay, all around. (Applause.) I will go further and say that I am in favor of votes for women. (Applause.) If you had a vote, and the privilege of the ballot, you have the organization, and you would make some of our political friends sit up and take notice. (Applause.)

I am glad that some of our legislators are coming around to our way of thinking; and I think we will have more of them coming around. You have even members of the Board of Education here to-night. Well, I don't care to say anything about the Board of Education, but I have my own opinion of them, and the least said about them, the better. (Laughter.) I have another cause of my own with the gentlemen, and have had for a long time—the janitors. You know something about the janitor system; which is a disgrace to the City of New York and to the Board of Education; and political influence is responsible for that situation.

Then why do they question about giving you a few more millions of dollars for equal pay? We have had administrations in the past in this city, that would steal that amount in a few months. (Laughter.) There is no getting away from that. I am telling you what I have said from a truck in this city, and I will say it again.

Now, my friends, I represent a labor organization. I am president of the International Brotherhood of State Firemen, and also delegate of the Central Federation of this State.

If the labor organizations have their say, you can bet your last dollar that you would have them with you, ninety per cent.

My friends, there is too little consideration given to women in this country. I know there is a prejudice against women entering the industrial field; I myself feel that way to a certain extent. But there are other fields, other lines of business, where they are a necessity, where they should be in the great majority. And if it is true, as one of your speakers has said to-night, that the best of them are not going into teaching, I don't blame them. It is a sad state of affairs, because the children—my children and every other man's children—should have the best, and the best is none too good for the future American citizens. (Applause.) I have five children attending school, and they are taught by women. I want them to be taught by women. These women I depend on for the molding of the young minds and character of my children—of all children in our public schools; and the women who do this work are entitled to a great deal more than they are getting now. It was said here a few moments ago that hod carriers got two dollars a day. Why, my friends, a hod carrier in this city gets $3.40. (Laughter.)

Only last night I learned of a girl who came home last week and threw her pay envelope down and it showed she drew twenty-five dollars for her week's work in a mill. I asked, "Do they make that much?" and she said, "They don't like to have us make $25 a week, but we get on an average $21 to $23." Now, this girl probably spent a few months in learning to become a weaver, and these teachers have to devote years to preparing themselves for their work; and then what do they get for it? There is no encouragement, and I don't wonder that the clever young women refuse to go in and work for the Board of Education. There is not a woman teaching in New York, that if she turned her attention in other directions, would not earn more money, and get along better.

I would like to make a good talk to you, but it is late. You may depend on it, when you go to Albany, or anywhere else where we can help you, we will be with you, and you will have our sympathy and support, and may God speed your success. (Applause.)

Hon. Alfred E. Smith:—Miss Strachan, ladies and gentlemen: At this late hour, it is not my purpose to make a speech. I feel like one of the Committee on "Equal Pay," and I think I ought to report as to what has happened and what has not happened since our last dinner. Unfortunately we have gotten into a situation where we have not been able to do anything for about four or five months. I think it will be remedied before long. We got into that position on this account: The well known and well defined policy of the Governor with regard to the right of localities to fix salaries, has been the principal stumbling block. In other words, in the proposed charter, the Governor wants eliminated from the Charter all reference to salary. That applies to the police and fire departments, and the school teachers. He wants the locality of Greater New York, as he does all other localities of this kind in the State left with entirely free hands to fix the salary of every person that draws money from the public treasury. That, of course, necessitates the repeal of the Davis bill. And the more I hear about the question of equal pay, the more I am convinced that the Davis act should be repealed. (Applause.) I think that this infernal situation that we are up against today, came about in connection with the Davis law, and that it should never have gone on the statute books, because it provided for this inequality, this injustice we are fighting, and waging this battle against to-day. (Applause.) Now, as to the arguments against our proposition, there are really none. Two classes of men we have to contend with. Only last Tuesday

I looked over across the table in Albany to my friend Foley; I lit a cigar and fell back in the chair; we were having it all over again. For the fortieth time I heard the arguments of the male school teachers. Their opposition to the proposition is a very simple one. It is entirely selfish. But it can be understood in a few minutes. They do not want the cost of education in this city to get so large that it may prevent them from getting more pay at some future time. (Applause.)

There is another fellow that comes along to help him out. That is the man that is making the real trouble for us. He is the man that is what you call a professional kicker against everything. He is president of some taxpayers' association some place, and he represents a large body of citizens that buy a house at $5 down and $1.25 a week; and until paid for, he is against everything, unless it is some immediate improvement on the block where his house stands, the expense of which is to be borne by the city at large. (Applause.)

Now, to-night I see the thing in a better light than I saw it this time a year ago. If the charter is enacted into law, there is no doubt about the repeal of the Davis bill, and it will not be enacted into law unless it contains the simple little provision that Senator Gledhill told you about—the night it took us until three o'clock in the morning to have it put into the charter. It doesn't say equal pay; but it says that the Board of Estimate and Apportionment, with the co-operation of the Board of Aldermen, shall fix the salaries, and in no instance shall that salary differ because of the sex of the incumbent. (Applause.)

I see the thing in a brighter light to-night, for another reason. I have the greatest confidence in the present Mayor of the City of New York. (Applause.) I believe he has taken hold of the affairs of this great city in a way that has instantly made him a national figure. (Applause.) And I do not think he can possibly be consistent with that record so far accomplished, if he allows his term of office to expire without giving some attention to this great question that has agitated the State for four years back. (Applause.) And I think, I feel, I hope, that when we meet again, one year from now, we will not be reporting upon the question; but we will be congratulating each other upon its accomplishment. (Applause.)

HON. THEODORE SUTRO:—Of course there is an enormous amount that might be said on this subject. I agree with Grady and the other speakers that have addressed you this evening. The bare annunciation of the proposition seems to prove itself: "Equal pay for equal work." Why, how can any argument be used for that? Suppose you put it the other way: Unequal pay for equal work. Isn't that an absurdity on its face? The principles of political economy have been invoked by the learned Commission appointed by Mayor McClellan in his dying hours (laughter) of supply and demand.

Now they say the women teachers are crowding out the men. I do not imagine that the school board would like to have this reflection cast upon them; that they seek inferior instruction because it is cheaper; that they seek women because they work for less, which naturally presupposes inferior work, in the most important work that the community can be engaged in, the rearing and educating of her future citizens. Besides, the old maxim, the old doctrine of Adam Smith in his "Wealth of Nations," which he enunciated 150 years ago, has been exploded as false. It may be applied to sugar and dry goods, perhaps, but not to human beings. That the labor market is entirely regulated by supply and demand, I have no time to go into.

Then there is the talk about saving so many millions to the city. I say to you ladies, whether it costs a million or twenty millions more to back up your efforts in trying to uphold our Republic, the price is cheap, but I haven't time to go into that subject either. (Applause.)

The subject I do want to say a word or two about is the absurd proposition, that of the "living wage," especially of the "family wage." Now, what does that mean? Is the State a charitable organization. (Applause.) Has the State a right to use our money for the purpose of supporting a family? If that is true, then is it right for the State to do its work improperly? If it is going to support the family, it ought to support the whole family, not a part of it. Therefore the salary of the male teacher ought to be gauged by the size of the family, and each one ought to get a different salary. If a man has twelve children, he certainly ought to have more pay than a man who has but two, even though both men be in the same grade, and are of the same efficiency. (Applause.)

I read a communication in the "Evening Post," in which a learned gentleman says, that the family wage is so important that even a young man, though he is not married, ought to receive the family wage, in order to enable him to marry. Now, what is that for a proposition? (Laughter.) I understand the women teachers are not permitted to marry. Therefore the State penalizes marriage, by prohibiting their marriage, and it sets a premium against marriage by giving the young unmarried man the same as the married man. (Applause.) I claim, ladies and gentlemen, that if that proposition is carried to its last analysis, the salary of each individual teacher ought to vary from time to time. When the first-born appears, it should be so-and-so much, and when the next one comes, there should be so much increase, and where there are twelve, it should be twelve times as much. If it is the purpose of the State to give a family wage, each member of the family ought to be supported, and not merely a part of it.

Now, that of itself is a barren argument. Still, it is the most frequently used argument I have heard in connection with this question.

The proposition which is advanced in that direction reminds me of a story—and it is a true story—of a millionaire physician in this city, who married the daughter of a multi-millionaire. When the first-born appeared in the house, the grandfather was so elated that he sent his daughter a check for fifty thousand dollars, and he promised to repeat that with every new-comer. I don't know whether I ought to continue the story in this presence, but it is a fact—I knew the gentleman—he had the largest number of children in a short time of any man that ever I heard of. And the result of that generosity on the part of the grandfather was, that this eminent surgeon celebrated so constantly and so hilariously the frequent arrivals of fifty thousand dollar checks, that he finally drank himself to death. (Laughter.)

Let that be a warning to the school board of what their proposition of unequal pay, what they mean by family wage, will result in. Let it also be a warning, and even a greater warning, to the male teachers themselves, as to what a future awaits them if their salary is kept on the family wage basis.

As to the question of cost, it would be far better if the city were to pay these teachers better and not build such expensive and luxurious school-houses. They could then pay the women teachers at least the same wages that are paid to the hod-carriers and other laborers that work on the buildings; and this they are not receiving to-day, because a hod-carrier, as I gather it from the report of the Commissioner of Education, receives $2 a day. As far as I have looked into the question, the average pay of the woman teacher in the United States is only $1.50 a day, which is the pay of the ordinary laborer.

The best place is to look always for an object lesson in these matters, and now, there is one district in this country, and it is a district where the proposition of equal pay has been successfully carried on. That is, the District of Columbia, where there is no distinction between the pay of men and women; where the question of unequal pay does not arise; where the teachers are slected as men or women are needed; and not from any motives of economy; and I hope that the system will continue there for all time to come. Now, I want to say in closing, this: that most maxims are false; they really are; they generally state an untruth. Now, I don't. The statement that "might makes right" is, in my opinion, absolutely absurd I think quite the converse is true. I have never yet found that right didn't make might in the end. And, ladies, the right is on your side, and the might will come into your hands eventually, and the victory will be yours. (Applause.)

MR. SIOSSON:—Instead of making a speech, I simply want to assure you of my great pleasure at being here with you, and my very great surprise that I am permitted to be here to eat this dinner with you. Because I know something already of the customs of these coast people, and I know it is not customary for the two sexes to dine together. I was very much afraid when I was invited, that I should find that this was one of those banquet halls where they have a gallery, and that the men would be put up in the gallery, where we would simply have to watch the ladies eat, listen to their speeches, and with our bright eyes, rain influence down upon them. (Laughter.) This is one of the most peculiar customs I have encountered here. You know that we of the interior tribes do not have this custom. In the hills, men and women associate together very frequently and very commonly. In Wyoming, where I came from, men and women are fond of being together (laughter). They like each other. They quite commonly go so far as to marry. (Laughter.) They marry much more commonly there than among the coast tribes (laughter). They go to the same schools; they go to church together, and they use the same books; they talk the same language, and understand each other, to a certain extent. They share, indeed, a common life; not segregated as here. They even go to the polls together. (Applause.)

We have, as a consequence, of course, no such question as that which agitates the people of New York, in regard to unequal pay for equal work. (Applause.) Equal pay for equal work is simply a corollary of equal suffrage. (Applause.)

I simply want to call your attention to one fact in physical geography which I have not seen in the text books. That is, the fact that men and women get further apart as one travels eastward. It is just as if one started at the pole, and the lines of longitude gradually separated as they went towards the equator. At least they say they do that way; I have never tried it. But I know that the other is true, because through coming from the west towards the east, in New York I found a definite line of demarcation between men and women. The women teachers eat by themselves; and the men teachers, if they have a disposition to eat, eat by themselves. (Laughter.) There is quite a difference, as I said, here, and suppose you go further and cross the sea. Suppose you go to France; there the men and women practically belong to a different race, from different training and education. The man may have been very liberal in his ideas, and his wife has been differently trained;

one may perhaps be an atheist, and the other may perhaps be a bigamist (Laughter.) At any rate, they have learned a different style of thinking, so a man is not on speaking terms with his wife, however much they may love each other. One has been enjoying freedom of the world, while perhaps the other has been immured in a convent school. If we go still further, say we go to Turkey, we find the women, creatures of the harem and we find the men, brutes. Suppose we go still further, and we visit New Caledonia, there the difference is greater still, for the woman is a slave, and the man a brute. It is simply a matter of longitude. In New Caledonia, it is considered improper for a brother and a sister to eat together; in New York it is considered improper for a brother and a sister to go to school together. It is simply a question of longitude. You have even in this town separate books of instruction; you have a school where masculine geography is taught, and a school where feminine geography is taught.

I hear there is some talk about changing the name of Normal College. It seems to me in some way it would be a bad change, because that name means so much. It has such a value for its historical interest because the training of what we call the normal woman was by our ancestors considered to be abnormal. They considered it was undesirable for woman to learn Latin and Greek; that it was impossible, because of her limited intellect, that she should learn mathematics. They considered it improper for her to learn physiology; they considered it useless for her to learn political economy. But in these later days, those things have become so commonly recognized as part of women's education, that the place where they were imparted was very appropriately named "Normal College." (Applause.)

REV. MAURICE HARRIS:—I come from a people who have always placed the teacher in a very high rank. In fact, one of the adages of our sages runs: "He who honors his teacher, honors God."

Ladies, you are teachers, but in another sense than in the school-room, you are carrying on a campaign of education. You will find out, ladies, that the best way of reaching the truth of a great project, or cause, is to establish its relationship to other causes. Very few causes stand isolated and alone. They are each a part of larger truths. In the effort you are making, it is not merely a matter of the equal pay of teachers; it is not merely a matter of equal pay between men and women in other walks of life, it is not only an economic question; it is a social one. Not socialistic, but sociological. And when you are fighting for this equality of pay, it is part of a larger effort for equality, for which woman has been fighting from the beginning. It is a chapter in the story of your emancipation, that began in the olden time, in the time when woman was subordinate; when woman was humiliated; when if she was a power, she was a power behind the throne, but rarely on it. And yet when we read in history, the story of the achievement of woman when she had so little chance, when she had so little power, we find that whenever there was a great man, there was always a great woman behind him. (Applause.) I don't mean in the French sense, that whenever there was mischief, you had to seek the woman; but whenever there was greatness, you had to seek the woman. If it was Alfred the Great, King of England; or Samuel, the great prophet, or Francis Bacon, the great philosopher, we are always told that a great mother in each of these instances explained the genius of the individual. Behind Mohammed, we find Kadisha. And if these are instances of what woman has achieved in her subordinate, and in a sense, enslaved condition, imagine what she may not achieve in the coming day, in the era of her thorough emancipation. In making this effort for equal pay, you are not only fighting for pay, you are not only fighting for teachers, you are fighting for equality, and for womankind. (Applause.) And please understand, ladies, that when you are fighting, if you are fighting, you are not fighting as against men, the men are with you, fighting for and with you. It is impossible for us to dissociate our interests. A man cares as much for the welfare of his daughters as for the welfare of his sons. And if you study the story of the great struggle for the emancipation of women, you will find how much men have done for the achievement of that cause.

But, ladies, just a word of warning. In seeking equality, in seeking to be brought to the level of man, take care that it means being brought up to the level of man, and not being brought down to the level of man. However much you may win, I don't want you to win this equality in a way that you may lose more than you gain. I would never wish that time to pass away when man should no longer need to put around woman his chivalry or protection; that he should say she is equal and alone, and she does not need me, and she need not look to the man, as she naturally does to-day, for his support, for his guidance, for his seat in the car. (Laughter.) For those attentions that we give to women explain the whole story of knighthood and chivalry, because whenever the time shall come that woman is so much the equal of man that man shall say "that obligation is over; I need not do this for her, or that"; then it would seem to me that one of the most beautiful sentiments in life will have passed away.

One word more. You will find, ladies, in life, that whenever we work hard for anything, we do not always achieve quite the thing that we are working for. Life is so full of unexpected surprises. It works out in ever so many unexpected ways. Providence fulfills itself in mysterious ways. But when we do work hard for a cause, and loyally, and devotedly, though we may not always achieve the thing we set out to achieve, we find because we have loyally tried, that something else has arisen, something unexpected has been achieved, far more precious than the thing we originally set out for.

Now, you have gone into this fight. You have been defeated on a few occasions, but you have never known that you were defeated. (Applause.) And when we don't know that we are defeated, we are not defeated. (Applause.) You are getting on in this struggle, and every year, at your banquet, there is going to be reported progress toward that achievement. It may possibly be, ladies, that in the ultimate outcome, something different may result than that which you expect, than that for which you are working. I said this is a campaign of education. It is part of the great sociological question, and all sorts of unexpected vistas of the relation of woman in the world and in life, may be the result of your effort, and through your fight. And if you may not in the end just achieve this particular thing, your effort may achieve a something for womankind far larger, and far more valuable.

That you may achieve what you are seeking, and that you may achieve a something more precious still is my heartfelt wish to you to-night. (Applause.)

## PART THREE—CHAPTER ONE

### DEMOCRACY EDITORIALS

Now, if we could get Grace Strachan to go tiger shooting in India, while Mr. Roosevelt is after lions in Africa, it looks as though we might have a little peace for a while.—Brooklyn *Times.*

### DEAL JUSTLY WITH THE 14,000 WOMEN TEACHERS IN MANHATTAN SCHOOLS

This morning, at ten o'clock, in the City Hall, the Mayor of New York will be called upon to veto or approve a legislative bill which deeply concerns the 17,000 teachers and the 800,000 school children of the greater city.

It is Senate bill No. 1210, and it is designed to give the women teachers of New York the same pay as that now received by the men teachers for the same work.

This is now the law in Chicago and other large cities of the country. It was the law, working to excellent effect, in the fine schools of Brooklyn before Brooklyn was consolidated with New York.

This Senate bill No. 1210 is the successor of three substantially similar bills which in three successive years have been passed by overwhelming majorities in the Legislature at Albany. In 1907 the Senate voted it by 45 to 1, the Assembly by 105 to 15. It was vetoed by Governor Hughes. In 1908 the Senate approved the bill by a two-thirds majority, but it was smothered in the House against the expressed wish of 104 out of 150 members that it be brought to a ballot. In the session of 1909, just closed, the Senate voted the bill by 38 to 3, and the House by 127 to 14.

It awaits now the approval of the Mayor and the Governor.

*Behind the Woman's bill, then, there stand in cordial approval three overwhelming majorities of the State Legislature,* 14,000 *of the* 17,000 *teachers of the greater city, a practically unanimous Board of Aldermen, the autographed signatures of* 20,000 *taxpayers of New York, a long list of the leading merchants, business men and publicists of the city, and of a nearly unanimous array of federated labor unions representing more than* 200,000 *citizens and voters.*

Opposed to the bill there appears in the open several organizations of men and taxpayers and a majority of the Board of Education who with almost unseemly haste, after a discussion of four minutes and thirty-seven seconds, disposed of this vital measure

Representatives of the Board of Education and of the men's associations will be present this morning to ask the mayor to veto the bill, and Miss Grace Strachan, at the head of the 14,000 teachers and the other organizations, will earnestly urge the mayor to approve the measure.

If the mayor approves the bill, only the governor's signature will be needed to make it a law. If the mayor vetoes the bill it falls dead until another legislature convenes to revive it.

*The American most sincerely trusts that the mayor will have the wisdom, justice and courage to give the bill his emphatic approval.*

Surely it would seem proper and just that where three successive legislatures, fresh from the people, have so represented the people in their overwhelming approval, and where so many taxpayers, citizens and laboring men have heartily endorsed the measure of common justice and good policy, that one man, as the mayor, or as the governor, should not again deny the people what the people have so repeatedly and emphatically asked and demanded, through their representatives.

*The New York American plants itself first upon the general and primary proposition that the salaries doled out to teachers, male and female, in New York and elsewhere throughout the schools of the country, are a distinct stigma upon the justice, gratitude and common sense of the American people.*

*That those who perform the holiest and noblest service to the Republic should be the poorest paid of all its workers, is a travesty upon the judgment and justice of the people.*

The woman teacher in New York begins at a salary of $600.00! The women in charge of the public comfort stations have $750.00! The scrubwoman appointed by the city gets $750.00! The telephone girl in the mayor's office gets $1,300.00 a year, with no other requirement but to be eighteen years old! The woman teacher, with her six or more years of expensive preparation at school, must work between seven and eight years at her supreme task before she begins to earn what the policeman and the fireman start with.—New York *American*, May 11, 1909.

## TWO BRAVE WOMEN DESERVE WHAT MEN RECEIVE

Those big-chested, broad-shouldered, manly men who have been fighting against equal pay for women teachers, and as vigorously fighting for bigger pay for themselves, all on the ground of the necessity for avoiding the de-energizing of boys by too much contact with the feminine quality in the school room, will do well to read the story this morning of the cool, brave nerve of Principal Mary McClay and Vice-Principal Linda Henderson, of Public School No. 91, which saved perhaps 2500 children from panic and death.

And then, perhaps these manly masculines may be big enough and broad enough, inside, to realize and to confess that New York children, boys or girls, could not possibly learn any manlier lessons of courage and strength and resource than these brave teachers illustrated in that perilous hour, and that it is a shame to rate the dollar worth of these splendid women below the level of men upon the false basis of feminine weakness and timidity.

Go to, thou male teacher, and be just!—New York *American*, May 25, 1909.

## EQUAL PAY FOR EQUAL WORK IS MERELY EDUCATIONAL JUSTICE

The women teachers of New York have called a great mass meeting at Carnegie Hall to-night to bring the whole matter of EQUAL PAY for EQUAL WORK before the public, and to invite full and fair discussion of the merits of this great question before the assembling of the legislature and the organization of the new municipal administration.

It is the fair and noble thing to do. The meeting should have a great attendance and be followed by great results.

The *American's* cordial support of the policy of equal pay for equal work has been a cardinal doctrine of its municipal policy.

Behind the women's earnest and absolutely just appeal there stand fourteen thousand of the seventeen thousand teachers of New York, three successive ballots of three successive State Legislatures in overwhelming approval, a practically unanimous vote of the Board of Aldermen, the autographed signatures of twenty thousand legal taxpayers, a long list of leading merchants, business men and publicists, the City Federation of Women's Clubs and an array of federated labor unions that include two hundred and twenty thousand workingmen of New York. All these and Justice!

In opposition there is gathered a hopeless minority of teachers, one or two special associations of citizens, and a majority vote of the Board of Education after hasty and inadequate consideration—these and an unjust and foolish prejudice!

How magnificent the disparity between the woman's just cause and the prejudiced opposition that fights it!

And to the noble minds of honest men and women the disparity of the argument is just as great in favor of the women.

Upon the one side is justice, equity, the open record of equal service, good public policy, legislative and popular approval, and the acceptable experience of other great cities of the country.

Upon the other side is sex prejudice, speculative apprehension and the sodden cry of money.

Patrick McCarren, with whom *The American* rarely agreed, but

HON. ROBERT S. CONKLIN,
FATHER OF ASSEMBLY "EQUAL PAY" BILLS OF 1907 AND 1908.

whose ability it never questioned, frankly and explicitly declared after his long experience with the school systems of the metropolis that "women make the best teachers in the world." And this sentiment *The American* heartily approves. They are natural teachers, pre-destined by instinct and equipment to deal with children. It is a tradition ancient as the race and now accepted in every theory of heredity that most if not all the great men of the world have received their great qualities from the character and training of great mothers. And this great fact shrivels into an absurdity the apprehension that women in the schools "would effeminize the children." Woman's spirit and her ideals are inspiring to all youth.

It is the contact of boy with boy, the Junior Republic of education, that makes men, and not more the teacher behind the desk. It was the Iron Duke of Wellington who said that "the battle of Waterloo was won on the football fields of Rugby."

The money argument is ignoble and unworthy of this great city dealing with its noblest and mightiest problem. Miss Strachan made clear the fact that the four-mill tax needed for the increase in the wage was a part of the original charter. It was reduced during the Low administration to three mills. The result has been insufficient to meet the school needs ever since, and we are likely under any circumstances to return to the four-mill tax.

But what does it count in this world-metropolis—this sum of three and one-half millions of dollars—against the greater thing, to establish justice, to properly pay good teachers, to renew a good spirit in the schools, and to inspire the children of to-day, who are the citizens of to-morrow? The issue is too vast and too vital to be decided by this sordid weight of money flung into the scale against justice, a great civic policy, and the future of the children.

When the people remember the multiplied millions that have been squandered without protest in the greed of corporations and the graft of politicians in New York, it sounds infinitely small and insincere, this sodden cry of a politician's parsimony.

The great meeting of to-night should go far to fix public opinion in favor of EQUAL PAY FOR EQUAL WORK.—New York *American,* December 17, 1909.

Whether men are better qualified to teach grown-up boys or should be employed in certain school classes is not the question. Different classifications of work may properly pay different salaries. These are questions outside the present movement. What the women teachers ask now is, that in the same grade and for the same kind of work the same rate of pay shall be set for men and women alike. We do not see how that proposition can be justly disputed. A teacher should not be penalized simply because she is a woman.—*Irish-American,* December 24, 1909.

## GRAFT AND MUNICIPAL ECONOMY

Some very distinguished public servants and others are busying themselves in opposing fair play to women teachers on the ground that the city cannot afford to be just.

Neither this city nor any other can afford to be unjust—there being no other extravagance known to man that is quite so high priced.

But take a good look at this.

These eminent gentlemen say the Equal Pay bill is likely to cost the city $6,000,000. It will do nothing of the kind, but suppose it did.

The corporations owe the city of New York $27,000,000 in back taxes.

The graft and waste already uncovered in the city departments amount to more than $6,000,000 a year.

The graft in the Catskill water project will be about $60,000,000.

How do these items foot up?

We do not hear the eminent gentlemen objecting to any of these expenditures. It is only when the women teachers—among the most important and worst paid of public servants—ask for a little justice that the vision of economy arises at the City Hall.

Politician contractors must have their graft, corporations must steal their taxes, heads of city departments must be supplied with automobiles and the women teachers can go whistle for the money they earn.

Is that the way of it?

If we should stop a small part of the graft we could deal justly with these women, build the schoolhouses we need, provide playgrounds, tear down the Lung Block and be decent.

How about stopping the graft, anyway? We can if we want to.—*Call*, New York City, May 17, 1909.

## SALARIES IN THE CLASSROOM

Senator McCarren's bill for the equalization of teachers' salaries in the public schools of New York City provides for the elimination of the adjectives "male" and "female" from the law under which the payrolls are made up. If the bill should be enacted the salaries now paid only to men would be paid to all teachers doing the same work, regardless of their sex.

If the wages of men in the public school service are fair recompense for the labor performed, such a measure as Senator McCarren's would end the injustice which the city now practices towards the women in its teaching corps. Of the fairness and propriety of the salary schedule for men no question has been raised.

At any rate, the ridiculous discrimination against teachers on account of their sex ought to be ended.—Editorial New York *Sun*, February 12, 1907.

## OUR TEACHERS AT ALBANY

The representatives of the male teachers of this city did not cut much of a figure at Albany yesterday. They were in an awkward situation as they faced the Assembly Committee and put forward their arguments against the increase of the pay of their women colleagues in the presence of more than 300 of the latter, all dressed in their very best clothes.

Poor Mr. Wellnesley, he could not help it. There was a suggestion of the dog in the manger when he argued as follows: "This bill says that women teachers shall have equal pay for equal work, but it says nothing about a woman being able to get more than a man. [Loud laughter.] We men teachers want to be protected so we can't be reduced."

This argument brought from Mrs. N. C. Lennan a little later the triumphant response that as assistant principal she got the magnificent salary of $1600 a year, though she had to supervise the work of a man who received $2400, all because of the trifling accident of an accident.

But for true frankness Mr. Cort surpassed all his fellow-protestants. He did not mince matters. "If this bill becomes law," he said, "it will defer the increase in the men's pay." In other words, the self-seeking male persons opposed what their opponents called a simple act of justice on the ground that it would tend to prevent the commission of a further injustice. This contention suggests that there is a good deal to be said for the theory that the reasoning processes of women are different from those of persons of the other sex.

As far as the home rule argument put forward by a representative of the Corporation Counsel's office is concerned—that this city is the only one in the state in the case of which the legislature has authority to fix salaries—the ladies and their friends might well retort that they had nothing to do with that. It was natural that they should accept conditions as they found them and fight with the weapons that they had ready to their hands. If the city refused to do them justice, and if the law gave them an appeal to the lawmaking body of the Commonwealth, why should they not make it, and if not, why not?

To ask where the extra money is to come from is to beg the question. *If an injustice is done to competent, hard working and faithful servants of the city, simply because they are women and not men, all right minded persons will be in favor of having it put an end to, and hang the expense.*—From the *Evening Sun*, Wednesday, February 27, 1907.

## THE EQUAL PAY BILL VETO

It was plain to everybody that the mayor would veto the bill equalizing the pay of men and women teachers in the public schools, or providing "pay for position." But the tone of his memorandum shows that the women have won a substantial victory.

To begin with, emphasis is laid by his Honor on the fact that, according to certain experts, the proposed change would add $6,000,000 a year to the budget. But, in spite of the other fact that this side of the question was aired at the hearing, and on other occasions, it is clear that it is a very weak argument. "Give us justice. That is all we ask," say the women. "Oh, but it would be so expensive," say the men. A very lame and ridiculous rejoinder. Besides, sordid as the defence is, it would be more conclusive if we lived in a city and state in which strict economy was regarded as one of the things earnestly sought after by persons in office.

Well, the ladies don't get the money, not just yet. They must go on paying a tax on the accident of birth. They may command in the schoolroom, but, when the time for remuneration comes around, must realize that in this best regulated of all possible worlds doublet and hose is superior to petticoat.

Now, in a case like this, the main thing is to get attention. The women court inquiry, investigation. From the beginning their appeal has been to the record of work done. The mayor announces that he will appoint a commission to investigate the whole question in all its aspects. It is safe to predict this will cause jubilation in the camp of the women and gloom among the men in the department.

In the meantime, the opponents of the measure might cast about for some new arguments, for there is reason to believe that they will be needed before long.—*Sun,* May 12, 1909.

Whenever we have had an opportunity to explain our cause to any judge, from the lowest court to the highest, we have found him on our side.—Miss Strachan on the Mayor's Committee of Inquiry.

Those who demand equal pay for equal work are in the position of making an appeal to reason. Their opponents appeal to prejudice.—*Evening Sun,* June 9, 1909.

## WOMEN, STATUS AND CONTRACT

The greatest jurist of the last century held that the most important step in modern progress was taken when man passed from a condition of status to that of contract; when he began to make his own bargains, instead of having them made for him, as a member of a clan or family or class.

The contention of the women teachers, as set forth in the letter printed in another column, virtually amounts to this, that, in so far as there is discrimination against them, on the ground of sex, their relation with the community is not contractual, while that of the men is.

If women are allowed to compete freely with men in any trade, profession or calling, and if there is discrimination against them in this matter of remuneration, it is plain that the disability of which they complain is contrary to the general tendency in the direction of equality which began with the first married woman's property act. For to set up a married woman as a person with property rights apart from her husband was a revolutionary proceeding destructive of all discipline and submission.—*Sun,* January 31, 1910.

## DIRT CHEAP

In the course of the discussion in the Board of Education yesterday on the resolution of Mr. Somers providing for equal pay for equal work in the department, one of the opponents of the proposal put his case this way:

We appoint very few men teachers now—the positions go to women. It is cheaper for the city to have women teachers. The cost is everything. If men and women had equal pay we would appoint more men and fewer women teachers.

So at last we have an explanation of the activity of the men instructors. They labor day and night to show the injustice of giving a woman the salary that belongs to the office she holds.

But it is not because they are selfish or self-seeking. Not at all. The worthy males look forward to the time when there will be no expensive, otherwise male, teachers. For, just as according to Gresham's law, bad money drives out good, so cheap teachers will drive out dear teachers. The altruists will be completely happy when economy, and no other consideration whatever, is the beginning and end of the city's policy.—*Evening Sun,* March 17, 1910.

## DR. ALLEN ON UNEQUAL PAY

Dr. William Allen went to scoff and remained to bray. It was at a meeting of the Women's Republican Club that he appeared as an advocate of unequal pay for equal work in the public schools. Some of the women present being earnest supporters of Miss Grace Strachan in what they call a fight for justice, were irritated. We fail to see why they should have been. The good Doctor is the best imaginable ally of his opponents.

It is a great mistake when you have such a bad case as Dr. Allen to give your reasons for the faith that is in you. How much more convincing it would have been if he had confined himself to the triumphant theory that women ought not to be as well paid as the men because they were women. There is no conceivable answer to that.

But no. The dear man digs up an economic theory. The woman teacher must get less than the male "for the same reason that you pay your cook what you have to pay her and no more. It sounds cruel, but it is only the working out of the great law of supply and demand."

What he doesn't see, won't see, or can't see, is just this, that by giving the men more pay *qua* men, the dear old principle of supply and demand is made inoperative. It is as if the male sex were an infant industry that had to be protected. For if it is assumed that equality would drive the men out of the service, then it follows, of course, that they and their friends do not think that they would have a chance if it were a case of a fair field and no favor.

Dr. Allen pointed out that the waste of Tammany Hall was a negligible quantity compared to the waste of energy that went on in groups like the one assembled before him. Of course women are never more ridiculous than when, instead of devoting all their energy to coddling some manly man, they give some of their attention to the task of righting a wrong or putting an end to an injustice.—*Evening Sun,* December 16, 1909.

## THE TEACHERS SALARIES BILL

The bill which gives to female teachers the same salaries for same services as are given to male teachers, has passed the Senate with only a single vote against it. Before it can become a law it must pass the Assembly. However, it is quite likely that it will pass that body without amendment. The bill is now known as the White compromise bill. The difference between the one which has just received the sanction of the Senate and that which was originally introduced is of little consequence. The essential or underlying principle was the same in both. And that is that there should be like compensation for like service; that, in this respect there should be no difference of sexes.

This is as it should be. There was manifest injustice in this preference of sexes. If women were employed as teachers it was because they could perform the services required quite as well as men. If they could not, then their employment was not justified. But it was justified. The moment that justification was made then it was clear that either the men were paid a larger sum than was proper for the performance of a similar service, or the women were not paid enough if the pay of the men was proper. Consideration determined that the men teachers were not too highly paid. Consequently it followed that the women teachers were inadequately remunerated. *The bill in question simply does justice.*—Brooklyn *Eagle,* April 16, 1907.

## WOMEN TEACHERS

The charge, often made, that women teachers tend to "feminize" boys is vigorously refuted by Professor John Dewey, one of our foremost psychologists and educators. "There is," he said, "no more efficient body of workers in America than the great army of its women teachers." And to the "feminizing" charge he replied, "Where are our effeminate boys, if you please? I have not been able to discover them." He calls the whole theory "an English pipe-dream."

Professor Dewey's point is an excellent one. It is quite certain that our system of education is not producing effeminate boys. The reason for women's good effect on children is stated by Professor Dewey. It is that women have as much executive skill and are capable of as high intellectual work as men. Whatever their limitations are, they are due to unfavorable social conditions, which may be changed, and not to their natural infirmity. Dr. Dewey insists that in New York to-day there are women better fitted to hold important administrative posts in educational matters than the present male incumbents, and that there should be women professors in all the universities.—*Press,* November 10, 1909.

## MORAL ASTIGMATISM

We imagine that disinterested people will read with a feeling of mixed censure and amusement the statement made by the men teachers of the elementary schools, in a pamphlet addressed to the Board of Education, in regard to the subject of equal pay for men and women teachers.

They, the men, have come out against equal pay. Perfectly natural action, based on naive selfishness, is likely to provoke a smile, mixed with unfavorable criticism. The men are afraid, no doubt, that if the women receive more pay they (the men) will not receive so much, or that, at any rate, their pay will not be so likely to be raised.

One of the arguments used by the men teachers against equal pay is that such a system would tend to prevent the women marrying, that it would "involve the establishment of a preferred celibate class." In other words, these men fear a system by which women may no longer feel themselves forced to marry for economic reasons. They say, in effect, "keep down the salaries of women, for if we give them an opportunity for independence they won't marry us."

Any action such as this on the part of the men teachers which tends to limit the growing independence of women is reactionary and shortsighted. The fact that so many women are led to marry in order to improve their material condition is hateful to our ideals.

It is probably true that, under a system of equal pay, where services should be paid for irrespective of sex, some women who now marry would remain single. But there are some men to-day who remain single because of relative economic independence, which they desire to maintain. These men are, however, relatively few. Women are as instinctive and as normal as men are, and independence which they feared to lose would prevent very few from marrying when they could make marriages which were attractive to them. Independence of women would improve marriage, since fewer women would marry because of necessity. By the same means divorce would be decreased, and human happiness would have a boom.

But these wide considerations do not appeal to a body of men teachers whom their "interests" have made morally astigmatic. Especially from teachers, perhaps, we should demand some element of altruism and sympathy with social progress.—*Press*, February 21, 1910.

## "DISCRIMINATION" AS AN ISSUE; WHAT IT MEANS IN THE MUSICAL WORLD.

If the United States stands, and has stood, for anything, it is against that discrimination which has existed from time immemorial in other countries, and which is based on prejudice, which in turn is based on ignorance. The United States, ever since its Constitution was formed, and even before that, upheld the great principle that a man or a woman shall be regarded "on the merits," and not be condemned or brushed aside on account of race or religion or previous condition; that, indeed, in this country humanity should have a fresh start, better conditions, and, above all, greater opportunities.

In nothing has this spirit shown itself more convincingly than in the laws passed in our various States, and also by the National Government, regarding women. The laws make it impossible for a man to transfer his real estate, if he be married, except with the consent of his wife, for the law recognizes the fact that in the acquisition of property the wife and mother has contributed at least a share.

For years, as we know, in the most advanced country in Europe, in England, a woman could acquire no property, even by her own efforts, after she was married. It was in the husband's power to come in and seize and sell it whenever it so pleased him. While in this and other respects we are in this country in advance of other nations, it must be admitted that there are still serious prejudices existent which, it is hoped, a more enlightened age will remove.

One of these prejudices is the accepted dictum that no Catholic could ever become President of the United States. Another is the unjust social prejudice against the Hebrew. Another is the unreasoning prejudice against Asiatics, even when they are highly educated, cultured and refined. We still have the disabilities under which women labor when they perform the work of men, but do not get the pay of men. Finally, we have the social prejudice against teachers who are—shameful to us as it is—regarded as little better than servants.

The movement to remove the disabilities of women is world-wide. It is active in such far-off countries as China, Persia, Turkey; it is active in France, Belgium; it is making headway in England; it has started to become active in this country. Back of it all is the basic principle of "justice," namely, that there shall be no discrimination against a person's work or social condition or legal rights on account of sex.

An instance of this movement was afforded in the appearance before the Mayor of the City of New York, the other day, of Miss Grace C. Strachan, superintendent of schools in Brooklyn, who came before the Mayor as the representative of 14,000 female teachers in New York City and Brooklyn, to attend a public hearing of a bill which had recently passed both houses of the legislature by overwhelming majorities, as it had already done twice before, to equalize the pay of the teachers in the schools of Greater New York. . . .

In the first place, the bill did not ask for more pay for the teachers. What it demanded was "justice," namely, that the women teachers should be paid what the job was worth when they did the same work as the men.

Now, there are some 14,000 female teachers in Greater New York, and some 3000 men teachers. It has been urged in some papers that the women are not entitled to the same pay as men because they are not as competent. It logically follows, therefore, that the great City of New York, the greatest city in the United States, which we consider the greatest country in the world, is deliberately giving its children inferior teachers, simply because they are cheaper, which convicts it of a crime.

If, on the other hand, it is admitted, as it should be, that the women teachers are fully as competent as the men—and as I will assert, with many others, in the earlier stages they are far more competent than men—then the city is convicted of gross injustice, for it is convicted of paying the women for work which is as good as the men's less than the men, simply because they are women!

And let us not forget that higher pay for the women means to induce a higher grade, a more educated, more intelligent type of woman to enter the school-teaching business. It needs no argument to show that this means more for the progress of the city than can be accomplished by the expenditure of money in any other possible direction, for if a nation is finally based on the home, and the home is based on the individual, the training of the individual citizen is the very foundation of our civilization, certainly the foundation of possible progress and evolution to higher and better conditions.

The argument which is made by some that legislation from Albany is not the proper way to get at the issue is a quibble, for the reason that it is well known that no appeal to the Board of Estimate on behalf of the women would have had the slightest effect.

And it is only because the legislature has again and again passed this bill and made the officials of New York realize that there is a great public sentiment back of it that the mayor has finally been forced by public opinion, evidently against his will, to appoint a commission to get at the facts, although in the appointment of the commission he evades the main issue, which is one of simple justice.

It is to the credit of the trades unions that they long ago maintained the principle of equal pay for equal work, and insisted, in every industry where they were powerful, that if the women did the work as well as the men, as competently as the men, as thoroughly as the men, they should get the same pay as the men.

It has been said by some that one of the reasons why women should accept a lower wage for the same work than men is that the man is generally responsible, as the head of the family, for many mouths, where the woman has only herself to care for.

This, again, is a quibble, but even if true would not touch the issue of justice. The average woman teacher, it would be found on investigation, has as a rule from two to three dependent upon her. Either it is a widowed mother, a sick sister, a helpless father, or she is struggling alone to help her little brothers and sisters to an education and to an opening in life.

It can be safely said that not 5 per cent. of the teachers in Greater New York are in a position where they can spend the money they earn upon themselves—and in the name of common sense and fair play, what is the money they get?

Do people realize that these women teachers, who are so bound up with all that is best and noblest in our social life, are, in the great majority of cases, receiving less salary than the janitors of the buildings in which they do their teaching?

The members of the musical world are interested in this fight by the women teachers for justice, for, as I have shown, they themselves suffer gravely from discrimination. And so it will be well for them not merely to take an interest in so far as the issue affects their particular profession, but whenever they can, by word, by deed, by vote where possible, to struggle against discrimination of whatever kind, wherever it is found.

In doing this they will ultimately help themselves, and take their stand with those of the higher intelligence, the broader mind, the larger sympathies, who are struggling for humanity's uplift against which all the forces of prejudice, of ignorance, of class, of graft and greed will ever be arrayed.—John C. Freund, *Musical America*, May 29, 1909.

## BATTLING FOR THE RIGHT

A fight not unlike that for the standard is on in New York City over the question of "Equal work, equal pay." Nor is it knights in armor who contend. It is women on one side, backed by some big-minded men, with men on the other. For a long time those familiar with the work of schools are well aware of a fact that is so prominent that it strikes out all over the system and that is the fact that the best school work on the whole is done by women. This being so it is hard to understand the policy, short-sighted and unfair, that pays them less wages than are paid to men for an equal amount of the same kind of work. It takes a long time for social justice to catch up with what is called, for want of a better name, natural justice. But it does in the end. . . .

That such a time is to come, is on the way hither, is just as certain as sunrise and sunset. We welcome these women to the ranks of the republic's best friends, for those are its best friends who fight the battles of righteousness; and one of these battles is about equal wages for equal work; and Miss Grace Strachan is its heroine and leader. That she is to win in the end is just as sure as justice. Only a little longer delay is possible. Petty men pass, poltroons, time or party-serving politicians pass—principles remain.—The *Catholic Times*, June 2, 1909.

## "EQUAL PAY FOR EQUAL WORK"

On April 24th, twelve hundred teachers were gathered at a banquet given in the famous Hotel Waldorf-Astoria, in New York City. They were representatives, and their friends, of a local organization of women teachers having an active membership of about twelve thousand, or more than twice the number of the active members of the National Education Association. It is probably the largest teachers' union in the world and owes its vitality chiefly to the magnificent leadership of Miss Grace C. Strachan, one of the district superintendents of schools in New York.

The Interborough Association of Women Teachers—that is the name—was reared on the single idea of "equal pay for equal work." In New York City the teachers in a number of the higher grammar grades are men. Their salaries are larger than those of the women teaching the same grades. A woman earning advancement to a principalship does not receive the pay of a man occupying a like position, and the maximum to which she can attain is considerably less than that held out to her brothers. The Interborough

Association was formed to do away with this discrimination between the sexes.

An interesting discussion resulted. The opponents of the Association made much of the plea that the women have only themselves to support, while the men are usually heads of families, with several people to take care of. The question naturally suggested itself, why unmarried men were receiving as much as the married ones. Furthermore, it could be demonstrated that the burden of responsibility resting upon most of the women is quite as heavy in every way as that resting upon the male supporters of dependents.

Another retort was that the men supplied a something that the pupils, especially the boys, were much in need of, and which women could not give. This something was characterized in various ways. Manliness is probably the best word for it. The manly example, the male attitude of looking at things, masculine reasoning and forcefulness are no doubt strong educational factors. How essential they are to successful elementary school work is a difficult question to answer. . . .

There is another matter involved. School inspectors and superintendents and other supervisors and examiners base their judgment of teachers upon results that have nothing to do with "manliness." It would seem to be only just that there should be a standard, measured by which the difference between the work of men and women teachers would become evident. Competition between the sexes could then be placed on a basis of fairness. It is just possible that some women teachers supply more training in "manliness" than some men who receive better pay because of the assumption of the superiority of the latter. . . .—*School Journal*, (Ossian Lang), March 7, 1909.

## TEACHERS AS SUPPORTERS OF DEPENDENTS

The arguments brought forward to promote the advancement of teachers' salaries must be framed with extreme caution, lest there be unpleasant reaction along unguarded lines. The arraignment of women against men, or of men against women, is an especially unwise procedure. There is no doubt about the reality of the justice behind the demands for a better remuneration of the teacher's services. Do not let us permit this to be obscured by fruitless discussions about the economic value of the sexes in the market places of the world.

Those women teachers of New York City who regard Miss Strachan as their leader have a strong claim in their insistence upon "equal pay for equal work." The men who are trying to weaken the cause of these women are bound to fail. The plea that the man supports a family, while the woman has only herself to take care of, can easily be shown to be without real foundation in fact, besides having nothing to do with the real issue. The truth is, that most teachers—men and women alike—have not only themselves to take care of, but contribute also to the support of dependent relatives. Times have changed. Arguments based on conditions that have passed away can be of no avail when the searchlight of intelligence is turned upon them.

Men are excluded from wage-earning pursuits at an earlier age than they were in former days. Women have become the competitors of men in nearly all lines. Meanwhile, the number of dependent parents has grown to large proportions, and the care of them has fallen largely upon the children. To what extent the burden has been shifted to the lot of the daughters, I am not prepared to state. I do know that there are few women teachers who are free of family responsibilities which consume a portion of their earnings. I have heard of these few, but I have never met them.

Two or three typical examples will make the point clear.

One of the best salaried women is principal of an Eastern training school for teachers. She receives something like $2,500 a year. In the fifteen years I have known her there never was a time when she did not carry on some university work for self-improvement and to keep abreast of the times in pedagogical sociology and psychology. She subscribes to the most helpful periodicals, and spends a portion of every vacation at a summer school. She dresses well, as becomes her office, and pays the ordinary taxes which social life exacts of cultured women. She has supported her widowed mother almost from the day when she began to teach, and has borne the expense of the education of her younger sisters. In her school are many poor pupils who have received substantial aid from her. And this is the type of the noble woman teacher of whom there are thousands in the common school service.

A young woman of twenty-two became supervisor of music in a Western city at a salary of $900. She had drawn only one monthly check when her father lost his position, and in spite of every endeavor could find no permanent employment because of aged appearance and feeble health. The daughter reduced her personal expenses to the lowest possible point, and contributed the balance of her money to the support of the family. She felt compelled to look for a better salaried place in the East, near the home of her parents. The $1,100 she was paid shrank considerably under the increased demands the new office made upon her purse. She undertook evening school and vacation school work to supply her family with the necessities of life. The strain proved too much for her young life. She, too, is a type.

A teacher in a city school receives $400 a year. A widowed mother and two small sisters are dependent upon her for support. After school hours she has private pupils. The intelligence, energy, pluck, and resourcefulness of this teacher would bring her twenty dollars a week in a commercial life. But she wants to teach.

And so she tries to earn enough by outside work to enable her to stay in the common school service. The city that pays her $400 gives the janitor of the school $1,200. But he has a wife and two children to support.

Now consider that there are not a few who receive only $300 or less a year, and these, too, have calls for financial aid. Yet, the teacher who is worried about the daily bread cannot possibly give the best strength to the work. In no other occupation is the drain upon the vital forces so constant. Irritability has serious effects upon the developing characters of the pupils. An atmosphere of cheerful serenity is the most favorable condition for the education of the young, and that is naturally dependent upon the personality of the teacher. Worry is conducive neither to cheerfulness nor serenity. The communities that keep their teachers poor are depriving their own children of a most valuable part of education.

It costs money to keep in touch with the progress of the world. A person of cultivation has many necessary expenses that others manage to do without. The very office of the teacher makes certain special demands that involve expense which are not required of either the bricklayer or the paperhanger. Attendance at educational conventions is most desirable for efficiency, and that necessitates further expense. School communities do not seem to have these considerations in mind when fixing the salaries of teachers.

Here is a line of arguments that tell.—*The School Journal,* Ossion Lang, Editor, September 21, 1907.

## COST

The cost of the proposed law has been carefully estimated at about six million dollars, and at no hearing either before the local School Board or the Senate or Assemblies Cities Committee has a single taxpayer or tax-paying organization protested. Instead, the advocates of the proposed legislation are in receipt of endorsements from hundreds of thousands of voters and taxpayers, to say nothing of numerous organizations.—N. Y. *Tribune.*

## PAY THE WOMEN LIKE MEN

The *Wall Street Journal* has been requested to speak favorably of the proposed amendment to the Davis law. This law makes the salaries of women employed as teachers in New York city from 50 to 70% of those of men occupying corresponding positions. It is proposed by amendment to make the salaries equal.

The *Wall Street Journal* cheerfully responds to this request. In the field of teaching women are in a true vocation, and are the equals of men. There can be no doubt whatever that they perform their duties with at least equal fidelity and ability as compared with male teachers. Performing corresponding duties with equal fidelity and ability they should be paid the salaries paid to men.

There is no other item of public expense which is more justified by economic results and none which gives a larger dividend of prosperity than education, and there is nothing that will contribute more to education than the employment of good teachers, women as well as men, adequately paid on a basis of equality.—*Wall Street Journal,* February 25, 1907.

## THE EQUAL PAY FIGHT ONCE MORE

Miss Grace C. Strachan is at any rate a courageous fighter. All sorts of dire things were threatened against her because she went to Albany and induced many teachers to go with her in order to fight for equal pay for equal work in the public schools without regard to sex. The Board of Education and the Tammany Mayor foamed and frothed about home rule, when they meant Tammany rule, and the Governor, accepting the time-worn slogan at its face value in the mouths of these valiant political trenchermen, although he paid no attention to it when his own pet Public Utilities bill knocked home rule higher than Gilroy's kite, finally defeated the measure.

And they would have been still under the feet of the politicians if the Legislature had not listened to the appeal of the teachers to a petition protesting against the repeal of the Davis bill.

Just the same home-rule howl was raised against these most just and equitable measures, the latter of which is not unfitly spoken of as the Magna Charta of the Public Schools, but it did not avail, because its utter insincerity was then clearly understood in the Executive Chamber at Albany. And it was fully as insincere when it was raised this year against the equal pay for equal work bill.

At least the women teachers are without redress in that direction, however the case may stand against the male teachers. These latter are now alarmed about the Davis bill, a measure they never could have succeeded in passing without the aid of the women teachers. The home-rule cry, in whooping up which they so vigorously joined last year in order to defeat the equal pay for equal work bill, is being started again, this time with the design of repealing the Davis bill, so that the teachers of both sexes may be once more under control of Tammany.

To ward off the impending blow, the very male teachers who worked so bitterly against the equal pay for equal work bill of last year are now trying to get the signatures of the women teachers to a petition protesting against the repeal of the Davis bill.

Miss Strachan meets the men teachers in militant style.

Remembering the warfare they conducted against the women teachers last winter at Albany, she issued a statement yesterday addressed to the women teachers, in which she says, among other things:

"You know that many of the very men who are seeking your signatures did all in their power to prevent our success last year, even being guilty of threats of unjust treatment of their subordinates and of misrepresentation of facts. Why, then, should you concern yourselves over the advisability of signing papers sent around by any association other than the Interborough Association of Women Teachers, the largest and strongest association of teachers in the world?"

Here is no note of surrender, but a courageous defiance not only of their opponents of last year among the men teachers and principals, but of the politicians and others behind them who think, or pretend to think, a woman is not entitled to as much pay as a man for doing precisely the same kind of work. However, the leader of the women teachers adds that if they desire to sign the petition for the retention of the Davis bill they should do so only when a clause is added making provision for an amendment giving equal pay for equal work without regard to sex. Following a great historical example, the women are evidently going to fight it out on that line if it takes all summer.—The *Standard-Union*, Brooklyn, Saturday Evening, December 14, 1907.

Author's Note—The Tammany leaders have favored the women teachers' bills and all the Tammany members of the Legislature have voted for them, with the exception of one Bronx Assemblyman, who was defeated for re-election, November, 1909.

Miss Grace Strachan makes it plain that what the women teachers are fighting for is not more salary, but equal pay for equal work. Three million dollars a year increase voted by the Board of Education two years ago, but refused by the Board of Estimate, was not what the members of Miss Strachan's organization asked for, nor does $6,000,000 a year proposed now meet the principle for which they are striving. It is not a question of more or less money, but of the maintenance or abolition of a discrimination expressly based upon sex and nowhere expressly based upon qualifications.—Brooklyn *Standard-Union*, July 16, 1909.

## ON THE FEMALE TEACHERS' MOVEMENT

Last Thursday night there was a mass meeting of women teachers at Cooper Union in the interest of the equalization of salaries. The opponents of that idea were also out in force and distributed circulars, part of which read as follows:

"When a woman not charged with a home, not contributing to the family life of the nation, enters the industrial field, she is entitled to compensation as an individual only. She is not entitled to the same pay as the man whose just wage is the family wage."

We doubt if there was a better argument presented by the female teachers themselves than in this extract from the objections of their opponents. The circular quoted speaks of the "just" wage of the man of family, but there is really no wage to-day that is based upon the necessary support of a family. And it is for this very reason that the wage of the man no longer suffices to keep the family that women have been forced to seek employment in industry and in the professions. In fact, the only wage known to-day is the individual wage, and that wage is regulated by the competition between the individuals, male and female, of the one family, aye, even the children of the family enter into the competition.

No more than cattle are paid for in the "Cattle Market" at the "family price" of the bull, are wage earners, among whom teachers take their place, paid for in the "Labor Market" at the family price of the male.

Woman, until the growth of the factory system, was nothing more nor less than a domestic servant, part of whose household duties consisted in spinning, weaving, making clothes, etc., etc. Woman was a producer, though mainly for the consumption of her own family, and when the household production developed into factory production she had to follow it to the factory, just as the handicraft man had to abandon his little shop and follow the developed tool into the factory.

In domestic servitude in the family woman received no "pay," in the present day sense, she shared in the general product. And now that she has "freedom" to work, the exploiters bargain to hold her to the no-cash basis that was a feature of her domestic servitude.

So real a fact is it that individual production, and not production by the head of the family, has become the order of the day that where women do not go out and work you find them bringing work home, or taking lodgers or boarders, in order to hold up their individual end of the family production.

We are glad to see the women school teachers organizing in an effort to better their condition. What is needed among women is a keener sense of solidarity. They are yet suffering from the long heritage of isolation endured by their mothers. All the real advantages that exploited woman may gain will only be secured by joining hands with her exploited brother man and wrenching such advantages from the exploiting class

—be they Boards of Education or Boards of Directors of corporations.—*Weekly People*, New York City, February 8, 1908.

Mayor McClellan is right. He says he vetoed the women teachers' bill because it was his "sacred duty to do so." So it was. A Democratic or a Republican official is a personage who directly and indirectly has pledged his sacred word to safeguard the interests of the capitalist class. The capitalist class is the taxpayer. The taxes it pays come, it is true, from wealth produced by the proletariat, but it is a wealth that the proletariat is plundered of in the shop. It follows that the higher the taxes all the more has the capitalist class to disgorge in the shape of taxes The equalization of salaries bill amounted to higher taxation. The sacredly pledged Mayor vetoed the bill. True McClellan! All credit to our God-fearing Mayor!—*People*, New York City, May 29, 1909.

## THE TEACHERS' SALARIES

A month's study of the problem of equal pay for teachers in the public schools has sufficed only to convince Mayor McClellan's commission that a deliberate investigation of the whole subject must be made if any satisfactory result is to be obtained. So extensive is the field and so complex the factors that nothing but a superficial survey was possible in the time at command. That glaring inequalities exist the commission had no difficulty in finding out. The further the matter was probed the more apparent became the need of something like a complete reconstruction of the entire system of compensation. Simple justice and the city's best interests alike demand that every man and woman employed in training our children shall be fairly treated, and that arbitrary distinctions, the outgrowth of custom, shall be abolished.

But discernment of the absurdities and injustice of the prevailing system is one thing—a thing of which any reasonable person of ordinary intelligence is capable—and discovery of a practicable means for removing these obstacles to rational administration is quite another. The mayor's commission, recognizing this difficulty, has contented itself with putting forward, merely tentatively, various alternative plans. No recommendation accompanies them. Admittedly none of them goes to the heart of the matter. They serve rather to make clear the difficulties in the way of arriving at a thorough solution. What is required if this object is to be achieved is a painstaking inquiry by a body of candid and competent investigators, which should include women as well as men, who will give the time necessary to get all the facts upon which to base a sound judgment.

This duty devolves upon the incoming administration, and the sooner it is undertaken the better for the good name and the welfare of the city.—*The Globe,* December 29, 1909.

## WOMEN SHOULD RECEIVE THE SAME PAY AS MEN IF THEY DO THE SAME WORK

The resolution now before the Board of Education, providing that women teachers shall be paid the same salaries as men teachers when they do the same work, should not be held up very long. It should be passed without any debate. Equal pay for equal work is sound common sense, and unequal pay for doing the same thing is unfair and absurd on the face of it. If a man receive $2,000 a year for teaching arithmetic to a room full of boys and he throws up his job and a woman is put in his place and does the same work as he does, and just as well, why should she receive $1,200 a year? It is not only an injustice to the women teachers, but it comes close to being an affront, inasmuch as the board members say in effect that they do not believe that women do the work as well as men do—while we and all the world know that in the public schools, especially those attended by the youngest children, women teachers are the more capable and patient and conscientious.—*Telegraph,* Dec. 25, 1909.

## EQUALIZING THE SALARY OF MALE AND FEMALE TEACHERS

If a male teacher receives $1,200 a year it is presumable that his service is worth that sum. If a female teacher receives for the same amount and quality of work $1,000, that reduction amounts to taxing her $200 for being a woman, and is neither equity nor chivalry.—Madison Square Presbyterian Church, Rev. C. H. Parkhurst, Pastor, May 19, 1907.

## TEACHERS' SALARIES

All over the country questions affecting public schools are alive and stirring. Among these questions those which concern salaries for teachers have, in a number of cities, for several years been especially acute. The Legislature of New York is now considering a bill to equalize the payment of men and women teachers for equal pay. At present a man may receive a higher salary than a woman who is his official superior and the supervisor of his work. A woman as principal of a school may receive less than a man may receive among the youngest children in the very lowest grade, where, by the way, he ought not to be allowed at all, and where he is put usually only for incompetence in the upper grades. Such flagrant injustice in the long run is flagrantly bad economy, for nothing is more important to all the people than that the schools should have the best teachers who can be secured, whether men or women. Those who object to equality talk about the way the money is spent, the men usually being married and the women not, but such a paternal ground for fixing salaries hardly requires an answer A deeper argument is that, in a region like New York, if money is spent in raising salaries it will not be spent on sorely needed buildings and increase of teaching force. This objection may be valid for the moment, but only for the moment. It does not touch the final principle, and the just principle should be in some way recognized and established, even if the full effect must be unfortunately postponed.—*Collier's*, February 22, 1908.

## THE SCHOOLMARM

New York's 12,000 women teachers have no votes, and therein doubtless they are "inferior" to the 2000 men teachers. Therein, doubtless, lies a part of their inability to get equal pay for equal work from the Board of Education, and the manifest difficulty of their cause before the legislature. Their appeal is to the generosity and justice of the city, not to anybody's political interest.

The people should realize the injustice of the presumption which underlies a system that starts a woman teacher in at $600 and a man teacher at $900, and raises the woman's pay $40 a year and the man's pay $105. It is assumed that the woman teacher is a bird of passage—a schoolmarm one day and a blushing bride the next, while the man teacher will be on the job for life. But it is very much the other way. Many women are electing school teaching as a permanent vocation. Most of the veteran teachers whose former pupils gather from time to time to do them honor are women.

Men make teaching a crutch at least as much as women do. They pursue their studies for the law and other professions, and meanwhile boil the pot by teaching. The initial inequality between the pay of men and women is deepened by the fact that many day teachers also teach in the night schools. With less endurance than men, and under a social scruple or danger that makes it unwise for them to undertake a night school in some parts of the city, women have this additional means of livelihood largely withdrawn from them.

While the compensation of all other classes of city employees is being raised, the woman teacher, who belongs to no political club, whose guiding principles are efficiency and the devoted care of her charges rather than influence, is passed by. She is ground between the upper and nether millstone of an inequitable and insufficient salary and the increased cost of living. Give the schoolmarm a square deal! As the chosen guardian of the rising generation she has a better title to it than anyone else.—*The Evening Mail,* Thursday, March 7, 1907.

The dinner of the school teachers last Saturday night was a most enlightening affair. It ought to have taught the few men present that the women are filling a place in the concerns of this country, little dreamt of a few years ago. When the Civil War called the men of the North to battle there were not men enough to do the work at home. Every industry languished for the lack of men, and women were called upon to take their places. The call was promptly heeded, and women appeared laboring in places where no man ever thought to see them. They were joyfully welcomed, and by their conduct, their thrift, and their competence, won from the American man that degree of homage that has set him above all of the men of other nations; in his respect for women. And the most important work done by women at that time was in public schools. Did they do their work well or ill? Incompetence cannot thrive. The spirit of humanity will not submit to costly and worthless experiments. If the women had not proved themselves capable of teaching children they would long ago have disappeared from the public schools. But instead of disappearing they have waxed in numbers and in usefulness.—*Democracy,* May 1, 1909.

At a meeting of the Men Teachers and Principals' Association held a week ago, Profesor Shumway made an effort to show that women teachers should not receive as much pay as men teachers for the same kind of work. He made these points:

"Wages must be just to employer and employee; that wage is just when sufficient to hold efficient labor; that it should be big enough to give the worker a living wage; that the necessary masculine wage is an unnecessary feminine wage; that it would be unjust to women to give them enough pay to make their places of value to men, for then they would be driven out of the schools; that if women succeed in driving out the men then they would have no call to raise a cry for the equalizing of pay and that this would work to their harm."

It seems to us that the professor has entirely missed any good reason for refusing women the same pay as that given to men for the same kind of work. It is certain that women are as necessary in our schools as the men. They depend upon each other. Without the women there could be no proper basis for the men to work upon. It would be like trying to build a house upon the shifting sand. Men cannot drive women out of the schools and women cannot drive the men out. The women have won their places in our educational system by hard, honest and competent work. The question of a living wage doesn't enter into the matter at all, if the professor will excuse us for saying so. There is no sentiment in business, and any corporation, municipal or otherwise, that seeks to do business on a sentimental basis will soon have a receiver in charge of his affairs.

What is the market price of labor? That is the only question. In the matter of public teaching the market price of teachers is fixed by the public. It has no variable quantity because it depends upon a monopoly. Then the question comes: What is the value of this labor to the corporation? In this case the corporation is the people of the state; and the people, represented in Senate and Assembly, have declared that the labor performed by the women is worth as much as the same kind of labor performed by the men. Wherefore this is the market price of this kind of labor and the women should benefit by this decision.

There are men in this country getting one hundred thousand dollars a year. Is this a living wage? Of course it is much more than any man needs to live upon, but he gets it because that is the market price. There are men getting seven dollars a week. Is this a living wage? No. Yet it is the market price. Who has set the market price? The consumer. And so the consumer in the matter of the women school teachers, or in other words the people, say that she ought to get the same pay as men. Then the professor says that if men be driven out of the public schools the women could not get more pay because then she could not raise the cry of equal pay. How can men be driven out because women have their pay raised? This statement is interesting only because it hasn't any foundation to support it. It is a phenomenon.

Being of the male species ourselves we do not want to think that there is any man whose livelihood depends upon the work of under-paid women. And so, with all courtesy to the professor, we are constrained to believe that he is wholly mistaken in the view he takes and we desire to assure him that the women school teachers will be receiving the same pay as men for the same kind of work before he or we are eighteen months older.—*Democracy,* May 29, 1909.

It is only reasonable to assume that the women school teachers have won their fight for equal pay. The battle has been fought with much honor and courage on the part of the women and with much sycophancy, dodging, and insincerity on the part of the men who have opposed their claim for fair treatment. It is an axiom to say that in the end right will prevail, but right very often has a mighty hard fight of it before it does prevail. Wrong is often strong and many fisted, and it is often aided by a line of persons, some thick-witted, some stubborn, some wicked, some blind, who battle against the right. There is never much difficulty in convincing the clear-eyed and clear-brained of the right, but when it comes to teaching the stupid, to win over the stubborn, to beat the wicked and to open the eyes of the blind, then real difficulties are met. If the women school teachers had a weaker cause, less courage, less courtesy, and less character, they would have despaired and future generations of teachers would have suffered. But they had every one of the qualities that make for success, and so, naturally, they succeed. The beginning of the year 1910 is the beginning of a new era for them. It will see the women school teachers getting the same pay as the men teachers for the same kind of work; it will see the women school teachers growing in numbers and efficiency; it will see a marked improvement in the public school system, and it will see a big advance toward the uplifting of the poor. The fact that the women school teachers have had to fight for so many years for justice that would involve an additional expenditure of less than six million dollars a year, while many men in public life engaged in public work directly and indirectly, become millionaires in a few years, has always seemed to us to be an alarming symptom. The work the women school teachers do is the most important work done by any of the public employees. Their work is not only for to-day but for all time. Its effect will be seen when every person living now will have passed away. It is work that will advance the nation in all of the sciences and arts, and in the deeper things, such as love of country, honesty, good living, and general knowledge. The meeting of the teachers last night was a good indication of the appreciation the people have of their work.—*Democracy,* Dec. 18, 1909.

## "JOURNAL" EDITORIALS

## SALARIES OF WOMEN THAT TEACH IN PUBLIC SCHOOLS

### What Excuse Is There For Underpaying Them? The Legislature Should Repair the Injustice!

Women that teach in New York's public schools are trying to get from the Legislature of the State, decent, fair treatment, and they ought to get it.

In the schools the first thing to be thought of is the children.

If children taught by women are not well taught, if the women's work is not as well done as in classes governed by men, then the women should be replaced by men.

The difficulty in getting fair treatment, common everyday justice, for the women teachers illustrates the general unwillingness of human beings to accept a plain truth.

A few centuries ago everybody thought it was right for one human being to own another, no matter what his color.

Fifty years ago in this country we thought it was right for one human being to own another, provided the slave had a black skin, or a black ancestor that made his skin yellow.

It seemed then proper that one man with a white skin should be paid for his work properly, and another man with a black skin paid nothing at all—unless with a whip.

That idea we have dropped. A long war, which cost millions of lives and thousands of millions of dollars, drummed into American skulls the truth that it doesn't pay to keep slaves, and that it isn't right.

If white men and black men do the same kind of work now, we give them the same kind of pay.

It is too bad we haven't sense of justice enough to do the same thing for women.

Nobody would dream of saying in this country, "I'll pay an Irishman nine cents, and a German eight cents for the same kind of work." It would seem ridiculous.

Then why pay a male human being two dollars and a female human being one dollar for identical work?

If men can do the school work better than the women, then men only should be employed, in justice to the children.

And if the women can do the work as well as the men, and they can, unless it be in the management of the very biggest and roughest boys, then the women should be paid as well as the men.—New York *Evening Journal* (Editorial).

## SENSELESS OPPOSITION TO THE TEACHERS' SALARY BILL

That the White bill, giving equal pay for equal work to New York teachers, is to be smothered in the Assembly was a statement made and applauded at the meeting of men teachers held at Terrace Garden Saturday. The cheering of such an announcement is incomprehensible to the average man, but, for the matter of that, so is the opposition to the measure. To the ordinary chivalrous, fair-minded American, the chief principle embodied in the White bill is one of simple justice, and the fight made on it is so out of keeping with the spirit of to-day that it has in it an element of barbarism.

Is compensation given for sex or for service rendered? If a certain piece of work is worth a certain amount of money, does it matter whether the one who does the work is a man or a woman? In buying a bushel of wheat or a loaf of bread, do we stop to inquire as to the sex of the farmer or baker? If any distinction is made, chivalry would suggest that the woman should be favored. To discriminate against her simply because she is a woman is not only unfair, but unmanly.

There was one gratifying note at the Terrace Garden meeting. It was the promise implied, if not stated, by members of the board, that if the White bill is killed there will be an advance of salaries all along the line. Promises are good, even if given only in hints and not in open, manlike statements. The salaries of teachers certainly should be advanced, and radically. Yet the majority of people would prefer legal enactments to that effect rather than vague intimations from a body that has had power to make such an increase for years, but has shown little desire to take such action until a fight is on to prevent women from receiving plain justice.

If there are defects in the White bill they are easily cured by amendment. The main idea is of enough worth that it should not be lost because of minor details. For this principle of equal pay for equal work the campaign should be waged until its success is assured.—*Journal,* 1907.

## THE EFFORT TO GET FAIR TREATMENT FOR WOMEN SCHOOL TEACHERS

### It Is Honorable, Necessary. It Should Be Persisted In

Last year a determined effort was made by women who teach in New York City's public schools to obtain fair treatment from the Legislature. Their demand was that a woman able to do as good work as a man should for the same work receive the same pay as the man. This newspaper endeavored to assist the teachers, and the Legislature decided in their favor. Governor Hughes, however, decided against the teachers.

Now a set of imposing resolutions has been adopted by the Board of Education censuring the teachers for their activity, which is called pernicious. An especial attack is made upon Miss Grace C. Strachan, District Superintendent of New York City.

The Board of Education is much grieved because it thinks that some of the women have been neglecting their duty.

On behalf of the teachers we wish to tell the Board of Education that the teachers that went to Albany were working in the best interests of the children, of all the people, as well as of the teachers themselves.

As for the attack on Miss Strachan personally, that is peculiarly uncalled for.

Miss Strachan did spend thirty-four days in hard work trying to get justice for the teachers.

And Miss Strachan couldn't possibly have made a cent by the passage of the law for which she worked.

Miss Strachan as district superintendent was not included in those that would have been benefited by the law. She was working simply from a sense of duty to help other teachers, and to help the city.

In addition, Miss Strachan reported every day's absence from duty, she worked overtime and at night to make up for such absence, and she was engaged, as she herself truly said in her report to the board, "in a cause destined to uplift the moral standards of the school system, and hence of the community, the State, the nation, and the world—the establishment of justice for the women workers in our public schools."

We should like to ask the members of the Board of Education who condemn Miss Strachan and the other teachers how many of them ever worked hard for thirty-four days to help other people; how many of them ever took the trouble to go to Albany day after day, when they couldn't possibly make a cent by doing that, and when all the satisfaction they could get was in knowing that they had done their duty?

## NOT ONLY EQUAL PAY BUT DECENT PAY TO TEACHERS

Not only the women teachers of New York, but the schools are entitled to congratulations on the first victory for the principle of equal pay for equal work. The fact that there was but one vote in the State Senate against the bill giving women the same salaries as men teachers, and that this one vote was not dictated by opposition to the main feature of the measure, but to a minor proposition, not only reflects credit on the Senate, but makes it certain that the bill will become a law. This is good as far it goes, but the principle should be extended to all other women in the employ of the city. Salary should be determined by the character of the position and not by the sex of the occupant. Discrimination does not cease to be discrimination because practised against a woman or against all women. Plain and simple justice is not a matter of sex distinction.—*Journal.*

## WHY THE CITY IS TOO POOR TO PAY THE TEACHERS FAIRLY

The school teachers of this city, notoriously underpaid, asked the Legislature for salaries more nearly commensurate with their valuable services. The Legislature granted their request. The Governor vetoed the bill.

The teachers next applied to the Board of Education, which had promised to "do something."

Recently a member of that Board named Jonas had this to say:

"We should not allow a single increase of salary. The condition of the city's finances does not warrant it. The Board of Estimate is not only responsible, but it will be called to account if a single increase of salary is allowed."

Exactly. The Board of Estimate is in constant terror lest it be called to account for allowing an advance of teachers' salaries.

Yet it summons abundant fortitude when it wants to buy a theatre for $230,000 and sell it back to the same crowd for $11,500. It has plenty of courage when raising the salaries of worthless appointees of McClellan. It is calm and untroubled when passing Bridge terminal deals or a thousand and one other operations by which the municipal treasury is almost daily looted.

The condition of the city's finances does not warrant giving fair pay to school teachers, upon whom rests the gravest and highest responsibility for the future of this country.

Yet it seems to warrant every sort of extravagance an extravagant and incompetent administration can indulge in.

Even at a time when the credit of the city is stretched till it cracks, the condition of its finances apparently warrants throwing away $2,000,000 by awarding the contract for the Ashokan dam to the highest bidder when the lowest bidder is a man of proven responsibility and experience.

The present administration has made many promises about what it was going to do for the schools.

In practice it has denied the teachers decent pay, deprived thousands of children of the privilege of going to school at all, and done absolutely nothing adequately to increase either the capacity or the efficiency of the city's educational system.

This is a matter that appeals directly to every parent, as it should to every citizen.

Upon the school children of to-day depends the welfare of the city to-morrow.

Do you who pay taxes prefer to have your money spent in fair salaries for the women who educate your children or in real estate deals which enrich a few grafting politicians?

Do you think that a Board of Estimate which can smugly defend the Montauk Theatre deal would actually have anything to fear from public opinion if it permitted the Board of Education to make the schools of New York worthy of the greatest city in the world?—*Journal,* August, 1907.

## ONE TRIUMPH FOR "EQUAL PAY"

The City of Buffalo is to be congratulated upon possessing the sense of justice and decency to establish the principle of "equal pay for equal work," which has been denied the women teachers of the City of New York. It is only a question of time when American fairness and chivalry will force the adoption of this measure everywhere. When that time arrives it will be no slight gratification to the citizens of Buffalo that they were among the pioneers in the work, just as it will be a like source of regret to the people of Greater New York that they permitted the second city in the State to get ahead of them in bringing about this inevitable reform.

The case is even worse with the metropolis, for not only did its city government throw every possible obstacle in the way of the Equal Pay bill, but refused a three-million-dollar appropriation for a general advance of teachers' salaries. There was plenty of money to add a salary grab of $116,000 in the Comptroller's office, and for even greater extravagance and graft in other departments, but not a cent to furnish a decent wage for those who educate the young. The women teachers cannot vote and are not a part of the political machine. Therefore they receive scant consideration or courtesy from the present "Mayor" of this city and his associates.

The pluck and courage shown by the Interborough Association of Women Teachers, in the face of rebuffs received from the Governor, the "Mayor" and the Comptroller, will arouse universal admiration, at least in all except the three gentlemen named. Not only do the members refuse to recede from their demands, but they propose to repeat the fight by which they won the Legislature last year. It is not exactly complimentary to modern ideas of chivalry that men leave them to make this fight for plain justice.—New York *Journal,* December 7, 1907.

## PAY TEACHERS ACCORDING TO THEIR VALUE

### They Are the Most Useful of Public Servants, and It Is Not Only Stupid but Infamous to Deny Them Justice



There is no more important duty in America than that performed by the teachers in the public schools—the manufacturing of good American citizens out of the raw material of good American boys.

The future of the republic depends on the success of the

teachers. To interfere with that success by parsimony is nothing short of criminal.

The Mayor of New York now has under advisement the Equal Pay bill, which provides that the women in the schools of this city shall receive the same pay as men engaged in the same work.

To veto such a bill would be to give notice to parents that the education of their children is considered of small importance by a public servant who is taking their money on the pretense of looking after their interests.

The Legislature has passed the bill. If vetoed by the Mayor it cannot be re-enacted for another year. In the meantime the outrageous injustice to the women teachers will continue—the shame of grossly underpaying the most useful of all public servants will remain with New York City.

It is the duty of the teacher to insure the future greatness of this country by turning out young men and young women who are able enough, and honest enough, and patriotic enough to be first-class citizens.

For the larger part of every week day the future citizens are in their hands, to be made or marred, according to the ability and earnestness of the teachers.

Originally parents educated their own children, giving the best that was in them to make the new generation wiser and better than the old.

It has now become necessary to delegate this work to others.

But it remains the greatest work of civilization—more important than any other art or profession—infinitely more useful to the republic than the labors of the doctor, who treats physical ailments, or of the judge, who is called in to settle the differences of opinion that arise between citizen and citizen.

We pay our judges big salaries, and vast veneration, and use them mostly to decide disputes—chiefly in matters of money.

We pay our teachers very small salaries, and use them, nine months in the year, to shape the whole course of human progress, through their direction of the minds of those who are to make human progress.

The shame of that is enough, as all fair-minded people will admit. The machinist, called in to tinker a refractory motor under an automobile, is paid better than the instructor who cares for the mind, and, incidentally, the soul of a growing human child.

As further proof of callousness to the even-handed justice that figures so often in public oratory and so seldom anywhere else, we pay men teachers far better than women teachers for identically the same work.

Usually the women do their work better. They have more sympathy, more undestanding of child nature, less aptitude to become swollen with importance because they know how to read and to spell a little better than their pupils.

The idea of public schools, free to the children of rich and poor, was the idea that made the United States a great nation. American schools are good—better than those of any other country.

But they can be made better still. The public schools should, in fact, be made so good that no parent, however rich could afford to send his children to a private school.

School superintendents should be men of as much ability and fitness for their positions as railroad superintendents, and should receive better pay.

School teachers should be the best paid class of public servants, as well as the most efficient.

And the fact that the work that they have been doing has been under-valued and under-rewarded for so long is all the more reason that it should be recognized and adequately paid now.

It will be time to talk economy when some legislature passes a bill to stop waste of public money on condemnation jobs, the gift of valuable franchises to greedy corporations, the purchase of rotten equipment for the Fire Department.

Economy aimed at impairing the efficiency of the public schools is no economy at all, but sheer criminal folly.

Naturally the teachers are interested in the bill. They have a right not to beg for justice, but demand it.

But important as is this measure to the teachers, it is far more important to every citizen. To the teacher it means only a fair return for their brains and time. To the citizen it means raising the schools toward the level on which they belong, and declaring publicly that the people of New York care as much for its future citizenship as they do for the future of the corporations that are seeking to grab its streets.—New York *Evening Journal*, May 13, 1909.

## WRITTEN FOR THE EVENING JOURNAL DEC. 8, 1909

By Dr. C. H. Parkhurst



The women teachers in our public schools are again exploiting the question of equal pay for equality (in quantity and quality) of service. This is to some extent a part of the great question that is now being agitated by her sex, and in part it is a question by itself.

Assuming that a piece of work done by a woman, whether in school or anywhere else, is the exact equivalent, in every respect, of the same piece of work done by a man, it is difficult to see the abstract justice of discriminating between the two in the matter of compensation.

### THE ONLY QUESTION IS WHETHER THEIR DEMAND IS JUST

If, for example, a man receives fifteen hundred dollars per annum for a given amount of instruction and of a given quality, and a woman receives fourteen hundred for its exact duplicate, in amount and quality, either he receives more than his services are worth or she receives less than they are worth; and if she receives less than they are worth she is by so much defrauded. It appears impossible to discover means by which any different conclusion can be arrived at.

It is not a question whether it would cost six million dollars more per annum, or twelve million, to meet the demand of the women teachers. The only question is whether their demand is a just one. If the people of the city at large understand the ins and outs of the problem, they will not willingly be partners to any dealing with these women that is not a just dealing.

If a given teacher's service is worth fifteen hundred dollars, the disposition of the town, whatever the disposition of the Board of Education, will be to pay it, and not to scale down her compensation on the ground of her sex. Saying nothing about the ungallantry of it, it is inequitable.

### EVERY PERSON, EVERY SERVICE, EVERY THING HAS ITS VALUE

Every person, every service, every thing, in fact, has its value. It may not always be easy to determine exactly what that value is, but, once determined, a consistent price should be put upon it. Granted that that is not the principle upon which compensations are ordinarily determined, custom is no excuse for injustice.

Out in Pasadena people pay for their electricity three cents for each kilowatt hour, and the manager of the system says: "We can make money at this figure, pay interest on the bonds, and establish a sinking fund."

The New York Edison Company charge ten cents for the same service. They charge it because they can get it, not because it is worth it. That is the way things generally go; but because it is usual for us to get all we can for what we sell, and to pay as little as we can for what we buy, does not justify either the seller or the buyer.

If the city is so poor as to be unable to pay these women teachers all they are worth, that is one thing, and under those circumstances the fair course to pursue will be to scale down the salary of the male teachers a little and scale up that of the women to meet it.

But if the town has the needed funds at command, as it undoubtedly has, and if the demand of the women is just, as it is claimed to be, then all they have got to do is to continue to stand squarely on the justice of that demand and eventually it will be conceded to them, and the more gentle and refined the persistency with which they press their claim the sooner the concession will be made. There are, however, two very delicate questions involved, and which require to be settled in advance.

The first is whether the women teachers are not already receiving all that their services are worth. It seems a little ungracious to raise that inquiry, but it is being raised, and that, too, by people whose judgment is to be respected. Their sense of justice would certainly (?) make them as unwilling to receive more than they earn as to receive less.

#### INCREASED SALARIES WILL ATTRACT BETTER TEACHERS

The second question is really included in the first, and is this—whether, taking the whole year through, there is not that feature of their physical constitution that positively prohibits that uninterrupted solidity of service possible to be rendered by the male.

These two questions are propounded only for the purpose of not leaving out of the investigation anything that is suitable to be included in it.

There is one further point that has perhaps not suggested itself to the teachers who are demanding an increase of salary, which is this: That if their compensation is increased, that increase will attract to the service a class of teachers correspondingly more competent than those that are employed here at present, so that if the claim that is now urged is conceded, the least qualified of those now upon the force will naturally find themselves supplanted, and instead of obtaining an addition to their salary, will lose all that they now have.

C. H. PARKHURST.

## DR. PARKHURST AND THE EQUAL PAY QUESTION

Miss Strachan, President of the Interboro Teachers' Association, Replies to the Article by Dr. Parkhurst Published in the Last Column of This Paper.



Dr. Parkhurst writes to-day on the question as to equal pay for women teachers. The Evening Journal believes that the city should set an example in common justice and honesty and pay the women for equal service as the men are paid. This will be better for the women and better for the men as well, although some of the men do not know it. We publish Dr. Parkhurst's extremely thoughtful and judicial article and present here the view of the women teachers presented by Miss Strachan:

BY MISS GRACE C. STRACHAN

Dr. Parkhurst in his article raises only two points that can be discussed as having any bearing on the question of whether or not women teaching in our public schools should receive equal pay with the men teachers.

In regard to the question of the women teachers being overpaid, I want to say that in order to be a teacher nowadays one first must have been graduated from a four years' course in a high school, and after having taken a two years' course in a training school for teachers, must have passed a very difficult examination for a license.

These requirements have raised the average age of the teacher at the beginning of her service to twenty-one years. The day has entirely gone when girls could begin to teach in the public schools of our city at the ages of fourteen, fifteen and sixteen. Yet our teachers receive the munificent salary in the first year of $600. This amount is increased annually, if the teacher stands well in the various examinations, by $40 a year for sixteen years. At this rate a woman is thirty-eight years of age, who, continuing to teach in the public schools, receives $1,240 a year.

I believe that a study of the City Record for June last will show that women telephone operators employed by the city received as much as $1,300 a year, and that women stenographers received salaries ranging from $600 to $2,400 a year, the majority of them receiving from $1,200 to $1,500.

In order to obtain these positions, these girls have to fulfill no other requirement than the Civil Service age requirement of at least eighteen years, and a simple educational test. They may never have attended school beyond the fifth year of our elementary course.

Even the matrons in the various stations throughout the city receive $750 a year.

Besides, the women teachers feel that the question whether they are receiving more money than they are worth is not a valid subject for discussion in this campaign for equal pay, because the male teachers occupying identical positions are receiving from fifty to a hundred per cent. more than the women teachers, yet the same men teachers are besieging the

Board of Education, the Charter Revision Committee and the Charter Legislative Committe for more pay.

In answer to the second question, I have no long list of statistics to offer to prove that women are as constant in attendance as the male teachers.

I can only say that in my own case I was absent only two days out of the first twelve years of my teaching, and that absence was due to a combination of grip and toothache. I know another teacher who was not absent or late once in her first seventeen years of teaching.

In my capacity of district superintendent, when examining teachers for a renewal of license, or for a certificate of approval of service, I always ask this question:

"How often have you been late or absent from school in the past three years?"

And it is not at all unusual for me to receive the answer: "Not once."

I am sure that there is no department of the public service where the employees render such faithful attendance as the women teachers do in the public school system of the greater city.

## OUT-OF-TOWN EDITORIALS

No doubt the fact that as a rule the teachers of the common schools are underpaid and that the salaries doled out to women have been so low as to offer small temptation to male competition has had much to do with bringing about the preponderance of women teachers. But it is certain that it is not an unhealthy preponderance. The most unsatisfactory feature of the employment of women grows out of the fact that very few enter upon the profession of teaching as a permanent occupation. The disparity in wages of the sexes is altogether wrong. For the like service there should be the like pay, and no female wageworker in any field of endeavor more honestly earns her pay than the teacher.—Philadelphia *Record*, 1907.

## PAY FOR SERVICE RENDERED

In New York equal pay for teachers has long been agitated. Governor Hughes stands in the way, but the women expect to triumph despite his opposition. Naturally, such a question has brought out many conflicting opinions. Whether a teacher has to support one person with his or her earnings or half a dozen should have nothing to do with the question. What the taxpayers want are the best teachers that can be obtained, whether men or women. School boards should make no distinction based either on sex or the number of teachers' dependent relatives. If the teacher engaged fills the bill that teacher, whether man or woman, should be paid all that the taxpayers of the employing community are able to pay for such services. So far as teachers are concerned the public should never be a charitable institution.—San Francisco *Bulletin*.

The proposition for equal pay for men and women teachers has again failed in New York. A fellow writes to one of the papers suggesting that the next effort at equalization of teachers' pay be made by going after the pay of the men teachers in the hope of slicing it down to the figure paid the women teachers. There are more ways than one of going at a subject to bring about the desired end. That man understands how to enlist support for the movement to raise the women teachers' pay.—*Vindicator*, Youngstown, Ohio, May 19, 1909.

## EDUCATIONAL COMMENT

Equal Pay.—It has been left for the New York teacher to contend for a principle of momentous importance to the entire working world of the public service, a principle as certain to redress the wrongs of the men who work as to remedy the injustices to the women.

It was left for the New York schoolma'ams to take up the fight for equal pay and to protest against this short-sighted lowering of the standard of the public service, and official branding of woman's labor as cheap labor. For if there is to be sex discrimination in labor, even to the statute books, the temporary competition of women workers in new fields who lower the rate of wage throughout the labor market will become a fixed and persistent condition. Every cry for more economy in the schools, in the public service everywhere, and in the industries will result in driving out more men workers and installing more women in their place. This has already been the case in the schools.

Sex discrimination in labor is a boomerang that rebounds to the injury of those who launch it forth. As related to the schools, if we are "feminizing" our schools, as has been charged, and if the schoolmaster abroad, who was so great an institution in the first century or so of American national life, has well-nigh disappeared, his elimination has been largely due to the economy of women's labor. However cheap women's labor in the school may be in its money value, it is good labor and of high educational value; and the better it is and the higher its quality the stronger the argument for equal pay for it as a matter of justice to the men as well as to the women.—Albany *Argus*, November 7, 1907.

## TEACHERS' WAGES

Steadily the demand for uniform wages for teachers, male and female, is gaining ground, despite the fact that it has received temporary setbacks here and there. It is generally known, we believe, that "The Citizen" is no advocate of woman suffrage; it subscribes nothing to the doctrine of equal rights in all things, but it has always declared that where a woman does a man's work, she should receive a man's pay. We fully believe with Elbert Hubbard that:

"The one-price system is a matter of ethics. It has come to stay. We also believe in paying a like wage for a similar service.

"This question has come to Albany for legal decision: Shall not women teachers be paid the same as men for doing the same grade and quality of work? Most of the states in the union have not even dared bring it up.

"If we were having our first look at the question we would say it was too childish a matter for consideration—there is only one side to it. In a hundred years it will be ridiculed as a relic of barbarism. But to-day it is a fight that must be decided by the legislature and an executive.

"When woman began to teach, to earn a little money and have a degree of independence, it was so great a joy that she accepted the gift of the gods without question as to whether she were receiving all that was her due. She had nothing to measure up her present condition with but her past, and all was favorable.

"But as the years went by and doors great and small flew open at her touch she drew points of comparison and the injustice of man's drawing the line where God had not, worked into her heart.

"At first woman was given only the less responsible positions in teaching. Now she is a co-worker with man—co-ordinates him.

"And I have seen no argument brought forward by the male teacher that touched upon the justice of paying one human being more than another for the same effort and the same results. The men have ostensibly fallen back on Bobby Burns and i'ween i'faith, 'A mon's a mon for a' that.'"—Atlanta *Citizen.*

## "EQUAL PAY FOR EQUAL WORK"

Once more the cry for more pay has been raised in New York by the female teachers in the public schools. These very unreasonable persons say that when they do identically the same work that men do they ought to receive equal pay. A whole lot of people throughout the State will sympathize with them in their claims. There is really no convincing argument against the contention except the financial one, "We can't afford it." A great city which is teaching its young the great lessons of justice and fair play can hardly afford to set the example of lowering womanhood. In a free-for-all foot race where women and men were admitted there would be no question about awarding the whole prize to the woman in the case if she happened to win the race. And there is no reason why the woman who does effectual work in instilling knowledge into the minds of the young should not receive just as much as the man who has been doing the same work, and in many instances probably not as well as the woman. To be sure the Governor has vetoed one bill which provided for equal pay for equal work, but if New York shows a disposition to be fair and treat its employees with justice it is hardly probable the State Executive will interfere. It might be a good idea for the city to use the money which has been paid to the fellows with easy jobs toward rewarding the teachers of the public schools who are accomplishing something. There may be a difference of opinion as to the desirability of giving the woman the ballot, but there can be no just ground for offering a man $900 for doing certain specific things and a woman only $600 for doing the same things and doing them just as well.—Rochester *Union and Advertiser*, Feb. 4, 1910.

## "EQUAL SALARY" BILL

The persistent fight made last year in the Legislature by the women teachers of New York city was not in vain. If it did nothing else, it has focused the attention of the people upon the inequality of salaries paid to men and women teachers. We believe it will do more than that. We believe it was the entering wedge, the leaven that shall in time make for better conditions and better pay for the whole teaching staff of the State. It cannot possibly be otherwise. That is, if school boards and authorities have the intelligence we believe they have. Woman is no longer a slave or a plaything. Here in America she is treated as an equal in nearly all respects to man. In some cases, however, especially in the line of endeavor to battle with the world and earn her own living, the idea is still clung to that she is inferior and therefore should receive an inferior salary. This idea is gradually wearing away. And nothing will hasten it more than united effort on their part—effort such as the Interborough Teachers' Association made at Albany last year. Knowing they are right, they should rush on to the goal of "equal pay for equal work."—The Dutchess County *Democrat and People's Plain Spokesman*, January 18, 1908.

## ALL EYES NOW ON SENATOR WHITE'S BILL

### "Equal Pay for Equal Work" Measure up for Action

*The Onondaga Representative will Move the Passage of His Pet Bill this Week—It Seems Certain the Senate will Pass It*

Albany, March 23.—Senator Horace White will move the passage of the New York city school teachers' "Equal Pay" bill this week, and from a poll made of the Senate last week the indications are that it will pass by a very comfortable majority. Only five votes were cast against it last year in the Upper House. The passing of a resolution by the New York city Board of Aldermen last week favoring the passage of the bill has strengthened the teachers' cause among many Senators and Assemblymen who have heretofore been classed as "doubtful."

No bill that has come up before the Legislature in recent years has been subject to so much public discussion on the platform and in the press as the "Equal Pay" bill. It has been discussed from one end of the State to the other. Chambers of Commerce, Boards of Trade, women's clubs, men's clubs, labor organizations, school teachers' clubs and even in the Grange the question of "equal pay for equal work" has been the subject of public discussions, especially in New York and Brooklyn.

"The White Bill" once passed the Senate and House, but did not pass the Governor. A well founded rumor has been in circulation in Albany for several weeks that the Governor has quietly told his friends that he does not want Senator White's bill put up to him again. The reason is very plain.

Ever since the Interborough Association of Women Teachers, led by Miss Grace C. Strachan, began the fight for "Equal Pay for Equal Work" the Governor and the Senators and Assemblymen have been bombarded with requests to come to the rescue of the women teachers who have been so unjustly discriminated against by the New York city Board of Education. From Chancellor James R. Day of Syracuse University down to the humblest citizen of New York and Brooklyn the capitol has been flooded with petitions to help the women teachers. The bill has been strongly endorsed in every city from Long Island to Dunkirk and from Ogdensburg to Elmira.

The friends of Governor Hughes intimate that he hesitates this year at flying in the face of public opinion by vetoing Senator White's bill. A veto in a Presidential campaign that will be at fever heat about the time that all thirty-day bills have to be signed or allowed to become laws would work to the disadvantage of the Governor, say his friends, and those who are close to him are working hard to prevent the bill from reaching him. Failing in that they will advise him to allow it to become a law in view of the fact that so many prominent men and women in Greater New York and elsewhere have petitioned for the signing of the "White Bill." Among the hundreds of organizations outside of Greater New York that have asked the Governor to sign the bill are the New York State Workingmen's Federation of Labor, the New York State Locomotive Enginemen and Firemen and the Trades Assemblies in Rochester, Syracuse, Elmira, Troy, Albany, Utica, Yonkers, Poughkeepsie, Jamestown, Binghamton, Schenectady and other cities.

Those who are closely following the movements of Senator White's pet bill say that it has a better chance of becoming a law this year than it did last. One who has been instrumental in shaping the destinies of the "Equal Pay" bill said to-day that there is more inside politics being played in behalf of this measure than thought.—Utica *Observer*, March 23, 1908.

## TEACHERS FIGHTING FOR GOOD CAUSE

With right and justice behind them, the women teachers of Greater New York are again knocking at the door of the Senate and Assembly and also at the door of Governor Hughes for their "Equal Salary" bill. The Governor last year put this question up to the New York City Board of Education, but the board has taken no notice as yet of the Governor's words and it would seem that it is the duty of the Legislature and the Governor to compel the board to pay the women teachers the same salaries as are paid to the men, as both are doing the same class of work—Editorial Plattsburgh *Republican*, February 8, 1908.

## NOT BENEVOLENT

The public schools are not an eleemosynary institution. They are not to be administered as public benevolence. They are a part of the regulated machinery of the community, and any disposition to treat them as benevolent factors is a perversion of the fact and intention, as well as the conditions of support of the schools.—Baltimore *American*.

## EQUAL PAY FOR EQUAL WORK

Certain periods in the world's history are referred to as "Dark Ages." When one reflects on the present inequality of men and women in political and industrial life, the historians of the future will probably characterize the century now passing as the "Age of Injustice."

The spirit of American rights is proclaimed in the magnificent protest, which says: "Taxation without representation is tyranny." Yet the majority of American women pay taxes without representation, and women can be hanged by laws in the making of which they have no voice.

Wherever women, as a class, are degraded in political, industrial or social life the men have a correspondingly low standard. Therefore the contention for "Equal Pay for Equal Work" will be the great factor for a better industrial condition for men, for where women's wages are low the men are correspondingly poorly paid.

This question of "Equal Pay for Men and Women Teachers" was defeated at a special meeting of the New York board of education held this week. The vote was 23 to 16, against the measure. Fifteen men and one woman voted in favor of it. Twenty men and three women voted against it.

Mr. Stern said to equalize the women's pay would cost the city from $7,000,000 to $11,000,000 annually. Admitted that this is a very large increase, but if it was an increase for men would it not be considered? Then why should men in the same grades in the schools doing exactly the same work, often not as good, receive a much larger salary than women do? If economy is the slogan, make the pay equal, regardless of sex.

Mr. Martin said: "The schedule prepared by the Interborough Association of Women Teachers should be called not 'equal pay for equal work' but 'equal pay for equal age,' as it based its increase on length of service." The Interborough Association of Teachers should realize the value of experience in dealing with children, and also the fact that the teachers recognize that time brings knowledge and matures the mind. This certainly should not militate against the teachers' graded scale, but rather it should be a recognized tribute to their sense of justice. Evidently Mr. Martin is not logical. Moreover the graduate scale is not the whole contention, but the fact that the men in the same grades are receiving much larger salaries than are the women for the same work, and the question is "Why?"

Again Mr. Martin said "that these teachers take the attitude that we (the board of education) must give it to them." Why not? Is not that the exact attitude that was assumed by our Revolutionary ancestors in their appeal to England? It was very effective, and the present one will prove to be equally so.

Commissioner Barrett said "the fact that one-twelfth of the teachers receive a certain salary is not a good reason that the other eleven-twelfths should receive the same salary." If they do exactly the same work, why should they not receive the same salary?

When Mayor McClellan appointed three women on the board of education last fall, many thought the millennium for women had arrived. While appreciative of the ex-mayor's act in recognizing women, many deplored the fact that three society women who never knew what it was to need or earn a dollar, had been selected to represent 15,000 teachers, who are engaged daily in the most difficult work of disciplining and educating about 50 children each crowded in one room. These children represent all classes in the community, possess all degrees of ability and lack of it, and have a variety of temperaments and different degrees of morality. These teachers meet all conditions at least five hours each day in school, and when one considers the price of food and the number often depending upon them for support, it is conceivable that they sometimes lack the comforts of life to which they are entitled. That even one woman member of the New York board of education, Mrs. Christine Towns, voted for equal pay is to her credit, and she is to be congratulated.

The great need in industrial success is the unity of interests of men and women. It is one of the enigmas of modern life that the literal striking of a woman would brand the offender as a social outcast, while in an economic way, the deadliest blows may be struck at her with impunity, while it is a fact that no class in the community is a greater barrier to better industrial conditions for men than are the women who do not believe in "equal pay for equal work."

## EQUAL PAY FOR WOMEN

The New York board of education has just rejected the plea of the women teachers in the public schools of that city for equal pay for equal work, as compared with men. The justice of this demand by the women teachers is readily apparent; but their case is no exception to the rule in the public school system of the country. Women teachers rarely in any city or state get the same salary for the same work, often done very much better than men teachers perform it.

The wisdom of women competing with men in some walks of professional life may well be disputed, but in the school room there is work to be done which women are pecularly well fitted to perform. Even here there are duties which cannot be best discharged by women, but these are exceptional. In the graded schools of the country the great majority of the teachers are women, and the faculties of the high schools contain at least an equal number of women and men. Under what possible theory of justice is a woman paid less than a man for the same work?

The question is not whether a man should do the work. That has been settled by the universal recognition of women's paramount qualification for certain departments of instruction. There certainly is something grotesque, to say the least, in the inequity of making the male teacher's salary larger than that of the woman teacher who works in the next room at the same task.

## PART IV—CHAPTER I

### LETTERS

Personally, however, I have never been able to see any good reason why a person who performs the same kind of work equally as well should be paid any less because she happens to be a woman. I am perfectly willing that you should use my name, but it must not be as the President of the Brooklyn League, only in my individual capacity.

GEORGE W. BRUSH (Ex-Senator).

I am very much in sympathy with your movement. I have learned through much experience that there are many things that women can do equally as well as men, and whenever a woman performs a service as well as a man I believe she should have the same pay. I have often said that the best teacher I ever had in my life was a woman, and strange to say, the subjects that she taught were higher mathematics.

GAGE E. TARBELL.

Jan. 30, 1908.

Any time I can be of service to your cause I will do anything in my power.

CHARLES J. TAYLIABUE.

Feb. 8, 1908.

If I can aid the movement in any way I hereby write myself down as awaiting instruction.

THOS. J. CUMMINGS.

Jan. 29, 1908.

I gladly accept the honor of again saying a good word in favor of the equalization salary bill. (In re the Mayor's hearing, May 11, 1909.)

WILLIAM A. COKELEY, Bronx.

May 5, 1909.

It has been a pleasure for me to do what I can in the interest of your cause.

NATHANIEL H. LEVI.

I heartily endorse the White Bill equalizing teachers' salaries and I most respectfully and earnestly urge you to approve the bill.

As the present injustice originated with the Legislature in the Davis Law, I believe that the proposed White Bill in correcting this injustice in no way interferes with the principle of home rule.

Respectfully yours,
W. E. VERITY,
President, Brooklyn Lumber Company.

To Gov. Hughes, May 1, 1907.

Sir: At the hearing on the Teachers' Bill this morning, it seemed to me that no very strong argument was advanced in opposition. The "home rule" objection might be reasonable, if the teachers had not already appealed to the Board of Education and failed to get a square deal. The gross disproportion in the schedule of salaries between men and women is too glaring to be successfully ignored in a profession for which women are so eminently fitted. Simple justice for a most faithful body of public servants demands the relief sought by this bill.

As a taxpayer I would esteem it a privilege to bear my share of the resultant cost. The opportunity is yours to see that the scales of justice are balanced evenly.

Very respectfully,
ALBERT E. DAVIS.

To Mayor McClellan, May 11, 1909.

I am deeply interested in the success of any progressive movement such as yours is.

In my mind, it is merely a matter of time before you achieve what you are striving for, because the trend of our civilization is to insure deserving equality.

"Equal pay for equal work" is logically fair and square, and you will undoubtedly win to it soon.

With my best wishes,
ARTHUR L. GILLAM.

Mar., 1910.

I wrote to Mayor McClellan that I was strongly in favor of equal pay for equal work and asked him to sign the bill.

FRED. NATHAN.

May 10, 1909.

I have followed your efforts in the newspapers and have been very sorry to see that you have met with a temporary defeat. Continue your efforts and you must, in time, succeed. The only way to get there is never to take a "knock-out blow," especially when you are in the right.

W. G. McADOO.

May 12, 1910.

You have evidently been misinformed as to our not being in favor of the Teachers' Bill. We not only signed the petition but wrote a letter to Mayor McClellan endorsing the bill.

FREDERICK LOESER & CO.

The movement has my entire sympathy and I hope you will be successful in your endeavor to have the salaries of men and women teachers equalized. To claim that a man should have more pay than a woman because he may have more people dependent upon him is as absurd as to claim that a man with six children should have more pay than one with none. Neither the City nor any other employer should consider anything but whether the person is fitted to fill the place, salary being based on the work performed and not on sex.

ARTHUR GIBB.
(Frederick Loeser & Co.)

Mar. 5, 1908.

The opponents of the equal salaries bill seem to place their reliance for a veto on two things, "the expense to the city" and the "principle of home rule."

The first is, of course, a mere pretense. You are not asking for a mere increase in salary, but for justice. In regard to the second, stress is laid upon the fact that Governor Hughes has vetoed two bills that conflicted with the principle, and your friends, the enemy, hope that the Mayor will look upon your bill as a violation of the same principle.

As to the two bills referred to, it may be said that they are political dickers, pure and simple, and the governor does not look with favor upon such interesting items, but, in the case of your bill, your grievance was first presented to the "home rulers," who have power in the matter, and they, to use a common but comprehensive expression, turned it down. In such a case, the principle of home rule should not prevail. There is not, in any sense, any politics in your bill, and it cannot consistently be vetoed on the ground held in the other two vetoes.

It is to be hoped that both the Mayor and the governor will look upon the matter in this light.

The enclosed "pome," cut from the Home Edition of the Globe of May 3, is a disgraceful production, and I should think that "Dr." Cronson and the members of his Association would be ashamed of themselves.

E. O. STRATTON.

May 5, 1905.

SHAW & CO.,

REAL ESTATE AGENTS AND BROKERS.

I most heartily endorse the equal pay bill, firmly believing that the servant is worthy of his hire. Trusting you will be successful,

Yours truly,

HENRY M. VELDERS.

Shaw & Co.

Mar. 26, 1908.

THE CLERGY

I have long been satisfied that the teachers in our public schools do not receive an adequate compensation. It is a position of such transcendent importance in its bearing upon the citizenship of the future that it is poor economy upon the part of the City to stint the salaries of those who are entrusted with the manners and instruction of its children; and if women render the same service as men they should receive the same pay.

Believe me, very truly yours,

DAVID H. GREER,

Bishop Episcopalian Diocese of New York.

Feb. 24, 1908.

I am glad to add my name to the list of those who sympathize with your cause. I wish you and the teachers every success in this movement. The teachers' proposition, which you are so ably defending, is just and ought to be granted.

WILLIAM A. COURTNEY,

Bishop, New York Apostolate.

To one that has taught or that observes thoughtfully it is obvious that the part performed in a community by a genuine teacher yields in importance to none and is approached by few. It is the teacher who, as a rule, leavens the human lump that is in time to crystallize into manhood and citizenship. We do not honor them sufficiently. When we pay them adequately it is somewhat grudgingly. We are willing for others to earn as much as they can. We are disposed to pay teachers as little as we can.

What we have said is true of teachers generally. Pedagogical ability is not a matter of sex, but of intellectual and moral quality. A good teacher is good indifferently to gender. This being so there ought to be no distinction on grounds of sex in our treatment of them.

And yet we have found it necessary to wage an organized fight in our Legislature in behalf of equal pay for women teachers.

From the Jewish standpoint, the McCarren-Conklin bill is imperative. While the teacher in Israel was usually a man the spirit of Judaism would accord the same dignity and desert to a woman. Every consistent Jew should favor such a measure.

Opposition to equal pay to both sexes is bad economics. Remuneration should be proportioned to work or product. From this standpoint some men are less deserving than their professional sisters. It is wide of the mark and ludicrous to argue that a woman needs less and should therefore receive less. Women do not always need less, but often are compelled by our inconsiderate masculine discrimination to adapt themselves to less. On several reasonable grounds women need more than men, but chiefly because of their greater dependency. If need is to be a criterion of wages the salaries of men themselves should not be uniform. The needs of men are diverse.

Refusal to pay women of equal competence equally with men is a vestige of that primitive social state where man was master and woman subordinate. The age of masculine assumption is a regrettable historic memory. Its spirit of brutal male domination should also be throttled. It is a boast of our civilization to have emancipated woman. Let us make good our claim. Let us not glory in a hollow pretense. We grant women equal opportunities and privileges. Let us consistently award them equal pay.

RABBI ALEXANDER LYONS, Brooklyn.

Extract from sermon, March 22, 1907.

I hold that "the laborer is worthy of his hire," and I do not see any justice in a deviation from that on the ground of sex. Women who perform the duties of professorships in our best colleges receive compensation on a par with men, and I have not heard eminent educators, or any other persons, raise objections. This, it seems to me, answers the contention of some that, while women should receive equal pay with men who teach younger children, they should not where higher branches are taught.

It is generally agreed that women are far more capable than men in dealing with children under the age of fifteen years. Why, then, do they not receive more than men teachers who deal with pupils of the same age?

The main argument of the men teachers appears to be that men are heads of families, and, therefore, have greater expenses to meet. Along with this is the advancement of the contention that the family is the unit of the nation, the father the head of it, and nothing should be done to impair his place in the sociological scale.

To this I answer that, while the theory is not to be denied, the fact is that in innumerable instances women are the mainstay of families. I believe women who teach generally aid in the support of their families.

Another thing: It is a fact that a large number of the women teachers in this city have come here from other places and have to support themselves just as the bachelor teachers—and how many of them there are!—do. I do not argue that the men do not deserve all they get; I mean simply to insist that women should not be discriminated against because they are women.

Of course, it would cost the city a great deal more money to pay women teachers salaries equal to men's. But here is no place for economy. Instead, a cut should be made in other city departments where men hold down sinecures due to political pull. Men teachers have votes, too, and there is the rub, in some degree. Many politicians fear to estrange men teachers' votes by upholding the cause of women who toil in our public schools.

It is all a matter of common justice—this equal pay demand. It is a principle already established in some cities in this and other states, and in time I hope and believe that equal pay will be the rule in the public schools of the greatest of American cities.

ROBERT E. JONES,
Canon, Cathedral of St. John the Divine.

Glad to be a vice-president. (Carnegie Hall Mass Meeting.)

CHARLES P. FAGNANI, D. D.

Dec. 1909.

Dr. Aked has received your letter of yesterday's date, requesting him to act as Honorary Vice-President. He has instructed me to say "with pleasure."

DUNCAN J. McMILLAN.

Dec. 1909.

My sympathies are with you.

(Rev.) W. N. ACKLEY.

I heartily believe in your worthy cause. Your efforts for justice and righteousness will ultimately prevail, and I wish you every success in your laudable endeavors.

Invoking the Divine blessing upon you and all associated with you in your demands for justice. I remain,

Sincerely yours,
(Rev.) GEORGE ADAMS.

Feb. 29, 1908.

I am writing to assure you of my thorough sympathy for your cause, or the cause of anyone, who makes bold to say: "What's mine is mine." I have watched the matter anxiously, confident Governor Hughes would favor you, provided the bill presented truly set forth the situation; and, so far as I have been able to observe, the best argument, emanating from the camp of the opposition, is that it will cost some odd millions of dollars more for the state to sustain the schools, should your request be granted.

Assuming this to be true, then someone in the past has been paid too much as someone has been paid too little—that was a degenerate past, before "knighthood was in flower." We can hardly expect those who are paid too much to become generous and turn over the extra to those who were paid too little; but *we do expect justice and equity for the future.* We who believe in the Golden Rule, as a corollary therefrom, believe we should pay a woman as much for a spool of silk, an apple pie, or an education, as we pay a man for the above mentioned features of graceful existence.

Those who do not appear to believe in the Golden Rule say this reform will cost millions, therefore drop it. One might as well say it will cost money to build bridges and subways for our vast city, therefore do not build them; it will cost millions to maintain courts of justice, therefore do not maintain them. I know of no worthy cause that succeeds without effort or cost—such an argument is unworthy of the most ordinary politician. If the thing is right, we'll have it; if not, we'll drop it.

As I understand it, you want the pay to balance the job, without reference to sex, race, religion or previous condition of servitude, on the part of the incumbent.

Do not worry, you will have that as truly as water runs down hill. There are oceans of injustice in the world; but the world is growing better all the time.

And, "I doubt not, through the ages, one unceasing purpose runs; and the minds of men will broaden, with the process of the sums."

Therefore, be not over-anxious, just keep busy and that better day will come.

You recall what Lincoln said about "fooling the people"—that is as true to-day as when first uttered.

Your cause is a splendid one—such reforms always cost sacrifice commensurate with the value of success; eventually the puerile arguments sink into oblivion, and the just cause has an honored past in the drama of civilization.

Sincerely,
LYNN P. ARMSTRONG, Pastor,
Cuyler Presbyterian Church, Brooklyn.

Feb. 15, 1908.

I am in full sympathy with you in this fight for "Equal Pay."
(Rev.) J. G. BACCHUS, Brooklyn.

I am heartily in favor of the Equal Pay Measure which you are so ably and eloquently advocating. *Were we dependent on men for the education of our children most of the schools would be*

Hon. Reuben L. Gledhill,
Father of Senate "Equal Pay Bill," 1909.

*closed to-morrow.* My observation and careful study of the question compel the conviction that the male teachers have no monopoly of brains or brilliance. The work of the average male teacher is not one whit superior to that of the average female teacher. Then why discriminate? In Plato's Republic woman occupies an inferior place because she is a woman. The American Republic will not be guilty of such an ancient and inexcusable anachronism.

All argument based on feminine mental and pedagogical inferiority is too puerile to be seriously combated. That based on increased taxation should be met by the frank rebuttal that a *glaring injustice is never ultimately economical,* and by the very important fact that the larger amount of the budget for equal pay would only mean a few extra cents per capita of the vast body of taxpayers. Personally, I can begrudge nothing to the noble men and women who consecrate themselves to the glorious task of educating the children of our city. New York holds her head too proudly high to discount the female teachers who are of more value than her sky scrapers.

Yours faithfully,
AUGUSTUS E BARNETT,
Tremont Methodist Episcopal Church, Bronx.

March 17, 1908.

I would be happy to attend this evening. I approve its object, but other engagements prevent attendance.

JONATHAN BARSTOW,
Pastor Second Ave. Baptist Church.

I appreciate the importance of the work you have undertaken, and believe in the righteousness of your cause.

L. W. BATTEN,
Rector, St. Mark's Church, New York.

Thank you for the information you sent me.

I believe in the principle of compensation. "The laborer is worthy of his hire," and every laborer deserves adequate compensation for the service he renders.

I should be glad to see the salary question adjusted in such a way that the standard would be not age or sex but service.

JOHN L. BELFORD,
Pastor, Roman Catholic Church—The Nativity.

March 11, 1908.

Our warmest sympathies are with your meeting and its object.

W. W. BELLINGER.
Vicar, St. Agnes' Chapel.

Dec., 1909.

I thoroughly believe in the justice of the proposed bill that provides "that where men and women are appointed to position of the same grade or rank, they shall receive the same pay," and can not understand how any man of the true modern spirit can oppose it.

WILLIAM M. BRUNDAGE.
Pastor, Unity Church, Brooklyn.

Feb. 26, 1908.

I have already expressed my belief in the justice of this simple claim: that whenever equal work is done by teachers, sex should have no deterrent influences, but equal pay should be given to all. I trust this plain, straightforward statement will aid your cause. I wish that there were more men in the teaching profession and better pay for all concerned in it.

Yours ever,
S. PARKES CADMAN,
Central Congregational Church, Brooklyn.

I am in fullest sympathy with your movement. There has recently come to my notice a case in our city, where a lady principal receives only about half as much salary as a gentleman in a nearby school, who supervises fewer teachers by several. I fully believe great injustice is being done the noble band of "women teachers" in our great city. I trust the meeting to-night will prove a great popular movement in the right direction and that your cause will prevail with Governor and Mayor alike.

J. W. CAMPBELL, Pastor,
Washington Heights Methodist Episcopal Church.

——— I trust that your bill will become a law. The sex of a teacher as regards proper compensation, is as irrelevant as the sex of an animal in a beautiful painting, or the sex of the painter in a true piece of art. The value of a teacher's services lies not in sex, but in pedagogic results. I do not see what sex has to do with education in the realm of economics. I do see what it involves in the realm of morals.

SYDNEY HERBERT COX, Pastor,
The Church of the Evangel, Congregational, Flatbush.

It has been a source of perplexity to me to understand why there should be any controversy at all about the question, referred to in your note. It seems to me perfectly obvious that it is *sheer injustice* to give a woman who does the same work as a man less compensation than he receives, *only because she is a woman.* I have kept somewhat in touch with the discussion and I do not recollect a single good reason advanced for beclouding the simple unimpeachable principle of equal pay for equal work. I am most heartily in sympathy with the movement to give the women teachers their rights in the premises. I recall reading somewhere that the effect of the success of this agitation would be to confer such a condition of independence upon the women teachers as to deter them from marriage. That I believe to be rot; insanely amusing rot, but rot just the same. Even if it were so I cannot but think it a piece of singular good fortune that would keep them from linking their lives with those of some of the specimens who plume themselves on being the "lords of creation." I fear I am far too obscure to be of much service for the triumph of your cause. I can only say that I am unreservedly in favor of putting an end to this long standing and shameful inequality. The legislature must somehow be made to realize that there are votes behind your demands. That is the consideration which seems to be most potent with most of those who make our laws.

JOSEPH F. DELANY, Rector,
St. Malachy's Roman Catholic Church.

Mar. 17, 1908.

By all means consider me heartily in favor of the school teachers' demands. Any word or effort of mine that may assist you in your honest endeavors to obtain what to me seems simply "justice," count as yours to have and to use at any time. With best wishes in Christ.

JOHN H. DOOLEY, Roman Catholic Rector,
Corpus Christi Chapel, New York.

(To Mayor McClellan.)
Honorable Sir:

In signing the "Gledhill-Foley Teachers' Bill," I am certain you will be actuated by the American spirit of justice. I am convinced that you are persuaded that where skill, labor or commodities are bought and sold, equivalent compensation should be given for equal service, irrespective of the sex, color, race or nationality of the producer.

By giving the above named Bill your approval, I believe you will commend your sense of exact right.

Yours cordially,
JOHN DONALDSON, Pastor,
Union Course Baptist Church.

May 9, 1909.

"Every problem of life must find its final solution in the light of the fatherhood of God, the brotherhood of man, and according to the practical application of the Golden Rule every contention, every cause, every issue, must be viewed in this light and settled upon this basis. World-wide problems, national issues, local issues, personal matters, must all be settled upon this basis. Perfectly germain to this line of thought is that matter of vital importance to the women teachers in our public schools, and it should be regarded as a matter of vital importance to us all. I need not reflect upon the intelligence of this large congregation by pausing, even for a moment, to explain what the White bill is. I need only to assume that you are posted, and well posted, upon all such matters as are of common interest to us. You know that the chief objection to the passing of the McCarren-Conklin bill which the noble army of women teachers have endorsed has been this: It means an increase of nine millions of dollars which our taxpayers must meet. A number of other objections have been made, but this seems to be the most formidable and persistent of them all. The objection cannot be justified in fact, and sustained by principle. It would mean an increase of about six millions to our taxpayers and not nine millions as has been claimed. It does mean that our women teachers shall have simple justice done them, nothing more, nothing less. It means that a woman shall be paid just as much as a man for the same service, equally well, if not better, rendered. It means that our people, who must finally settle everything, are not willing that so many of the best and influential persons that we have, our women teachers, shall continue to suffer an injustice simply because they happen to be women. Our mothers and sisters who can influence the voters, our politicians who hold their positions according to the decrees of the voters, our noble Governor of the State of New York, of whom we are justly proud, all these should be heard from and in the name of chivalry, in the name of grateful parents who appreciate the intellectual and moral worth of these women, in the name of a cause broader than any creed, in the name of justice, let us settle this matter which ought to be settled only in one way, and that in the right way. Settle this and everything else according to the Golden Rule, and always behave as the children of God."—Extract from sermon, Rev. Luther B. Dyott, United Congregational Church, Brooklyn.

I am in fullest sympathy with your effort to secure (regardless of sex) equal pay for positions of the same grade or rank.

W. R. ESTES, Pastor,
Union Methodist Episcopal Church, Brooklyn.

March 6, 1908.

I wish I could be with you, and give you all the sympathy and aid in my power.

WALTER A. A. GARDURI, Rector.
Protestant Episcopal Church, West Houston Street.

I believe in your work and wish you success.

(Rev.) GEORGE C. GROVES, Jr.,
Holy Cross Mission, Brooklyn.

Mar. 4, 1908.

The Parkside Christian Socialist Fellowship heartily endorses the "Equal Pay Bill" supported by the Interborough Association of Women Teachers.

B. C. HAMMOND.
Parkside Church, Presbyterian,
Lenox Road, Flatbush.

March 26, 1908.

I am in most hearty accord with the efforts of the teachers in New York City to secure for their work the same compensation that is paid to men for the same work. I never could see any reason why there should be any discrimination. In a city so large and wealthy as is ours there can be no excuse for such injustice. I have found from observation that quite a large percentage of women teachers have others dependent upon them for support. For this reason they should be fairly compensated for their labor. I sincerely hope that the efforts which your society is making may be successful.

RICHARD HARTLEY, Pastor,
Hope Baptist Church, New York.

Feb. 13, 1908.

——— The movement has my entire sympathy and approbation.

JOHN J. HEISCHMANN, D. D., Pastor,
St. Peter's Evangelical Lutheran Church, Brooklyn.

Mar. 20, 1907.

I do not think that the knowledge that I am in hearty agreement with you will add very materially to the weight of your argument, unless there is some truth in the old saying that "many a meikle mak's a muckle."

However, let me assure you that, speaking for myself, I can see no reason why the female teachers of our schools who are called upon to do exactly the same work as the male teachers should not get salaries on the same scale. This, I think, is fundamental, and, simple as it seems, the whole burden of your argument will need to be directed to the enlightenment of the citizens of the State upon this one point. Once our citizens become possessed with the idea of the injustice of the two scales, relief will follow. If my voice can aid any in the rising cry, I am ready to shout. Wishing you the success you deserve in your effort, I am,

JAMES BOYD HUNTER, Pastor,
Anderson Memorial Reformed Church, New York.

Mar. 9, 1908.

I will drop everything at the shortest notice and go anywhere at your call for your cause.

ALEXANDER IRVINE,
Church of the Ascension.

Dec., 1909.

Wishing you abundant success.

T. J. LACEY, Rector,
Church of the Redeemer.

Dec., 1909.

You may quote me as being in hearty sympathy with the principle of "equal pay for equal service."

M. A. LAYTON, Pastor,
DeKalb Avenue Methodist Episcopal Church.

You may quote me anywhere as believing, that since, after years of demonstration, it is proved beyond a doubt that women make as effective teachers in the public schools as men, I am strongly of the opinion that when they do precisely the same work, and carry identical burdens, and show essentially the same results, that men and women should receive the same pay.

CHARLES EDWARD LOCKE,
Hanson Place Methodist Episcopal Church.

March 5, 1908.

I heartily approve your movement and endorse the principle upon which it is based.

My convictions have grown out of thirty-five years' experience in school work in various capacities,—as teacher, City Superintendent, County Superintendent, College President, and other official positions. During my nine years' pastorate in this city, I have kept close touch with the public schools in an unofficial capacity. I am confirmed in the conviction that it is unfair and unjust to require a man and a woman to do the same amount and character in the same community upon different stipends. The evil is aggravated when the discrimination is against the sex which our civilization has always delighted to honor. And it seems almost pusillanimous when we remember that the favored sex has exclusive power in fixing the salaries. It is unmanly and un-American to discriminate against a helpless class, however they may be differentiated, whether by race, color, or sex.

DUNCAN J. McMILLAN, Pastor,
New York Presbyterian Church, New York City.

I am in full sympathy with your movement.

(Rev.) D. J. McWILLIAM.

My sympathy is with you.

(Rev.) G. MAINE.

I am with you. Your contention is so just that it will ultimately prevail.

REV. EDWARD McGUFFEY.

Dec., 1909.

With the purpose of your movement I am indeed in hearty sympathy. Woman has become economically free. This is a fact. The recognition of the fact by law makers and law administrators and by the public generally, is only a question of time. Equal pay for equal work is one step in this direction. Work for it, and when you get it, as you will in time, take up the next step.

JOHN HOWARD MELISH, Rector.
Church of the Holy Trinity, Brooklyn.

Mar. 4, 1908.

I am very glad to go on record as favoring the "Equal Pay Bill." I have not heard a single argument against it which was worth repeating. It seems to me a question of common justice and withal of good economics. We need the best teachers we can procure for the children who are to become our citizens. To my mind, in the lower grades of our public schools, the woman is the greater power in training the boys for political and the girls for social influence. Especially in the congested districts of the city—like our East Side—the children need "mothering." Too frequently they do not receive it in the home. The woman teacher not only supplies this element, but is in no wise inferior to the man in her educational equipment and ability. I say this after careful consideration of the question.

G. ERNEST MERRIAM, Pastor,
Fourteenth Street Presbyterian Church, N. Y.

April 11, 1908.

I am in thorough sympathy with your movement and have advocated it on numerous occasions. Permit me to congratulate you on the same methods you are employing to enforce the demands of justice. We are living in an age when public opinion is the great ruling force in all departments of life. If we can educate and crystallize this all-pervading force, justice will come of itself, without revolutionary tactics of any kind. "Whoever fights, whoever falls, justice conquers evermore."

GROVER G. MILLS, Pastor,
Pilgrim Chapel, Brooklyn.

Feb. 29, 1908.

"Equal pay for equal work" is common justice, both within and without the public schools. I, for one, cannot see why ability and efficiency should be discriminated against when dressed in gowns instead of pantaloons. You surely are right, so go ahead!

L. K. MOORE, Pastor,
Eighteenth Street M. E. Church, Brooklyn.

Mar. 10, 1908.

I am an ex-public school teacher, and I have always been strongly in favor of the movement for which you are working.

HENRY MOTTET, Rector.
Church of the Holy Communion, New York.

Jan. 23, 1908.

I believe that a woman doing equal work with a man should be paid the same compensation.

FRANK PAGE, Rector.
St. John's Church, Brooklyn.

Jan. 22, 1908.

In payment for service rendered the question of sex should not exclude honesty. Because I believe in the necessity of justice and the essentialness of honorable treatment, your claim of "equal pay for equal work" appeals to me with the power of right and the persuasiveness of truth.

Success to your cause.

THOMAS EDWARD POTTERTON, Pastor,
Church of Our Father, Brooklyn.

I wish you success.

PAUL H. SCHNATZ, Pastor,
Martha Memorial Reformed Church.

I desire to assure you of my deep sympathy with your cause and my firm conviction as to the righteousness of its principles. Last year I went to Albany to the public hearing before the Governor, representing the women teachers of Richmond Borough, but you will recollect I had no opportunity to speak at the hearing because of the lack of time. I have written two or three times to my friend, Governor Hughes, urging his interest and support. If I can in any way help the cause for which you are so heroically struggling, I shall be glad to do so.

REV. CHARLES SCHWEIKERT.

You may count on me as heartily in favor of the success of the cause which you represent.

I trust that you and your associates will not grow discouraged and give over your efforts, for you will assuredly yet win a memorable and justly deserved victory. Your cause is just and righteous, and men, although they are proverbially narrow when dealing in money matters with women, still they yet will see their error and grant your claim. Moral progress will not much longer tolerate delay. So-called logic may make crooked paths to get around the fixed principle—"Equal pay for equal work," but common sense and right reason will yet lead a reluctant public opinion to right conclusions, and all the fair-minded will rejoice that the women have finally come into their own!

G. E. STROWBRIDGE, Pastor,
Washington Square Methodist Episcopal Church.

Feb. 5, 1908.

It has always seemed to me that efficiency and not sex should determine compensation for service. The general principle enunciated by the Great Teacher when he sent forth those who were to be teachers "the laborer is worthy of his hire," is as true to-day as then, and if you shall find strong incentive for best possible equipment for your work and for the attainment of the highest success in your calling, you must be given to understand that all the rights and emoluments of your calling are available to you.,

May your cause prevail.

D. B. THOMPSON, Pastor,
Park Avenue Methodist Episcopal Church, N. Y.

April 8, 1908.

I hope you will be successful in your efforts toward receiving "Equal Pay for Equal Work."

FRANK M. TOWNLEY, Rector,
St. Bartholomew's Church.

I am in sympathy with the movement for equal pay, and I think the plea is just, though in the present state of finance this might mean the reduction of the salaries of the male teaching force.

F. TRACEY,
The Church of the Redeemer, Brooklyn.

Jan. 23, 1908.

There is no sex in teaching, and there ought to be none in pay.

DR. HENRY VAN DYKE.

As to the use of my name, I am perfectly willing to be quoted as heartily in favor of a just compensation for services rendered, whether by men or women, and as heartily opposed to any discrimination in the matter of compensation, on the ground of difference in sex or anything else. Work should be recompensed according to its quality and quantity, whether the worker be man or woman, even though the man be the head of a household and the woman have no one else dependent upon her.

(REV.) NEWELL WOOLSEY WELLS,
Brooklyn.

Feb. 29, 1908.

I am in hearty sympathy with the effort of your Association.

T. J. WHITAKER, Pastor.
Bushwick Avenue Baptist Church, Brooklyn.

Jan. 22, 1908.

I am very much in favor of "Equal Pay" legislation.

A. ARCESE, Rector.
St. Lucy's Roman Catholic Church, Brooklyn.

Jan. 20, 1908.

I am in deep sympathy with the movement and in favor of the proposed bill.

LEIGHTON WILLIAMS,
Amity House, New York City.

## EDITORS, LITTERATEURS AND ARTISTS

Mr. Hearst has given instructions to all of his newspapers and to all of his editorial writers, to fight persistently on the side of the teachers and of the public school children. Mr. Hearst has said to me repeatedly that he considers the welfare of the public school children, and generous, appreciative treatment of public school teachers, the most important individual thing in our public life.

The articles which you see in the paper, similar to the one of which you speak, are written in accordance with Mr. Hearst's personal and often-repeated instructions.

A. BRISBANE,
Editor, New York *Journal.*

Sept. 26, 1907.

I am very much interested in the work that women teachers do, unquestionably the most important daily work that is done in the world. I shall be glad to talk to your membership for a few minutes, as you suggest, if you want me to, but I am a pretty bad talker.

A. BRISBANE,
Editor, New York *Journal.*

May 23, 1908.

Dear Miss Ennis:

Your very kind favor has been forwarded to me. I am heartily in sympathy with the movement on the part of the Interborough Association of Women Teachers to secure the full salaries paid to men teachers. My feelings have been expressed on this subject at various times, and I hope are well known in Brooklyn. I certainly shall feel proud to be casually mentioned as an enthusiastic believer in your cause. If I felt that any word from me would aid you, I would be present at your meeting, and also volunteer to go to Albany to state your case, from my heart to the Legislative Committees. Do not be discouraged. Great battles for the right are not won easily. Common sense tells every rational man that teaching is an art that woman can practice as well if not with more success, than men. A man ought to be paid more money for carrying a hod or mixing mortar than a woman could earn at the same work, because she is unfitted for the labor, but she should be paid exactly what he receives,—if she be competent for the job.

With the most sincere hope for and belief in your success,

I am, yours faithfully,

Mar. 2, 1908. JULIUS CHAMBERS.

My Dear Miss Corney:

After studying over your question for nearly a month, I can make but one answer and that is it should be the quality of the work done and not the sex of the worker which should govern the price.

DAN BEARD.

(Author of "Field and Forest Handy Book," "The American Boy's Handy Book," "The Outdoor Handy Book," "The Jack of All Trades," etc. E. C.)

Dear Miss Corney.

I have always believed that women should receive the same pay for the same work as men do. If a life is saved or a good deed performed, does God ask whether it was a man or a woman? You might as well pay more or less for services performed by those of different religious belief or political faith. A result obtained should be paid for without regard to who performed it. The rain falls alike on the just and unjust—if they haven't sense enough to go in out of the rain. Many women have those depending upon them for support the same as men. It certainly costs more to dress a woman than it does a man, especially when she is single. If it doesn't, it ought to.

R. F. OUTCAULT,

(Creator of Buster Brown)

April 9, 1908. E. C.

I need hardly say I am entirely in sympathy with your movement. This sex bar is becoming quite ridiculous.

FORBES-ROBERTSON.

I do not think the pay for any position in the public service should depend upon whether the occupant is a man or a woman. I shall therefore be glad to be included among your vice-presidents.

NORMAN HAPGOOD.
Editor, *Colliers Weekly.*

Dec., 1909.

Israel Zangwill in a London speech denounced the flagrant injustice of denying women equal recognition with men in their work in the profession.

## "EQUAL PAY"

Under the rule of commercialism, labor receives only the current rate of wages. If sex makes labor cheaper, only the sex price will be paid in general business accordingly as we find that we can secure the service we need from either the potential father or the potential mother. Individual merit often rises above the limitations of sex, as thus. You may prefer an efficient woman in some particular line or capacity, even if nature at intervals interrupts her office attendance, to a man who, though even a little more efficient perhaps, is less faithful in the imperative routine because of the sin which doth most easily beset males. (Need I name it?)

So we shall have to leave business to work out its own problems, for it will always do so, even if strange Government policies are sometimes adopted with a view to making water run up hill without a pump. But although Government was first established as a selfish measure of mutual protection of the units of a community, it has grown to a moral ideal. It is ideals alone that make life worth living, and it is reality alone that justifies the modern multifariousness of the activities of Government. Granting that almost self-evident proposition, the logical deduction is that the payments of Government for its machinery and the operators of it should be on a more moral basis than that of the individual units of a community, each struggling in the battle of bread-winning on the principle of "all's fair * * * in war," but keeping truce in the communal organization. We aim to have a perfect Government even if our private lives are not aimed at perfection. And perfect Government demands that labor shall be paid under a scheme of equality; that qualification and merit shall be the test for allotting wages or other forms of remuneration—not color, nor religion, nor fashion, nor SEX.

The women teachers whose cause you have so long and so ably advocated, Miss Strachan, have special claims, in my opinion, in the controversy that will never be settled till it is settled right. Personally, however, I prefer to argue on the one line herebefore mentioned—"Equal Pay." The very shibboleth is conclusive of all discussion.

JAMES S. H. UMSTED.

## "EQUAL PAY FOR EQUAL WORK"

A reply to a circular entitled "Equal Pay For Equal Work" which male teachers had distributed outside Cooper Union on the occasion of our mass meeting, January 30, 1908.

By Miss Lina E. Gano, Manhattan Vice-President, Interborough Association of Women Teachers.

"The laborer is worthy of his hire."—Luke, X-7.

Many women are laborers; "so recognized by our statutes, and firmly so established by consent" of modern society, their male relatives and shifting economic conditions.

Because of peculiar adaptations woman has found her "natural and advantageous sphere of effort in activities" associated with the training and education of youth. Because of peculiar economic and social conditions of modern life, many women have found this "natural sphere of effort in activities beyond the threshold of the home."

"Money in the form of salary, wages, etc., also as the price of marketable products, is, after all, but the mere convenience of civilization by which mankind" and womankind "may easily interchange their peculiar individual products or benefits for desirable necessities or benefits held by others."

The above facts are some of the fundamental truths in our social and economic systems.

The family is one of several social units recognized by prominent authorities. See Gidding's Historical Sociology. Seventy-five per cent. of the women teachers of New York City find themselves the heads of families which they have inherited. For the support and maintenance of said families they are forced to pay the full market price for foods, shelter, clothing, transportation, physician's services, amusements, etc.

The family in ancient Greece and Rome was probably the economic unit. The wife, the children and all other property constituted the family wealth—oikos. This is no longer true. The fact that women are recognized as independent units in the industrial world, with independent responsibilities, proves the failure of the acient scheme under modern conditions.

The statutes of the State of New York recognize the man and the woman as separate economic units even when they are one in marriage. The married woman has the right to her own earnings and to her own inherited wealth. Married or single, the woman may make contracts and be held responsible for the same under statute law governing similar transactions in any case. She may buy or sell in the open market of the City, the State, or the Nation, and enjoy all the protection and immunities of property accorded to other citizens. She is also forced to recognize the duties and responsibilities of other property owners. She may hold real estate in her own right and must pay her full pro-rata of taxes for state and local protection. She may enter any service or profession for which she is eligible without hindrance or discrimination of statute law, except that of teaching the youth of the State.

By the Constitution, the women of the State of New York are recognized as citizens, or political units; by statute law they are recognized as industrial and economic units. To confuse ancient and mediaeval economic standards with modern standards, or to confuse social units with industrial units is either the result of ignorance or perversion.

"The more clearly we look into the daily lives, habits and occupations of the great mass of society, that in some form or other is obliged to work for and earn its own living, the more clearly do we perceive that the so-called work" of the individual is the combined work of the individual and those who minister to the individual's necessities. "The wife prepares meals and helps in maintaining the home of the husband"; the woman who goes out into the working world must trust the same to servants, often careless, extravagant and incompetent.

The wages of an individual, then, should be the wages fitted to the requirements for the service, the results of the service and the supply of said individuals in the open market. For any class in any service to ask or petition for more is to ask for special protection and consideration from society. It is a pitiful exhibition on the part of those claiming the protection and an unjust reflection upon others of the same class who are ready to meet the conditions. Granting the special protection, forces the employer, the City or State of New York, into the attitude of an eleemosynary institution. To the credit of American manhood and our civil administration it is fair to say that there is but one department of the public service of the City of New York where discrimination in favor of men as against women is asked. It is also fair to state that the economic standards of every profession except that of teaching, are measured by conditions of to-day as opposed to those of Ancient Rome and Mediaeval Europe. This may perhaps account for the measure of contempt sometimes felt for the teaching service, by those who know and recognize that economics is a "shifting science."

When, therefore, a woman, often charged with a home and always contributing to the life of the nation, enters the industrial field, she is entitled to the compensation of other individuals in the same field. She is entitled to the same pay as the man whose just wage is what he is worth. It is right that she should receive as much as any other employee, meeting the same requirements and producing equivalent results, particularly when we remember the helpless members of her family or the incompetent servants upon whom she must depend for necessities.

The pay that men teachers receive by the existing schedule is certainly not extravagant, but compared with women gives them in many cases double pay for the same work.

These considerations are in distinct contradiction to the requirements of the civil service system in every other department of the City or State service. Any legislation that continues these discriminations and "inflicts arbitrary, artificial and unnatural conditions" in economic life, is not in the interest of justice or equity, but in the interest of a special class. It is class legislation of the grossest type.

The demand for unequal pay by men teachers is based upon the mistaken notion that woman is not yet an entity, and ignoring the fact that the Constitution and statute law have recognized her as such in making her a political and industrial unit with accompanying responsibilities.

When the wife made the cloth and the clothes, knit the stockings and the gloves, brewed the ale, made the cheese, the butter and the bread for the family, cured the meats and all table delicacies, and combined the qualifications of a teacher with those of a physician, and when the husband provided the shelter and contributed the raw materials for all of his so-called natural dependents, the family was an economic unit. But conditions have changed.

This work is now done outside the home by women as well as men who are skilled in the various industries and professions. Each of these individuals has his or her own burdens and problems as an individual. Each receives a renumeration as an individual. The woman does very much the same kind of work as before, only the ways of doing the work and the methods of remuneration have changed. In other words, society has come to recognize the woman and the man as individuals and as economic units rather than parts of units. Each individual comes very near living an individual life but with certain obligations to render to dependents and to the great social structure. Women as well as men have become bread winners and have been forced to assume the responsibilities and obligations formerly assumed by the so-called heads of families. In some industries and several professions there is no discrimination against women if the service rendered is satisfactory, but in the teaching profession many localities make a discrimination varying from 30 per cent. to 50 per cent. because of sex and no corresponding discrimination in their favor from landlords, grocers, public service corporations, etc.

These social and economic conditions have come in spite of any theories that we may individually entertain. As Professor Farnum, of Yale, has recently said, "We are living in a highly dynamic period. We are so accustomed to change that we sometimes do not realize all that it means or the rate of the change of the present day." But the family as an economic unit has passed. In the industrial and commercial world, persons are paid for efficiency of service. Salaries and wages are not determined by the size of families.

Systems of economics also reflect these changes. Each historic period has had some economic ideal which passed for a law in its time. In the Feudal period society was wedded to the theory that the economic status of every class was measured by its relation to the land. Legislation was class legislation and reflected the position of the classes to landed estates. But in turn many of these ideas and ideals were outgrown. The Davis Law, however, which fixes the salaries of teachers in the City of New York is a relic of this mediaeval class legislation.

By this law, men secured protection which removed them and their services from the open market and fixed a wage for a class from 30 per cent. to 60 per cent. greater than for another class (women) for whom they also legislated.

After the Feudal theories came the theory of government control and government interference in all industrial and commercial enterprises, as evidenced in France and England for two or more centuries before the French Revolution. Again the economic, political and legislative ideas went hand in hand until they were overthrown by one of the most notable struggles in history.

Then gradually came freedom from government control, freedom for labor, freedom to combine and in time freedom for trade and the announcement that the "law of supply and demand" would at last settle the economic questions of the world. It was thought that John Stuart Mill had said the last word on the subject of competition. When Bagehot doubted whether competition always worked perfectly and when Walker dared to advocate governmental interference in industry, they were consigned to the place from which we all hope to escape. But as President Hadley of Yale has recently said, "Modern economics as a science is being freed from the remorseless logic of John Stuart Mill. Even this system is passing. The old

HON. MIRABEAU L. TOWNS,
CHAIRMAN, CARNEGIE HALL MASS MEETING, DECEMBER 17, 1909.

economic orthodoxy is gone, and may I add, no one knows this better than American men. The doctrine of supply and demand is not accepted by society. Our American financial system is a very definite protest against the logic of a few economists whose teachings American men have never heeded. Then why quote this antiquated doctrine to women and ask them to conform to a theory that society has overthrown for men. Professor Dewey, of the Massachusetts Institute of Technology, in his Presidential address before the American Economic Association, made a plea for more accurate and scientific observation of facts before any theory of economics could be established with justice and intelligence for all. He insisted upon the futility of teaching theory while there is no unanimity as to the facts upon which these theories are based. For example, exactly opposite statements were made concerning the panic of 1907, by eminent authorities. In the remorseless theory of supply and demand not all of the facts are known—the theory is based upon partial knowledge. In fact, no economic theory is yet to be trusted. There is much propaganda for the sake of promoting the theory of some interested party or parties.

But at last men have come to realize that for men competition is not merely a struggle for existence. They insist that for men, at least, society shall draw up the rules of the game and hence by organization, agitation and legislation they are able to escape the bitter theory of supply and demand. Society must establish social justice. New ideas of justice and equality are being recognized. A new economic philosophy must be formulated and women bearing the burdens of men and rendering to society a service equally valuable must not be asked to conform to an economic code, that the other half of the race has outgrown.

LINA E. GANO,
Manhattan Vice-President,
Interborough Association Women Teachers.

I have made some inquiries as to the attitude of universities in the matter of salaries paid to women instructors. The question does not come up here at Cornell, where the instructing staff, with a single exception, is made up of men, but so far as I have been able to learn in universities where both men and women are eligible for appointment "the salary paid goes with the grade of the position, and is not subject to variation by reason of sex." Cornell does appoint freely women to fellowships, and I have never heard a suggestion that the income paid should be made to vary with the sex of the incumbent.

I am not so well informed as I should like to be concerning particular local conditions which you face, but as regards the general principle that the position should determine the salary, I am in hearty accord with you.

GEORGE P. BRISTOL,
Director, Summer Session,
Cornell University.

Jan. 16, 1908.
To Miss Lina E. Gano.

My sympathies are and always have been with you in your great movement for right and justice—for Equal Pay for Equal Work, which is really a self-evident principle. The only arguments against it are expediency and an "economy which squanders."

THOMAS HUNTER,
President Emeritus, Normal College.

I am with you in the great work.

WILLIAM HARKNESS,
Ex-Member, Board of Education.

As to the matter in general, I do believe in equal pay for equal work. I think, however, that the whole situation as regards the schools and the economic conditions of the city is not a simple but a complex problem, and I am not yet ready at this time to express an opinion either pro or con with regard to any particular line of action. I should want to investigate it very carefully and take counsel of men and women in whose judgment I rely.

Sincerely yours,
CHARLES SPRAGUE SMITH.

Feb. 6, 1908.

My Dear Miss Strachan—You are doubtless aware of the fact that I have resigned from the Board of Education, my resignation to take effect March 1. I had intended to resign in January, but wished to remain long enough to vote upon and place myself on record as in favor of Mr. Somers' resolution. By dating my resignation as far ahead as March 1, when I sent it to the Mayor in January, I thought I should have ample time for the resolution to be acted on, but Mr. Somers' absence has unexpectedly postponed action.

I wish to assure you that I keenly regret my inability to avail myself of the privilege and the honor of recording myself with the progressive minority of the board, and I desire again to emphasize my unequivocal position in favor of the principle of equal pay for men and women teachers who perform the same work.

I have found it necessary to resign for the reason that I could not afford to give the time required for conscientious performance of the work of the board. My one cause for anxiety now is that those who do not know me well may possibly class me with the non-progressive element which still entertains the ideas and habit of mind of more than a half century ago.

I shall esteem it a favor if you will let my position be freely known, in any way and through any medium that you may deem advisable. The cause with which you are so prominently and unselfishly identified is absolutely certain to be victorious and you have the satisfaction of knowing that those in opposition are fighting a losing battle, for the reason that they are fighting against the inevitable progress of civilized ideas and the perfectly clear and well-defined trend of future progress.

With great respect,
Very truly yours,
(Signed) ARTHUR HOLLICK.

I never have understood why persons should not receive pay without regard to sex for the same work and service. We make no discrimination in Syracuse University because of sex, either in the privileges of the students or in the salaries of any employed. In our College of Fine Arts we have a number of women on the faculty.

Very truly yours,
JAMES R. DAY,
Chancellor, Syracuse University.

You have had my fullest sympathy in your fight for the cause of right and justice from the first, and you can rely on my support till the end, which I have no doubt will be victory. I have given careful attention to the controversy, and have failed to find a single logical argument against your reasonable demands.

It is a pleasure to find our most intellectual men now ranging themselves upon your side.

JOSEPH HETHERINGTON,
Dec., 1909. Chairman, Local School Board, District 42.

I have always believed that whenever a woman does the same work as a man and does it equally well, she should receive a man's wages. This is a general principle.

(Signed) CHAS. R. SKINNER,
Ex-Member Congress; formerly Supt. Public Instruction, State of New York; Ex-Pres., National Association of Teachers.

March 24, 1908.

I believe heartily in the general principle of equal pay for equal work. I believe further, that women teachers in the City of New York should, in general, receive more pay than they are at present receiving, but I am not able, as yet at least, to give assent to the principle of "equal pay" for teachers as that principle is now interpreted.

WALTER L. HERVEY,
The Board of Examiners,
Dept. of Education, New York.

Dec. 19, 1909.

Salaries should be adjusted—not on a physiological basis, but on a pedagogical one. The Board of Education has said that women are eligible to the positions of principals and assistant principal. To pay different salaries to incumbents of the same positions is to employ teachers as farmers employ their help—half a man (a boy), half pay. Or as sailors are employed "able-bodied" men and "ordinary" sailors.

2d.—A woman principal gets a maximum salary of $2500 and is responsible for the work of the entire school, while a man teacher in her school with a class of 30 to 35 pupils is paid $2400.

Is it possible that $100 difference is consistent?

An assistant principal gets a maximum of $1600 and shares the principal's responsibility for the school, while a man teacher with a class of 30 to 35 whom she supervises, is paid $2400. Is it consistent to pay a supervisor $800 less than a subordinate?

Both a principal and an assistant principal must have superior qualifications, and prove those qualifications by a professional examination—such examination being wholly pedagogical and not physiological.

These two positions are used as illustrations of every other.

M. H. BARTLETT.

We extend our hearty endorsement. We employ a number of teachers in our school and reward them for their services according to their ability and regardless of sex. We believe a woman teacher is a more important factor than a man teacher in the educational field. Naturally, her sympathies are nearer the hearthstone and she is more patient; therefore, her influence with children has a greater tendency to aid in training the young mind. With these advantages, she is equal to or greater than the man. A woman in her effort to support herself deserves and should have, at all times, the support of the sterner sex.

ESTEY AND GARDNER,
Merchants and Bankers School, New York.

* * * I am, however, in accord with the principle that the position filled should have a salary fixed without regard to the

sex of the holder, provided that the logical consequences of this doctrine be accepted, to wit, that equal pay demands equal work in every respect and equal responsibility.

F. C. BYRNES,
Board of Examiners,
Department of Education,
New York.

Jan. 30, 1908.

Ever since the Interborough Association of Women Teachers commenced their campaign for "Equal Pay for Equal Work," I have been much interested in the movement, for it seemed to me in every way worthy of the considerate and favorable attention of the school authorities, as well as of the people of this great City, and if the demands of my professional life had not been so insistent and exhaustive, I would have been glad to have added my voice and my efforts (feeble though they might have been) in furthering such a just cause.

I am not speaking particularly of any of the details of the plans proposed by your Association, or by some of its friends, but of "the general principle which it seems to me is thoroughly in accord with that other and equally true principle 'a square deal.'"

I wish your Association all success in its efforts in behalf of the women teachers of this City, for I believe they will not only benefit the women teachers, but the men teachers as well, and above and beyond all individuals, that great system which is the bulwark of our free institutions.

Faithfully yours,
HENRY N. TIFFT.
Lawyer and Ex-President,
Board of Education.

March 3, 1908.

Do you know that Horace Mann said he "would as soon place an elephant to brooding chickens as he would a man to teach little children"?

I endorse the above. As "the workman is worthy of his hire," let the women's salaries be commensurate with work accomplished, but do not pull down the salaries of the men to equalize.

Yours sincerely,
I. B. POUCHER, A. M., Pd. D.,
Principal, State Normal and Training School.

Feb. 25, 1907.

Hon. Member of Assembly,

My Dear Mr. Lee:

Your reason for not favoring the Equal Pay Bill, viz., "The

city cannot afford it this year," sets me wondering if you really know what it really will cost—or, are you depending upon the men for your estimate?

If so, I beg to state you are laboring under a very false impression.

Our leader, Miss Strachan, formerly head teacher of mathematics in the Brooklyn Training School, has proved conclusively, using city records, that the extra mill tax will aggregate a sum of over six millions of dollars.

This is ample to meet the requirements of the bill.

Perhaps you feel that the individual taxpayer cannot afford it. Has he said so?

Assuredly not. Consider, if you will, the weighty significance of the many boards of trade, tax-payers' associations, dry goods establishments, labor unions, clubs, noted men and women—not to mention the thousands and thousands of signatures willingly given by taxpayers throughout the entire city—that have signified their loyal support to this most worthy cause.

Does not all this forcibly manifest the desire of the people to pay cheerfully, in the cause of justice, the cost, each year, say of a few theater or opera tickets?

"Taxation without representation is tyranny."

Taxation with representation unheeding the demands of the people is, well, what is it? Better or worse than tyranny?

Let us consider for a moment the unit of the state—the family.

If a dear one is stricken with some serious physical illness, what is it we immediately do, no matter how humble the circumstances or how empty the purse?

We hail the very best physician, employ a high-salaried nurse, purchase expensive medicines, follow this, in many cases, with consultations, operations, and health-seeking journeys, realizing that no effort or expense is too great to restore health.

If it be a mental disease the same course is pursued.

How about an insidious moral disease like injustice? Is not prompt and efficient treatment of vital importance here also?

Surely the representatives of the largest city of the new world, and the leading state of the Union, should set the example, and once having had their eyes opened to the "glaring inequalities" that have existed for some eight years in the payment of the city's and state's best servants—the teachers,—proceed to put a speedy end to such conditions.

Countless centuries—aye, back even as far as Plato—have proved beyond question that the corner stone of every true and lasting republic is justice.

Mar. 26, 1908. ANNA L. McGUIRE.

## THE EQUAL PAY QUESTION

Miss Jeliffe of the Girls' High School Presents Logical Arguments on Behalf of Her Sex

To the Editor of the Brooklyn Eagle:

Women are employed in the public school system of Greater New York in numbers overwhelming as compared with the number of men. There are three possible causes for this: First, they are better teachers; second, it costs the city less to employ them; third, they are more willing to enter a profession in which the amount of work, the amount of drudgery, the amount of monotony is so large compared with resulting emolument and renown.

The first hypothesis is a debatable one. It is probable that the capacities of men and women as regards teaching balance very fairly, except in the matter of patience and willingness to dwell on detailed drill work. In this last, I think, it will be generally considered that women excel.

The second reason is manifestly true at present. Now, if there is no choice between the teaching capacities of men and women, then the pay should not show partiality. If New York feels, on the other hand, that men are better teachers, then the Board of Education, despite the enormous appropriation of city funds, is supplying an inferior article to the people of New York City on the ground of cheapness. Surely New York City should object to this. If the city is, however, satisfied with the quality of the work and with the results obtained by the present educational force, should it not then, in justice, pay that force what it considers the fair wage in the case of a man? Fully as many women now have to be supporting factors in families as do men. Only less satisfactory work on their part should, therefore, occasion less satisfactory pay.

In the third place, the Board of Education employs more women, partly because more women fit themselves for this profession. This state of affairs would seem to indicate that men are not so much drawn to the profession as women are. They are not drawn to it, possibly, because they feel in themselves no fitness for it, or because it is a badly paid profession, or because it offers no resulting renown comparable to work required.

Suppose the first reason to be the true reason; then women are granted as superior teachers, and should receive superior, not inferior, pay. Suppose the second reason be true: then surely the woman has a right to complain, for she is worse paid than the man. If, however, the third reason be the correct one, then a woman who willingly undergoes the work, and foregoes the renown, should at least get material compensation adequate to her efforts; and she asks not for pay superior to a man's, but simply equal to his.

It would seem, then, that the question is reduced to the following: Since men do not willingly enter the profession, either from lack of capacity or because the emolument and renown are not sufficient to be tempting, and since the burden of education—the factor acknowledged as most potent in modern civilization—is left on the shoulders of the women teachers, New York City should feel it simple justice to pay said women teachers a wage equal to that which she would consider as fair for a man.

ELIZABETH M. JELIFFE.

Girls' High School, Brooklyn, May 14, 1907.

Dear Senator Grady.

As principal for nearly thirteen years of one of the largest grammar schools for boys in Manhattan, and as a public school teacher for nearly double that period, permit me to address you in reference to the bill for the equalization of salaries of school teachers.

According to the reports published in this morning's newspapers, a large meeting of male principals and male teachers was held yesterday for the purpose of voicing their opposition to the bill. One of the points presented in the series of resolutions introduced and adopted at this meeting was that in Germany, 88 per cent. of the teachers were males, and in France, 60 per cent. of the teachers were males. Where women are concerned, Germany and France are hardly the standards to present to an American community. Yet it was certainly in keeping with the selfish, unmanly, boorish spirit which actuated these male teachers and male principals, that such a comparison should be made. Anyone at all conversant with the status of Woman in the countries named, might well be astonished that women are permitted to have any place at all in the schools. It must certainly be taken as a great concession, or condescension, that women should be permitted to have any hand in the school-training of German or French boys and girls.

Another point upon which particular stress was laid at this meeting of male principals and male teachers, was the effeminization of the schools, a most terrible calamity threatening the whole school system of the Greater New York. This dread disease has been hinted at elsewhere and recently; but whether as a playful euphemism, or as a cloak to hide some real conditions of decay in our school system, deponent sayeth not. It must be admitted that there are symptoms of decay, symptoms which have been apparent for years back; but while your male teachers and your male principals say it is too much Woman in the schools, there are Men Teachers and Men Principals—and others—who aver that the marking system has let loose upon the schools a horde of mollycoddles who will reel off pedagogics and psychology by the yard, but are as soft as putty in the hands of the ordinary New York school-boy.

Of thirty-two teachers in my school, twenty-one are Women. Among these women are a dozen who are the equals of any dozen male teachers in the system, and are vastly superior to a dozen dozen of the bunch of male teachers who exploited themselves yesterday so uproariously.

If a woman will do as effective work as a man will do, she should be paid a wage equal to the wage paid to the man. This principle is already recognized in two departments of the Board of Education, in direct contradiction to a statement by Dr. Conroy. There are three women District Superintendents, each of whom is getting a salary similar to the salary of the men District Superintendents. In the Truancy Department are six women Attendance Officers, each of whom is getting a salary equal to the salary of any of the men Attendance Officers.

So there you are.

Pay for Service, not pay for Sex.

You are at liberty to make such use of this letter as you see fit.

JOSEPH J. CASEY.

Hon. George B. McClellan,
Mayor of the City of New York.

* * * If I convey the idea from what I have written that women teachers can do the work that men teachers do, and do it equally as well—a doctrine that I firmly believe and have always believed—it is not for the purpose of having you fall in with that idea, but to accept it as an axiom and to apply it to the principle—pay for service, not pay for sex.

I think you are broad minded enough to accept the principle. The question of salary, therefore, becomes an ethical one which should not be measured by dollars and cents "Fiat justitia, ruat coelum" cannot find an apter application than here.

In conclusion permit me to say that I am Principal of Public School 83 in East 110th Street, with a corps of thirty-two teachers, twenty-one of whom are women. I have, therefore, reason and experience for everything I have written.

JOSEPH J. CASEY.

May, 1909.

I wish you God-speed in your efforts for "Equal pay for Equal work." I have been with women in the public schools—

whose influences were soothing, refining, uplifting; under whose inspiration, noble characters were formed or developed. Perhaps it was my fortune to have been among such women. I have been with men, gross, treacherous, shallow, whose influences tended to stunt the moral growth—moral, in its broadest sense—of the sensitive natures entrusted to their moulding. Perhaps it was my mishap to have been among such men. We form our judgments according to our experiences, and my experiences, reaching back longer than you might care to know, are responsible for my adhesion to your cause. Very respectfully yours,

April 6, 1910. JOSEPH J. CASEY.

## CALIFORNIA SCHOOL TEACHERS

To the Editor of *The Sun*—Sir: "Poor little New York," as a Los Angeles paper recently called the metropolis, was never known (according to an eastern publication) to originate a reform nor an improvement of importance. She does, however, sometimes adopt the more advanced ideas of other cities and "go them one better," enlarging upon them with all the resources at her command.

Just now she is suffering throes of anguish over the school salary question, that was settled long ago, peaceably, fairly and with no wild cries from a public about to be ruined, by the laws of one of the younger States of the Union.

When I went to California to live, in 1878, I found that three grades of certificates were issued by the State to teachers, after rigorous examination, and each grade commanded a fixed salary. It made no difference whether the teacher was male or female, each position had its allotted pay, and could be secured by any one duly qualified. The schools of that far-away State were then ranked among the best in this country, and they have kept pace with the times. There has been no worrying about "lack of masculine influence on the growing boy," no injury to men teachers, no inordinate taxation; in fact, the arrangement has always been accepted as a matter of course, with that broad and generous treatment of women which is characteristic of western communities, and it amuses Californians now to read of the tempest, the dire forebodings aroused by an effort to accomplish, in the greatest city of the United States, what is to them a thing scarcely admitting of argument.

"Poor little New York" indeed! "Poor" in her professed inability to "meet the expense." "Little" in her frantic clinging to rulings of a bygone era. Can't she brush down the cobwebs, broaden her mental horizon and keep step with the progressive people of this twentieth century?—Clara S. Ellis, New York, May 9, 1907.

## SUPPLY AND DEMAND IN EDUCATION

It might be suggested to Mr. Edgar L. Levey, whose recent letter to the New York *Sun* was quoted at length in the *Educational Review* for February, that neither abuse of one's opponents nor dogmatic assertion constitutes argument. Perhaps the "grotesque propaganda" of the women teachers "excites disgust," perhaps their supporters are guilty of "opportune sycophancy," the taxpayers of "flaccid indifference," the public of "stupid unconcern," but no set of people who are whole-heartedly convinced of the justice of their cause may be denominated "hypocrites"—except, of course, in a Levitical sense.

"The Interborough Association of Women Teachers," says Mr. Levey, "would have the city ignore the law of supply and demand. Shall this law also be ignored in all the other city departments in the fixing of salaries? Shall it also be ignored in the purchase of materials and supplies? What limit, if any, shall be set to this new standard of privilege which is to turn our bureaucracy into a veritable aristrocracy?"

In this statement Mr. Levey compares things which are not comparable—rather an elementary mistake in logic. The years of special training required of teachers, as well as the exacting and, the old-fashioned among us still think, holy nature of their work, would seem to put them in a different class from the unskilled laborers employed by the city—snow-shovelers, for example. Nor can they be lumped with "materials and supplies" any more than you can multiply nights by cats and get eternal bliss.

The law of supply and demand, the fetish of commercialists in education, is continually being modified or even set aside in its own particular domain, that of trade. Sweat-shop labor is cheap, the commodities produced by it may be obtained at a ridiculously low price, and yet there are many persons who cheerfully pay more for the same article out of considerations of humanity, or, perhaps, dread of infectious disease. Child labor is cheap and the supply on the increase, but the statutes of many states make its use illegal. There is, too, even in the world of trade, such a thing as ultimate gain to be set over against the immediate receipt of dollars and cents. And so, shorter working hours, sanitary conditions in workrooms, holidays, have come to modify the rigidity of the law of supply and demand.

In so complex a matter as education the rigidity of the law must be still further modified. Why is a Sabbatical year given in many colleges? Plenty of professors could be obtained to work year in and year out with long hours and large classes, until they degenerated into mechanical drudges. But here the college administration is wise and sees that leisure for travel, wider reading, periods of uninterrupted research increase a teacher's worth and so benefit the college. Nor would the city "violate the specific pledge of trusteeship toward its taxpayers proclaimed in the charter" if it were to increase the salaries of its women teachers so that they might be enabled to secure more of the daily comforts of life than a hall bedroom implies and make reasonable provision for old age.

As to Mr. Levey's hint—evidently thrown in for good measure—that women teachers use a large part of their salary for "mere pin money," the present writer showed in a letter to the *Evening Post,* dated, February 20, 1908, that in one of the city high schools ninety-one per cent. of the women had one or more persons dependent upon her, either wholly or in part. In most cases it was an aged father or mother, in some the education of younger brothers or sisters. One woman held herself largely responsible for the five children of a dead brother, and another took entire care of a bed-ridden mother and aged aunt. Nor, as was there said, is this outlay in the nature of an investment (unless it be treasure in heaven). A man looks to his children for support in old age, but those for whom a woman cares—for the most part—will be gone when she is old and needs help.

"If," says Mr. Levey, "women in the public schools can properly perform all the functions of men at a smaller wage, then in the interest of honest and economical government by all means get rid of the men. But this is not claimed." It is precisely what *is* claimed and all that is claimed. Otherwise, "Equal Pay for Equal Work" would be the fallacy Mr. Levey calls it. Women are doing the same grade of work as men and are doing it as satisfactorily. They are doing as much work, in some cases even more (see a letter by the present writer, also to the *Evening Post,* dated December 14, 1908). Nor was there ever any question of their equal or superior fitness until the matter came to be one of dollars and cents. It is, therefore, a violation of the law of supply and demand to have any men teachers in the public schools. Why are they there? Because, contrary to the law of supply and demand, it is thought that the influence of men, at least some men, is needed in education, and also—this is never omitted—they are needed to superintend athletics, which, by the way, could be looked after much better by a paid coach.

In conclusion we are told that for the city "to yield to these demands (of the women teachers) means an immense obstacle to the solution of its many pressing problems of civic progress and development." This would be serious if it were true. Two measures of relief suggest themselves: first, instead of putting up more school buildings at an enormous cost and packing children into them like sardines to justify the expense, smaller and less expensive buildings might be put up, or buildings already standing might be bought and turned into schoolrooms. It does not take much fitting up to make a schoolroom, given a real teacher, a class of children, and a blackboard, if, that is to say, education is the primary object in view and not the creation of huge educational machines too large for one man to handle. Second, and this is a hard saying, if sinecures held by politicians (like Cicero, nomina non nomino) were lopped off; if appropriations, repairs, and supplies were lifted out of the realm of farce; as, for instance, certain Windsor chairs worth about sixty cents, for which the city paid twenty-two dollars and a half each; if, in a word, the interests of taxpayers were protected against graft, "honest" and otherwise, the city would save enough money to meet, and more than meet, the just demands of the women teachers. Here is a possibility of "civic progress and development," and, at the present writing, it almost seems as though it were going to be realized. ELIZABETH DU BOIS PECK.

## PROFESSION OR "JOB."

To the Editor of *The Evening Post*—Sir: A few years ago teaching was, at least occasionally, spoken of as a profession, and its members compared, in respect to income, with ministers, doctors, lawyers, or artists. In all of these last-named professions women come into competition with men to a greater or less extent. Men have the advantage of custom and of numbers, but, in the last analysis, income is dependent on the training, experience, and skill, not at all on sex. Last spring a writer in the *Evening Post* gave a long table in which the "wage" of teachers was compared with that of clerks, stenographers, paper-box makers, and others. With no disparagement to these occupations, it seems economically sound to argue that the special training required of the teacher should put his calling upon a somewhat higher plane, and make such comparisons inappropriate.

Now, in the issue of the *Evening Post* for February 17 I read this statement, signed E. S. S.: "Economic law and the well-being of society set the wage of the adult male at the 'living wage' of the family—this quite regardless whether the individual man is even married." That is to say, society owes every "adult male," no matter how ignorant, no matter how dull, no matter how depraved, every "adult male," enough money to support a family—even if he has no family. I do not so understand economic law. The work of the world comes, in the long run, into the hands of those who can do it best. This is true from the philosopher and inventor, at one end of the line, to the coal-heaver at the other. The more highly specialized the work is, the more it depends on fitness alone. Here is the reason that E. S. S. and those like him are anxious to be classed with stenographers and box-makers, rather than physicians or writers. We can see that in making a paper box the fact that a man is a father might have weight, as it would not in operating for appendicitis, for instance, or writing an article on high finance.

The question of equal pay has been argued again and again, logically, economically, sometimes even politely. But all the diverse arguments reduce themselves to just two propositions. The first is, Are women as fit in every way as men, for the position of teacher in the public schools? and the second, Granted their equal fitness, is it economically sound to make their salaries equal?

(1) Woman's equal fitness as a teacher was not seriously questioned by the male members of the profession until it became a matter of dollars and cents. Men teachers sat in their classrooms, in the good old days, and read the morning paper; in difficult cases of discipline, they called on the woman in the next room for aid, or resorted to corporal punishment, sometimes even distressingly severe (I am not giving imaginary instances). Again, a serious comparison of the results of examinations in classes of the same grade taught by men and by women has always shown equal intellectual fitness on the part of the women. And the children themselves have paid as much respect to their women as to their men teachers. This is important. Children know whether a teacher is just, sincere, and interested in their welfare, or the reverse. They are even shrewder judges of ability and character than their elders.

For the last few months I have never heard the subject of equal pay argued to a finish but the male disputant, beaten by facts and statistics from one outpost of argument to another, at last took refuge in athletics. Women may be able to teach mathematics, English, Latin, but where are they in athletics? "Down and out." And what are mathematics, English and Latin in comparison with athletics? It is that their children may become proficient in shooting, football, and cross-country running that the taxpayers of this city foot the enormous school bills.

(2) Is it economically sound to make the salaries equal? Here is where the "family" comes in. Is a man, because he has a family, or may have a family, to receive money for that family rather than for his services? The statement has been made that 80 per cent. of the men teachers in the high schools of this city are married. In one of the high schools (for which the statistics are at hand), the number of women with some family obligation is 91 per cent. "That is as it should be," says E. S. S. "A single woman should be productive to society as well as self-supporting." "A single woman"—"ah, there's the rub!" But I have known instances in which the duty of supporting an aged father or mother stood in the way of a woman's marriage, while her brother, so fortunate as to be an "adult male," had married and was raising the aforesaid "family." Again, as has been said, a man looks to his children for support in old age; the money he spends on them is an investment for the future, while

those for whom a woman cares—for the most part—will be gone when she is old and needs help. . . .

Finally, although the "gross inequalities" in the salaries of men and women teachers are well known, perhaps it is not so well known that when a vacancy is to be filled or a first appointment made to one of the higher positions, a man is selected even for a girls' school (where there are no athletics) though a woman may precede him on the eligible list, may have been waiting longer, etc., etc. As a case in point, five years ago next June, the present writer received a first assistant's license along with two men and two other women. After four years, when one man had been appointed and the other refused to take a position offered, but none of the women appointed, a second examination in the subject was held, to which men only were admitted, and of the nine men who qualified, all but one were appointed before the first woman from the previous list, although she stood second on that list, received an appointment.

The case of the men teachers seems from first to last a piece of special pleading. What if they lack knowledge of their subject, ability to make all clear, a high sense of honor—they are fathers, or may be. This is taking the city's money under false pretences. Just as between a man and a woman physician, income from practice is a matter of special fitness, so it should be between the man and woman teacher. Let this fitness be discovered by examinations, oral and written, by tests of character, by what you please, and then let the one that "makes good" have the position. Let it be a matter of who can "make good," for the taxpayers have a right to the best.

E. H. DuBOIS, Ph. D.,<br>
The Morris High School.

New York, February 20.

April 11th, 1910.

To the Editor of the *Outlook*,<br>
New York City.

Dear Sir:—The *Outlook* of April second had an editorial on "Equal Pay for Equal Work."

At an official meeting, the Board of Education of the City of New York voted against equal pay, the vote standing twenty-three to sixteen. To say that the decision is final is to be absolutely unacquainted with the movement. Four years ago no one in the board supported the proposition. Now after four years of agitation, the Board of Education itself, not a fraction of one committee, gave the matter a serious and dignified consideration and sixteen members supported it. "Revolutions do not go backward." If in four years the women teachers can gain sixteen supporters, are they going to stop? The vote then is not in any way final. It is a great encouragement.

The three ladies who voted against the women teachers were

new appointees. Their position in the community had shut them out from all contact with the common schools. Therefore not as a matter of judgment, because judgment implies knowledge, but as a matter of custom they followed man's judgment. It takes an independent and courageous woman to help other women.

One objection the *Outlook* presented is that "men and women cannot do equal work." Two men cannot do equal work. There are in the schools some very inefficient male teachers and some of loose habits, yet they get the same pay as efficient male teachers. Women teachers in the City of New York have been assigned over and over again positions identical with male teachers. Their work has been given the highest possible rating again and again by male principals and male superintendents. Over against the *Outlook's* present opinion these other opinions have been reiterated for years. No one ever questioned the equality of woman's work until she asked equal pay for it.

The *Outlook* said one speaker's words were felicitous. The speaker was a new member, new to the board, new to America, and full of more new ideas than the *Outlook* may know. He is not always so hostile to women. Of course women teachers of experience whom he gallantly called in this same speech "semi-derelicts," awaken his loudest condemnation. But let the hotels of New York City turn out a man and his pseudo wife, and this generous member may open his doors to the pair. This new member's entire speech was filled with complete ignorance of the school question.

Next the article said: "The ablest men cannot do as good work in teaching a kindergarten as a competent woman." That is a matter of opinion. A man invented the kindergarten system. The *Outlook* confuses matters of fact and matters of opinion. It goes on to say: "The ablest woman cannot do as good work in superintending a school of boys from fourteen to eighteen as a competent man." The *Outlook* thinks so. It is a matter of fact that the development of the playgrounds and recreation centers was in the hands of a woman until she died. These activities controlled boys of the age mentioned, and this work is spoken of most highly by the associates and the official superiors of this woman. Further than this it is a matter of fact that "superintending a school of boys from fourteen to eighteen" has nothing to do with the equal pay question. Such a school is a boys' high school and is, and always has been, in the charge of a male principal. The superintending of a group of schools containing boys, or girls, is in the hands of a number of persons, men and women, and these superintendents receive equal pay already.

In its third objection the *Outlook* was in error. Briefly it says, if equal pay were given "many women teachers would be discharged." Discharged? Even the women teachers of New York City enjoy the provision of Section 1089 of the Charter of the

City of New York. The women teachers do die or retire, but they are not discharged, for they cannot be, except for cause, and being a woman is not a cause for dismissal.

The second part of the *Outlook's* third reason says: "Women are now doing work which men could do better." How does the *Outlook* know this? It is a mere assertion. If it were a matter of fact what an arraignment of the Board of Education! The board is consciously giving the boys of this city a cheap bargain-counter education.

The third part of the *Outlook's* third objection says that equalizing by lowering men's salaries would lead to an exodus of men from the schools and under wholly feminine influence there would be an "exodus of many male pupils." [1] Is the *Outlook* sure of this? There were men in the schools before the Davis law raised the men's salaries to their present proportions; and the boys in large numbers leave those schools which are now wholly managed by men.

PRESS COMMITTEE,
Interborough Association of Women Teachers.

## AN OPEN LETTER TO THE CLERGYMEN OF NEW YORK CITY.

We, the women teachers of New York City, twelve thousand in number, appeal to you, the clergymen of our city, and ask you to bring our appeal to the notice of your congregations by reading this letter to them. We do not ask you to support our claim or to advocate it, but only to publish it so that the men and women of your churches may pass upon the justice of our cause.

For four years we have tried to get from our city government Equal Pay for Equal Work, and we have striven to put the profession of teaching on a Civil Service basis so that the work in our schools shall be paid for irrespective of the sex of the worker.

Side by side with the men teachers we teach the *same subjects* to the *same pupils* from the *same text-books* through the *same hours* reaching the *same results* under the *same standards.*

In all the years of our struggle for justice it has never been successfully maintained that our work is inferior. On the contrary, it has been well-nigh universally acknowledged that schools and classes governed and taught by women compare favorably with those governed and taught by men and that women bring to the care and training of the young a motherly sympathy, patience and devotion that make them peculiarly successful in the high calling of education.

Is it just that we should be paid so much less than our male co-

[1] See Professor Thorndike's conclusion in chapter on Feminization.—G. C. S.

laborers for the same work? Does New York supply us with any of the necessities or decencies of life for less? Are our rents and taxes less? Can we obtain food and clothing for less? Are our doctors and lawyers' fees less? Can we live for less in this most expensive of all cities by pleading that we are paid less for our work as the city's servants?

Our obligations, too, are as heavy as those of the men in respect to life's burdens and responsibilities. On us, too, rests oftentimes the care of the aged and infirm; on us, too, devolves the generous duty of helping younger relatives to secure an adequate education; on us, too, falls the expense of maintaining a home for those who could not, unassisted, escape indigence and suffering. There are few indeed of our profession who do not share an already insufficient salary with those who are more or less dependent on them.

In our work, in our expenses, in all of life's obligations our burdens are as heavy as the men's. Only in our pay is there a striking and unjust difference and it is this intolerable injustice we are striving to remove.

Nor are we asking our city to do the impossible. New York is rich enough, its revenues are vast enough to do justice to all of its employees if its money were wisely and economically managed, and expended solely for the public good. Other cities and other states have placed their schools on a Civil Service basis with Equal Pay, and surely New York, the richest and most powerful city of the United States, can afford to do what poorer municipalities have already done.

We, the women teachers of New York City, base our appeal to you, the clergymen of New York City, on the closer relation existing between the work of pastor and teacher. Without the Church Ideal, which is righteousness, and the School Ideal, which is good citizenship, the State could not endure. We are the lay preachers of the community. Day in and day out in connection with our work in the school-room we teach our boys and girls truth, honesty, justice, reliability, self-control, obedience to the laws and devotion to duty in private and in public life.

We are serving the city faithfully to the best of our ability and strength. *All we ask of the city in return is Justice—the justice of Equal Pay for Equal Work.*

Will not you, who believe that Justice is a law of the universe, give a little space to our cause?

JOSEPHINE A. RICE, Chairman.
CARRIE A. HAWTHORNE,
HELEN LOUISE COHEN,
JENNIE V. NAUGHTON,
GRACE C. STRACHAN,

Committee representing Interborough Association of Women Teachers.

Mr. Oliver, Superintendent of Schools in San Francisco, said while visiting here in 1907: "In San Francisco we pay both men and women teachers on the same schedules. We do not believe that a man is any better as a teacher than a woman. In fact, we haven't much use for men teachers." When told of the women teachers' fight here, he said, "I wish them all success."

Following are some of the educational associations that have formally endorsed "Equal Pay":

The Teachers' Association of Troy, Frances J. Galvin, secretary, March 13, 1908; Local School Board, District 27; Local School Board, District 26; Syracuse Grade Teachers' Association; Bronx Teachers' Association. Society of Women Class Teachers; Public Education Society; New York City Teachers' Association; Heads of Department Association, Manhattan; Association of Women Principals, Manhattan; Women Principals' Association, Brooklyn; Brooklyn Teachers' Association; Brooklyn Class Teachers' Organization; Queens Teachers' Association; Women High School Teachers' Association.

Brooklyn, N. Y., March 11, 1908.

MISS GRACE C. STRACHAN,
Pres. Interborough Association of Women Teachers,
293 Henry Street, Brooklyn.

My dear Miss Strachan:—Your suggestion of a debate upon the essential principle involved in the equal pay movement was received yesterday. While thanking you for the courtesy, and appreciating the spirit in which the proposition is made, we believe, for the following reasons, that no beneficial result would follow such a public joint debate.

The question is one that affects us as teachers in a way very different from the way in which the public deems that it affects the public. While we as teachers have the question so prominently in mind during the present agitation, we are apt to feel that the public is deeply sympathetic. The public is interested somewhat in the care of all of its servants, more interested in the results attained in this particular department, and least interested in such matters as affect only the peculiar interests of factions of its serving body. Therefore, the audience that would listen to a debate such as the one proposed would be composed only of those who have a direct pecuniary interest in the question involved.

This movement has already engendered much of bitterness, due to the natural differences in temperament of the factions. Since this bitterness has hampered materially the work in the schools, it has been the policy of our organization to avoid a discussion that inevitably leads to personalities.

Finally, while appreciating the excellent influence that you personally have exerted over the adherents to this cause, but at the same time bearing in mind the composition of the audience as indicated above, as well as experiences under similar circumstances, we believe that few arguments in opposition to the principle would be heard by any one not very close to the speaker.

Believing that a declination to participate in the matter of your suggestion demanded a reply that would give the reasons for such refusal, and believing that we are all appreciative of the growth of dignity in the attitude of both factions, I thank you.

Very truly yours,

HENRY C. MOORE,

Pres. Association of Male Teachers of Brooklyn and Queens.

Brooklyn, N. Y., April 8, 1910.

To the New York *Press*:—On March 23, 1910, you printed on your editorial page some remarks and a picture of "John Martin of Grymes Hill, Stapleton, S. I., who recently was appointed a member of the Board of Education by Mayor Gaynor."

Permit me to state, as President of the Interborough Association of Women Teachers, that the figures quoted by Mr. Martin are taken from the schedules proposed by the Board of Education, which schedules the Interborough Association of Women Teachers has opposed. Mr. Martin's criticism, therefore, should be directed against the Board of Education of which he is a part. It is unfortunate that a member of the Board of Education should speak publicly and write for publication before being acquainted with facts.

Among other things he is quoted as saying, "The only positions for which the schedules of the Interborough Association provide 'one salary for one and the same position' are the city superintendent and his associate city superintendents, the district superintendents, and the members of the Board of Examiners." The Interborough Association has never included any of the above-named officials in the schedules, as they are paid without reference to sex. I might add "without reference to age either." Mr. Martin's references to *age* indicate a further ignorance of the schedules of the Board of Education, not only of this city but practically of all cities: almost every Civil Service schedule takes note of experience. Mr. Martin confuses "age of schedule" with "age of teacher."

The only connection the Interborough Association has had with the salary of superintendents has been that instigated by myself—a district superintendent—to prevent the adding of $1000 to the salary of district superintendents. I believe the claims of district superintendents for a higher salary are sound, reasonable, and just; but the injustice which the women teachers are suffering is the greatest and the most dangerous evil in our salary schedules and should be the first remedied.

GRACE C. STRACHAN,

President of the Interborough Association of Women Teachers.

## LETTERS—LAWYERS

Enclosed you will find resolutions which were adopted last evening at our club at my request and with the hearty co-operation of Mr. Curry, the leader of our district. I hope the women teachers of our city will get justice and you can always count upon me to use my influence in their behalf.

March 26, 1908. JOHN J. HALLIGAN.

## FAVORS WOMEN TEACHERS—E. A. TUTTLE WILL GIVE $1000 TO A FUND TO ENABLE THEM TO ORGANIZE FOR INCREASED PAY

To the Editors of the Brooklyn *Eagle*:—I see by the papers that the Board of Education is preparing to have an investigation of the alleged use of funds raised by the women teachers to assist in obtaining legislation to give them the same pay as men for the same services. I also see some strong language used regarding the improper use of funds and the neglect of duty on the part of the women teachers. I have also read Governor Hughes' veto message, a most remarkable piece of reasoning.

I want to enter a protest against what I deem gross injustice toward the women teachers, and also I want to protest against that form of equity and justice which is based upon the doctrine that "might makes right." Oh, mighty man! it is hard to surrender the prerogative of beating woman. Time was when men could not only beat and enslave, but could also kill women. While that may not be lawful now, man still adheres to the refinement of the same principle, and still beats woman—by denying her the right to vote, the right to be paid equally with men for performing equal services, the right to make a living in some avocations, the right of equality anywhere if it interferes with men's selfish interests.

The governor's message on the equal pay bill denies justice and equity to some thousands of women teachers in Greater New York because, forsooth, all the women teachers throughout the state, nurses and attendants in other public or quasi-public institutions, did not join in the request for justice, and equity, and that by signing the bill he would not administer justice and equity to everybody alike.

Consider only for a moment how futile an effort would have been by teachers in small communities to have secured legislation on this subject, and consider what a hue and cry would have been raised if the women teachers of New York City had endeavored to organize the women teachers of the state as well as other female workers, to have them join in an effort to secure equal pay for equal services. It is rarely that universal justice is done by any act of legislation, but if a large measure of justice and right be accomplished by a single act of legislation, it is no valid objection that it is not universal in its operations.

Now, as to the proposed or threatened action of our highly developed board of education. Is there a man on that board who honestly believes that the women teachers of this city have used money improperly to influence legislation in their behalf? If so let him who is without fault cast the first stone. I doubt if any man in this community believes that any person threatening suspensions or dismissals of the women teachers because they sought to obtain justice and fair treatment would hesitate or refrain from using methods and means far less defensible than any used by the women teachers to accomplish any selfish purpose for gain or advancement.

Many years ago I taught school for several years. I believe I know something of the character and ability of women teachers. I believe in nine positions out of ten the average woman teacher will do better work than the average man teacher. I believe the women teachers to be the most poorly paid and poorly appreciated public servants in this country. I believe also, that the men teachers are not properly paid nor appreciated, but I despise the men teachers of this city, in so far as they have shown a selfish, greedy and unmanly opposition to the equal pay bill.

I do not often care to express my feelings in a letter to a newspaper, but I feel so bitterly indignant over the injustice and oppression that have been disclosed in connection with this equal pay matter that I cannot refrain from recommending to the teachers of this city and this state that they organize at once, in this city and throughout the state, so that they may meet the weighty objections of our governor's veto message, and also that they may no longer have to beg for common justice and fair dealing, but so that they may stand erect and demand and secure their rights in this matter. I will gladly contribute $1000 to a fund to be used to defray the necessary expenses of an organization of the women teachers of this city and state, to the end that they may compel selfish, greedy man to give them what is their right, and what, if decency prevailed, would be given them without waiting for the enactment of a law.

I am a rank outsider; I have absolutely no personal interest in this contest, but I believe it is time that decent men in this city rallied to the support of the women teachers, when all they ask is fair treatment and the application of simple justice and equity.

EZRA A. TUTTLE.

150 Broadway, Manhattan, June 14, 1907.

I am heartily in sympathy with your movement. So far the only opportunity I have had for comparing women's work with that of my own sex has been along the lines of stenographers, and although men are more rapid, they are undoubtedly to my mind inferior to women for the ordinary purposes of office work. . . .

My wife, who feels as strongly on the subject as I do, will be glad to give you any help she can.

February 28, 1908. EDMOND KELLY.

I am heartily in accord with your movement and believe that if women are qualified to teach at all, they should receive the same pay as men. Sex should make no difference, or if at all it should be in woman's favor. There was an assistant principal, a lady, in the high school I attended who had the love and respect of every pupil in the school, and three male principals ran their courses in the school while the assistant principal remained until old age compelled her retirement, and her teachings are remembered by her scholars to this day, while the teachings of the principals are forgotten. Her quiet, unassuming manner, her dignified but firm insistence that work must be performed by the scholar, and her judicious approval of work well done, won the esteem of every scholar in her class. Cling to the one idea—"Equal Pay for Equal Work"—you will win.

February 4, 1908. SEWARD BAKER.

Whether the salary be fixed by the legislature or by the municipal government (and I believe it should be fixed entirely by the municipal government, if we are ever to obtain home rule), women should receive the same pay as men for the same service.

February 4, 1908. WILLIAM M. IVINS.

I am in full sympathy with your movement. There is absolutely no reason, either good or bad, why a woman who does the same work as a man, in an equally efficient manner, should not receive the same pay that a man does. To attempt to prove the contrary is as absurd as it would be for a mathematician to sit down and try to prove two and two do not make four, but that they make five.

January 30, 1908. HENRY A. POWELL.

I believe in equal pay for equal work and hope you may meet with success in the matter.

March 3, 1908. EDWARD L. COLLIER,
Lawyer, ex-member Board of Education.

All who are animated by the spirit of justice and fair play must admire, prize and applaud your heroic effort to blot from the statute books of this state unjust laws which deny frail women equal compensation for similar services rendered by men in our public schools. Such laws are simply a survival of that barbaric age which deprived women of their property rights to enrich their lord and master and his creditors. Chivalric men have united with public spirited women and wiped out most of this heritage from barbarous ages. There should be no discrimination in the wages of those who work in plastic clay or on the plastic minds of our boys and girls. Justice is blind and in the matter of pay it should recognize no sex and see only merit and excellence in its public servants.

Trusting that you will triumph in your unremitting toil for this betterment of your co-workers.

EDWARD EVERETT WARNER,
March 26, 1908. Attorney-at-Law.

I am very glad to be identified with this movement.

J. EDWARD SWANSTROM,
Ex-President, Board of Education.

I am with the women teachers to the end of their battle.

GEORGE FREDERICK ELLIOTT.

Now, as ever, you may command my services in the laudable campaign of "Equal Pay for Equal Work."

WILLOUGHBY DOBBS,
Ex-member of Assembly.

Wishing your cause every success.

JAMES A. BLANCHFIELD.

Your communication of the 26th ultimo received. I am in favor of the movement for just salary schedules for the supervising and teaching staff of our public school system and hope the legislature will take such action as may be necessary to accomplish the result for which you are working. Sincerely,

April 8, 1908. HOWARD PENDLETON, JR.

I assure you that I sympathize heartily with the movement and shall be pleased to avail myself of every possible opportunity—no matter how humble the effort—to advance the good couse.

FRANK X. McCAFFRY,
January 20, 1908. Brooklyn.

The teachers have made a magnificent uphill fight against tremendous odds, and have laid a foundation for success hereafter that a veto this year can only postpone. It would be most unusual to carry through in one campaign such a revolution as you have started, but the revolution is bottomed on righteousness, and a veto will be only an additional reason for further effort.

May 29, 1907. HORACE E. DEMING.

I believe in equal rights to all and special privileges to none. If a woman does the same work as a man, be it in the coal mines of Pennsylvania or in the public schools of the State of New York, she is entitled to the same pay. If my daughter does the same work as my son she should have the same compensation. Why discriminate against a woman because of her sex? I therefore glory in the effort of the 13,000 female school teachers of Greater New York who are conducting a campaign for equal rights; for equal pay for the same work; and it ill becomes men, like Dr. Parkhurst, blinded by partisanship, to defame them, and charge them with having "entered into an unholy alliance with the gamblers." To these noble women I say God bless you, God speed you in the effort you are making to right a great wrong, and in the only way in which you can do it, by the ballot.

Your fathers, your brothers, your old pupils who have profited by your instruction and are better men and women by reason thereof, are with you in this fight, and hope and pray that you will relax no effort until the polls close, to accomplish the purpose for which you have banded yourselves together. Don't be frightened with the untruthful, ill-tempered charge of Mr. Parkhurst, that you have "entered into an unholy alliance with the gamblers," but gently, quietly and sweetly ask your maligners and those whom you find are being influenced by them, why it is that the popular demand of last winter that Wall Street gambling should be checked was sidetracked at Albany? Everyone concedes that it is a far greater evil than race track gambling. Ask them why it is that Governor Hughes in his hundreds of speeches the last three months has not breathed a word against the Wall Street gamblers.

It certainly looks to me as if the "unholy alliance with the gamblers" was with others than you.

November 2, 1908. FRANKLIN COUCH.

I have just read the governor's veto message as printed in this morning's *Times*. I note that he agrees with everyone of our arguments. He find no question of "Home Rule" involved, nor of "Mandatory" legislation. He admits the existence of gross inequalities and that these should be removed.

He asserts that the legislature is the proper body to which to appeal to correct the inequalities. *But* he says the principle involved—"equal pay for equal work"—should be applied to one city or one locality, or to one branch of the state service. The state should apply it to all branches of the state service or to none of them.

This is a plausible argument and a sound one in the abstract, but if literally applied in practice would have prevented the accomplishment of almost every change for the better in governmental policy.

It is really an obstructionist argument and its fallacy should be pointed out in debate, if the legislature will permit debate when the bill comes again before it after the veto. The way to begin is to begin, and if one waits to begin till one can do it all, one will wait indefinitely.

If the legislature does not pass the bill over the veto, the governor's message should be a call to arms for a new campaign to be waged in every city in the state for the application of the principle of simple justice in the payment of women in the State Civil Service.

The way has now been cleared for an effective campaign on this one definite, clear-cut proposition—equal pay for equal service, the same pay for the same work.

May 30, 1907. HORACE E. DEMING.

I deeply regret that the women teachers are obliged to continue this struggle for equal pay, when your demands are based on the soundest principles of equity. I fail to comprehend how people in authority can be so unjust in this so-called age of enlightenment and civilization. The teachers should bear in mind that no victory for justice, equal rights, or liberty, has ever been achieved against the strcnger oppressors in society and in official positions without a bitter and protracted struggle, usually not without resort to force. I trust you will present your claims again to the Legislature this year and that the Bill, when passed, will receive the approval of the present Mayor, who has been trained to recognize pure justice and to administer it under the aw. If the Mayor and the Governor again refuse to approve an Act of the Legislature in your behalf, I hope there is a sufficiently strong spirit of unity, mutual interest, mutual protection and courage among the women teachers to enforce their demands, as they can easily do, without further begging the authorities to do them justice.

Mar. 21, 1910. EZRA A. TUTTLE, Attorney.

*To the Editor of the New York Times*:

Will you permit me space in your paper to say that your comment upon the Governor's veto of the teachers' equal pay bill two years ago seems to justify an absolutely indefensible position? The ground taken in supporting that veto, and the grounds taken by the Governor in vetoing the bill, were that the bill should be general in character, should apply to all school teachers all over the State, likewise employes in the hospitals and other institutions, and employes in general under the local or State Government. When analyzed, this position means that you must never do right unless you can do universal right; you must never do justice unless you can do universal justice; you must never correct any evil unless you can correct all evil.

Such reasoning is absolutely unworthy of your paper or of the Governor of this State, and I hope that the Governor's mind has been so enlightened by the very reasonable, consistent, and praiseworthy persistency of the women teachers during the last three sessions of the Legislature that he may appreciate a principle of pure and absolute equity. The women teachers ask no favors, they do not ask for higher salaries; they ask to be paid the same as men for doing the same work. If they are not capable of filling positions in our schools, it is inexcusable that they should be appointed to such positions; but if they are capable of filling positions, filled also by men, they should have the same pay as the men, and it seems idle to repeat an argument which is so plain and indisputable.

We can understand why a "peanut politician" seeking favors of voters and political bosses of greater and lesser degree should veto a bill which might impose some additional expense and some increased taxation, but if these same politicians would refrain from "grafting" and the foolish and unnecessary expenditure of millions in the administration of the City Government, and would devote a fraction of that money to the proper payment of the school teachers, both men and women, it would greatly redound to the honor and advancement of our city.

If it were not for the efficient, devoted, self-sacrificing performance of duty by the women teachers of this city our condition in a few years would revert to that of the heathen, and we would have no city, no homes, no civilization. . . .

As a graduate of a normal school of this State thirty-four years ago, and as a teacher for some years—many years ago—and as a practicing lawyer in this city for more than twenty-five years, and as a taxpayer in this city, I want to raise my voice in defense of what seems to me the most iniquitous oppression on the part of men, for no reason that I can understand, unless it may be that we regard might to be synonymous with right and because men make the laws—and men do the voting—and men govern the school board—and men employ the teachers—and men fix the salaries—that men may do any injustice that they please to the women teachers, and because the women are powerless they must submit, and forsooth be disciplined and punished for even requesting that equity and justice be done them.

New York, May 4, 1909. EZRA A. TUTTLE.

## ARGUMENT IN FAVOR OF THE "EQUAL PAY BILL"

Three points present themselves conspicuously in favor of the passage of the bill which equalizes the salaries of men and women teachers: First, the nature and operation of an eligible list, established on a Civil Service basis, such as that from which the teachers in the public schools of New York City are appointed; second, the recognition of important changes in economic conditions, relating to the occupation of women in remunerative lines; and, third, the fact that the present law regulating public school salaries is a gross instance of class legislation.

First: The object of an eligible list established as a result of competitive examination, is to insure a given standard of merit in candidates for a position, and to eliminate from appointment every consideration but that of merit. This is plainly shown in the operation of eligible lists in other civic departments, especially in those relating to clerks and stenographers. There is no line of occupation open to women in which overcrowding and consequent competition operate more flagrantly to lower remuneration; but as soon as these workers are placed upon an eligible list this competition ceases, and all, men and women alike, are placed upon an equal footing. To introduce an element of competition among the candidates on such a list is to defeat one of the great ends of justice for which the list exists.

It is worthy of note that in other departments of the school system than the day schools, namely, in the evening schools and summer schools, men and women are paid equally for positions of equal rank; and also worthy of note that the present plan in the day schools operates to keep men out of the system, as the Board of Education has frequently appointed women in preference to men as a matter of economy.

Second: The entrance of women in large numbers into fields of remunerative occupation is often referred to by men as a willful turning away from the conventional lines of home life and duties. Those of us who have been studying these questions through intimate association with large numbers of women so employed, are impressed with the fact that in a large majority of cases, probably for two-thirds of those concerned, these women have others wholly or partially dependent upon them; in short, their work in remunerative fields, so far from being a repudiation of home ties, is an expression of devotion to home and family.

This indicates some sweeping changes in economic conditions whereby masculine support is failing, as it has never before done in the history of the world, and the burden of support is being shifted to the shoulders of women. Men themselves are not to blame for these conditions, changes in methods of business, such as the combinations of capital whereby manufacturers and dealers on a small scale are forced out of business; changes in methods of manufacturing, whereby men trained and experienced in certain lines of work are suddenly confronted with conditions requiring adaptation to altered methods; the lowering of the age limits for employment, whereby many of our largest corporations discharge their old employees and will not engage new employees over the age of thirty-five years, thus making the employment of men of middle age and beyond very difficult; the increased cost of living and especially the large amount of cash required since primitive methods of manufacture of clothing and food at home have become obsolete;—these and other conditions are making an entirely new environment for the support of families. Women are stepping into the gap, often at the cost of supreme self-sacrifice, with a nobility that has never been surpassed or perhaps equalled in the history of the world. Whether the condition be temporary or is to be permanent none of us at present know; but it is a condition in which both men and women should stand shoulder to shoulder, and in which it is inconceivable that one should say to the other—"You shall work at a disadvantage, and I shall reserve certain privileges to myself, simply because I am a man."

Third: The present statute which provides that men in our public day schools shall receive from 50% to 100% more for positions of equal rank and grade is gross class legislation favoring one set of workers at the expense of another. It is inconceivable that this state government should grant a franchise to a corporation which franchise should contain a provision that the men employed by the corporation must receive from 50% to 100% more than women for positions of equal rank. It is inconceivable that a law could be placed on our statute books, providing for the extension of this obnoxious principle to all civic employees. Imagine the people of this Commonwealth for one instant tolerating the bare suggestion that all men in city or state employ should be thus favored. Such a thing could not be. If such a law would be wrong for the whole, surely it is wrong for a part.

CHARLES F. KINGSLEY.

From the outset of the movement to secure for the women who teach in the public schools the same salary as that received by men who do teaching of the same kind and character, I have believed that you should succeed.

I have followed the varying stages of the movement with much interest and I think you have constantly gained ground in the public mind and have won over to your side many people who, when the question was first mooted, had no sympathy with your efforts.

I trust that the public authorities having this matter in charge may, before long, do whatever is necessary to solve this problem in such manner as to give equal pay for like service to all who work in the public schools regardless of sex.

Sincerely yours,

March 30, 1910. DANIEL F. COHALAN.

Dear Madam.

In reply to your printed inquiry addressed to me as the Fusion candidate for Alderman in the Ninth Assembly District (Manhattan), asking whether I believe that all city employees whose appointment is made from an eligible list, should be paid according to the position held without regard to the sex of the employee, I beg to state that when I buy any commodity I do not expect its price to be regulated by the fact that the producer of the commodity is a woman or a man. I buy the goods and I pay the price. Labor is a commodity like any other, and if an individual or a community contracts for a certain amount of human effort and time, I see no reason why the sex of the persons rendering that labor should be made a basis of discrimination.

If I am elected alderman I shall be glad to hear from you further, as I consider our schools far more important than subways, and shall do what I can to wipe out the disgrace of unutilized school sites and insufficient school accommodations.

Very respectfully,

Oct. 20, 1909. GERALD VAN CASTEEL,
Counsellor-at-law.

Dear Madam:

I am in receipt of a letter from your Association requesting a reply to the question:

"Do you believe that all city employees whose appointment is made from an eligible list, should be paid according to the position held, without regard to the sex of the employee?"

In answer thereto, I would state that as a general proposition I believe that the salary should attach to the position.

I have had no occasion to give special consideration to the application of the principle to the positions of teachers in the public schools, but as I understand that the qualifications and the character of work required are the same for men and women alike, I should, under the circumstances, favor the equalization of their salaries.

Respectfully yours,

Oct. 25, 1909. JOHN F. GALVIN.

Dear Madam:

In placing myself on record as being in favor of your movement I wish to state that I do so after having made a most careful examination of the same.

How a distinction can be lawfully made, so that the teachers of the evening schools and the summer schools of this City, whether male or female, are paid according to the grades taught by them respectively; and how the attendance officers of the Department of Education of this City are paid according to their work regardless of sex; and yet the women teachers in the day schools of this city are discriminated against in this respect, I cannot understand. All of said departments are under the direct supervision of the Department of Education of this city.

I may say, after having spoken to many taxpayers concerning this matter, I find few who oppose your application, and in almost every instance my interview developed the fact that those few who were opposed to your measure were not sufficiently familiar with it to discuss the situation intelligently. The name of your measure commonly called "The Women Teachers Equal Pay Bill," is possibly misleading, for according to my understanding the women teachers are not asking for "equal pay" in so many words. What they seek, as I understand it, is a graduated scale of salaries to be paid according to the class taught, regardless of sex; conceding that the teachers of the male classes are entitled to greater remuneration for their services than the teachers of the female classes.

It is well known that the male teachers of this city are in charge of the male classes in our public schools and in consequence thereof they would naturally continue to receive more for their services than the female teachers, with the exception of those few female teachers who are performing identically the same labor, teaching the same grade in the male department. In that respect I feel that they are performing the same work as their brethren, and are entitled to the same pay.

In no department other than the Department of Education is there a discrimination made against women holding positions nor does such a condition exist in our State and National offices. In fact as above indicated it exists only in certain branches of the said Department of Education of this city.

That this is class legislation, there can be no doubt, and where the legislature of this State permits the same to continue, I feel that the taxpayers are being deprived of the good work which teachers are capable of rendering and which is being discouraged by this controversy; for it must be conceded by students of labor that where a question is pending undetermined and in controversy, the same work cannot possibly be obtained as where satisfaction exists.

I have expressed myself at length upon this subject for the reason that I do not wish to be misunderstood. My opponent, the Republican candidate for re-election to the Assembly from the 18th Assembly District of Brooklyn, opposed your bill in the last Assembly, and that caused me to investigate this issue more closely than I would otherwise have possibly done. I find that he fathered the Women's equal suffrage bill and am at a loss to understand how he can in one breath favor women's equality so far as the right of franchise,—the greatest right in this country, is concerned—and in the next breath oppose women's rights in respect of their earning capacity, when they are performing identically the same work as their brother teachers.

Very truly yours,
MILTON G. BUCKY,
Counsellor-at-Law.

Seventeen hundred male teachers object to thirteen thousand female teachers receiving equal emolument for the same class work. Why? It certainly could not hurt these men, nor decrease their pay; but animated by a spirit of intolerance and narrow-mindedness they raise objection to an act of justice, threatening to use their ballots against the legislative friends of the women teachers.

Every one of these thirteen thousand women teachers has the power to influence in their just cause, say, an average of six votes, with father, brothers, relatives and friends, or 78,000 votes in Greater New York. This is a low estimate, for all broad-minded, liberal-thinking men are with the women teachers in the fight for their rights; and partisan lines can be forgotten in a just and noble cause.

The seventeen hundred male teachers may appeal to blind partisan prejudice, dividing between the existing parties, but as their influence is insignificant, their arguments fallacious, their animus contemptible, and their labors indicative of the bigotry of a darker age, they will not have followers.

My New York grammar school experience, and also that of all my friends with whom I have discussed the subject, left me with grateful recollection of the female teachers, and appreciation of their painstaking care and deep interest.

The weaknesses, selfishness, lack of ability and frequent injustice, of the male teachers I knew as a boy, were apparent to every scholar, and contempt was often expressed by such soubriquets as "Pop," "Poppy," "Bully," etc.

I am most heartily in favor of the Teachers' Equal Pay Bill.

P. E. DOWE,
Ex-president Commercial Travelers' National League.

That equal service is entitled to equal reward is quite as susceptible to proof as is the statement that two and two equal four.

If men are more capable teachers than women, then women must necessarily suffer if the pay be equal. The city will, or should, employ the strongest teachers the salaries will procure.

Is the opposition of the male teacher to the equalization of pay therefore dictated by chivalrous sentiments? While not

Hon. James A. Foley,
Father of Assembly "Equal Pay Bill" of 1909.

entirely practical, it would be at least graceful and pleasing. I regret to say, however, that I recently discussed the matter with two male teachers and they told me that they objected to an increase of pay for the women teachers because they (the male teachers) had intended to ask for increased salaries for themselves.

This, then, is the cause of their indigestion!

Wishing you justice and success, synonymous terms in this case.

March 30, 1908. JOHN T. GILROY.

## LETTERS—JUDGES

I have watched the efforts of your Association to obtain favorable legislation, and I have been, and am, in sympathy with this effort because I can see no reason why sex alone should give rise to inequality of compensation. I do not think there is any body of public servants more devoted to duty than are the school teachers of Greater New York, and I wish them all success in obtaining satisfactory legislative recognition of their ability and fidelity.

PETER A. HENDRICK,
January 23, 1908. Justice, Supreme Court.

I sympathize with your move.

FRANK C. LAUGHLIN,
Justice, Supreme Court.

It was a pleasure to sign and transmit to the Committees of Senate and Assembly the postals enclosed in your letter. I will directly communicate with the members I know. I wish you success in your efforts.

Please command me whenever you think I can be of service to you.

LUKE D. STAPLETON,
April 21, 1909. Justice, Supreme Court.

I am in thorough sympathy with your movement to secure Equal Pay for Equal Work for the school teachers of New York.

SAMUEL SEABURY,
December, 1909. Justice, Supreme Court.

Your invitation to join the demonstration in favor of equal pay received. In my judgment your efforts to that end should be successful.

January 26, 1908. HOWARD J. FORKER, Justice.

Wishing you success in all your undertakings and especially in this one.

January 20, 1908. PATRICK KEADY, Justice.

Call on me for anything that I can do to aid you in your cause.

January 13, 1908. JOHN F. HYLAN, Magistrate.

## CITY, COUNTY, STATE, NATIONAL OFFICERS AND POLITICAL LEADERS

I am in favor of the bill, and sincerely hope it will become a law at this session.

JOHN, D. GUNTHER,
March 2, 1908. Alderman, 57th Dist., Brooklyn.

I am most heartily in favor of the Teachers' Equal Pay bill, believing that it is but an act of justice to a superior body of public servants.

I can at the same time assure you of the support of my party associates in the Assembly. As a member of the Rules Committee I shall be in favor of reporting it to the House.

You are at liberty to use this letter in any manner you see fit.

DANIEL D. FRISBIE,
April 22, 1909. Democratic Leader, Assembly.

On Monday night, April 13, 1908, the Kings County Independence League unanimously indorsed the Teachers' Equal Pay bill. ALFRED J. BOULTON.

Assuring you of my hearty co-operation in and sympathy for your movement, and wishing your Association every success in its undertaking.

January 17, 1908. (SENATOR) WILLIAM SOHMER.

I am glad the Teachers' Equal Pay Bill passed the Legislature, almost unanimously. It speaks well for the intelligence and sense of justice of the respective members of the Assembly and the Senate of the State of New York. Of course, the Mayor and the Governor should approve the bill. I will do everything in my power to bring this about, and to that end have written very strong letters to Mayor McClellan and Governor Hughes, and I cannot see how they can possibly refuse again to sign the bill in the face of the overwhelming public sentiment in its favor.

WM. SULZER,
May 3, 1909. Member, House of Representatives.

I am in entire sympathy with your movement, and have always strongly believed in the principles of your association.

I never yet have been able to see how, under any circumstances, it is fair that when equally efficient work is done by women as by men, in any walk of life, they should not receive the same compensation.

J. VAN VECHTEN OLCOTT,

April 23, 1909. Member, House of Representatives.

I have always been in favor of the Bill, "Equal Pay for Teachers," and when the bill is on final passage I shall voice the sentiments of every member of my Club who are to a man in favor of the Teachers Equal Pay Bill.

THOMAS J. M'MANUS.

March 21, 1908.

I am in favor of the principle of equalization of teachers' salaries and the only difficulty in my mind is the question of expense—can the city afford it?

C. H. FULLER,

February 21, 1907. Member, Senate.

I was Mayor of Syracuse from 1895 to 1902, and during that period our Charter was changed three times, and the changes radically affected the school system of Syracuse.

I always found Senator White, of Syracuse, the Chairman of the Senate Cities Committee, to be in favor of doing justice to the women teachers.

I am not familiar with present demands of the teachers, and if you will inform me when we meet next, I should only be too glad to do what little lies in my power to help you and your Organization.

January 31, 1908. JAMES K. M'GUIRE.

I am in hearty accord with you in your desire to improve the condition of the women teachers by securing for them "equal pay for equal work." Justice, not charity, should be the motto. I sincerely hope your bill becomes a law at this session of the Legislature.

M. A. FITZGERALD,

January 24, 1908. Deputy Secretary of State.

The teachers have a good cause—one that strongly appeals to all classes of people—and I hope it will win. You have my very best wishes for success.

JOHN S. WHALEN,

January 27, 1908. Secretary of State.

I cannot emphasize too strongly my sympathy with you and all connected with you in the movement that you have undertaken. It is through the kindness, patience and intelligence of women like you and those associated with you that the first teachings of men like myself and all those in public life were attained. What we were taught by you we have never forgotten, and that the pay of the women teachers should not be the same as that of the men is something which I cannot understand. It is an injustice, and any little influence which I may possess you are at liberty to call on if you think that in any manner I can further the cause of justice—for such I consider your fight.

With very best wishes for your ultimate success, I remain as always, "A Friend of the Women Teachers."

GEORGE F. SCANNELL,
February 4, 1908. Superintendent of Highways.

Your movement, to put the teaching force of the public schools in the City of New York (male teachers and women teachers) on an equal footing, has my hearty support and whatever aid I may be able to render you I will gladly give.

With best wishes for the success of your undertaking.

JULIUS HAUSER,
January 17, 19908. State Treasurer.

It affords me great pleasure to write to Governor Hughes in behalf of the White Bill. I hope the Governor will sign the bill.

LAWRENCE T. LEE,
May 22, 1907. Department of Commerce and Labor.

I am unalterably in favor of the principle that where men and women are appointed to positions in the same grade or rank they should receive the same pay. The character of the work, and not the sex of the worker, should fix the compensation. If, as is claimed, there is not money enough to pay the teaching force required, which I for one do not believe, then the women teachers should not be the only sufferers. The argument that there are greater demands upon men than upon women is entirely irrelevant. If it were valid, it would require that the bachelor should receive less pay than the man with ten children, and the thrifty man much less pay than the spendthrift. I am in favor of legislation providing for equal pay for equal work regardless of sex, on a ground entirely outside of its being required by justice—on the ground that it is involved in the very fundamental conception of democracy, which requires equality of opportunity and equality of the rewards of genuine labor based upon the character of the work performed.

J. D. BELL,
March 6, 1908. Corporation Counsel for Brooklyn.

Wish you success.

MICHAEL STAPLETON,
Alderman, 2d Dist., Manhattan.

Hon. William E. Morris bids me to assure you of his sympathy with the movement.

D. S. M'CORMICK,
Cor. Sec. Tammany Hall, 35th Assembly Dist.

I am in hearty sympathy with you and your fellow teachers in your just appeal. If I can facilitate or aid in your just endeavor in any way possible, you have only to let me know to secure my earnest help.

JAMES S. CLARKSON,
January 17, 1908. United States Custom Service.

Wishing you all success.

HERMAN RINGE,
January 18, 1908. Secretary, Borough of Queens.

I am in hearty sympathy with the good cause. I am in favor of your bill and will assist in its passage in any way possible.

WILLIAM DUANE,
February 29, 1908. Deputy Chief.

I am in hearty accord with your cause and wish it every success.

JOHN HETHERINGTON,
Assistant District Attorney.

My sympathies are positively with you in your noble fight for justice and fair play. I taught school for seven years in a district and under a system where equal pay was obtained. The results were admirable and the system attained a high degree of perfection.

M. F. CONRY,
Congressman, New York.

I consider it a duty as well as a pleasure to attend your Mass Meeting.

JOHN D. M'EWEN,
Republican Leader, Queens.

I am uncompromisingly for equal pay for equal work.

CHARLES FREDERICK ADAMS.

You may use my name as you see fit, if it will help your cause for Justice.

JOSEPH H. deBRAGGA.

I am firmly convinced of the justice of your cause, and will support it when the opportunity to do so presents itself.

P. J. M'GRATH,
Member of Assembly.

I hope that you will meet with every success in your work. There are no employees of the city who render greater service to the community than do the school teachers.

R. WALDO,
Commissioner, Fire Department.

March 29, 1910.

I am in thorough sympathy with the movement which has for its object equal pay for equal work, without regard as to whether it is a man or a woman who does the work. This, it seems to me, should apply not only to teaching, but to any other work in the public service or in private business.

Those who employ men and women to work either with their hands or their brains are buying a commodity, and it is not a square deal to pay less to a woman for that commodity than to a man, just because circumstances and traditions make it possible to discriminate in favor of the man. It is neither common sense nor common justice, nor in accordance with economic rules. On the contrary, it is rank injustice to the one who receives the lesser compensation. It is discrimination against the so-called weaker sex for which there is no just or legitimate excuse.

In recent years many women have taken up important branches of work which it had previously been thought could only be performed by men, and, in countless instances, they are just as successful as men. This, of course, has always been largely true of teachers. All of these women and all men who are moved by a sense of justice, rather than by selfish motives, should congratulate you and your associates on what you have done to bring about a change for the better for your sex.

February, 1910.

WILLIAM LEARY.

## BRYAN ENDORSES WOMEN TEACHERS' "EQUAL PAY" MOVEMENT

Col. William Jennings Bryan has come forth rather unexpectedly as an ally of the "equal pay for equal work" movement, which is being propelled to all parts of this country by thousands of women teachers. This fact became known yesterday when Col. Bryan was approached by a representative of the 13,000 women teachers of this city who are fighting to have the legislature equalize the salary standards of the men and the women teachers employed in the public schools here.

Mr. Bryan said he was not familiar with the local school situation, but he authorized this statement to be made:

"I believe in the general principle of equal pay for equal work, and I believe that the position should carry the salary, irrespective of the sex of the incumbent."

Mr. Bryan was then asked this question:

"Do you think that if the legislature was responsible for the present unjust discrepancies in the salaries of women teachers and men teachers, it should be appealed to to rectify these discrepancies?"

"As I said," replied Mr. Bryan, "I am not familiar with the local situation, but I believe that when any body, legislative or otherwise, is responsible for conditions which need rectifying, that body should be appealed to for relief.—New York *Evening Telegram*, 1907.

I am heartily in favor of the Association's efforts for more remuneratory salaries for the women teachers, thereby increasing the efficiency and raising to a higher standard the teachers of our Public Schools.

Please allow me to congratulate you on the disinterested work you are doing so well and which is bound to meet with the success it so well deserves.

With best wishes.

February 5, 1908. JOHN J. MURPHY.

The earnest conscientious effort of yourself and members of your association to establish the principle of equal pay for equal work is bound to be successful, even though it has received a temporary set-back.

With best wishes.

April 7, 1910. JAMES F. HOEY.

## WOMEN'S CLUBS

I am with you and your colleagues heart and soul, and you have my best wishes for your ultimate success,

(MRS. E. J.) JEANIE D. GRANT,

March 5, 1908. President, Chiropean.

Assure you of my hearty sympathy with the work you are doing.

(MRS. N. E.) LOUISE D. HULBERT,
February 9, 1908. First Vice-President, National Society of the Empire State.

You have my best wishes for your success and any time that I can be of any service, I hope you will call upon me.

HELEN ARTHUR,
March 2, 1908. Lawyer.

I'm with you, of course, absolutely. You are bound to win out in time, because you are right. Everything in the way of logical argument is on your side, to say nothing of just plain every day common justice.

January, 1908. KATHERINE D. BURNETTE, M. D.

Wishing you success.

ELLA L. BLAIR,
December, 1909. President, State Federation of Women's Clubs.

Equal pay for equal work is a grand rallying cry, and with your great organization so splendidly efficient you surely must succeed.

(MRS. T. E.) ELLEN A. LONERGAN,
Second Vice-President, Chicago Women's
January 26, 1908. Club of N. Y. City.

Will do all in my power to help you.

(MRS. STEPHEN D.) AGNES L. STEPHENS,
January, 1908. Director, State Federation Woman's Clubs.

Best wishes for success.

January, 1908. MRS. S. DICKINSON LEWIS.

I most heartily endorse the work in which you and your associates are so nobly and faithfully engaged. I trust you will gain your object this winter. Rights are not adjusted in a day, particularly the rights for Woman, but success will come eventually and women will have equal pay with men, not only as teachers, but in every work they undertake.

(MRS. THOMAS H.) LUCY E. WHITNEY.
January 18, 1908.

I am heartily in sympathy with the purpose of this meeting and assure you of my co-operation and all the influence I may have. Hoping the Women Teachers may be successful this time.

MARY J. MACNUTT,
January 20, 1908. President, Minerva.

I am now, as I have always been, a strong advocate of equal pay for equal work. Any movement toward this end among teachers has my warm sympathy and support.

MRS. HARLOW R. BROWN,
Pres. School Settlement Association,
Sec. Local School Board, Dist. 31.

This movement for "equal pay" is very significant. It is based upon a just foundation, and the result should prove rightful and normal.

Heartily wishing you a successful Bill passage.

MARY MOORE ORR,
January 31, 1908. Sec. Local School Board, Dist. 27.

Good wishes to you.
January, 1908. VIRGINIA C. GILDERSLEEVE.

I am in favor of and in entire sympathy with your movement. I have not heard that Mrs. Humphrey Ward, Edith Wharton, and other women writers are offered lower royalties because of their sex.

As to men with family responsibilities requiring larger salaries than women, I would say there are too many women nobly shouldering heavy responsibilities for this to be just ground for discriminating against them.

I am ignorant as to whether bachelors receive less salary than benedicts.

"Equal pay for equal work" is the only reasonable conclusion.

February 7, 1908. MARGARET W. HUGHAN.

I am always ready to do whatever I can to help you in the splendid work.

MARY G. HAY,
December, 1909. Vice-President, General Federation of Women's Clubs.

It is a principle of which I most thoroughly approve.
December, 1909. JESSIE ASHLEY.

The Daughters of the Empire State are more than willing to

endorse the "Equal Pay Bill," and if there is anything further we can do, command us.

(MRS. GERARD) MARY W. BANCKER.
January, 1908. President.

The Chiropean endorses the "Equal Pay Bill" supported by the Interborough Association of Women Teachers and asks the Legislature to pass and the Mayor and the Governor to approve the same.

JULIA F. RING, Secretary.
(Largest women's club in Brooklyn.)

The Little Mothers' Aid Association and its Auxiliaries, at its regular meeting held March 5th, heartily endorsed the resolution for the Women Teachers' Equal Pay Bill—and sent letters to that effect to the Governor, their Senator, and Assemblyman Conklin.

With every wish for your ultimate success.

EMILIE VAN BEIL, Secretary.
MRS. CLARENCE BURNS, President.
March 7, 1908.

Whereas, The Women's Republican Association of the State of New York believe in the principle of equal pay for equal work, and whereas requirements for both preparation and work are the same for women as for men school teachers in the City of New Yok, while the pay is far in excess for the men teachers and whereas discrimination because of sex is unfair and unwarranted,

Resolved, That we endorse the amendment to the Davis Law known as "The Teachers' Equal Pay Bill," and pray that our request be granted.

MRS. JAMES G. WENTZ, President.
MISS HELEN VARICK BOSWELL,
First Vice-President.
MRS. CLARENCE BURNS, Chr., Ex.
MRS. EDWARD P. SWAN, Secretary.
March 10, 1908.

It is a thing my heart and soul is in. Wishing you every success.

MRS. R. A. BENEDICT.

I am most heartily in favor of your aims.

MRS. H. S. STOWE.

Our Society is in sympathy with your effort to secure Equal Pay for Equal Work.

JANETTE L. BOYNTON.

I am with the teachers every inch!

MARTHA WENTWORTH SUFFREN.

Wishing your cause the greatest success.

LUCY CRAPO WINTER.

I have full sympathy with the proposition of Equal Pay for Equal Work.

IDA M. TARBELL.

## ENDORSEMENTS BY.

Society for Political Study; Phalo Club; Optima Club; Equality League of Self-Supporting Women; Philemon Literary Club of Tottenville, of the City of New York; The Woman's League of New York State of the City of New York; Professional Women's League; College Women's Club; Sorosis; Chicago Women's Club of New York City; Woman's League, of New York State; West End Woman's Republican Association; The Woman's Press Club, New York City; Brooklyn Woman Suffrage Association; State Federation of Women's Clubs, New York; New York City Federation of Women's Clubs; Women's Democratic Club; National Daughters Empire State; Washington Heights Chapter, Daughters of American Revolution; Equality League of Self-Supporting Women.

## MISCELLANEOUS

Extending to the Association my best wishes.

HENRY THOMPSON.

April 4, 1910. Commissioner of Water Supply, Gas and Electricity.

There is no organization—and no woman—to whom we all give greater respect and good will, than your Association and Miss Strachan.

HELEN VARICK BOSWELL,

April 5, 1910. President, The Women's Forum.

I desire at this time to say to you that your cause has, I believe, the support of every sane and honest taxpayer, and like all causes that are right it will win in the near future.

Yours very truly, with best wishes for the success of your cause,

CLEMENT J. DRISCOLL,

April 9, 1910. Political Editor, N. Y. *Journal.*

With all good wishes and a "God bless you" in your work for womanhood.

March 30, 1910. CHARLOTTE ERRANI.

In accepting we desire to express the hope . . . that every object of the Interborough may be fulfilled in the near future.

EDWARD D. FARRELL.
April 2, 1910. Ex-District Superintendent of Schools.

I'll be at the Dinner. It will give me an added opportunity of showing as far as my official position will allow that I'm an ardent *advocate* of equal pay for our women teachers. With all good wishes, and again regretting that I can't do as much for you in this matter as I could wish, I am

MATTHEW C. GLEESON, Chaplain. U. N. S.

Mrs. Markham (herself an old teacher) and I will be happy to attend the Dinner on the sixteenth of April. You already know that we are both in sympathy with the labors of teachers and their aspirations.

March 25, 1910. EDWIN MARKHAM.

You have made a brave fight and I hope you will not grow discouraged with this defeat (the vote in Board of Education.) You are a strong body of women and must stand together.

MARY E. TRAUTMAN.
March 21, 1910. Health Protective Association.

I hope that any time our club, the National California, or I can be of any use to you or your great Association you will command us. I personally am at your service for all things.

April 3, 1910. ENO. W. VIVIAN (Mrs. Thomas J.)

Trust you will meet with the success that you so well deserve.

HENRY P. MOLLOY,
April 14, 1910. County Clerk.

I am called to Philadelphia and it is imperative, or believe me, I would be with your fine body of women. I had hoped to hear such speeches as would put to shame the action of the Board of Education not long since, and when members of that board were of our own sex. Be firm, and remember that Right always wins. It may take some time, but it will win.

ALICE FISCHER HARCOURT.

In sympathy I am fully.

ARTHUR DAY.
April 14, 1910. Vice-Pres. Savoy Trust Co.

I hope that your efforts to secure equal pay may be crowned with success.

DANIEL HARRIS,
President, Workingmen's Federation of the State of New York.
April 15, 1910.

Nor need I add since you know my record in regard to all the matters in which you have been interested, how much of success I wish you in all your undertakings.

JOHN F. AHEARN.
Father of the "Ahearn Bill."
April 6, 1910.

Nothing would give me more pleasure than to meet face to face the brave women who are fighting the battle of equal pay for equal work.

April 6, 1910. RACHEL FOSTER AVERY.

Wishing you and your co-workers every success.

FRANCIS P. BENT,
Vice-Chairman, Board of Aldermen.
March 31, 1910.

Please accept my cordial good wishes for the success of your cause, and believe me.

April 2, 1910. GEORGE W. BRUSH, M. D., Ex-Senator.

Assure you that I will gladly help you to attain for women teachers that which you desire, *i.e.*,—equal pay—in any way I can.

April 12, 1910. JOHN H. CAMPBELL.

I wish you all kinds of good luck and if I can do you any good at any time please call on me.

D. T. CORNELL.
Real Estate and Auctioneer.
April 4, 1910.

Feel very confident that your cause will ultimately triumph. Let me assure you of my best wishes for the accomplishment of all your aims.

April 13, 1910. ALFRED B. HALL.

I will congratulate you on the fact, though you may not realize it, that your fight for equal pay is almost won. Let a few more cities do what Milwaukee did on April 5th, and you will get anything you want.

April 12, 1910. B. C. HAMMOND.

Kindly fill my place with someone who needs converting.

March 30, 1910. ALGERNON S. HIGGINS.

I trust that the long battle for justice may never be abandoned by the Association until full justice is established.

FLORENCE KELLEY.
March 30, 1910. Consumers' League.

Wishing you every success, and that the occasion will be an enjoyable as well as a profitable one.

April 4, 1910. DANIEL A. McCORMICK.

Otherwise I would be most happy to be present, to testify by my presence, to the high regard in which I hold the Association and its aims.

MRS. DONALD McLEAN,
April 4, 1910. President, Daughters of American Revolution.

I trust you will have a very pleasant social gathering and hope much good may result.

March 24, 1910. MONS. P. F. O'HARE.

Wishing you and the members of the Association success.

Dr. ANTONIO PISANI,
March 19, 1910. Commissioner, Board of Education.

I wish your Association every success.

DANIEL J. RIORDAN,
April 5, 1910. U. S. Representative.

Wishing you success in your laudable efforts, I have the honor to remain,

THOMAS F. SMITH.
March 30, 1910. Secy., Tammany Hall.

With kind regards, and best wishes for the Women Teachers' Association,

April 4, 1910. SAM A. SCRIBNER.

Of course, you know I am deeply interested in your work.

J. E. SULLIVAN.
April 11, 1910. Commissioner, Board of Education.

Wishing you success in your work.

REV. CHAS. A. CASSIDY,
St. Peter's Rectory, New Brighton.

My best wishes will be with them, albeit I myself must that day be in Washington.

ALFRED HENRY LEWIS, 457 W. 14th St.

Assuring the Association of my warmest sympathy.

CHAS. H. HYDE, City Chamberlain.

MISCELLANEOUS

C. A. BECKER, M. D.
JOHN B. BYRNE, M. D.
FRANK LeC. DOWE, M. D.
GEORGE C. OWENS, M. D.
WILLIAM H. CARY, M. D.

I am very glad to lend my individual support to your cause.

J. RICHARD KEVIN, M. D.

I am in thorough sympathy. Woman suffers injustice in many ways under our industrial system and semi-barbarous civilization, but denying her equal pay for equal service with men is the rankest and most apparent injustice of all.

DAVID ALLYN GORTON, M. D.

The professions of Law and Medicine do not discriminate against women in the remuneration for equal service, and I see no reason why women teachers should not receive the same salary as men for the same work.

Feb. 6, 1908. WM. L. LOVE, M. D.

I hope you will succeed and I have no doubt you will, when those that are now blind see the "true light."

EDWARD H. GREEN, Brooklyn Navy Yard.

Your cause should receive the hearty co-operation of all those who believe in the supremacy of our country and wish to maintain it. "Equal pay" for our school teachers is just as much a right that should be maintained to-day, as was "Equal Rights" when our Republic was founded.

Feb. 26, 1908 MAURICE KAHN.

LETTER—FOURTH ANNUAL BANQUET—APRIL 16, 1910

I had expected to be present and, with the time permitted me, to endeavor once again to impress upon the membership of your great Association the undeniable justice of its cause and to urge a confident reliance, that, in the near future, governmental conditions, already foreshadowed and easily discerned, guarantee the recognition of the sound principle of political economy, that for identical work. simple justice requires there shall be identical pay, without regard to the particular sex of the individual by whom such work is performed.

I know how utterly disheartening it is to have one's position misrepresented in any way in which your opponents have dealt with this question. I know how indignant your membership must be that, in urging a just cause, they find themselves antagonized only by the forces of selfishness and expediency. And yet, I would have the women teachers remember that they are meeting with only the experience which precedes the triumph of every endeavor to impress simple justice upon the laws of the Nation and State.

When the day seems darkest, when the outlook is apparently least promising, when, after repeated failure, despair threatens dominion, then, it is that loyalty and energy, united in determined effort, gain their triumph.

With every good wish for the membership of your Association, I am with special grateful acknowledgments to yourself,

Very truly yours,

April 14, 1910. THOS. F. GRADY.

## LETTER SENT BY MAJOR EDWARD R. GILMAN, ONE OF THE SPEAKERS LISTED FOR THE FOURTH ANNUAL BANQUET, WHO WAS UNABLE TO ATTEND

We are living in an age of marvelous progress—the greatest age in the history of the world—the age of the telephone, the telegraph, the wireless, the electric motor, the subway, and even the aeroplane; but wonderful as are all these great inventions, the greatest discovery of the century has not yet occurred; but it is sure to come. The new discovery is the light that will come and give women justice. The century will not be complete in all its great achievements until it has undone the injustice that has been done to women since the world began, until it has put her on an equality with man. We shall be not far above barbarians until this has been accomplished. We have made some little progress in the State of New York. Women can at least own property and we are beginning to allow them to hold certain executive positions. They are demonstrating their entire fitness for these positions. Why we should divide our teachers into two classes simply because one wears skirts and the other pants, I cannot understand. The teachers should be paid according to the services they render, irrespective of sex, creed, or age. Age, creed, or the color of one's hair should not enter into the question of compensation, nor should the question of sex. The only things to be considered are ability and fitness.

There is no argument at all in the matter from my standpoint, but I would go a great deal further than merely giving "Equal Pay" to women. I should make women the only teachers of our boys and girls. They are better fitted for this work than men are. Men are all right as teachers after the children have reached a certain age, but women are the only proper teachers for the young and also for the girls. The male in the animal race is generally a polygamous brute, and while in the human race he is naturally faithful to his mate and willing and anxious to provide for his offspring, yet he is not inclined to assume the burdens of its daily teaching. The mother chicken will take care of her brood even to the point of losing her life, but the rooster knows not his own. The tom cat even kills its young. All through animal life the male cares little for its offspring, while the mother provides for it, brings it up, and teaches it how to sustain itself. It is a law of nature, and in the human race it is even more pronounced. Man is always willing to help provide for his family,—often to work like a dog to do it. He is most generous and noble in this respect, but he does not know how to bring up his children Nature did not intend him to do so. He is born without that instinct and he cannot acquire it. Woman is born with ability to educate and bring up children. It is inborn in her heart and soul. She is their natural educator. There is a gentleness and sympathy about a woman that appeals to every child, and is almost always lacking in man. I know I felt it when I was a boy in school. I liked my men teachers, but I had no sympathy with them. I was devoted to my women teachers. Their real genuine interest in me was like that of my own mother. You can lead a horse to water, but you cannot make him drink. You can drive a child to school, but you cannot make him work unless he is interested in his work. Women can secure this interest better than men.

I wish it were in my power to reorganize the whole plan for teachers. I would have women exclusively for the girls and boys until they had reached an age where perhaps a man teacher could train them as well or better than a woman. The majority of the members of the Board of Education should be women. I would have no woman on that Board of Education who did not believe that women were equal to men. I would not consider sex in the matter of the pay of school teachers. I would pay liberal salaries to all teachers, as the education of our children is the most important thing to our city, and the best talent is none too good.

Some people believe that the greatest aid to humanity is the school of religion, since it aims to teach us how to save our souls in eternity; others think that the school of medicine and surgery is the greatest because it relieves suffering and prolongs and often saves lives; but I say the greatest blessing to humanity is the school teacher, because when education is universal, we will know how to live correctly in this world and how to prepare ourselves for the world beyond. Education is the foundation of the future success of our city, state, and nation, and in the great City of New York with its conglomerate population from all parts of the world, sprinkled with socialistic and anarchistic minds, it is of the utmost importance that the education of the new generation should be of the very best and that a spirit of public pride and patriotism should be instilled into the children of to-day—the citizens of to-morrow.

The work of the educator is the most important work in the

world. It is the noblest calling, yet the poorest paid. It is of fundamental importance to the future welfare of our country. Our city does not hesitate to spend large sums freely for fire and police protection and for the mere amusement of the public. Parks, public libraries, bath houses, recreation piers, and bands of music are all maintained at the expense of the city to amuse or benefit the public, but we growl and kick as if the taxpayers were being sandbagged and robbed if we give a teacher half a living salary.

Now you have my sentiments. If I were so fortunate as to be able to go to your dinner, I would not say much other than along these lines, except perhaps to say this—that the women on the Board of Education who voted against "Equal Pay" should be called upon to resign immediately because they publicly admitted in that vote that women were not equal to men, and having so admitted, the only thing for them to do is resign. They were appointed to represent women, not to be dictated to by men. They have failed in their duty and they should leave the Board. As a citizen and a taxpayer I would call upon them to resign immediately, for having admitted that they were not men's equal; they should not serve on the same Board on an equality with men.

There is just one more thing that I would like to say and that I would say with pleasure: That all the people in this great city should fight with you and for your cause until you have won the fight,—a noble cause that should appeal to every man who believes in a "square deal" to his fellow men. Let us give a "square deal" also to women who are entitled to all our rights, and to my mind, two more: The right of man's sympathy and of man's protection.

## PART FIVE—CHAPTER ONE

## ENDORSEMENTS

By a "club to club" canvass among civic, labor and tax-payers' organizations, we secured endorsements for our "equal pay" bill from more than 300,000 voters.

Scores of organizations have been won over to the "equal pay for equal work" cause by the women's representatives, who secured hearings from three to five associations every week and explained the women teachers' bill in open meeting.

I am confident we would have secured even more endorsements were it not for the fact that many of the men teachers were members of the organizations we addressed. In several cases they prevented prompt endorsement of our bill by moving that the organization's action upon it be postponed until a later meeting.

An instance of this character took place at a meeting of the Flushing Association, when John Holley Clark, principal of the local high school, moved that the association's action upon the "equal pay" bill be postponed until the next meeting. Mr. Baumeister, a teacher, seconded this motion, and it was carried.

Despite the opposition of the men teachers, however, we have secured the support of sixty-five civic, labor and tax-payers' organizations, representing more than 200,000 voters. (See list following.)

We are especially pleased with the endorsements of the Board of Aldermen, as several members of the Board of Education opposed to our bill laid great stress on the anti-corporal punishment attitude of the Board of Aldermen at the recent hearing on corporal punishment. One of the members, Commissioner Robert L. Harrison, said the Board of Aldermen was very close to the people and represented their views better, perhaps, than any other body in the city.

Now that the Aldermen have unanimously endorsed the "equal pay" bill, we are hopeful that the Board of Education may regard the Aldermen's action as reflecting the attitude of the people and assist us, instead of fighting our salary measure.

The following is an extract from our reply to Senator Fuller in 1908: "Again is Senator Fuller mistaken in the following statement: 'And I speak now with the authority of not only New York City individual citizens, but of taxpayers' associations, who have considered this matter, having held joint debate between the women and the men, and I have in my hand a circular stating that the feelings of these various associations are against the bill. Here are some of them: Flatbush Taxpayers' Association, the Prospect Heights Citizens' Association; South Brooklyn Board of Trade; the Downtown Taxpayers' Association; the Park Board of Trade; the Fulton Street Board of Trade; the North Side Board of Trade; the Old Jones Park, and the Central and Smith Street Associations; and the Twenty-third Ward Property Owners' Association.' While it is true that last year the Downtown Taxpayers' Association and the Fulton Street Board of Trade did grant us a hearing, I challenge Senator Fuller to refute the statement that not one of the Associations named has heard the men and the women in joint debate on this year's Bill. Of those named only the North Side Board of Trade gave us even a partial hearing and that was before its Committee on Education. I challenge him further to refute the statement that at the meeting of the Flatbush Taxpayers' Association which passed a resolution disapproving our bill, there were present only about 5% of the membership. I am informed by one of the prominent members of said association that probably 40 of the 982 members were present, and that several of these were male teachers. I am informed also by a prominent member of the Prospect Heights Association that a male principal and a male high school teacher, both members of said association, were given full and free privilege of speaking against our bill, though our request for a hearing was not granted. In the South Brooklyn

Board of Trade there are also many male teachers. Furthermore, Senator Travis spoke before this Board in opposition to our bill.

"Moreover, side by side with the short list of associations supplied by Senator Fuller, we can place a list of endorsements of two hundred and fifty civic, political, and taxpaying associations, business firms and labor unions, not the least of which is the unanimous endorsement of the Board of Aldermen of the City of New York, given at its stated meeting on March 18, 1908; also thousands of individual endorsements obtained from citizens ranging in rank from millionaires to laborers, whose names have been cheerfully given in support of our bill. These form a conclusive refutation of the implication that taxpayers generally are opposed to the women teachers. *In fact, it is generally believed that if the question under discussion could be submitted to the voters of the City of New York, the women teachers would win by an overwhelming majority.*

"GRACE C. STRACHAN, *President*,
"Interborough Association of Women Teachers."

BOARD OF ALDERMAN—LABOR UNIONS

The Board of Aldermen of the City of New York at its stated meeting, March 18, 1908, unanimously endorsed the Women Teachers' Equal Pay Bill by passing the following resolution:

WHEREAS, Education is a State function, and the Board of Education in the City of New York is a corporate body created by State legislation to carry out said State function in the City of New York, and since the salaries of teachers in the City of New York are regulated by statute law known as "The Davis Law," enacted in 1900 by State legislation; and

WHEREAS, Salaries for teachers in the City of New York are made under the provisions of said Davis Law and by said Board of Education of the City of New York; and

WHEREAS, According to by-laws made by the Board of Education the requirements for women are the same as those for men, and positions of the same grade are given to both men and women; and

WHEREAS, The salaries given to women doing the same grade of work are from 30 to 100 per cent. less than those given to men in the same grade; and

WHEREAS, Said Davis Law is the only statute law in the State of New York which discriminates against women as economic and industrial units, because of sex; be it

*Resolved*, That the Board of Aldermen of the City of New York endorse the amendment to the Davis Law, known as "The Teachers' Equal Pay Bill," since said amendment proposes to establish the principle that the position shall carry the salary in the public schools of the City of New York, and since its provisions greatly extend the power of the local authorities in the matter of schedules for every grade of the public school system, and since said bill carries a four-mill clause providing a tax of four mills upon assessed valuation of property as against the present three-mill provision, and also since said bill carries the provision that 93 per cent. of said fund shall be devoted to the salaries of teachers of the public day schools; also be it

*Resolved,* That copies of this resolution be forwarded to Governor Hughes and the Senate and Assembly of the State of New York.

Adopted by the Board of Aldermen, March 18, 1908, a majority of all the members elected voting in favor thereof.

P. J. Scully, Clerk.
Compared and Correct. D. M. C.

Fee paid Mar. 24, 1908.
Jones, Cashier.

Extracts from address of Daniel F. Harris, President of Workingmen's Federation of New York State at the annual convention held in Syracuse, Sept. 17, 1907.

The bill to increase and equalize the pay of New York City School Teachers did not have smooth sailing. It was opposed by the Board of Education, also by a number of male teachers. Endeavors were also made to cause a division among the teachers themselves. In spite of all the opposition the bill passed both houses, but was vetoed by the Mayor of New York.

The bill was again passed over the veto, but was subsequently vetoed by the Governor.

The attempt on the part of the Board of Education to victimize the leaders in this fight for equal rights deserves condemnation, to say the least, and we trust that the day is not far distant when equal pay for equal work will be the rule and not the exception in all branches of industry regardless of sex.

*To Whom it May Concern:*

Whereas, The Consolidated Board of Business Agents of the Building Trades of New York and Vicinity, fully believe that the Amendment to the Davis Law, introduced by Assemblyman Robert S. Conklin, January 29, 1908, known as Assembly Bill 463 or "The Teachers Equal Pay Bill," is equitable and just;

Whereas, That all labor performed by either a Male of Female Teacher in our Public Schools, should be on equal or a "Prevailing Rate of Wages" schedule, irrespective of sex; and,

Whereas, That Bill 463 proposes to establish the principle that the position shall carry the salary in the Public Schools of the City of New York;

*Be it Resolved,* That we, the Consolidated Board of Business Agents of the Building Trades of New York and Vicinity, fully endorse and go on record, as advocating the passage of Assembly Bill 463, which will do away with the present discrimination in salaries of our Teachers, and give to those who fulfill their duties, one hundred cents for a dollar's worth of labor performed, no matter whether by a Male or a Female Teacher.

[Consolidated Board of Business Agents of N. Y. and Vicinity.
Organized June, 1906.
labore omnia vincit.]
[Seal.]

Respectfully submitted by Consolidated Board of Business Agents Resolution Committee,

Paul Sperling,
Frank Hirtzel,
Joseph LaMonte,
Richard Mortan,
James Lennon.

Attest: Roswell D. Tompkins,
Board Secretary.

March 6, 1908.
Representing 115,000 voters.

The Board of Delegates of the Building Trades of Brooklyn and Vicinity endorses the "Equal Pay Bill" supported by the Interborough Association of Women Teachers and asks the Legislature to pass, and the Mayor and Governor to approve the same.

Our association takes this action because it believes:

(a) That salary is the wage for service rendered;

(b) That when two people—one a man, and the other a woman—fulfill the same requirements, pass the same examinations, and are then appointed to *the same position, they should receive the same pay.*

(c) That the present law as incorporated in Section 1091, of the Charter of the City of New York, in indicating salaries for "male" teachers from fifty to one hundred per cent. higher than those for "female" teachers in the same positions, is the cause of great injustice to thousands of the City's best servants, and

(d) That the majority of the taxpayers are willing to pay *one dollar* more per thousand dollars, to supply the money required to give these faithful servants "a square deal."

Charles Burns, Secretary.

Representing 75,000 members.

## INTERNATIONAL BROTHERHOOD OF LOCOMOTIVE ENGINEERS

There is not a locomotive engineer, nor an electric motorman that would be willing to see a woman run an engine or motor for less than the standard wages; consequently we are a unit in wishing that you succeed in obtaining your just dues, viz., as much as a man gets for the same work.

Yours fraternally,

M. C. Baldwin, F. A. E.

Property Owners' Association of the Twenty-third Ward, Bronx, March 2, 1908.

Chas. Baxter, Chairman Executive Board,
By instruction of John Hoffer, President.

## SHOULD HAVE EQUAL WAGES

A well-attended meeting of the Brooklyn Economic Society was held at its headquarters, Fulton and Cranberry Streets, yesterday afternoon. The subject up for discussion was: "Should Women Teachers Receive the Same Salary as Male Teachers?" After a very animated discussion the affirmative side was sustained.—*Eagle,* December, 1907.

Extract from Minutes of the Regular Meeting of the City Island Board of Trade held at Library Guilding, City Island, March 16, 1908:

"On motion, duly made, seconded and carried, it was resolved that L. B. Bigelow be appointed a delegate to the Taxpayers' Alliance of the Bronx, which meets March 27, 1908, at Masonic Hall, 177th St. and 3d Ave., the Bronx, and that he be instructed to cast a vote in favor of the Women Teachers' Equal Pay Bill, now pending before the Legislature of New York State."

Leander B. Bigelow,
Secretary City Island Board of Trade.

Brownville Taxpayers' Association appointed Dr. N. J. Coyne, Jacob Marman, Isaac Allen and Saul C. Lavine, a committee to favor the Gledhill-Foley Teachers' Equal Pay Bill at the hearing before Mayor McClellan, May 11, 1909.

The following is a copy of a resolution adopted by the Board of Trustees of the Civic League of the Bronx:

*Resolved,* By the Board of Trustees of the Civic League of the Bronx that the State and City authorities be respectfully urged to approve of the bill known as the Equal Pay Bill for Women Teachers, for the following reasons:

Under the present salary schedule, a woman receives $600 the first year ($660 to teach boys) while a man is paid $900—half as much again for the same work.

In the 9th year (7th year, if boys), with the experience gained, a woman receives no more than a man without experience in his first year.

In the 13th year a man receives twice as much as a woman who has been the same number of years in the service.

After teaching 17 years a woman teacher receives less than a man in his 5th year.

Both have to follow the same course of study and conform to the same requirements, standards, and teaching qualifications.

Equal pay, regardless of sex, has already been adopted by several large cities. It is a matter of simple justice to a faithful body of public servants.

*Resolved,* That a copy of the foregoing, duly attested by the President and Secretary, be transmitted to the members of the Legislature, the Mayor and the Governor, and to the public press of this City.

Wishing you success, I am very sincerely yours,

ALBERT E. DAVIS, President.

March 9, 1908.

## THE SOUTH SIDE CIVIC LEAGUE OF JAMAICA, N. Y.

I am directed to inform you that at the last meeting of our Civic League the following resolution has been adopted:

WHEREAS, This Civic League while not in favor of the bill now before the Legislature, amending the Davis' salary schedule for school teachers; be it

*Resolved,* That this Civic League does endorse the principle of equal pay for equal services to all civil employees.

Yours truly,
SAMUEL SANDERS, President.
G. MAINE, Cor. Sec'y.

April 10, 1908.

## TAXPAYERS' LEAGUE OF RICHMOND HILL

Member of the United Civic Associations of the Borough of Queens and the Allied Civic Associations, 4th Ward, Borough of Queens.

RICHMOND HILL, N. Y., March 24, 1908.

At a well attended meeting of this League on the 17th inst., the Women Teachers' Equal Pay Bill was endorsed by a good sized majority.

I have accordingly notified Governor Hughes and Assemblyman De Groot.

[Seal.]

## CENTRAL LABOR UNION

BOROUGHS OF BROOKLYN AND QUEENS, COMPRISING THE FOLLOWING:

Pattern Makers; Park Employees; Piano & Organ, No. 27; Plumbers, No. 1; Pressman, No. 26; Pressman, No. 51; Painters, No. 670; Painters, No. 1006; Riggers No. 11561; Theatrical Employees, No. 4; Steamfitters' Association, No. 1; United Brewery Workers Local, No. 24, of the City of New York; White Stone Workers, No. 41; Compact Labor Club; Machinists, No. 401; Reliance Labor Club; Upholsterers' Union, Local 39, U. I. U. of N. Y.; Plumbers and Gasfitters, Local No. 498, N. Y.; Bricklayers' Union, No. 35; Typographical Union, No. 6; Central Federated Union; Local 476, U. B. of C. & J. of America; Local 375, Carpenters & Joiners of America, 243-47; Sheep Butchers' Protective Union, Local No. 10, B. B. W. of America; Carpenters' Local Union, 309, U. B. of C.; United Brotherhood of Carpenters and Joiners of America; District Assembly, No. 220, Knights of Labor, this organization numbers over 10,000 members; New York State Brotherhood of Locomotive Firemen and Enginemen; New York State Allied Printing Trades Council; Amalgamated Association of Street and Electrical Railway Employees of America; Auburn Trades Assembly; Oneida Trades and Labor

Assembly; Norwich Trades Assembly; Jamestown Central Labor Council; Batavia Trades Council; Local 497 United Brotherhood of Carpenters and Joiners of America; Wine, Liquor and Beer Dealers' Association, 28th District; United Brotherhood of Carpenters, Local 382; Local 724 of the United Brotherhood of Carpenters and Joiners; L. U. 848, Brotherhood Painters, Dec. and P. of America; Indorsed by L. N., No. 11, A. S. M. W. I. A.; Textile Workers' Industrial Union of U. S.; Inside Electrical Workers of Greater New York; Piano Makers' Union, Local 16; Longshoremen's Union Protective Association, Branch No. 4; New York District Council, Brotherhood of Painters, of the City of New York; Workingmen's Federation, New York State; International Brotherhood of Teamsters' Joint Council; Association of Janitors and Engineers; The Workmen's Educational Association; Metal Spinners of New York and Vicinity; Troy Trades Assembly.

## SIMILAR RESOLUTIONS WERE PASSED BY

Central Flatbush Taxpayers' Association; Taxpayers' and Rentpayers' Association of the 30th and 31st Wards, Brooklyn; East Morrisania Taxpayers' or Property Owners' Association; Third Ward Property Owners' Association, Bronx; The Heights Taxpayers' Association, Bronx, endorses the "Equal Pay Bill" supported by the Interborough Association of Women Teachers and asks the Legislature to pass, and the Mayor and the Governor to approve the same; Ocean Hill Board of Trade; 24th Ward Board of Trade; The Grand Street Board of Trade, Brooklyn; West End Board of Trade, Brooklyn; Ridgewood Board of Trade; N. Y. District Council, Brotherhood of Painters, of the City of New York; The 26th Ward Board of Trade, Brooklyn, endorses the "Equal Pay Bill" supported by the Interborough Association of Women Teachers and asks the Legislature to pass, and the Mayor and the Governor to approve the same; Grocery Clerks, No. 1100; Retail Clerks, No. 1132; Engineers, No. 56; Engineers, No. 319; Elevators' Conductors, No. 2; Electrical Workers, inside; Electrical Workers, No. 270; Electrical Workers, No. 419; Electrical Workers, No. 522; Flour & Cereal, No. 3; Foundry Employees, No. 9; Marine Firemen; Flint Glass Workers, No. 1; Glass Bottle Blowers, No. 52; Flint Glass, No. 69; United Hatters, No. 7; United Hatters, No. 8; Horse Shoers, No. 7; Plumbers' Laborers, No. 155; Moulders, No. 445; Moulders, No. 22; Moulders, No. 96; Musicians, No. 310; Metal Polishers, No. 12; Mailers, No. 6; Mailers, No. 9463; Teamsters, No. 375; Teamsters, No. 499; Teamsters, No. 592; Teamsters, No. 763; Teamsters' Milk Routemen's Union; Typographical, No. 6; Upholsterers, No. 121; Waiters, No. 2; Wood Workers, No. 249; Bartenders, No. 70; Wire Weavers; Actors' Union, No. 2; Bookkeepers and Accountants; Bill Posters, No. 33; Boot & Shoe Workers, No. 160; Brush Makers, No. 6; Brewery Workers, No. 59; Pipe Caulkers & Tappers; Calcium Light Operators, No. 35; Cigar Makers, No. 37; Cigar Makers, No. 87; Clothing Cutters, No. 5; Street Car Employees, No. 283; Metropolitan Association of Retail Druggists; The New York Branch of the American Pharmaceutical Association; Hudson River Pharmaceutical Association; The Manhattan Pharmaceutical Association; New York German Apothecary Association; Upholsterers, No. 3.

*Resolved,* That this Association known as Sheet Metal Workers, L. U. No. 11 of the City of New York endorse the amendment to the Davis Law known as "The Teachers' Equal Pay Bill."

MANHATTAN LODGE, I. A. OF M.
LOCAL NO. 402 OF THE CITY OF NEW YORK,

## CARRIAGE AND WAGON WORKERS INTERNATIONAL UNION

It is one of our fundamental principles that women should receive equal pay for equal work.

I wish to state personally that I will do anything in my power to aid you in getting "The Teachers' Equal Pay Bill" made a law. I am writing a letter to the Senator and Assemblyman from this district asking them to give it their support, and I will endeavor to have some of my friends from this district (the 35th Assem.) to do the same.

If I can aid you in any other manner, if you will me know in what way, I will be only too glad to do so, and will feel it an honor if I can be of assistance to your organization in the slightest degree.

John D. Atherton, Sec. No. 5.

March 9, 1908.

Hon. Michael J. Flaherty, ex-Sheriff; Charles E. Gehring.

New York, March 23, 1908.

The Taxpayers Alliance,
Hon. A. C. Hottenroth, President.

*My Dear Sir.*—According to motion prevailing at the last regular meeting of the Alliance, referring the matter of the Davis Bill, or Equal Pay Bill, to the Local Associations, I would respectfully state that the delegates from the Bedford Park Taxpayers' Association to your honorable body, were instructed to oppose the measure, at your special meeting on Wednesday evening, 25th inst.

As I, personally, am in favor of equal pay for equal work, and feeling that the opposition shown at the meeting of the B. Pk. Taxpayers' Association did not voice the sentiment of our membership (there being but about one-fifth present) I would strenuously protest again my name being used as an opponent to the measure, and if any record is kept of the friends of the movement, I wish my name recorded among them.

No plausible reason, has, as yet, been brought out why the Governor should not sign the bill, excepting that the applicants are women.

No self-respecting man, if he loves his mother, would advance such a reason.

We are living in a free and enlightened country (not a monarchy) where all are equal, and where the services of one, male or female, should be worth the same as another, particularly in our school system, in parallel grades.

With assurances of my esteem,

I am yours very truly,

Daniel A. McCormick.

N. B.—I would add that *no* notice of *this special business* was sent to the members of the B. P. T. Assn. D. A. McC.

The following business firms have formally endorsed our Equal Pay Bill:

Abraham & Straus; A. Alexander; Arnold & Co.; H. M. Baum; Ludwig, Bauman & Co.; L. M. Blumstein; Bonwit, Teller & Co.; Buckley-Newhall Co.; Alfred Cammeyer; John Daniell Sons & Sons; Frazin & Oppenheim & Co.; Fisher Bros.; Greenhut & Co.; Hackett, Carhart & Co.; Kalmus Bros.; Thomas Kelly; Klauber Bros. & Co.; E. C. Batten; W. L. Boyde; John Wanamaker; Koch & Sons; James McCreery & Co.; Mahler Bros.; T. A. & L. Y. Newman; O'Neill-Adams Co.; John D. O'Neill & Sons; Oppenheim, Collins & Co.; P. Morton Oppenheim & Co.; J. Parsleys Sons; M. Philipsborn Co.; Saks & Co.; Simpson, Crawford Co.; The 14th Street Store; A. A. Vantine; John B. Van Wagenen; Young Bros.; Bloomingdale Bros.

## CLUBS—POLITICAL

### INDEPENDENCE LEAGUE

Whereas, The Independence League stands for the principle of "Equal rights for all and special privileges to none"; and

Whereas, The Interborough Association of Women Teachers are now The communcations of the Interborough Association of Women Teachers receive "equal pay for equal work"; and

WHEREAS, We believe that when the same requirements are fulfilled, the same examination passed and the same positions assigned, the same remuneration should be received, regardless of sex; therefore, be it

*Resolved,* That the Independence League of the Twenty-second Assembly District, County of Kings, endorse the amendment to the Davis Law, known as the "Teachers' Equal Pay Bill," as the amendment proposes to establish the principle that the position—not the sex—shall carry the salary; also be it

*Resolved,* That copies of the resolution be forwarded to Governor Hughes, and the Senator and Assemblyman of the 10th Senatorial District, and 22d Assembly District.

S. J. TRAPANIC, Secretary,
ALFRED HUGHES, Leader.

A similar resolution was passed by the Tamaror Club, and signed by Roswell D. Williams, Peter J. Falligan, John T. Maquire, John S. Dunn, Jr., John M. Wilson, David W. Dowling.

Also by the Seneca Club: George E. LaMont, Secretary; James I. Atchison, president, and forwarded with following letter:

NEW YORK, March 6, 1908.

The endorsement of the Women Teachers' Equal Pay Bill passed unanimously last evening at the meeting of the Seneca Club, which is the Democratic political club of the Twenty-fifth Assembly District, Manhattan.

The endorsement was unanimous and many kind words were spoken in behalf of the women teachers in their fight for equal pay rights.

With best wishes for your success,

JAMES I. ATCHISON, President,
GEORGE E. LA MONT, Secretary,
GEO. F. SCANNELL.

Your communication of the 19th inst. addressed to the Queens County Republican Committee, requesting the endorsement of that organization, was received, and on motion it was referred to the Legislative Committee, which is the customary action in such matters. That committee has given your matter its consideration and heartily endorses your petition, and at the next regular meeting will report its action to the whole committee, which will, no doubt, confirm the endorsement.

Assuring you of my best wishes for the success of your undertaking, I remain,

Mar. 21, 1908. JOHN D. MCEWEN,
Chairman of Legislative Committee.

The communications of the Interborough Association of Women Teachers' recently addressed to Congressman William S. Bennet, were personally presented by him to the Republican District Committee of the Nineteenth Assembly District Borough of Manhattan, at its last meeting; whereupon a resolution was offered and unanimously carried, whereby said District Committee placed itself on record as favoring the passage of the bill now in the Legislature, which provides among other things, that where men and women are appointed to positions of the same grade or rank, that they shall receive the same pay.

ANDREW F. MURRAY,
Chairman of the Nineteenth Assembly District.

March 3, 1908.

*Dear Madam.*—This is to certify that the members of the North End Democratic Club of the 35th Assembly District have approved and endorsed the resolutions of the Women Teachers' Association for equal pay for equal work.

DANIEL A. MCCORMICK, Secretary.

The Patrick F. Lynch Democratic Association of the Twenty-third Assembly District unanimously endorsed the McCarren Bill, increasing the teachers' salaries.

The Amsterdam Democratic Club, at a regular meeting held at its Club House and Auditorium, at No. 131 West 64th street, New York, N. Y., the 20th day of December, 1909, on motion of Hon. John B. Adger Mullally, which was duly seconded by Hon. Joseph Gordon and others and unanimously carried,

*Resolved,* That the Amsterdam Democratic Club is in most hearty sympathy with the Interborough Association of Women Teachers in its effort to secure some measure of justice for Women Teachers, especially in respect to the matter of their inadequate, unfair and unequal compensation; and that this Club, recognizing the great debt, which can not be measured in material terms, due to the women who teach our little ones, wishes the officers and members of the Women Teachers' Association Godspeed in their undertakings and God's richest blessings individually and collectively.

Attest: ALBERT E. WALKER, Secretary.

WHEREAS, The Socialist party the world over stands for the principle of equal rights, without distinction as to color, creed or sex, and

WHEREAS, In matters of education we demand that the State should afford to every child the opportunity for harmonious development of all its faculties, therefore be it

*Resolved,* That we heartily endorse the struggle of the women teachers of the City of New York in their demand of "Equal Pay for Equal Work";

*Resolved,* That we stand ready to co-operate with any movement honestly endeavoring to bring our educational system nearer to our ideal of true education.

Approved at the regular meeting of the Executive Committee, S. P., Local New York, March 23, 1908.

Attest: MOSES OPPENHEIMER,
FRANCIS M. GILL,
Sub-Committee of the Executive Committee.

## SIMILAR RESOLUTIONS WERE PASSED BY:

Tammany Hall General Committee, 30th Assembly District, Wm. J. Sinnott, Executive Member; The John F. Curry Association of the City of New York; Progress Republican Club; The Jefferson Club, 5th Assembly District, Brooklyn; Ætna Club of Brooklyn; Alpha Republican Club, 15th Assembly District, Brooklyn; Jeffersonian Democratic Club; Manhattan Single Tax Club; Mount Morris Democratic Club; East Side Clinic for Children, Adelaide Wallerstein, M. D., President; East Side Clinic; Columbus Lodge No. 24, Order of True Friends; Arbeiter Maenerchor, N. Y.; Maenerchor Des Mobelarbeiter, 243-247 East 84th St., Manhattan; Socialistic Liedertafel, N. Y.

## THE "EQUAL PAY" BILL WAS ALSO ENDORSED BY:

Sterling Republican Club, Manhattan; Bedford Political Equality League; Queens County Democratic Central Committee; The North End Democratic Association of the Bronx, 35th Assembly District; Pensa Club; Bushwick Political Equality Club; President Rubinstein Club; 6th Assembly District Democratic Club; P. F. Lynch, 23d Assembly District Club; Independence League, 12th Assembly District; Independence League, First Assembly District; Independence League, Fourth Assembly District; Interborough Council (consists of Presidents of Borough Teachers' Associations); Jackson Association, 34th Assembly District; 18th Assembly District Republican Club; Seneca Club of Kings County; Wampanoag Club, 32d Assembly District; Jefferson Club, 5th Assembly District; Third Ward Republican Club; Independence League, 20th District; South Brooklyn Republican Club; Court Vittorio Emanuele II, N. 435 F. or A.; Arthur H. Murphy Association, Bronx (34th Assembly District); St. Veronica C. Club, 451 Hudson St., City of New York; Kings County Democratic Party, First Assembly District; Kings County Political Equality League.

# PART SIX—CHAPTER ONE

## DOCUMENTS

*To the Members of the Charter Revision Commission:*
Hon. William M. Ivins, Chairman.

*Sirs.*—The twelve thousand members of the Interborough Association of Women Teachers of the City of New York, representing every grade and department of the public school service from kindergarten to district superintendent, inclusive, is unanimous in its petition that you recommend such a revision of the Chapter on Education as will secure:

A.—Salary for position, regardless of sex of incumbent;
B.—State protection of minimum salaries;
C.—Greater minimum than "three mills" as required in Section 1064 of the Charter.

### I

### C.—Greater Minimum than "Three Mills" as Required in Section 1064 of the Charter

In connection with request "C," we beg you to consider the following extract from "Memorandum on Senate Bill 1218" (familiarly known as the "White Bill" or the "Teachers' Equal Pay Bill") submitted to Governor Hughes by Horace E. Deming:

"The State has never hesitated, either in New York or in the other States of the Union, to take effective measures to *compel a given locality* to raise by taxation sufficient funds to maintain a proper system of education. When the State standard of what should be expended for education, in view of the general interests of the public, is higher than the local standard the locality sometimes fails to raise enough money by taxation to support the schools according to the State standard. To meet this niggardliness on the part of the local taxing officers, resort is sometimes had to the conferring of direct powers of taxation on boards of education, or to mandatory legislation directing that such and such a per cent. of the annual tax levy in the locality shall be devoted to school purposes.

"When the Greater City of New York was created the experiment was tried of having the Board of Estimate and Apportionment act upon the budget which the Board of Education prepared, setting forth the needs of the department of education. Experience soon made it clear that the Board of Estimate and Apportionment would not willingly allow a sufficient sum adequately to support education in New York. The Legislature was compelled, therefore, to state a minimum figure and to order that at least that amount should be collected in the City of New York and devoted to the purposes of education. This is the origin of the four-mill provision contained in the so-called Davis Law of 1900, now incorporated in section 1064 of the New York Charter.

"When the City authorities announced that property in New York would thereafter be assessed at one hundred per cent. of its market value, it was thought that the four-mill provision would produce more money than was needed, and the City authorities asked the Legislature, therefore, to reduce the four mills to three. This was done in 1903. But the raising of the assessed values to one hundred per cent. of the market value never really materialized, and the three-mill provision has proved insufficient."

Hence our request for the restoration of the fourth mill.

II

B—State Protection of Minimum Salaries

In connection with request "B," we ask you to consider that the State in its Constitution makes *mandatory* the establishing of common schools and the education of its children therein. We believe, therefore, that the State should also make *mandatory* the minimum wage to be paid its servants in this department.

It is within the memory of every member of your Honorable Body that prior to the enactment of the "Davis Law," teachers could not know from year to year, sometimes even from month to month, what salaries they would receive, the demands of Dock, Bridge, Street, Police, Fire and other departments always being considered superior to those of teachers' salaries. It is evident that teachers cannot do their best work under such conditions. It is useless for them to plan to improve themselves by study, as they cannot be sure of being financially able to carry out said plans. The great strides forward which the teachers of our city have made since the State has protected them in minimum salaries are patent to all acquainted with our school system.

The following extracts from the "Memorandum in Support of Senate Bill 1218" submitted to Governor Hughes by Horace E. Deming are convincing on this point:

Page 4: "From time immemorial education has been in the special care of the State. Education is a State function. No State in the Union has ever surrendered this function, or has abdicated the right to exercise the function.

"The Constitution of the State of New York, in Article IX, declares that the Legislature shall provide for the *maintenance* and *support* of a system of free common schools wherein all the children of this State may be educated—all the children of this State; not some of them, but *all* of them."

Page 5: "The Gunnison case, decided by the Court of Appeals in 1903 (176 N. Y., 11), states very clearly the precise legal status of the Board of Education. The decision is by a unanimous court, consisting of Chief Judge Parker and Judges Gray, Barlett, Haight, Cullen, Werner and O'Brien, unanimously affirming a decision of the Appellate Division, Second Department, made by Goodrich, P. J., and Bartlett, Woodward, Jenks and Hirschberg, JJ., Justice Hirschberg writing the opinion at the Appellate Division and Justice O'Brien in the Court of Appeals."

Extract from said opinion: "It is apparent from the general drift of the argument that the learned counsel for the defendant is of the opinion that the employment of the teachers in the public schools and the general conduct and management of the schools is a city function, in the same sense as it is in the case of the care of the streets or the employment of police and the payment of their salaries and compensation. But that view of the relations of the City to public education, if entertained, is an obvious mistake."—"These corporate powers are expressly conferred upon this defendant by the City Charter (Section 1062) . . . The only purpose for which the defendant was created a corporate body was to conduct a system of public education in a designated division of the State, and manage and control the schools therein. This obviously includes the employment and payment of teachers, and none of these powers or functions are conferred upon the City as such."

We believe the above justifies our appeal for State protection of minimum salaries.

III is included in Part I.

## ANSWER TO MAYOR McCLELLAN'S VETO MESSAGE ON SENATE BILL 1218

### SUMMARY OF OBJECTIONS

1. Bill is *mandatory* and places enormous expense on the taxpayers.
2. Local authorities have the powers the bill gives them.
3. The bill is class legislation pure and simple.
4. The bill destroyes the elasticity of the present school system.

Any unprejudiced student of Senate Bill 1218 must acknowledge that it is mandatory in a far less degree than Section 1091 of the Charter which it seeks to amend.

In eliminating all definite and distinct schedules it leaves the making of salary schedules entirely to the Board of Education, stipulating only some broad general principles, which have been generally recognized as just and practical.

Therefore, inasmuch as this bill restores in great measure the "Home Rule," taken from the city by the enactment of the Davis Law in 1900, it would seem the part of wisdom and good citizenship to assist in this restoration.

"The enormous expense to the taxpayers" is fully covered by the "four mill provision" (page 7, lines 1-6). The Davis Law (1900) contained this identical provision. In 1902, the Board of Education asked the Legislature to reduce the "four" to "three," because it estimated that a three mill fund would be sufficient if Controller Grout's plan to assess taxes on a hundred per cent. valuation should be carried out. Since this "par value" plan never materialized, it is only fair to restore the "mill" taken away from the teachers' salary fund, in anticipation thereof.

### SECOND OBJECTION

"Local authorities have the powers the bill gives them."

The local authorities, as represented in the Board of Education, refused to grant the principle that women employed in the same grade should be paid under the same schedule. Hence the appeal to "Albany." Furthermore, the local authorities have *not* the power to amend the charter of the City of New York and remove therefrom the words "male" and "female" as applied to teachers. Previous to the passage of the Davis Law there was no discrimination in salaries on account of sex, in the school systems of Brooklyn and other parts of the present City of New York. Should not the Legislature, therefore, be permitted to make restitution to the citizens it then injured?

### THIRD OBJECTION

"The bill is class legislation favoring certain grades of women."

It is a deplorable fact that the "local authorities" seem unable to state the facts in this connection.

Mr. Stern, representing the Board of Education at a hearing on this bill before the Assembly Cities Committee on April 23. 1907, said there was a man teacher in the 1A grade receiving $2,160. At the hearing before Mr. McClellan, Monday May 6, 1907, the said Mr. Stern, representing the said Board of Education, read a letter from Mr. Maxwell, City Superintendent, in which Mr. Maxwell referred to the 519 men from the 2B through the 6B. Out of their own mouths, therefore, have the opponents of the bill—and Mr. McClellan bases his veto on *their* arguments and *their* estimates—condemned their own arguments on class legislation and discrimination against primary teachers to ridicule and scorn. Yet notwithstanding the above statements that there are men all through the grades from 1A upwards, and notwithstanding the fact that the White Bill provides for equal salaries for men and women employed in any one schedule, these opponents, determined to defeat "the women" at any cost, claim that the bill favors "women in certain grades and not in others."

In this connection, the Mayor also writes, "but in those grades where there are no men the salaries remain unchanged." It seems pitiable that a man holding the high office of executive in the largest city in America should exhibit either such gross carelessness or ignorance. The bill distinctly provides changes in the salaries of women "in those grades where there are no men" by raising the present first year minimum of from $600 to $720, and by reducing the period of serving for a maximum from 17 years to 12 years. Furthermore, should the Mayor's Board of Education acting under the White Bill if enacted into law, fail to use some of the money provided by the additional mill, in raising the maximum salaries in such grades, it would be guilty of misuse of the powers conferred upon it, and another appeal to Albany would be justified.

In this arguments, the Mayor cancels his first objection with his third, and reduces both to zero. Proof: In expanding on his first objection he sets forth the $9,000,000 estimate set forth by the Men Principals' and Teachers' Association, and the Board of Education. (No disrespect is meant by thus placing the Board second. It is done to indicate that the information received is that neither the Board of Education nor the Board of Estimate has made any official estimate and that the figures quoted by the opponents of the bill and by the Mayor were largely compiled by a volunteer force of male principals and teachers who were permitted access to the records by the Board of Education). Now this $9,000,000 estimate is obtained by assumming that the Board will pay *all the teachers from the kindergarten* through the 8A grade under the $900, $2,160 schedule. Therefore, there can be no "class legislation" considered. For if the "equalizing" is to affect simply the women working in schedules secured *by the Davis Law* to male teachers, only positions above the 6B grade should be used in the "equalizing estimate," and even the figures of our opponents make this estimate only $1,858,035. So, it clearly appears that "class legislation" and "$9,000,000" invalidate objections one and three.

Continuing on this line, a line which the opponents of this bill have found most effective because by it they have misled a few "primary teachers," the Mayor cites more of the estimates submitted by the Male Principals' and Teachers' Association, and says there are "about 6,500 teachers from 1A to 4B" and "according to provisions of this law the salaries of the 5,000 women teachers in the first eight grades will remain unchanged, inasmuch as there are no men serving in those schedules." If as quoted above there are about 6,500 teachers in grades from 1A to 4B, and if 5,000 of them are women, is it not reasonable to suppose that the other 1,500 are men? But Mr. Maxwell says, "519 men from 2B to 6B." Again Mr. Maxwell's latest annual report shows only 1,701 men in the entire system. So the answer to the problem: Find the number of women in the first eight grades, is, if based on the foregoing figures, *Reductio ad absurdam,* and therefore any arguments based thereon are absurd.

### FOURTH OBJECTION

"The Bill would destroy in a large measure the elasticity of the present system and thus seriously impair the efficiency of the service. At present, as there is no difference in salary between the various grades up to 7A it is possible to assign the various teachers to those grades below 7A for which they are best fitted."

The proponents of the bill challenge any one to find in Senate Bill 1218 any provision which prevents the Board of Education from making the same salary schedule cover all the "various grades up to 7A." The proponents know that no such provision can be found in the bill, hence objection four is also absurd.

The Mayor's message, in connection with his veto of Senate Bill 1218, is conspicuously like the argument made by Mr. Stern at the hearing May 6,

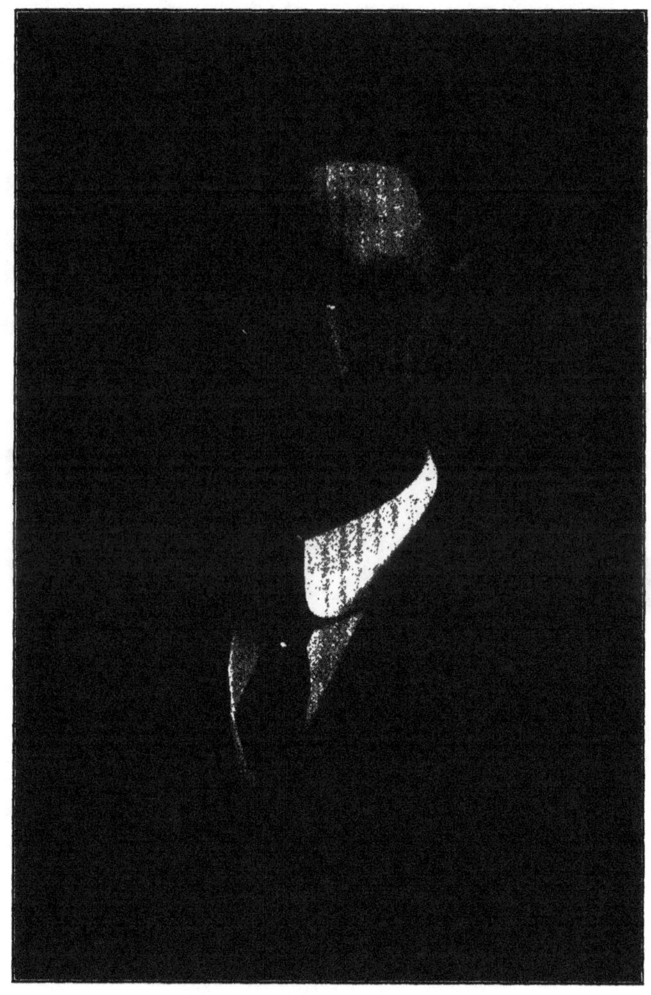

Hon. Arthur S. Somers,
Father of "Equal Pay" Resolution in Board of Education,
Dec. 22, 1909.

1907. A search of the "minutes of the Legislative hearings" of 1900 would disclose that Mr. Stern's arguments in opposing the Davis Bill were no more reliable or logical than are those he uses in opposing the White Bill. Then he estimated that a teacher's salary under the Davis Law would become $13,500, and that the cost of the Davis Law to the city would be $26,000,000.

Knowing, as he so well does, that the present Schedule VI, in so far as it affects the salary of a male teacher in any grade below the 7A, beyond assuring said male teacher of an initial salary of $900 and an annual increment of $105, is not protected by law, and can be changed at any meeting of the Board of Education, Mr. Stern nevertheless makes an arbitary and wholly unauthorized division between the 4A and 4B grades, and contemplates paying all teachers down through the 4B a salary of $2160 after 12 years of service, thus forecasting an average annual increase of 56%, and further contemplates when he pleads for the "primary teachers"—not, mind you, when he hold up $9,000,000, to the taxpayers—*leaving the maximum of $1240 for teachers below the 4B unchanged.* Is it surprising in the face of such decisions that out of 66 cases in which teachers have appealed to the courts, from the decisions of the Committee on By-Laws and Legislation—of which Mr. Stern is the most conspicuous member—that upwards of 62 have been won by the teachers? Is it not sad, however, that teachers should be obliged to spend upwards of a hundred thousand dollars to get through the Courts of Justice the rights which their employer, the City, through its Board of Education, denies them?

## AN ACT

To amend the Greater New York charter in relation to the fixing and regulating of the salaries of members of the supervising and the teaching staff of the public schools in the city of New York, and to the general school fund.

*The People of the State of New York represented in Senate and Assembly do enact as follows:*

SECTION 1. Section ten hundred and ninety-one of the Greater New York charter, as re-enacted by chapter four hundred and sixty-six of the laws of nineteen hundred and one is hereby amended to read as follows:

*Board of Education; Power to Fix Salaries; Method; Regulating.*

1091. The Board of Education shall *subject to the following rules and regulation* have power to adopt *and shall* adopt by-laws, fixing *and regulating* the salaries of all members of the supervising and the teaching staff *of the public schools in the City of New York and establishing schedules of such salaries.*

1. *The salaries of men and women in the supervising and teaching staff* (and the salaries of all principals and teachers) shall be *fixed and regulated* by merit, grade of class taught, length of service and experience in teaching or supervising (only a combination of these considerations) *and no discrimination or difference in the amount of salary paid men and women shall be made on account of their difference in sex;*

2. *The schedules of salaries shall be uniform* (such by-laws shall establish a uniform schedule of salaries for the supervising and the teaching staff) throughout all boroughs; (which schedule shall provide for an equal annual increasement, etc., etc., as in

3. *The first year's salary of a member of the teaching staff shall not be less than seven hundred and twenty dollars;*

4. *No member of the teaching staff shall suffer a reduction of salary because of his or her transfer from an elementary school to a high school or a training school;*

5. *The difference between the yearly salary of a teacher of a boys' class and that of a teacher of a girls' class of corresponding grade who have had the same number of years teaching experience shall not exceed one hundred and eighty dollars;*

6. *Each schedule shall establish an initial minimum annual salary and equal annual increments thereafter not to exceed twelve until the maximum annual salary prescribed in the schedule shall be attained and no such increment shall be less than the smallest annual increment paid to male teachers in the public elementary schools in the City of New York at the time of the passage of this act;*

7. *All increases in the salary of a member of the supervising or the teaching staff shall cease with the fifth year and again with the ninth year of the member's service unless and until the service of such member shall have been approved after inspection and investigation as meritorious and fit by a majority of a board consisting of the district superintendent assigned to the district or school in which such member is serving and the member of the board of superintendents,* and in every such case said board so constituted as aforesaid shall approve or disapprove at least forty days before the date when the increase of salary conditioned upon said board's approval will be due, (provided, however, that none of the aforesaid members of the supervising and teaching staff of any of

Take in pp. 5, 6, 7 to and including "per annum" 1.14, p. 7, but omitting all italicized words and sentences and all bracket signs except the bracket sign after said "per annum")

8. Each member of the supervising and the teaching staff shall, under the by-laws adopted in conformity with the provisions of this section, at once have all the rights to which such member is entitled by reason of merit, grade of class taught, length of service, and experience in teaching or supervising;

9. The board of examiners shall issue to a principal who has or a teacher who has had experience in schools other than the *public* schools (of) *in* the City of New York, a certificate stating (that the experience of such teacher is equivalent to a certain) *the* number of years of *service and* the experience in the *elementary, or as the case may be, in the high or training* schools in (of) the city *to which the service and experience of the holder of the certificate is equivalent and such certificate shall be final and conclusive as to the rating of the holder thereof for length of service and experience on becoming a member of the supervising or the teaching staff of the public schools in the City of New York;* (the board of examiners shall

Take in 1. 1. 20-26 p. 6 and to and including "in such certificates" on 1. 6 p. 8,)

10. No salary (now paid to) *of* any member of the supervising *or* (and) the teaching staff of (any of) the public schools in the City of New York *at the time this act goes into effect and who continue such member thereafter* shall be reduced by the operation of this section.

(and the aforesaid annual equal increment for each etc. etc. etc. take in 1. 1. 10-16, p. 8, omitting italicized words and bracket signs.)

The board of estimate and apportionment of the City of New York shall appropriate for the general school fund for the year nineteen hundred and nine and annually for each year thereafter an amount equivalent to not less than four mills on every dollar of assessed valuation of the real and personal estate in the City of New York liable to taxation; and at least ninety-three percentum of the amount appropriate for the general school shall be set aside for the payment of the salaries of the members of the supervising and the teaching staff of the regular public day schools in the City of New York.

2. All acts and parts of acts inconsistent with the provisions of this act are hereby repealed.

3. This act shall take effect January first nineteen hundred and nine.

## THE DAVIS-SMITH BILL—1909

AN ACT

To establish uniform compensation to all holding appointments after competitive examination, in the several departments of government.

The People of the state of New York represented in the Senate and Assembly do enact as follows:

Section 1. In all state, county, and municipal departments of government, there shall be but one salary for one and the same position whose incumbent is appointed from an eligible list after competitive examination.

Section 2. All acts and parts of acts in so far as inconsistent with this act are hereby repealed.

Section 3. This act shall take effect October first, one thousand nine hundred and nine.

N. B.—Never reported out of committee.

## GLEDHILL-FOLEY BILL—1909

AN ACT

To amend the Greater New York charter, in relation to the fixing and regulating of the salaries of members of the supervising and the teaching staff of the public schools in the city of New Work, and to the general school fund.

The People of the State of New York, represented in Senate and Assembly, do enact as follows:

Section 1. Section ten hundred and ninety-one of the Greater New York charter, as re-enacted by chapter four hundred and sixty-six of the laws of nineteen hundred and one, is hereby amended to read as follows:

Board of Education: Power to Fix Salaries; Method; Regulating.

Sec. 1091 The board of education shall subject to the following rules and restrictions have power to adopt and shall adopt by-laws fixing and regulating the salaries of all members of the supervising and the teaching staff of the public schools in the city of New York and establishing schedules of such salaries.

There shall be a uniform schedule of salaries for the supervising and the teaching staff throughout all boroughs, providing for initial salaries and annual increment thereof as follows:

1. In kindergartens and grades of the first six years,

a. The initial salary of a teacher shall be: in a girls' class, seven hundred and twenty dollars per annum; in grades of the first and second years, in a boys' class, seven hundred and eighty dollars; in grades of the third and fourth years, in a mixed class, seven hundred and eighty dollars, and in a boys' class, eight hundred and fifty-two dollars; and in grades of the fifth and sixth years, in a mixed class, seven hundred and ninety-two dollars, and in a boys' class, nine hundred dollars; increasing by annual increments of seventy-five dollars until the thirteenth year, when the maximum shall be reached.

b. The initial salary of an assistant to principal supervising grades of the first six years shall be: in a girls' school, eighteen hundred dollars; in a mixed school, nineteen hundred and forty dollars; and in a boys' school, twenty-one hundred dollars; increasing by annual increments of one hundred fifty dollars until the third year, when the maximum shall be reached.

c. The initial salary of a principal of at least twenty classes in grades of the first six years shall be; in a girls' school, twenty-four hundred and fifty dollars; in a mixed school, twenty-six hundred dollars, and in a boys' school, twenty-seven hundred and fifty dollars; increasing by annual increments of two hundred and fifty dollars until the fourth year, when the maximum shall be reached.

2. In schools including or consisting of the grades of the seventh and eighth years.

a. The initial salary of a teacher in grades of the seventh and eighth years shall be: in a girls' school, $1140; in a mixed school, $1290; and in a boys' school, $1440; increasing by annual increments of $150 until the third year, when the maximum shall be reached.

b. The initial salary of an assistant to principal supervising in grades of the seventh and eighth years shall be: in a girls' school, $1950; in a mixed school, $2100; and in a boys' school, $2250; increasing by annual increments of $150 until the third year, when the maximum shall be reached.

c. The initial salary of a principal having twenty-five or more teachers in the grades of the seventh and eighth years shall be: in a girls' school, $2700; in a mixed school, $2850; and in a boys' school, $3000; increasing by annual increments of $250 until the fourth year, when the maximum shall be reached.

3. In schools including or consisting of the seventh, eighth and ninth years,

a. The initial salary of a teacher in the grades of the seventh, eighth and ninth years shall be; in a girls' school, $1140; in a mixed school, $1290; and in a boys' school, $1440; increasing by annual increments of $150 until the third year when the maximum shall be reached.

b. The initial salary of an assistant to principal supervising in the grades of the seventh, eighth and ninth grades shall be; in a girls' school, $2150; in a mixed school, $2300; and in a boys' school, $2450; increasing by annual increments of $150 until the third year, when the maximum shall be reached.

c. The initial salary of a principal having twenty-five or more teachers in the grades of the seventh, eighth and ninth years shall be: in a girls' school, $3200; in a mixed school $3350; and in a boys' school, $3500; increasing by annual increments of $250 until the third year, when the maximum shall be reached.

4. In high schools and training schools for teachers,

a. The initial salary of a junior teacher shall be: in a girls' school, $900; in a mixed school, $1000; and in a boys' school, $1100; increasing by annual increments of $100 until the third year, when the maximum shall be reached.

b. The initial salary of an assistant teacher shall be: in a girls' school, $1250; in a mixed school, $1400; and in a boys' school, $1550; increasing by annual increments of $150 until the ninth year, when the maximum shall be reached.

c. The initial salary of a first assistant shall be: in a girls' school $2600; in a mixed school, $2750; and in a boys' school, $2900; increasing by annual increments of $200 until the fourth year, when the maximum shall be reached.

d. The salary of a principal supervising at least twenty-five teachers shall be $5000; of one supervising sixty or more teachers, not more than $5500.

5. All increase in the salary of a member of the supervising or the teaching staff shall cease with the fifth year and again with the ninth year of the member's service unless and until the service of such member shall have been approved after inspection and investigation as meritorious and fit by a majority of a board consisting of the district superintendent assigned to the district or school in which such member is serving and the member of the board of superintendents, and in every such case said board so constituted as aforesaid shall approve or disapprove at least forty days

before the date when the increase of salary conditioned upon said board's approval will be due.

6. No salary of any member of the supervising or the teaching staff of the public schools in the city of New York shall be reduced by the operation of these schedules; and this provision shall be construed to protect all salary contracts now in operation so that no losses shall ensue by reason of alteration of the annual increments; and it recommends, further, that each member of the supervising and the teaching staff shall at once become entitled to all the emolument in accordance with above schedule to which said person is entitled by reason of merit, experience, and position held; but the board of education may limit the expense of putting these schedules into effect by making the highest salary to be paid to any teacher or supervisor in the year 1910 and each year thereafter until the maximum salary shall have been reached, the salary in the proposed schedule which is equal to or next higher than the amount that would be obtained by adding two of the annual increments in said schedule to the salary due said teacher or supervisor under the present schedule.

7. Principals of elementary schools having at least twelve classes on the date of the adoption of these schedules shall receive all the emoluments and benefits of said schedule, but no principal of an elementary school appointed after such date shall receive the salary fixed by said schedules, except those in charge of schools having at least twenty classes.

8. The board of estimate and apportionment of the city of New York shall appropriate for the general school fund for the year nineteen hundred and nine and annually for each year thereafter an amount equivalent to not less than four mills on every dollar of assessed valuation of the real and personal estate in the city of New York liable to taxation; and at least ninety-three per centum of the amount appropriated for the general school fund shall be set aside for the payment of the salaries of the members of the supervising and the teaching staff of the regular public day schools in the city of New York.

9. All acts and parts of acts inconsistent with the provisions of this act are hereby repealed.

10. This act shall take effect January first, nineteen hundred and ten.

## THAT PART OF REPORT OF THE CONCILIATION COMMITTEE NOT INCLUDED IN GLEDHILL-FOLEY BILL

The undersigned, acting individually, and not in any representative capacity, as members of a committee which has had for its purpose the consideration and preparation of plans whereby the standards of education in this city may be advanced, and the many divergent and often opposing interests of the members of the teaching profession may be harmonized, and that this may be done without placing too heavy a burden upon the taxpayer, respectfully submit the following report:

The committee approves a plan of organization which would confine the elementary school to the kindergarten and the grades of the first six years of the present elementary school course; would establish an intermediate school, called in the report the *sub-high school,* for the grades of the seventh, eighth and ninth years; and would limit the high school to grades of the tenth, eleventh and twelfth years.

## SPECIAL SALARY RECOMMENDATIONS

The committee believes that an ideal school should be limited to 20 or 30 classes and deplores the organization of excessively large schools; but it recognizes the necessity which demands these in many sections of this city and recommends that in recognition of the greater responsibility and the heavier burden an additional salary of not more than $500 per annum shall be paid to principals supervising sixty or more teachers.

After much consideration and discussion this committee has decided that, in view of the evident intention of the board of education to establish vocational schools in the very near future, and in view of the consequent necessity for a special adjustment of the salaries relating to special subjects, it is best at this time to recommend no definite salaries for directors, assistant directors, and teachers of special subjects; but this committee does recommend that there be revision of the present salary schedules of said directors, assistant directors, and teachers, and that the general plan of the schedule recommended above be followed in such revision.

The committee recommends that the initial salary of a clerk in an elementary school shall be $600 per annum, increasing by annual increments of $60 until the sixth year, when the maximum will be reached.

The committee recommends that substitutes in elementary schools shall receive not less than $3 per diem.

The committee recommends that the salary of no teacher shall be reduced by reason of transfer from elementary to sub-high, high, or training schools.

## GENERAL RECOMMENDATIONS.

The committee recommends the restoration of the "four mill tax."

The committee recommends that all provisions relating to the tenure of office in the present charter be continued.

The committee recommends that in the grades of the first six years the classes be mixed classes.

The committee recommends that no salary of any member of the supervising or the teaching staff of the public schools in the city of New York shall be reduced by the operation of these schedules; and this provision shall be construed to protect all salary contracts now in operation so that no losses shall ensue by reason of alteration of the annual increments; and it recommends, further, that each member of the supervising and the teaching staff shall at once become entitled to all the emolument in accordance with above schedule to which said person is entitled by reason of merit, experience, and position held; but the Board of Education may limit the expense of putting these schedules into effect by making the highest salary to be paid to any teacher or supervisor in the year 1910 and each year thereafter until the maximum salary shall have been reached, the salary in the proposed schedule which is equal to or next higher than the amount that would be obtained by adding two of the annual increments in said schedule to the salary due said teacher or supervisor under the present schedule.

The committee recommends that principals of elementary schools having at least twelve classes on the date of the adoption of these schedules shall receive all the emoluments and benefits of said schedule; but no principal of an elementary school appointed after such date shall receive the salary fixed by said schedules, except those in charge of schools having at least twenty classes.

The committee recommends that such changes be made in the pension law as will do equal justice to all members of the teaching and supervising force.

The committee recommends that the present charter provisions for determining fitness and merit of teachers shall be retained in full force and effect.

The committee recommends that from time to time and in such sub-high schools as the school authorities may deem expedient there may be established industrial or vocational courses in addition to the regular course leading to the high school and college.

The members of the committee deem it proper to state that they have held many sessions of protracted length since December 18, 1908, during which every pertinent phase of the question under discussion was thoroughly considered, with the foregoing results. They further deem it proper to note that Mr. Magnus Gross and Mr. James J. Sheppard have been members of this committee and have participated in its deliberations, but resigned before the completion of its work.

The signatures of the committee do not necessarily mean that each member is entirely in favor of every detail of the report; and some may not have felt themselves competent to judge in instances where knowledge of technicalities was demanded; but they do mean that the committee believe that the report expresses the best method of conciliating the teachers of the city and that the committee feel strongly that conciliation is absolutely necessary for the good of the schools.

March 2, 1909.

Respectfully submitted,

(Sd.) Katharine D. Blake.
(Sd.) Charles O. Dewey.
(Sd.) W. B. Gunnison.
(Sd.) Katharine A. McCann.
(Sd.) Annie B. Moriarity.
(Sd.) Mary Moore Orr.
(Sd.) Frank K. Perkins.
(Sd.) Mariam Sutro Price.
(Sd.) Grace C. Strachan.
(Sd.) J. Edw. Swanstrom.
(Sd.) Kate E. Turner, *Secretary.*
(Sd.) Henry N. Tifft, *Chairman.*

Under Section 44, 3A of the By-Laws of the Board of Education, the following permission had to be obtained:

May 8, 1909.

Miss Grace C. Strachan,
No. 1308 Pacific St.,
Brooklyn, N. Y.

Dear Madam:

In accordance with your request, permission is hereby granted to you to attend the hearing on the Gledhill-Foley bill before his Honor, the Mayor, on Tuesday, May 11, 1909, at ten o'clock A. M.

Very truly yours,
Egerton L. Winthrop, Jr.,
President, Board of Education.

By-Laws, Board of Education:

Sec. 44, sub. 3A. Absence from duty on the part of the City Superintendent of Schools, any Associate Superintendent or District Superintendent, or any other member of the supervising or teaching staff, or any member of the board of Examiners, or other salaried officer or employee of the Board of Education, for the purpose of advocating or opposing any legislative or other measure or proposition affecting the public schools or the public school system, before any official or body having jurisdiction in the matter, is prohibited, except by express permission of the Board of Education or of its President, or, in the absence of the President, of the Vice-President; and the Board of Education may cause charges to be preferred against any person violating this provision. Absence in pursuance of permission granted under the provisions of this sub-division shall not be considered absence from duty. (This subdivision was adopted Oct. 23, 1907.)

April 7, 1910.

Mr. Egerton L Winthrop, Jr.,
President, Board of Education.

My dear Mr. Winthrop,

I respectfully submit the following resolution:

WHEREAS, Mr. Abraham Stern has:

(1) voted against the Interborough Association of Women Teachers on every occasion possible since its organization in February, 1906;

(2) appeared and spoken in opposition to it at Albany at the hearing before the Assembly Committee on Affairs of Cities and before Governor Hughes;

(3) appeared and spoken against it at two public hearings before Mayor McClellan and at least one public hearing of the Charter Legislative Commission;

(4) attended and addressed at least one meeting of the Association of Men Teachers and Principals where plans were being made to defeat the aims of the Interborough Association of Women Teachers;

(5) traveled to Albany with the representatives of the associations of male teachers and principals and other opponents of the Interborough Association of Women Teachers;

(6) attended and addressed at least one meeting of a so-called Primary Teachers' League managed by male teachers opposed to the Interborough Association of Women Teachers,

(7) and been throughout the existence of our association a member of the Committee on By-Laws of the Board of Education which has reported unfavorably on every proposition and resolution affecting the Interborough Association of Women Teachers;

AND WHEREAS, Mr. Robert L. Harrison has:

(1) voted against the Interborough Association of Women Teachers on every occasion possible since its organization in February, 1906;

(2) appeared and spoken in opposition to it at Albany at the hearing before the Assembly Committee on Affairs of Cities and before Governor Hughes;

(3) appeared and spoken against it at two public hearings before Mayor McClellan and at least one public hearing of the Charter Legislative Commission;

(4) traveled to Albany with the representatives of the Associations of Male Teachers and Principals and other opponents of the Interborough Association of Women Teachers;

(5) and been throughout the existence of our association a member of the Committee on By-Laws of the Board of Education which has reported unfavorably on every proposition and resolution affecting the Interborough Association of Women Teachers;

AND WHEREAS, Mr. George W. Wingate has:

(1) voted against the Interborough Association of Women Teachers on every occasion possible since its organization in February, 1906;

(2) and been throughout the existence of our association a member of the Committee on By-Laws of the Board of Education which has reported unfavorably on every proposition and resolution affecting the Interborough Association of Women Teachers;

AND WHEREAS, Mr. John Green has:

(1) voted against the Interborough Association of Women Teachers on every occasion possible since its organization in February, 1906;

AND WHEREAS, Mr. Egerton L. Winthrop, Jr., as President of the Board of Education is ex-officio member of all committees;

AND WHEREAS, Mr. Winthrop has:

(1) voted gainst the Interborough Association of Women Teachers on every occasion possible since its organization in February, 1906;

(2) appeared and spoken against it at two public hearings before Mayor McClellan and at least one public hearing of the Charter Legislative Commission;

AND WHEREAS, President Winthrop has appointed Mr. Abraham Stern, Mr. Robert L. Harrison, Mr. George W. Wingate, Mr. John Greene and Mr. A. S. Somers as the Teachers' Commission of the Board of Education;

AND WHEREAS, The vote on the "Somers Resolution" at the Special Meeting of the Board of Education held on March 16, 1910, was twenty-three to sixteen against the Interborough Association of Women Teachers;

THEREFORE, RESOLVED: That the Interborough Association of Women Teachers regrets that the Teachers' Salaries Commission as above constituted does not more fairly represent the Board of Education on this question of salaries.

Yours very truly,
GRACE C. STRACHAN,
President, Interborough Association
of Women Teachers.

## DEPARTMENT OF EDUCATION

### THE CITY OF NEW YORK

### Examination for License as Teacher of Shopwork in Elementary Schools

Office of the Board of Examiners,
Park Avenue and 59th Street,
New York, September 30, 1909.

A written examination of applicants for license as teacher of shopwork in the elementary schools of the City of New York will be conducted by the Board of Examiners on Thursday and Friday, March 3 and 4, 1910, commencing at 9.30 A. M., in Room 422, Hall of the Board of Education, Park Avenue and 59th Street, Borough of Manhattan. An oral eaxmination will be given at the call of the Board of Examiners.

No person will be eligible for this license whose age on March 3, 1910, is under eighteen or over thirty-five eyars. Under this provision an applicant will be regarded as eligible up to and including the day preceding his thirty-sixth birthday.

Each applicant must have the qualifications indicated under (*a*), (*b*), or (*c*), following:

(*a*) Graduation from a satisfactory high school or institution of equal or higher rank, or an equivalent academic training, or the passing of an academic examination; and the completion of a satisfactory course of professional training of at least two years in shopwork.

(*b*) Graduation from a college course recognized by the Regents of the University of the State of New York, which includes satisfactory courses in the principles of education and in shopwork.

(*c*) Two years of successful experience as substitute teacher of shopwork in the schools of the City of New York, together with the completion of a satisfactory professional course in shopwork.

The completion of a course of 90 hours in principles and practice of shopwork teaching at a recognized institution shall be regarded as a satisfactory course in shopwork within the meaning of clause (*c*).

Candidates who, prior to July 1, 1910, will have established eligibility under any one of the preceding heads may enter this examination.

The written examination will be upon mechanical and freehand drawing, constructive and applied design, geometry, the principles and practice of shopwork, methods of instruction, and class management.

The oral examination will include tests of technical skill and knowledge. A practical test of ability to teach will also form a part of the examination.

In the written and the oral answers to examination questions, an applicant must give evidence of his ability to use the English language correctly.

All documents submitted as evidence of scholarship, training or experience, must be originals, and must be accompanied by duplicate copies. The filing of such documents is optional. No diplomas will be received, except in cases where the institution is no longer in existence.

NOTE: The academic examination required of certain applicants under class (a) will be conducted by the Board of Examiners on January 24, 1910, and again in May, 1910. A separate circular giving particulars will be forwarded on request.

All persons in doubt as to their eligibility, and desiring information respecting the matter, may communicate with the Board of Examiners not later than February 15, 1910.

A certificate of physical fitness made after examination *by one of the physicians of the Board of Education* will be required in the case of each applicant. No person will be licensed who has not been vaccinated within eight years, unless the examining physician recommends otherwise.

The licenses issued under these regulations hold for the period of one year, and may be renewed for two successive years, without examination, in case the work of the holder is satisfactory. At the close of the third year of continuous successful service, the City Superintendent may make the license permanent.

Section 67, subdivision 12, of the By-Laws of the Board of Education, reads as follows:

"No married woman shall be appointed to any teaching or supervising position in the day public schools unless her husband is incapacitated from physical or mental disease to earn a livelihood, or has continuously abandoned her for not less than three years prior to the date of appointment, provided proof satisfactory to the Board of Superintendents is furnished to establish such physical or mental disability or abandonment."

The salary for men is $900 the first year, with an annual increase of $105 for meritorious service, to a maximum of $2160; for women, $900 the first year, with an annual increase of $100, to a maximum of $1200. Credit is allowed for outside experience of sufficient length and satisfactory character, in accordance with a fixed schedule.

NOTE: The examination will begin *promptly* at the time stated above, and no applicant who is late will be allowed to enter the examination room.

WILLIAM H. MAXWELL,
City Superintendent of Schools.

## THE AUTHOR

Grace Charlotte Strachan was born in Buffalo, New York, and was graduated from the Buffalo Normal School. After teaching in elementary and high schools there she came to Brooklyn, at the request of Prof. Franklin W. Hooper, then a member of the Board of Education. Before securing appointment here, she had to obtain licenses B and A. In the examination for the first she stood highest in a list of nearly three hundred candidates.

After a year at Public School No. 11, Miss Strachan was appointed to the faculty of the Training School for Teachers. Two years later she was appointed Principal of Public School No. 42, which was made a branch of the training School for Teachers. She held this position four years. Thus for six years Miss Strachan was connected with the teachers in training, and she has since found many of her "old girls" in the schools she has supervised. She was elected associate superintendent of schools in Brooklyn, July 3, 1900, and under the new charter became district superintendent of schools of the City of New York.

While principal of Public School No. 42, Miss Strachan taught in Evening High School, and later served as principal of Evening School No. 85.

As principal she was especially noted for her work in developing the character of her pupils. The boys and girls organized into companies elected their own officers, and took practically entire charge of the school grounds, recesses, dismissals, and fire drills. She also organized an Anti-Cigarette League.

The value of school-room decoration in the development of character was impressed upon the teachers, and soon the building, though old and dingy, became one of the most attractive schoolhouses in the city.

As district superintendent, Miss Strachan has probably come into contact with more pupils and teachers than any other superintendent during the past ten years, on account of frequent changes of assignment.

She is now in charge of districts 33 and 35, which register upwards of 32,000 children, mostly of foreign birth or parentage. As a result of the preponderance of foreigners and of the overcrowded conditions of the district, there are thousands of over-age children. Her division superintendent recently said that there were no other districts in the city where the "special" children were being so well cared for. The first class for deaf children in Brooklyn was established in one of her schools last February, and plans are ready for the establishment of classes for the blind, crippled and anaemic children, as soon as money for the transportation of such children is secured.

In May, 1909, 2,500 pupils from her districts gave an exhibition of folk dancing and wand, Indian club, and dumb bell exercises, which was declared by Mr. Egerton L. Winthrop, Jr., President of the Board, Superintendent Meleney, and other distinguished visitors, the best of its kind they had ever seen.

On the occasion of her re-election in January, 1910, rumors that she might be punished for her work in connection with the Interborough Association of Women Teachers proved unfounded. The Brooklyn *Eagle* of January 10, 1910, commenting on these rumors, said "Her name has been mentioned, indeed, in connection with the city superintendency and with an associate superintendency."

Miss Strachan's work as the leader of the women teachers in their campaign for "equal pay" is familiar to any one who reads the newspapers. She believes that success is at hand, and that it will be won in the most dignified and desirable way—through the Board of Education and the Board of Estimate and Apportionment.

www.ingramcontent.com/pod-product-compliance
Lightning Source LLC
LaVergne TN
LVHW011247110826
845149LV00001B/65

* 9 7 8 1 4 1 8 1 8 9 0 9 9 *